Stanley Gibbons
Commonwealth Stamp Catalogue

Brunei, Malaysia and Singapore

3rd edition

STANLEY GIBBONS LTD
London and Ringwood

By Appointment to Her Majesty The Queen
Stanley Gibbons Ltd, London
Philatelists

Published by Stanley Gibbons Ltd
Editorial, Publications Sales Offices
and Distribution Centre:
7 Parkside, Christchurch Road, Ringwood,
Hants BH24 3SH

2nd Edition – 2004
3rd Edition – 2010

British Library Cataloguing in Publication Data.
A catalogue record for this book is available from the British Library.

ISBN-10: 0-85259-734-7
ISBN-13: 978-0-85259-734-7

Item No. 2879-09

Printed by Latimer Trend & Company Ltd,
Plymouth

Contents

Information and Guidelines

These notes reflect current practice in compiling the Stanley Gibbons Commonwealth Catalogues.

The Stanley Gibbons Stamp Catalogue has a very long history and the vast quantity of information it contains has been carefully built up by successive generations through the work of countless individuals. Philately is never static and the Catalogue has evolved and developed over the years. These notes relate to the current criteria upon which a stamp may be listed or priced. These criteria have developed over time and may have differed somewhat in the early years of this catalogue. These notes are not intended to suggest that we plan to make wholesale changes to the listing of classic issues in order to bring them into line with today's listing policy, they are designed to inform catalogue users as to the policies currently in operation.

PRICES

The prices quoted in this Catalogue are the estimated selling prices of Stanley Gibbons Ltd at the time of publication. They are, unless it is specifically stated otherwise, for examples in fine condition for the issue concerned. Superb examples are worth more; those of a lower quality considerably less.

All prices are subject to change without prior notice and Stanley Gibbons Ltd may from time to time offer stamps below catalogue price. Individual low value stamps sold at 399 Strand are liable to an additional handling charge. Purchasers of new issues should note the prices charged for them contain an element for the service rendered and so may exceed the prices shown when the stamps are subsequently catalogued. Postage and handling charges are extra.

No guarantee is given to supply all stamps priced, since it is not possible to keep every catalogued item in stock. Commemorative issues may, at times, only be available in complete sets and not as individual values.

Quotation of prices. The prices in the left-hand column are for unused stamps and those in the right-hand column are for used.

A dagger (†) denotes that the item listed does not exist in that condition and a blank, or dash, that it exists, or may exist, but we are unable to quote a price.

Prices are expressed in pounds and pence sterling. One pound comprises 100 pence (£1 = 100p).

The method of notation is as follows: pence in numerals (e.g. 10 denotes ten pence); pounds and pence, up to £100, in numerals (e.g. 4.25 denotes four pounds and twenty-five pence); prices above £100 are expressed in whole pounds with the '£' sign shown.

Unused stamps. Great Britain and Commonwealth: the prices for unused stamps of Queen Victoria to King George V are for lightly hinged examples. Unused prices for King Edward VIII, King George VI and Queen Elizabeth issues are for unmounted mint.

Some stamps from the King George VI period are often difficult to find in unmounted mint condition. In such instances we would expect that collectors would need to pay a high proportion of the price quoted to obtain mounted mint examples. Generally speaking lightly mounted mint stamps from this reign, issued before 1945, are in considerable demand.

Used stamps. The used prices are normally for stamps postally used but may be for stamps cancelled-to-order where this practice exists.

A pen-cancellation on early issues can sometimes correctly denote postal use. Instances are individually noted in the Catalogue in explanation of the used price given.

Prices quoted for bisects on cover or large piece are for those dated during the period officially authorised.

Stamps not sold unused to the public (e.g. some official stamps) are priced used only.

The use of 'unified' designs, that is stamps inscribed for both postal and fiscal purposes, results in a number of stamps of very high face value. In some instances these may not have been primarily intended for postal purposes, but if they are so inscribed we include them. We only price such items used, however, where there is evidence of normal postal usage.

Cover prices. To assist collectors, cover prices are quoted for issues up to 1945 at the beginning of each country.

The system gives a general guide in the form of a factor by which the corresponding used price of the basic loose stamp should be multiplied when found in fine average condition on cover.

Care is needed in applying the factors and they relate to a cover which bears a single of the denomination listed; if more than one denomination is present the most highly priced attracts the multiplier and the remainder are priced at the simple figure for used singles in arriving at a total.

The cover should be of non-philatelic origin; bearing the correct postal rate for the period and distance involved and cancelled with the markings normal to the offices concerned. Purely philatelic items have a cover value only slightly greater than the catalogue value for the corresponding used stamps. This applies generally to those high-value stamps used philatelically rather than in the normal course of commerce. Low-value stamps, e.g. ¼d. and ½d., are desirable when used as a single rate on cover and merit an increase in 'multiplier' value.

First day covers in the period up to 1945 are not within the scope of the system and the multiplier should not be used. As a special category of philatelic usage, with wide variations in valuation according to scarcity, they require separate treatment.

Oversized covers, difficult to accommodate on an album page, should be reckoned as worth little more than the corresponding value of the used stamps. The condition of a cover also affects its value. Except for 'wreck covers', serious damage or soiling reduce the value where the postal markings and stamps are ordinary ones. Conversely, visual appeal adds to the value and this can include freshness of appearance, important addresses, old-fashioned but legible handwriting, historic town-names, etc.

The multipliers are a base on which further value would be added to take account of the cover's postal historical importance in demonstrating such things as unusual, scarce or emergency cancels, interesting routes, significant postal markings, combination usage, the development of postal rates, and so on.

Minimum price. The minimum catalogue price quoted is 10p. For individual stamps prices between 10p. and 95p. are provided as a guide for catalogue users. The lowest price charged for individual stamps or sets purchased from Stanley Gibbons Ltd is £1

Set prices. Set prices are generally for one of each value, excluding shades and varieties, but including major colour changes. Where there are alternative shades, etc., the cheapest is usually included. The number of stamps in the set is always stated for clarity. The prices for sets containing *se-tenant* pieces are based on the prices quoted for such combinations, and not on those for the individual stamps.

Varieties. Where plate or cylinder varieties are priced in used condition the price quoted is for a fine used example with the cancellation well clear of the listed flaw.

Specimen stamps. The pricing of these items is explained under that heading.

Stamp booklets. Prices are for complete assembled booklets in fine condition with those issued before 1945 showing normal wear and tear. Incomplete booklets and those which have been 'exploded' will, in general, be worth less than the figure quoted.

Repricing. Collectors will be aware that the market factors of supply and demand directly influence the prices quoted in this Catalogue. Whatever the scarcity of a particular stamp, if there is no one in the market who wishes to buy it cannot be expected to achieve a high price. Conversely, the same item actively sought by numerous potential buyers may cause the price to rise.

All the prices in this Catalogue are examined during the preparation of each new edition by the expert staff of Stanley Gibbons and repriced as necessary. They take many factors into account, including supply and demand, and are in close touch with the international stamp market and the auction world.

Commonwealth cover prices and advice on postal history material originally provided by Edward B Proud.

GUARANTEE

All stamps are guaranteed originals in the following terms:

If not as described, and returned by the purchaser, we undertake to refund the price paid to us in the original transaction. If any stamp is certified as genuine by the Expert Committee of the Royal Philatelic Society, London, or by BPA Expertising Ltd, the purchaser shall not be entitled to make any claim against us for any error, omission or mistake in such certificate.

Consumers' statutory rights are not affected by the above guarantee.

The recognised Expert Committees in this country are those of the Royal Philatelic Society, 41 Devonshire Place, London W1G, 6JY, and BPA Expertising Ltd, PO Box 1141, Guildford, Surrey GU5 0WR. They do not undertake valuations under any circumstances and fees are payable for their services.

MARGINS ON IMPERFORATE STAMPS

Superb | Very fine | Fine | Average | Poor

GUM

Unmounted | Very lightly mounted | Lightly mounted | Mounted/ large part original gum (o.g.). | Heavily mounted small part o.g.

CENTRING

Superb | Very fine | Fine | Average | Poor

CANCELLATIONS

Superb | Very fine | Fine | Average | Poor

Superb | Very fine

Fine | Average | Poor

CONDITION GUIDE

To assist collectors in assessing the true value of items they are considering buying or in reviewing stamps already in their collections, we now offer a more detailed guide to the condition of stamps on which this catalogue's prices are based.

For a stamp to be described as 'Fine', it should be sound in all respects, without creases, bends, wrinkles, pin holes, thins or tears. If perforated, all perforation 'teeth' should be intact, it should not suffer from fading, rubbing or toning and it should be of clean, fresh appearance.

Margins on imperforate stamps: These should be even on all sides and should be at least as wide as half the distance between that stamp and the next. To have one or more margins of less than this width, would normally preclude a stamp from being described as 'Fine'. Some early stamps were positioned very close together on the printing plate and in such cases 'Fine' margins would necessarily be narrow. On the other hand, some plates were laid down to give a substantial gap between individual stamps and in such cases margins would be expected to be much wider.

An 'average' four-margin example would have a narrower margin on one or more sides and should be priced accordingly, while a stamp with wider, yet even, margins than 'Fine' would merit the description 'Very Fine' or 'Superb' and, if available, would command a price in excess of that quoted in the catalogue.

Gum: Since the prices for stamps of King Edward VIII, King George VI and Queen Elizabeth are for 'unmounted' or 'never hinged' mint, even stamps from these reigns which have been very lightly mounted should be available at a discount from catalogue price, the more obvious the hinge marks, the greater the discount.

Catalogue prices for stamps issued prior to King Edward VIII's reign are for mounted mint, so unmounted examples would be worth a premium. Hinge marks on 20th century stamps should not be too obtrusive, and should be at least in the lightly mounted category. For 19th century stamps more obvious hinging would be acceptable, but stamps should still carry a large part of their original gum—'Large part o.g.'—in order to be described as 'Fine'.

Centring: Ideally, the stamp's image should appear in the exact centre of the perforated area, giving equal margins on all sides. 'Fine' centring would be close to this ideal with any deviation having an effect on the value of the stamp. As in the case of the margins on imperforate stamps, it should be borne in mind that the space between some early stamps was very narrow, so it was very difficult to achieve accurate perforation, especially when the technology was in its infancy. Thus, poor centring would have a less damaging effect on the value of a 19th century stamp than on a 20th century example, but the premium put on a perfectly centred specimen would be greater.

Cancellations: Early cancellation devices were designed to 'obliterate' the stamp in order to prevent it being reused and this is still an important objective for today's postal administrations. Stamp collectors, on the other hand, prefer postmarks to be lightly applied, clear, and to leave as much as possible of the design visible. Dated, circular cancellations have long been 'the postmark of choice', but the definition of a 'Fine' cancellation will depend upon the types of cancellation in use at the time a stamp was current—it is clearly illogical to seek a circular datestamp on a Penny Black.

'Fine', by definition, will be superior to 'Average', so, in terms of cancellation quality, if one begins by identifying what 'Average' looks like, then one will be half way to identifying 'Fine'. The illustrations will give some guidance on mid-19th century and mid-20th century cancellations of Great Britain, but types of cancellation in general use in each country and in each period will determine the appearance of 'Fine'.

As for the factors discussed above, anything less than 'Fine' will result in a downgrading of the stamp concerned, while a very fine or superb cancellation will be worth a premium.

Combining the factors: To merit the description 'Fine', a stamp should be fine in every respect, but a small deficiency in one area might be made up for in another by a factor meriting an 'Extremely Fine' description.

Some early issues are so seldom found in what would normally be considered to be 'Fine' condition, the catalogue prices are for a slightly lower grade, with 'Fine' examples being worth a premium. In such cases a note to this effect is given in the catalogue, while elsewhere premiums are given for well-centred, lightly cancelled examples.

Stamps graded at less than fine remain collectable and, in the case of more highly priced stamps, will continue to hold a value. Nevertheless, buyers should always bear condition in mind.

The Catalogue in General

Contents. The Catalogue is confined to adhesive postage stamps, including miniature sheets. For particular categories the rules are:

(a) Revenue (fiscal) stamps or telegraph stamps are listed only where they have been expressly authorised for postal duty.
(b) Stamps issued only precancelled are included, but normally issued stamps available additionally with precancel have no separate precancel listing unless the face value is changed.
(c) Stamps prepared for use but not issued, hitherto accorded full listing, are nowadays foot-noted with a price (where possible).
(d) Bisects (trisects, etc.) are only listed where such usage was officially authorised.
(e) Stamps issued only on first day covers or in presentation packs and not available separately are not listed but may be priced in a footnote.
(f) New printings are only included in this Catalogue where they show a major philatelic variety, such as a change in shade, watermark or paper. Stamps which exist with or without imprint dates are listed separately; changes in imprint dates are mentioned in footnotes.
(g) Official and unofficial reprints are dealt with by footnote.
(h) Stamps from imperforate printings of modern issues which occur perforated are covered by footnotes, but are listed where widely available for postal use.

Exclusions. The following are excluded:

(a) non-postal revenue or fiscal stamps;
(b) postage stamps used fiscally (although prices are now given for some fiscally used high values);
(c) local carriage labels and private local issues;
(d) bogus or phantom stamps;
(e) railway or airline letter fee stamps, bus or road transport company labels or the stamps of private postal companies operating under licence from the national authority;
(f) cut-outs;
(g) all types of non-postal labels and souvenirs;
(h) documentary labels for the postal service, e.g. registration, recorded delivery, air-mail etiquettes, etc.;
(i) privately applied embellishments to official issues and privately commissioned items generally;
(j) stamps for training postal officers.
(k) Telegraph stamps

Full listing. 'Full listing' confers our recognition and implies allotting a catalogue number and (wherever possible) a price quotation.

In judging status for inclusion in the catalogue broad considerations are applied to stamps. They must be issued by a legitimate postal authority, recognised by the government concerned, and must be adhesives valid for proper postal use in the class of service for which they are inscribed. Stamps, with the exception of such categories as postage dues and officials, must be available to the general public, at face value, in reasonable quantities without any artificial restrictions being imposed on their distribution.

For errors and varieties the criterion is legitimate (albeit inadvertent) sale through a postal administration in the normal course of business. Details of provenance are always important; printers' waste and deliberately manufactured material are excluded.

Certificates. In assessing unlisted items due weight is given to Certificates from recognised Expert Committees and, where appropriate, we will usually ask to see them.

Date of issue. Where local issue dates differ from dates of release by agencies, 'date of issue' is the local date. Fortuitous stray usage before the officially intended date is disregarded in listing.

Catalogue numbers. Stamps of each country are catalogued chronologically by date of issue. Subsidiary classes are placed at the end of the country, as separate lists, with a distinguishing letter prefix to the catalogue number, e.g. D for postage due, O for official and E for express delivery stamps.

The catalogue number appears in the extreme left-column. The boldface Type numbers in the next column are merely cross-references to illustrations.

Once published in the Catalogue, numbers are changed as little as possible; really serious renumbering is reserved for the occasions when a complete country or an entire issue is being rewritten. The edition first affected includes cross-reference tables of old and new numbers.

Our catalogue numbers are universally recognised in specifying stamps and as a hallmark of status.

Illustrations. Stamps are illustrated at three-quarters linear size. Stamps not illustrated are the same size and format as the value shown, unless otherwise indicated. Stamps issued only as miniature sheets have the stamp alone illustrated but sheet size is also quoted. Overprints, surcharges, watermarks and postmarks are normally actual size. Illustrations of varieties are often enlarged to show the detail. Stamp booklet covers are illustrated half-size, unless otherwise indicated.

Designers. Designers' names are quoted where known, though space precludes naming every individual concerned in the production of a set. In particular, photographers supplying material are usually named only where they also make an active contribution in the design stage; posed photographs of reigning monarchs are, however, an exception to this rule.

CONTACTING THE CATALOGUE EDITOR

The editor is always interested in hearing from people who have new information which will improve or correct the Catalogue. As a general rule he must see and examine the actual stamps before they can be considered for listing; photographs or photocopies are insufficient evidence.

Submissions should be made in writing to the Catalogue Editor, Stanley Gibbons Publications at the Ringwood office. The cost of return postage for items submitted is appreciated, and this should include the registration fee if required.

Where information is solicited purely for the benefit of the enquirer, the editor cannot undertake to reply if the answer is already contained in these published notes or if return postage is omitted. Written communications are greatly preferred to enquiries by telephone or e-mail and the editor regrets that he or his staff cannot see personal callers without a prior appointment being made. Correspondence may be subject to delay during the production period of each new edition.

The editor welcomes close contact with study circles and is interested, too, in finding reliable local correspondents who will verify and supplement official information in countries where this is deficient.

We regret we do not give opinions as to the genuineness of stamps, nor do we identify stamps or number them by our Catalogue.

TECHNICAL MATTERS

The meanings of the technical terms used in the catalogue will be found in our *Philatelic Terms Illustrated.*

References below to (more specialised) listings are to be taken to indicate, as appropriate, the Stanley Gibbons *Great Britain Specialised Catalogue* in five volumes or the *Great Britain Concise Catalogue*.

1. Printing

Printing errors. Errors in printing are of major interest to the Catalogue. Authenticated items meriting consideration would include: background, centre or frame inverted or omitted; centre or subject transposed; error of colour; error or omission of value; double prints and impressions; printed both sides; and so on. Designs *tête-bêche*, whether intentionally or by accident, are listable. *Se-tenant* arrangements of stamps are recognised in the listings or footnotes. Gutter pairs (a pair of stamps separated by blank margin) are not included in this volume. Colours only partially omitted are not listed. Stamps with embossing omitted are reserved for our more specialised listings.

Printing varieties. Listing is accorded to major changes in the printing base which lead to completely new types. In recess-printing this could be a design re-engraved; in photogravure or photolithography a screen altered in whole or in part. It can also encompass flat-bed and rotary printing if the results are readily distinguishable.

To be considered at all, varieties must be constant.

Early stamps, produced by primitive methods, were prone to numerous imperfections; the lists reflect this, recognising re-entries, retouches, broken frames, misshapen letters, and so on. Printing technology has, however, radically improved over the years, during which time photogravure and lithography have become predominant. Varieties nowadays are more in the nature of flaws and these, being too specialised for this general catalogue, are almost always outside the scope.

In no catalogue, however, do we list such items as: dry prints, kiss prints, doctor-blade flaws, colour shifts or registration flaws (unless they lead to the complete omission of a colour from an individual stamp), lithographic ring flaws, and so on. Neither do we recognise fortuitous happenings like paper creases or confetti flaws.

Overprints (and surcharges). Overprints of different types qualify for separate listing. These include overprints in different colours; overprints from different printing processes such as litho and typo; overprints in totally different typefaces, etc. Major errors in machine-printed overprints are important and listable. They include: overprint inverted or omitted; overprint double (treble, etc.); overprint diagonal; overprint double, one inverted; pairs with one overprint omitted, e.g. from a radical shift to an adjoining stamp; error of colour; error of type fount; letters inverted or omitted, etc. If the overprint is handstamped, few of these would qualify and a distinction is drawn. We continue, however, to list pairs of stamps where one has a handstamped overprint and the other has not.

Varieties occurring in overprints will often take the form of broken letters, slight differences in spacing, rising spaces, etc. Only the most important would be considered for listing or footnote mention.

Sheet positions. If space permits we quote sheet positions of listed varieties and authenticated data is solicited for this purpose.

De La Rue plates. The Catalogue classifies the general plates used by De La Rue for printing British Colonial stamps as follows:

VICTORIAN KEY TYPE

Die I

1. The ball of decoration on the second point of the crown appears as a dark mass of lines.
2. Dark vertical shading separates the front hair from the bun.
3. The vertical line of colour outlining the front of the throat stops at the sixth line of shading on the neck.
4. The white space in the coil of the hair above the curl is roughly the shape of a pin's head.

Die II

1. There are very few lines of colour in the ball and it appears almost white.
2. A white vertical strand of hair appears in place of the dark shading.

3. The line stops at the eighth line of shading.
4. The white space is oblong, with a line of colour partially dividing it at the left end.

Plates numbered 1 and 2 are both Die I. Plates 3 and 4 are Die II.

GEORGIAN KEY TYPE

Die I

A. The second (thick) line below the name of the country is cut slanting, conforming roughly to the shape of the crown on each side.
B. The labels of solid colour bearing the words "POSTAGE" and "& REVENUE" are square at the inner top corners.
C. There is a projecting "bud" on the outer spiral of the ornament in each of the lower corners.

Die I

A. The second line is cut vertically on each side of the crown.
B. The labels curve inwards at the top.
C. There is no "bud" in this position.

Unless otherwise stated in the lists, all stamps with watermark Multiple Crown CA (w **8**) are Die I while those with watermark Multiple Crown Script CA (w **9**) are Die II. The Georgian Die II was introduced in April 1921 and was used for Plates 10 to 22 and 26 to 28. Plates 23 to 25 were made from Die I by mistake.

2. Paper

All stamps listed are deemed to be on (ordinary) paper of the wove type and white in colour; only departures from this are normally mentioned.

Types. Where classification so requires we distinguish such other types of paper as, for example, vertically and horizontally laid; wove and laid bâtonné; card(board); carton; cartridge; glazed; granite; native; pelure; porous; quadrillé; ribbed; rice; and silk thread.

Wove paper

Laid paper

Granite paper

Quadrillé paper

Burelé band

The various makeshifts for normal paper are listed as appropriate. The varieties of double paper and joined paper are recognised. The security device of a printed burelé band on the back of a stamp, as in early Queensland, qualifies for listing.

Descriptive terms. The fact that a paper is handmade (and thus probably of uneven thickness) is mentioned where necessary. Such descriptive terms as "hard" and "soft"; "smooth" and "rough"; "thick", "medium" and "thin" are applied where there is philatelic merit in classifying papers.

Coloured, very white and toned papers. A coloured paper is one that is coloured right through (front and back of the stamp). In the Catalogue the colour of the paper is given in italics, thus:
black/*rose* = black design on rose paper.

Papers have been made specially white in recent years by, for example, a very heavy coating of chalk. We do not classify shades of whiteness of paper as distinct varieties. There does exist, however, a type of paper from early days called toned. This is off-white, often brownish or buffish, but it cannot be assigned any definite colour. A toning effect brought on by climate, incorrect storage or gum staining is disregarded here, as this was not the state of the paper when issued.

"Ordinary" and "Chalk-surfaced" papers. The availability of many postage stamps for revenue purposes made necessary some safeguard against the illegitimate re-use of stamps with removable cancellations. This was at first secured by using fugitive inks and later by printing on paper surfaced by coatings containing either chalk or china clay, both of which made it difficult to remove any form of obliteration without damaging the stamp design.

This catalogue lists these chalk-surfaced paper varieties from their introduction in 1905. Where no indication is given, the paper is "ordinary".

The "traditional" method of indentifying chalk-surfaced papers has been that, when touched with a silver wire, a black mark is left on the paper, and the listings in this catalogue are based on that test. However, the test itself is now largely discredited, for, although the mark can be removed by a soft rubber, some damage to the stamp will result from its use.

The difference between chalk-surfaced and pre-war ordinary papers is fairly clear: chalk-surfaced papers being smoother to the touch and showing a characteristic sheen when light is reflected off their surface. Under good magnification tiny bubbles or pock marks can be seen on the surface of the stamp and at the tips of the perforations the surfacing appears "broken". Traces of paper fibres are evident on the surface of ordinary paper and the ink shows a degree of absorption into it.

Initial chalk-surfaced paper printings by De La Rue had a thinner coating than subsequently became the norm. The characteristics described above are less pronounced in these printings.

During and after the Second World War, substitute papers replaced the chalk-surfaced papers, these do not react to the silver test and are therefore classed as "ordinary", although differentiating them without recourse to it is more difficult, for, although the characteristics of the chalk-surfaced paper remained the same, some of the ordinary papers appear much smoother than earlier papers and many do not show the watermark clearly. Experience is the only solution to identifying these, and comparison with stamps whose paper type is without question will be of great help.

Another type of paper, known as "thin striated" was used only for the Bahamas 1s. and 5s. (Nos. 155a, 156a, 171 and 174) and for several stamps of the Malayan states. Hitherto these have been described as "chalk-surfaced" since they gave some reaction to the silver test, but they are much thinner than usual chalk-surfaced papers, with the watermark showing clearly. Stamps on this paper show a slightly 'ribbed' effect when the stamp is held up to the light. Again, comparison with a known striated paper stamp, such as the 1941 Straits Settlements Die II 2c. orange (No. 294) will prove invaluable in separating these papers.

Glazed paper. In 1969 the Crown Agents introduced a new general-purpose paper for use in conjunction with all current printing processes. It generally has a marked glossy surface but the degree varies according to the process used, being more marked in recess-printing stamps. As it does not respond to the silver test this presents a further test where previous printings were on chalky paper. A change of paper to the glazed variety merits separate listing.

Green and yellow papers. Issues of the First World War and immediate postwar period occur on green and yellow papers and these are given separate Catalogue listing. The original coloured papers (coloured throughout) gave way to surface-coloured papers, the stamps having "white backs"; other stamps show one colour on the front and a different one at the back. Because of the numerous variations a grouping of colours is adopted as follows:

Yellow papers

(1) The original *yellow* paper (throughout), usually bright in colour. The gum is often sparse, of harsh consistency and dull-looking. Used 1912–1920.
(2) The *white-backs*. Used 1913–1914.
(3) A bright lemon paper. The colour must have a pronounced greenish tinge, different from the "yellow" in (1). As a rule, the gum on stamps using this lemon paper is plentiful, smooth and shiny, and the watermark shows distinctly. Care is needed with stamps printed in green on yellow paper (1) as it may appear that the paper is this lemon. Used 1914–1916.
(4) An experimental *orange-buff* paper. The colour must have a distinct brownish tinge. It is not to be confused with a muddy yellow (1) nor the misleading appearance (on the surface) of stamps printed in red on yellow paper where an engraved plate has been insufficiently wiped. Used 1918–1921.
(5) An experimental *buff* paper. This lacks the brownish tinge of (4) and the brightness of the yellow shades. The gum is shiny when compared with the matt type used on (4). Used 1919–1920.
(6) A *pale yellow* paper that has a creamy tone to the yellow. Used from 1920 onwards.

Green papers

(7) The original "green" paper, varying considerably through shades of blue-green and yellow-green, the front and back sometimes differing. Used 1912–1916.
(8) The *white backs*. Used 1913–1914.
(9) A paper blue-green on the surface with *pale olive* back. The back must be markedly paler than the front and this and the pronounced olive tinge to the back distinguish it from (7). Used 1916–1920.
(10) Paper with a vivid green surface, commonly called *emerald-green*; it has the olive back of (9). Used 1920.
(11) Paper with *emerald-green* both back and front. Used from 1920 onwards.

3. Perforation and Rouletting

Perforation gauge. The gauge of a perforation is the number of holes in a length of 2 cm. For correct classification the size of the holes (large or small) may need to be distinguished; in a few cases the actual number of holes on each edge of the stamp needs to be quoted.

Measurement. The Gibbons *Instanta* gauge is the standard for measuring perforations. The stamp is viewed against a dark background with the transparent gauge put on top of it. Though the gauge measures to decimal accuracy, perforations read from it are generally quoted in the Catalogue to the nearest half. For example:

Just over perf 12¾ to just under 13¼ = perf 13
Perf 13¼ exactly, rounded up = perf 13½
Just over perf 13¼ to just under 13¾ = perf 13½
Perf 13¾ exactly, rounded up = perf 14

However, where classification depends on it, actual quarter-perforations are quoted.

Notation. Where no perforation is quoted for an issue it is imperforate. Perforations are usually abbreviated (and spoken) as follows, though sometimes they may be spelled out for clarity. This notation for rectangular stamps (the majority) applies to diamond shapes if "top" is read as the edge to the top right.

P 14: perforated alike on all sides (read: "perf 14").
P 14×15: the first figure refers to top and bottom, the second to left and right sides (read: "perf 14 by 15"). This is a compound perforation. For an upright triangular stamp the first figure refers to the two sloping sides and second to the base. In inverted

triangulars the base is first and the second figure to the sloping sides.

P 14–15: perforation measuring anything between 14 and 15: the holes are irregularly spaced, thus the gauge may vary along a single line or even along a single edge of the stamp (read: "perf 14 to 15").

P 14 *irregular*: perforated 14 from a worn perforator, giving badly aligned holes irregularly spaced (read: "irregular perf 14").

P *comp(ound)* 14×15: two gauges in use but not necessarily on opposite sides of the stamp. It could be one side in one gauge and three in the other; or two adjacent sides with the same gauge. (Read: "perf compound of 14 and 15".) For three gauges or more, abbreviated as "P 12, 14½, 15 *or compound*" for example.

P 14, 14½: perforated approximately 14¼ (read: "perf 14 or 14½"). It does *not* mean two stamps, one perf 14 and the other perf 14½. This obsolescent notation is gradually being replaced in the Catalogue.

Imperf: imperforate (not perforated)

Imperf×P 14: imperforate at top ad bottom and perf 14 at sides.

P 14×*imperf*: perf 14 at top and bottom and imperforate at sides.

Such headings as "P 13×14 (*vert*) and P 14×13 (*horiz*)" indicate which perforations apply to which stamp format—vertical or horizontal.

Some stamps are additionally perforated so that a label or tab is detachable; others have been perforated for use as two halves. Listings are normally for whole stamps, unless stated otherwise.

Imperf×perf

Other terms. Perforation almost always gives circular holes; where other shapes have been used they are specified, e.g. square holes; lozenge perf. Interrupted perfs are brought about by the omission of pins at regular intervals. Perforations merely simulated by being printed as part of the design are of course ignored. With few exceptions, privately applied perforations are not listed.

In the 19th century perforations are often described as clean cut (clean, sharply incised holes), intermediate or rough (rough holes, imperfectly cut, often the result of blunt pins).

Perforation errors and varieties. Authenticated errors, where a stamp normally perforated is accidentally issued imperforate, are listed provided no traces of perforation (blind holes or indentations) remain. They must be provided as pairs, both stamps wholly imperforate, and are only priced in that form.

Stamps imperforate between stamp and sheet margin are not listed in this catalogue, but such errors on Great Britain stamps will be found in the *Great Britain Specialised Catalogue*.

Pairs described as "imperforate between" have the line of perforations between the two stamps omitted.

Imperf between (horiz pair): a horizontal pair of stamps with perfs all around the edges but none between the stamps.

Imperf between (vert pair): a vertical pair of stamps with perfs all around the edges but none between the stamps.

Imperf between (vertical pair)

Imperf horizontally (vertical pair)

Where several of the rows have escaped perforation the resulting varieties are listable. Thus:

Imperf vert (horiz pair): a horizontal pair of stamps perforated top and bottom; all three vertical directions are imperf—the two outer edges and between the stamps.

Imperf horiz (vert pair): a vertical pair perforated at left and right edges; all three horizontal directions are imperf—the top, bottom and between the stamps.

Straight edges. Large sheets cut up before issue to post offices can cause stamps with straight edges, i.e. imperf on one side or on two sides at right angles. They are not usually listable in this condition and are worth less than corresponding stamps properly perforated all round. This does not, however, apply to certain stamps, mainly from coils and booklets, where straight edges on various sides are the manufacturing norm affecting every stamp. The listings and notes make clear which sides are correctly imperf.

Malfunction. Varieties of double, misplaced or partial perforation caused by error or machine malfunction are not listable, neither are freaks, such as perforations placed diagonally from paper folds, nor missing holes caused by broken pins.

Types of perforating. Where necessary for classification, perforation types are distinguished.

These include:

Line perforation from one line of pins punching single rows of holes at a time.

Comb perforation from pins disposed across the sheet in comb formation, punching out holes at three sides of the stamp a row at a time.

Harrow perforation applied to a whole pane or sheet at one stroke.

Rotary perforation from toothed wheels operating across a sheet, then crosswise.

Sewing machine perforation. The resultant condition,

clean-cut or rough, is distinguished where required.

Pin-perforation is the commonly applied term for pin-roulette in which, instead of being punched out, round holes are pricked by sharp-pointed pins and no paper is removed.

Mixed perforation occurs when stamps with defective perforations are re-perforated in a different gauge.

Punctured stamps. Perforation holes can be punched into the face of the stamp. Patterns of small holes, often in the shape of initial letters, are privately applied devices against pilferage. These (perfins) are outside the scope except for Australia, Canada, Cape of Good Hope, Papua and Sudan where they were used as official stamps by the national administration. Identification devices, when officially inspired, are listed or noted; they can be shapes, or letters or words formed from holes, sometimes converting one class of stamp into another.

Rouletting. In rouletting the paper is cut, for ease of separation, but none is removed. The gauge is measured, when needed, as for perforations. Traditional French terms descriptive of the type of cut are often used and types include:

Arc roulette (percé en arc). Cuts are minute, spaced arcs, each roughly a semicircle.

Cross roulette (percé en croix). Cuts are tiny diagonal crosses.

Line roulette (percé en ligne or *en ligne droite).* Short straight cuts parallel to the frame of the stamp. The commonest basic roulette. Where not further described, "roulette" means this type.

Rouletted in colour or coloured roulette (percé en lignes colorées or *en lignes de coleur).* Cuts with coloured edges, arising from notched rule inked simultaneously with the printing plate.

Saw-tooth roulette (percé en scie). Cuts applied zigzag fashion to resemble the teeth of a saw.

Serpentine roulette (percé en serpentin). Cuts as sharply wavy lines.

Zigzag roulette (percé en zigzags). Short straight cuts at angles in alternate directions, producing sharp points on separation. US usage favours "serrate(d) roulette" for this type.

Pin-roulette (originally *percé en points* and now *perforés trous d'epingle*) is commonly called pin-perforation in English.

4. Gum

All stamps listed are assumed to have gum of some kind; if they were issued without gum this is stated. Original gum (o.g.) means that which was present on the stamp as issued to the public. Deleterious climates and the presence of certain chemicals can cause gum to crack and, with early stamps, even make the paper deteriorate. Unscrupulous fakers are adept in removing it and regumming the stamp to meet the unreasoning demand often made for "full o.g." in cases where such a thing is virtually impossible.

5. Watermarks

Stamps are on unwatermarked paper except where the heading to the set says otherwise.

Detection. Watermarks are detected for Catalogue description by one of four methods: (1) holding stamps to the light; (2) laying stamps face down on a dark background; (3) adding a few drops of petroleum ether 40/60 to the stamp laid face down in a watermark tray; (4) by use of the Stanley Gibbons Detectamark, or other equipment, which work by revealing the thinning of the paper at the watermark. (Note that petroleum ether is highly inflammable in use and can damage photogravure stamps.)

Listable types. Stamps occurring on both watermarked and unwatermarked papers are different types and both receive full listing.

Single watermarks (devices occurring once on every stamp) can be modified in size and shape as between different issues; the types are noted but not usually separately listed. Fortuitous absence of watermark from a single stamp or its gross displacement would not be listable.

To overcome registration difficulties the device may be repeated at close intervals *(a multiple watermark)*, single stamps thus showing parts of several devices. Similarly, a *large sheet watermark* (or *all-over watermark*) covering numerous stamps can be used. We give informative notes and illustrations for them. The designs may be such that numbers of stamps in the sheet automatically lack watermark: this is not a listable variety. Multiple and all-over watermarks sometimes undergo modifications, but if the various types are difficult to distinguish from single stamps notes are given but not separate listings.

Papermakers' watermarks are noted where known but not listed separately, since most stamps in the sheet will lack them. Sheet watermarks which are nothing more than officially adopted papermakers' watermarks are, however, given normal listing.

Marginal watermarks, falling outside the pane of stamps, are ignored except where misplacement caused the adjoining row to be affected, in which case they may be footnoted.

Watermark errors and varieties. Watermark errors are recognised as of major importance. They comprise stamps intended to be on unwatermarked paper but issued watermarked by mistake, or stamps printed on paper with the wrong watermark. Varieties showing letters omitted from the watermark are also included, but broken or deformed bits on the dandy roll are not listed unless they represent repairs.

Watermark positions. The diagram shows how watermark position is described in the Catalogue. Paper has a side intended for printing and watermarks are usually impressed so that they read normally when looked through from that printed side. However, since philatelists customarily detect watermarks by looking at the back of the stamp the watermark diagram also makes clear what is actually seen.

Illustrations in the Catalogue are of watermarks in normal positions (from the front of the stamps) and are actual size where possible.

Differences in watermark position are collectable varieties. This Catalogue now lists inverted, sideways inverted and reversed watermark varieties on Commonwealth stamps from the 1860s onwards except where the watermark position is completely haphazard.

Great Britain inverted and sideways inverted watermarks can be found in the *Great Britain Specialised Catalogue* and the *Great Britain Concise Catalogue*.

Where a watermark comes indiscriminately in various positions our policy is to cover this by a general note: we do not give separate listings because the watermark position in these circumstances has no particular philatelic importance.

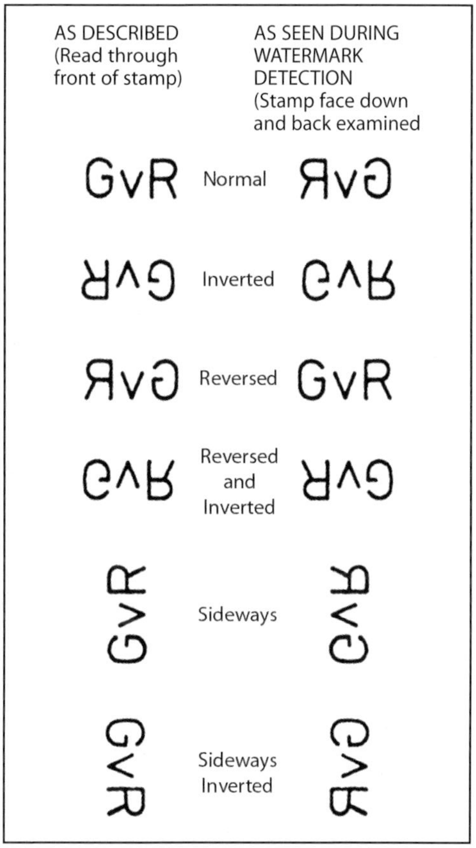

Standard types of watermark. Some watermarks have been used generally for various British possessions rather than exclusively for a single colony. To avoid repetition the Catalogue classifies 11 general types, as under, with references in the headings throughout the listings being given either in words or in the form ("W w **9**") (meaning "watermark type w **9**"). In those cases where watermark illustrations appear in the listings themselves, the respective reference reads, for example, W **153**, thus indicating that the watermark will be found in the normal sequence of illustrations as (type) **153**.

The general types are as follows, with an example of each quoted.

W	*Description*	*Example*
w **1**	Large Star	St. Helena No. 1
w **2**	Small Star	Turks Is. No. 4
w **3**	Broad (pointed) Star	Grenada No. 24
w **4**	Crown (over) CC, small stamp	Antigua No. 13
w **5**	Crown (over) CC, large stamp	Antigua No. 31
w **6**	Crown (over) CA, small stamp	Antigua No. 21
w **7**	Crown CA (CA over Crown), large stamp	Sierra Leone No. 54
w **8**	Multiple Crown CA	Antigua No. 41
w **9**	Multiple Script CA	Seychelles No. 158
w **9***a*	do. Error	Seychelles No. 158a
w **9***b*	do. Error	Seychelles No. 158b
w **10**	V over Crown	N.S.W. No. 327
w **11**	Crown over A	N.S.W. No. 347

CC in these watermarks is an abbreviation for "Crown Colonies" and CA for "Crown Agents". Watermarks w **1**, w **2** and w **3** are on stamps printed by Perkins, Bacon; w **4** onwards on stamps from De La Rue and other printers.

w **1**
Large Star

w **2**
Small Star

w **3**
Broad-pointed Star

Watermark w **1**, *Large Star*, measures 15 to 16 mm across the star from point to point and about 27 mm from centre to centre vertically between stars in the sheet. It was made for long stamps like Ceylon 1857 and St. Helena 1856.

Watermark w **2**, *Small Star* is of similar design but measures 12 to 13$^{1}/_{2}$mm from point to point and 24 mm from centre to centre vertically. It was for use with ordinary-size stamps such as Grenada 1863–71.

When the Large Star watermark was used with the smaller stamps it only occasionally comes in the centre of the paper. It is frequently so misplaced as to show portions of two stars above and below and this eccentricity will very often help in determining the watermark.

Watermark w **3**, *Broad-pointed Star*, resembles w **1** but the points are broader.

w **4**
Crown (over) CC

w **5**
Crown (over) CC

Two *Crown (over) CC* watermarks were used:
w **4** was for stamps of ordinary size and w **5** for those of larger size.

w **6**
Crown (over) CA

w **7**
CA over Crown

Two watermarks of *Crown CA* type were used, w **6** being for stamps of ordinary size. The other, w **7**, is properly described as *CA over Crown*. It was specially made for paper on which it was intended to print long fiscal stamps: that some were used postally accounts for the appearance of w **7** in the Catalogue. The watermark occupies twice the space of the ordinary Crown CA watermark, w **6**. Stamps of normal size printed on paper with w **7** watermark show it *sideways*; it takes a horizontal pair of stamps to show the entire watermark.

w **8**
Multiple Crown CA

w **9**
Multiple Script CA

Multiple watermarks began in 1904 with w **8**, *Multiple Crown CA,* changed from 1921 to w **9**, *Multiple Script CA*. On stamps of ordinary size portions of two or three watermarks appear and on the large-sized stamps a greater number can be observed. The change to letters in script character with w **9** was accompanied by a Crown of distinctly different shape.

It seems likely that there were at least two dandy rolls for each Crown Agents watermark in use at any one time with a reserve roll being employed when the normal one was withdrawn for maintenance or repair.

Both the Mult Crown CA and the Mult Script CA types exist with one or other of the letters omitted from individual impressions. It is possible that most of these occur from the reserve rolls as they have only been found on certain issues. The MCA watermark experienced such problems during the early 1920s and the Script over a longer period from the early 1940s until 1951.

During the 1920s damage must also have occurred on one of the Crowns as a substituted Crown has been found on certain issues. This is smaller than the normal and consists of an oval base joined to two upright ovals with a circle positioned between their upper ends. The upper line of the Crown's base is omitted, as are the left and right-hand circles at the top and also the cross over the centre circle.

Substituted Crown

The *Multiple Script CA* watermark, w **9**, is known with two errors, recurring among the 1950–52 printings of several territories. In the first a crown has fallen away from the dandy-roll that impresses the watermark into the paper pulp. It gives w **9a**, *Crown missing*, but this omission has been found in both "Crown only" (*illustrated*) and "Crown CA" rows. The resulting faulty paper was used for Bahamas, Johore, Seychelles and the postage due stamps of nine colonies

w **9a**: Error, Crown missing

w **9b**: Error, St. Edward's Crown

When the omission was noticed a second mishap occurred, which was to insert a wrong crown in the space, giving w **9b**, St. Edward's Crown. This produced varieties in Bahamas, Perlis, St. Kitts-Nevis and Singapore and the incorrect crown likewise occurs in (Crown only) and (Crown CA) rows.

w **10**
V over Crown

w **11**
Crown over A

Resuming the general types, two watermarks found in issues of several Australian States are: w **10**, *V over Crown*, and w **11**, *Crown over A*.

w **12**
Multiple St. Edward's Crown Block CA

w **13**
Multiple PTM

The *Multiple St. Edward's Crown Block CA* watermark, w **12**, was introduced in 1957 and besides the change in the Crown (from that used in Multiple Crown Script CA, w **9**) the letters reverted to block capitals. The new watermark began to appear sideways in 1966 and these stamps are generally listed as separate sets.

The watermark w **13**, *Multiple PTM*, was introduced for new Malaysian issues in November 1961.

w **14**
Multiple Crown CA Diagonal

By 1974 the two dandy-rolls (the "upright" and the "sideways") for w **12** were wearing out; the Crown Agents therefore discontinued using the sideways watermark one and retained the other only as a stand-by. A new dandy-roll with the pattern of w **14.** *Multiple Crown CA Diagonal,* was introduced and first saw use with some Churchill Centenary issues.

The new watermark has the design arranged in gradually spiralling rows. It is improved in design to allow smooth passage over the paper (the gaps between letters and rows had caused jolts in previous dandy-rolls) and the sharp corners and angles, where fibres used to accumulate, have been eliminated by rounding.

This watermark has no "normal" sideways position amongst the different printers using it. To avoid confusion our more specialised listings do not rely on such terms as "sideways inverted" but describe the direction in which the watermark points.

w **16**
Multiple Crown Script CA Diagonal

A new Crown Agents watermark was introduced during 1985, w **16**, *Multiple Crown Script CA Diagonal.* This was very similar to the previous w **14**, but showed "CA" in script rather than block letters. It was first used on the omnibus series of stamps commemorating the Life and Times of Queen Elizabeth the Queen Mother.

6. Colours

Stamps in two or three colours have these named in order of appearance, from the centre moving outwards. Four colours or more are usually listed as multicoloured.

In compound colour names the second is the predominant one, thus:

orange-red = a red tending towards orange;
red-orange = an orange containing more red than usual.

Standard colours used. The 200 colours most used for stamp identification are given in the Stanley Gibbons Stamp Colour Key. The Catalogue has used the Stamp Colour Key as standard for describing new issues for some years. The names are also introduced as lists are rewritten, though exceptions are made for those early issues where traditional names have become universally established.

Determining colours. When comparing actual stamps with colour samples in the Stamp Colour Key, view in a good north daylight (or its best substitute; fluorescent "colour matching" light). Sunshine is not recommended. Choose a solid portion of the stamp design; if available, marginal markings such as solid bars of colour or colour check dots are helpful. Shading lines in the design can be misleading as they appear lighter than solid colour. Postmarked portions of a stamp appear darker than normal. If more than one colour is present, mask off the extraneous ones as the eye tends to mix them.

Errors of colour. Major colour errors in stamps or overprints which qualify for listing are: wrong colours; one colour inverted in relation to the rest; albinos (colourless impressions), where these have Expert Committee certificates; colours completely omitted, but only on unused stamps (if found on used stamps the information is footnoted) and with good credentials, missing colours being frequently faked.

Colours only partially omitted are not recognised, Colour shifts, however spectacular, are not listed.

Shades. Shades in philately refer to variations in the intensity of a colour or the presence of differing amounts of other colours. They are particularly significant when they can be linked to specific printings. In general, shades need to be quite marked to fall within the scope of this Catalogue; it does not favour nowadays listing the often numerous shades of a stamp, but chooses a single applicable colour name which will indicate particular groups of outstanding shades. Furthermore, the listings refer to colours as issued; they may deteriorate into something different through the passage of time.

Modern colour printing by lithography is prone to marked differences of shade, even within a single run, and variations can occur within the same sheet. Such shades are not listed.

Aniline colours. An aniline colour meant originally one derived from coal-tar; it now refers more widely to colour of a particular brightness suffused on the surface of a stamp and showing through clearly on the back.

Colours of overprints and surcharges. All overprints and surcharges are in black unless stated otherwise in the heading or after the description of the stamp.

7. Specimen Stamps

Originally, stamps overprinted SPECIMEN were circulated to postmasters or kept in official records, but after the establishment of the Universal Postal Union supplies were sent to Berne for distribution to the postal administrations of member countries.

During the period 1884 to 1928 most of the stamps of British Crown Colonies required for this purpose were overprinted SPECIMEN in various shapes and sizes by their printers from typeset formes. Some locally produced provisionals were handstamped locally, as were sets prepared for presentation. From 1928 stamps were punched with holes forming the word SPECIMEN, each firm of printers using a different machine or machines. From 1948 the stamps supplied for UPU distribution were no longer punctured.

Stamps of some other Commonwealth territories were overprinted or handstamped locally, while stamps of Great Britain and those overprinted for use in overseas postal agencies (mostly of the higher denominations) bore SPECIMEN overprints and handstamps applied by the Inland Revenue or the Post Office.

De La Rue & Co. Ltd.

Bradbury, Wilkinson & Co. Ltd.

Waterlow & Sons Ltd.

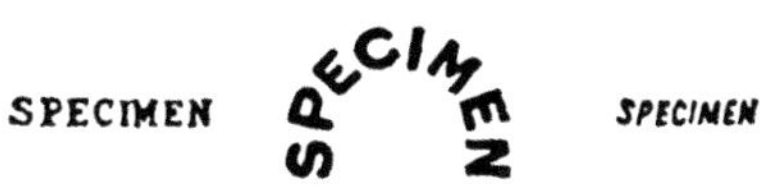

Great Britain overprints

Some of the commoner types of overprints or punctures are illustrated here. Collectors are warned that dangerous forgeries of the punctured type exist.

The *Stanley Gibbons Commonwealth Catalogues* record those Specimen overprints or perforations intended for distribution by the UPU to member countries. In addition the Specimen overprints of Australia and its dependent territories, which were sold to collectors by the Post Office, are also included.

Various Perkins Bacon issues exist obliterated with a "CANCELLED" within an oval of bars handstamp.

Perkins Bacon "CANCELLED" Handstamp

This was applied to six examples of those issues available in 1861 which were then given to members of Sir Rowland Hill's family. 75 different stamps (including four from Chile) are recorded with this handstamp although others may possibly exist. The unauthorised gift of these "CANCELLED" stamps to the Hill family was a major factor in the loss of the Agent General for the Crown Colonies (the forerunner of the Crown Agents) contracts by Perkins Bacon in the following year. Where examples of these scarce items are known to be in private hands the catalogue provides a price.

For full details of these stamps see *CANCELLED by Perkins Bacon* by Peter Jaffé (published by Spink in 1998).

All other Specimens are outside the scope of this volume.

Specimens are not quoted in Great Britain as they are fully listed in the Stanley Gibbons *Great Britain Specialised Catalogue*.

In specifying type of specimen for individual high-value stamps, "H/S" means handstamped, "Optd" is overprinted and "Perf" is punctured. Some sets occur mixed, e.g. "Optd/Perf". If unspecified, the type is apparent from the date or it is the same as for the lower values quoted as a set.

Prices. Prices for stamps up to £1 are quoted in sets; higher values are priced singly. Where specimens exist in more than one type the price quoted is for the cheapest. Specimen stamps have rarely survived even as pairs; these and strips of three, four or five are worth considerably more than singles.

8. Luminescence

Machines which sort mail electronically have been introduced in recent years. In consequence some countries have issued stamps on flourescent or phosphorescent papers, while others have marked their stamps with phosphor bands.

The various papers can only be distinguished by ultraviolet lamps emitting particular wavelengths. They are separately listed only when the stamps have some other means of distinguishing them, visible without the use of these lamps. Where this is not so, the papers are recorded in footnotes or headings.

For this catalogue we do not consider it appropriate that collectors be compelled to have the use of an ultraviolet lamp before being able to identify stamps by our listings. Some experience will also be found necessary in interpreting the results given by ultraviolet. Collectors using the lamps, nevertheless, should exercise great care in their use as exposure to their light is potentially dangerous to the eyes.

Phosphor bands are listable, since they are visible to the naked eye (by holding stamps at an angle to the light and looking along them, the bands appear dark). Stamps existing with or without phosphor bands or with differing numbers of bands are given separate listings. Varieties such as double bands, bands omitted, misplaced or printed on the back are not listed.

Detailed descriptions appear at appropriate places in

the listings in explanation of luminescent papers; see, for example, Australia above No.363, Canada above Nos. 472 and 611, Cook Is. above 249, etc.

For Great Britain, where since 1959 phosphors have played a prominent and intricate part in stamp issues, the main notes above Nos. 599 and 723 should be studied, as well as the footnotes to individual listings where appropriate. In general the classification is as follows.

Stamps with phosphor bands are those where a separate cylinder applies the phosphor after the stamps are printed. Issues with "all-over" phosphor have the "band" covering the entire stamp. Parts of the stamp covered by phosphor bands, or the entire surface for "all-over" phosphor versions, appear matt. Stamps on phosphorised paper have the phosphor added to the paper coating before the stamps are printed. Issues on this paper have a completely shiny surface.

Further particularisation of phosphor – their methods of printing and the colours they exhibit under ultraviolet – is outside the scope. The more specialised listings should be consulted for this information.

9. Coil Stamps

Stamps issued only in coil form are given full listing. If stamps are issued in both sheets and coils the coil stamps are listed separately only where there is some feature (e.g. perforation or watermark sideways) by which singles can be distinguished. Coil stamps containing different stamps *se-tenant* are also listed.

Coil join pairs are too random and too easily faked to permit of listing; similarly ignored are coil stamps which have accidentally suffered an extra row of perforations from the claw mechanism in a malfunctioning vending machine.

10. Stamp Booklets

Stamp booklets are now listed in this catalogue.

Single stamps from booklets are listed if they are distinguishable in some way (such as watermark or perforation) from similar sheet stamps.

Booklet panes are listed where they contain stamps of different denominations *se-tenant*, where stamp-size labels are included, or where such panes are otherwise identifiable. Booklet panes are placed in the listing under the lowest denomination present.

Particular perforations (straight edges) are covered by appropriate notes.

11. Miniature Sheets and Sheetlets

We distinguish between "miniature sheets" and "sheetlets" and this affects the catalogue numbering. An item in sheet form that is postally valid, containing a single stamp, pair, block or set of stamps, with wide, inscribed and/or decorative margins, is a miniature sheet if it is sold at post offices as an indivisable entity. As such the Catalogue allots a single MS number and describes what stamps make it up. The sheetlet or small sheet differs in that the individual stamps are intended to be purchased separately for postal purposes. For sheetlets, all the component postage stamps are numbered individually and the composition explained in a footnote. Note that the definitions refer to post office sale—not how items may be subsequently offered by stamp dealers.

12. Forgeries and Fakes

Forgeries. Where space permits, notes are considered if they can give a concise description that will permit unequivocal detection of a forgery. Generalised warnings, lacking detail, are not nowadays inserted, since their value to the collector is problematic.

Forged cancellations have also been applied to genuine stamps. This catalogue includes notes regarding those manufactured by "Madame Joseph", together with the cancellation dates known to exist. It should be remembered that these dates also exist as genuine cancellations.

For full details of these see *Madame Joseph Forged Postmarks* by Derick Worboys (published by the Royal Philatelic Society London and the British Philatelic Trust in 1994) or *Madame Joseph Revisited* by Brian Cartwright (published by the Royal Philatelic Society London in 2005).

Fakes. Unwitting fakes are numerous, particularly "new shades" which are colour changelings brought about by exposure to sunlight, soaking in water contaminated with dyes from adherent paper, contact with oil and dirt from a pocketbook, and so on. Fraudulent operators, in addition, can offer to arrange: removal of hinge marks; repairs of thins on white or coloured papers; replacement of missing margins or perforations; reperforating in true or false gauges; removal of fiscal cancellations; rejoining of severed pairs, strips and blocks; and (a major hazard) regumming. Collectors can only be urged to purchase from reputable sources and to insist upon Expert Committee certification where there is any kind of doubt.

The Catalogue can consider footnotes about fakes where these are specific enough to assist in detection.

ACKNOWLEDGMENTS

We are grateful to individual collectors, members of the philatelic trade and specialist societies and study circles for their assistance in improving and extending the Stanley Gibbons range of catalogues. The addresses of societies and study circles relevant to this volume are:

Malaya Study Group
Membership Secretary: Mr D. Tett,
PO Box 34,
Wheathampstead, Herts AL4 8JY

Sarawat Specialists Society
Secretary: Dr J. Higgins
The Stone House, 31 Grimston Road
South Woolton, Kings Lynn, Norfolk PE30 3HT

Abbreviations

Printers

A.B.N. Co.	American Bank Note Co, New York.
B.A.B.N.	British American Bank Note Co. Ottawa
B.D.T.	B.D.T. International Security Printing Ltd, Dublin, Ireland
B.W.	Bradbury Wilkinson & Co, Ltd.
Cartor	Cartor S.A., La Loupe, France
C.B.N.	Canadian Bank Note Co, Ottawa.
Continental	Continental Bank Note Co. B.N. Co.
Courvoisier	Imprimerie Courvoisier S.A., La-Chaux-de-Fonds, Switzerland.
D.L.R.	De La Rue & Co, Ltd, London.
Enschedé	Joh. Enschedé en Zonen, Haarlem, Netherlands.
Harrison	Harrison & Sons, Ltd. London
P.B.	Perkins Bacon Ltd, London.
Questa	Questa Colour Security Printers Ltd, London
Walsall	Walsall Security Printers Ltd
Waterlow	Waterlow & Sons, Ltd, London.

General Abbreviations

Alph	Alphabet
Anniv	Anniversary
Comp	Compound (perforation)
Des	Designer; designed
Diag	Diagonal; diagonally
Eng	Engraver; engraved
F.C.	Fiscal Cancellation
H/S	Handstamped
Horiz	Horizontal; horizontally
Imp, Imperf	Imperforate
Inscr	Inscribed
L	Left
Litho	Lithographed
mm	Millimetres
MS	Miniature sheet
N.Y.	New York
Opt(d)	Overprint(ed)
P or P-c	Pen-cancelled
P, Pf or Perf	Perforated
Photo	Photogravure
Pl	Plate
Pr	Pair
Ptd	Printed
Ptg	Printing
R	Right
R.	Row
Recess	Recess-printed
Roto	Rotogravure
Roul	Rouletted
S	Specimen (overprint)
Surch	Surcharge(d)
T.C.	Telegraph Cancellation
T	Type
Typo	Typographed
Un	Unused
Us	Used
Vert	Vertical; vertically
W or wmk	Watermark
Wmk s	Watermark sideways

(†) = Does not exist

(–) (or blank price column) = Exists, or may exist, but no market price is known.

/ between colours means "on" and the colour following is that of the paper on which the stamp is printed.

Colours of Stamps

Bl (blue); blk (black); brn (brown); car, carm (carmine); choc (chocolate); clar (claret); emer (emerald); grn (green); ind (indigo); mag (magenta); mar (maroon); mult (multicoloured); mve (mauve); ol (olive); orge (orange); pk (pink); pur (purple); scar (scarlet); sep (sepia); turq (turquoise); ultram (ultramarine); verm (vermilion); vio (violet); yell (yellow).

Colour of Overprints and Surcharges

(B.) = blue, (Blk.) = black, (Br.) = brown, (C.) = carmine, (G.) = green, (Mag.) = magenta, (Mve.) = mauve, (Ol.) = olive, (O.) = orange, (P.) = purple, (Pk.) = pink, (R.) = red, (Sil.) = silver, (V.) = violet, (Vm.) or (Verm.) = vermilion, (W.) = white, (Y.) = yellow.

Arabic Numerals

As in the case of European figures, the details of the Arabic numerals vary in different stamp designs, but they should be readily recognised with the aid of this illustration.

٠	١	٢	٣	٤	٥	٦	٧	٨	٩
0	1	2	3	4	5	6	7	8	9

Features Listing

An at-a-glace guide to what's in the Stanley Gibbons catalogues

Area	Feature	Collect British Stamps	Stamps of the World	Thematic Catalogues	Comprehensive Catalogue, Parts 1-22 (including Commonwealth and British Empire Stamps and country catalogues)	Great Britain Concise	Specialised catalogues
General	SG number	√	√	√	√	√	√
General	Specialised Catalogue number						√
General	Year of issue of first stamp in design	√	√	√	√	√	√
General	Exact date of issue of each design				√	√	√
General	Face value information	√	√	√	√	√	√
General	Historical and geographical information	√	√	√	√	√	√
General	General currency information, including dates used	√	√	√	√	√	√
General	Country name	√	√	√	√	√	√
General	Booklet panes				√	√	√
General	Coil stamps				√		√
General	First Day Covers	√				√	√
General	Brief footnotes on key areas of note	√	√	√	√	√	√
General	Detailed footnotes on key areas of note				√	√	√
General	Extra background information				√	√	√
General	Miniature sheet information (including size in mm)	√	√	√	√	√	√
General	Sheetlets				√		
General	Stamp booklets				√	√	√
General	Perkins Bacon "Cancelled"				√		
General	PHQ Cards	√				√	√
General	Post Office Label Sheets					√	
General	Post Office Yearbooks	√				√	√
General	Presentation and Souvenir Packs	√				√	√
General	*Se-tenant* pairs	√			√	√	√
General	Watermark details - errors, varieties, positions				√	√	√
General	Watermark illustrations	√			√	√	√
General	Watermark types	√			√	√	√
General	Forgeries noted				√		√
General	Surcharges and overprint information	√	√	√	√	√	√
Design and Description	Colour description, simplified		√	√			
Design and Description	Colour description, extended	√			√	√	√
Design and Description	Set design summary information	√	√	√	√	√	√
Design and Description	Designer name				√	√	√
Design and Description	Short design description	√	√	√	√	√	√

Area	Feature	Collect British Stamps	Stamps of the World	Thematic Catalogues	Comprehensive Catalogue, Parts 1-22 (including Commonwealth and British Empire Stamps and country catalogues)	Great Britain Concise	Specialised catalogues
Design and Description	Shade varieties				√	√	√
Design and Description	Type number	√	√		√	√	√
Illustrations	Multiple stamps from set illustrated	√			√	√	√
Illustrations	A Stamp from each set illustrated in full colour (where possible, otherwise mono)	√	√	√	√	√	√
Price	Catalogue used price	√	√	√	√	√	√
Price	Catalogue unused price	√	√	√	√	√	√
Price	Price - booklet panes				√	√	√
Price	Price - shade varieties				√	√	√
Price	On cover and on piece price				√	√	√
Price	Detailed GB pricing breakdown	√			√	√	√
Print and Paper	Basic printing process information	√	√	√	√	√	√
Print and Paper	Detailed printing process information, e.g. Mill sheets				√		√
Print and Paper	Paper information				√		√
Print and Paper	Detailed perforation information	√			√	√	√
Print and Paper	Details of research findings relating to printing processes and history						√
Print and Paper	Paper colour	√	√		√	√	√
Print and Paper	Paper description to aid identification				√	√	√
Print and Paper	Paper type				√	√	√
Print and Paper	Ordinary or chalk-surfaced paper				√	√	√
Print and Paper	Embossing omitted note						√
Print and Paper	Essays, Die Proofs, Plate Descriptions and Proofs, Colour Trials information						√
Print and Paper	Glazed paper				√	√	√
Print and Paper	Gum details				√		√
Print and Paper	Luminescence/Phosphor bands - general coverage	√			√	√	√
Print and Paper	Luminescence/Phosphor bands - specialised coverage						√
Print and Paper	Overprints and surcharges - including colour information	√	√	√	√	√	√
Print and Paper	Perforation/Imperforate information	√	√		√	√	√
Print and Paper	Perforation errors and varieties				√	√	√
Print and Paper	Print quantities				√		√
Print and Paper	Printing errors				√	√	√
Print and Paper	Printing flaws						√
Print and Paper	Printing varieties				√	√	√
Print and Paper	Punctured stamps - where official				√		
Print and Paper	Sheet positions				√	√	√
Print and Paper	Specialised plate number information						√
Print and Paper	Specimen overprints (only for Commonwealth & GB)				√	√	√
Print and Paper	Underprints					√	√
Print and Paper	Visible Plate numbers	√			√	√	√
Print and Paper	Yellow and Green paper listings				√		√
Index	Design index	√			√	√	

Stanley Gibbons Publications

1 Commonwealth & British Empire Stamps 1840–1970

Commonwealth Country Catalogues
Australia and Dependencies (5th edition, 2009)
Bangladesh, Pakistan & Sri Lanka (1st edition, 2004)
Belize, Guyana, Trinidad & Tobago (1st edition, 2009)
Brunei, Malaysia & Singapore (3rd edition, 2009)
Canada (3rd edition, 2008)
Central Africa (2nd edition, 2008)
Cyprus, Gibraltar & Malta (2nd edition, 2008)
East Africa with Egypt and Sudan (1st edition, 2006)
Eastern Pacific (1st edition, 2007)
Falkland Islands (3rd edition, 2008)
Hong Kong (2nd edition, 2007)
India (including Convention and Feudatory States) (3rd edition, 2009)
Indian Ocean (1st edition, 2006)
Ireland (4th edition, 2008)
Leeward Islands (1st edition, 2007)
New Zealand (3rd edition, 2009)
Northern Caribbean, Bahamas & Bermuda (2nd edition, 2009)
St. Helena & Dependencies (3rd edition, 2007)
Southern Africa (2nd edition, 2007)
West Africa (1st edition, 2009)
Western Pacific (2nd edition, 2009)
Windward Islands and Barbados (1st edition, 2007)

Foreign Countries
2 ***Austria & Hungary*** (7th edition, 2009)
3 ***Balkans*** (5th edition, 2009)
4 ***Benelux*** (5th edition, 2003)
5 ***Czechoslovakia & Poland*** (6th edition, 2002)
6 ***France*** (6th edition, 2006)
7 ***Germany*** (8th edition, 2007)
8 ***Italy & Switzerland*** (7th edition, 2010)
9 ***Portugal & Spain*** (5th edition, 2004)
10 ***Russia*** (6th edition, 2008)
11 ***Scandinavia*** (6th edition, 2008)
12 ***Africa since Independence A-E*** (2nd edition, 1983)
13 ***Africa since Independence F-M*** (1st edition, 1981)
14 ***Africa since Independence N-Z*** (1st edition, 1981)
15 ***Central America*** (3rd edition, 2007)
16 ***Central Asia*** (4th edition, 2006)
17 ***China*** (7th edition, 2006)
18 ***Japan & Korea*** (5th edition, 2008)
19 ***Middle East*** (7th edition, 2009)
20 ***South America*** (4th edition, 2008)
21 ***South-East Asia*** (4th edition, 2004)
22 ***United States*** (6th edition, 2005)

Great Britain Specialised Catalogues
Volume 1 ***Queen Victoria*** (15th edition, 2008)
Volume 2 ***King Edward VII to King George VI*** (13th edition, 2009)
Volume 3 ***Queen Elizabeth II Pre-decimal issues*** (11th edition, 2006)
Volume 4 ***Queen Elizabeth II Decimal Definitive Issues – Part 1*** (10th edition, 2008)
Volume 5 ***Queen Elizabeth II Decimal Special Issues*** (3rd edition, 1998 with 1998-99 and 2000/1 Supplements)

Thematic Catalogues
Stanley Gibbons Catalogues for use with ***Stamps of the World.***
Collect Aircraft on Stamps (2nd edition, 2009)
Collect Birds on Stamps (5th edition, 2003)
Collect Chess on Stamps (2nd edition, 1999)
Collect Fish on Stamps (1st edition, 1999)
Collect Fungi on Stamps (2nd edition, 1997)
Collect Motor Vehicles on Stamps (1st edition 2004)

Other Publications
Philatelic Terms Illustrated (4th edition, 2003)
Collect British Stamps (61st edition, 2010)
Great Britain Concise Stamp Catalogue (24th edition, 2009)
How to Identify Stamps (4th edition, 2007)
Collect Channel Islands and Isle of Man Stamps (25th edition, 2009)
Great Britain Numbers Issued (3rd edition, 2008)
Enjoy Stamp Collecting (7th edition, 2006)

For other titles, and further details on the above, please see *www.stanleygibbons.com*

International Philatelic Glossary

English	French	German	Spanish	Italian
Agate	Agate	Achat	Agata	Agata
Air stamp	Timbre de la poste aérienne	Flugpostmarke	Sello de correo aéreo	Francobollo per posta aerea
Apple Green	Vert-pomme	Apfelgrün	Verde manzana	Verde mela
Barred	Annulé par barres	Balkenentwertung	Anulado con barras	Sbarrato
Bisected	Timbre coupé	Halbiert	Partido en dos	Frazionato
Bistre	Bistre	Bister	Bistre	Bistro
Bistre-brown	Brun-bistre	Bisterbraun	Castaño bistre	Bruno-bistro
Black	Noir	Schwarz	Negro	Nero
Blackish Brown	Brun-noir	Schwärzlichbraun	Castaño negruzco	Bruno nerastro
Blackish Green	Vert foncé	Schwärzlichgrün	Verde negruzco	Verde nerastro
Blackish Olive	Olive foncé	Schwärzlicholiv	Oliva negruzco	Oliva nerastro
Block of four	Bloc de quatre	Viererblock	Bloque de cuatro	Bloco di quattro
Blue	Bleu	Blau	Azul	Azzurro
Blue-green	Vert-bleu	Blaugrün	Verde azul	Verde azzuro
Bluish Violet	Violet bleuâtre	Bläulichviolett	Violeta azulado	Violtto azzurrastro
Booklet	Carnet	Heft	Cuadernillo	Libretto
Bright Blue	Bleu vif	Lebhaftblau	Azul vivo	Azzurro vivo
Bright Green	Vert vif	Lebhaftgrün	Verde vivo	Verde vivo
Bright Purple	Mauve vif	Lebhaftpurpur	Púrpura vivo	Porpora vivo
Bronze Green	Vert-bronze	Bronzegrün	Verde bronce	Verde bronzo
Brown	Brun	Braun	Castaño	Bruno
Brown-lake	Carmin-brun	Braunlack	Laca castaño	Lacca bruno
Brown-purple	Pourpre-brun	Braunpurpur	Púrpura castaño	Porpora bruno
Brown-red	Rouge-brun	Braunrot	Rojo castaño	Rosso bruno
Buff	Chamois	Sämisch	Anteado	Camoscio
Cancellation	Oblitération	Entwertung	Cancelación	Annullamento
Cancelled	Annulé	Gestempelt	Cancelado	Annullato
Carmine	Carmin	Karmin	Carmín	Carminio
Carmine-red	Rouge-carmin	Karminrot	Rojo carmín	Rosso carminio
Centred	Centré	Zentriert	Centrado	Centrato
Cerise	Rouge-cerise	Kirschrot	Color de ceresa	Color Ciliegia
Chalk-surfaced paper	Papier couché	Kreidepapier	Papel estucado	Carta gessata
Chalky Blue	Bleu terne	Kreideblau	Azul turbio	Azzurro smorto
Charity stamp	Timbre de bienfaisance	Wohltätigkeitsmarke	Sello de beneficenza	Francobollo di beneficenza
Chestnut	Marron	Kastanienbraun	Castaño rojo	Marrone
Chocolate	Chocolat	Schokolade	Chocolate	Cioccolato
Cinnamon	Cannelle	Zimtbraun	Canela	Cannella
Claret	Grenat	Weinrot	Rojo vinoso	Vinaccia
Cobalt	Cobalt	Kobalt	Cobalto	Cobalto
Colour	Couleur	Farbe	Color	Colore
Comb-perforation	Dentelure en peigne	Kammzähnung, Reihenzähnung	Dentado de peine	Dentellatura e pettine
Commemorative stamp	Timbre commémoratif	Gedenkmarke	Sello conmemorativo	Francobollo commemorativo
Crimson	Cramoisi	Karmesin	Carmesí	Cremisi
Deep Blue	Blue foncé	Dunkelblau	Azul oscuro	Azzurro scuro
Deep bluish Green	Vert-bleu foncé	Dunkelbläulichgrün	Verde azulado oscuro	Verde azzurro scuro

English	French	German	Spanish	Italian
Design	Dessin	Markenbild	Diseño	Disegno
Die	Matrice	Urstempel. Type, Platte	Cuño	Conio, Matrice
Double	Double	Doppelt	Doble	Doppio
Drab	Olive terne	Trüboliv	Oliva turbio	Oliva smorto
Dull Green	Vert terne	Trübgrün	Verde turbio	Verde smorto
Dull purple	Mauve terne	Trübpurpur	Púrpura turbio	Porpora smorto
Embossing	Impression en relief	Prägedruck	Impresión en relieve	Impressione a relievo
Emerald	Vert-eméraude	Smaragdgrün	Esmeralda	Smeraldo
Engraved	Gravé	Graviert	Grabado	Inciso
Error	Erreur	Fehler, Fehldruck	Error	Errore
Essay	Essai	Probedruck	Ensayo	Saggio
Express letter stamp	Timbre pour lettres par exprès	Eilmarke	Sello de urgencia	Francobollo per espresso
Fiscal stamp	Timbre fiscal	Stempelmarke	Sello fiscal	Francobollo fiscale
Flesh	Chair	Fleischfarben	Carne	Carnicino
Forgery	Faux, Falsification	Fälschung	Falsificación	Falso, Falsificazione
Frame	Cadre	Rahmen	Marco	Cornice
Granite paper	Papier avec fragments de fils de soie	Faserpapier	Papel con filamentos	Carto con fili di seta
Green	Vert	Grün	Verde	Verde
Greenish Blue	Bleu verdâtre	Grünlichblau	Azul verdoso	Azzurro verdastro
Greenish Yellow	Jaune-vert	Grünlichgelb	Amarillo verdoso	Giallo verdastro
Grey	Gris	Grau	Gris	Grigio
Grey-blue	Bleu-gris	Graublau	Azul gris	Azzurro grigio
Grey-green	Vert gris	Graugrün	Verde gris	Verde grigio
Gum	Gomme	Gummi	Goma	Gomma
Gutter	Interpanneau	Zwischensteg	Espacio blanco entre dos grupos	Ponte
Imperforate	Non-dentelé	Geschnitten	Sin dentar	Non dentellato
Indigo	Indigo	Indigo	Azul indigo	Indaco
Inscription	Inscription	Inschrift	Inscripción	Dicitura
Inverted	Renversé	Kopfstehend	Invertido	Capovolto
Issue	Émission	Ausgabe	Emisión	Emissione
Laid	Vergé	Gestreift	Listado	Vergato
Lake	Lie de vin	Lackfarbe	Laca	Lacca
Lake-brown	Brun-carmin	Lackbraun	Castaño laca	Bruno lacca
Lavender	Bleu-lavande	Lavendel	Color de alhucema	Lavanda
Lemon	Jaune-citron	Zitrongelb	Limón	Limone
Light Blue	Bleu clair	Hellblau	Azul claro	Azzurro chiaro
Lilac	Lilas	Lila	Lila	Lilla
Line perforation	Dentelure en lignes	Linienzähnung	Dentado en linea	Dentellatura lineare
Lithography	Lithographie	Steindruck	Litografía	Litografia
Local	Timbre de poste locale	Lokalpostmarke	Emisión local	Emissione locale
Lozenge roulette	Percé en losanges	Rautenförmiger Durchstich	Picadura en rombos	Perforazione a losanghe
Magenta	Magenta	Magentarot	Magenta	Magenta
Margin	Marge	Rand	Borde	Margine
Maroon	Marron pourpré	Dunkelrotpurpur	Púrpura rojo oscuro	Marrone rossastro
Mauve	Mauve	Malvenfarbe	Malva	Malva
Multicoloured	Polychrome	Mehrfarbig	Multicolores	Policromo
Myrtle Green	Vert myrte	Myrtengrün	Verde mirto	Verde mirto
New Blue	Bleu ciel vif	Neublau	Azul nuevo	Azzurro nuovo
Newspaper stamp	Timbre pour journaux	Zeitungsmarke	Sello para periódicos	Francobollo per giornali

English	French	German	Spanish	Italian
Obliteration	Oblitération	Abstempelung	Matasello	Annullamento
Obsolete	Hors (de) cours	Ausser Kurs	Fuera de curso	Fuori corso
Ochre	Ocre	Ocker	Ocre	Ocra
Official stamp	Timbre de service	Dienstmarke	Sello de servicio	Francobollo di
Olive-brown	Brun-olive	Olivbraun	Castaño oliva	Bruno oliva
Olive-green	Vert-olive	Olivgrün	Verde oliva	Verde oliva
Olive-grey	Gris-olive	Olivgrau	Gris oliva	Grigio oliva
Olive-yellow	Jaune-olive	Olivgelb	Amarillo oliva	Giallo oliva
Orange	Orange	Orange	Naranja	Arancio
Orange-brown	Brun-orange	Orangebraun	Castaño naranja	Bruno arancio
Orange-red	Rouge-orange	Orangerot	Rojo naranja	Rosso arancio
Orange-yellow	Jaune-orange	Orangegelb	Amarillo naranja	Giallo arancio
Overprint	Surcharge	Aufdruck	Sobrecarga	Soprastampa
Pair	Paire	Paar	Pareja	Coppia
Pale	Pâle	Blass	Pálido	Pallido
Pane	Panneau	Gruppe	Grupo	Gruppo
Paper	Papier	Papier	Papel	Carta
Parcel post stamp	Timbre pour colis postaux	Paketmarke	Sello para paquete postal	Francobollo per pacchi postali
Pen-cancelled	Oblitéré à plume	Federzugentwertung	Cancelado a pluma	Annullato a penna
Percé en arc	Percé en arc	Bogenförmiger Durchstich	Picadura en forma de arco	Perforazione ad arco
Percé en scie	Percé en scie	Bogenförmiger Durchstich	Picado en sierra	Foratura a sega
Perforated	Dentelé	Gezähnt	Dentado	Dentellato
Perforation	Dentelure	Zähnung	Dentar	Dentellatura
Photogravure	Photogravure, Heliogravure	Rastertiefdruck	Fotograbado	Rotocalco
Pin perforation	Percé en points	In Punkten durchstochen	Horadado con alfileres	Perforato a punti
Plate	Planche	Platte	Plancha	Lastra, Tavola
Plum	Prune	Pflaumenfarbe	Color de ciruela	Prugna
Postage Due stamp	Timbre-taxe	Portomarke	Sello de tasa	Segnatasse
Postage stamp	Timbre-poste	Briefmarke, Freimarke, Postmarke	Sello de correos	Francobollo postale
Postal fiscal stamp	Timbre fiscal-postal	Stempelmarke als Postmarke verwendet	Sello fiscal-postal	Fiscale postale
Postmark	Oblitération postale	Poststempel	Matasello	Bollo
Printing	Impression, Tirage	Druck	Impresión	Stampa, Tiratura
Proof	Épreuve	Druckprobe	Prueba de impresión	Prova
Provisionals	Timbres provisoires	Provisorische Marken. Provisorien	Provisionales	Provvisori
Prussian Blue	Bleu de Prusse	Preussischblau	Azul de Prusia	Azzurro di Prussia
Purple	Pourpre	Purpur	Púrpura	Porpora
Purple-brown	Brun-pourpre	Purpurbraun	Castaño púrpura	Bruno porpora
Recess-printing	Impression en taille douce	Tiefdruck	Grabado	Incisione
Red	Rouge	Rot	Rojo	Rosso
Red-brown	Brun-rouge	Rotbraun	Castaño rojizo	Bruno rosso
Reddish Lilac	Lilas rougeâtre	Rötlichlila	Lila rojizo	Lilla rossastro
Reddish Purple	Poupre-rouge	Rötlichpurpur	Púrpura rojizo	Porpora rossastro
Reddish Violet	Violet rougeâtre	Rötlichviolett	Violeta rojizo	Violetto rossastro
Red-orange	Orange rougeâtre	Rotorange	Naranja rojizo	Arancio rosso
Registration stamp	Timbre pour lettre chargée (recommandée)	Einschreibemarke	Sello de certificado lettere	Francobollo per raccomandate
Reprint	Réimpression	Neudruck	Reimpresión	Ristampa
Reversed	Retourné	Umgekehrt	Invertido	Rovesciato

English	French	German	Spanish	Italian
Rose	Rose	Rosa	Rosa	Rosa
Rose-red	Rouge rosé	Rosarot	Rojo rosado	Rosso rosa
Rosine	Rose vif	Lebhaftrosa	Rosa vivo	Rosa vivo
Roulette	Percage	Durchstich	Picadura	Foratura
Rouletted	Percé	Durchstochen	Picado	Forato
Royal Blue	Bleu-roi	Königblau	Azul real	Azzurro reale
Sage green	Vert-sauge	Salbeigrün	Verde salvia	Verde salvia
Salmon	Saumon	Lachs	Salmón	Salmone
Scarlet	Écarlate	Scharlach	Escarlata	Scarlatto
Sepia	Sépia	Sepia	Sepia	Seppia
Serpentine roulette	Percé en serpentin	Schlangenliniger Durchstich	Picado a serpentina	Perforazione a serpentina
Shade	Nuance	Tönung	Tono	Gradazione de colore
Sheet	Feuille	Bogen	Hoja	Foglio
Slate	Ardoise	Schiefer	Pizarra	Ardesia
Slate-blue	Bleu-ardoise	Schieferblau	Azul pizarra	Azzurro ardesia
Slate-green	Vert-ardoise	Schiefergrün	Verde pizarra	Verde ardesia
Slate-lilac	Lilas-gris	Schierferlila	Lila pizarra	Lilla ardesia
Slate-purple	Mauve-gris	Schieferpurpur	Púrpura pizarra	Porpora ardesia
Slate-violet	Violet-gris	Schieferviolett	Violeta pizarra	Violetto ardesia
Special delivery stamp	Timbre pour exprès	Eilmarke	Sello de urgencia	Francobollo per espressi
Specimen	Spécimen	Muster	Muestra	Saggio
Steel Blue	Bleu acier	Stahlblau	Azul acero	Azzurro acciaio
Strip	Bande	Streifen	Tira	Striscia
Surcharge	Surcharge	Aufdruck	Sobrecarga	Soprastampa
Tête-bêche	Tête-bêche	Kehrdruck	Tête-bêche	Tête-bêche
Tinted paper	Papier teinté	Getöntes Papier	Papel coloreado	Carta tinta
Too-late stamp	Timbre pour lettres en retard	Verspätungsmarke	Sello para cartas retardadas	Francobollo per le lettere in ritardo
Turquoise-blue	Bleu-turquoise	Türkisblau	Azul turquesa	Azzurro turchese
Turquoise-green	Vert-turquoise	Türkisgrün	Verde turquesa	Verde turchese
Typography	Typographie	Buchdruck	Tipografia	Tipografia
Ultramarine	Outremer	Ultramarin	Ultramar	Oltremare
Unused	Neuf	Ungebraucht	Nuevo	Nuovo
Used	Oblitéré, Usé	Gebraucht	Usado	Usato
Venetian Red	Rouge-brun terne	Venezianischrot	Rojo veneciano	Rosso veneziano
Vermilion	Vermillon	Zinnober	Cinabrio	Vermiglione
Violet	Violet	Violett	Violeta	Violetto
Violet-blue	Bleu-violet	Violettblau	Azul violeta	Azzurro violetto
Watermark	Filigrane	Wasserzeichen	Filigrana	Filigrana
Watermark sideways	Filigrane couché liegend	Wasserzeichen	Filigrana acostado	Filigrana coricata
Wove paper	Papier ordinaire, Papier uni	Einfaches Papier	Papel avitelado	Carta unita
Yellow	Jaune	Gelb	Amarillo	Giallo
Yellow-brown	Brun-jaune	Gelbbraun	Castaño amarillo	Bruno giallo
Yellow-green	Vert-jaune	Gelbgrün	Verde amarillo	Verde giallo
Yellow-olive	Olive-jaunâtre	Gelboliv	Oliva amarillo	Oliva giallastro
Yellow-orange	Orange jaunâtre	Gelborange	Naranja amarillo	Arancio giallastro
Zig-zag roulette	Percé en zigzag	Sägezahnartiger Durchstich	Picado en zigzag	Perforazione a zigzag

British P.O. in Siam

(Bangkok)

An overseas postal service for foreign residents was operated by the British Consulate at Bangkok from 1858. Mail was despatched by steamer to Singapore and from 1876 onwards was increasingly franked with Straits Settlements stamps. These were initially cancelled on arrival at Singapore, but later an oval postmark inscribed "BRITISH CONSULATE BANGKOK" was used. In 1883 a circular "BANGKOK" datestamp was introduced for use with Nos. 1/23. Both cancellations can also be found used on Hong Kong stamps between 1881 and 1885.

(Currency. 100 cents = 1 Straits dollar)

Stamps of Straits Settlements (see Malaysia) cancelled with oval postmark inscribed "BRITISH CONSULATE BANGKOK" around Royal Arms.

1882. Wmk Crown CC (Nos. 11/15, 33, 35).

Z1	2c. brown	£425
Z2	4c. rose	£425
Z3	6c. dull lilac	£475
Z4	8c. orange-yellow	£425
Z5	10c. on 30c. claret (thin "0") (No. 33)	£1100
Z6	10c. on 30c. claret (thick "10") (No. 34)	£1100
Z7	10c. on 30c. claret (thin "1", thick "0") (No. 35)	£1300
Z8	12c. blue	£650

Subsequent Straits Settlements values to 8c. watermarked Crown CA are known used at Bangkok in 1883 and 1884. During this period the stamps overprinted "B" were on sale at the British Post Office.

PRICES FOR STAMPS ON COVER

The issues of the British Post Offices in Siam are worth from × 100 the prices quoted for used stamps when on cover.

B (1) B (2)

1882 (May)–**85**. *Stamps of Straits Settlements optd with T* **1** *or* **2**.

	(a) On No. 9 of 1867.		
1	32c. on 2a. yellow (1885)	£35000	
	(b) On Nos. 11/13, 14a, 15/17 and 19 of 1867–72 and Nos. 48/9 of 1882. Wmk Crown CC.		
2	2c. brown	£3500	£1500
3	4c. rose	£3250	£1300
	a. Opt double	—	£7500
4	5c. purple-brown	£375	£425
5	6c. lilac	£250	£120
	a. Opt Type **2**	†	£1200
6	8c. orange	£2500	£225
7	10c. slate	£450	£150
8	12c. blue	£1000	£475
	a. Opt Type **2**	†	£750
9	24c. green	£700	£150
	a. Opt Type **2**	†	£1000
10	30c. claret	£45000	£30000
11	96c. grey	£7500	£3000
	(c) On Nos. 59/60 of April 1883.		
12	2c. on 32c. pale red (*Wide* "S")	£2750	£2750
13	2c. on 32c. pale red (*Wide* "E")	£3500	£3500
	(d) On Nos. 50/3 of 1882 and Nos. 63/7 of 1883–84. Wmk Crown CA.		
14	2c. brown	£500	£350
	a. Opt Type **2**	†	£1000
15	2c. pale rose (1883)	60·00	45·00
	a. Opt inverted	—	£13000
	b. Opt double	£2750	£2750
	c. Opt treble	£10000	
16	4c. rose (1883)	£650	£325
	a. Opt Type **2**	†	£1000
17	4c. pale brown (1883)	80·00	70·00
	a. Opt double	£3500	
	b. Broken oval	£1100	£1100
18	5c. blue (1884)	£275	£170
19	6c. lilac (1884)	£190	£110
20	8c. orange (1883)	£170	65·00
	a. Opt inverted	£24000	£13000
21	10c. slate (1883)	£170	85·00
22	12c. brown-purple (1883)	£325	£150
23	24c. yellow-green (1884?)	£6000	£3000

Opt Type **2** differs from Type **1** in having the two loops of the "B" almost equal in size with wider internal dimensions. The Type **2** overprints are generally placed higher than Type **1**. It is believed that the two types were both supplied to Bangkok in May 1882.

The prices quoted for the overprint double errors, Nos. 3a, 15b and 17a, are for stamps showing two clear impressions of the overprint. Examples showing partial doubling, on these and other values, are worth a small premium over the price quoted for normal stamps.

No. 17b shows the edge of the central oval broken above the "O" of "POSTAGE". It occurs on R. 10/5 of the lower right pane.

The use of these stamps ceased on 30 June 1885. Siam joined the Universal Postal Union on 1 July 1885.

Brunei

Sultan Hashim Jalil-ul-alam Akamudin, 1885–1906

(Currency. 100 cents = 1 Straits, later Malayan and Brunei, dollar)

For many years the status of the 1895 issue remained uncertain to such an extent that the 1906 provisionals on Labuan were taken to be the first issue of Brunei.

The 1895 "Star and Crescent" design stamps were, from their first appearance, considered bogus or, at best, as an issue made purely for philatelic purposes. Research into the background of the events surrounding the set led to the publication, in 1933, of the original agreement between Sultan Hashim and J. C. Robertson, dated 20 August 1894, which made clear that the stamps fulfilled a genuine postal purpose. Although Robertson and his partners intended to exploit the philatelic sales for their own benefit, the agreement testifies, as does other evidence, to the use of the stamps by the Sultan for his postal service. As Brunei did not, at that time, belong to any local or international postal union, the stamps were only valid within the state or on mail to Labuan or Sarawak. Items for further afield required franking with Labuan stamps in addition. Although most covers surviving are addressed to Robertson's associates, enough commercial covers and cards exist to show that there was, indeed, a postal service.

PRICES FOR STAMPS ON COVER TO 1945

Nos. 1/10 are rare used on cover.

Nos. 11/22	*from* × 30
Nos. 23/33	*from* × 25
Nos. 34/50	*from* × 10
Nos. 51/9	*from* × 12
Nos. 60/78	*from* × 8

The Sarawak Government maintained a post office at the coal mining centre of Brooketon, and the stamps of SARAWAK were used there from 1893 until the office was handed over to Brunei in February 1907.

1 Star and Local Scene

(Litho in Glasgow)

1895 (22 July). P 13–13½.

1	**1**	½c. brown	4·25	20·00
2		1c. brown-lake	3·50	15·00
3		2c. black	4·00	16·00
4		3c. deep blue	3·75	14·00
5		5c. deep blue-green	6·50	17·00
6		8c. plum	6·50	38·00
7		10c. orange-red	8·00	35·00
		a. Imperf (pair)	£2000	
8		25c. turquoise-green	75·00	90·00
9		50c. yellow-green	21·00	£100
10		$1 yellow-olive	23·00	£110
1/10 *Set of* 10			£140	£400

BRUNEI. BRUNEI.

BRUNEI. (2) TWO CENTS. (3) 25 CENTS. (4)

Line through "B" (R. 5/10)

(Optd by Govt Printer, Singapore)

1906 (1 Oct). Nos. 117/26 of Labuan (see North Borneo), optd with T **2**, or surch as T **3** or **4** (25c.), in red. P 13½ or 14 (1c.).

11	1c. black and purple	38·00	55·00
	a. Error. Opt in black	£2250	£2750
	b. Line through "B"	£550	
	c. Perf 13½–14, comp 12–13	£180	
12	2c. on 3c. black and sepia	4·25	14·00
	a. "BRUNEI" double	£3750	£2500
	b. "TWO CENTS" double	£5000	
	c. Line through "B"	£180	
13	2c. on 8c. black and vermilion	27·00	80·00
	a. "TWO CENTS" double	£12000	
	b. "TWO CENTS" omitted (in vert pair with normal)	£13000	
	c. Line through "B"	£500	
14	3c. black and sepia	35·00	85·00
	a. Line through "B"	£500	
15	4c. on 12c. black and yellow	5·00	5·00
	a. Line through "B"	£190	
16	5c. on 16c. green and brown	45·00	75·00
	a. Line through "B"	£600	
17	8c. black and vermilion	10·00	32·00
	a. Line through "B"	£350	
18	10c. on 16c. green and brown	6·50	22·00
	a. Line through "B"	£300	
19	25c. on 16c. green and brown	£100	£120
	a. Line through "B"	£1100	
20	30c. on 16c. green and brown	£100	£120
	a. Line through "B"	£1100	
21	50c. on 16c. green and brown	£100	£120
	a. Line through "B"	£1100	
22	$1 on 8c. black and vermilion	£100	£120
	a. Line through "B"	£1100	
11/22 *Set of* 12		£500	£750

Only one sheet of the 1c. received the black overprint.

The surcharges were applied in settings of 50. Nos. 13a/b occur from one sheet on which the surcharge from the second impression of the setting was misplaced to give two surcharges on row five and none on row ten.

Examples of all values are known showing a forged Brunei postmark dated "13 JUL".

Sultan Mohamed Jemal-ul-Alam, 1906–1924

PRINTERS. All Brunei stamps from Nos. 23 to 113 were recess-printed by De La Rue.

5 View on Brunei River

1907 (26 Feb)–**10**. Wmk Mult Crown CA. P 14.

23	**5**	1c. grey-black and pale green	2·25	11·00
		x. Wmk reversed	15·00	
		xs. Ditto, optd "Specimen"	40·00	
24		2c. grey-black and scarlet	2·50	3·75
		x. Wmk reversed	32·00	
25		3c. grey-black and chocolate	10·00	22·00
		x. Wmk reversed	40·00	
26		4c. grey-black and mauve	7·50	10·00
		a. Grey-black and reddish purple (1910)	60·00	45·00
		w. Wmk inverted	£200	
		x. Wmk reversed	70·00	
27		5c. grey-black and blue	50·00	90·00
		x. Wmk reversed	£100	£160
		y. Wmk inverted and reversed	£250	
28		8c. grey-black and orange	7·50	23·00
29		10c. grey-black and deep green	4·50	5·00
30		25c. pale blue and ochre-brown	32·00	48·00
31		30c. violet and black	25·00	22·00
		x. Wmk reversed	£250	

32		50c. green and deep brown	15·00	22·00
33		$1 red and grey	60·00	90·00
23/33 *Set of* 11			£190	£300
23s/33s Optd "Specimen" *Set of* 11			£275	

I

II

I Double plate. Lowest line of shading on water is dotted.

II Single plate. Dotted line of shading removed.

Stamps printed in two colours are as I.

1908 (12 June)–**22**. Colours changed. Double or single plates. Wmk Mult Crown CA. P 14.

34	**5**	1c. green (I)	80	2·25
35		1c. green (II) (1911)	60	2·00
		a. "A" missing from wmk	£225	
		b. "C" missing from wmk	£225	
36		2c. black and brown (5.4.11)	4·00	1·25
		w. Wmk inverted	90·00	
37		3c. scarlet (I)	6·50	1·25
		a. Substituted crown in wmk	£700	
38		3c. scarlet (II) (1916)	£110	38·00
39		4c. claret (II) (17.4.12)	4·75	75
40		5c. black and orange (1916)	7·00	7·00
41		8c. blue and indigo-blue (10.08)	7·00	11·00
42		10c. purple/*yellow* (II) (11.12)	4·00	1·75
		a. On pale yellow (1922)	3·50	4·00
		as. Optd "Specimen"	50·00	
		w. Wmk inverted	£160	
		x. Wmk reversed	£130	
		y. Wmk inverted and reversed	£325	£325
43		25c. deep lilac (II) (30.5.12)	6·00	20·00
		a. Deep dull purple (1920)	14·00	20·00
44		30c. purple and orange-yellow (18.3.12)	9·00	13·00
45		50c. black/*green* (II) (1912)	28·00	65·00
		a. On blue-green (1920)	8·50	35·00
46		$1 black and red/*blue* (18.3.12)	23·00	48·00
47		$5 carmine/*green* (I) (1910)	£170	£250
48		$25 black/*red* (I) (1910)	£550	£1000
34/47 *Set of* 12			£225	£350
34s/48s Optd "Specimen" *Set of* 13			£550	

The used price for No. 48 is for a cancelled-by-favour example, dated before December 1941; there being no actual postal rate for which this value could be used. Examples dated after 1945 are worth much less.

For illustration of the substituted watermark crown see Catalogue Introduction.

Retouch

Normal

(**6**)

RETOUCHES. We list the very distinctive 5c. Retouch (top left value tablet, R. 1/8), but there are others of interest, notably in the clouds.

1916. Colours changed. Single plates. Wmk Mult Crown CA. P 14.

49	**5**	5c. orange	17·00	23·00
		a. "5c." retouch	£500	£600
50		8c. ultramarine	6·00	30·00
49s/50s Optd "Specimen" *Set of* 2			£110	

MALAYA-BORNEO EXHIBITION OVERPRINTS. These were produced from a setting of 30 examples, applied twice to overprint the complete sheet of 60 stamps. Three prominent overprint flaws exist, each occurring on all the stamps in two vertical rows of the sheet.

Short "I" (all stamps in 2nd and 8th vertical rows)

Broken "E" (all stamps in 4th and 10th vertical rows)

Broken "N" (all stamps in 6th and 12th vertical rows)

(Optd by Govt Printer, Singapore)

1922 (31 Mar). Optd with T **6**, in black.

51	**5**	1c. green (II)	7·00	38·00
		a. Short "I"	10·00	50·00
		b. Broken "E"	10·00	50·00
		c. Broken "N"	10·00	50·00
52		2c. black and brown	7·00	45·00
		a. Short "I"	10·00	60·00
		b. Broken "E"	10·00	60·00
		c. Broken "N"	10·00	60·00
53		3c. scarlet (II)	8·00	50·00
		a. Short "I"	13·00	75·00
		b. Broken "E"	13·00	75·00
		c. Broken "N"	13·00	75·00
54		4c. claret (II)	14·00	50·00
		a. Short "I"	19·00	75·00
		b. Broken "E"	19·00	75·00
		c. Broken "N"	19·00	75·00
55		5c. orange (II)	19·00	55·00
		a. "5c." retouch (and short "I")	£500	£950
		b. Short "I"	25·00	85·00
		c. Broken "E"	25·00	85·00
		d. Broken "N"	25·00	85·00
56		10c. purple/*yellow* (II)	6·50	55·00
		a. Short "I"	14·00	85·00
		b. Broken "E"	14·00	85·00
		c. Broken "N"	14·00	85·00
57		25c. deep dull purple (II)	14·00	80·00
		a. Short "I"	30·00	£130
		b. Broken "E"	30·00	£130
		c. Broken "N"	30·00	£130
		d. "C" missing from wmk	£1200	
		x. Wmk reversed	£325	
58		50e. black/*blue-green* (II)	45·00	£150
		a. Short "I"	80·00	£225
		b. Broken "E"	80·00	£225
		c. Broken "N"	80·00	£225
59		$1 black and red/*blue*	70·00	£190
		a. Short "I"	£120	£275
		b. Broken "E"	£120	£275
		c. Broken "N"	£120	£275
51/9 *Set of* 9			£160	£600

Examples of all values are known showing a forged Brunei postmark dated "13 JUL".

Sultan Ahmed Tajudin Akhazul Khairi Wadin, 1924–1950

7 Native houses, Water Village

1924 (Feb)–**37**. Printed from single plates as Type **II**, except 30c. and $1 as Type **I**. Wmk Mult Script CA. P 14.

60	**5**	1c. black (9.26)	1·00	75
		a. "A" of "CA" missing from wmk	£750	
61		2c. brown (3.24)	1·00	8·00
62		2c. green (3.33)	2·00	1·00
63		3c. green (3.24)	1·00	6·50
64		4c. maroon (3.24)	1·50	1·25
65		4c. orange (1929)	2·00	1·00
66		5c. orange-yellow* (3.24)	7·50	1·75
		a. "5c." retouch	£250	£130
67		5c. grey (1931)	19·00	12·00
		a. "5c." retouch	£500	£425
68		5c. chocolate (1933)	19·00	1·00
		a. "5c." retouch	£275	65·00
69	**7**	6c. intense black** (3.24)	14·00	10·00
		x. Wmk reversed		
70		6c. scarlet (1931)	7·00	11·00
71	**5**	8c. ultramarine (9.27)	6·00	5·00
72		8c. grey-black (1933)	16·00	75
73		10c. purple/*yellow* (3.37)	19·00	27·00
74	**7**	12c. blue	4·50	9·00
		a. Pale greenish blue (1927)	£130	£200
75	**5**	25c. slate-purple (1931)	13·00	13·00
76		30c. purple and orange-yellow (1931)	22·00	16·00
77		50c. black/*emerald* (1931)	12·00	15·00
78		$1 black and red/*blue* (1931)	24·00	75·00
60/78 *Set of* 19			£170	£190
60s/78s (*ex* 10c.) Optd (Nos. 60/1, 63/4, 66, 69, 71, 74) or Perf "Specimen" *Set of* 18			£425	

*For 5 c, orange, see No. 82. No. 66 is a "Wet" printing and No. 82 a "Dry".

**For 6c. black, see No. 83. Apart from the difference in shade there is a variation in size, No. 69 being 37¾ mm long and No. 83 39 mm.

The 2c. orange and 3c. blue-green in Type **5**, and the 6c. greenish grey, 8c. red and 15c. ultramarine in Type **7** were not issued without the Japanese Occupation overprint, although unoverprinted examples exist. It is believed that these 1941 printings were produced and possibly perforated, by other firms in Great Britain following bomb damage to the De La Rue works at the end of 1940 (*Price for set of 5, £475 un*).

During the life of this issue De La Rue changed the method of production from a "Wet" to a "Dry" process. Initially the stamps were printed on ungummed paper which was dampened before being put on the press. Once the paper had dried, and contracted in the process, the gum was then applied. "Dry" printings, introduced around 1934, were on pre-gummed paper. The contraction of the "Wet" printings was considerable and usually involves a difference of between 0.5 mm and 1 mm when compared with the larger "Dry" printings. The following stamps occur from both "Wet" and "Dry" versions: 1c., 2c. green, 4c. orange, 5c. chocolate, 6c. scarlet, 8c. grey-black, 10c. and 25c.

Stamps of this issue can be found either line or comb perforated.

The 10c. was also perforated "Specimen" but was not distributed by the UPU.

Brunei was occupied by the Japanese Army in January 1942 and remained under Japanese administration until liberated by the 9th Australian Division in June 1945.

After the cessation of hostilities with the Japanese Postal services were re-introduced by the British Military Administration. Post offices under B.M.A. control were opened at Brunei Town and Kuala Belait on 17 December 1945 where B.M.A. overprints on the stamps of NORTH BORNEO and SARAWAK were used until the reappearance of Brunei issues on 2 January 1947.

Redrawn clouds (R. 1/1 of No. 80*ab* only)

1947 (2 Jan)–**51**. Colours changed and new values. Wmk Mult Script CA. P 14.

79	**5**	1c. chocolate	50	2·00
		a. "A" of "CA" missing from wmk	£1100	
80		2c. grey	60	5·50
		a. Perf 14½×13½ (25.9.50)	2·00	4·50
		ab. Black (27.6.51)	2·00	6·50
		ac. Redrawn clouds	75·00	
81	**7**	3c. green	1·00	5·50
82	**5**	5c. orange*	80	1·50
		a. "5c." retouch	65·00	90·00
		b. Perf 14½×13½ (25.9.50)	4·00	16·00
		c. Ditto "5c." retouch	£130	£250
83	**7**	6c. black*	1·00	4·50
84	**5**	8c. scarlet	50	1·25
		a. Perf 13 (25.1.51)	55	9·50
85		10c. violet	2·25	30
		a. Perf 14½×13½ (25.9.50)	2·00	5·50
86		15c. ultramarine	1·75	70
87		25c. deep claret	2·75	1·25
		a. Perf 14½×13½ (25.1.51)	3·00	9·50
88		30c. black and orange	2·50	1·00
		a. Perf 14½×13½ (25.1.51)	2·00	15·00
89		50c. black	4·00	80
		a. Perf 13 (25.9.50)	1·75	18·00
90		$1 black and scarlet	10·00	1·25
91		$5 green and red-orange (2.2.48)	18·00	20·00
92		$10 black and purple (2.2.48)	75·00	30·00
79/92 *Set of* 14			£110	65·00
79s/92s Perf "Specimen" *Set of* 14			£275	

*See also Nos. 66 and 69.

The 1, 2, 3, 5, 6, 10 and 25c. values utilised the plates of the pre-war issue and were line perforated until the introduction of the 14½×13½ comb machine for some values in 1950–51. The 8, 15, 50c., $1, $5 and $10 were from new plates with the sheets comb perforated. The 30c. was initially a pre-war plate, but it is believed that a new plate was introduced in 1951.

8 Sultan Ahmed Tajudin and Water Village

1949 (22 Sept). Sultan's Silver Jubilee. Wmk Mult Script CA. P 13.

93	**8**	8c. black and carmine	1·25	1·25
94		25c. urple and red-orange	1·25	1·60
95		50c. black and blue	1·25	1·60
93/5 *Set of* 3			3·25	4·00

8a Hermes, Globe and Forms of Transport

8b Hemispheres, Jet-powered Vickers Viking Airliner and Steamer

8c Hermes and Globe

8d U.P.U. Monument

1949 (10 Oct). 75th Anniv of Universal Postal Union. Wmk Mult Script CA.

96	8c. carmine (p 13½-14)	1·00	1·50
97	15c. deep blue (p 11×11½)	3·50	1·50
98	25c. magenta (p 11×11½)	1·00	1·50
99	50c. blue-black(p 13½-14)	1·00	1·25
96/9 *Set of* 4		6·00	5·25

Sultan Sir Omar Ali Saifuddin-Wasa'adul Khairi Wadin, 1950-1967

9 Sultan Omar Ali Saifuddin

10 Native houses, Water Village

1952 (1 Mar)–**58**. Wmk Mult Script CA. P 13.

100	**9**	1c. black	10	50
101		2c. black and orange	10	50
102		3c. black and lake-brown	10	30
103		4c. black and green	10	20
104		6c. black and grey	50	10
105		8c. black and crimson	50	60
		a. *Black and crimson-lake* (15.2.56)	11·00	20
106		10c. black and sepia	15	10
107		12c. black and violet	6·00	10
108		15c. black and pale blue	3·25	10
109		25c. black and purple	2·50	10
		a. *Black and reddish purple* (8.10.53)	4·50	90
110		50c. black and ultramarine	2·50	10
		a. *Black and blue* (22.6.55)	8·00	10
111	**10**	$1 black and green	1·50	1·40
		a. *Black and bronze-green* (23.7.58)	6·50	3·00
112		$2 black and scarlet	4·50	2·50
113		$5 black and maroon	20·00	8·50
		a. *Black and brown-purple* (15.2.56)	26·00	8·50
100/13 *Set of* 14			38·00	13·00

No. 106 exists in coils constructed from normal sheets.

See also Nos. 118/31.

11 Brunei Mosque and Sultan Omar

(Recess B.W.)

1958 (24 Sept). Opening of Brunei Mosque. W w **12**. P 13½.

114	**11**	8c. black and myrtle-green	20	65
115		15c. black and carmine	25	15
116		35c. black and deep lilac	30	90
114/16 *Set of 3*			65	1·50

12 "Protein Foods"

(Des M. Goaman. Photo Harrison)

1963 (4 June). Freedom from Hunger. W w **12**. P 14×14½.

117	**12**	12c. sepia	2·75	1·00

1964–72. As Nos. 100/13, but W w **12**. Glazed paper ($2, 5) or ordinary paper (others).

118	**9**	1c. black (17.3.64)	50	70
		a. Glazed paper. Grey (28.11.69)	2·25	2·75
		ab. *Slate grey* (30.6.72)	15	2·25
119		2c. black and orange (17.3.64)	1·50	20
		a. Glazed paper (27.5.70)	2·50	10
120		3c. black and lake-brown (10.11.64)	1·50	60
		a. Glazed paper (27.5.70)	2·50	10
121		4c. black and green (12.5.64)	30	10
		a. Glazed paper (6.3.70)	50	10
		ab. *Black and emerald* (19.11.71)	1·75	4·00
122		6c. black and grey (12.5.64)	3·00	10
		a. *Black* (28.11.69)	8·00	8·50
		b. Glazed paper (28.11.69)	35	30
		ba. *Light grey* (19.11.71)	2·00	3·75
123		8c. black and crimson-lake (12.5.64)	1·00	10
		a. Glazed paper (27.5.70)	1·00	15
		ab. *Black and brown-red* (19.11.71)	3·75	4·50
124		10c. black and sepia (12.5.64)	65	10
		a. Glazed paper (31.3.70)	2·75	10
		ab. *Grey and pale brown* (coil) (11.10.71)	3·50	4·75
125		12c. black and violet (12.5.64)	1·50	10
		a. Glazed paper (5.11.70)	14·00	1·00
126		15c. black and pale blue (12.5.64)	55	10
		a. Glazed paper (28.11.69)	65	20
127		25c. black and purple (12.5.64)	7·50	10
		a. Glazed paper (18.5.70)	14·00	7·50
		ab. Glazed paper. *Black and reddish violet* (30.4.71)	15·00	1·25
128		50c. black and ultramarine (10.11.64)	2·50	10
		a. *Black & brt ultramarine* (17.3.69)	7·50	1·50
		b. Glazed paper (5.11.70)	16·00	4·00
		ba. *Grey and indigo* (21.12.71)	12·00	4·00
129	**10**	$1 black and bronze-green (14.5.68)	3·00	6·00
		a. Glazed paper (5.11.70)	9·00	7·00
130		$2 black and scarlet (5.11.70)	38·00	20·00
131		$5 black and maroon (5.11.70)	45·00	35·00
118/29 *Set of 12*			20·00	7·00
118ab/29a, 130/1 *Set of 14*			£120	65·00

Printings of the 6 and 15c. issued on 28 November 1969 were on both ordinary and glazed paper, the 6c. on ordinary producing a distinct shade.

No. 124a exists in coils constructed from normal sheets.

The 2c., 3c., 4c., 6c., 8c., 10c., 12c. and 15c. were reissued between 1972 and 1974 with W w **12** sideways.

13 I.T.U. Emblem

(Des M. Goaman. Litho Enschedé)

1965 (17 May). I.T.U. Centenary. W w **12**. P 11×11½.

132	**13**	4c. mauve and orange-brown	35	10
133		75c. orange-yellow and light emerald	1·00	75

14 I.C.Y. Emblem

(Des V. Whiteley. Litho Harrison)

1965 (25 Oct). International Co-operation Year. W w **12**. P 14.

134	**14**	4c. reddish purple and turquoise-green	20	10
135		15c. deep bluish green and lavender	55	35

15 Sir Winston Churchill and St. Paul's Cathedral in Wartime

(Des Jennifer Toombs. Photo Harrison)

1966 (24 Jan). Churchill Commemoration. W w **12**. P 14.

136	**15**	3c. black, cerise, gold and new blue	30	1·00
137		10c. black, cerise, gold and deep green	1·50	20
138		15c. black, cerise, gold and brown	1·75	35
139		75c. black, cerise, gold and bluish violet	4·25	3·00
136/9 *Set of 4*			7·00	4·00

16 Footballer's Legs, Ball and Jules Rimet Cup

(Des V. Whiteley. Litho Harrison)

1966 (4 July). World Cup Football Championship. W w **12** (side ways). P 14.

140	**16**	4c. violet, yellow-green, lake & yell-brn	20	15
141		75c. chocolate, blue-grn, lake & yell-brn	80	60

17 W.H.O. Building

(Des M. Goaman. Litho Harrison)

1966 (20 Sept). Inauguration of W.H.O. Headquarters, Geneva. W w **12** (sideways). P 14.

142	**17**	12c. black, yellow-green and light blue.	40	65
143		25c. black, light purple and yellow-brown	60	1·25

18 "Education"

19 "Science"

20 "Culture"

(Des Jennifer Toombs. Litho Harrison)

1966 (1 Dec). 20th Anniv of U.N.E.S.C.O. W w **12** (sideways). P 14.

144	**18**	4c. slate-violet, red, yellow and orange	35	10
145	**19**	15c. orange-yellow, violet and deep olive	75	50
146	**20**	75c. black, bright purple and orange	2·50	6·00
144/6 *Set of 3*			3·25	6·00

Sultan Sir Hassanal Bolkiah Mu'izzadin Waddaulah, 1967

21 Religious Headquarters Building

(Des and photo Harrison)

1967 (19 Dec). 1400th Anniv of Revelation of the Koran. W w **12** (sideways). P 12½.

147	**21**	4c. multicoloured	10	10
148		10c. multicoloured	15	10
149	–	25c. multicoloured	20	30
150	–	50c. multicoloured	35	1·50
147/50 *Set of 4*			70	1·75

Nos. 149/50 are as T **21** but have sprigs of laurel flanking the main design (which has a smaller circle) in place of flagpoles.

22 Sultan of Brunei, Mosque and Flags

(Des V. Whiteley. Photo Enschedé)

1968 (9 July). Installation of Y.T.M. Seri Paduka Duli Pengiran Temenggong. T **22** and similar multicoloured design. P 14×13 (12c.) or 13×14 (others)

151		4s. Type **22**	15	80
152		12s. Sultan of Brunei, Mosque and Flags (horiz)	40	1·60
153		25s. As Type **22**	55	2·00
151/3 *Set of 3*			1·00	4·00

23 Sultan of Brunei

24 Sultan of Brunei

(Des V. Whiteley. Litho D.L.R.)

1968 (15 July). Sultan's Birthday. W w **12** (sideways). P 12.

154	**23**	4c. multicoloured	10	50
155		12c. multicoloured	20	85
156		25c. multicoloured	30	1·40
154/6 *Set of 3*			55	2·50

(Des V. Whiteley. Photo Harrison)

1968 (1 Aug). Coronation of the Sultan of Brunei. W w **12** (sideways). P 14½×14.

157	**24**	4c. multicoloured	15	25
158		12c. multicoloured	25	50
159		25c. multicoloured	40	75
157/9 *Set of 3*			70	1·40

25 New Building and Sultan's Portrait

26 New Building and Sultan's Portrait

(Photo Enschedé)

1968 (29 Sept). Opening of Language and Literature Bureau. W w **12** (sideways). P 13½ (10c.) or 12½×13½ (others).

160	**25**	10s. multicoloured	20	1·75
		a. Tête-bêche (pair)	40	3·50
161	**26**	15s. multicoloured	20	35
162		30s. multicoloured	45	90
160/2 *Set of 3*			75	2·75

The above were scheduled for release in 1967, and when finally issued had the year altered by overprinting.

27 Human Rights Emblem and struggling Man

28 Sultan of Brunei and W.H.O. Emblem

(Des V. Whiteley. Litho Harrison)

1968 (16 Dec). Human Rights Year. W w **12**. P 14.

163	**27**	12c. black, yellow and green	10	20
164		25c. black, yellow and blue	15	25
165		75c. black, yellow and dull purple	45	1·75
163/5 *Set of 3*			65	2·00

(Des V. Whiteley. Litho Format)

1968 (19 Dec). 20th Anniv of World Health Organization. P 14.

166	**28**	4c. yellow, black and cobalt	30	30
167		15c. yellow, black and deep bluish violet	55	65
168		25c. yellow, black and pale yellow-olive	65	1·25
166/8 *Set of 3*			1·40	2·00

29 Deep Sea Oil-Rig, Sultan of Brunei and inset portrait of Pengiran Di-Gadong

(Des adapted by V. Whiteley. Photo Enschedé)

1969 (10 July). Installation (9th May, 1968) of Pengiran Shahbandar as Y.T.M. Seri Paduka Duli Pengiran Di-Gadong Sahibol Mal. W w **12**. P 14×13.

169	**29**	12s. multicoloured	85	50
170		40s. multicoloured	1·25	2·00
171		50s. multicoloured	1·25	2·00
169/71 *Set of 3*			3·00	4·00

30 Aerial View of Parliament Buildings

(Des Harrison. Litho D.L.R.)

1969 (23 Sept). Opening of Royal Audience Hall and Legislative Council Chamber. P 15.

172	**30**	12s. multicoloured	20	25
173		25s. multicoloured	30	45
174	–	50s. rose-red and bluish violet	60	3·50
172/4 *Set of 3*			1·00	3·75

Design:—50c. Elevation of new buildings.

32 Youth Centre and Sultan's Portrait

(Des V. Whiteley. Litho D.L.R.)

1969 (20 Dec). Opening of the New Youth Centre. W w **12**. P 15×14½.

175	**32**	6c. flesh, slate-lilac and black	20	1·00
176		10c. olive-yellow, grey-green and blackish brown	25	10
177		30c. yellow-olive, yellow-brown and black	70	1·00
175/7 *Set of 3*			1·00	1·90

33 Soldier, Sultan and Badge

34 Badge, and Officer in Full-dress Uniform

(Des Maj. M. A. Bowman. Adapted V. Whiteley. Litho Questa)

1971 (3 May). Tenth Anniv of Royal Brunei Malay Regiment. Multicoloured designs, each with Badge and Sultans portrait as T **33**. W w **12** (sideways on 15 and 75c.). P 14½.

178		10s. Type **33**	80	30
179		15s. Bell 205 UH-1H Iroquois helicopter (horiz)	1·75	70
180		75s. *Pahlawan* (patrol boat) (horiz)	3·25	7·00
178/80 *Set of 3*			5·25	7·00

(Des Supt. T. Swan. Litho Format)

1971 (14 Aug). 50th Anniv of Royal Brunei Police Force. T **34** and similar vert designs. Multicoloured. W w **12** (sideways). P 14½.

181		10s. Type **34**	50	30
182		15s. Badge and Patrol Constable	60	90
183		50s. Badge and Traffic Constable	1·10	6·00
181/3 *Set of 3*			2·00	6·50

35 Perdana Wazir, Sultan of Brunei and view of Water Village

(Des and litho Harrison)

1971 (27 Aug). Installation of the Yang Teramat Mulia as the Perdana Wazir (1970). T **35** and similar horiz designs showing different views of Brunei Town. W w **12**. P 14.

184	**35**	15c. multicoloured	40	50
185	–	25c. multicoloured	70	1·00
186	–	50c. multicoloured	1·40	5·00
184/6 *Set of 3*			2·25	6·00

36 Pottery

(Des C. Abbott. Litho Questa)

1972 (29 Feb). Opening of Brunei Museum. T **36** and similar horiz designs. Multicoloured. W w **12** (sideways). P 13½.

187		10s. Type **36**	30	10
188		12s. Straw-work	40	20
189		15s. Leather-work	45	20
190		25s. Cold-work	1·25	1·25
191		50s. Museum Building (58×21 mm)	2·25	5·50
187/91 *Set of 5*			4·25	6·50

37 Brunei Museum, Queen Elizabeth and Sultan of Brunei

(Des locally. Photo Enschedé)

1972 (29 Feb). Royal Visit. T **37** and similar horiz designs each with portraits of Queen and Sultan. Multicoloured. W w **12** (sideways*). P 13×13½.

192		10s. Type **37**	70	20
193		15s. Native houses	95	55
		w. Wmk Crown to right of CA		
194		25s. Mosque	2·00	1·60
195		50s. Royal Assembly Hall	3·75	7·00
192/5 *Set of 4*			6·75	8·50

*The normal sideways watermark shows Crown to left of CA, *as seen from the back of the stamp.*

38 Secretariat Building

(Des Harrison. Litho J.W.)

1972 (4 Oct). Renaming of Brunei Town as Bandar Seri Begawan. T **38** and similar horiz designs. W w **12** (sideways). P 13½.

196		10c. multicoloured	20	15
197		15c. green, light yellow and black	25	15
198		25c. ultramarine, lemon and black	45	50
199		50c. rosine, pale turquoise-blue and black	75	2·25
196/9 *Set of 4*			1·50	2·75

Views:—15c. Dural Hana Palace; 25c. Old Brunei Town; 50c. Town and Water Village.

39 Blackburn Beverley C1 parachuting Supplies

(Des Trident Artists. Litho Questa)

1972 (15 Nov). Opening of R.A.F. Museum, Hendon. T **39** and similar horiz design. Multicoloured. W w **12** (sideways on 75c.). P 14×13½ (25c.) or 13½×14 (75c.).

200		25c. Type **39**	1·75	1·25
201		75c. Blackburn Beverley C1 landing	3·25	4·75

1972 (17 Nov)–**74**. As Nos. 119/26, but W w **12** (sideways*). Glazed paper.

202	**9**	2c. black and orange (9.5.73)	3·25	8·50
203		3c. black and lake-brown	1·75	40
204		4c. black and green	50	1·00
205		6c. black and grey	2·75	30
206		8c. black and brown-red (9.5.73)	3·50	7·00
207		10c. black and sepia	80	50
		a. *Black and bistre-brown* (24.7.74)	80	3·50
		aw. Wmk Crown to right of CA	6·50	
208		12c. black and violet	1·50	2·50
209		15c. black and pale blue	1·75	2·25
202/9 *Set of 8*			14·00	20·00

*The normal sideways watermark shows Crown to left of CA, *as seen from the back of the stamp.*

40 Girl with Traditional Flower-pot, and Boy with Bowl and Pipe

(Des (from photograph by D. Groves) and photo Harrison)

1972 (20 Nov). Royal Silver Wedding. Multicoloured; background colour given. W w **12**. P 14×14½.

210	**40**	12c. carmine-red	10	10
		w. Wmk inverted	26·00	
211		75c. deep myrtle-green	20	50

41 Interpol H.Q., Paris

(Des Shamir Bros. Litho Harrison)

1973 (7 Sept). 50th Anniv of Interpol. T **41** and similar horiz design. W w **12** (inverted on 50c.). P 14×14½.

212		25s. bright green, purple and dull blue-black	1·50	1·25
213		50s. pale greenish blue, ultramarine & carm	1·50	1·25

The 50c. shows a different view of the H.Q.

42 Sultan, Princess Anne and Capt. Phillips

(Des PAD Studio. Litho Fomat)

1973 (14 Nov). Royal Wedding. W w **12**. P 14.

214	**42**	25s. multicoloured	15	10
215		50s. multicoloured	15	25

43 Churchill Painting

44 Sultan Sir Hassanal Bolkiah Muizzaddin Waddaulah

(Des C. Abbott. Litho Questa)

1973 (31 Dec). Opening of Churchill Memorial Building. T **43** and similar vert design. Multicoloured. W w **12** (sideways). P 14×13½.

216		12s. Type **43**	10	20
217		50s. Churchill Statue	30	1·40

(Des Staff Artists, Dept of Language and Literature. Photo Harrison)

1974 (15 July*). Multicoloured; background colour given. W w **12** (sideways†). P 13½×14½.

218	**44**	4s. turquoise-green	20	20
219		5s. pale blue	20	30
220		6s. olive	3·25	6·50
221		10s. lavender	30	10
222		15s. light brown	2·50	40
223		20s. stone	30	20
		w. Wmk Crown to right of CA	1·60	
224		25s. sage-green	40	15
225		30s. bright blue	40	15
226		35s. grey	40	20
227		40s. bright purple	40	20
228		50s. cinnamon	40	20
229		75s. light yellow-green	60	3·50
230		$1 pale salmon	1·50	3·50
231		$2 greenish yellow	2·25	11·00
232		$5 silver	3·00	18·00
233		$10 gold	5·00	32·00
218/33 *Set of 16*			19·00	65·00

*This was the London release date. The stamps were not put on sale locally until 29 August 1974, but First Day Covers were cancelled with the 15 July date.

†The normal sideways watermark shows Crown to left of CA, *as seen from the back of the stamp.*

See also Nos. 244/59 and 260/2.

45 Aerial View of Airport

(Des Harrison. Litho B.W.)

1974 (18 July). Inauguration of Brunei International Airport. T **45** and similar horiz design. Multicoloured. W w **12** (sideways on 75c.). P 14×14½ (50c.) or 12½×13 (75c.).

234	50c. Type **45**	1·25	1·00
235	75c. Sultan in Army uniform, and airport (48×36 mm)	1·50	1·50

46 U.P.U. Emblem and Sultan

(Des J.W. Litho Harrison)

1974 (28 Oct). Centenary of Universal Postal Union. W w **12** (sideways). P 14½.

236	**46**	12c. multicoloured	20	20
237		50c. multicoloured	40	1·40
238		75c. multicoloured	50	1·75
236/8 *Set of 3*			1·00	3·00

47 Sir Winston Churchill

(Des C. Abbott. Litho Questa)

1974 (30 Nov). Birth Centenary of Sir Winston Churchill. T **47** and similar horiz design. Multicoloured. W w **14** (sideways). P 14.

239	12s. Type **47**	25	20
240	75s. Churchill smoking cigar (profile)	45	1·40

A set of four, 12, 20, 25 and 75c., was prepared during this period to mark the opening of new port facilities at Muara, but these stamps were never issued.

48 Boeing 737 and R.B.A. Crest

(Des PAD Studio. Litho Enschedé)

1975 (14 May). Inauguration of Royal Brunei Airlines. T **48** and similar horiz designs. Multicoloured. No wmk. P 12½×12.

241	12c. Type **48**	1·00	25
242	35c. Boeing 737 over Bandar Seri Begawan Mosque	1·75	1·75
243	75c. Boeing 737 in flight	2·50	4·00
241/3 *Set of 3*		4·75	5·50

1975 (13 Aug)–**78**. As Nos. 218/33, but W w **14** (sideways*).

244	**44**	4s. turquoise-green	30	3·00
245		5s. pale blue	30	3·00
246		6s. olive	6·00	7·00
247		10s. lavender	30	10
		a. *Pale bluish violet* (19.4.77)	30	10
248		15s. light brown	60	1·75
249		20s. stone	60	1·50
250		25s. sage-green	70	1·50
		a. *Grey-olive* (25.5.78)	60	1·75
251		30s. bright blue	35	2·00
		w. Wmk Crown to right of CA	1·75	
252		35s. grey	45	2·00
253		40s. bright purple	55	2·25
254		50s. cinnamon	90	60
		a. Blue omitted†	75·00	
		w. Wmk Crown to right of CA	8·00	
255		75s. light yellow-green	80	3·50
256		$1 pale salmon	1·50	3·50
		w. Wmk Crown to right of CA	4·00	6·50
257		$2 greenish yellow	4·00	9·50
258		$5 silver	5·50	18·00
259		$10 gold	27·00	35·00
244/59 *Set of 16*			45·00	85·00

*The normal sideways watermark shows Crown to left of CA, *as seen from the back of the stamp.*

†The blue colour on the 50c. value is only evident in the bluish green stripes of the sash and on several of the medal ribbons.

1976 (12 Apr). As Nos. 221 and 223/4 but W w **12** (upright).

260	**44**	10s. lavender	3·75	1·50
261		20s. stone	3·75	4·00
262		25s. sage-green	3·75	5·50
260/2 *Set of 3*			10·00	11·00

10
sen

(**49**)

50 Royal Coat of Arms

(Surchd by Govt Printer, Brunei)

1976 (16 Aug). No. 246 surch with T **49** in silver.

263	**44**	10s. on 6s. olive	1·75	1·75
		a. Surch on No. 220	2·50	1·75

(Des S. Abbott. Litho D.L.R.)

1977 (7 June). Silver Jubilee. T **50** and similar vert designs. Multicoloured. W w **14**. P 13½×14.

264	10s. Type **50**	15	15
265	20s. Imperial State Crown	20	20
	a. Silver omitted	£250	
266	75s. Queen Elizabeth (portrait by Annigoni)	45	60
264/6 *Set of 3*		70	85

51 The Moment of Crowning

52 Royal Crest

(Des J. Cooter. Litho Enschedé)

1978 (2 June). 25th Anniv of Coronation. T **51** and similar vert designs. Multicoloured. W w **14**. P 13½×13.

267	10s. Type **51**	15	10
268	20s. Queen in Coronation regalia	20	20
	w. Wmk inverted	75·00	
269	75s. Queen's departure from Abbey	55	80
267/9 *Set of 3*		80	1·00

(Des local artist; adapted BG Studio. Litho Cartor)

1978 (1 Aug). Tenth Anniv of Sultan's Coronation. T **52** and similar vert designs. W w **14** (inverted). P 12.

270	10s. black, scarlet and greenish yellow	20	10
271	20s. multicoloured	40	25
272	75s. multicoloured	1·10	3·50
270/2 *Set of 3*		1·50	3·50
MS273	182×77 mm. Nos. 270/2	12·00	16·00

Designs:—20s. Coronation ceremony; 75s. Royal Crown.

53 Human Rights Emblem and struggling Man

54 Smiling Children

(Des V. Whiteley; adapted L. McCombie. Litho Questa)

1978 (10 Dec). Human Rights Year. W w **14**. P 14½.

274	**53**	10s. black, yellow and scarlet	15	10
275		20s. black, yellow and violet	20	35
276		75s. black, yellow and bistre	40	2·50
274/6 *Set of 3*			70	2·75

Type **53** is similar to the design used for the 1968 Human Rights Year issue.

(Des L. Curtis. Litho Harrison)

1979 (30 June). International Year of the Child. T **54** and similar horiz design. W w **14** (sideways). P 14.

277	10s. multicoloured	20	10
278	$1 black and dull green	80	2·50

Design:—$1 I.Y.S. emblem.

55 Earth Satellite Station

56 Hegira Symbol

(Des A. Theobald. Litho Questa)

1979 (23 Sept). Telisai Earth Satellite Station. T **55** and similar horiz designs. Multicoloured. W w **14** (sideways). P 14.

279	10s. Type **55**	20	15
280	20s. Satellite and antenna	30	40
281	75s. Television camera, telex machine and telephone	60	2·75
279/81 *Set of 3*		1·00	3·00

(Litho Secura, Singapore)

1979 (21 Nov). Moslem Year 1400 AH Commemoration. W w **14**. P 13×13½.

282	**56**	10s. black, yellow and emerald	10	15
283		20s. black, yellow and light blue	15	30
284		75s. black, yellow and violet	45	2·25
282/4 *Set of 3*			60	2·25
MS285 178×200 mm. Nos. 282/4			3·00	7·50
		w. Wmk inverted	3·00	7·50

57 Installation Ceremony

58 Royal Umbrella and Sash

(Des BG Studio. Litho Questa)

1980 (8 Nov). First Anniv of Prince Sufri Bolkiah's Installation as First Wazir. T **57** and similar vert design. Multicoloured. W w **14**. P 13½.

286	10s. Type **57**	15	10
287	75s. Prince Sufri	85	2·25

Nos. 286/7 have blue borders.

(Des BG Studio. Litho Secura, Singapore)

1980 (6 Dec). First Anniv of Prince Jefri Bolkiah's Installation as Second Wazir. Vert designs as T **57**. Multicoloured. W w **14**. P 13½.

288	10s. Installation ceremony	15	10
	w. Wmk inverted	38·00	
289	75s. Prince Jefri	85	2·25

Nos. 288/9 have green borders.

(Des BG Studio. Litho Security Printers (M), Malaysia)

1981 (18 Jan*). Royal Regalia (1st series). T **58** and similar multicoloured designs. P 13½×13 (50s.) or 12½×11½ (others).

290	10s. Type **58**	20	15
291	15s. Sword and Shield	35	25
292	20s. Lance and Sheath	40	40
293	30s. Betel-leaf Container	60	1·25
294	50s. Coronation Crown (23×40 mm)	1·25	5·00
290/4 *Set of 5*		2·50	6·25
MS295 98×142 mm. Nos. 290/4		5·00	8·00

*This is the local release date. The Crown Agents released the stamps on 19 January. See also Nos. 298/303, 314/19 and 320/5.

59 I.T.U. and W.H.O. Emblems

60 Shield and Broadsword

(Litho Security Printers (M), Malaysia)

1981 (17 May). World Telecommunications and Health Day. P 13×13½.

296	**59**	10s. black and bright crimson	50	25
297		75s. black, chalky blue & pale violet-bl..	2·25	5·00

(Des BG Studio. Litho Security Printers (M), Malaysia)

1981 (15 July). Royal Regalia. (2nd series). T **60** and similar multicoloured designs. P 12.

298	10s. Type **60**	10	10
299	15s. Blunderbuss and Pouch	20	20
300	20s. Crossed Lances and Sash	30	30
301	30s. Sword, Shield and Sash	40	75
302	50s. Forked Lance	60	2·50
303	75s. Royal Drum (29×45 mm)	80	4·50
298/303 *Set of 6*		2·10	7·50

61 Prince Charles as Colonel of the Welsh Guards

62 Fishing

(Des J.W. Litho Format)

1981 (29 July). Royal Wedding. T **61** and similar vert designs. Multicoloured. W w **14**. P 14.

304	10s. Wedding bouquet from Brunei	15	15
305	$1 Type **61**	35	1·50
306	$2 Prince Charles and Lady Diana Spencer	50	2·50
	w. Wmk inverted	15·00	
304/6 *Set of 3*		90	3·75

(Des local artist. Litho Secura, Singapore)

1981 (16 Oct). World Food Day. T **62** and similar vert design. Multicoloured. P 12×11½.

307 10s. Type **62** ... 50 15
308 $1 Farm produce and machinery ... 4·50 7·50

63 Blind Man and Braille Alphabet

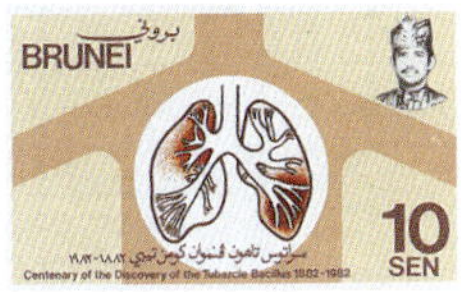

64 Drawing of Infected Lungs

(Des local artist. Litho Security Printers (M), Malaysia)

1981 (16 Dec). International Year for Disabled Persons. T **63** and similar vert designs. Multicoloured. W w **14**. P 12.

309 10s. Type **63** ... 65 20
w. Wmk inverted ... 16·00
310 20s. Deaf people and sign language ... 1·50 80
a. Wmk sideways ... 2·00 2·00
311 75s. Disabled person and wheelchairs ... 3·00 6·75
309/11 *Set of 3* ... 4·75 7·00

(Des local artist. Litho Security Printers (M), Malaysia)

1982 (24 May). Centenary of Robert Koch's Discovery of Tubercle Bacillus. T **64** and similar horiz design. Multicoloured. W w **14**. P 12 (10s.) or 13½ (75s.).

312 10s. Type **64** ... 50 25
313 75s. Magnified tubercle bacillus and microscope ... 3·00 6·50

(Des PAD Studio. Litho Security Printers (M), Malaysia)

1982 (31 May). Royal Regalia (3rd series). Multicoloured designs as T **60**. W w **14** (sideways). P 13½ (75s.) or 12×11½ (others).

314 10s. Ceremonial Ornament ... 10 10
315 15s. Silver Betel Caddy ... 20 20
316 20s. Traditional Flower-pot ... 25 30
317 30s. Solitary Candle ... 50 90
318 50s. Golden Pipe ... 70 2·50
319 75s. Royal Chin Support (28×45 *mm*) ... 90 4·00
314/19 *Set of 6* ... 2·40 7·25

(Des BG Studio. Litho Security Printers (M), Malaysia)

1982 (15 July). Royal Regalia (4th series). Multicoloured designs as T **60**. W w **14** (sideways*). P 12 (75s.) or 12×11½ (others).

320 10s. Royal Mace ... 25 10
321 15s. Ceremonial Shield and Spears ... 35 30
322 20s. Embroidered Ornament ... 45 40
323 30s. Golden-tasselled Cushion ... 75 1·50
324 50s. Ceremonial Dagger and Sheath ... 1·25 3·50
325 75s. Religious Mace (28×45 *mm*) ... 1·60 4·50
w. Wmk Crown to left of CA ... 22·00
320/5 *Set of 6* ... 4·25 9·25

*The normal sideways watermark shows Crown to right of CA, *as seen from the back of the stamp*.

65 Brunei Flag

(Des Siti Zaleha Haji Kaprawi. Litho Secure, Singapore)

1983 (14 Mar). Commonwealth Day. T **65** and similar horiz designs. P 13×13½.

326 10s. multicoloured ... 15 80
a. Horiz strip of 4. Nos. 326/9 ... 1·75 4·50
327 20s. bright blue, black and buff ... 20 90
328 75s. bright blue, black and bright green ... 45 1·40
329 $2 bright blue, black and lemon ... 1·10 2·00
326/9 *Set of 4* ... 1·75 4·50

Designs:—20s. Brunei Mosque; 75s. Machinery; $2 Sultan of Brunei.

Nos. 326/9 were printed together, *se-tenant*, in horizontal strips of four throughout the sheet.

66 "Postal Service"

67 Football

(Litho Secura, Singapore)

1983 (15 Aug). World Communications Year. T **66** and similar horiz designs. P 13½.

330 10s. multicoloured ... 15 10
331 75s. yellow, orange-brown and black ... 60 75
332 $2 multicoloured ... 1·75 2·25
330/2 *Set of 3* ... 2·25 2·75

Designs:—75s. "Telephone Service"; $2 "Communications".

(Litho Security Printers (M), Malaysia)

1983 (23 Sept). Official Opening of Hassanal Bolkiah National Stadium. T **67** and similar multicoloured designs. P 12.

333 10s. Type **67** ... 55 15
334 75s. Athletics ... 2·25 1·50
335 $1 View of stadium (44×27 mm) ... 2·75 4·00
333/5 *Set of 3* ... 5·00 5·00

68 Fishermen and Crustacea

(Litho Secura, Singapore)

1983 (23 Sept). Fishery Resources. T **68** and similar horiz designs. Multicoloured. P 13½×14.

336 10s. Type **68** ... 1·50 15
337 50s. Fishermen with net ... 3·75 1·50
338 75s. Fishing trawler ... 4·00 4·25
339 $1 Fishing with hook and tackle ... 4·25 4·75
336/9 *Set of 4* ... 12·00 9·75

INDEPENDENT

From No. 349 onwards issues are inscribed "BRUNEI DARUSSALAM".

69 Royal Assembly Hall

(Des Haji Salleh bin Haji Ibrahim (No. 346) Pengiran Haji Muhammed bin Pengiran Duraman (No. **MS**348) or Sid Zaleha Haji Kaprawi (others). Litho Cartor)

1984 (1 Jan). Independence. T **69** and similar designs. P 13.

340 10s. pale stone and bright orange ... 20 10
341 20s. flesh and brown-red ... 30 20
342 35s. rose-pink and plum ... 60 60
343 50s. pale blue and new blue ... 1·75 1·25
344 75s. bright yellow-green and emerald ... 1·75 2·00
345 $1 light brownish grey and light brown ... 2·00 2·50
346 $3 multicoloured ... 7·00 10·00
340/6 *Set of 7* ... 11·50 14·00
MS347 150×120 mm. Nos. 340/6 ... 12·00 16·00
MS348 Two sheets each 150×120 mm. containing 4 stamps (34×69 mm.). (a) 25s.×4 grey-black and new blue (Signing of the Brunei Constitution). (b) 25s.×4 multicoloured (Signing of Brunei-U.K. Friendship Agreement) *Set of 2 sheets* ... 2·25 4·50

Designs:—34×25 mm. 20s. Government Secretariat Building; 35s. New Supreme Court; 50s. Natural gas well; 75s. Omar Ali Saifuddin Mosque; $1 Sultan's Palace; 68×24 mm. $3 Brunei flag and map of South-East Asia.

70 Natural Forests and Enrichment Planting

(Des Awang Nor Ariffin bin Md. Yassin. Litho Secura, Singapore)

1984 (21 Apr). Forestry Resources. T **70** and similar horiz designs, Multicoloured. P 13½×14.

349	10s. Type **70**	1·00	25
350	50s. Forests and water resources	2·50	2·25
351	75s. Recreation forests	3·25	4·50
352	$1 Forests and wildlife	4·75	6·00
349/52 *Set of* 4		10·00	11·50

71 Sultan Omar Saifuddin 50s. Stamp of 1952

(Recess and litho D.L.R.)

1984 (22 Oct). Philakorea International Stamp Exhibition, Seoul. T **71** and similar vert designs. Multicoloured. P 13.

353	10s. Type **71**	50	15
354	75s. Brunei River view 10s. stamp of 1907	1·50	2·25
355	$2 Star and view ½s. stamp of 1895	2·50	6·50
353/5 *Set of* 3		4·00	7·75
MS356	Three sheets, 117×100 mm, each containing one stamp as Nos. 353/5 *Set of* 3 *sheets*	3·75	7·00
	a. Line perf 14 at left *Set of* 3 *sheets*	4·50	8·00

The stamps within the miniature sheets were perforated by means of a three-sided comb gauging 13 and completed by a line perforation at left. Normally this line perforation is also 13, but on **MS**356a it measures 14.

72 United Nations Emblem

73 Young People and Brunei Flag

(Des Awang Nor Ariffin bin Md. Yassin (No. 357, 359), Haji Salleh bin Haji Ibrahim (358) or Siti Zaleha Haji Kaprawi (360). Litho Cartor)

1985 (23 Sept). Admission of Brunei to World Organizations (1st issue). T **72** and similar horiz designs. W w **17** (sideways*). P 13.

357	50s. black, gold and pale greenish blue	50	70
358	50s. multicoloured	50	70
359	50s. multicoloured	50	70
360	50s. multicoloured	50	70
357/60 *Set of* 4		1·75	2·50
MS361	110×151 mm. Nos. 357/60	4·00	4·00
	w. Wmk reading upwards	4·00	4·00

Designs—No. 357, Type **72**; No. 358, Islamic Conference Organization logo; No. 359, Commonwealth logo; No. 360 A.S.E.A.N. emblem.

*The normal sideways version of the watermark shows the words reading downwards.

See also Nos. 383/7.

(Des Siti Zaleha Haji Kaprawi. Litho Security Printers (M), Malaysia)

1985 (17 Oct). International Youth Year. T **73** and similar horiz designs. Multicoloured. P 12.

362	10s. Type **73**	2·00	30
363	75s. Young people at work	5·50	7·00
364	$1 Young people serving the community	6·00	7·50
362/4 *Set of* 3		12·00	13·00

74 Palestinian Emblem

75 Early and Modern Scout Uniforms

(Des Haji Salleh bin Haji Ibrahim. Litho Secura, Singapore)

1985 (29 Nov). International Palestinian Solidarity Day. P 12×12½.

365	**74**	10s. multicoloured	2·25	20
366		50s. multicoloured	4·75	1·50
367		$1 multicoloured	6·50	3·75
365/7 *Set of* 3			12·00	5·00

(Des Awang Nor Ariffin bin Md. Yassin. Litho Secura, Singapore)

1985 (14 Dec). National Scout Jamboree. T **75** and similar vert designs. Multicoloured. P 13½.

368	10s. Type **75**	60	10
369	20s. Scout on tower signalling with flag	90	40
370	$2 Jamboree emblem	2·75	3·25
368/70 *Set of* 3		3·75	3·25

76 Sultan Sir Hassanal Bolkiah Mu'izzaddin Waddaulah

77

(Des Awang Nor Ariffin bin Md. Yassin. Photo Harrison)

1985 (23 Dec)–**86**. W w **77**. P 13½×14½ (10 to 75s.) or 14 ($1 to $10).

371	**76**	10s. multicoloured	30	10
372		15s. multicoloured	30	10
373		20s. multicoloured	40	10
374		25s. multicoloured	40	15
375		35s. multicoloured (15.1.86)	55	20
376		40s. multicoloured (15.1.86)	60	25
377		50s. multicoloured (15.1.86)	70	35
378		75s. multicoloured (15.1.86)	90	50
379		$1 multicoloured (23.2.86)	1·25	70
		a. Wmk sideways	—	1·50
380		$2 multicoloured (23.2.86)	2·75	1·75
		a. Wmk sideways	—	2·75
381		$5 multicoloured (23.2.86)	4·25	5·00
		a. Wmk sideways	—	7·00
382		$10 multicoloured (29.3.86)	8·00	11·00
		a. Wmk sideways	—	14·00
371/82 *Set of* 12			18·00	18·00

Nos. 379/82 are larger, size 32×39 mm. The sideways watermark printings of the dollar values, which are only known used, may date from around 1995.

(Des Awang Nor Ariffin bin Md. Yassin. Litho Cartor)

1986 (30 Apr). Admission of Brunei to World Organizations (2nd issue). Horiz designs as T **72**. W w **17** (sideways). P 13.

383	50s. black, gold and bright yellow-green	50	60
384	50s. black, gold and bright pinkish mauve	50	60
385	50s. black, gold and orange-red	50	60
386	50s. black, gold and dull ultramarine	50	60
383/6 *Set of* 4		1·75	2·10
MS387	105×155 mm. Nos. 383/6. Wmk upright	1·50	4·00

Designs:—No. 383, World Meteorological Organization emblem; 384, International Telecommunication Union emblem; 385, Universal Postal Union emblem; 386, International Civil Aviation Organization emblem.

78 Soldiers on Assault Course and Bell 205 UH-1H Iroquois Helicopter

79 Tunggul Charok Buritan, Alam Bernaga (Alam Besar), Pisang-Pisang and Sandaran

(Des Awang Nor Ariffin bin Md. Yassin. Litho Secura, Singapore)

1986 (31 May). 25th Anniv of Brunei Armed Forces. T **78** and similar horiz designs. Multicoloured. P 13½.

388	10s. Type **78**	4·25	4·25
	a. Horiz strip of 4. Nos. 388/91	19·00	19·00
389	20s. Operating computer	4·50	4·50
390	50s. Anti-aircraft missile, MBB-Bolkow Bo 105L helicopter and missile boat	6·00	6·00
391	75s. Army commanders and parade	6·50	6·50
388/91 *Set of 4*		19·00	19·00

Nos. 388/91 were printed together, *se-tenant*, in horizontal strips of four throughout the sheet, forming a composite design.

(Des Awang Nor Ariffin bin Md. Yassin. Litho Secura, Singapore)

1986 (15 July). Royal Ensigns (1st series). T **79** and similar vert designs. P 12.

392	10s. black, greenish yellow and red	30	10
393	75s. multicoloured	1·10	1·10
394	$2 black, greenish yellow and green	2·25	2·75
392/4 *Set of 3*		3·25	3·50

Designs:—75s. Ula-Ula Besar, Sumba Layang and Payong Haram; $2 Panji-Panji, Chogan Istiadat (Chogan Di-Raja) and Chogan Ugama.

(Des Awang Nor Ariffin bin Md. Yassin. Litho Secura, Singapore)

1986 (30 Sept). Royal Ensigns (2nd series). Vert designs as T **79**. P 12.

395	10s. multicoloured	30	10
396	75s. black, red and greenish yellow	1·10	1·10
397	$2 multicoloured	2·25	2·75
395/7 *Set of 3*		3·25	3·50

Designs:—10s. Dadap, .Tunggul Kawan, Ambal, Payong Ubor-Ubor, Sapu-Sapu Ayeng and Rawai Lidah; 75s. Payong Tinggi and Payong Ubor-Ubor Tiga Ringkat; $2 Lambang Du li Yang Maha Mulia and Mahligai.

80 Stylised Peace Doves

81 Drug Addict in Cage and Syringe (poster by Othman bin Ramboh)

(Des Zainal Abidin Haji Ibrahim. Litho Security Printers (M), Malaysia)

1986 (24 Oct). International Peace Year. T **80** and similar horiz designs. Multicoloured. P 12.

398	50s. Type **80**	75	75
399	75s. Stylised hands and "1986"	1·00	1·10
400	$1 International Peace Year emblem and arms of Brunei	1·25	1·50
398/400 *Set of 3*		2·75	3·00

(Litho Security Printers (M), Malaysia)

1987 (15 Mar). National Anti-drug Campaign. Children's Posters. T **81** and similar vert designs. Multicoloured. P 12.

401	10s. Type **81**	1·50	35
402	75s. Drug addict and noose (Arman bin Mohd. Zaman)	3·00	4·25
403	$1 Blindfolded drug addict and noose (Abi din bin Hj. Rashid)	3·50	5·50
401/3 *Set of 3*		7·25	9·00

82 Cannon ("badil")

83 Map showing Member Countries

(Des Haji Salleh bin Haji Ibrahim. Litho Security Printers (M), Malaysia)

1987 (15 July). Brassware (1st series). T **82** and similar vert designs. Multicoloured. P 12.

404	50s. Type **82**	50	50
405	50s. Lamp ("pelita")	50	50
406	50s. Betel container ("langguai")	50	50
407	50s. Water jug ("kiri')	50	50
404/7 *Set of 4*		1·75	1·75

See also Nos. 434/7.

(Des Zainal Abidin bin Haji Ibrahim. Litho Security Printers (M), Malaysia)

1987 (8 Aug). 20th Anniv of Association of South East Asian Nations. T **83** and similar horiz designs. Multicoloured. P 14×13½.

408	20s. Type **83**	35	20
409	50s. Dates and figures "20"	60	50
410	$1 Flags of member states	1·25	1·25
408/10 *Set of 3*		2·00	1·75

84 Brunei Citizens

(Des Pengiran Haji Muhammad bin Pengiran Duraman. Litho Secure, Singapore)

1987 (29 Sept). 25th Anniv of Language and Literature Bureau (1986). T **84** and similar horiz designs. Multicoloured. P 13×12½.

411	10s. Type **84**	50	40
	a. Horiz strip of 3. Nos. 411/13	3·00	2·75
412	50s. Flame emblem and hands holding open book	1·00	75
413	$2 Scenes of village life	1·75	2·00
411/13 *Set of 3*		3·00	2·75

Nos. 411/13 were printed together, *se-tenant*, in horizontal strips of three throughout the sheet, each strip forming a composite design taken from a mural.

85 *Artocarpus odoratissima*

(Litho Security Printers (M), Malaysia)

1987 (31 Oct). Local Fruits (1st series). T **85** and similar horiz designs. Multicoloured. P 12.

414	50s. Type **85**	75	70
	a. Horiz strip of 4. Nos. 414/17	2·75	2·50
415	50s. *Canarium odontophyllum mig*	75	70
416	50s. *Litsea garciae*	75	70
417	50s. *Mangifera foetida lour*	75	70
414/17 *Set of 4*		2·75	2·50

Nos. 414/17 were printed together, *se-tenant*, in horizontal strips of four throughout the sheet.

See also Nos. 421/4, 459/62, 480/2 and 525/8.

86 Modern House

87 Wooden Lathe

(Litho Security Printers (M), Malaysia)

1987 (28 Nov). International Year of Shelter for the Homeless. T **86** and similar horiz designs, each showing modern Brunei housing. P 13×12½.

418	50s. multicoloured	40	50
419	75s. multicoloured	55	65
420	$1 multicoloured	80	90
418/20	*Set of 3*	1·60	1·90

(Des Awang Nor Ariffin bin Md. Yassin. Litho Security Printers (M), Malaysia)

1988 (30 Jan). Local Fruits (2nd series). Horiz designs as T **85**. Multicoloured. P 12.

421	50s. *Durio spp*	95	1·25
	a. Horiz strip of 4. Nos. 421/4	3·50	4·50
422	50s. *Durio oxleyanus*	95	1·25
423	50s. *Durio graveolens* (blue background)	95	1·25
424	50s. *Durio graveolens* (white background)	95	1·25
421/4	*Set of 4*	3·50	4·50

Nos. 421/4 were printed together, *se-tenant*, in horizontal strips of four throughout the sheet.

(Des Awang Padzil bin Haji Abroad. Litho Security Printers (M), Malaysia)

1988 (29 Feb). Opening of Malay Technology Museum. T **87** and similar vert designs. Multicoloured. P 12.

425	10s. Type **87**	15	10
426	75s. Crushing sugarcane	55	70
427	$1 Bird scarer	70	85
425/7	*Set of 3*	1·25	1·50

88 Beragi Bunga Sakah-Sakah don Bunga Cengkih Cloth

89 Sultan reading Proclamation

(Des Awang Nor Ariffin bin Md. Yassin. Litho Security Printers (M), Malaysia)

1988 (30 Apr). Handwoven Material (1st series). T **88** and similar horiz designs showing different patterns. Multicoloured. P 12.

428	10s. Type **88**	10	10
429	20s. Jong Sarat cloth	15	15
430	25s. Si Pugut cloth	20	25
431	40s. Si Pugut Bunga Berlapis cloth	30	35
432	75s. Si Lobang Bangsi Bungs Belitang Kipas cloth	55	80
428/32	*Set of 5*	1·10	1·50
MS433	150×204 mm. Nos. 428/32	3·00	4·50

See also Nos. 442/7.

(Des Haji Salleh bin Haji Ibrahim. Litho Security Printers (M), Malaysia)

1988 (30 June). Brassware (2nd series). Vert designs as T **82**. Multicoloured. P 12.

434	50s. Lidded two-handled pot ("periok")	60	75
435	50s. Candlestick ("lampong")	60	75
436	50s. Shallow circular dish with stand ("gangsa")	60	75
437	50s. Repousse box with lid ("celapa")	60	75
434/7	*Set of 4*	2·25	2·75

(Des Awang Nor Ariffin bin Md. Yassin. Litho Security Printers (M), Malaysia)

1988 (1 Aug). 20th Anniv of Sultan's Coronation. T **89** and similar vert designs. Multicoloured. P 14 (20, 75s.) or 12½×13 ($2).

438	20s. Type **89**	25	15
439	75s. Sultan reading from Koran	1·00	60
440	$2 In Coronation robes (26×63 mm)	2·25	1·60
438/40	*Set of 3*	3·25	2·10
MS441	164×125 mm. Nos. 438/40	3·00	2·50

In No. **MS**441 the perforations of the stamps are as Nos. 438/40 except for the 75s. which is perforated 13 at right.

(Des Awang Nor Ariffin bin Md. Yassin. Litho Security Printers (M), Malaysia)

1988 (29 Sept). Handwoven Material (2nd series). Horiz designs as T **88**. Multicoloured. P 12.

442	10s. Beragi cloth	15	10
443	20s. Bertabur cloth	20	20
444	25s. Sukma Indra cloth	25	35
445	40s. Si Pugut Bunga cloth	40	75
446	75s. Beragi Si Lobang Bangsi Bunga Cendera Kesuma cloth	75	1·40
442/6	*Set of 5*	1·60	2·50
MS447	150×204 mm. Nos. 442/6	3·50	4·50

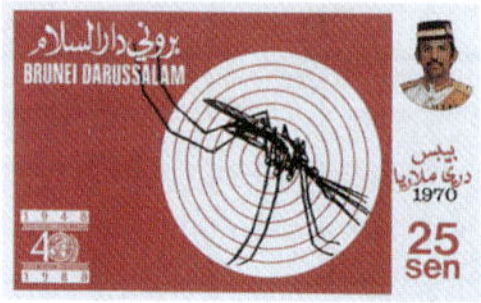

90 Malaria-carrying Mosquito

(Litho Cartor)

1988 (17 Dec). 40th Anniv of World Health Organization. T **90** and similar horiz designs. Multicoloured. P 14×13½.

448	25s. Type **90**	1·25	30
449	35s. Man with insecticide spray and sample on slide	1·40	45
450	$2 Microscope and magnified malaria cells	3·25	2·00
448/50	*Set of 3*	5·50	2·50

91 Sultan and Council of Ministers

92 Dove escaping from Cage

(Des Awang Nor Ariffin bin Md Yassin. Litho Security Printers (M), Malaysia)

1989 (23 Feb). Fifth Anniv of National Day. T **91** and similar multicoloured designs. P 12.

451	20s. Type **91**	15	10
452	30s. Guard of honour	20	15
453	60s. Firework display (27×55 *mm*)	45	40
454	$2 Congregation in mosque	1·50	1·75
451/4	*Set of 4*	2·10	2·10
MS455	164×124 mm. Nos. 451/4	2·25	2·75

(Des Haji Salleh bin Haji Ibrahim. Litho Secure. Singapore)

1989 (1 Apr). "Freedom of Palestine". T **92** and similar horiz design., Multicoloured. P 13½.

456	20s. Type **92**	50	20
457	75s. Map and Palestinian flat;	2·00	1·25
458	$1 Dome of the Rock, Jerusalem	2·75	1·50
456/8	*Set of 3*	4·75	2·75

(Des Awang Nor Ariffin bin Md. Yassin. Litho Secura, Singapore)

1989 (31 Oct). Local Fruits (3rd series). Horiz designs as T **85**. Multicoloured. P 12.

459	60s. *Daemonorops fissa*	2·00	2·50
	a. Horiz strip of 4. Nos. 459/62	7·25	9·00
460	60s. *Eleiodoxa conferta*	2·00	2·50
461	60s. *Salacca zalacca*	2·00	2·50
462	60s. *Calamus ornatus*	2·00	2·50
459/62	*Set of 4*	7·25	9·00

Nos. 459/62 were printed together, *se-tenant*, in horizontal strips of four throughout the sheet.

93 Oil Pump

(Des Brunei Shell Petroleum Co. Litho Secura, Singapore)

1989 (28 Dec). 60th Anniv of Brunei Oil and Gas Industry. T **93** and similar horiz designs. Multicoloured. P 13½.

463	20s. Type **93**	2·50	30
464	60s. Loading tanker	4·00	2·25
465	90s. Oil well at sunset	4·50	3·00
466	$1 Pipe laying	4·75	3·00
467	$2 Oil terminal	8·00	9·00
463/7 *Set of 5*		21·00	16·00

94 Museum Building and Exhibits

(Des Awang Padzil bin Haji Abroad ($1), Mobil Yamin bin Haji Abd. Momin (others). Litho Security Printers (M), Malaysia)

1990 (1 Jan). 25th Anniv of Brunei Museum. T **94** and similar horiz designs. Multicoloured. P 12.

468	30s. Type **94**	1·50	70
469	60s. Official opening, 1965	2·25	2·25
470	$1 Brunei Museum	3·00	4·00
468/70 *Set of 3*		6·00	6·25

95 Letters from Malay Alphabet

96 Tarsier in Tree

(Des Pengiran Haji Muhammad bin Pengiran Duraman. Litho Security Printers (M), Malaysia)

1990 (15 July). International Literacy Year. T **95** and similar horiz designs. Multicoloured. P 12.

471	15s. Type **95**	80	40
472	90s. English alphabet	3·50	4·25
473	$1 Literacy Year emblem and letters	3·50	4·25
471/3 *Set of 3*		7·00	8·00

(Des Haji Salleh bin Haji Ibrahim Litho Security Printers (M), Malaysia)

1990 (29 Sept). Endangered Species. Western Tarsier. T **96** and similar vert designs. Multicoloured. P 12 (20s.) or 12½×13 (others).

474	20s. Western Tarsier on branch	1·25	45
475	60s. Western Tarsier feeding	2·50	3·00
476	90s. Type **96**	3·50	4·50
474/6 *Set of 3*		6·50	7·25

97 Symbolic Family

98 Proboscis Monkey on Ground

(Litho Security Printers (M), Malaysia)

1990 (1 Dec). Worldwide Campaign against AIDS. T **97** and similar vert designs. Multicoloured. P 12½.

477	20s. Type **97**	3·00	60
478	30s. Sources of infection	4·00	2·00
479	90s. "AIDS" headstone surrounded by skulls	9·50	8·50
477/9 *Set of 3*		15·00	10·00

(Litho Security Printers (M), Malaysia)

1990 (31 Dec). Local Fruits (4th series). Horiz designs as T **85**. Multicoloured. P 12.

480	60s. *Willoughbea sp.* (brown fruit)	3·00	3·75
	a. Horiz strip of three. Nos. 480/2	8·00	10·00
481	60s. *Ripe Willoughbea sp.* (yellow fruit)	3·00	3·75
482	60s. *Willoughbea angustifolia*	3·00	3·75
480/2 *Set of 3*		8·00	10·00

Nos. 480/2 were printed together, *se-tenant*, in horizontal strips of three throughout the sheet.

(Des Haji Salleh bin Hajji Ibrahim. Litho Cartor)

1991 (30 Mar). Endangered Species. Proboscis Monkey. T **98** and similar vert designs. Multicoloured. P 13½×14.

483	15s. Type **98**	1·50	60
484	20s. Head of monkey	1·60	70
485	50s. Monkey sitting on branch	3·00	3·25
486	60s. Female monkey with baby climbing tree	3·25	3·75
483/6 *Set of 4*		8·50	7·50

99 Junior School Classes

100 Young Brunei Beauty

(Des Awang Nor Ariffin bin Md Yassin. Litho, Secura Singapore)

1991 (29 Sept). Teachers' Day. T **99** and similar horiz design. Multicoloured. P 13½×14.

487	60s. Type **99**	2·25	2·50
488	90s. Secondary school class	2·75	3·50

(Des Awang Padzil bin Haji Abroad. Litho Security Printers (M), Malaysia)

1991 (1 Oct). Fishes. Brunei Beauty. T **100** and similar horiz designs. Multicoloured. P 12½.

489	30s. Type **100**	1·50	85
490	60s. Female fish	2·50	4·00
491	$1 Male fish	3·00	4·75
489/91 *Set of 3*		6·25	8·75

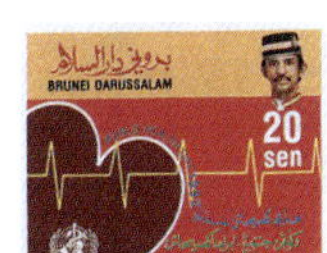

101 Graduate with Family

102 Symbolic Heart and Trace

(Des A. Mansur. Litho Cartor)

1991 (30 Nov). Happy Family Campaign. T **101** and similar vert designs. Multicoloured. P 13.

492	20s. Type **101**	70	50
493	60s. Mothers with children	1·75	2·00
494	90s. Family	2·00	3·25
492/4 *Set of 3*		4·00	5·25

(Des Siti Zaleha Haji Kaprawi. Litho Cartor)

1992 (7 Apr). World Health Day. T **102** and similar horiz designs showing heart and heartbeat trace. P 13.

495	20s. multicoloured	2·25	50
496	50s. multicoloured	4·00	2·50
497	75s. multicoloured	6·00	6·50
495/7 *Set of 3*		11·00	8·50

The 75s. is larger, 48×27 mm.

103 Map of Cable System

(Des Awang Nor Ariffin bin Md. Yassin. Litho Security Printers (M), Malaysia)

1992 (28 Apr). Launching of Singapore-Borneo-Philippines Fibre Optic Submarine Cable System. T **103** and similar horiz designs. P 12.

498	20s. Type **103**	3·00	50
499	30s. Diagram of Brunei connection	3·00	1·50
500	90s. Submarine cable	6·00	6·50
498/500 *Set of 3*		11·00	7·75

104 Modern Sculptures

105 "A.S.E.A.N. 25" and Logo

(Des Awang Nor Ariffin bin Md. Yassin. Litho Enschede)

1992 (30 June). Visit A.S.E.A.N. Year. T **104** and similar horiz designs. Multicoloured. P 13½×14.

501	20s. Type **104**	2·75	3·00
	a. Horiz strip of 3. Nos. 501/3	8·00	8·75
502	60s. Traditional martial arts	3·00	3·25
503	$1 Modern sculptures (different)	3·25	3·50
501/3 *Set of 3*		8·00	8·75

Nos. 501/3 were printed together, *se-tenant*, in horizontal strips of three throughout the sheet with the backgrounds forming a composite design.

(Des Mobil. Yamin bin Haji Abd. Momin. Litho Questa)

1992 (8 Aug). 25th Annie of A.S.E.A.N (Association of South East Asian Nations). T **105** and similar vert designs. Multicoloured. P 14.

504	20s. Type **105**	1·25	65
505	60s. Headquarters building	2·75	2·75
506	90s. National landmarks	3·50	4·50
504/6 *Set of 3*		6·75	7·00

106 Sultan in Procession

107 Crested Wood Partridge

(Des Awang Padzil bin Haji Ahmad. Litho Enschedé)

1992 (5 Oct). 25th Anniv of Sultan's Accession. T **106** and similar vert designs. Multicoloured. P 14×13½.

507	25s. Type **106**	1·50	2·00
	a. Horiz strip of 5. Nos. 507/11	6·75	9·00
508	25s. Brunei International Airport	1·50	2·00
509	25s. Sultan's Palace	1·50	2·00
510	25s. Docks and Brunei University	1·50	2·00
511	25s. Mosque	1·50	2·00
507/11 *Set of 5*		6·75	9·00

Nos. 507/11 were printed together, *se-tenant*, in horizontal strips of five throughout the sheet, each strip forming a composite design.

(Des Awang Padzil bin Haji Abroad. Litho Enschedé)

1992 (30 Dec). Birds (1st series). T **107** and similar vert designs. Multicoloured. P 14×13½.

512	30s. Type **107**	1·00	50
513	60s. Asiatic Paradise Flycatcher	2·00	2·25
514	$1 Great Argus Pheasant	2·25	3·00
512/14		4·75	5·25

(Des Awang Padzil bin Haji Ahmad (60s.), Kassim bin Haji Ismail (others). Litho Enschedé)

1993 (2 Jan). Birds (2nd series). Vert designs as T **107**. Multicoloured. P 14×13½.

515	30s. Long-tailed Parakeet	1·00	50
516	60s. Magpie Robin	2·00	2·25
517	$1 Blue-crowned Hanging Parrot	2·50	3·00
515/17 *Set of 3*		5·00	5·25

(Des Kassim bin Haji Ismail. Litho Enschedé)

1993 (3 May). Birds (3rd series). Multicoloured designs as T **107**. P 13½×14 (horiz) or 14×13½ (vert).

518	30s. Chesnut-breasted Malkoha	1·25	50
519	60s. White-tamped Shams	2·25	2·50
520	$1 Black and Red Broadbill (vert)	3·00	3·50
518/20 *Set of 3*		6·00	6·00

108 National Flag and "10"

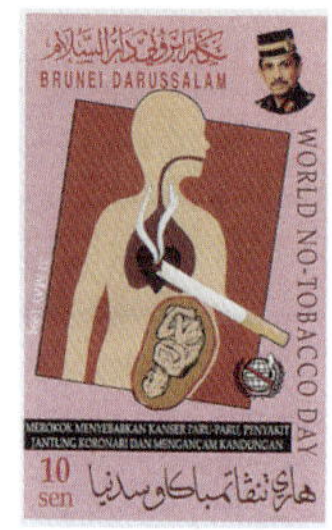

109 Cigarette burning Heart and Deformed Baby in Womb

(Des Awang Nor Ariffin bin Md. Yassin. Litho Cartor)

1994 (16 June). Tenth Anniv of National Day. T **108** and similar vert designs. Multicoloured. P 13.

521	10s. Type **108**	1·25	1·25
	a. Horiz strip of 4. Nos. 521/4	5·00	5·50
522	20s. Symbolic hands	1·25	1·40
523	30s. Previous National Day symbols	1·40	1·50
524	60s. Coat of arms	1·75	1·90
521/4 *Set of 4*		5·00	5·50

Nos. 521/4 were printed together, *se-tenant*, in horizontal strips of four throughout the sheet.

(Des Ali bin Haji Abd Rahim. Litho Cartor)

1994 (8 Aug). Local Fruits (5th issue). Horiz designs as T **85**, but each 36×26 mm. Multicoloured. P 13½.

525	60s. *Nephelium mutabile*	85	1·40
526	60s. *Nephelium xerospermoides*	85	1·40
527	60s. *Nephelium* spp	85	1·40
528	60s. *Nephelium macrophyllum*	85	1·40
525/8 *Set of 4*		3·00	5·00

(Lithe Enschedé)

1994 (1 Sept). World No Tobacco Day. T **109** and similar vert designs. Multicoloured. P 14×13½.

529	10s. Type **109**	40	20
530	15s. Symbols of smoking over crowd of people	40	20
531	$2 Globe crushing cigarettes	3·00	5·00
529/31 *Set of 3*		3·50	5·00

110 Raja Isteri (wife of Sultan) in Guide Uniform

111 Turbo-prop Airliner on Runway

(Des Awang Nor Ariffin bin Md. Yassin. Litho Enschedé)

1994 (7 Oct). 40th Anniv of Brunei Girl Guides' Association. T **110** and similar vert designs. Multicoloured. P 14×13½.

532	40s. Type **110**	2·00	2·00

a. Horiz strip of 5. Nos. 532/6 9·00 9·00
533 40s. Guide receiving award 2·00 2·00
534 40s. Guide reading 2·00 2·00
535 40s. Group of guides 2·00 2·00
536 40s. Guides erecting tent 2·00 2·00
532/6 *Set of 5* 9·00 9·00

Nos. 532/6 were printed together, *se-tenant*, in horizontal strips of five throughout the sheet.

(Des Mobil Yamin bin Haji Abd Momin. Litho Cartor)

1994 (18 Nov). 20th Anniv of Royal Brunei Airlines. T **111** and similar horiz designs. Multicoloured. P 13½.

537 10s. Type **111** 1·00 45
538 20s. Jet airliner on runway 1·50 45
539 $1 Jet airliner in the air 3·50 4·50
537/9 *Set of 3* 5·50 4·75

112 Malay Family

113 Aerial View of City, 1970

(Des Awang Padzil bin Hap Ahmad. Litho Cartor)

1994 (30 Dec). International Day against Drug Abuse and Trafficking. T **112** and similar vert designs. P 13½×14.

540 20s. Type **112** 1·10 1·60
a. Horiz strip of 3. Nos. 540/2 3·75 5·50
541 60s. Chinese family 1·40 1·90
542 $1 Doctor, police officers and members of youth organizations 1·75 2·50
540/2 *Set of 3* 3·75 5·50

Nos. 540/2 were printed together, *se-tenant*, in horizontal strips of three throughout the sheet, each strip forming a composite design.

(Des Awang Padzil bin Haji Abroad. Litho Cartor)

1995 (4 Oct). 25th Anniv of Bandar Seri Begawan. T **113** and similar horiz designs. Multicoloured. P 13½.

543 30s. Type **113** 1·50 45
544 50s. City in 1980 2·00 1·50
545 $1 City in 1990 2·75 4·00
543/5 *Set of 3* 5·50 5·50

114 United Nations General Assembly

115 Students in Laboratory

(Des Mobil Yamin bin Haji Abd Momin. Litho Walsall)

1995 (24 Oct). 50th Anniv of United Nations. T **114** and similar vert designs. Multicoloured. P 14½×14.

546 20s. Type **114** 50 25
547 60s. Security Council in session 1·00 90
548 90s. United Nations Building, New York (27×44 mm) 1·50 2·50
546/8 *Set of 3* 2·75 3·25

(Des Mahadi bin Haji Matzain. Litho Cartor)

1995 (28 Oct). Tenth Anniv of University of Brunei. T **115** and similar vert designs. Multicoloured. P 13×13½.

549 30s. Type **115** 45 35
550 50s. University building 70 70
551 90s. Sultan visiting University 1·25 2·25
549/51 *Set of 3* 2·10 3·00

116 Police Officers

117 Telephones

(Des Awang Nor Ariffin bin Md. Yassin. Litho Enschede)

1996 (10 Feb). 75th Anniv of Royal Brunei Police Force. T **116** and similar vert designs. Multicoloured. P 13½×13.

552 25s. Type **116** 1·50 60
553 50s. Aspects of police work 2·00 1·50
554 75s. Sultan inspecting parade 2·50 3·50
552/4 *Set of 3* 5·50 5·00

(Litho Cartor)

1996 (17 May). World Telecommunications Day. Children's Paintings. T **117** and similar vert designs. Multicoloured. P 13½.

555 20s. Type **117** 85 40
556 35s. Telephone dial and aspects of telecommunications 1·40 60
557 $1 Globe and aspects of telecommunications 3·50 4·00
555/7 *Set of 3* 5·25 4·50

118 Sultan and Crowd

119 Sultan Hassanal Bolkiah Mu'izzaddin Waddaulah

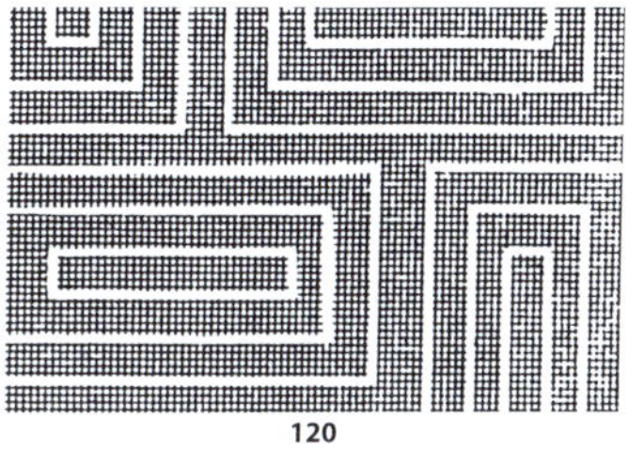

120

(Des Awang Nor Ariffin bin Md. Yassin. Litho Carter)

1996 (15 July). 50th Birthday of Sultan Hassanal Bolkiah Mu'izzaddin Waddaulah. T **118** and similar vert designs. Multicoloured. P 13×13½.

558 50s. Type **118** 1·40 1·75
559 50s. Sultan in ceremonial dress 1·40 1·75
560 50s. Sultan receiving dignitaries at mosque 1·40 1·75
561 50s. Sultan with subjects 1·40 1·75
558/61 *Set of 4* 5·00 6·25
MS562 152×100 mm. $1 Sultan in ceremonial dress (different). P 13 2·25 3·00

A larger miniature sheet, 176×128 mm, containing five vertical $50 values was produced in a limited printing for presentation purposes.

FLUORESCENT SECURITY MARKING. All issues from No. 563 onwards carry a fluorescent security marking, unless otherwise stated. This takes the form of a single impression of the Postal Service logo only visible under U.V. light. The size and the colour of the fluorescent ink varies according to the printer involved.

(Litho Enschedé)

1996 (9 Oct). T **119** and similar vert design. W **120**. P 14×13½.

563	**119**	10s. multicoloured	20	10
564		15s. multicoloured	25	25
565		20s. multicoloured	30	25
566		30s. multicoloured	40	35
567		50s. multicoloured	70	50
568		60s. multicoloured	80	60
569		75s. multicoloured	1·00	70
570		90s. multicoloured	1·25	90
571	–	$1 multicoloured	1·50	1·00
572	–	$2 multicoloured	2·75	2·25
573	–	$5 multicoloured	6·50	6·50
574	–	$10 multicoloured	12·00	12·00
563/74 *Set of* 12			25·00	23·00

Design: (27×39 mm)—$1 to $10 Sultan in ceremonial robes.

121 Black-naped Tern

122 *Acanthus ebrocteatus*

(Des Siti Zaleha Haji Kaprawi. Litho Enschede)

1996 (11 Nov). Birds (4th series). Sea Birds. T **121** and similar vert designs. Multicoloured. P 14×13½.

575	20s. Type **121**	75	50
576	30s. Roseate Tern	75	50
577	$1 Bridled Tern	1·75	2·75
575/7 *Set of* 3		3·00	3·50

No. 576 is inscribed "ROSLATE TERN" in error.

(Des J. Esther Lee. Litho Security Printers (M), Malaysia)

1997 (29 May). Mangrove Flowers. T **122** and similar horiz designs. Multicoloured. P 12.

578	20s. Type **122**	45	25
579	30s. *Lumnitzera littorea*	50	35
580	$1 *Nypa fruticans*	1·40	2·50
578/80 *Set of* 3		2·10	2·75

123 *Heterocentrotus mammillatus*

(Des J. Esther Lee. Litho Southern Colour Print, Dunedin)

1997 (15 Dec). Marine Life. T **123** and similar horiz designs. Multicoloured. P 12.

581	60s. Type **123**	70	1·00
582	60s. *Linckia laevigata* (starfish)	70	1·00
583	60s. *Oxycomanthus bennetti* (plant)	70	1·00
584	60s. *Bohadschia argus* (sea slug)	70	1·00
581/4 *Set of* 4		2·50	3·50

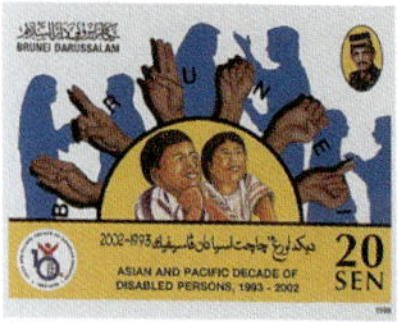

124 Children and Sign Language

(Des Padzil bin Haj Ahmed* Litho Cartor)

1998 (31 May). Asian and Pacific Decade of Disabled Persons, 1993–2002. T **124** and similar horiz designs. Multicoloured. P 13×13½.

585	20s. Type **124**	55	25
586	50s. Woman typing and firework display	1·00	1·00
587	$1 Disabled athletes	1·75	2·50
585/7 *Set of* 3		3·00	3·25

125 Sultan performing Ceremonial Duties

126 A.S.E.A.N. Architecture and Transport

(Des Awang Nor Ariffin bin Md. Yassin. Litho Security Printers (M), Malaysia)

1998 (1 Aug). 30th Anniv of Coronation of Sultan Hassanal Bolkiah Mu'izzaddin Waddaulah. T **125** and similar horiz designs. Multicoloured. P 12.

588	60s. Type **125**	1·00	50
589	90s. Sultan on Coronation throne	1·40	1·60
590	$1 Coronation parade	1·50	1·60
588/90 *Set of* 3		3·50	3·25
MS591 150×180 mm. Nos. 588/90		3·50	4·00

(Des Siti Zaleha Haji Kaprawi. Litho Enschedé)

1998 (8 Aug). 30th Anniv of Association of South-east Asian Nations. T **126** and similar vert designs. Multicoloured. P 13½.

592	30s. Type **126**	1·25	1·25
593	30s. Map of Brunei and city scenes	1·25	1·25
594	30s. Flags of member nations	1·25	1·25
592/4 *Set of* 3		3·25	3·25

127 Crown Prince at Desk

128 Koran, Civil Servants and Handshake

(Des Mobil Yamin bin Haji Abd Momin. Litho Security Printers (M), Malaysia)

1998 (10 Aug). Proclamation of Prince Al-Muhtadee Billah as Crown Prince. T **127** and similar vert designs. Multicoloured. P 12.

595	$1 Type **127**	1·00	1·00
596	$2 Crown Prince in military uniform	1·75	2·75
597	$3 Crown Prince's emblem	2·25	3·75
595/7 *Set of* 3		4·50	6·75
MS598 175×153 mm. Nos. 595/7		5·50	7·00

(Des Awang Nor Ariffin bin Md Yassin. Litho Cartor)

1998 (29 Sept). Fifth Anniv of Civil Service Day. T **128** and similar vert designs. Multicoloured. P 13×13½.

599	30s. Type **128**	60	30
600	60s. Symbols of progress	1·00	75
601	90s. Civil servants at work	1·50	2·00
599/601 *Set of* 3		2·75	2·75

129 Blue-eared Kingfisher

130 Water Village, Bandar Seri Begawan

(Des J. Esther Lee. Litho Cartor)

1998 (11 Nov). Birds (5th series). Kingfishers. T **129** and similar vert designs. Multicoloured. P 13½×13.

602	20s. Type **129**	1·00	60
603	30s. Common Kingfisher	1·25	60
604	60s. White-collared Kingfisher	2·00	1·50
605	$1 Stork-billed Kingfisher	2·50	3·00
602/5 *Set of 4*		6·00	5·25

(Des Siti Zaleha Haji Kaprawi. Litho Cartor)

1999 (23 Feb). 15th Anniv of National Day. T **130** and similar vert designs. Multicoloured. P 13.

606	20s. Type **130**	50	20
607	60s. Modern telecommunications and air travel	1·50	1·10
608	90s. Aspects of modern Brunei	2·00	2·25
606/8 *Set of 3*		3·50	3·25
MS609 118×85 mm. Nos. 606/8		3·50	4·00

131 Rifle-shooting

132 Clasped Hands and Globe

(Litho Southern Colour Print, Dunedin)

1999 (7 Aug). 20th South-east Asia Games, Brunei. T **131** and similar square designs. Multicoloured. P 14½.

610	20s. Type **131**	65	75
	a. Horiz strip of 5. Nos. 610/14	3·00	3·25
611	20s. Golf and tennis	65	75
612	20s. Boxing and judo	65	75
613	20s. Squash and table tennis	65	75
614	20s. Swimming and canoe racing	65	75
615	20s. Hockey and cycling	65	75
	a. Horiz strip of 5. Nos. 615/19	3·00	3·25
616	20s. Basketball and football	65	75
617	20s. High jumping, shot putting and running	65	75
618	20s. Snooker	65	75
619	20s. Bowling	65	75
610/19 *Set of 10*		6·00	6·50
MS620 110×73 mm. $1 Various sports		2·00	3·25

Nos. 610/14 and 615/19 were each printed together, *se-tenant*, in horizontal strips of five throughout separate sheets.

(Des Awang Nor Ariffin bin Md. Yassin. Litho Southern Colour Print, Dunedin)

1999 (9 Oct). 125th Anniv of Universal Postal Union. T **132** and similar vert designs. Multicoloured. P 14.

621	20s. Type **132**	60	25
622	30s. "125" and logos	70	30
623	75s. Aspects of postal service	1·50	2·25
621/3 *Set of 3*		2·50	2·50

133 Modern Building and Children using Computer

134 Sultan Mohamed Jemal-ul-Alam and Traditional Buildings, 1901–20

(Litho Security Printers (M), Malaysia)

2000 (1 Feb). New Millennium. T **133** and similar vert designs. Multicoloured. Phosphorised paper. P 14×13½ (with two elliptical holes on each vertical side).

624	20s. Type **133**	75	75
	a. Horiz strip of 6. Nos. 624/9	4·00	4·00
625	20s. Royal Palace, tree and people using computer	75	75
626	20s. Aerial view of mosque and factory	75	75
627	20s. Plan of Parterre Gardens	75	75
628	20s. Container ships and airliner	75	75
629	20s. Satelite dish aerials	75	75
624/9 *Set of 6*		4·00	4·00
MS630 221×121 mm. Nos. 624/9		4·00	4·00

Nos. 624/9 were printed together, *se-tenant*, as horizontal strips of six in sheets of 30 with the backgrounds of each strip forming a composite design.

(Des B.K. Network. Litho Security Printers (M), Malaysia)

2000 (23 Feb). Brunei in the 20th Century. T **134** and similar vert designs. Multicoloured. Phosphorised paper. P 13½ (with one elliptical hole on each vertical side).

631	30s. Type **134**	1·00	1·00
	a. Horiz strip of 5. Nos. 631/5	4·50	4·50
632	30s. Sultan Ahmed Tajudin, oil well and Brunei police, 1921–40	1·00	1·00
633	30s. Signing of the Constitution and Brunei Mosque, 1941–60	1·00	1·00
634	30s. Oil installation, satellite dish, Royal Brunei Airlines and bank note, 1961–80	1·00	1·00
635	30s. Sultan on throne, international organisation emblems and crowd with trophy, 1981–99	1·00	1·00
631/5 *Set of 5*		4·50	4·50

Nos. 631/5 were printed together, *se-tenant*, in horizontal strips of five throughout the sheet.

135 Sultan Hashim Jalil-ul-Alam, 1885–1906

136 *Rafflesia pricei*

(Des Siti Zaleha Haji Kaprawi. Litho Security Printers (M), Malaysia)

2000 (15 July). The Sultans of Brunei. T **135** and similar vert designs. Multicoloured. Phosphorised paper. P 13½.

636	60s. Type **135**	1·40	1·40
	a. Horiz strip of 5. Nos. 636/40	6·00	6·00
637	60s. Sultan Mohamed Jemal-ul-Alam, 1906–24	1·40	1·40
638	60s. Sultan Ahmed Tajudin, 1924–50	1·40	1·40
639	60s. Sultan Omar Ali Saifuddin, 1950–67	1·40	1·40
640	60s. Sultan Hassanal Bolkiah, 1967	1·40	1·40
636/40 *Set of 5*		6·00	6·00
MS641 190×99 mm. Nos. 636/40. P 14½×14		4·50	6·00

Nos. 636/40 were printed together, *se-tenant*, in horizontal strips of five throughout the sheet.

(Des Siti Khairuleena Bte Abdullah. Litho Southern Colour Print, New Zealand)

2000 (2 Oct). Local Flowers. T **136** and similar horiz designs. Multicoloured. P 14.

642	30s. Type **136**	75	30
643	50s. *Rhizanthes lowi*	1·25	1·25
644	60s. *Nepenthes rafflesiana*	1·40	1·40
642/4 *Set of 3*		3·00	2·75

137 Information Technology

138 Green Turtle

(Des Abdull Rahman Ahmad. Litho Cartor)

2000 (15 Nov). Asia-Pacific Economic Cooperation. Heads of Government Meeting. T **137** and similar vert designs. Multicoloured. P 13.

645	20s. Type **137**	70	70
	a. Booklet pane of 1 with margins all round	70	
646	30s. Small and medium businesses	70	95
	a. Booklet pane of 1 with margins all round	95	
647	60s. Tourism	1·75	1·75
	a. Booklet pane of 1 with margins all round	1·75	
645/7 *Set of 3*		3·00	3·00
MS648 150×108 mm. Nos. 645/7		3·00	3·50

(Litho Cartor)

2000 (16 Nov). Turtles. T **138** and similar horiz designs. Multicoloured. P 13.

649	30s. Type **138**	1·00	1·00
	a. Horiz strip of 3. Nos. 649/51	2·75	2·75
650	30s. Hawksbill Turtle	1·00	1·00
651	30s. Olive Ridley Turtle	1·00	1·00
649/51 *Set of 3*		2·75	2·75

Nos. 649/51 were printed together, *se-tenant*, in horizontal strips of three throughout the sheet.

139 Tourist Canoe on River

(Litho Enschedé)

2001 (14 Mar). "Visit Brunei Year". T **139** and similar horiz designs. Multicoloured. P 14.

652	20s. Type **139**	1·25	75
653	30s. Traditional water village	1·25	75
654	60s. Carved building façade	2·25	2·75
652/4 *Set of 3*		4·25	3·75

140 Sultan in Army Uniform

141 First Aid Demonstration

(Des Siti Zaleha Haji Kaprawi. Litho Security Printers (M), Malaysia)

2001 (15 July). 55th Birthday of Sultan Hassanal Bolkiah Muizzaddin Waddaulah. T **140** and similar vert designs. Multicoloured. Phosphorised paper. P 12.

655	55s. Type **140**	1·40	1·40
	a. Horiz strip of 5. Nos. 655/9	6·25	6·25
656	55s. Sultan in Air Force uniform	1·40	1·40
657	55s. Sultan in traditional dress	1·40	1·40
658	55s. Sultan in Army camouflage jacket	1·40	1·40
659	55s. Sultan in Navy uniform	1·40	1·40
655/9 *Set of 5*		6·25	6·25
MS660 100×75 mm. 55s. Sultan and Bandar Seri Begawan (40×71 mm)		2·25	2·50

Nos. 655/9 were printed together, *se-tenant*, in horizontal strips of five, in sheet of 25.

(Litho Security Printers (M), Malaysia)

2001 (5 Aug). International Youth Camp. T **141** and similar vert designs. Multicoloured. W **138** (sideways) of Malaysia. Phosphorised paper. P 12.

661	30s. Type **141**	1·00	1·00
	a. Horiz strip of 3. Nos 661/3	2·75	2·75
662	30s. Brunei guides and tent demonstration	1·00	1·00
663	30s. Scouts with cooking pot	1·00	1·00
661/3 *Set of 3*		2·75	2·75
MS664 110×77 mm. Nos. 661/3		2·75	3·25

Nos. 661/3 were printed together, *se-tenant*, in horizontal strips of three forming a composite design.

142 Islamic Regalia

(Des Abdul Rahman bin Haji Mohammad. Litho Security Printers (M), Malaysia)

2001 (18 Aug). First Islamic International Exhibition, Brunei. T **142** and similar horiz designs. Multicoloured. W **138** (sideways) of Malaysia. Phosphorised paper. P 12.

665	20s. Type **142**	80	80
	a. Horiz strip of 4. Nos. 665/8	3·00	3·00
666	20s. Exhibition centre	80	80
667	20s. Computer communications	80	80
668	20s. Opening ceremony	80	80
665/8 *Set of 4*		3·00	3·00

Nos. 665/8 were printed together, *se-tenant*, in horizontal strips of four.

143 Forest Walkway

144 "Children encircling Globe" (Urska Golob)

(Des K. Mirzoyev. Litho Cartor)

2001 (1 Sept). Visit Brunei (2nd series). T **143** and similar horiz designs. Multicoloured. P 13½.

669	20s. Type **143**	85	85
	a. Horiz strip of 4. Nos. 669/72	3·00	3·00
670	20s. Waterfall	85	85
671	20s. Jerudong Theme Park	85	85
672	20s. Footbridges across lake	85	85
669/72 *Set of 4*		3·00	3·00

Nos. 669/72 were printed together, *se-tenant*, in horizontal strips of four throughout the sheet.

(Litho Security Printers (M), Malaysia)

2001 (9 Oct). UN Year of Dialogue among Civilisations. T **144** and similar vert designs. Multicoloured. Phosphorised paper. P 12.

673	30s. Type **144**	1·00	1·00
	a. Horiz strip of 4. Nos. 673/6	3·50	3·50
674	30s. Quotation marks illustrated with faces..	1·00	1·00
675	30s. Cubist portrait and Japanese girl	1·00	1·00
676	30s. Coloured leaves	1·00	1·00
673/6 *Set of 4*		3·50	3·50

Nos. 673/6 were printed together, *se-tenant*, in horizontal strips of four throughout the sheet.

145 Male and Female Bulwer's Pheasants

146 Early and Modern Telephone Systems

(Des K. Ismail. Litho Security Printers (M), Malaysia)

2001 (1 Nov). Endangered Species. Bulwer's Pheasant. T **145** and similar horiz designs. Multicoloured. W **138** of Malaysia. Phosphorised paper. P 12.

677	30s. Type **145**	1·10	1·10
	a. Horiz strip of 4. Nos. 677/80	4·00	4·00
678	30s. Male pheasant	1·10	1·10

679	30s. Female pheasant with chicks	1·10	1·10
680	30s. Female pheasant	1·10	1·10
677/80	*Set of 4*	4·00	4·00

Nos. 677/80 were printed together, *se-tenant*, in horizontal strips of four throughout the sheet.

2002 (17 May). 50th Anniv of Department of Telecommunications (JTB). T **146** and similar vert designs. Litho. Multicoloured. P 12.

681	50s. Type **146**	1·40	1·40
	a. Horiz strip of 3. Nos. 681/3	3·75	3·75
682	50s. JTB Golden Jubilee emblem	1·40	1·40
683	50s. Computer networks	1·40	1·40
681/3	*Set of 3*	3·75	3·75

Nos. 681/3 were printed together, *se-tenant*, in horizontal strips of three throughout the sheet.

147 50th Anniversary Logo

148 Modern Housing, Water Village

(Litho Security Printers (M), Malaysia)

2002 (1 Aug). 50th Anniv of Survey Department. T **147** and similar vert designs. Multicoloured. Phosphorised paper. P 12.

684	50s. Type **147**	1·40	1·40
	a. Horiz strip of 3. Nos. 684/6	3·75	3·75
685	50s. Survey Department Offices	1·40	1·40
686	50s. Theodolite and thermal map	1·40	1·40
684/6	*Set of 3*	3·75	3·75

Nos. 684/6 were printed together, *se-tenant*, in horizontal strips of three throughout the sheet.

(Litho National Security Printers, Malaysia)

2002 (5 Oct). Tenth Anniv of Yayasan Sultan Haji Hassanal Bolkiah Foundation. T **148** and similar vert designs. Multicoloured. Phosphorised paper. P 12½.

687	10s. Type **148**	50	50
	a. Horiz strip of 4. Nos. 687/90	1·75	1·75
688	10s. Mosque and interior	50	50
689	10s. School and computer class	50	50
690	10s. University of Brunei	50	50
687/90	*Set of 4*	1·75	1·75

Nos. 687/90 were printed together, *se-tenant*, in horizontal strips of four in sheets of 20.

149 Anti-Corruption Bureau Headquarters

(Litho National Security Printers, Malaysia)

2002 (19 Nov). 20th Anniv of Anti-Corruption Bureau. T **149** and similar square designs. Multicoloured. Phosphorised paper. P 13.

691	20s. Type **149**	85	85
	a. Horiz strip of 3. Nos. 691/3	2·25	2·25
692	20s. Skyscrapers and mosque	85	85
693	20s. Anti-Corruption Bureau posters	85	85
691/3	*Set of 3*	2·25	2·25

Nos. 691/3 were printed together, *se-tenant*, in horizontal strips of three in sheets of 15.

HAVE YOU READ THE NOTES AT THE BEGINNING OF THIS CATALOGUE?

These often provide answers to the enquiries we receive

150 *Melastoma malabathricum*

2003 (25 Dec). Flowering Medicinal Plants. T **150** and similar vert designs. Multicoloured. Litho. P 12½.

694	20s. Type **150**	80	80
	a. Horiz strip of 4. Nos. 694/7	3·00	3·00
695	20s. *Etlingera solaris*	80	80
696	20s. *Dillenia suffruticosa*	80	80
697	20s. *Costus speciosus*	80	80
694/7	*Set of 4*	3·00	3·00

Nos. 694/7 were printed together, *se-tenant*, in horizontal strips of four throughout the sheet.

151 Drums and Musicians

152 Sultan of Brunei and UN Emblem

(Litho National Security Printers, Malaysia)

2003 (31 Dec). ASEAN—Japan Exchange Year. T **151** and similar horiz designs. Multicoloured. P 13.

698	20s. Type **151**	70	70
	a. Horiz strip of 3. Nos. 698/700	1·90	1·90
699	20s. Woodworker and handicrafts	70	70
700	20s. Exchange Year logo	70	70
698/700	*Set of 3*	1·90	1·90

Nos. 698/700 were printed together, *se-tenant*, in horizontal strips of three throughout the sheet.

2004 (23 Feb). 20th Anniv of National Day. T **152** and similar vert designs. Multicoloured. Litho. P 12.

701	20s. Type **152**	70	70
	a. Horiz strip of 4. Nos. 701/4	2·50	2·50
702	20s. In military uniform	70	70
703	20s. Reading speech at National Day celebration	70	70
704	20s. Emblem	70	70
701/4	*Set of 4*	2·50	2·50
MS705	185×140 mm. Nos. 701/4	2·75	3·00

Nos. 701/4 were printed together, *se-tenant*, in horizontal strips of four throughout the sheet.

153 Brunei 1895 ½s. Stamp

154 Crown Prince Al-Muhtadee Billah Bolkiah and Sarah Salleh

2004 (27 Mar). Brunei Darussalam National Philatelic Society. T **153** and similar vert designs. Multicoloured. Litho. P 12½.

706	25s. Type **153**	75	75
	a. Horiz strip of 3. Nos. 706/8	2·00	2·00
707	25s. Magnifying glass, perforation gauge, tweezers and stamps	75	75

708 25s. Postmarks, stamp catalogue and first day covers 75 75
706/8 *Set of 3* .... 2·00 2·00

Nos. 706/8 were printed together, *se-tenant*, in horizontal strips of three throughout the sheet.

(Litho Security Printers (M), Malaysia)

2004 (9 Sept). Royal Wedding. P 12.

709 **154** 99s. multicoloured .... 1·60 1·75
a. Horiz pair. Nos. 709/b and central label .... 3·00 3·50
b. With dark shading between portraits .... 1·60 1·75

Nos. 709/b were printed together, *se-tenant* , as horizontal pairs separated by a central label in sheets of 10 (5×2). The shading of the tapestry background to the portraits differs between the two stamps.

No. 709 has a bright area at the closest point between the two portraits, but No. 709b has blackish brown shading in that area.

155 Sultan of Brunei and Jame'Asr Hassanal Bolkiah Mosque

157 Parcels and Letters travelling around Globe

156 General Post Office, Bandar Seri Begawan

2006 (15 July). 60th Birthday of Sultan Hassanal Bolkiah Muizzaddin Waddaulah. T **155** and similar vert designs showing montage of images, all with portrait of Sultan at top right. Multicoloured (except $60), panel colours given. Litho. Phosphorised paper. P 13×12½.

710 60s. Type **155** (mauve) .... 1·00 1·00
a. Horiz strip of 6. Nos. 710/15 .... 5·50 5·50
711 60s. Sultan, palace and crowd with flags (Venetian red) .... 1·00 1·00
712 60s. Sultan and urban and agricultural scenes (orange-yellow) .... 1·00 1·00
713 60s. Sultan speaking at 9th ASEAN?Japan Summit and at APEC 2000 (salmon) .... 1·00 1·00
714 60s. Sultan meeting woman (bright yellow-green) .... 1·00 1·00
715 60s. Sultan in military uniform (turquoise-blue) .... 1·00 1·00
710/15 *Set of 6* .... 5·50 5·50
MS716 166×120 mm. Nos. 710/15 .... 5·50 6·00
MS717 148×137 mm. $60 Montage of five black and white photographs of Sultan as young man, at Coronation, seated on throne and wearing crown and military uniform (black and grey) (99×90 mm). P 13½ .... 42·00 48·00

Nos. 710/15 were printed together, *se-tenant* , in horizontal strips of six stamps throughout the sheet.

2006 (11 Oct). Centenary of Postal Services Department. Multicoloured. Litho. (a) T **156** and similar horiz designs. Phosphorised paper. P 13½.

718 100s. Type **156** .... 1·40 1·60
a. Horiz strip of 4. Nos. 781/21 .... 5·00 5·75
719 100s. Kuala Belait Post Office .... 1·40 1·60
720 100s. Tutong Post Office at the District Office, Tutong .... 1·40 1·60
721 100s. Bangar Post Office at the District Office, Temburong .... 1·40 1·60
718/21 *Set of 4* .... 5·00 5·75
MS722 115×115 mm. Nos. 718/21 .... 5·00 5·75

(b) T **157** and similar vert designs showing children's drawings. P 13×12½.

MS723 95×145 mm. 100s.×6 Type **157**; Postman; Globe, letter, house and aircraft; Air mail letters, postbox and post office; Letters, globe and families in Brunei and China; Globe and national flags ('EVERYONE REACHING EVERYWHERE') .... 7·00 8·00

Nos. 718/21 were printed together, *se-tenant*, in horizontal strips of four stamps throughout the sheet.

158 *Balistapus undulates* (orangestriped triggerfish)

159 Sultan Hassanal Bolkiah Mu'izzaddin Waddaulah

(Des Awang Ali bin Hj. Litho Security Printers (M), Malaysia)

2007 (6 Feb). Marine Life. T **158** and similar horiz designs. Multicoloured. Phosphorised paper. P 13½.

724 60s. Type **158** .... 1·25 1·25
725 60s. *Taenionotis triacanthus* (leaf scorpionfish) .... 1·25 1·25
MS726 100×70 mm. $1 *Nautilus pompilus* (chambered nautilus); $1 *Ostracion meleagris* (spotted boxfish) .... 3·50 3·50

Stamps in similar designs were issued by Malaysia.

(Des Pg Hj Mohd Yamin PSJ Pg Hj Adbul Momin. Litho Enschedé)

2007 (22 Feb). T **159** and similar vert designs. Multicoloured. Fluorescent markings. P 13½ (10 to 90s.) or 13½×14 ($1 to $10).

727 **159** 10s. multicoloured 10 10
728 15s. multicoloured 20 20
729 20s. multicoloured 25 25
730 30s. multicoloured 35 35
731 50s. multicoloured 60 60
732 60s. multicoloured 70 70
733 75s. multicoloured 90 90
734 90s. multicoloured .... 1·10 1·10
735 – $1 multicoloured .... 1·25 1·25
736 – $2 multicoloured .... 2·40 2·40
737 – $5 multicoloured .... 6·00 6·00
738 – $10 multicoloured .... 12·00 12·00
727/38 *Set of 12* .... 23·00 23·00

Nos. 735/8 are as Type **159** but larger, 27×40 mm.

160 Bubungan Dua Belas

2007 (23 July). Centenary of Bubungan Dua Belas (House of Twelve Roofs, former British High Commissioner's Residence), Bukit Subok. T **160** and similar horiz designs. Multicoloured. Litho. P 13½.

739 30s. Type **160** 90 35
740 60s. Bubungan Dua Belas (seen from above) .... 1·60 1·25
741 £1 Bubungan Dua Belas, 1907 .... 2·50 3·00
739/41 *Set of 3* .... 4·50 4·25
MS742 150×90 mm. Nos. 739/41 .... 4·50 4·75

161 Public Works Department Headquarters

162 Secretariat Building, Brunei

(Des Hj Husni Hj Damit and Hjh Marwani Hj Mohd Aarif)

2007 (30 Aug). Centenary (2006) of Public Works Department. T **161** and similar square designs. Multicoloured. Litho. Phosphorised paper. P 13½.

743	75s. Type **161**	1·00	1·25
	a. Horiz strip of 3. Nos. 743/5	2·75	3·25
744	75s. Engineers Office, (PWD Headquarters), Subok, 1906	1·00	1·25
745	75s. "100" and PWD logo	1·00	1·25
743/5 *Set of 3*		2·75	3·25

Nos. 743/5 were printed together, *se-tenant* , in horizontal strips of three stamps throughout the sheet. The official date of issue was 30 August 2007 but these stamps appear to have been distributed earlier by the Crown Agents.

2007 (21 Nov). 40th Anniv of ASEAN (Association of South-east Asian Nations). Ancient and Modern Architecture. T **162** and similar horiz designs. Multicoloured. Litho. P 13½.

746	20s. Type **162**	1·10	1·10
	a. Sheetlet. Nos. 746/55	10·00	10·00
747	20s. Yangon Post Office, Myanmar	1·10	1·10
748	20s. National Museum of Cambodia	1·10	1·10
749	20s. Malacañang Palace, Philippines	1·10	1·10
750	20s. Fatahillah Museum, Jakarta, Indonesia	1·10	1·10
751	20s. National Museum of Singapore	1·10	1·10
752	20s. Lao Typical House	1·10	1·10
753	20s. Vimanmek Mansion, Bangkok, Thailand	1·10	1·10
754	20s. Malayan Railway Headquarters Building, Kuala Lumpur, Malaysia	1·10	1·10
755	20s. Presidential Palace, Hanoi, Vietnam	1·10	1·10
746/55 *Set of 10*		10·00	10·00

Nos. 746/55 were printed together, *se-tenant* , in sheetlets of ten stamps. Similar designs were issued by the ten member countries, Indonesia, Malaysia, Philippines, Singapore, Thailand, Vietnam, Laos, Myanmar and Cambodia.

163 Istana Majlis

(Des Awang Abd Ajihis bin Haji Terawih. Litho Secura, Singapore)

2008 (24 Apr). Centenary of Transition of the Capital City from Kampung Air to Mainland. T **163** and similar horiz designs. Multicoloured. Phosphorised paper. P 13.

756	20s. Type **163**	60	40
757	30s. Istana Kota	70	40
758	60s. Bandar Brunei Mula-Mula Dirona di Darat, 1906	1·40	1·25
759	100s. Modern city of Bandar Seri Begawan	2·25	2·75
756/9 *Set of 4*		4·50	4·25
MS760 130×130 mm. Nos. 756/9		4·50	4·50

164 Sultan saluting

165 Sultan Omar Ali Saifuddin outside Mosque, 1958

2008 (1 Aug). 40th Anniv of Coronation of Sultan Hassanal Bolkiah Mu'izzadin Waddaulah. T **164** and similar vert designs. Multicoloured. Litho. P 12 (**MS**766) or 12½ (others).

761	40s. Type **164**	60	60
	a. Horiz strip of 4. Nos. 761/4	2·25	2·25
762	40s. Coronation ceremony	60	60
763	40s. Crowning of Sultan	60	60
764	40s. Crowned Sultan seated in chair	60	60
761/4 *Set of 4*		2·25	2·25
MS765 160×100 mm. Nos. 761/4		3·25	3·75
MS766 159×100 mm. $40 Crowned Sultan on throne and courtiers (44×69 mm)		35·00	40·00

Nos. 761/4 were printed together, *se-tenant*, in horizontal strips of four stamps throughout the sheet.

2008 (26 Sept). 50th Anniv of Omar Ali Saifuddien Mosque. T **165** and similar vert designs. Multicoloured. Litho. P 14½×14.

767	50s. Type **165**	85	95
	a. Horiz strip of 4. Nos. 767/70	3·00	3·50
768	50s. Sultan Hassanal Bolkiah Mu'izzadin Waddaulah	85	95
769	50s. Sultan and courtiers inside Mosque	85	95
770	50s. Aerial view of Mosque	85	95
767/70 *Set of 4*		3·00	3·50
MS771 150×80 mm. Nos. 767/70		3·00	3·50
MS772 199×110 mm. $50 Omar Ali Saifuddin Mosque (44×71 mm). P 13½		40·00	45·00

Nos. 767/70 were printed together, *se-tenant*, in horizontal strips of four stamps throughout the sheet.

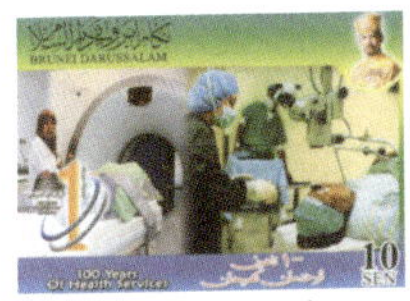

166 Scanner and Medical Staff

167 Montage of Buildings

2008 (9 Oct). Centenary of Health Services in Brunei. T **166** and similar horiz designs. Multicoloured. Litho. P 13.

773	10s. Type **166**	25	25
774	10s. Nurse with mother and baby	25	25
775	$1 First government hospital in Brunei town	1·75	2·00
773/5 *Set of 3*		2·00	2·25

2009 (23 Feb). National Day Silver Jubilee (25th Anniv of Independence). T **167** and similar multicoloured designs; background colours given. Litho. P 13.

776	25s. Type **167**	55	55
	a. Sheetlet. Nos. 776/83	4·00	4·00
777	25s. Montage of buildings (different) (bright green)	55	55
778	25s. Military parade, helicopter (on ground) and buildings (cerise)	55	55
779	25s. Montage of buildings (different) (pale yellow)	55	55
780	25s. Oil refinery, oil well, storage tanks and docks (lavender)	55	55
781	25s. Dancers and processions with national flags (bright purple)	55	55
782	25s. Women using mobile phone and laptop computer, modern buildings and airliner (reddish-brown)	55	55
783	25s. Anniversary emblem	55	55
784	25s. As Type **167** but blue border	55	55
	a. Sheetlet. Nos. 784/91	4·00	4·00
785	25s. As No. 777 but blue border	55	55
786	25s. As No. 778 but blue border	55	55
787	25s. As No. 779 but blue border	55	55
788	25s. As No. 780 but blue border	55	55
789	25s. As No. 781 but blue border	55	55
790	25s. As No. 782 but blue border	55	55
791	25s. As No. 783 but blue border	55	55
776/91 *Set of 16*		8·00	8·00
MS792 180×140 mm. $25 Sultan Hassanal Bolkiah Mu'izzadin Waddaulah, Sultan Omar Ali Saifuddin and Bandar Seri Begawan city (101×71 mm)		27·00	29·00

Nos. 776/83 and 784/91 were each printed together, *se-tenant*, in sheetlets of eight stamps with enlarged illustrated margins.

STAMP BOOKLETS

1976 (23 Feb). Buff card cover showing Sultan's arms. Panes attached to cover by selvedge.

SB1	$1 booklet containing four 5s. and eight 10s. (Nos. 245, 247) in blocks of 4	7·00

B **1** Post Office Emblem

1986. Black and bright scarlet printed cover as type B **1**, 80×51 mm. Stitched.

SB2	$1 booklet containing four 10s. and four 15s. (Nos. 371/2) in blocks of 4	3·00

B **2**

2000 (15 Nov). Asia-Pacific Economic Cooperation. Heads of Government Meeting. Multicoloured cover as Type B **2**, 100×120 mm. Stitched.

SB3	$1.10 containing booklet pane Nos. 645a/7a	3·00

B **3** Old and New Capital City

2008 (24 Apr). Centenary of Transition of the Capital City from Kampung Air to Mainland. Multicoloured covers, 119×69 mm, as Type B **3**.

SB4	80c. booklet containing strip of four 20s. (No. 756)	2·40
SB5	$1.20 booklet containing strip of four 30s. (No. 757)	2·75
SB6	$2.40 booklet containing strip of four 60s. (No. 758)	5·50
SB7	$4 booklet containing strip of four 100s. (No. 759)	9·00

JAPANESE OCCUPATION OF BRUNEI

Japanese forces landed in Northern Borneo on 15 December 1941 and the whole of Brunei had been occupied by 6 January 1942.

Brunei, North Borneo, Sarawak and, after a short period, Labuan, were administered as a single territory by the Japanese. Until September-October 1942, previous stamp issues, without overprint, continued to be used in conjunction with existing postmarks. From the Autumn of 1942 onwards unoverprinted stamps of Japan were made available and examples can be found used from the area for much of the remainder of the War. Japanese Occupation issues for Brunei, North Borneo and Sarawak were equally valid throughout the combined territory but not, in practice, equally available.

PRICES FOR STAMPS ON COVER

Nos. J1/16	*from* × 8
Nos. J17/20	—

(**1**) ("Imperial Japanese Government")

(**2**) ("Imperial Japanese Postal Service $3")

1942 (Oct)–**44**. Stamps of Brunei handstamped with T **1** in violet to blue. Wmk Mult Script CA (except Nos. J18/19, Mult Crown CA). P 14.

J1	5	1s. black	8·00	23·00
		a. Red opt	£110	£130
J2		2s. green	50·00	£110
J3		2s. orange (1943)	4·75	9·00
J4		3s. blue-green	28·00	75·00
		a. Opt omitted (in pair with normal)	£3000	
J5		4s. orange	3·25	13·00
J6		5s. chocolate	3·75	13·00
		a. "5s." retouch	£150	£375
J7	7	6s. greenish grey (P 14×11½) (1944)	40·00	£225
J8		6s. scarlet	£550	£550
J9	5	8s. grey-black	£700	£850
J10	7	8s. red	6·50	12·00
		a. Opt omitted (in pair with normal)	£2000	
J11	5	10s. purple/*yellow*	9·00	26·00
J12	7	12s. blue	28·00	26·00
		a. Red opt	£325	£425
J13		15s. ultramarine (1944)	20·00	26·00
J14	5	25s. slate-purple	25·00	50·00
		a. Red opt	£450	£550
J15		30s. purple and orange-yellow	95·00	£180
J16		50s. black/*emerald*	38·00	60·00
		a. Red opt	£475	
J17		$1 black and red/*blue* (1944)	55·00	70·00
		a. Red opt	—	£1000
J18		$5 carmine/*green* (1944)	£900	£2250
J19		$25 black/*red* (1944)	£900	£2250

The overprint varies in shade from violet to blue, and being handstamped, exists inverted, double, double one inverted and treble.

Nos. J3, J4, J7, J10 and J13 were not issued without the overprint (See footnote below Brunei No. 78).

1944 (11 May). No. J1 surch with T **2** in orange-red.

J20	5	$3 on 1s. black	£7500	£7500
		a. Surch on No. 60 of Brunei	£9000	

Three separate handstamps were used to apply Type **2**, one for the top line, one for the bottom and the third for the two central characters.

Malaysia

The Federation of Malaya was formed on 1 February 1948 by the former Straits Settlements of Malacca and Penang, the four Federated Malay States and the five Unfederated States. It did not, however, issue any stamps until it became an independent member of the Commonwealth in 1957.

The philatelic history of the component parts of the federation is most complex.

The method adopted is to show the general issues for the area first, before dealing with the issues for the individual States. The section is divided as follows:

I. STRAITS SETTLEMENTS
II. FEDERATED MALAY STATES
III. MALAYAN POSTAL UNION
IV. MALAYA (BRITISH MILITARY ADMINISTRATION)
V. MALAYAN FEDERATION
VI. MALAYSIA
VII. MALAYAN STATES—Johore, Kedah, Kelantan, Malacca, Negri Sembilan (with Sungei Ujong), Pahang, Penang, Perak, Perlis, Sabah, Selangor, Trengganu
VIII. JAPANESE OCCUPATION OF MALAYA 1942–45
IX. THAI OCCUPATION OF MALAYA 1943–45
X. LABUAN
XI. SABAH
XII. JAPANESE OCCUPATION OF NORTH BORNEO
XIII. SARAWAK
XIV. JAPANESE OCCUPATION OF SARAWAK

I. STRAITS SETTLEMENTS

The three original Settlements, Malacca, Penang (with Province Wellesley) and Singapore (with Christmas Island), were formed into a Crown Colony on 1 April 1867. The Cocos (Keeling) Islands were transferred to Straits Settlements on 7 February 1886. Labuan was attached to the Colony in 1896, becoming the fourth Settlement in 1906, but was transferred to North Borneo in 1946.

The first known prestamp cover with postal markings from Penang (Prince of Wales Island) is dated March 1806 and from Malacca, under British civil administration, February 1841. The civil post office at Singapore opened on 1 February 1823.

The stamps of India were used at all three post offices from late in 1854 until the Straits Settlements became a separate colony on 1 September 1867.

The Indian stamps were initially cancelled by dumb obliterators and their use in the Straits Settlements can only be identified from complete covers. In 1856 cancellations of the standard Indian octagonal type were issued, numbered "B 109" for Malacca, "B 147" for Penang and "B 172" for Singapore.

CURRENCY. Before 1867 official accounts of the East India Company administration for the Straits Settlements were kept in rupees, although the vast majority of commercial transactions used Spanish American silver dollars, supplies of which reached Malaya via the Philippines.

This confusing situation was rapidly amended when the Straits Settlements became a Crown Colony on 1 April 1867 and Spanish American dollars were declared to be the only legal currency. In 1874 American trade dollars and Japanese yen were also accepted, but in 1890 recognition of the Spanish American dollars was restricted to those from the Mexican mints. A shortage of silver coinage led to the introduction of silver British trade dollars in 1895 which also circulated in Hong Kong and Labuan.

Dollar banknotes first appeared in 1899, but Mexican dollars were not finally replaced until the issue of silver Straits Settlements dollars in 1903, the gold value of which was set at 2s.4d. in January 1906.

A

B

C

The Penang and Singapore octagonals were replaced by a duplex type, consisting of a double-ringed datestamp and a diamond-shaped obliterator containing the office number, in 1863 and 1865 respectively.

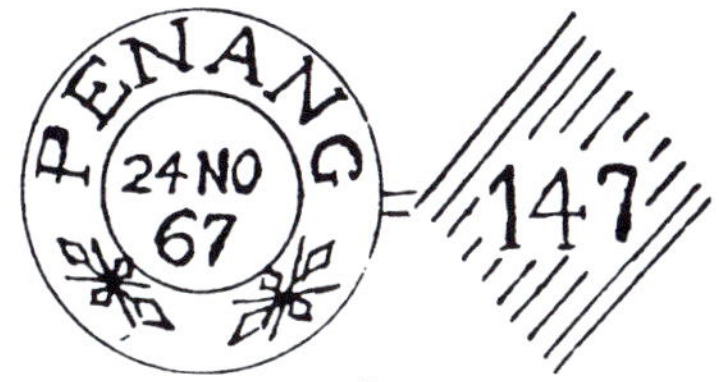

D

E

PRICES. Catalogue prices in this section are for stamps with clearly legible, if partial, examples of the postmarks.

EAST INDIA COMPANY ADMINISTRATION
MALACCA

Stamps of INDIA *cancelled with Type* A.

1854. (Nos. 2/34).

Z1	½a. blue (Die I)	£1500
Z2	1a. red (Die I)	£1300
Z3	1a. dull red (Die II)	£1300
Z4	2a. green	£1700
Z4*a*	4a. blue and pale red (Head Die I) (*cut-to-shape*)	£1700
Z5	4a. blue and red (Head Die II) (*cut-to-shape*)	£1700
Z5*a*	4a. blue and red (Head Die III) (*cut-to-shape*)	£1700

1855. (Nos. 35/6).

Z6	8a. carmine (Die I)/*blue glazed*	£600

1856–64. (Nos. 37/49).

Z7	½a. pale blue (Die I)	£400
Z8	1a. brown	£300
Z8*a*	2a. dull pink	£425
Z9	2a. yellow-buff	£325
Z10	2a. yellow	£350
Z10a	4a. black	£600
Z11	4a. green	£550
Z12	8a. carmine (Die I)	£400

1860. (Nos. 51/3).

Z13	8p. purple/*bluish*	£950
Z14	8p. purple/*white*	£500

1865. (Nos. 54/65).

Z15	4a. green	£550

PENANG

Stamps of INDIA *cancelled with Type* B.

1854. (Nos. 2/34).

Z20	½a. blue (Die I)	£500
Z21	1a. red (Die I)	£180
Z21a	1a. red (Die II)	£1700
Z22	2a. green	£325
Z23	4a. blue and pale red (Head Die I)	£1800
Z24	4a. blue and red (Head Die II)	£1800
Z25	4a. blue and red (Head Die III)	£1200

1855. (Nos. 35/6).

Z26	4a. black/*blue glazed*	£100
Z27	8a. carmine (Die I)/*blue glazed*	90·00
	a. Bisected (4a.) (1860) (on cover)	£75000

1856–64. (Nos. 37/49).

Z28	½a. pale blue (Die I)	£100
Z29	1a. brown	60·00
Z30	2a. dull pink	85·00
Z31	2a. yellow-buff	80·00
Z32	2a. yellow	80·00
Z33	2a. orange	80·00
Z34	4a. black	60·00
Z35	8a. carmine (Die I)	75·00

1860. (Nos. 51/3).

Z36	8p. purple/*white*	£180

Stamps of INDIA *cancelled with Type* D.

1854. (Nos. 2/34).

Z38	1a. red (Die I)	£3000

1856–64. (Nos. 37/49).

Z39	½a. pale blue (Die I)	£225
Z40	1a. brown	65·00
Z40a	2a. yellow-buff	85·00
Z41	2a. yellow	75·00
Z42	4a. black	65·00
Z43	4a. green	£190
Z44	8a. carmine (Die I)	70·00

1860. (Nos. 51/3).

Z45	8p. purple/*white*	£100
Z46	8p. mauve	£110

1865. (Nos. 54/65).

Z47	8p. purple	
Z48	1a. deep brown	65·00
Z49	2a. yellow	75·00
Z50	4a. green	£200
Z51	8a. carmine (Die I)	

1866–67. (Nos. 69/72).

Z52	4a. green (Die 1)	£225

OFFICIAL STAMP

1866–67. (No. O2).

Z54	½a. pale blue	

SINGAPORE

Stamps of INDIA *cancelled with Type* C.

1854. (Nos. 2/34).

Z60	½a. blue (Die I)	£190
Z61	1a. red (Die I)	£140
Z62	1a. dull red (Die II)	£140
Z63	1a. red (Die III)	£1500
Z64	2a. green	90·00
	a. Bisected (1a.) (1857) (on cover)	£150000
Z65	4a. blue and pale red (Head Die I)	£1500
Z66	4a. blue and red (Head Die II)	£1500
Z67	4a. blue and red (Head Die III)	£850

1855. (Nos. 35/6).

Z68	4a. black/*blue glazed*	42·00
	a. Bisected (2a.) (1859) (on cover)	£12000
Z69	8a. carmine/*blue glazed*	42·00
	a. Bisected (4a.) (1859) (on cover)	£75000

1856–66. (Nos. 37/49).

Z70	½a. pale blue (Die I)	50·00
Z71	1a. brown	25·00
	a. Bisected (½a.) (1859) (on cover)	£80000
Z72	2a. dull pink	45·00
Z73	2a. yellow-buff	38·00
Z74	2a. yellow	40·00
Z75	2a. orange	45·00
Z76	4a. black	25·00
	a. Bisected (2a.) (1859) (on cover)	£30000
Z77	4a. green	£140
Z78	8a. carmine (Die I)	35·00
	a. Bisected (4a.) (1866) (on cover)	£75000

1860–61. (Nos. 51/3).

Z79	8p. purple/*bluish*	£600
Z80	8p. purple/*white*	75·00
	a. Bisected diagonally (4p.) (1861) (on cover)	£80000
Z81	8p. mauve	85·00

1865. (Nos. 54/65).

Z82	½a. blue (Die I)	60·00
Z83	8p. purple	£150
Z84	1a. deep brown	45·00
Z85	2a. yellow	48·00
Z86	2a. orange	48·00
Z87	4a. green	£120
Z88	8a. carmine (Die I)	£275

1866–67. (Nos. 69/72).

Z89	4a. green (Die I)	£150
Z90	6a.8p. slate	£375

OFFICIAL STAMPS

1866–67. (Nos. O6/14).

Z91	½a. pale blue	£550
Z92	2a. yellow	£700

Stamps of INDIA *cancelled with Type* E.

1856–64. (Nos. 37/49).

Z100	1a. brown	£300
Z101	2a. yellow	£400
Z102	4a. black	£400
Z103	8a. carmine (Die I)	£400

1860. (Nos. 51/3).

Z104	8p. purple/*white*	£425

1865. (Nos. 54/65).

Z105	2a. yellow	£375
Z106	2a. orange	£375
Z107	4a. green	£450

PRICES FOR STAMPS ON COVER

Nos. 1/9	*from* × 20
No. 10	—
Nos. 11/19	*from* × 12
Nos. 20/1	*from* × 30
Nos. 22/39	*from* × 15
Nos. 41/6	*from* × 25
No. 47	—
Nos. 48/9	*from* × 12
Nos. 50/3	*from* × 20
Nos. 54/62	*from* × 30
Nos. 63/71	*from* × 15
No. 72	—
Nos. 73/80	*from* × 30
Nos. 82/7	*from* × 20
Nos. 88/94	*from* × 15
Nos. 95/105	*from* × 8
Nos. 106/9	*from* × 20
Nos. 110/21	*from* × 6
No. 122	—
Nos. 123/6	*from* × 5
Nos. 127/38	*from* × 4
Nos. 139/40	—
Nos. 141/51	*from* × 15
Nos. 152/67	*from* × 4
Nos. 168/9	—
Nos. 193/212	*from* × 3
Nos. 213/15	—
Nos. 216/17	*from* × 10
Nos. 218/40*a*	*from* × 3
Nos. 240*b*/*d*	—
Nos. 241/55	*from* × 15
Nos. 256/9	*from* × 4
Nos. 260/98	*from* × 3
Nos. D1/6	*from* × 20
No. F1	—

PRINTERS. All Straits Settlements issues were printed in typography by De La Rue & Co, Ltd, London, *unless otherwise stated.*

USED PRICES. The prices quoted for Nos. 1/9 are for fine used examples. Those showing parts of commercial "chops" are worth less.

CROWN COLONY

(Currency. 100 cents = 1 Spanish American dollar)

THREE HALF CENTS
(**1**)

32 CENTS
(**2**)

1867 (1 Sept). Nos. 54, 59, 61, 69 and 73 of India surch as T **1** or **2** (24c., 32c.) by De La Rue. W **13** (Elephant's head) of India. P 14.

1	1½c. on ½a. blue (Die I) (R.)	90·00	£200
2	2c. on 1a. deep brown (R.)	£140	80·00
3	3c. on 1a. deep brown (B.)	£130	85·00
4	4c. on 1a. deep brown (Bk.)	£250	£250

5	6c. on 2a. yellow (P.)	£600	£250
6	8c. on 2a. yellow (G.)	£190	42·00
7	12c. on 4a. green (R.)	£950	£300
	a. Surch double	£2750	
8	24c. on 8a. rose (Die II) (B.)	£450	80·00
9	32c. on 2a. yellow (Bk.)	£350	90·00

The 32c. was re-issued for postal use in 1884.

No. 7a. is only known unused.

1869. (?) No. 1 with "THREE HALF" deleted and "2" written above, in black manuscript.

10	2 on 1½c. on ½a. blue	£15000	£5000

This stamp has been known from very early days and was apparently used at Penang, but nothing is known of its history.

5

6

7

8

9

1867 (Dec)–**72**. Ornaments in corners differ for each value. Wmk Crown CC. P 14.

11	**5**	2c. brown (6.68)	38·00	5·50
		a. Yellow-brown	40·00	5·50
		b. Deep brown	£100	15·00
		w. Wmk inverted	£450	£160
12		4c. rose (7.68)	65·00	9·50
		a. Deep rose	80·00	13·00
		w. Wmk inverted	£190	
13		6c. dull lilac (1.68)	£100	18·00
		a. Bright lilac	£120	18·00
		w. Wmk inverted	†	£225
14	**6**	8c. orange-yellow	£180	14·00
		a. Orange	£180	14·00
		w. Wmk inverted	£400	£140
15		12c. blue	£140	7·00
		a. Ultramarine	£160	9·50
		w. Wmk inverted	£425	
16	**7**	24c. blue-green	£130	6·00
		a. Yellow-green	£300	21·00
		w. Wmk inverted	†	£250
17	**8**	30c. claret (12.72)	£275	13·00
		w. Wmk inverted	†	£400
18	**9**	32c. pale red	£500	65·00
		w. Wmk inverted	†	£300
19		96c. grey	£300	50·00
		a. Perf 12½ (6.71)	£2250	£225

Five Cents. (10)   Seven Cents. (11)

1879 (May). Nos. 14a and 18 surch with T **10** and **11**.

20	**6**	5c. on 8c. orange	£100	£160
		a. No stop after "Cents"	£850	£950
		b. "F i" spaced	£900	£1000
21	**9**	7c. on 32c. pale red	£130	£170
		a. No stop after "Cents"	£1300	£1500

The no stop error occured once in the setting.

10 cents. (12)

10 (*a*)   10 (*b*)   10 (*c*)   10 (*d*)

10 (*e*)   10 (*f*)   10 (*g*)   10 (*h*)

10 (*i*)   10 (*j*)   10 (*jj*)   10 (*k*)   10 (*l*)

(*a*) "1" thin curved serif and thin foot, "0" narrow.

(*b*) "1" thick curved serif and thick foot: "0" broad. Both numerals heavy.

(*c*) "1" as (*a*); "0" as (*b*).

(*d*) "1" as (*a*) but thicker; "0" as (*a*).

(*e*) As (*a*) but sides of "0" thicker.

(*f*) "1" as (*d*); "0" as (*e*).

(*g*) As (*a*) but "0" narrower.

(*h*) "1" thin, curved serif and thick foot; "0" as (*g*).

(*i*) "1" as (*b*); "0" as (*a*).

(*j*) "1" as (*d*); "0" as (*g*) but raised.

(*jj*) "1" as (*a*) but shorter, and with shorter serif and thicker foot; "0" as (*g*) but level with "1".

(*k*) "1" as (*jj*); "0" as (*a*).

(*l*) "1" straight serif; "0" as (*g*).

1880 (Mar). No. 17 surch with T **12** (showing numerals (a) to (jj)).

22	10c. on 30c. claret (*a*)	£450	90·00
23	10c. on 30c. claret (*b*)	£425	85·00
24	10c. on 30c. claret (*c*)	£8000	£850
25	10c. on 30c. claret (*d*)	£3250	£275
26	10c. on 30c. claret (*e*)	£13000	£1700
27	10c. on 30c. claret (*f*)	£13000	£1700
28	10c. on 30c. claret (*g*)	£4750	£500
29	10c. on 30c. claret (*h*)	£13000	£1700
30	10c. on 30c. claret (*i*)	£13000	£1700
31	10c. on 30c. claret (*j*)	£13000	£1700
32	10c. on 30c. claret (*jj*)	£13000	£1700

Nos. 22/32 come from the same setting of 60 (6×10) containing twenty examples of No. 22 (R. 1/1-2, 1/4, 1/6, 2/1-6, 3/1, 3/3, 3/5, 4/1, 4/3-4, 10/1, 10/3-5), twenty-two of No. 23 (R. 4/6, 5/1-6, 6/1-6, 7/1, 8/2-4, 9/1-5), six of No. 25 (R. 1/5, 3/2, 3/4, 4/2, 4/5, 10/2), four of No. 28 (R. 7/2-5), two of No. 24 (R. 9/6, 10/6) and one each of Nos. 26 (R. 3/6), 27 (R. 1/3), 29 (R. 7/6), 30 (R. 8/1), 31 (R. 8/6) and 32 (R. 8/5).

No. 23 is known with large stop after "cents" and also with stop low.

1880 (Apr). No. 17 surch as T **12**, but without "cents.", showing numerals (a) to (c), (g) to (i), (k) and (l).

33	10. on 30c. claret (*a*)	£200	50·00
	w. Wmk inverted	†	£250
34	10 on 30c. claret (*b*)	£225	50·00
	w. Wmk inverted	†	£250
35	10 on 30c. claret (*c*)	£700	£110
	w. Wmk inverted	†	£475
36	10 on 30c. claret (*g*)	£1700	£325
	aw. Wmk inverted	†	£950
36*b*	10 on 30c. claret (*h*)	†	£16000
37	10 on 30c. claret (*i*)	£4750	£850
38	10 on 30c. claret (*k*)	£4750	£850
39	10 on 30c. claret (*l*)	£4750	£850

Nos. 33/9 were surcharged from an amended setting of 60 (6×10) of which 59 positions have been identified. Of those known No. 33 occurs on twenty-four (R. 6/1-6, 7/1-6, 8/1-6, 9/1-2, 9/6, 10/1-3), No. 34 on twenty-one (R. 1/2-6, 2/1-6, 3/1-6, 4/3-5, 5/6), No. 35 on eight (R. 1/1, 4/2, 4/6, 5/1-5), No. 36 on three (R. 9/3-5) and Nos. 37 (R. 10/6), 38 (R. 10/4) and 39 (R. 10/5) on one each. R. 4/1 remains unidentified.

The existence of No. 36*b*, known as a single example from the 6th vertical column, and a stamp in the Royal Collection with "1" as (*b*) and "0" as (*g*) suggests that there may have been another setting.

5 cents. (13)   5 cents. (14)   5 cents. (15)

1880 (Aug). No. 14a surch with T **13** to **15**.

41	**13**	5c. on 8c. orange	£150	£180
42	**14**	5c. on 8c. orange	£140	£170
43	**15**	5c. on 8c. orange	£550	£650

Surcharged in a setting of 60 (6×10) with T **13** on rows one to four, T **14** on rows five to nine and T **15** on row ten.

10 cents. (16)   5 cents. (17)

1880–81. Nos. 13, 15/a and 17 surch with T **16**.

44	10c. on 6c. lilac (11.81)	70·00	6·00
	a. Surch double	—	£2750
45	10c. on 12c. ultramarine (1.81)	75·00	16·00
	a. Blue	55·00	9·00
46	10c. on 30c. claret (12.80)	£400	90·00

A second printing of the 10c. on 6c. has the surcharge heavier and the "10" usually more to the left or right of "cents".

1882 (Jan). No. 12 surch with T **17**.

47	5c. on 4c. rose	£275	£300

18

19

1882 (Jan). Wmk Crown CC. P 14.

48	**18**	5c. purple-brown	95·00	£100
49	**19**	10c. slate	£425	65·00
		s. Optd "Specimen"	£500	

1882. Wmk Crown CA. P 14.

50	**5**	2c. brown (Aug)	£300	48·00
51		4c. rose (April)	£130	8·50
52	**6**	8c. orange (Sept)	3·75	1·00
		w. Wmk inverted	†	£325
53	**19**	10c. slate (Oct)	8·00	1·25
		w. Wmk inverted		

For the 4c. in deep carmine see No. 98.

20a "S" wide **20b** "E" and "S" wide **20c** "N" wide

20d All letters narrow **20e** "EN" and "S" wide **20f** "E" wide

1883 (Apr). Nos. 52 and 18 surch with T **20a/f.**

54	**20a**	2c. on 8c. orange	£250	£110
55	**20b**	2c. on 8c. orange	£250	£110
56	**20c**	2c. on 8c. orange	£250	£110
57	**20d**	2c. on 8c. orange	£140	80·00
		a. Surch double	£3000	£1100
58	**20e**	2c. on 8c. orange	£1600	£600
59	**20a**	2c. on 32c. pale red	£800	£200
		a. Surch double	†	£2000
60	**20f**	2c. on 32c. pale red	£1100	£275
		a. Surch double		

The 8c. was surcharged using one of two triplet settings, either 54 + 55 + 56 or 57 + 57 + 57, applied to rows 2 to 10. A single handstamp, either No. 57 or No. 58, was then used to complete row 1. The 32c. was surcharged in the same way with a triplet of 59 + 60 + 59 and a single handstamp as No. 60.

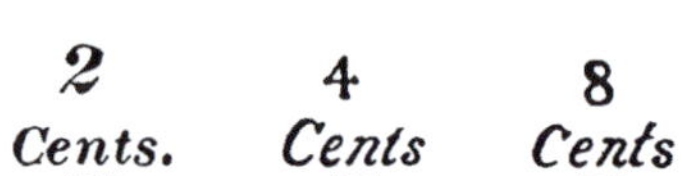

(21) (22) (23)

1883 (June–July). Nos. 51 and 15 surch with T **21**.

61	2c. on 4c. rose	80·00	90·00
	a. "s" of "Cents" inverted	£1400	£1600
62	2c. on 12c. blue (July)	£350	£160
	a. "s" of "Cents" inverted	£5500	£3000

The inverted "S" error occurred once in the setting of 60.

Broken oval above "O" of "POSTAGE" (Lower right pane R. 10/5)

1883 (July)–**91**. Wmk Crown CA. P 14.

63	**5**	2c. pale rose	38·00	3·75
		a. Bright rose (1889)	10·00	85
64		4c. pale brown	40·00	3·00
		a. Broken oval	£350	75·00
		b. Deep brown	48·00	4·00
		ba. Broken oval	£475	£110
		w. Wmk inverted	£160	£100
65	**18**	5c. blue (8.83)	15·00	1·00
		w. Wmk inverted	†	£300
66	**5**	6c. lilac (11.84)	25·00	13·00
		a. Violet	2·00	7·50
		w. Wmk inverted	—	£180
67	**6**	12c. brown-purple	65·00	15·00
68	**7**	24c. yellow-green (2.84)	75·00	8·50
		a. Blue-green	7·00	4·50
		w. Wmk inverted	†	£275
69	**8**	30c. claret (9.91)	15·00	17·00
		w. Wmk inverted	£110	75·00
70	**9**	32c. orange-vermilion (1.87)	10·00	3·50
		w. Wmk inverted	65·00	65·00
71		96c. olive-grey (7.88)	75·00	55·00
63*a*/71 *Set of 9*			£200	95·00
63s/5s, 67s Optd "Specimen" *Set of 4*			£1200	

Most examples of the 4c. in shades of olive-bistre are thought to be colour changelings.

For the 4c. in deep carmine and 12c. in claret see Nos. 98 and 102.

1884 (Feb–Aug). Nos. 65, 15 and 67 surch with T **22** or **23**.

72	**18**	4c. on 5c. blue (Aug)	£3250	£4000
73		4c. on 5c. blue (R.) (Aug)	£130	£100
74	**6**	8c. on 12c. blue	£700	£150
		w. Wmk inverted	†	£600
75		8c. on 12c. brown-purple (Aug)	£450	£140
		b. "s" of "Cents" low (R. 5/1)	£4000	£1500

1884 (Aug). No. 65 surch with T **20d/f.**

76	**20d**	2c. on 5c. blue	£140	£150
77	**20e**	2c. on 5c. blue	£140	£150
		a. Pair, with and without surch		
		b. Surch double		
78	**20f**	2c. on 5c. blue	£140	£150

Surcharged as a triplet, 77 + 76 + 78. On No. 76 "TS" are dropped below the line.

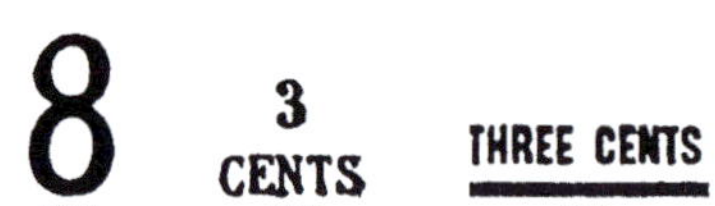

(24) (25) (26)

1884 (Sept). No. 75 additionally surch with large numeral as T **24** in red.

80	**6**	8 on 8c. on 12c. dull purple	£375	£400
		a. Surch *T* **24** double	£5500	
		b. Surch *T* **23** in blue	£9000	
		c. "s" of "Cents" low	£3000	£3500

Examples as No. 75, but with Type **23** in blue, were further surcharged in error.

A similar "4" surcharge in red on No. 73 exists from a trial printing of which seven examples are known, all used on an official's correspondence (*Price £28000 used*).

1885. No. 65 and T **9** in new colour, wmk Crown CA, surch with T **25** or **26**.

82	**25**	3c. on 5c. blue (Sept)	£140	£225
		a. Surch double	£3000	
83	**26**	3c. on 32c. pale magenta (Dec)	4·00	4·00
		a. Deep magenta	1·50	1·00
		s. Optd "Specimen"	£225	

The surcharge on No. 82 was applied locally by a triplet setting. No. 83 was surcharged by De La Rue in complete panes.

(27) (28)

1886 (Apr). No. 48 surch with T **27**.

84	**18**	3c. on 5c. purple-brown	£200	£225

The surcharge on No. 84 was applied by a triplet setting.

1887 (July). No. 65 surch with T **28**.

85	**18**	2c. on 5c. blue	32·00	75·00
		a. "C" of "Cents" omitted	—	£3750
		b. Surch double	£1400	£1300

The surcharge on No. 85 was applied by a triplet setting.

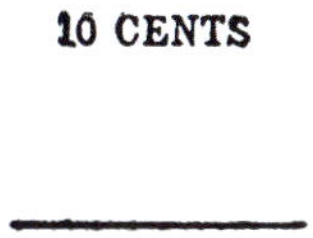

(29)

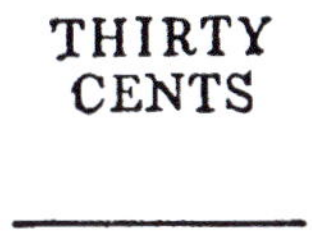

(30)

1891 (Nov). Nos. 68 and 70 surch with T **29** and **30**.

86	**7**	10c. on 24c. yellow-green	5·00	1·25
		a. Narrow "0" in "10" (R. 4/6)	28·00	30·00
		w. Wmk inverted	75·00	80·00
87	**9**	30c. on 32c. orange-vermilion	11·00	3·50
		w. Wmk inverted		

The "R" of "THIRTY" and "N" of "CENTS" are found wide or narrow and in all possible combinations.

(31)

(32)

1892. Stamps of 1882–91 (wmk Crown CA) surch with T **31**.

88	1c. on 2c. bright rose (Mar)	2·00	3·75
89	1c. on 4c. brown (Apr)	5·00	5·50
	a. Surch double	£1600	
	b. Broken oval	£150	£160
	w. Wmk inverted	£190	
90	1c. on 6c. lilac (Feb)	1·40	7·50
	a. Surch double, one inverted	£2000	£1800
	w. Wmk inverted	£190	
91	1c. on 8c. orange (Jan)	1·00	1·75
92	1c. on 12c. brown-purple (Mar)	5·00	9·00
88/92 *Set of 5*		13·00	25·00

The three settings used for Nos. 88/92 contained various combinations of the following varieties: "ON" of "ONE" and "N" of "CENT" wide; "O" wide, "N" of "ONE" narrow and "N" of "CENT" wide; "O" narrow and both letters "N" wide; "ON" narrow and "N" of "CENT" wide; "O" wide and both letters "N" narrow; "ON" wide and "N" of "CENT" narrow; "ON" and "N" of "CENT" narrow; "O" narrow; "N" of "ONE" wide and "N" of "CENT" narrow. Antique "N" and "E" letters also occur.

1892–94. Colours changed. Wmk Crown CA. P 14. Surch with T **32** and **26** by De La Rue.

93	**6**	1c. on 8c. green (3.92)	1·00	1·50
94	**9**	3c. on 32c. carmine-rose (6.94)	2·25	70
		a. Surch omitted	£4000	
93s/4s Optd "Specimen" *Set of 2*			£130	

No. 94a comes from a sheet found at Singapore on which all stamps in the upper left pane had the surcharge omitted. Five vertical inter-panneau pairs still exist with the surcharge omitted on the upper stamps (*Price* £35000 *unused*). The only used example of the error is on cover.

33

34

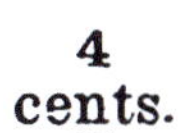

(35)

Normal

Malformed "S"

Repaired "S"

The malformed "S" occurs on R. 7/3 of the left pane from Key Plate 2. It is believed that the repair to it took place in mid-1898. Both states may occur on other stamps in Types **33** and **34**. Stamps subsequently printed from Key Plate 3 showed the "S" normal.

1892 (Mar)–**99**. Wmk Crown CA. P 14.

95	**33**	1c. green (9.92)	5·50	70
		a. Malformed "S"	£475	£160
		b. Repaired "S"	£450	£150
96		3c. carmine-rose (2.95)	12·00	40
		a. Malformed "S"	£650	£170
97		3c. brown (3.99)	10·00	60
		a. Repaired "S"	£550	£160
		b. Yellow-brown	9·00	60
98	**5**	4c. deep carmine (7.99)	9·00	1·25
		a. Broken oval	£200	90·00
99	**18**	5c. brown (6.94)	10·00	1·00
100		5c. magenta (7.99)	2·25	2·00
101	**6**	8c. ultramarine (6.94)	4·50	50
		a. Bright blue	7·50	80
102		12c. claret (3.94)	20·00	9·00
103	**33**	25c. purple-brown and green	32·00	7·00
		a. Malformed "S"	£1000	£425
		b. Repaired "S"	£900	£400
		c. Dull purple and green	30·00	7·00
104		50c. olive-green and carmine	21·00	2·50
		a. Repaired "S"	£950	£375
105	**34**	$5 orange and carmine (10.98)	£325	£250
		a. Repaired "S"	£4000	£4000
95/105 *Set of 11*			£400	£250
95s/101s, 103s/5s Optd "Specimen" *Set of 10*			£600	

1898 (26 Dec). T **18** and **6** surch with T **35** at Singapore.

106	4c. on 5c. brown (No. 99)	2·75	4·75
107	4c. on 5c. blue (No. 65)	6·00	16·00
	a. Surch double	—	£3000
108	4c. on 8c. ultramarine (No. 101)	1·75	2·75
	a. Surch double	£1300	£1200
	b. Bright blue (No. 101*a*)	1·25	1·00
106/8*b Set of 3*		9·00	20·00

Nos. 107 and 108*b* exist with stop spaced 1½ mm from the "S" (R. 10/6).

(36)

37

38

1899 (Mar). T **18** (wmk Crown CA. P 14), surch with T **36** by De La Rue.

109	4c. on 5c. carmine	1·00	30
	a. Surch omitted	£35000	
	s. Optd "Specimen"	48·00	
	x. Wmk reversed	90·00	

No. 109a is only known unused.

1902 (Apr)–**03**. Wmk Crown CA. P 14.

110	**37**	1c. grey-green (7.02)	2·75	3·00
		a. Pale green	4·50	3·25
111		3c. dull purple and orange	3·50	20
		w. Wmk inverted	£650	£325
112		4c. purple/*red* (9.02)	4·75	30
113	**38**	5c. dull purple (8.02)	5·50	85
114		8c. purple/*blue*	4·50	20
115		10c. purple and black/*yellow* (9.02)	25·00	1·50
116	**37**	25c. dull purple and green (8.02)	14·00	6·50
117	**38**	30c. grey and carmine (7.02)	18·00	8·00
118	**37**	50c. deep green and carmine (9.02)	20·00	20·00
		a. Dull green and carmine	23·00	23·00
119	**38**	$1 dull green and black (9.02)	23·00	75·00
120	**37**	$2 dull purple and black (9.02)	75·00	75·00
121	**38**	$5 dull green and brown-orange (10.02)	£200	£170
122	**37**	$100 purple and green/*yellow* (3.03) (F.C. £225)	£13000	
		s. Optd "Specimen"	£600	
110/21 *Set of 12*			£350	£325
110s/21s Optd "Specimen" *Set of 12*			£375	

(Currency 100 cents = 1 Straits, later Malayan, dollar)

39

40

41

42

(Des N. Trotter and W. Egerton)

1903 (Dec)–**04**. Wmk Crown CA. P 14.

123	**39**	1c. grey-green	2·25	8·00
124	**40**	3c. dull purple (1.04)	11·00	4·50
125	**41**	4c. purple/*red* (4.04)	8·00	30
		w. Wmk inverted	†	£325
126	**42**	8c. purple/*blue* (7.04)	50·00	1·25
123/6 *Set of* 4			65·00	12·50
123s/6s Optd "Specimen" *Set of* 4			£160	

1904 (Aug)–**10**. Wmk Multiple Crown CA. Ordinary paper (1c. to $1 and $5) or chalk-surfaced paper ($2, $25, $100). P 14.

127	**39**	1c. deep green (9.04)	4·25	10
		a. Chalk-surfaced paper (12.05)	14·00	1·50
		aw. Wmk inverted	£130	80·00
128	**40**	3c. dull purple	2·50	30
		a. Chalk-surfaced paper (8.06)	14·00	1·75
		aw. Wmk inverted	£140	90·00
		b. Plum (2.08)	9·50	1·75
129	**41**	4c. purple/*red* (11.04)	17·00	75
		a. Chalk-surfaced paper (10.05)	17·00	1·25
		aw. Wmk inverted	90·00	70·00
130	**38**	5c. dull purple (12.06)	17·00	2·25
		a. Chalk-surfaced paper (12.06)	21·00	9·50
		ay. Wmk inverted and reversed	†	£400
131	**42**	8c. purple/*blue* (8.05)	40·00	1·50
		a. Chalk-surfaced paper (12.05)	38·00	2·75
132	**38**	10c. purple and black/*yellow* (8.05)	8·00	80
		a. Chalk-surfaced paper (11.05)	12·00	3·00
133	**37**	25c. dull purple and green (1.05)	48·00	30·00
		a. Chalk-surfaced paper (11.05)	50·00	28·00
134	**38**	30c. grey and carmine (3.05)	48·00	2·50
		a. Chalk-surfaced paper (3.06)	55·00	2·75
135	**37**	50c. dull green and carmine (10.05)	60·00	17·00
		a. Chalk-surfaced paper (11.06)	35·00	15·00
136	**38**	$1 dull green and black (3.05)	65·00	28·00
		a. Chalk-surfaced paper (3.06)	55·00	20·00
137	**37**	$2 dull purple and black (10.05)	£110	90·00
138	**38**	$5 dull green and brown-orange (10.05)	£275	£190
		a. Chalk-surfaced paper (1.08)	£225	£160
139	**37**	$25 grey-green and black (7.06)	£2000	£2000
		s. Optd "Specimen"	£325	
140		$100 purple and green/*yellow* (6.10) (F.C. £350)	£14000	
127/38a *Set of* 12			£550	£300

STRAITS
SETTLEMENTS.
(**43**)

Straits Settlements.
(**44**)

STRAITS
SETTLEMENTS.

FOUR CENTS.
(**45**)

1906 (20 Dec)–**07**. T **18** of Labuan (Nos. 117 etc.) optd with T **43** or **44** (10c.) or additionally surch with T **45**, in black (No. 145), claret (No. 151) or brown-red (others) at Singapore. P 13½–14.

141	1c. black and purple (P 14½–15)	70·00	£180
	a. Perf 14	£400	£550
	b. Line through "B"	£800	
142	2c. black and green	£400	£475
	a. Perf 14½–15	£180	£325
	b. Perf 13½–14 comp 12–13	£1300	£1300
	c. Line through "B"	£1400	
143	3c. black and sepia (1.07)	20·00	90·00
	a. Line through "B"	£425	
144	4c. on 12c. black and yellow	2·75	8·00
	a. No stop after "CENTS" (R. 1/8, 6/8)	£550	
	b. Line through "B"	£250	£350
145	4c. on 16c. green and brown (Blk.)	7·00	8·50
	a. "STRAITS SETTLEMENTS" in both brown-red and black	£650	£750
	b. Ditto. In vert pair with normal	£7000	
	c. Line through "B"	£275	£375
146	4c. on 18c. black and pale brown	2·75	8·00
	a. No stop after "CENTS" (R. 1/8, 6/8)	£375	
	b. "FOUR CENTS" and bar double	£10000	
	c. "FOUR CENTS" and bar 1½ mm below normal position (pair with normal)	£2000	
	d. Line through "B"	£250	£350
147	8c. black and vermilion	4·50	8·00
	a. Line through "B"	£250	£375
148	10c. brown and slate	8·50	9·00
	a. No stop after "Settlements" (R. 1/4, 6/4)	£475	
	b. Line through "B"	£325	£350
149	25c. green and greenish blue (1.07)	24·00	42·00
	a. Perf 14½–15	£100	£150
	b. Perf 13½–14 comp 14½–15	£425	
	c. Line through "B"	£450	
150	50c. dull purple and lilac (1.07)	21·00	70·00
	a. Line through "B"	£475	
151	$1 claret and orange (Claret) (1.07)	48·00	£120
	a. Perf 14½–15	£850	
	b. Line through "B"	£800	£1300
141/51 *Set of* 11		£350	£800

Nos. 141/51 were overprinted by a setting of 50 (10×5) applied twice to the sheets of 100. The "FOUR CENTS" surcharges were applied separately by a similar setting.

No. 145a shows impressions of Type **43** in both brown-red and black. It is known from one complete sheet and the top half of another.

No. 146b occurred on row 5 from one sheet only. No. 146c occurred on R. 4/10 and 9/10 of the first printing.

The line through "B" flaw occurs on R. 5/10 of the basic stamp. For illustration see Labuan.

46

47

1906 (Sept)–**12**. Wmk Mult Crown CA. Ordinary paper (1c. to 10c.) or chalk-surfaced paper (21c. to $500). P 14.

152	**39**	1c. blue-green (3.10)	23·00	1·10
153	**40**	3c. red (6.08)	5·50	10
154	**41**	4c. red (7.07)	7·50	2·50
155		4c. dull purple (2.08)	6·00	10
		a. Chalk-surfaced paper (1.12)	11·00	2·75
		as. Optd "Specimen"	£120	
156		4c. claret (9.11)	2·75	80
157	**38**	5c. orange (4.09)	2·75	2·50
158	**42**	8c. blue	4·25	60
159	**38**	10c. purple/*yellow* (7.08)	11·00	1·00
		a. Chalk-surfaced paper (5.12)	20·00	12·00
160	**46**	21c. dull purple and claret (11.10)	6·50	38·00
161	**37**	25c. dull and bright purple (7.09)	18·00	8·00
162	**38**	30c. purple and orange-yellow (11.09)	50·00	4·25
163	**46**	45c. black/*green* (11.10)	2·50	4·00
164	**37**	50c. black/*green* (4.10)	6·50	5·00
165	**38**	$1 black and red/*blue* (10.10)	15·00	5·50
166	**37**	$2 green and red/*yellow* (12.09)	24·00	24·00
167	**38**	$5 green and red/*green* (11.09)	£130	75·00
		w. Wmk inverted	£1200	£500
168	**47**	$25 purple and blue/*blue* (5.11)	£1900	£1500
		s. Optd "Specimen"	£475	
169		$500 purple and orange (5.10) (F.C. £750)	£110000	
		s. Optd "Specimen"	£2500	
152/67 *Set of* 16			£275	£160
153s/67s Optd "Specimen" *Set of* 15			£850	

Beware of dangerous forgeries of No. 169.

48

49

50

51

52

53

54

Break in scroll (R. 1/12)

Broken crown and scroll (R. 2/12)

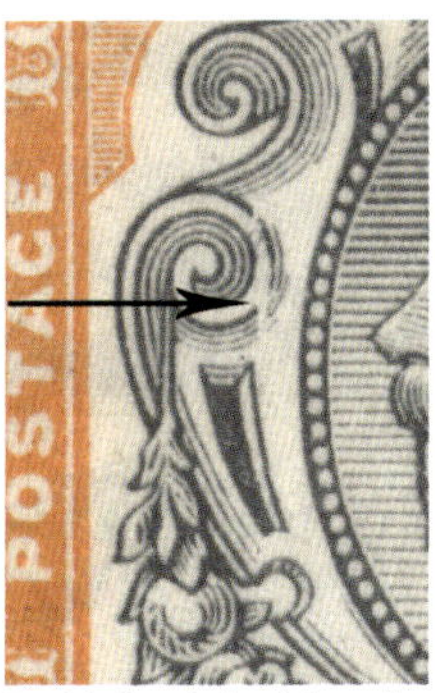

Break in lines below left scroll (R. 4/9. Ptgs from May 1920)

Damaged leaf at bottom right (R. 5/6. Ptgs from April 1918)

1912–23. $25, $100 and $500 as T **47**, but with head of King George V. Die I (5, 10, 25, 30, 50c., $1, $2, $5). Wmk Mult Crown CA. Ordinary paper (Nos. 193/6, 198/201, 203) or chalk-surfaced paper (others). P 14.

193	**48**	1c. green (9.12)	9·00	1·25
		a. Pale green (1.14)	8·50	1·25
		b. Blue-green (1917)	8·50	1·75
		bw. Wmk inverted	†	£400
194		1c. black (2.19)	2·25	1·00
		w. Wmk inverted	†	£400
195	**52**	2c. green (10.19)	1·75	50
		w. Wmk inverted	£550	
196	**49**	3c. red (2.13)	3·25	1·25
		a. Scarlet (2.17)	2·50	10
		y. Wmk inverted and reversed	£375	
197	**50**	4c. dull purple (3.13)	2·00	60
		a. Wmk sideways	†	£2500
		w. Wmk inverted	†	£400
198		4c. rose-scarlet (2.19)	2·25	15
		aw. Wmk inverted	†	£400
		b. Carmine	1·75	20
199	**51**	5c. orange (8.12)	2·00	50
		a. Yellow-orange	3·50	1·00
200	**52**	6c. dull claret (3.20)	2·00	50
		a. Deep claret	6·50	2·75
		aw. Wmk inverted	£275	£300
201		8c. ultramarine (3.13)	3·25	80
		w. Wmk inverted	†	£425
202	**51**	10c. purple/*yellow* (9.12)	1·50	1·00
		aw. Wmk inverted	†	£400
		b. White back (1913)	1·50	1·10
		bs. Optd "Specimen"	50·00	
		c. On lemon (1916)	18·00	1·25
		cs. Optd "Specimen"	75·00	
		d. Wmk sideways	†	£4000
203		10c. deep bright blue (1918)	7·50	1·00
		a. Bright blue (1919)	4·00	50
204	**53**	21c. dull and bright purple (11.13)	8·50	9·50
205	**54**	25c. dull purple and mauve (7.14)	16·00	13·00
		aw. Wmk inverted	£180	£200
		b. Dull purple and violet (1919)	70·00	16·00
207	**51**	30c. dull purple and orange (12.14)	8·00	4·00
		w. Wmk inverted	†	£550
208	**53**	45c. black/*green* (*white back*) (12.14)	6·50	18·00
		a. On blue-green, olive back (7.18)	4·00	23·00
		as. Optd "Specimen"	60·00	
		b. On emerald back (6.22)	3·25	13·00
209	**54**	50c. black/*green* (7.14)	6·00	3·50
		a. On blue-green, olive back (1918)	19·00	8·00
		aa. Wmk sideways	†	
		b. On emerald back (1921)	12·00	9·50
		c. Die II. *On emerald back* (1922)	3·00	4·00
		cs. Optd "Specimen"	65·00	£5000
210	**51**	$1 black and red/*blue* (10.14)	13·00	12·00
		w. Wmk inverted	£200	£200
211	**54**	$2 green and red/*yellow, white back* (1914)	14·00	48·00
		a. Green and red/yellow (1915)	13·00	48·00
		as. Optd "Specimen"	65·00	
		b. On orange-buff (1921)	65·00	80·00
		c. On pale yellow (1921)	70·00	90·00
212	**51**	$5 green and red/*green, white back* (11.13)	£100	48·00
		a. Green and red/green (1915)	£100	75·00
		as. Optd "Specimen"	£100	
		b. On blue-green, olive back (1918)	£170	£100
		bw. Wmk inverted		
		c. On emerald back (1920)	£225	£120
		d. Die II. *On emerald back* (1923)	£110	80·00
		ds. Optd "Specimen"	£110	
213	–	$25 purple and blue/*blue*	£1700	£475
		a. Break in scroll	£3500	
		b. Broken crown and scroll	£3500	
		e. Break in lines below scroll	£3500	
		f. Damaged leaf at bottom right	£3500	
		s. Optd "Specimen"	£400	
214	–	$100 black and carmine/*blue* (8.12) (F.C. £200)	£7000	
		a. Break in scroll	£12000	
		b. Broken crown and scroll	£12000	
		e. Break in lines below scroll		
		f. Damaged leaf at bottom right		
		s. Optd "Specimen"	£800	
215	–	$500 purple and orange-brown (8.12) (F.C. £500)	£70000	
		a. Break in scroll	£90000	
		b. Broken crown and scroll	£95000	
		f. Damaged leaf at bottom right		
		s. Optd "Specimen"	£3000	
193/212 *Set of* 19			£180	£140
193s/212s Optd "Specimen" *Set of* 19			£800	

The 6c. is similar to *T* **52**, but the head is in a beaded oval as in *T* **53**. The 2c., 6c. (and 12c. below) have figures of value on a circular ground while in the 8c. this is of oval shape.

RED CROSS

2c.

(55)

MALAYA-
BORNEO
EXHIBITION.

(56)

1917 (1 May). Surch with T **55**.

216	**49**	3c. + 2c. scarlet	2·75	30·00
		a. No stop (R. 2/3)	£450	£850
217	**50**	4c. + 2c. dull purple	3·75	30·00
		a. No stop (R. 2/3)	£500	£850

Nos 216/17 were sold at face, plus 2c. on each stamp for Red Cross funds.

Nos. 216a and 217a occur in the first setting only.

Type I

Type II

The duty plate for the 25c. value was replaced in 1926. In Type II the solid shading forming the back of the figure 2 extends to the top of the curve; the upturned end of the foot of the 2 is short; two background lines above figure 5; c close to 5; STRAITS SETTLEMENTS in taller letters.

1921–33. Wmk Mult Script CA. Ordinary paper (1c. to 6c., 10c. (No. 230), 12c.) or chalk-surfaced paper (others). P 14.

218	**48**	1c. black (3.22)	60	10
219	**52**	2c. green (5.21)	60	10
		w. Wmk inverted	42·00	
		x. Wmk reversed	†	—
		y. Wmk inverted and reversed		
220		2c. brown (3.25)	7·00	2·75

221	**49**	3c. green (9.23)	1·50	80
		w. Wmk inverted	42·00	55·00
222	**50**	4c. carmine-red (9.21)	2·00	4·75
		y. Wmk inverted and reversed	†	£325
223		4c. bright violet (8.24)	60	10
		w. Wmk inverted	42·00	
224		4c. orange (8.29)	1·00	10
225	**51**	5c. orange (Die I) (5.21)	2·25	15
		a. Wmk sideways	†	£3500
		bw. Wmk inverted	42·00	
		bx. Wmk reversed	†	—
		c. Die II (1922)	2·25	1·25
226		5c. brown (Die II) (1932)	3·00	10
		a. Die I (1933)	5·00	10
		ab. Face value omitted	£24000	
227	**52**	6c. dull claret (10.22)	2·00	15
		w. Wmk inverted	40·00	48·00
228		6c. rose-pink (2.25)	25·00	9·50
229		6c. scarlet (1.27)	2·50	10
230	**51**	10c. bright blue (Die I) (1921)	1·75	3·50
		w. Wmk inverted	42·00	70·00
231		10c. purple/*pale yellow* (Die I) (1923)	2·50	10·00
		a. Die II (11.26)	2·50	30
		b. Purple/bright yellow (Die II) (1932)	17·00	3·00
		ba. Die I (1933)	10·00	10
232	**52**	12c. bright blue (1.22)	1·25	20
		w. Wmk inverted	42·00	
233	**53**	21c. dull and bright purple (2.23)	6·00	50·00
234	**54**	25c. dull purple and mauve (Die I, Type I) (1921)	29·00	80·00
		a. Die II, Type I (1923)	12·00	3·75
		b. Die II, Type II (1927)	5·00	1·75
235	**51**	30c. dull purple and orange (Die I) (1921)	24·00	48·00
		a. Die II (1922)	2·00	1·25
236	**53**	35c. dull purple and orange-yellow (8.22)	12·00	6·00
		a. Dull purple and orange	3·50	4·50
237		35c. scarlet and purple (4.31)	10·00	4·50
238	**54**	50c. black/*emerald* (9.25)	1·75	40
239	**51**	$1 black and red/*blue* (Die II) (1921)	6·00	65
240	**54**	$2 green and red/*pale yellow* (Die II) (1923)	10·00	8·00
240*a*	**51**	$5 green and red/*green* (Die II) (1926)	90·00	32·00
240*b*	–	$25 purple and blue/*blue* (5.23)	£850	£150
		ba. Break in scroll	£1800	
		bb. Broken crown and scroll	£1800	£1100
		be. Break through lines below left scroll		
		bf. Damaged leaf at bottom right		
		bs. Optd "Specimen"	£275	
240*c*	–	$100 black and carmine/*blue* (5.23) (F.C. £150)	£6500	£2250
		ca. Break in scroll	£10000	
		cb. Broken crown and scroll	£10000	
		ce. Break through lines below left scroll		
		cf. Damaged leaf at bottom right		
		cs. Optd "Specimen"	£650	
240*d*	–	$500 purple and orange-brown (4.23) (F.C. £500)	£48000	
		da. Break in scroll	£60000	
		db. Broken crown and scroll	£65000	
		de. Break through lines below left scroll		
		df. Damaged leaf at bottom right		
		ds. Optd "Specimen"	£2500	
218/40*a* *Set of 24*			£170	£110
218s/40as (*ex* 6c. rose-pink) Optd or Perf (Nos. 224s, 226s, 237s) "Specimen" *Set of 23*			£700	

Nos. 240*b/d* are as Type **47**, but with portrait of George V.

No. 226ab was caused by a progressive inking failure, resulting in the value being completely omitted on R.10/10 of a single sheet.

The 2c. green was reissued in 1927, and exists with "Specimen" overprint 15.5×1.75 mm instead of the 14.5×2.5 mm of the original issue (*Price*, £65).

An 8c. in carmine was prepared but not issued (Optd "Specimen" £450).

The paper of Nos. 231*b*/ba is the normal *pale yellow* at the back, but with a bright yellow surface.

In 1926 new Key and Duty plates were made of 100 (10×10) instead of the usual 60 (6×10).

SETTINGS OF TYPE 56. Nos. 241/55 were produced using a typeset block of 12 (6×2) overprints from which ten stereos were taken to provide a forme for the complete sheet of 120. Two such formes were prepared of which the second was only used for a limited number of Straits Settlements sheets in addition to the Kedah and Trengganu issues.

Several constant varieties occur on the original typeset block of 12 and so appear ten times on sheets printed from both Settings I and II. These include:

Oval last "O" in "BORNEO" (R. 1/3 of typeset block of 12)

Raised stop after "EXHIBITION" (R. 2/2 of typeset block of 12)

Small second "A" in "MALAYA" (R. 2/6 of typeset block of 12).

The two formes also produced constant varieties in each setting which include:

Setting I

No hyphen (Left pane. R. 7/1 or 9/2)

No stop (Left and right panes. Either on R. 10/4 (right pane) or, for some sheets, on other stamps from even numbered horizontal rows in the 4th vertical column (both panes))

Third "I" in "EXHIBITION" omitted (R. 8/5, 10/5 (left pane)). This must have occurred very late in the use of this setting and is only found on the 5c. and 10c.

Setting II

No stop (Left pane. R. 1/5)

"EXH.BITION" (Left pane. Stamps from even numbered horizontal rows in the 3rd vertical column)

1922 (31 Mar). Malaya-Borneo Exhibition, Singapore. Optd with T **56**.

(a) Wmk Mult Crown CA (Nos. 195, 198/9, 201, 205, 208a, 210, 211b and 212b).

241	**52**	2c. green	30·00	80·00
		b. Oval last "O" in "BORNEO"	65·00	£140
		c. Raised stop after "EXHIBITION"	65·00	£140
		d. Small second "A" in "MALAYA"	65·00	£140
		e. No hyphen	£225	
		f. No stop	85·00	£170
242	**50**	4c. rose-scarlet	8·50	23·00
		b. Oval last "O" in "BORNEO"	18·00	48·00
		c. Raised stop after "EXHIBITION"	18·00	48·00
		d. Small second "A" in "MALAYA"	18·00	48·00
		e. No hyphen	80·00	
		f. No stop	22·00	55·00
		h. "EXH.BITION"	80·00	
243	**51**	5c. orange	6·50	19·00
		b. Oval last "O" in "BORNEO"	14·00	40·00
		c. Raised stop after "EXHIBITION"	14·00	40·00
		d. Small second "A" in "MALAYA"	14·00	40·00
		e. No hyphen	55·00	
		f. No stop	16·00	45·00
		h. "EXH.BITION"	55·00	
244	**52**	8c. ultramarine	1·75	8·50
		b. Oval last "O" in "BORNEO"	5·50	18·00
		c. Raised stop after "EXHIBITION"	5·50	18·00
		d. Small second "A" in "MALAYA"	5·50	18·00
		e. No hyphen	38·00	
		f. No stop	6·50	20·00
		h. "EXH.BITION"	38·00	
245	**54**	25c. dull purple and mauve	3·50	42·00
		b. Oval last "O" in "BORNEO"	9·50	80·00
		c. Raised stop after "EXHIBITION"	9·50	80·00
		d. Small second "A" in "MALAYA"	9·50	80·00
		e. No hyphen	48·00	
		f. No stop	11·00	90·00
		h. "EXH.BITION"	48·00	
246	**53**	45c. black/*blue-green* (*olive back*)	3·00	32·00
		b. Oval last "O" in "BORNEO"	9·00	65·00
		c. Raised stop after "EXHIBITION"	9·00	65·00
		d. Small second "A" in "MALAYA"	9·00	65·00
		e. No hyphen	45·00	
		f. No stop	10·00	75·00
247	**51**	$1 black and red/*blue*	£350	£1100
		b. Oval last "O" in "BORNEO"	£650	
		c. Raised stop after "EXHIBITION"	£650	
		d. Small second "A" in "MALAYA"	£650	
		e. No hyphen		
		f. No stop	£750	
248	**54**	$2 green and red/*orange-buff*	26·00	£130
		a. *On pale yellow* (No. 211c)	65·00	£170
		b. Oval last "O" in "BORNEO"	60·00	£275
		c. Raised stop after "EXHIBITION"	60·00	£275
		d. Small second "A" in "MALAYA"	60·00	£275
		e. No hyphen	£275	
		f. No stop	70·00	£300
		h. "EXH.BITION"	£750	
249	**51**	$5 green and red/*blue-green* (*olive-back*)	£325	£550
		b. Oval last "O" in "BORNEO"	£500	
		c. Raised stop after "EXHIBITION"	£500	
		d. Small second "A" in "MALAYA"	£500	
		e. No hyphen	£1600	
		f. No stop	£600	

(b) Wmk Mult Script CA (Nos. 218/19, 222, 225b, 230 and 239).

250	**48**	1c. black	3·00	18·00
		b. Oval last "O" in "BORNEO"	8·00	30·00
		c. Raised stop after "EXHIBITION"	8·00	30·00
		d. Small second "A" in "MALAYA"	8·00	30·00
		e. No hyphen	45·00	
		f. No stop	9·50	35·00
		h. "EXH.BITION"	45·00	
251	**52**	2c. green	2·50	15·00
		b. Oval last "O" in "BORNEO"	6·50	28·00
		c. Raised stop after "EXHIBITION"	6·50	28·00
		d. Small second "A" in "MALAYA"	6·50	28·00
		e. No hyphen	38·00	
		f. No stop	7·50	30·00
		h. "EXH.BITION"	38·00	
252	**50**	4c. carmine-red	3·50	42·00

		b. Oval last "O" in "BORNEO"	9·00	80·00
		c. Raised stop after "EXHIBITION"	9·00	80·00
		d. Small second "A" in "MALAYA"	9·00	80·00
		e. No hyphen	45·00	
		f. No stop	10·00	80·00
253	**51**	5c. orange (Die II)	2·75	50·00
		b. Oval last "O" in "BORNEO"	8·00	95·00
		c. Raised stop after "EXHIBITION"	8·00	95·00
		d. Small second "A" in "MALAYA"	8·00	95·00
		e. No hyphen	45·00	
		f. No stop	9·50	£110
		g. Third "I" in "EXHIBITION" omitted	£1900	
254		10c. bright blue	2·25	26·00
		b. Oval last "O" in "BORNEO"	7·00	55·00
		c. Raised stop after "EXHIBITION"	7·00	55·00
		d. Small second "A" in "MALAYA"	7·00	55·00
		e. No hyphen	38·00	
		f. No stop	8·00	65·00
		g. Third "I" in "EXHIBITION" omitted	£800	
255		$1 black and red/*blue* (Die II)	20·00	£140
		b. Oval last "O" in "BORNEO"	50·00	£300
		c. Raised stop after "EXHIBITION"	50·00	£300
		d. Small second "A" in "MALAYA"	50·00	£300
		e. No hyphen		
		f. No stop	60·00	£325
		h. "EXH.BITION"		
242/55 *Set of* 11			£350	£900

Examples of most values are known with part strikes of a forged Singapore postmark dated "AU 1 1910".

56a Windsor Castle

Damaged turret (Plate "1" R. 5/6)

(Des H. Fleury. Recess Waterlow)

1935 (6 May). Silver Jubilee. Wmk Mult Script CA. P 11×12.

256	**56a**	5c. ultramarine and grey	3·00	30
257		8c. green and indigo	3·00	3·25
258		12c. brown and deep blue	3·00	6·50
		j. Damaged turret	£600	
259		25c. slate and purple	3·25	8·50
256/9 *Set of* 4			11·00	17·00
256s/9s Perf "Specimen" *Set of* 4			£190	

57

58

1936 (1 Jan)–**37**. Chalk-surfaced paper. Wmk Mult Script CA. P 14.

260	**57**	1c. black (1.1.37)	1·25	20
261		2c. green (1.2.36)	1·50	70
262		4c. orange (15.6.36)	2·25	70
263		5c. brown (1.8.36)	1·00	30
264		6c. scarlet (1.2.36)	1·25	1·10
265		8c. grey	2·75	70
266		10c. dull purple (1.7.36)	2·25	60
267		12c. bright ultramarine (1.9.36)	2·00	2·50
268		25c. dull purple and scarlet (1.2.36)	1·25	50
269		30c. dull purple and orange	1·25	3·25
270		40c. scarlet and dull purple	1·25	2·50
271		50c. black/*emerald* (1.9.36)	4·50	1·25
272		$1 black and red/*blue* (1.7.36)	19·00	1·75
273		$2 green and scarlet (1.4.36)	50·00	10·00
274		$5 green and red/*emerald* (1.1.37)	£130	10·00
260/74 *Set of* 15			£200	32·00
260s/74s Perf "Specimen" *Set of* 15			£425	

57a King George VI and Queen Elizabeth

(Des and recess D.L.R.)

1937 (12 May). Coronation. Wmk Mult Script CA. P 11×11½.

275	**57a**	4c. orange	1·00	10
276		8c. grey-black	1·25	10
277		12c. bright blue	2·75	1·00
275/7 *Set of* 3			4·50	1·10
275s/7s Perf "Specimen" *Set of* 3			£160	

1937–41. Chalk-surfaced paper. Wmk Mult Script CA. P 14 or 15×14 (15c.).

		(a) Die I (printed at two operations).		
278	**58**	1c. black (1.1.38)	9·00	10
279		2c. green (6.12.37)	18·00	20
280		4c. orange (1.1.38)	22·00	20
281		5c. brown (19.11.37)	20·00	30
282		6c. scarlet (10.1.38)	11·00	50
283		8c. grey (26.1.38)	38·00	10
284		10c. dull purple (8.11.37)	9·00	10
285		12c. ultramarine (10.1.38)	9·00	50
286		25c. dull purple and scarlet (11.12.37)	42·00	1·10
287		30c. dull purple and orange (1.12.37)	20·00	2·00
288		40c. scarlet and dull purple (20.12.37)	15·00	2·25
289		50c. black/*emerald* (26.1.38)	11·00	10
290		$1 black and red/*blue* (26.1.38)	15·00	20
291		$2 green and scarlet (26.1.38)	32·00	9·50
292		$5 green and red/*emerald* (26.1.38)	25·00	5·00
		(b) Die II (printed at one operation).		
293	**58**	2c. green (28.12.38)	50·00	40
294		2c. orange (*thin striated paper*) (6.10.41)	2·00	15·00
295		3c. green (*ordinary paper*) (5.9.41)	9·00	4·00
296		4c. orange (29.10.38)	80·00	10
297		5c. brown (18.2.39)	29·00	10
298		15c. ultramarine (*ordinary paper*) (6.10.41)	7·50	10·00
278/98 *Set of* 18			£275	45·00
278s/92s 294s/5s, 298s Perf "Specimen" *Set of* 18			£550	

Die I. Lines of background outside central oval touch the oval and the foliage of the palm tree is usually joined to the oval frame. The downward-pointing palm frond, opposite the King's eye, has two points.

Die II. Lines of background are separated from the oval by a white line and the foliage of the palm trees does not touch the outer frame. The palm frond has only one point.

Nos. 295 and 298 were printed by Harrison and Sons following bomb damage to the De La Rue works on 29 December 1940.

The 6c. grey, 8c. scarlet and $5 purple and orange were only issued with the BMA overprint, but the 8c. without overprint is known although in this state it was never issued (*Price* £15).

STAMP BOOKLETS

1914–19. Black on blue (No. SB1) or grey (No. SB1b) covers, Stapled.

SB1	$1 booklet containing twenty-five 4c. dull purple (No. 197) in two blocks of 12 and one single	
	a. Containing 4c. rose-scarlet (No. 198) (1919)	
SB1*b*	$1 booklet containing four 1c., sixteen 3c. and twelve 4c. (Nos. 193, 196/7) in blocks of four	

1921. Black on blue cover. Stapled.

SB2	$1 booklet containing twenty-five 4c. (No. 222) in two blocks of 12 and one single	
	a. Contents as SB2, but four blocks of 6 and one single	

1922. Black on red cover. Stapled.

SB3	$1 booklet containing 5c. (No. 225) in block of 8 and 6c. (No. 227) in block of 10	£1700

1925–29. Black on red cover. Stapled.

SB4	$1.20 booklet containing thirty 4c. bright violet (No. 223) in blocks of 10	£3000
	a. Containing 4c. orange (No. 224) (1929)	£3250

1927. Black on grey (No. SB5), green (No. SB6) or blue (No. SB7) covers. Stapled.

SB5	$1 booklet containing 4c. and 6c. (Nos. 223, 229) in blocks of 10	£2250
SB6	$1.20 booklet containing twenty 6c. (No. 229) in blocks of 10	£2500
SB7	$1.20 booklet containing 2c., 4c. and 6c. (Nos. 219, 223, 229) in blocks of 10	£3250

1933. Black on buff cover. Stapled.

SB8	$1 booklet containing twenty 5c. (No. 226a) in blocks of 10	

1936. Stapled.

SB9	$1 booklet containing twenty 5c. (No. 263) in blocks of 10	
SB10	$1.30 booklet containing 5c. and 8c. (Nos. 263, 265) in blocks of 10	

1938. Black on buff (No. SB11) or black on green (No. SB12) covers. Stapled.

SB11	$1 booklet containing twenty 5c. (No. 281) in blocks of 10	£3500
SB12	$1.30 booklet containing 5c. and 8c. (Nos. 281, 283) in blocks of 10 and pane of airmail labels	£3750

POSTAGE DUE STAMPS

D 1

1924 (1 Jan)–**26**. Wmk Mult Script CA. P 14.

D1	D **1**	1c. violet	5·00	5·50
D2		2c. black	3·25	1·00
D3		4c. green (5.26)	2·00	4·00
D4		8c. scarlet	4·50	55
D5		10c. orange	6·00	85
D6		12c. bright blue	7·00	65
D1/6 *Set of* 6			25·00	11·00
D1s/6s *Set of* 6			£250	

For later issues of Postage Due stamps, see MALAYAN POSTAL UNION.

POSTAL FISCAL STAMPS

1938. T **47** but with head of King George VI and inscribed "REVENUE" at each side. Wmk Mult Script CA. P 14.

F1	$25 purple and blue/*blue*	£650	£425

No. F1 was regularly used for postal purposes in 1941, although no specific authorisation for such use has been discovered.

The Straits Settlements were occupied by the Japanese in 1942.

After the Second World War the stamps of MALAYA (BRITISH MILITARY ADMINISTRATION) were used. In 1946 Singapore became a separate Crown Colony and Labuan was transferred to North Borneo. Separate stamps were issued for Malacca and Penang, which both joined the Malayan Federation on 1 February 1948.

II. FEDERATED MALAY STATES

On 1 July 1896, the States of Negri Sembilan, Pahang, Perak and Selangor were organised on a federal basis to be known as the Federated Malay States. For the time being each State continued with individual issues, but stamps for the use of the Federation replaced these in 1900.

PRICES FOR STAMPS ON COVER

Nos. 1/13	*from* × 15
No. 14	—
Nos. 15/22	*from* × 10
Nos. 23/5	*from* × 3
No. 26	—
Nos. 27/50	*from* × 6
No. 51	—
Nos. 52/81	*from* × 5
No. 82	—
Nos. D1/6	*from* × 10

PRINTERS. All issues of the Federated Malay States were printed in typography by De La Rue & Co, Ltd, London, *unless otherwise stated*.

(**1**)

(**2**)

1900. Optd with T **1** (cent values) or **2** (dollar values).

(a) Stamps of Negri Sembilan (T **3**).

1	1c. dull purple and green	3·00	8·00
2	2c. dull purple and brown	29·00	65·00
3	3c. dull purple and black	2·75	4·25
4	5c. dull purple and olive-yellow	70·00	£170
5	10c. dull purple and orange	11·00	35·00
6	20c. green and olive	90·00	£100
7	25c. green and carmine	£250	£375
8	50c. green and black	95·00	£140
1/8 *Set of* 8		£500	£800
1s/8s Optd "Specimen" *Set of* 8		£190	

(b) Stamps of Perak (T **44** and **45**).

9	5c. dull purple and olive-yellow	23·00	65·00
10	10c. dull purple and orange	80·00	65·00
11	$1 green and pale green	£170	£250
	w. Wmk inverted	£950	£1000
12	$2 green and carmine	£150	£275
13	$5 green and ultramarine	£475	£700
14	$25 green and orange (F.C. £350)	£9500	
	s. Optd "Specimen"	£400	
11s/13s Optd "Specimen" *Set of* 3		£150	

The Negri Sembilan 3c. dull purple and black does not exist without overprint Type **1**.

The stamps of STRAITS SETTLEMENTS were used in Federated Malay States from 16 July 1900 until replaced by the 1900–1 issue.

3

4

1900–01. P 14.

(a) T **3**. Wmk Crown CA, sideways (1901).

15	1c. black and green	13·00	8·50
	a. Grey and green	4·00	1·00
	b. Grey-brown and green	11·00	30
16	3c. black and brown	17·00	4·75
	a. Grey and brown	6·00	35
	b. Grey-brown and brown	7·50	20
17	4c. black and carmine	22·00	8·00
	a. Grey and carmine	8·50	5·00
	b. Grey-brown and carmine	25·00	2·50
18	5c. green and carmine/*yellow*	2·50	3·00
19	8c. black and ultramarine	48·00	22·00
	a. Grey and ultramarine	22·00	8·00
	b. Grey-brown and ultramarine	27·00	3·75
20	10c. black and claret	£120	50·00
	a. Grey and claret	75·00	9·50
	b. Black and purple	£150	45·00
	c. Grey and purple	80·00	15·00
	d. Grey-brown and purple	85·00	7·00
21	20c. mauve and black	18·00	11·00
22	50c. black and orange-brown	£170	£130
	a. Grey and orange-brown	£100	55·00
	b. Grey-brown and orange-brown	90·00	45·00
15/22b *Set of* 8		£200	65·00
15s/22s Optd "Specimen" *Set of* 8		£200	

Later printings in 1903–4 show the two upper lines of shading in the background at the corner nearest to the "S" of "STATE" blurred and running into one another, whereas in earlier printings these lines are distinct. Two plates were used for printing the central design of *T* **3**. In Plate 1 the lines of background are regular throughout, but in Plate 2 they are lighter around the head and back of the tiger. The 5c. was the only value with single wmk to be printed from Plate 2. Stamps with multiple wmk were printed for a short time from Plate 1, and show the two blurred lines of background near "S" of "STATE," but the majority of these stamps were printed from Plate 2 and later plates.

(b) T **4**. Wmk Crown CC (1900).

23	$1 green and pale green	£130	£140
	w. Wmk inverted	†	—
24	$2 green and carmine	£140	£160
25	$5 green and bright ultramarine	£350	£375
	a. Green and pale ultramarine	£325	£325
26	$25 green and orange (F.C. £100)	£3000	£1600
	s. Optd "Specimen"	£300	
23s/5s Optd "Specimen" *Set of* 3		£160	

Two dies for 1c. green and 4c. scarlet

Die I. "Head" and duty plates. Thick frame line below "MALAY" and in the 1c. the "c" is thin whilst in the 4c. it is thick.

Die II. Single working plate. Thin frame line below "MALAY" and in the 1c. the "c" is thicker whilst in the 4c. it is thinner.

1904 (Aug)–**22**. T **3** and T **4** (dollar values). Wmk Mult Crown CA (sideways* on T **3**). Ordinary paper (1c. to 50c.) or chalk-surfaced paper ($1 to $25).

27	1c. grey and green (8.04)	75·00	8·50
	a. *Grey-brown and green*	38·00	70
28	1c. green (Die I) (8.7.06)	16·00	30
29	1c. green (Die II) (1908)	9·00	20
	a. *Yellow-green*	21·00	2·50
	aw. Wmk Crown to right of CA	60·00	9·50
	b. *Blue-green*	28·00	1·75
30	1c. deep brown (21.1.19)	2·25	90
	w. Wmk Crown to right of CA	†	£225
31	2c. green (18.2.19)	2·50	30
	w. Wmk Crown to right of CA	60·00	14·00
32	3c. grey and brown (10.04)	70·00	1·00
	a. *Grey-brown and brown* (12.05)	48·00	1·75
	ab. Chalk-surfaced paper	45·00	2·75
33	3c. brown (11.7.06)	9·50	15
34	3c. carmine (2.2.09)	4·50	10
	aw. Wmk Crown to right of CA	11·00	40
	b. *Scarlet* (1.17)	19·00	50
	bw. Wmk Crown to right of CA	30·00	4·50
35	3c. grey (29.10.18)	2·50	20
	w. Wmk Crown to right of CA	55·00	14·00
36	4c. grey and scarlet (8.04)	55·00	6·00
	a. Chalk-surfaced paper. *Grey and rose*	27·00	3·25
	b. *Grey-brown and scarlet*	45·00	3·25
	c. *Black and scarlet*	24·00	2·50
	d. *Black and rose*	6·50	80
	dw. Wmk Crown to right of CA	12·00	80
	e. *Black and deep rose (aniline)* (1909)	50·00	5·00
	f. *Jet black and rose* (1914)	29·00	2·75
37	4c. scarlet (Die I) (11.2.19)	3·50	4·75
38	4c. scarlet (Die II) (15.4.19)	1·75	15
	aw. Wmk Crown to right of CA	55·00	6·00
	b. Wmk upright (2.22)	£800	£375
39	5c. green and carmine/*yellow* (5.06)	12·00	3·00
	aw. Wmk Crown to right of CA	75·00	20·00
	b. Chalk-surfaced paper	32·00	6·00
	c. *Deep green and carmine/yellow*	15·00	3·50
	d. *On orange-buff* (1921)	18·00	10·00
	e. *On pale yellow* (4.22)	13·00	8·50
40	6c. orange (11.2.19)	2·75	3·25
41	8c. grey and ultramarine (2.05)	75·00	23·00
	aw. Wmk Crown to right of CA		
	b. *Grey-brown and ultramarine* (12.05)	19·00	4·25
	ba. Chalk-surfaced paper	80·00	14·00
	bb. Wmk upright (3.07)	9·00	4·75
42	8c. ultramarine (8.3.10)	13·00	1·00
	aw. Wmk Crown to right of CA	95·00	32·00
	b. *Deep blue* (1918)	16·00	1·25
43	10c. grey-brown and claret (5.04)	80·00	8·00
	a. Chalk-surfaced paper (1905)	£120	14·00
	b. *Black and claret*	30·00	65
	bw. Wmk Crown to right of CA	48·00	1·50
	c. *Grey-brown and purple* (1905)	75·00	3·25
	d. *Black and purple*	30·00	2·75
	dy. Wmk Crown to right of CA and reversed	†	£325
	e. *Jet-black and bright purple* (1914)	£100	5·00
44	10c. deep blue (3.6.19)	6·50	1·75
	a. *Bright blue*	6·50	1·00
	ab. Wmk inverted	†	—
	aw. Wmk Crown to right of CA	75·00	23·00
45	20c. mauve and black (3.05)	18·00	1·25
	a. Chalk-surfaced paper	13·00	3·00
	w. Wmk Crown to right of CA	90·00	23·00
46	35c. scarlet/*pale yellow* (25.8.22)	5·50	12·00
47	50c. grey and orange (3.05)	75·00	12·00
	aw. Wmk Crown to right of CA	£200	65·00
	b. Wmk inverted	†	—
	c. *Grey-brown and orange-brown* (1906)	50·00	11·00
	caw. Wmk Crown to right of CA	†	—
	cb. Chalk-surfaced paper. *Grey-brown and orange-brown*	55·00	7·50
	cbw. Wmk Crown to right of CA	†	80·00
	cc. *Grey and orange-brown*	65·00	11·00
	cd. *Black and orange-brown*	90·00	21·00
	ce. *Jet-black and orange-brown* (1914)	£130	25·00
48	$1 grey-green and green (10.07)	85·00	50·00
	a. *Green and pale green*	£110	50·00
	aw. Wmk inverted		
49	$2 green and carmine (4.12.07)	90·00	£120
	a. Printed on the gummed side		
	w. Wmk inverted		
	y. Wmk inverted and reversed	†	£800
50	$5 green and blue (1.08)	£225	£130
51	$25 green and orange (12.09) (F.C. £60)	£1300	£800
27/50 *Set of 22*		£600	£300
28s, 30s/1s, 33s/5s, 38s, 40s, 42s, 44s, 46s Optd "Specimen" *Set of 11*		£550	

*The normal sideways watermark shows Crown to left of CA, *as seen from the back of the stamp*. The watermark on No. 47b is vertical, inverted.

Nos. 29/*b*, 30, 31, 33, 34/*b* and 35 were printed from single working plates and all the rest from double plates.

Most examples of No. 47b have fiscal cancellations, but at least one is known postally used.

The 3c. scarlet (No. 34*b*) was surcharged '4/CENTS.' between horizontal lines in early 1918, but was never issued. The entire printing of five million stamps was sunk at sea, nevertheless a few examples do exist. (*Price, £5000, unused*).

1922–34. Wmk Mult Script CA (sideways* on T **3**). Ordinary paper (1c. to 10c. (No. 66), 12c., 20c. (No. 69a), 35c. (No. 72)) or chalk-surfaced paper (others).

52	**3**	1c. deep brown (1.8.22)	1·50	3·25
		w. Wmk Crown to right of CA	65·00	65·00
53		1c. black (12.6.23)	75	20
54		2c. brown (5.8.25)	6·50	9·00
55		2c. green (15.6.26)	3·00	10
		a. Wmk upright	£425	
56		3c. grey (27.12.22)	1·75	7·50
		w. Wmk Crown to right of CA	80·00	80·00
57		3c. green (22.1.24)	1·25	1·50
58		3c. brown (31.5.27)	3·00	50
		a. Wmk upright	£425	
59		4c. carmine-red (Die II) (27.11.23)	3·50	50
		w. Wmk Crown to right of CA	48·00	21·00
60		4c. orange (9.11.26)	1·50	10
		a. No watermark	£325	£225
		b. Wmk upright	£425	
		c. "A" of "CA" missing from wmk	†	£800
61		5c. mauve/*pale yellow* (17.3.22)	1·00	20
		w. Wmk Crown to right of CA	65·00	42·00
62		5c. brown (1.3.32)	3·50	10
63		6c. orange (2.5.22)	1·00	45
		w. Wmk Crown to right of CA	£100	
64		6c. scarlet (9.11.26)	1·50	10
		a. Wmk upright		
65		10c. bright blue (23.10.23)	1·25	8·00
		w. Wmk Crown to right of CA		
66		10c. black and blue (18.1.24†)	2·00	75
67		10c. purple/*pale yellow* (14.7.31)	3·75	40
68		12c. ultramarine (12.9.22)	1·25	10
		w. Wmk Crown to right of CA	75·00	35·00
		x. Wmk sideways reversed	£225	
69		20c. dull purple and black (*chalk-surfaced paper*) (3.4.23)	4·00	1·75
		a. Ordinary paper (29.12.26)	45·00	3·25
		b. Wmk inverted	†	£275
70		25c. purple and bright magenta (3.9.29)	2·75	1·75
71		30c. purple and orange-yellow (3.9.29)	3·25	3·75
72		35c. scarlet/*pale yellow* (6.11.28)	3·25	24·00
73		35c. scarlet and purple (29.9.31)	13·00	14·00
74		50c. black and orange (24.4.24)	13·00	13·00
		aw. Wmk Crown to right of CA	£140	
		b. *Black and orange-brown*	32·00	5·00
75		50c. black/*green* (16.6.31)	4·00	2·50
76	**4**	$1 pale green and green (2.2.26)	23·00	95·00
		a. *Grey-green and emerald* (5.10.26)	22·00	50·00
77	**3**	$1 black and red/*blue* (10.3.31)	12·00	4·00
78	**4**	$2 green and carmine (17.8.26)	30·00	85·00
79	**3**	$2 green and red/*yellow* (6.2.34)	48·00	40·00
80	**4**	$5 green and blue (24.2.25)	£140	£200
		w. Wmk inverted	£950	
81	**3**	$5 green and red/*green* (7.34)	£200	£200
82	**4**	$25 green and orange (14.2.28) (F.C. £100)	£1100	£1300
		s. Optd "Specimen"	£300	
52/81 *Set of 30*			£475	£600
52s/81s Optd or Perf (No. 62s, 67s, 70s/1s, 73s, 77s, 79s, 81s) "Specimen" *Set of 30*			£1300	

*The normal sideways watermark shows Crown to left of CA, *as seen from the back of the stamp*.

†No. 66 was released in London by the Crown Agents some months earlier but this is the official date of issue in the States.

Nos. 52, 56 and 59 were printed from single working plates and the rest from double plates.

No. 55 exists in coils constructed from normal sheets.

The 5c. mauve on white Script paper is the result of soaking early printings of No. 61 in water.

STAMP BOOKLETS

1909. Black on pink (Nos. SB1/2) or black on buff (No. SB3) covers. Stapled.

SB1	25c. booklet containing twenty-four 1c. (No. 29) in blocks of 6	£2000
	a. Black on green cover (1917)	
	b. Black on blue cover	£2000
SB2	73c. booklet containing twenty-four 3c. (No. 34) in blocks of 6	£2000
	a. Black on red cover (1917)	
	b. Black on blue cover	£2000
SB3	97c. booklet containing twenty-four 4c. (No. 36*d*) in blocks of 6	£2250

1919. Black on green (No. SB4) or black on pink (No. SB5) covers. Stapled.

SB4	49c. booklet containing twenty-four 2c. (No. 31) in blocks of 6	£5000
SB5	97c. booklet containing twenty-four 4c. (No. 37) in blocks of 6	£1800

1922. Black on buff cover (No. SB7). Stapled.

SB6	$1.21 booklet containing twenty-four 5c. (No. 61) in blocks of 6	£2750
SB7	$1.45 booklet containing twenty-four 6c. (No. 63) in blocks of 6	£2250

1926. As Nos. SB4, SB3 and SB7, but sold at face value without premium. Black on green (No. SB8), black on pink (No. SB9) or black on buff (No. SB10) covers. Stapled.

SB8	48c. booklet containing twenty-four 2c. (No. 55) in blocks of 6	
SB9	96c. booklet containing twenty-four 4c. (No. 60) in blocks of 6	£2250
SB10	$1.44 booklet containing twenty-four 6c. (No. 64) in blocks of 6	£2250

1926. Black on grey cover. Stapled.

SB11	$1 booklet containing 4c. and 6c. (Nos. 60, 64) each in block of 10	£2250

1927. Black on bluish green cover. Stapled.

SB12	$1.50 booklet containing 2c., 3c., 4c. and 6c. (Nos. 55, 58, 60, 64) each in block of 10	£2750

1927–30. Black on red (No. SB13), black on green (No. SB14) or black on blue (No. SB15) covers. Stapled.

SB13	$1.20 booklet containing thirty 4c. (No. 60) in blocks of 10	£2500
	a. Black on orange cover (1930)	
SB14	$1.20 booklet containing twenty 6c. (No. 64) in blocks of 10 (1928)	£3000
SB15	$1.20 booklet containing 2c., 4c. and 6c. (Nos. 55, 60, 64) each in block of 10 (1928)	£2250
	a. Black on white cover (1930)	

1934. Black on buff cover. Stapled.

SB16	$1 booklet containing twenty 5c. (No. 62) in blocks of 10	£2750

POSTAGE DUE STAMPS

D **1**

(Typo Waterlow)

1924 (1 Dec)–**26**. Wmk Mult Script CA (sideways*). P 15×14.

D1	D **1**	1c. violet	4·75	38·00
		w. Wmk Crown to left of CA (1926)	17·00	30·00
D2		2c. black	1·75	6·50
		w. Wmk Crown to left of CA (1926)	4·00	3·25
D3		4c. green (wmk Crown to left of CA) (27.4.26)	2·25	5·00
D4		8c. red	5·50	35·00
		w. Wmk Crown to left of CA (1926)	15·00	18·00
D5		10c. orange	9·00	17·00
		w. Wmk Crown to left of CA (1926)	27·00	22·00
D6		12c. blue	9·00	27·00
		w. Wmk Crown to left of CA (1926)	15·00	12·00
D1/6 *Set of 6*			29·00	75·00
D1s/6s Optd "Specimen" *Set of 6*			£200	

*The normal sideways watermark shows Crown to right of CA, *as seen from the back of the stamp.*

The issues of the Federated Malay States were replaced by stamps for the individual States from 1935 onwards.

III. MALAYAN POSTAL UNION

The Malayan Postal Union was organised in 1934 and, initially, covered the Straits Settlements and the Federated Malay States. Stamps of the Straits Settlements together with issues for the individual States continued to be used, but Malayan Postal Union postage due stamps were introduced in 1936.

Following the end of the Second World War the use of these postage dues spread throughout Malaya and to Singapore.

PRICES FOR STAMPS ON COVER TO 1945	
Nos. D1/6	*from* × 10
Nos. D7/13	*from* × 4

POSTAGE DUE STAMPS

D **1**

10

cents

(D **2**)

(Typo Waterlow until 1961, then D.L.R.)

1936 (June)–**38**. Wmk Mult Script CA. P 15×14.

D1	D **1**	1c. slate-purple (4.38)	10·00	70
D2		4c. green (9.36)	25·00	1·00
D3		8c. scarlet	14·00	2·75
D4		10c. yellow-orange	21·00	30
D5		12c. pale ultramarine (9.36)	22·00	14·00
D6		50c. black (1.38)	28·00	4·50
D1/6 *Set of 6*			£110	21·00
D1s/6s Perf "Specimen" *Set of 6*			£250	

For use in Negri Sembilan, Pahang, Perak, Selangor and Straits Settlements including Singapore.

1945–49. New values and colours. Wmk Mult Script CA. P 15×14.

D7	D **1**	1c. purple	3·25	2·00
D8		3c. green	6·50	4·00
D9		5c. scarlet	6·00	3·00
D10		8c. yellow-orange (1949)	13·00	14·00
		s. Perf "Specimen"	75·00	
D11		9c. yellow-orange	35·00	42·00
D12		15c. pale ultramarine	£110	28·00
D13		20c. blue (1948)	8·00	5·00
		s. Perf "Specimen"	75·00	
D7/13 *Set of 7*			£160	90·00

1951 (8 Aug)–**63**. Wmk Mult Script CA. P 14.

D14	D **1**	1c. violet (21.8.52)	70	1·60
D15		2c. deep slate-blue (16.11.53)	1·25	2·25
		a. Perf 12½ (15.11.60)	1·75	19·00
		ab. Chalk-surfaced paper (10.7.62)	1·50	12·00
		ac. Ditto. Imperf horiz (vert pair)	†	£13000
D16		3c. deep green (21.8.52)	27·00	14·00
D17		4c. sepia (16.11.53)	70	7·00
		a. Perf 12½ (15.11.60)	1·75	20·00
		ab. Chalk-surfaced paper. *Bistre-brown* (10.7.62)	1·00	17·00
D18		5c. vermilion	48·00	12·00
D19		8c. yellow-orange	2·25	5·50
D20		12c. bright purple (1.2.54)	1·25	6·00
		a. Perf 12½. Chalk-surfaced paper (10.7.62)	2·50	26·00
D21		20c. blue	6·50	6·50
		a. Perf 12½. *Deep blue* (10.12.57)	7·00	26·00
		ab. Chalk-surfaced paper (15.10.63)	6·00	40·00
D14/21 *Set of 8*			80·00	50·00

Nos. D7 to D21ab were for use in the Federation and Singapore.

1964 (14 Apr)–**65**. Chalk-surfaced paper. Wmk w **12** (sideways on 1c.). P 12½.

D22	D **1**	1c. maroon	30	18·00
		a. Perf 12. Wmk upright (4.5.65)	1·25	15·00
D23		2c. deep slate-blue	1·75	15·00
		a. Perf 12 (9.3.65)	1·00	21·00
D24		4c. bistre-brown	1·00	15·00
		a. Perf 12 (9.3.65)	1·50	15·00
D25		8c. yellow-orange (*p* 12) (4.5.65)	2·00	20·00
D27		12c. bright purple	1·50	20·00
		a. Perf 12 (4.5.65)	6·00	38·00
D28		20c. deep blue	2·50	35·00
		a. Perf 12 (4.5.65)	9·50	50·00
D22/8 *Set of 6*			7·50	£110

1964 (1 Dec). As No. D19 surch locally with Type D **2**.

D29	D **1**	10c. on 8c. yellow-orange	60	3·00

First supplies of this stamp differed from No. D19 in that they had been climatically affected but later a fresh printing of No. D19 was surcharged.

1966. Unsurfaced paper. Wmk w **12**. P 15×14.

D30	D **1**	50c. black	£1600	£1500

Nos. D22/9 were for use throughout Malaysia and Singapore. They were superseded on 15 August 1966 by the postage dues inscribed "MALAYSIA", but continued in use, together with No. D30, for Singapore until 31 January 1968 when they were replaced by Singapore Postage Dues.

IV. MALAYA (BRITISH MILITARY ADMINISTRATION)

Following the Japanese surrender on 2 September 1945 British troops landed in Malaya which was placed under a British Military Administration. The Director of Posts was ashore at Singapore on 6 September and had reached Kuala Lumpur by 13 September. Postal services in Singapore and Johore resumed on 17 September and had spread to the remainder of the country by 5 October. No stamps were initially available so all mail up to 1 oz. was carried free until the first overprinted stamps appeared on 19 October.

De La Rue had overprinted available stocks of pre-war Straits Settlements stamps earlier in 1945 and initial supplies of these London overprints were placed on sale from 19 October (Nos. 1, 2a, 4, 6a, 7 and 8a) with the 15c. and 25c. (Nos. 11 and 13a) issued later. A second consignment contained dollar values including the $5 purple and orange. Duplicate plates were subsequently sent to the Government Printing Office at Kuala Lumpur, where the overprinting of surviving local stocks of the 1c., 5c., 10c., 15c. (overprinted in black) and $5 green and red on emerald took place, and to Australia for those shipments which had been diverted there in 1941.

The stamps were used throughout all Malay States and in Singapore. From 1948 this general issue was gradually replaced by individual issues for each state. The last usage was in Kelantan where B M A overprints were not withdrawn until 10 July 1951.

B M A
MALAYA
(**1**)

1945 (19 Oct)–**48**. T **58** of Straits Settlements from Die I (double-plate printing) or Die II (single-plate printing) optd with T **1**. Wmk Mult Script CA. Chalk-surfaced paper. P 14 or 15×14 (No. 11).

1	1c. black (I) (R.)	4·75	70
	a. Ordinary paper	10	30
	b. Thin striated paper (8.46)	30·00	15·00
2	2c. orange (II) (8.7.47)	7·00	60
	a. Ordinary paper (19.10.45)	20	10
	b. Thin striated paper (7.46)	18·00	7·00
	w. Wmk inverted	†	£1600
3	2c. orange (I) (*ordinary paper*) (9.46)	28·00	4·50
4	3c. yellow-green (II) (*ordinary paper*)	2·25	50
	a. Blue-green (27.1.47)	7·50	4·25
	b. Chalk-surfaced paper. *Blue-green* (8.7.47)	17·00	1·00
5	5c. brown (II) (24.10.45)	70	1·00
6	6c. grey (II) (22.3.48)	22·00	5·00
	a. Ordinary paper (19.10.45)	30	20
	b. Thin striated paper (6.46)	18·00	10·00
7	8c. scarlet (II) (*ordinary paper*)	30	10
	a. Thin striated paper (6.46)	18·00	14·00
8	10c. purple (I) (12.45)	6·00	80
	a. Ordinary paper (19.10.45)	50	10
	b. Slate-purple (12.45)	6·00	30
	c. Magenta (22.3.48)	9·50	70
	d. Thin striated paper (8.46)	22·00	12·00
9	10c. purple (II) (28.7.48)	19·00	4·75
10	12c. bright ultramarine (I) (11.45)	1·75	11·00
11	15c. bright ultramarine (II) (*ordinary paper*) (11.45)	2·50	9·00
12	15c. bright ultramarine (II) (R.) (22.3.48)	35·00	1·50
	a. Ordinary paper (12.45)	75	20
	b. Blue (27.11.47)	65·00	85
	ba. Ordinary paper (8.7.47)	£150	16·00
13	25c. dull purple and scarlet (I) (22.3.48)	23·00	3·00
	a. Ordinary paper (12.45)	1·40	30
	ab. Opt double	£5500	
	ac. "A" of "CA" missing from watermark	†	£2500
	b. Thin striated paper (8.46)	20·00	7·00
14	50c. black/*emerald* (I) (R.) (12.45)	35·00	2·50
	a. Ordinary paper	75	10
15	$1 black and red (I) (*ordinary paper*) (12.45)	2·00	10
16	$2 green and scarlet (I) (*ordinary paper*) (12.45)	2·75	75
17	$5 green and red/*emerald* (I) (11.45)	90·00	£120
18	$5 purple and orange (I) (*ordinary paper*) (12.45)	3·75	3·00
1/18 *Set of* 15		95·00	£130
1s/11s, 13s/16s, 18s Perf "Specimen" *Set of* 14		£550	

The 8c. grey with "BMA" opt was prepared but not officially issued (*Price £375 unused*).

Nos. 3 and 9 do not exist without the overprint.

Initial printings on ordinary paper were produced by Harrison and Sons in 1941 following bomb damage to the De La Rue works on 29 December 1940.

For a description of the trin striated paper, see the introduction to this catalogue.

No. 8 with reddish purple medallion and dull purple frame is from a 1947 printing with the head in fugitive ink which discolours with moisture.

Postal forgeries of the 50c. value exist made by dyeing examples of the 1c. and then altering the face value to 50c.

In 1946 8c. and 15c. stamps in the Crown Colony Victory design were prepared for the Malayan Union, but not issued. Examples of the 8c. carmine from this issue exist from unofficial leakages (*Price £425 unused*).

V. MALAYAN FEDERATION

The Malayan Federation, formed on 1 February 1948 by Malacca, Penang, the four Federated Malay States and the five Unfederated States, became an independent member of the British Commonwealth on 31 August 1957.

Commemoratives and a limited series of definitives were issued by the Federation and were used concurrently with the stamps from the individual States.

1 Tapping Rubber

2 Federation coat of arms

3 Tin dredger

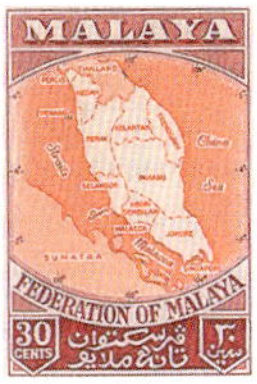

4 Map of the Federation

(Centre recess, frame litho (6c., 25c.); centre litho, frame recess (12c.); recess (30c.), D.L.R.)

1957 (5 May)–**63**. T **1**, **4** and similar designs. W w **12**. P 13×12½ (No. 4) or 13 (others).

1	6c. deep blue, red, yellow and grey-blue	50	10
	a. *Indigo, red, yellow and grey-blue* (20.6.61)	5·00	65
	b. *Indigo, red, yellow and slate-blue* (12.2.63)	4·00	65
	c. Yellow (star and crescent) omitted	75·00	
2	12c. red, yellow, blue, black and scarlet	1·25	1·00
3	25c. maroon, red, yellow and dull greenish blue	3·50	20
4	30c. orange-red and lake	1·25	20
	a. Perf 13. *Orange-red and deep lake* (20.6.61)	1·50	1·00
	ab. *Orange-red and lake* (10.7.62)	3·75	10
1/4 *Set of* 4		6·00	1·25

5 Prime Minister Tunku Abdul Rahman and Populace greeting Independence

(Des A. B. Seeman. Recess Waterlow)

1957 (31 Aug). Independence Day. Wmk Mult Script CA. P 12½.

5	**5**	10c. bistre-brown	65	10

6 United Nations Emblem

7 United Nations Emblem

(Recess D.L.R.)

1958 (5 Mar). U.N. Economic Commission for Asia and Far East Conference, Kuala Lumpur. W w **12**. P 13½ (12c.) or 12½ (30c.).

6	**6**	12c. carmine-red	30	80
7	**7**	30c. maroon	40	80

8 Merdeka Stadium, Kuala Lumpur

9 The Yang di-Pertuan Agong (Tuanku Abdul Rahman)

(Photo Harrison)

1958 (31 Aug). First Anniv of Independence. W w **12**. P 13½×14½ (10c.) or 14½×13½ (30c.).

8	**8**	10c. green, yellow, red and blue	15	10
9	**9**	30c. red, yellow, violet-blue and green	40	70

10 "Human Rights"

11 Malayan with Torch of Freedom

(Des J. P. Hendroff. Litho (10c.), photo (30c.) D.L.R.)

1958 (10 Dec). Tenth Anniv of Declaration of Human Rights.

(a) W w **12**. P 12½×13

10	**10**	10c. blue, black, carmine and orange	15	10

(b) Wmk Mult Script CA. P 13×12½

11	**11**	30c. deep green	45	60

12 Mace and Malayan Peoples

(Photo Enschedé)

1959 (12 Sept). Inauguration of Parliament. No wmk. P 13×14.

12	**12**	4c. rose-red	10	10
13		10c. violet	10	10
14		25c. yellow-green	75	20
12/14 *Set of 3*			85	30

13

14

(Recess D.L.R.)

1960 (7 Apr). World Refugee Year. W w **12**. P 13½ (12c.) or 12½×13 (30c.)

15	**13**	12c. purple	10	60
16	**14**	30c. deep green	10	10

HAVE YOU READ THE NOTES AT THE BEGINNING OF THIS CATALOGUE?

These often provide answers to the enquiries we receive

15 Seedling Rubber Tree and Map

16 The Yang di-Pertuan Agong (Tuanku Syed Putra)

(Photo Japanese Govt Ptg Wks)

1960 (19 Sept). Natural Rubber Research Conference and 15th International Rubber Study Group Meeting, Kuala Lumpur. T **15** and similar vert design. No wmk. P 13.

17		6c. yellow-green, black, orange and red-brown	20	1·25
18		30c. yellow-green, black, orange and bright blue	50	75

No. 18 is inscribed "INTERNATIONAL RUBBER STUDY GROUP 15th MEETING KUALA LUMPUR" at foot.

(Photo Harrison)

1961 (4 Jan). Installation of Yang di-Pertuan Agong, Tuanku Syed Putra. W w **12**. P 14×14½.

19	**16**	10c. black and blue	10	10

17 Colombo Plan Emblem

18 Malaria Eradication Emblem

(Photo Japanese Govt Ptg Works)

1961 (30 Oct). Colombo Plan Conference, Kuala Lumpur. P 13.

20	**17**	12c. black and magenta	35	2·75
21		25c. black and apple-green	80	2·25
22		30c. black and turquoise-blue	70	1·00
20/2 *Set of 3*			1·75	5·50

(Photo Harrison)

1962 (7 Apr). Malaria. Eradication. W w **13**. P 14×14½.

23	**18**	25c. orange-brown	20	40
24		30c. deep lilac	20	15
25		50c. ultramarine	40	80
23/5 *Set of 3*			70	1·25

19 Palmyra Palm Leaf

20 "Shadows of the Future"

(Photo Harrison)

1962 (21 July). National Language Month. W w **13** (upright or inverted). P 13½.

26	**19**	10c. light brown and deep reddish violet	15	10
27		20c. light brown and deep bluish green	60	1·25
28		50c. light brown and magenta	1·75	1·75
26/8 *Set of 3*			2·25	2·75

(Photo Enschedé)

1962 (1 Oct). Introduction of Free Primary Education. W w **13**. P 13½.

29	**20**	10c. bright purple	10	10
		w. Wmk inverted	45·00	
30		25c. ochre	50	1·25
31		30c. emerald	2·75	10
29/31 *Set of 3*			3·00	1·25

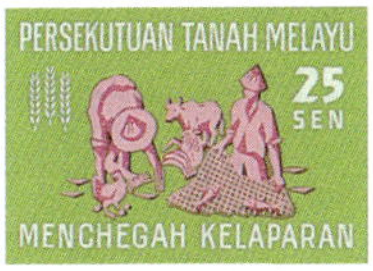

21 Harvester and Fisherman

22 Dam and Pylon

(Photo Courvoisier)

1963 (21 Mar). Freedom from Hunger. P 11½.

32	**21**	25c. carmine and apple-green	2·50	3·00
33		30c. carmine and crimson	2·75	1·50
34		50c. carmine and bright blue	2·50	3·00
32/4 *Set of 3*			7·00	6·75

(Photo Harrison)

1963 (26 June). Cameron Highlands Hydro-Electric Scheme. W w **13**. P 14.

35	**22**	20c. green and reddish violet	60	10
36		30c. blue-green and ultramarine	1·00	1·50

The definitive general issue for Malaysia and the low value sets for the individual states superseded the stamps of the Malayan Federation by 15 November 1965.

VI. MALAYSIA

On 16 September 1963, the Malayan Federation, Sabah (North Borneo), Sarawak and Singapore formed the Federation of Malaysia. Singapore left the Federation on 9 August 1965, and became an independent republic. Stamps of Singapore continued to be valid in Malaysia, and those of Malaysia in Singapore, until 1 February 1967.

Individual issues for the component States continued, but were restricted to low value definitives and the occasional "State" commemorative. The higher value definitives and the vast majority of commemoratives were issued on a "National" basis.

A. NATIONAL ISSUES

General issues for use throughout the Malaysian Federation.

1 Federation Map

2 Bouquet of Orchids

(Photo Harrison)

1963 (16 Sept). Inauguration of Federation. W w **13**. P 14½.

1	**1**	10c. yellow and bluish violet	40	10
		a. Yellow omitted	£250	
2		12c. yellow and deep green	1·00	60
3		50c. yellow and chocolate	1·40	10
1/3 *Set of 3*			2·50	65

(Photo Enschedé)

1963 (3 Oct). Fourth World Orchid Conference, Singapore. No wmk. P 13×14.

4	**2**	6c. multicoloured	1·25	1·25
5		25c. multicoloured	1·25	25

4 Parliament House, Kuala Lumpur

(Des V. Whiteley. Photo Harrison)

1963 (4 Nov). Ninth Commonwealth Parliamentary Conference, Kuala Lumpur. W w **13** (inverted). P 13½.

7	**4**	20c. deep magenta and gold	1·25	40
8		30c. deep green and gold	1·25	15

5 "Flame of Freedom" and Emblems of Goodwill, Health and Charity

6 Microwave Tower and I.T.U. Emblem

(Photo Harrison)

1964 (10 Oct). Eleanor Roosevelt Commemoration. W w **13**. P 14½×13½.

9	**5**	25c. black, red and greenish blue	20	10
10		30c. black, red and deep lilac	20	15
11		50c. black, red and ochre-yellow	20	10
9/11 *Set of 3*			55	30

(Photo Courvoisier)

1965 (17 May). I.T.U. Centenary. P 11½.

12	**6**	2c. multicoloured	40	1·50
13		25c. multicoloured	1·75	60
14		50c. multicoloured	2·25	10
12/14 *Set of 3*			4·00	2·00

7 National Mosque

8 Air Terminal

(Photo Harrison)

1965 (27 Aug). Opening of National Mosque, Kuala. Lumpur. W w **13**. P 14×14½.

15	**7**	6c. carmine	10	10
16		15c. red-brown	20	10
17		20c. deep bluish green	20	15
15/17 *Set of 3*			45	30

(Photo Harrison)

1965 (30 Aug). Opening of International Airport, Kuala Lumpur. W w **13**. P 14½×14.

18	**8**	15c. black, yellow-green and new blue	40	10
		a. Yellow-green omitted	30·00	
19		30c. black, yellow-green and magenta	60	20

9 Crested Wood Partridge

17 Sepak Raga (ball game) and Football

(Des A. Fraser-Brunner. Photo Harrison)

1965 (9 Sept). T **9** and similar vert designs. Multicoloured. W w **13**. P 14½.

20	25c. Type **9**	50	10
	w. Wmk inverted	3·50	
21	30c. Blue-backed Fairy Bluebird	60	10
	a. Blue (plumage) omitted	£300	
	b. Yellow omitted	£400	
	w. Wmk inverted	6·50	
22	50c. Black-nailed Oriole	1·25	10
	a. Yellow omitted	£180	
	b. Imperf (pair)	£200	
	c. Scarlet (inscr and berries) omitted	£100	
	w. Wmk inverted	14·00	
23	75c. Rhinoceros Hornbill	90	10
24	$1 Zebra Dove	1·50	10
	w. Wmk inverted	32·00	
25	$2 Great Argus Pheasant	4·25	30
	a. Imperf (pair)	£200	
	w. Wmk inverted	12·00	
26	$5 Asiatic Paradise Flycatcher	18·00	3·00
	w. Wmk inverted	38·00	
27	$10 Blue-tailed Pitta	48·00	13·00
	a. Imperf (pair)	£275	
20/7 *Set of 8*		65·00	14·00

All values except the 75c. and $10 exist with PVA gum as well as gum arabic, 21a and 22c exist on both papers.

(Des E. A. F. Anthony. Litho Japanese Govt Ptg Wks)

1965 (14 Dec). Third South East Asian Peninsular Games. T **17** and similar vert designs. P 13×13½.

28		25c. black and olive-green	40	1·25
29		30c. black and bright purple	40	20
30		50c. black and light blue	70	30
28/30 *Set of 3*			1·40	1·60

Designs:—30c. Running; 50c. Diving.

20 National Monument

21 The Yang di-Pertuan Agong (Tuanku Ismail Nasiruddin Shah)

(Photo Harrison)

1966 (8 Feb). National Monument, Kuala Lumpur. W w **13**. P 13½.

31	**20**	10c. multicoloured	50	10
		a. Blue omitted	£150	
32		20c. multicoloured	1·00	40

(Photo Japanese Govt Ptg Wks)

1966 (11 Apr). Installation of Yang di-Pertuan Agong, Tuanku Ismail Nastruddin Shah. P 13½.

33	**21**	15c. black and light yellow	10	10
34		50c. black and greenish blue	20	20

22 School Building

23 "Agriculture"

(Photo D.L.R.)

1966 (21 Oct). 150th Anniv of Penang Free School. W w **13** (sideways). P 13.

35	**22**	20c. multicoloured	70	10
36		50c. multicoloured	90	10

The 50c. is also inscr "ULANG TAHUN KE-150" at foot and bears a shield at bottom left corner.

(Des Enche Ng Peng Nam. Photo Japanese Govt Ptg Wks)

1966 (1 Dec). First Malaysia Plan. T **23** and similar horiz designs. Multicoloured. P 13½.

37		15c. Type **23**	20	10
38		15c. "Rural Health"	20	10
39		15c. "Communications"	1·90	15
40		15c. "Education"	20	10
41		15c. "Irrigation"	20	10
37/41 *Set of 5*			2·50	50

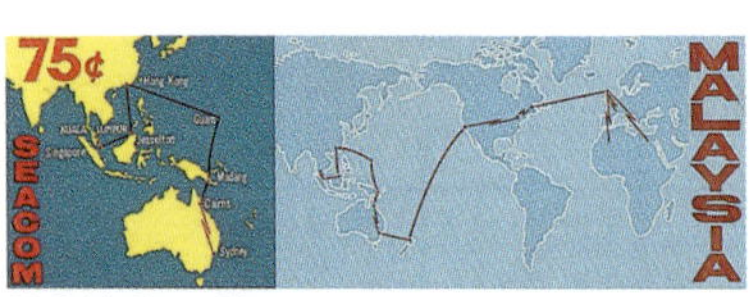

28 Cable Route Maps

(Des Enche Ng Peng Nam. Photo Japanese Govt Ptg Wks)

1967 (30 Mar). Completion of Malaysia–Hong Kong Link of SEACOM Telephone Cable. P 13½.

42	**28**	30c. multicoloured	80	50
43		75c. multicoloured	2·50	4·00

29 Hibiscus and Paramount Rulers

(Photo Harrison)

1967 (31 Aug). Tenth Anniv of Independence. W w **13**. P 14½.

44	**29**	15c. multicoloured	20	10
		w. Wmk inverted	4·00	
45		50c. multicoloured	1·25	80

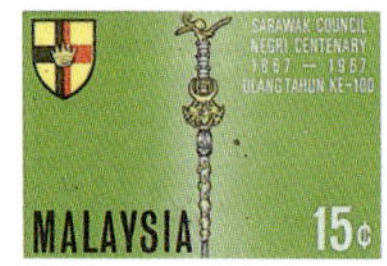

30 Mace and Shield

31 Straits Settlements 1867 8c. and Malaysia 1965 25c. Definitive

(Des Enche Ng Peng Nam. Photo Harrison)

1967 (8 Sept). Centenary of Sarawak Council. W w **13**. P 14½.

46	**30**	15c. multicoloured	10	10
47		50c. multicoloured	30	60

(Des Enche Ng Peng Nam. Photo Japanese Govt Ptg Works)

1967 (2 Dec). Stamp Centenary. T **31** and similar shaped designs. Multicoloured. P 11½.

48		25c. Type **31**	1·60	3·25
		a. Tête-Bêche (horiz pair)	3·00	6·50
49		30c. Straits Settlements 1867 24c. and Malaysia 1965 30c. definitive	1·60	2·75
		a. Tête-Bêche (horiz pair)	3·00	5·50
50		50c. Straits Settlements 1867 32c. and Malaysia 1965 50c. definitive	2·50	3·50
		a. tête-Bêche (horiz pair)	5·00	7·00
48/50 *Set of 3*			5·25	8·50

Nos. 48/50 were each printed in sheets with the stamps arranged horizontally tête-bêche.

34 Tapping Rubber, and Molecular Unit

37 Mexican Sombrero and Blanket with Olympic Rings

(Litho B.W.)

1968 (29 Aug). Natural Rubber Conference, Kuala Lumpur. T **34** and similar horiz designs. Multicoloured. W w **13**. P 12.

51		25c. Type **34**	30	10
52		30c. Tapping rubber, and export consignment	40	20
53		50c. Tapping rubber, and aircraft tyres	40	10
51/3 *Set of 3*			1·00	35

(Litho B.W.)

1968 (12 Oct). Olympic Games Mexico. T **37** and similar vert design. Multicoloured. W w **13**. P 12×11½.

54		30c. Type **37**	20	10
55		75c. Olympic rings and Mexican embroidery	55	20

39 Tunku Abdul Rahman against background of Pandanus Weave

40 Tunku Abdul Rahman against background of Pandanus Weave

(Photo Japanese Govt Ptg Wks)

1969 (8 Feb). Solidarity Week. T **39**/**40** and similar multicoloured design. P 13½.

56		15c. Type **39**	15	10
57		20c. Type **40**	45	1·25
58		50c. Tunku Abdul Rahman with pandanus pattern (horiz)	50	20
56/8 *Set of 3*			1·00	1·40

42 Peasant Girl with Sheaves of Rice

(Des Enche Hoessein Anas. Photo Harrison)

1969 (8 Dec). National Rice Year. W w **13**. P 13½.

59	**42**	15c. multicoloured	15	10
60		75c. multicoloured	55	1·50

43 Satellite tracking Aerial

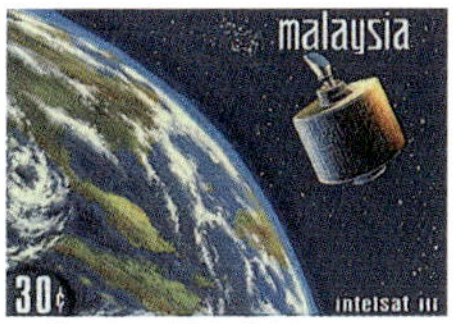

44 "Intelsat III" in Orbit

(Photo Enschedé)

1970 (6 Apr). Satellite Earth Station. W w **13**. P 14×13 (15c.) or 13½×13 (30c.)

61	**43**	15c. multicoloured	1·00	15
		a. Tête-Bêche (horiz pair)	2·00	2·50
62	**44**	30c. multicoloured*	1·00	2·50
63		30c. multicoloured*	1·00	2·50
61/3 *Set of 3*			2·75	4·75

No. 61 was issued horizontally tête-bêche in the sheets.

*Nos. 62/3 are of the same design, differing only in the lettering colours (No. 62 white; No. 63 gold).

45 *Euploea leucostictus*

46 Emblem

(Des V. Whiteley. Litho B.W. (to 1976) or Harrison)

1970 (31 Aug). Butterflies. T **45** and similar vert designs. Multicoloured. P 13×13½.

64	25c. Type **45**	1·00	10
65	30c. *Zeuxidia amethystus*	1·50	10
66	50c. *Polyura athamas*	2·00	10
67	75c. *Papilio memnon*	2·00	10
68	$1 *Appias nero* (16.11)	2·50	10
69	$2 *Trogonoptera brookiana* (16.11)	3·50	10
70	$5 *Narathura centaurus* (16.11)	5·00	3·75
71	$10 *Terinos terpander* (16.11)	17·00	5·00
64/71 *Set of 8*		30·00	8·50

See also Nos. 144/5.

(Litho Harrison)

1970 (7 Sept). 50th Anniv of International Labour Organization. P 14×13½.

72	**46**	30c. grey and new blue	10	20
73		75c. pink and new blue	20	30

47 U.N. Emblem encircled by Doves

50 The Yang di-Pertuan Agong (Tuanku Abdul Halim Shah)

(Des Enche Ng Peng Nam. Litho D.L.R.)

1970 (24 Oct). 25th Anniv of United Nations. T **47** and similar horiz designs. P 13×12½.

74	25c. gold, black and brown	35	40
75	30c. multicoloured	35	35
76	50c. black and dull yellow-green	40	75
74/6 *Set of 3*		1·00	1·40

Designs:—30c. Line of doves and U.N. emblem; 50c. Doves looping U.N. emblem.

(Des Union Art Corp. Photo Harrison)

1971 (20 Feb). Installation of Yang di-Pertuan Agong (Paramount Ruler of Malaysia). P 14½×14.

77	**50**	10c. black, gold and lemon	20	30
		a. Gold (value and inscr) omitted	£180	
78		15c. black, gold and bright mauve	20	30
79		50c. black, gold and new blue	70	1·60
77/9 *Set of 3*			1·00	2·00

51 Bank Negara Complex

(Photo Harrison)

1971 (15 May). Opening of Bank Negara Building. P 13½ (and around design).

80	**51**	25c. black and silver	2·50	2·75
81		50c. black and gold	1·75	1·25

52 Aerial view of Parliament Buildings

(Des Union Art Corp. Litho Harrison)

1971 (13 Sept). 17th Commonwealth Parliamentary Association Conference, Kuala Lumpur. T **52** and similar multicoloured design. P 13½ (25c.) or 12½×13 (75c.).

82	25c. Type **52**	1·25	50

83	75c. Ground view of Parliament Buildings (73×23½ mm)	2·75	1·75

53 Malaysian Carnival

54 Malaysian Carnival

55 Malaysian Carnival

(Des locally. Litho Harrison)

1971 (18 Sept). Visit A.S.E.AN.* Year. P 14½.

84	**53**	30c. multicoloured	1·60	55
		a. Horiz strip of 3. Nos. 84/6	4·25	5·50
85	**54**	30c. multicoloured	1·60	55
86	**55**	30c. multicoloured	1·60	55
84/6 *Set of 3*			4·25	5·50

*A.S.E.A.N.= Association of South East Asian Nations.

Nos. 84/6 were printed together, *se-tenant*, in horizontal strips of three throughout the sheet, forming a composite design.

56 Trees, Elephant and Tiger

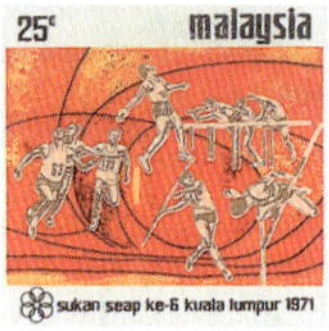

57 Athletics

(Des from children's drawings. Litho Harrison)

1971 (2 Oct). 25th Anniv of U.N.I.C.E.F. T **56** and similar multicoloured designs. P 12½.

87	15c. Type **56**	2·50	60
	a. Horiz strip of 5. Nos. 87/91	12·00	13·00
88	15c. Cat and kittens	2·50	60
89	15c. Sun, flower and bird (22×29 *mm*)	2·50	60
90	15c. Monkey, elephant and lion in jungle	2·50	60
91	15c. Spider and butterflies	2·50	60
87/91 *Set of 5*		12·00	13·00

Nos. 87/91 were issued in horizontal *se-tenant* strips of five throughout the sheet.

(Des Union Art Corp. Litho B.W.)

1971 (11 Dec). Sixth S.E.A.P.* Games, Kuala Lumpur. T **57** and similar horiz designs. Multicoloured. P 14½×14.

92	25c. Type **57**	45	40
93	30c. Sepak Raga players	60	50
94	50c. Hockey	1·75	95
92/4 *Set of 3*		2·50	1·75

*S.E.A.P. = South East Asian Peninsula.

58 Map and Tourist Attractions

59 Map and Tourist Attractions

60 Map and Tourist Attractions

(Des locally. Litho Harrison)

1972 (31 Jan). Pacific Area Tourist Association Conference. P 14×14½.

95	**58**	30c. multicoloured	3·00	1·50
		a. Horiz strip of 3. Nos. 95/7	8·00	9·00
96	**59**	30c. multicoloured	3·00	1·50
97	**60**	30c. multicoloured	3·00	1·50
95/7 *Set of 3*			8·00	9·00

Nos. 95/7 were printed together, *se-tenant*, in horizontal strips of three throughout the sheet forming a composite design.

61 Kuala Lumpur City Hall

(Des from colour transparencies. Litho Harrison)

1972 (1 Feb). City Status for Kuala Lumpur. T **61** and similar horiz design. Multicoloured. P 14½×14.

98	25c. Type **61**	1·25	1·25
99	50c. City Hall in floodlights	2·00	1·25

62 SOCSO Emblem

63 W.H.O. Emblem

(Des B.W. Litho Harrison)

1973 (2 July). Social Security Organisation. P 13½.

100	**62**	10c. multicoloured	15	15
101		15c. multicoloured	15	10
102		50c. multicoloured	40	1·40
100/2 *Set of 3*			65	1·50

(Des Union Advertising. Litho B.W.)

1973 (1 Aug). 25th Anniv of W.H.O. T **63** and similar vert design. P 13.

103	30c. multicoloured	50	25
104	75c. multicoloured	1·00	2·75

64 Fireworks, National Flag and Flower

65 Emblems of Interpol and Royal Malaysian Police

(Des Clover Associates. Litho Harrison)

1973 (31 Aug). Tenth Anniv of Malaysia. P 13½.

105	**64**	10c. multicoloured	40	25
106		15c. multicoloured	55	15
107		50c. multicoloured	1·90	1·60
105/7 *Set of 3*			2·50	1·75

(Des Union Advertising. Litho Harrison)

1973 (15 Sept). 50th Anniv of Interpol. T **65** and similar vert design. Multicoloured. P 13½.

108	25c. Type **65**	1·00	50
109	75c. Emblems within "50"	2·25	2·00

66 Boeing 737 and M.A.S. Emblem

(Des Art Dept, Malaysia Airline System. Litho Harrison)

1973 (1 Oct). Foundation of Malaysia Airline System. P 14½.

110	**66**	15c. multicoloured	35	10
111		30c. multicoloured	65	60
112		50c. multicoloured	95	1·60
110/12 *Set of 3*			1·75	2·10

67 Kuala Lumpur

(Des Malaysian Advertising Services. Litho B.W.)

1974 (1 Feb). Establishment of Kuala Lumpur as Federal Territory. P 12½×13.

113	**67**	25c. multicoloured	50	85
114		50c. multicoloured	1·00	1·75

68 Development Projects

69 Scout Badge and Map

(Des Malaysian Advertising Services. Litho Rosenbaum Bros, Vienna)

1974 (25 Apr). Seventh Annual Meeting of Asian Development Bank's Board of Governors, Kuala Lumpur. P 13½.

115	**68**	30c. multicoloured	25	50
116		75c. multicoloured	80	1·75

(Des Malaysian Advertising Services. Litho Harrison)

1974 (1 Aug). Malaysian Scout Jamboree. T **69** and similar multicoloured designs. P 13×13½ (15c.) or 14×13½ (others).

117	10c. Type **69**	60	1·00
118	15c. Scouts saluting and flags (46×24 mm)	95	30
119	50c. Scout badge	1·75	3·00
117/19 *Set of 3*		3·00	2·50

70 Coat of Arms and Power Installations

(Des Malaysian Advertising Services. Litho Harrison)

1974 (1 Sept). 25th Anniv of National Electricity Board. T **70** and similar multicoloured design. P 14 (30c.) or 14×14½ (75c.).

120	30c. Type **70**	30	50
121	75c. National Electricity Board Building (37×27 mm)	1·00	2·50

71 U.P.U. and Post Office Emblems within "100"

(Des Clover Associates. Litho Harrison)

1974 (9 Oct). Centenary of Universal Postal Union. P 14½×14.

122	**71**	25c. dull yell-grn, brt yell & lt rose-caret	20	35
123		30c. lt new blue, brt yell & lt rose-caret.	25	35
124		75c. brownish orange, bright yellow and light rose-carmine	65	1·75
122/4 *Set of 3*			1·00	2·25

72 Gravel Pump in Tin Mine

73 Hockey-players, World Cup and Federation Emblem

(Des Malaysian Advertising Service. Litho D.L.R.)

1974 (31 Oct). Fourth World Tin Conference, Kuala Lumpur. T **72** and similar horiz designs. Multicoloured. P 13½.

125	15c. Type **72**	1·75	20
126	20c. Open-cast mine	2·00	2·50
127	50c. Dredger within "ingot"	3·75	5·50
125/7 *Set of 3*		6·75	7·50

(Des Malaysian Advertising Services. Litho Harrison)

1975 (1 Mar). Third World Cup Hockey Championships. P 13½×13.

128	**73**	30c. multicoloured	90	60
129		75c. multicoloured	2·10	2·25

74 Congress Emblem

75 Emblem of M.K.P.W. (Malayan Women's Organisation)

(Des Malaysian Advertising Services. Litho Harrison)

1975 (1 May). 25th Anniv of Malaysian Trade Union Congress. P 14×14½.

130	**74**	20c. multicoloured	20	25
131		25c. multicoloured	25	30
132		30c. multicoloured	65	60
130/2 *Set of 3*			1·00	1·00

(Des Malaysian Advertising Services. Litho Harrison)

1975 (25 Aug). International Women's Year. P 14.

133	**75**	10c. multicoloured	15	25
134		15c. multicoloured	30	25
135		50c. multicoloured	1·25	2·25
133/5 *Set of 3*			1·50	2·50

76 Ubudiah Mosque, Kuala Kangsar

77 Plantation and Emblem

(Des Malaysian Advertising Services. Litho Harrison)

1975 (22 Sept). Koran Reading Competition. T **76** and similar horiz designs. Multicoloured. P 14.

136	15c. Type **76**	1·75	60
	a. Horiz strip of 5. Nos. 136/40	8·00	8·75
137	15c. Zahir Mosque, Alor Star	1·75	60
138	15c. National Mosque, Kuala Lumpur	1·75	60
139	15c. Sultan Abu Bakar Mosque, Johore Bahru	1·75	60
140	15c. Kuching State Mosque, Sarawak	1·75	60
136/40 *Set of 5*		8·00	8·75

The above were printed together, horizontally *se-tenant* throughout the sheet.

(Des E. Sulaiman bin Haji Hassan and E. Hoh Lian Yong. Litho Harrison)

1975 (22 Oct). 50th Anniv of Malaysian Rubber Research Institute. T **77** and similar horiz designs. Multicoloured. P 14×14½.

141	10c. Type **77**	40	15
142	30c. Latex cup and emblem	1·10	70
143	75c. Natural rubber in test-tubes	2·25	2·25
141/3 *Set of 3*		3·25	2·75

77a *Hebomoia glaucippe*

78 Scrub Typhus

(Photo Harrison)

1976 (19 Jan). Coil Stamps. T **77**a and similar horiz design. Multicoloured. P 13½.

144	10c. Type **77**a	2·75	7·00
145	15c. *Precis orithya*	2·75	7·00

(Des Lap Loy Fong (25c.), Lee Eng Kee (others). Litho Harrison)

1976 (6 Feb). 75th Anniv of the Institute of Medical Research. T **78** and similar vert designs. Multicoloured. P 14.

146	20c. Type **78**	40	15
147	25c. Malaria diagnosis	45	20
148	$1 Beri-beri	1·60	2·50
146/8	*Set of 3*	2·25	2·50

79 The Yang di-Pertuan Agong (Tuanku Yahya Petra)

80 State Council Complex

(Des Union Advertising. Photo Harrison)

1976 (28 Feb). Installation of Yang di-Pertuan Agong. P 14½×13½.

149	**79**	10c. black, bistre and yellow	25	10
150		15c. black, bistre and bright mauve	40	10
151		50c. black, bistre and ultramarine	2·25	2·50
149/51		*Set of 3*	2·75	2·50

(Des Aini bin Abdul Rahman. Litho Harrison)

1976 (17 Aug). Opening of the State Council Complex and Administrative Building, Sarawak. P 12½.

152	**80**	15c. grey-green and light yellow	35	10
153		20c. grey-green and light bright mauve	45	40
154		50c. grey-green and pale blue	1·00	1·40
152/4		*Set of 3*	1·60	1·75

81 E.P.F. Building

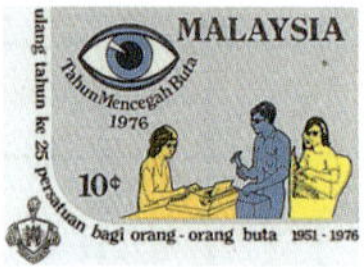

82 Blind People at Work

(Litho Harrison)

1976 (18 Oct). 25th Anniv of Employees' Provident Fund. T **81** and similar multicoloured designs. P 14½ (25c.) or 13½×14½ (others).

155	10c. Type **81**	15	10
156	25c. E.P.F. emblems (27×27 mm)	35	75
157	50c. E.P.F. Building at night	60	1·40
155/7	*Set of 3*	1·00	2·00

(Des Malayan Association for the Blind, Messrs Advertising Sales Promotion and Hexxon Grafic. Litho Harrison)

1976 (20 Nov). 25th Anniv of Malayan Association for the Blind. T **82** and similar horiz design. Multicoloured. P 13½×14½.

158	10c. Type **82**	15	15
159	75c. Blind man and shadow	1·25	2·75

83 Independence Celebrations, 1957

84 F.E.L.D.A. Village Scheme

(Des Hexxon Grafic. Photo Harrison)

1977 (14 Jan). First Death Anniversary of Tun Abdul Razak (Prime Minister). T **83** and similar horiz designs, each sepia and gold. P 14.

160	15c. Type **83**	1·50	60
	a. Horiz strip of 5. Nos. 160/4	6·50	7·25
161	15c. "Education"	1·50	60
162	15c. Tun Razak and map ("Development")	1·50	60
163	15c. "Rukunegara" (National Philosophy)	1·50	60
164	15c. A.S.E.A.N. meeting	1·50	60
160/4	*Set of 5*	6·50	7·25

The above were printed together, horizontally *se-tenant* throughout the sheet.

(Des Halim Teh and Basyuni Sumrah. Litho Harrison)

1977 (7 July). 21st Anniv of Federal Land Development Authority (F.E.L.D.A.). T **84** and similar horiz design. Multicoloured. P 13½×14.

165	15c. Type **84**	30	10
166	30c. Oil Palm settlement	80	2·00

85 Figure "10"

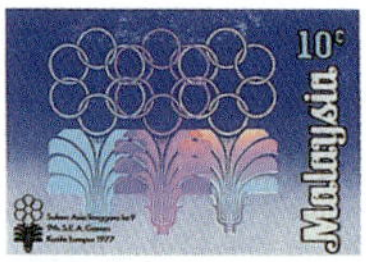

86 Games Logos

(Des Hexxon Grafic. Litho Harrison)

1977 (8 Aug). Tenth Anniv of A.S.E.A.N. (Association of South East Asian Nations). T **85** and similar horiz design. Multicoloured. P 13½×14½.

167	10c. Type **85**	10	10
168	75c. Flags of members	1·25	1·00

(Des PTM Communications & Co. Litho Harrison)

1977 (19 Nov). 9th South East Asia Games, Kuala Lumpur. T **86** and similar horiz designs. Multicoloured. P 13½×14½.

169	10c. Type **86**	15	15
170	20c. "Ball"	20	15
171	75c. Symbolic athletes	75	1·75
169/71	*Set of 3*	1·00	1·60

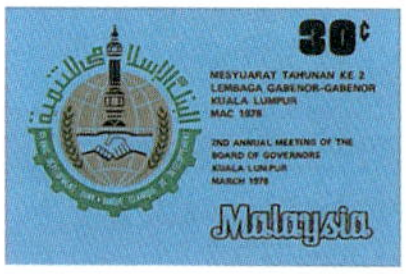

87 Islamic Development Bank Emblem

88 Mobile Post Office

(Des Queen's Advertising. Litho J.W.)

1978 (15 Mar). Islamic Development Bank Board of Governors Meeting, Kuala Lumpur. P 14.

172	**87**	30c. multicoloured	25	15
173		75c. multicoloured	75	85

(Des Hessen Grafic. Litho J.W.)

1978 (10 July). Fourth Commonwealth Postal Administrations Conference, Kuala Lumpur. T **88** and similar horiz designs. Multicoloured. P 13½×13.

174	10c. Type **88**	30	10
175	25c. G.P.O., Kuala Lumpur	75	2·00
176	50c. Postal delivery by motor-cycle	2·00	3·00
174/6	*Set of 3*	2·75	4·50

89 Boy Scout Emblem

90 Dome of the Rock, Jerusalem

(Des Aini bin Abdul Rahman. Litho J.W.)

1978 (26 July). Fourth Malaysian Boy Scout Jamboree, Sarawak, T **89** and similar horiz design. Multicoloured. P 13½×13.

177	15c. Type **89**	75	10
178	$1 Bees and honeycomb	2·75	3·25

(Des Union Advertising. Litho Harrison)

1978 (21 Aug). "Freedom for Palestine". P 12½.

179	**90**	15c. multicoloured	1·00	25
180		30c. multicoloured	1·75	2·50

91 Globe and Emblems

92 "Seratus Tabun Getah Ash" and Tapping Knives Symbol

(Litho Harrison)

1978 (30 Sept). Global Eradication of Smallpox. P 13½×14½.

181	**91**	15c. black, rosine and new blue	25	10
182		30c. black, rosine and yellowish green	40	30
183		50c. black, rosine and rose-pink	70	95
181/3 *Set of 3*			1·25	1·25

(Des Azmi bin Anuar. Litho J.W.)

1978 (28 Nov). Centenary of Rubber Industry. T **92** and similar horiz designs. P 13½×13.

184	10c. gold and blue-green	10	10
185	20c. ultramarine, brown & brt yellow-green	15	10
186	75c. gold and blue-green	65	1·00
184/6 *Set of 3*		80	1·00

Designs:—20c. Rubber tree seedling and part of "maxi stump"; 75c. Graphic design of rubber tree, latex cup and globe arranged to form "100".

93 Sultan of Selangor's New Palace

(Des Queen's Advertising. Litho Harrison)

1978 (7 Dec). Inauguration of Shah Alam New Town as State Capital of Selangor. T **93** and similar horiz designs. Multi coloured. P 13½×14½.

187	10c. Type **93**	15	10
188	30c. Shah Alam (aerial view)	30	15
189	75c. Shah Alam	65	2·00
187/9 *Set of 3*		1·00	2·00

94 Tiger

95 Multiple "POS" in Octagon

(Des Ong Soo Keat; adapted Malaysian Advertising Services. Litho Asher and Co, Melbourne)

1979 (4 Jan). Wildlife. Multicoloured designs as T **94**. W **95** (inverted on $10 or sideways* on others). P 14½.

190	30c. Type **94**	1·75	10
191	40c. Malayan Flying Lemur (*Cynocephalus variegatus*)	80	10
	w. Wmk top of letters to left	25·00	
192	50c. Lesser Malay Chevrotain (*Tragulus javanicus*)	1·75	10
193	75c. Leathery Pangolin (*Manis javanicus*)	1·00	10
194	$1 Malayan Turtle	1·50	10
195	$2 Malayan Tapir	1·50	10
196	$5 Gaur	4·50	2·00
197	$10 Orang-Utan (vert)	7·00	3·50
190/7 *Set of 8*		18·00	5·50

*The normal sideways watermark shows the top of the letters to right, as seen from the back of the stamp.

For these stamps without watermark, see Nos. 272/9.

96 View of Central Bank of Malaysia

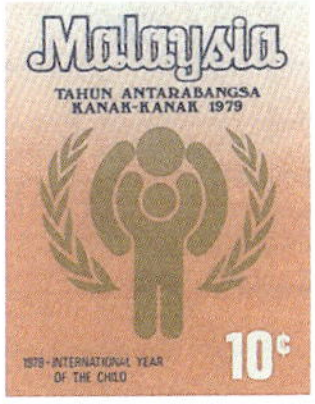

97 I.Y.C. Emblem

(Des Union Advertising. Litho J.W.)

1979 (26 Jan). 20th Anniv of Central Bank of Malaysia. T **96** and similar vert design showing view of bank building. P 13.

198	10c. multicoloured	10	10
199	75c. multicoloured	40	1·50

(Des Queen's Advertising. Litho Harrison)

1979 (24 Feb). International Year of the Child. T **97** and similar vert designs. P 14½×14.

200	10c. gold, blue and salmon	35	20
201	15c. mulicoloured	60	10
202	$1 multicoloured	3·00	4·00
200/2 *Set of 3*		3·50	4·00

Designs:—15c. Children of different races holding hands in front of globe; $1 Children taking part in various activities.

98 Dam and Power Station

99 Exhibition Emblem

(Des National Electricity Board. Litho Harrison)

1979 (19 Sept). Opening of Hydro-Electric Power Station, Temengor. T **98** and similar horiz designs showing views of power station and dam. P 13½×14½.

203	15c. multicoloured	20	15
204	25c. multicoloured	35	70
205	50c. multicoloured	55	1·40
203/5 *Set of 3*		1·00	2·00

(Des Malaysian Advertising Services. Litho J.W.)

1979 (20 Sept). World Telecommunications Exhibition, Geneva. T **99** and similar designs. P 14 (50c.) or 13 (others).

206	10c. orange, ultramarine and silver	15	50
207	15c. multicoloured	20	10
208	50c. multicoloured	75	2·50
206/8 *Set of 3*		1·00	2·75

Designs: (34×24 mm)—15c. Telephone receiver joining one half of World to the other. (39×28 mm)—50c. Communications equipment.

100 Tuanku Haji Ahmad Shah

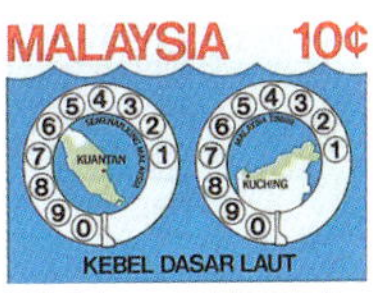

101 Pahang and Sarawak Maps within Telephone Dials

(Des Malaysian Advertising Services. Litho Harrison)

1980 (10 July). Installation af Yang di-Pertuan Agong (Tuanku Haji Ahmad Shah). P 14.

209	**100**	10c. black, gold and yellow	15	40
210		15c. black, gold and bright purple	20	10
211		50c. black, gold and new blue	75	2·00
209/11 *Set of 3*			1·00	2·25

(Des Malaysian Advertising Services. Litho J.W.)

1980 (31 Aug). Kuantan-Kuching Submarine Cable Project. T **101** and similar horiz designs. Multicoloured. P 13.

212	10c. Type **101**	15	40
213	15c. Kuantan and Kuching views within telephone dials	20	10
214	50c. Pahang and Sarawak Maps within telephone receiver	45	1·75
212/14 *Set of 3*		70	2·00

102 Bangi Campus

103 Mecca

(Des Malaysian Advertising Services. Litho J.W.)

1980 (2 Sept). Tenth Anniv of National University of Malaysia. T **102** and similar horiz designs. Multicoloured. P 13.

215	10c. Type **102**	15	20
216	15c. Jan Pantai Baru campus	20	10
217	75c. Great Hall	80	3·00
215/17	*Set of* 3	1·00	3·00

(Des Malaysian Advertising Services. Litho J.W.)

1980 (9 Nov). Moslem Year 1400 A.H. Commemoration. P 13.

218	**103**	15c. multicoloured	10	10
219		50c. multicoloured	30	1·50

The 50c. value is as T **103** but the inscriptions are in Roman lettering and the country name is to the left of the design.

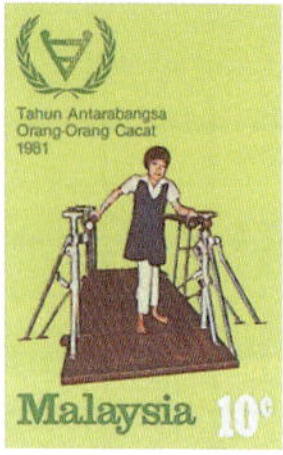

104 Disabled Child learning to Walk

105 Industrial Scene

(Des Malaysian Advertising Services. Litho J.W.)

1981 (14 Feb). International Year for Disabled Persons. T **104** and similar vert designs. Multicoloured. P 13½×13.

220	10c. Type **104**	30	30
221	15c. Disabled woman sewing	55	10
222	75c. Disabled athlete throwing javelin	1·50	3·50
220/2	*Set of* 3	2·10	3·50

(Des Malaysian Advertising Services. Litho J.W.)

1981 (2 May). Expo '81 Industrial Training Exposition, Kuala Lumpur and Seminar, Genting Highlands. T **105** and similar horiz designs. Multicoloured. P 13½×13.

223	10c. Type **105**	10	10
224	15c. Worker and bulldozer	15	10
225	30c. Workers at ship-building yard	25	35
226	75c. Agriculture and fishing produce, workers and machinery	65	2·25
223/6	*Set of* 4	1·00	2·50

106 "25"

(Des A. Yusof and Malaysian Advertising Services. Litho J.W.)

1981 (17 June). 25th Anniv of Malaysian National Committee for World Energy Conferences. T **106** and similar horiz designs. Multicoloured. P 13½×13.

227	10c. Type **106**	20	20
228	15c. Drawings showing importance of energy sources in industry	45	10
229	75c. Symbols of various energy sources	2·50	3·75
227/9	*Set of* 3	2·75	3·75

107 Drawing showing development of Sabah from Village to Urbanised Area

(Des Creative Concepts. Litho J.W.)

1981 (31 Aug). Centenary of Sabah. T **107** and similar horiz design. Multicoloured. P 12.

230	15c. Type **107**	50	15
231	80c. Drawing showing traditional and modern methods of agriculture	2·00	4·25

108 *Samanea saman*

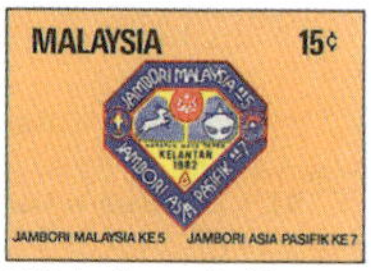

109 Jamboree Emblem

(Des Yusof bin Hadji Saman. Litho J.W.)

1981 (16 Dec). Trees. T **108** and similar multicoloured designs. P 14.

232	15c. Type **108**	55	10
233	50c. *Dyera costulata* (vert)	1·75	1·40
234	80c. *Dryobalanops aromatics* (vert)	2·00	4·25
232/4	*Set of* 3	3·75	5·25

(Des P. Lim (15c.), Datuk Syed Hashim bin Abdullah (others). Litho J.W.)

1982 (10 Apr). Fifth Malaysian/7th Asia-Pacific Boy Scout Jamboree. T **109** and similar horiz designs. Multicoloured. P 13½×13.

235	15c. Type **109**	35	10
236	50c. Malaysian flag and scout emblem	80	85
237	80c. Malaysian and Asia-Pacific scout emblems	1·25	4·25
235/7	*Set of* 3	2·25	4·75

110 A.S.E.A.N. Building and Emblem

111 Dome of the Rock, Jerusalem

(Litho JW.)

1982 (8 Aug). 15th Anniv Ministerial Meeting of A.S.E.A.N. (Association of South East Asian Nations). T **110** and similar horiz design. Multicoloured. P 14.

238	15c. Type **110**	15	10
239	$1 Flags of member nations	2·00	3·75

(Litho J.W.)

1982 (21 Aug). "Freedom for Palestine". P 13½.

240	**111**	15c. gold, blue-green and black	1·50	25
241		$1 silver, pale turquoise-green & blk	4·50	5·25

112 Views of Kuala Lumpur in 1957 and 1982

(Des Ministry of Information. Litho Rosenbaum Bros, Vienna)

1982 (31 Aug). 25th Anniv of Independence. T **112** and similar horiz designs. Multicoloured. P 14×13½.

242	10c. Type **112**	10	10
243	15c. Malaysian industries	15	15
244	50c. Soldiers on parade	40	55
245	80c. Independence ceremony	70	3·00
242/5	*Set of* 4	1·25	3·50
MS246	120×190 mm. Nos. 242/5 (with silver frame around centre vignette of 10c.)	15·00	11·00
	a. Without silver frame around centre vignette of 10c.	12·00	12·00

No. **MS**246a is from the second printing. It is without the narrow silver frame around the centre part of the 10c. design which is shown on Nos. 242 and **MS**246.

113 Shadow Play

(Des N. Ajib. Litho J.W.)

1982 (30 Oct). Traditional Games. T **113** and similar horiz designs. Multicoloured. P 13.

247	10c. Type **113**	55	30
248	15c. Cross Top	55	15
249	75c. Kite flying	2·25	4·75
247/9 *Set of 3*		3·00	4·75

114 Sabah Hats

(Litho Harrison)

1982 (26 Nov). Malaysian Handicrafts. T **114** and similar horiz designs. Multicoloured. P 13×13½.

250	10c. Type **114**	25	30
251	15c. Gold-threaded cloth	25	20
252	75c. Sarawak pottery	1·25	3·75
250/2 *Set of 3*		1·60	3·75

115 Gas Exploitation Logo

116 Flag of Malaysia

(Litho Security Printers (M), Malaysia)

1983 (22 Jan). Export of Liquefied Natural Gas from Bintulu Field, Sarawak. T **115** and similar horiz designs. Multicoloured. P 12.

253	15c. Type **115**	75	15
	a. Perf 13½	22·00	
254	20c. *Tenaga Satu* (liquid gas tanker)	1·50	70
	a. Perf 13½	35·00	
255	$1 Gas drilling equipment	3·50	6·50
	a. Perf 13½	50·00	
253/5 *Set of 3*		5·25	6·50

Other versions of these designs, some with different face value, were prepared, but not issued.

(Litho J.W.)

1983 (14 Mar). Commonwealth Day. T **116** and similar horiz designs. Multicoloured. P 13½×14.

256	15c. Type **116**	20	10
257	20c. The King of Malaysia	20	20
258	40c. Oil palm tree and refinery	25	45
259	$1 Satellite view of Earth	60	2·75
256/9 *Set of 4*		1·10	3·25

117 Nile Mouthbrooder

(Des and litho Security Printers (M), Malaysia)

1983 (15 June). Freshwater Fish (1st series). T **117** and similar horiz designs. Multicoloured. P 12.

260	20c. Type **117**	1·25	2·00
	a. Horiz pair. Nos. 260/1	2·50	4·00
	b. Perf 13½×14	10·00	5·00
	ba. Horiz pair. Nos. 260b/1b	20·00	10·00
261	20c. Common Carp	1·25	2·00
	b. Perf 13½×14	10·00	5·00
262	40c. Lampan Barb ("*Puntius gonionotus*")	1·75	2·75
	a. Horiz pair. Nos. 262/3	3·50	5·50
	b. Perf 13½×14	2·50	3·25
	ba. Horiz pair. Nos. 262b/3b	5·00	6·50
263	40c. Grass Carp ("*Ctenopharyngodon idellus*")	1·75	2·75
	b. Perf 13½×14	2·50	3·25
260/3 *Set of 4*		5·50	8·50

Nos. 260/1 and 262/3 were each printed together, *se-tenant*, in horizontal pairs throughout the sheet.

118 Lower Pergau River Bridge

(Des Malaysian Public Works Dept. Litho Security Printers (M), Malaysia)

1983 (11 July). Opening of East-West Highway. T **118** and similar horiz designs. Multicoloured. P 13½.

264	15c. Type **118**	80	15
265	20c. Perak river reservoir bridge	1·00	75
266	$1 Map showing East-West highway	3·75	6·50
264/6 *Set of 3*		5·00	6·75

119 Northrop F-5E Tiger II Fighter

120 Helmeted Hornbill

(Des and litho J.W.)

1983 (16 Sept). 50th Anniv of Malaysian Armed Forces. T **119** and similar horiz designs. Multicoloured. P 13.

267	15c. Type **119**	1·25	15
268	20c. Missile boat	1·75	45
269	40c. Battle of Pasir Panjang	2·25	2·50
270	80c. Trooping the Colour	3·25	6·00
267/70 *Set of 4*		7·75	7·75
MS271 130×85 mm. Nos. 267/70. P 13½		13·00	14·00

1983 (3 Oct)–**85**. As Nos. 190/7 but without wmk.

272	30c. Type **94** (1984)	4·50	1·25
273	40c. Malayan Flying Lemur (6.10.83)	3·75	75
274	50c. Lesser Malay Chevrotain (10.4.84)	5·00	75
275	75c. Leathery Pangolin (19.10.85)	4·75	7·50
276	$1 Malayan Turtle (5.10.83)	5·50	80
277	$2 Malayan Tapir	4·00	70
278	$5 Gaur (1985)	19·00	9·00
279	$10 Orang-Utan (vert) (3.84)	14·00	11·00
272/9 *Set of 8*		55·00	29·00

*There was no official release date for these stamps. Dates shown are the earliest recorded from postmarks and may be revised should earlier examples be reported.

(Des P. Ket. Litho Security Printers (M), Malaysia)

1983 (26 Oct). Hornbills of Malaysia. T **120** and similar vert designs. Multicoloured. P 13½.

280	15c. Type **120**	1·00	15
281	20c. Wrinkled Hornbill	1·25	50
282	50c. Long-crested Hornbill	2·00	2·00
283	$1 Rhinoceros Hornbill	3·25	5·50
280/3 *Set of 4*		6·75	7·50

121 Bank Building, Ipoh

122 Sky-scraper and Mosque, Kuala Lumpur

(Des P. Hoong. Litho Security Printers (M), Malaysia)

1984 (26 Jan). 25th Anniv of Bank Negara. T **121** and similar horiz design. Multicoloured. P 13½×14.

284	20c. Type **121**	40	30
285	$1 Bank building, Alor Setar	2·00	3·75

(Des Mara Institute of Technology. Litho Security Printers (M), Malaysia)

1984 (1 Feb). Tenth Anniv of Federal Territory of Kuala Lumpur. T **122** and similar multicoloured designs. P 13½×14 (80c.) or 14×13½ (others).

286	20c. Type **122**	80	20
287	40c. Aerial view	1·60	1·40
288	80c. Gardens and clock-tower (horiz)	2·50	6·50
286/8 *Set of 3*		4·50	7·25

123 Map showing Industries

124 Semenanjung Keris

(Litho Security Printers (M), Malaysia)

1984 (16 Apr). Formation of Labuan Federal Territory. T **123** and similar vert design. Multicoloured. P 13½×14.

289	20c. Type **123**	75	25
290	$1 Flag and map of Labuan	4·25	6·00

(Des P. Ket. Litho Harrison)

1984 (30 May). Traditional Malay Weapons. T **124** and similar vert designs. Multicoloured. P 13½×14.

291	40c. Type **124**	1·25	2·10
	a. Block of 4. Nos. 291/4	4·50	7·75
292	40c. Pekakak keris	1·25	2·10
293	40c. Jawa keris	1·25	2·10
294	40c. Lada tumbuk	1·25	2·10
291/4 *Set of 4*		4·50	7·75

Nos. 291/4 were printed in *se-tenant* blocks of four throughout the sheet.

125 Map of World and Transmitter

126 Facsimile Service

(Des Dept of Broadcasting. Litho Harrison)

1984 (23 June). 20th Anniv of Asia-Pacific Broadcasting Union. T **125** and similar horiz design. Multicoloured. P 13½×14½.

295	20c. Type **125**	40	25
296	$1 Clasped hands within "20"	2·00	5·00

(Des Mark Johan and Associates. Litho Security Printers (M), Malaysia)

1984 (29 Oct). Opening of New General Post Office, Kuala Lumpur. T **126** and similar horiz designs. Multicoloured. P 12.

297	15c. Type **126**	35	20
298	20c. New G.P.O. building	45	45
299	$1 Mailbag conveyor	2·00	4·75
297/9 *Set of 3*		2·50	4·75

127 Yang di Pertuan Agong (Tuanku Mahmood)

128 White Hibiscus

(Des P. Ket. Litho Security Printers (M), Malaysia)

1984 (15 Nov). Installation of Yang di Pertuan Agong (Tuanku Mahmood). T **127** and similar design. P 12.

300	**127**	15c. multicoloured	60	20
301		20c. multicoloured	65	20
302	–	40c. multicoloured	1·25	1·00
303	–	80c. multicoloured	2·50	5·00
300/3 *Set of 4*			4·25	5·75

Design: Horiz—40c., 80c. Yang di Pertuan Agong and Federal Crest.

(Litho Security Printers (M), Malaysia)

1984 (12 Dec). Hibiscus. T **128** and similar vert designs. Multicoloured. P 13½.

304	10c. Type **128**	50	30
305	20c. Red Hibiscus	1·00	20
306	40c. Pink Hibiscus	1·75	2·00
307	$1 Orange Hibiscus	2·75	5·75
304/7 *Set of 4*		5·50	7·50

129 Parliament Building

130 Banded Linsang

(Des P. Ket. Litho Security Printers (M), Malaysia)

1985 (30 Mar). 25th Anniv of Federal Parliament. T **129** and similar multicoloured design. P 13½×14 (20c.) or 14×13½ ($1).

308	20c. Type **129**	30	15
309	$1 Parliament Building (*different*) (horiz)	1·75	3·50

(Des P. Ket. Litho J.W.)

1985 (25 Apr). Protected Animals of Malaysia (1st series). T **130** and similar multicoloured designs. P 14.

310	10c. Type **130**	60	10
311	40c. Slow Loris (vert)	2·00	1·40
312	$1 Spotted Giant Flying Squirrel (vert)	4·00	6·50
310/12 *Set of 3*		6·00	7·50

See also Nos. 383/6.

131 Stylised Figures

132 Steam Locomotive No. 1, 1885

(Des Amir bin Osman. Litho Security Printers (M), Malaysia)

1985 (15 May). International Youth Year. T **131** and similar horiz design. Multicoloured. P 13.

313	20c. Type **131**	40	15
314	$1 Young workers	3·50	5·50

(Des AMW Communications Management. Litho Security Printers (M), Malaysia).

1985 (1 June). Centenary of Malayan Railways. T **132** and similar horiz designs. P 13.

315	15c. black, carmine-verm & pale orange	1·60	50
316	20c. multicoloured	1·75	60
317	$1 multicoloured	4·25	7·00
315/17 *Set of 3*		6·75	7·25
MS318	119×59 mm. 80c. multicoloured. P 13½×13	8·00	9·00

Designs: Horiz (as T **132**)—20c. Class 20 diesel-electric locomotive, 1957; $1 Hitachi Class 23 diesel-electric locomotive, 1983. (48×31 *mm*)—80c. Class 56 steam locomotive No. 564.18, *Seletar*, 1938.

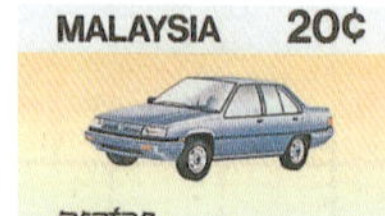

133 Blue Proton "Saga 1.3s"

134 Penang Bridge

(Des and litho J.W.)

1985 (9 July). Production of Proton "Saga" (Malaysian national car). T **133** and similar horiz designs. Multicoloured. P 14.

319	20c. Type **133**	80	15
320	40c. White Proton "Saga 1.3s"	1·40	1·00
321	$1 Red Proton "Saga 1.5s"	2·50	6·50
319/21 *Set of 3*		4·25	7·00

(Des Kathy's Design. Litho Security Printers (M), Malaysia)

1985 (14 Sept). Opening of Penang Bridge. T **134** and similar horiz designs. Multicoloured. P 12 ($1) or 13 (others).

322	20c. Type **134**	90	15
323	40c. Penang Bridge and location map	1·75	90
324	$1 Symbolic bridge linking Penang to mainland (40×24 mm)	3·50	6·00
322/4 *Set of 3*		5·50	6·50

135 Offshore Oil Rig

136 Sultan Azlan Shah and Perak Royal Crest

(Des Andamaz Enterprise. Litho Security Printers (M), Malaysia)

1985 (4 Nov). Malaysian Petroleum Production. T **135** and similar multicoloured designs. P 12.

325	15c. Type **135**	1·25	20
326	20c. Malaysia's first oil refinery (horiz)	1·40	50
327	$1 Map of Malaysian offshore oil and gas fields (horiz)	3·75	6·00
325/7 *Set of 3*		5·75	6·25

(Des Kathy's Design. Litho J.W.)

1985 (9 Dec). Installation of the Sultan of Perak. P 14.

328 **136**	15c. multicoloured	65	10
329	20c. multicoloured	75	25
330	$1 multicoloured	3·75	7·00
328/30 *Set of 3*		4·75	7·00

137 Crested Fireback Pheasant

139 Two Kadazan Dancers, Sabah

138

(Des P. Ket. Litho Security Printers (M), Malaysia)

1986 (11 Mar). Protected Birds of Malaysia. (1st series). T **137** and similar multicoloured designs. Phosphorised paper. W **138** (sideways on 40c.). P 13½.

331	20c. Type **137**	2·50	3·25
	a. Horiz pair. Nos. 33½	5·00	6·50
332	20c. Malaya Peacock-Pheasant	2·50	3·25
333	40c. Bulwer's Pheasant (horiz)	3·50	4·25
	a. Horiz pair. Nos. 333/4	7·00	8·50
	b. Perf 12	2·00	3·50
	ba. Horiz pair. Nos. 333b/4b	4·00	7·00
334	40c. Great Argus Pheasant (horiz)	3·50	4·25
	b. Perf 12	2·00	3·50
331/4 *Set of 4*		11·00	13·50

Nos. 331/2 and 333/4 were each printed together, *se-tenant*, in horizontal pairs throughout the sheets.

See also Nos. 394/7.

(Des AMC Advertising Agencies. Litho Questa)

1986 (14 Apr). Pacific Area Travel Association Conference, Malaysia. T **139** and similar vert designs. Multicoloured. P 15×14.

335	20c. Type **139**	85	1·25
	a. Horiz strip of 3. Nos. 335/7	2·25	3·50
336	20c. Dyak dancer and longhouse, Sarawak	85	1·25
337	20c. Dancers and fortress, Malacca	85	1·25
338	40c. Malay dancer and Kuala Lumpur	1·25	1·50
	a. Horiz strip of 3. Nos. 338/40	3·25	4·00
339	40c. Chinese opera dancer and Penang Bridge	1·25	1·50
340	40c. Indian dancer and Bain Caves	1·25	1·50
335/40 *Set of 6*		5·50	7·50

Nos. 335/7 and 338/40 were each printed together, *se-tenant*, in horizontal strips of three throughout the sheets.

140 Stylized Competitors

141 Rambutan

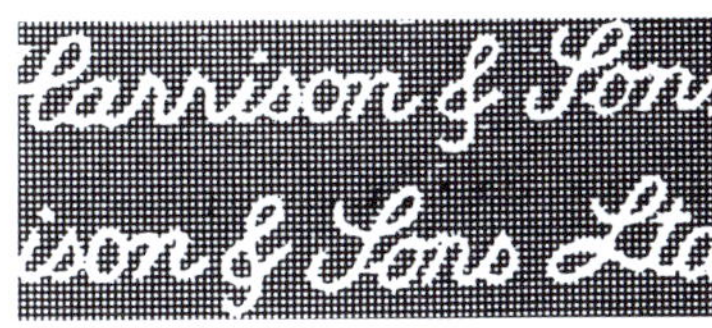

141a

(Des Design Excelsior. Litho Security Printers (M), Malaysia)

1986 (19 Apr). Malaysia Games. T **140** and similar multicoloured designs. Phosphorised paper. W **138** (sideways on 20c.). P 12.

341	20c. Type **140**	1·25	20
342	40c. Games emblems (vert)	2·25	2·00
343	$1 National and state flags (vert)	9·00	7·75
341/3 *Set of 3*		11·50	9·00

(Des P. Ket)

1986 (5 June)–**2000**. Fruits of Malaysia. T **141** and similar vert designs. Multicoloured. W **138**. P 12 (40c. to $1) or 13½×14 ($2, $5, $10).

(a) Litho Security Printers (M) Malaysia. Phosphorised paper.

344	40c. Type **141**	1·00	10
	aw. wmk inverted	11·00	
	b. Perf 13½x14 (1994)	1·75	10
	bw. wmk inverted	9·00	
345	50c. Pineapple	1·00	10
	aw. wmk inverted		
	b. Perf 13½×14 (1994)	1·75	10
	bw. wmk inverted	9·00	
346	80c. Durian	1·25	10
	aw. wmk inverted	6·50	
	b. Perf 13½×14 (1994)	2·00	10
347	$1 Mangosteen	1·50	10
	aw. wmk inverted	7·50	
	b. Perf 13½×14 (1994)	2·00	20
	bw. Wmk inverted		
347*c*	$2 Star Fruit (1999)	2·00	80
	cw. Wmk sideways		
347*d*	$5 Banana (9.2000)	4·50	1·90
	dw. Wmk inverted	15·00	
347*e*	$10 Mango (2002)	10·00	6·00
	ew. Wmk inverted	19·00	
344/7e *Set of 7*		19·00	8·50

(b) Photo Harrison. W **141**a. P 13½

348	$2 Star Fruit	2·00	10
	a. Black (inscrs and face value) omitted	£1500	
349	$5 Banana	4·50	50
350	$10 Mango	7·00	1·25
351	$20 Papaya	12·00	3·25
348/51 *Set of 4*		23·00	4·50

No. 348a occurs on row 9 of a sheet. Stamps in row 8 show the bottom inscription omitted and those from row 10 lack the top inscription and face value.

For stamps from this series denominated in 'sen' and 'RM' see Nos. 1095a/h.

$1 stamps in a wider format (26.5 mm against 25 mm) in deeper colours with a larger vignette and smaller inscriptions, perf 13½, are unapproved essays.

PHOSPHORISED PAPER. From No. 352 onwards all stamps were on phosphorised paper, unless otherwise stated.

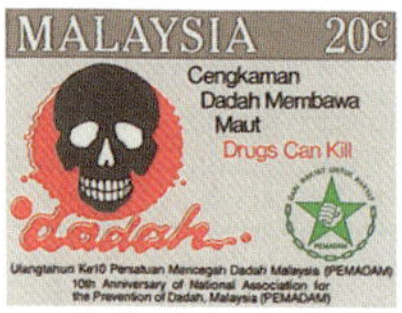

142 Skull and Slogan "Drugs Can Kill"

143 MAS Logo and Map showing Routes

(Des Kathy's Design. Litho Security Printers (M), Malaysia)

1986 (26 June). Tenth Anniv of National Association for Prevention of Drug Addiction. T **142** and similar multicoloured designs. W **138** (sideways on 20c., $1). P 13.

352	20c. Type **142**	1·50	30
353	40c. Bird and slogan "Stay Free From Drugs"	2·50	1·10
354	$1 Addict and slogan "Drugs Can Destroy" (vert)	3·75	5·00
352/4 *Set of 3*		7·00	5·75

(Des PTM Thompson Advertising. Litho Security Printers (M), Malaysia)

1986 (31 July). Inaugural Flight of Malaysian Airlines Kuala Lumpur–Los Angeles Service. T **143** and similar horiz designs. Multicoloured. W **138** (sideways). P 14×13½.

355	20c. Type **143**	2·50	20
356	40c. Logo, stylized aircraft and route diagram	3·50	80
357	$1 Logo and stylized aircraft	5·00	4·50
355/7 *Set of 3*		10·00	5·00

144 Building Construction

145 Old Seri Menanti Palace, Negri Sembilan

(Des M. Chin. Litho Security Printers (M), Malaysia)

1986 (3 Nov). 20th Anniv of National Productivity Council and 25th Anniv of Asian Productivity Organization (40c., $1). T **144** and similar multicoloured designs. W **138** (sideways on 40c., $1). P 13½×14 (20c.) or 14×13½ (others).

358	20c. Type **144**	85	25
359	40c. Planning and design (horiz)	1·40	1·25
360	$1 Computer-controlled car assembly line (horiz)	3·75	6·50
358/60 *Set of 3*		5·50	7·25

(Des P. Ket. Litho Security Printers (M), Malaysia)

1986 (20 Dec). Historic Buildings of Malaysia (1st series). T **145** and similar horiz designs. Multicoloured. W **138** (sideways). P 13.

361	15c. Type **145**	1·00	20
362	20c. Old Kenangan Palace, Perak	1·10	20
363	40c. Old Town Hall, Malacca	2·00	80
364	$1 Astana, Kuching, Sarawak	3·50	5·00
361/4 *Set of 4*		6·75	5·50

See also Nos. 465/8.

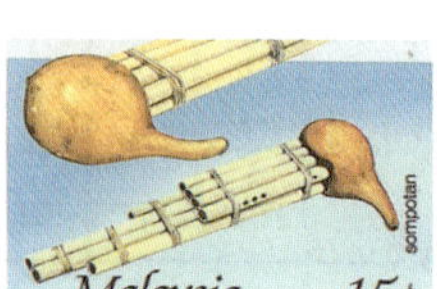

146 Sompotan (bamboo pipes)

(Des Kathy Wong. Litho Security Printers (M), Malaysia)

1987 (7 Mar). Malaysian Musical Instruments. T **146** and similar multicoloured designs. W **138** (sideways on 50, 80c.). P 12.

365	15c. Type **146**	1·40	10
366	20c. Sapih (four-stringed chordophone)	1·50	20
367	50c. Serunai (pipes) (vert)	2·50	60
368	80c. Rebab (three-stringed fiddle) (vert)	3·50	2·50
365/8 *Set of 4*		8·00	3·00

147 Modern Housing Estate

(Litho Security Printers (M), Malaysia)

1987 (6 Apr). International Year of Shelter for the Homeless. T **147** and similar horiz design. Multicoloured. W **138**. P 12.

369	20c. Type **147**	1·25	15
370	$1 Stylised families and houses	3·50	1·75

MACHINE LABELS. From 25 May 1987 gummed labels printed in red on yellow paper with an overall design of the postal logo were issued from a machine in Kuala Lumpur. Available face values ranged from 5c. to $15.

148 Drug Addict and Family

(Des Kathy's Design. Litho Security Printers (M), Malaysia)

1987 (8 June). International Conference on Drug Abuse, Vienna. T **148** and similar horiz designs. Multicoloured. W **138** (sideways). P 13.

371	20c. Type **148**	2·00	1·50
	a. Vert pair. Nos. 37½	4·00	3·00
372	20c. Hands holding drugs and damaged internal organs	2·00	1·50
373	40c. Healthy boy and broken drug capsule	2·75	1·75
	a. Vert pair. Nos. 373/4	5·50	3·50
374	40c. Drugs and healthy internal organs	2·75	1·75
371/4 *Set of 4*		8·50	6·00

Nos. 371/2 and 373/4 were printed together, *se-tenant*, in vertical pairs throughout the sheet, each pair forming a composite design.

149 Spillway and Power Station

(Des Kathy's Design. Litho Security Printers (M), Malaysia)

1987 (13 July). Opening of Sultan Mahmud Hydro-electric Scheme, Kenyir Trengganu. T **149** and similar horiz design. Multicoloured. W **138**. P 12.

375	20c. Type **149**	75	10
376	$1 Dam, spillway and reservoir	2·75	2·00

150 Crossed Maces and Parliament Building, Kuala Lumpur

151 Dish Aerial, Satellite and Globe

(Des R. Zahabuddin. Litho Security Printers (M), Malaysia)

1987 (1 Sept). 33rd Commonwealth Parliamentary Conference. T **150** and similar horiz design. Multicoloured. W **138**. P 12.

377	20c. Type **150**	25	10
378	$1 Parliament building and crossed maces emblem	1·25	1·25

(Des Mark Design. Litho Security Printers (M), Malaysia)

1987 (26 Oct). Asia/Pacific Transport and Communications Decade. T **151** and similar horiz designs. Multicoloured. W **138** (sideways). P 13.

379	15c. Type **151**	65	10
380	20c. Diesel train and car	2·00	75
381	40c. Container ships and lorry	2·50	1·60
382	$1 Malaysian Airlines Boeing 747, Kuala Lumpur Airport	4·75	7·00
379/82	*Set of* 4	9·00	8·50

152 Temminck's Golden Cat

153 Flags of Member Nations and "20"

(Des Ong Soo Kest. Litho Security Printers (M), Malaysia)

1987 (14 Nov). Protected Animals of Malaysia (2nd series). T **152** and similar horiz designs. Multicoloured. W **138** (sideways on 15, 20, 40c.). P 13.

383	15c. Type **152**	2·75	50
384	20c. Flatheaded Cat	2·75	50
385	40c. Marbled Cat	4·00	1·75
386	$1 Clouded Leopard	7·50	7·50
383/6	*Set of* 4	15·00	9·25

(Des P. Ket. Litho Security Printers (M), Malaysia)

1987 (14 Dec). 20th Anniv of Association of South East Asian Nations. T **153** and similar horiz design. Multicoloured. W **138**. P 13.

387	20c. Type **153**	35	10
388	$1 Flags of member nations and globe	1·25	1·50

154 Mosque and Portico

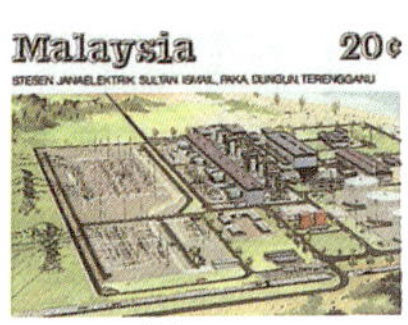

155 Aerial View

(Des R. Zahabuddin. Litho Security Printers (M), Malaysia)

1988 (11 Mar). Opening of Sultan Salahuddin Abdul Aziz Shah Mosque. T **154** and similar multicoloured designs. W **138** (sideways on 15, 20c.). P 12.

389	15c. Type **154**	30	10
390	20c. Dome, minarets and Sultan of Selangor	30	20
391	$1 Interior and dome (vert)	1·50	3·00
389/91	*Set of* 3	1·90	3·00

(Des Azmi bin Kassim. Litho Security Printers (M), Malaysia)

1988 (4 Apr). Sultan Ismail Hydro-electric Power Station, Paka, Trengganu. T **155** and similar horiz design. Multicoloured. W **138** (sideways). P 13.

392	20c. Type **155**	30	10
393	$1 Power station and pylons	1·40	1·50

156 Black-naped Blue Monarch

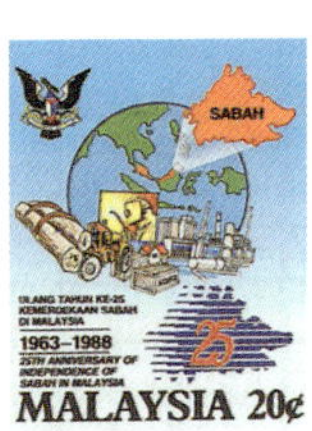

157 Outline Map and Products of Sabah

(Des Ong Soo Kest. Litho Security Printers (M), Malaysia)

1988 (30 June). Protected Birds of Malaysia (2nd series). T **156** and similar vert designs. Multicoloured. W **138**. P 13.

394	20c. Type **156**	1·75	2·25
	a. Horiz pair. Nos. 394/5	3·50	4·25
	w. Inverted wmk	11·00	
	wa. Horiz pair. Nos. 394w/5w	22·00	
395	20c. Scarlet-backed Flowerpecker	1·75	2·25
	w. Inverted wmk	11·00	
396	50c. Yellow-backed Sunbird	2·50	3·00
	a. Horiz pair. Nos. 396/7	5·00	5·75
	w. Inverted wmk	5·00	
	wa. Horiz pair. Nos. 396w/7w	10·00	
397	50c. Black and Red Broadbill	2·50	3·00
	w. Inverted wmk	5·00	
394/7	*Set of* 4	7·50	8·00

The two designs of each value were printed together, *se-tenant*, in horizontal pairs throughout the sheets.

(Des P. Ket. Litho Security Printers (M), Malaysia)

1988 (31 Aug). 25th Anniv of Sabah and Sarawak as States of Malaysia. T **157** and similar vert designs. Multicoloured. W **138**. P 13.

398	20c. Type **157**	65	80
	a. Horiz pair. Nos. 398/9	1·25	1·60
399	20c. Outline map and products of Sarawak	65	80
400	$1 Flags of Malaysia, Sabah and Sarawak (30×40 mm)	2·00	3·50
398/400	*Set of* 3	3·00	4·50

Nos. 398/9 were printed together, *se-tenant*, in horizontal pairs throughout the sheet.

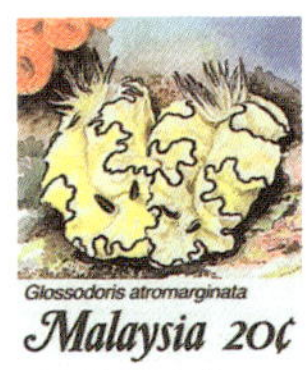

158 *Glossodoris atromarginata*

159 Sultan's Palace, Malacca

(Litho Security Printers (M), Malaysia)

1988 (17 Dec). Marine Life (1st series). T **158** and similar vert designs. Multicoloured. W 138. P 12.

401	20c. Type **158**	85	1·10
	a. Horiz strip of 5. Nos. 401/5	3·75	5·00
402	20c. Ocellate Nudibranch (*Phyllidia ocellata*)	85	1·10
403	20c. *Chromodoris annae*	85	1·10
404	20c. *Flabellina macassarana*	85	1·10
405	20c. Ruppell's Nudibranch (*Reyfria ruppeli*)	85	1·10
401/5	*Set of* 5	3·75	5·00
MS406	100×75 mm. $1 Blue-ringed Angelfish (50×40 mm). P 14	3·00	1·75

Nos. 401/5 were printed together, *se-tenant*, in horizontal strips of five throughout the sheet, forming a composite background design.

See also Nos. 410/13, 450/3, 492/7 and 559/62.

(Des P. Ket. Litho Security Printers (M), Malaysia)

1989 (15 Apr). Declaration of Malacca as Historic City. T **159** and similar multicoloured designs. W **138** (sideways on 20c.). P 13.

407	20c. Type **159**	35	30
408	20c. Independence Memorial Building	35	30
409	$1 Ports De Santiago Fortress (vert)	1·40	2·00
407/9	*Set of* 3	1·90	2·25

160 *Tetralia nigrolineata*

161 Map of Malaysia and Scout Badge

(Des P. Ket. Litho Security Printers (M), Malaysia)

1989 (29 June). Marine Life (2nd series). Crustaceans. T **160** and similar horiz designs. Multicoloured. W **138** (sideways). P 12.

410	20c. Type **160**	45	90
	a. Horiz pair. Nos. 410/11	90	1·75
	b. wmk upright		

ba. Horiz pair. Nos. 410b/11b
411 20c. *Neopetrolisthes maculatus* (crab) 45 90
b. wmk upright
412 40c. *Periclimenes holthuisi* (shrimp) 55 1·10
a. Horiz pair. Nos. 412/13 1·10 2·00
b. wmk upright
ba. Horiz pair. Nos. 412b/13b
413 40c. *Synalpheus neomeris* (shrimp) 55 1·10
b. wmk upright
410/13 *Set of 4* 1·75 3·75

Nos, 410/11 and 412/13 were each printed together, *se-tenant*, in horizontal pairs throughout the sheets.

(Des T. Teh Ching Seng. Litho Security Printers (M), Malaysia)

1989 (26 July). Seventh National Scout Jamboree. T **161** and similar multicoloured designs. W **138** (sideways on 10, 20c.). P 13.

414 10c. Type **161** 30 10
415 20c. Saluting national flag 60 25
416 80c. Scouts around camp fire (horiz) 1·40 3·00
w. wmk inverted 4·00
414/16 *Set of 3* 2·10 3·00

162 Cycling

163 Sultan Azlan Shah

(Litho Security Printers (M), Malaysia)

1989 (20 Aug). 15th South East Asian Games, Kuala Lumpur. T **162** and similar multicoloured designs. W 138 (sideways on 50c., $1). P 13.

417 10c. Type **162** 1·50 70
418 20c. Athletics 55 20
419 50c. Swimming (vert) 1·00 1·00
420 $1 Torch bearer (vert) 1·75 4·00
417/20 *Set of 4* 4·25 5·50

(Des R. Zahabuddin. Litho Security Printers (M), Malaysia)

1989 (18 Sept). Installation of Sultan Azlan Shah as Yang di Pertuan Agong. W **138** (sideways). P 13.

421 **163** 20c. multicoloured 20 15
422 40c. multicoloured 35 35
423 $1 multicoloured 1·00 2·75
421/3 *Set of 3* 1·40 3·00

164 Putra World Trade Centre and Pan-Pacific Hotel

165 Clock Tower, Kuala Lumpur City Hall and Big Ben

(Litho Security Printers (M), Malaysia)

1989 (18 Oct). Commonwealth Heads of Government Meeting, Kuala Lumpur. T **164** and similar multicoloured designs. W **138** (sideways on 50c.). P 13.

424 20c. Type **164** 20 10
a. wmk sideways
w. wmk inverted 2·25
425 50c. Traditional dancers (vert) 1·00 75
a. wmk upright 6·50
426 $1 National flag and map showing Commonwealth countries 2·25 3·00
a. wmk sideways 6·50
424/6 *Set of 3* 3·00 3·50

(Des AMC-Melewar Zecha Communications. Litho Security Printers (M), Malaysia)

1989 (2 Dec). Inaugural Malaysia Airlines "747" Non-stop Flight to London. T **165** and similar horiz designs. each showing Malaysia Airlines Boeing "747-400". Multicoloured. W **138**. P 13.

427 20c. Type **165** 2·25 2·25
a. Horiz pair. Nos. 427/8 4·50 4·50
428 20c. Parliament Buildings, Kuala Lumpur, and Palace of Westminster 2·25 2·25
429 $1 World map showing route 5·50 5·50
427/9 *Set of 3* 9·00 9·00

Nos. 427/8 were printed together, *se-tenant*, in horizontal pairs throughout the sheet.

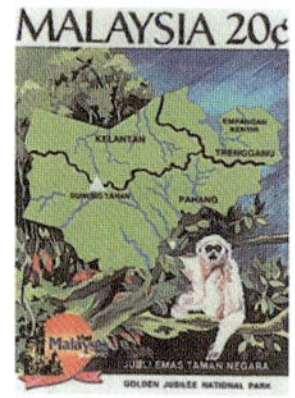

166 Sloth and Map of Park

167 Outline Map of South-east Asia and Logo

(Des Jermaine. Litho Security Printers (M), Malaysia)

1989 (28 Dec). Tenth Anniv of National Park. T **166** and similar vert design. Multicoloured. W **138**. P 12 (20c.) or 13 ($1).

430 20c. Type **166** 1·50 30
a. Perf 14½ 4·25 4·25
431 $1 Pair of Malay Ocellated Pheasants 4·50 5·00
a. Perf 14½ 5·50 6·00

(Des A. Kassim. Litho Security Printers (M), Malaysia)

1990 (1 Jan). Visit Malaysia Year. T **167** and similar horiz designs. Multicoloured. W **138** (sideways). P 12.

432 20 c. Type **167** 1·00 25
433 50 c. Traditional drums 1·25 1·25
434 $1 Scuba diving, windsurfing; and yachting 2·50 3·50
432/4 *Set of 3* 4·25 4·50

168 *Dillenia suffruticosa*

169 Monument and Rainbow

(Des T. Teh Chin Seng. Litho Security Printers (M), Malaysia)

1990 (12 Mar). Wildflowers (1st series). T **168** and similar vert designs. Multicoloured. W **138**. P 12.

435 15c. Type **168** 25 15
436 20c. *Mimosa pudica* 30 20
437 50c. *Ipmoea cornea* 60 90
438 $1 *Nymphaea pubescens* 80 2·75
435/8 *Set of 4* 1·75 3·50

See also Nos. 505/8.

(Des CD Advertising. Litho Security Printers (M), Malaysia)

1990 (14 May). Kuala Lumpur, Garden City of Lights. T 169 and similar multicoloured designs. W **138** (sideways on 40c., $1). P 12.

439 20c. Type **169** 25 20
440 40c. Mosque and skyscrapers at night (horiz) 55 55
441 $1 Kuala Lumpur skyline (horiz) 1·40 3·50
439/41 *Set of 3* 2·00 3·75

170 Seri Negara Building

171 Alor Setar

(Des T. Teh Chin Seng. Litho Security Printers (M), Malaysia)

1990 (1 June). First Summit Meeting of South-South Consultation and Co-operation Group, Kuala Lumpur. T **170** and similar horiz design. Multicoloured. W **138** (sideways). P 13.

442	20c. Type **170**	40	15
	w. Wmk top of SPM to right	3·00	
443	80c. Summit logo	1·40	2·50

The normal watermark shows the top of SPM pointing to the left on No. 442 and to the right on No. 443 *as seen from the back of the stamp.*

(Des Penerbit Hidayah. Litho Security Printers (M), Malaysia)

1990 (2 June). 250th Anniv of Alor Setar. T **171** and similar multicoloured designs. W **138** (sideways on 40c., $1). P 12.

444	20c. Type **171**	40	20
445	40c. Musicians and monument (vert)	50	40
446	$1 Zahir Mosque (vert)	1·25	3·75
444/6 *Set of 3*		1·90	4·00

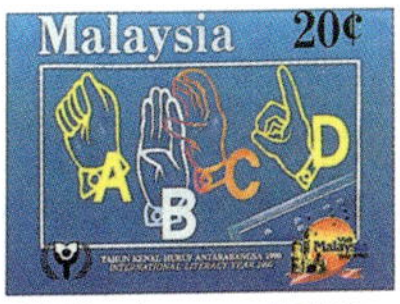

172 Sign Language Letters

173 Leatherback Turtle

(Des S. Senika. Litho Security Printers (M), Malaysia)

1990 (8 Sept). International Literacy Year. T **172** and similar multicoloured designs. W **138** (sideways on 20, 40c.). P 13 (40c.) or 12 (others).

447	20c. Type **172**	70	10
	a. Perf 13	13·00	
448	40c. People reading	1·00	40
449	$1 Symbolic person reading (vert)	2·50	3·50
447/9 *Set of 3*		3·75	3·50

(Des Ong Soo Kest. Litho Security Printers (M), Malaysia)

1990 (17 Nov). Marine Life (3rd series). Sea Turtles. T **173** and similar horiz designs. Multicoloured. W 138 (sideways). P 12.

450	15c. Type **173**	60	10
451	20c. Common Green Turtle	60	15
452	40c. Olive Ridley Turtle	1·25	80
	w. Wmk top of SPM to left	13·00	
453	$1 Hawksbill Turtle	2·25	3·75
	a. wmk inverted		
450/3 *Set of 4*		4·25	4·25

The normal watermark shows the top of SPM pointing to the left on Nos. 450 and 451 and to the right on Nos. 452 and 453 *as seen from the back of the stamp.*

174 Safety Helmet, Dividers and Industrial Skyline

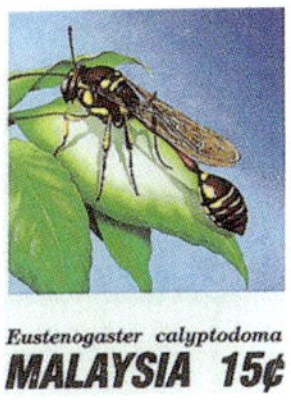

175 *Eustenogaster calyptodoma*

(Litho Security Printers (M), Malaysia)

1991 (25 Apr). 25th Anniv of MARA (Council of the Indigenous People). T **174** and similar horiz designs. Multicoloured. W **138** (sideways). P 12.

454	20c. Type **174**	15	10
455	40c. Documents and graph	30	35
456	$1 25th Anniversary logo	75	2·25
454/6 *Set of 3*		1·10	2·50

(Des Loh Wen Kong. Litho Security Printers (M), Malaysia)

1991 (29 July). Insects. (1st series). Wasps. T **175** and similar vert designs. Multicoloured. W **138** (sideways). P 12.

457	15c. Type **175**	25	30
	a. wmk upright	3·25	
458	20c. *Vespa affinis indonensis*	25	20
459	50c. *Sceliphorn javanum*	60	70
460	$1 *Ampulex compressa*	1·00	2·50
457/60 *Set of 4*		1·90	3·25
MS461	130×85 mm. Nos. 457/60. wmk sideways. P 14½×14	4·25	5·50
	a. wmk upright. P 12	10·00	12·00

15c. stamps from normal sheets (Nos. 457/a) show the wasp's left-hand feeler touching the edge of the design. On stamps of this value from the miniature sheet the feeler stops short of the edge.

See also Nos. **MS**714 and 1417/21.

176 Tunku Abdul Rahman Putra and Independence Rally

(Des Design Dimension. Litho Security Printers (M), Malaysia)

1991 (30 Aug). Former Prime Ministers of Malaysia. T **176** and similar horiz designs. Multicoloured. W **138**. P 12.

462	$1 Type **176**	70	1·25
463	$1 Tun Abdul Razak Hussein and jungle village	70	1·25
464	$1 Tun Hussein Orin and standard bearers.	70	1·25
462/4 *Set of 3*		1·90	3·50

177 Maziah Palace, Trengganu

178 Museum Building in 1891, Brass Lamp and Fabric

(Des A. Kassim. Litho Security Printers (M), Malaysia)

1991 (7 Nov). Historic Buildings of Malaysia (2nd series). T **177** and similar horiz designs. Multicoloured. W **138**. P 12.

465	15c. Type **177**	25	10
466	20c. Grand Palace, Johore	25	15
467	40c. Town Palace, Kuala Langat, Selangor	50	50
468	$1 Jahar Palace, Kelantan	1·00	2·75
465/8 *Set of 4*		1·75	3·25

(Des T. Teh Chin Song. Litho Security Printers (M), Malaysia)

1991 (21 Dec). Centenary of Sarawak Museum. T **178** and similar horiz design. Multicoloured. W **138**. P 12.

469	30c. Type **178**	30	15
470	$1 Museum building in 1991, vase and fabric	1·00	2·00

179 Rural Postman on Cycle

180 Hill Forest and Jelutong Tree

(Des Ismail & Associates. Litho Security Printers (M), Malaysia)

1992 (1 Jan). Inauguration of Post Office Corporation. T **179** and similar vert designs. Multicoloured. W **138** (sideways). P 12.

471	30c. Type **179**	60	85
	a. Horiz strip of 5. Nos. 471/5	2·75	3·75
472	30c. Urban postman on motorcycle	60	85
473	30c. Inner city post van	60	85
474	30c. Industrial post van	60	85
475	30c. Malaysian Airlines Boeing 747 and globe	60	85
471/5 *Set of 5*		2·75	3·75

Nos. 471/5 were printed together, *se-tenant*, in horizontal strips of 5 throughout the sheet.

(Des T. Teh Chin Seng. Litho Security Printers (M), Malaysia)

1992 (23 Mar). Tropical Forests. T **180** and similar horiz designs. Multicoloured. W **138** (sideways). P 12.

476	20c. Type **180**	35	10
477	50c. Mangrove swamp and Bakau Minyak tree	65	50
478	$1 Lowland forest and Chengal tree	1·10	2·50
476/8 *Set of 3*		1·90	2·75

181 Tuanku Ja'afar and Coat of Arms

182 Badminton Players

(Des TIARA CDP. Litho Security Printers (M), Malaysia)

1992 (18 Apr). 25th Anniv of Installation of Tuanku Ja'afar as Yang di-Pertuan Besar of Negri Sembilan. T **181** and similar horiz design. W **138** (sideways). P 12.

479	30c. Type **181**	30	20
480	$1 Palace, Negri Sembilan	1·00	2·25

(Des T. Teh Chin Seng. Litho Security Printers (M), Malaysia)

1992 (25 July). Malaysian Victory in Thomas Cup Badminton Championship. T **182** and similar multicoloured designs. W **138**. P 12.

481	$1 Type **182**	90	1·40
	w. wmk inverted	13·00	
482	$1 Thomas Cup and Malaysian flag	90	1·40
MS483	105×80 mm. $2 Winning team (76×28 mm). Wmk sideways	1·75	2·75

183 Women in National Costumes

184 Straits Settlements 1867 1½c. and Malaysian Federation 1957 10c. Stamps

(Des Image Productions. Litho Security Printers (M), Malaysia)

1992 (8 Aug). 25th Anniv of A.S.E.A.N. (Association of South East Asian Nations). T **183** and similar horiz designs. Multicoloured. W **138** (sideways). P 12.

484	30c. Type **183**	40	30
	a. wmk inverted		
485	50c. Regional flowers	65	75
486	$1 Traditional architecture	1·25	2·25
484/6 *Set of 3*		2·10	3·00

(Des Mega Dot. Litho Security Printers (M), Malaysia)

1992 (1 Sept). 125th Anniv of Postage Stamps and Kuala Lumpur '92 International Stamp Exhibition. T **184** and similar horiz designs. Multicoloured. W **138** (sideways). P 12.

487	30c. Type **184**	45	90
	a. Horiz pair. Nos. 487/8	90	1·75
488	30c. Straits Settlements 1867 2c. and Malaysia 1963 Federation Inauguration 12c.	45	90
489	50c. Straits Settlements 1868 4c. and Malaysia 1990 Kuala Lumpur 40c.	70	1·10
	a. Horiz pair. Nos. 489/90	1·40	2·10
	b. wmk inverted	4·75	
	ba. Horiz pair. Nos. 489b/90b	9·50	
490	50c. Straits Settlements 1867 12c. and Malaysia Kuala Lumpur '92 $2	70	1·10
	b. wmk inverted	4·75	
487/90 *Set of 4*		2·10	3·50
MS491	120×92 mm. $2 Kuala Lumpur '92 logo on Malaysian flag. P 13×13½	1·75	2·75
	a. Perf 12	20·00	24·00

Nos. 487/8 and 489/90 were printed together, *se-tenant*, in horizontal pairs throughout the sheets.

185 *Acropora*

186 Girls smiling

(Des Greenmild Advertising. Litho Security Printers (M), Malaysia)

1992 (21 Dec). Marine Life (4th series). Corals. T **185** and similar multicoloured designs. W **138**. P 12.

492	30c. Type **185**	80	1·10
	a. Horiz strip of 5. Nos. 492/6	3·50	5·00
493	30c. *Dendronephthya*	80	1·10
494	30c. *Dendrophyllia*	80	1·10
495	30c. *Sinularia*	80	1·10
496	30e. *Melithaea*	80	1·10
492/6 *Set of 5*		3·50	5·00
MS497	100×70 mm. $2 *Subergorgia* (38×28 mm). wmk sideways	2·50	4·00
	a. wmk upright	5·50	7·00

Nos. 492/6 were printed together, *se-tenant*, in horizontal strips of 5 throughout the sheet.

CURRENCY

From 1993 higher value stamps were denominated in Malaysian Ringgit ("RM") rather than dollars ("$"). Apart from No. 550, the lower values remained in cents "c" until December 1996 (**MS**626), when the designation was changed to "sen". To assist collectors, the currency shown in the listings reflects that shown on the stamp.

(Des Image Promotions. Litho Security Printers (M), Malaysia)

1993 (24 Apr). 16th Asian-Pacific Dental Congress. T **186** and similar horiz designs. Multicoloured. W **138** (sideways). P 12.

498	30c. Type **186**	50	75
	a. Horiz pair. Nos. 498/9	1·00	1·50
499	30c. Girls smiling with Koala Bear	50	75
500	50c. Dentists with Japanese, Malaysian and South Korean flags	1·00	1·00
	a. Horiz pair. Nos. 500/1	2·20	3·00
501	1r. Dentists with New Zealand, Thai, Chinese and Indonesian flags	1·25	2·00
498/501 *Set of 4*		3·00	4·00

Nos. 498/9 and 500/1 were each printed together, *se-tenant*, in horizontal pairs throughout the sheets.

187 View of Golf Course

188 *Alpinia rafflesiana*

(Des T. Teh Chin Seng. Litho Security Printers (M), Malaysia)

1993 (24 June). Centenary of Royal Selangor Golf Club. T **187** and similar multicoloured designs. W **138** (sideways on $1). P 12.

502	30c. Type **187**	60	20
503	50c. Old and new club houses	90	80
	w. wmk inverted	13·00	
504	1r. Bunker on course (horiz)	2·00	3·50
502/4 *Set of 3*		3·25	4·00

(Des TIARA CDP. Litho Security Printers (M), Malaysia)

1993 (2 Aug). Wildflowers (2nd series). Gingers. T **188** and similar vert designs. Multicoloured. W **138**. P 12.

505	20c. Type **188**	40	10
	w. Wmk inverted	11·00	
506	30c. *Achasma megalocheilos*	50	20
507	50c. *Zingiber spectabile*	90	80
508	1r. *Costus speciosus*	1·75	3·00
	w. wmk inverted	13·00	
505/8 *Set of 4*		3·25	3·75

189 Forest under Magnifying Glass

190 White-breasted Kingfisher

(Des CD Advertising. Litho Security Printers (M), Malaysia)

1993 (13 Sept). 14th Commonwealth Forestry Conference, Kuala Lumpur. T **189** and similar multicoloured designs. W **138** (sideways on 30c., 50c.). P 12.

509	30c. Type **189**	40	20
510	50c. Hand holding forest	65	70
511	1r. Forest in glass dome (vert)	1·40	2·75
	w. Wmk inverted	7·00	
509/11	*Set of 3*	2·25	3·25

Nos. 509/11 were re-issued on 1 October 1994 with the Bangkok '93 Stamp Exhibition logo incorporated in the designs. Such stamps were only available from the Malaysia stand at the exhibition and in very limited quantities from the philatelic bureaux.

(Des Ong Soo Kest. Litho Security Printers (M), Malaysia)

1993 (23 Oct). Kingfishers. T **190** and similar vert designs. Multicoloured. W **138**. P 12.

512	30c. Type **190**	1·75	2·00
	a. Horiz pair. Nos. 512/13	3·50	4·00
513	30c. Pair of Blue-eared Kingfishers	1·75	2·00
514	50c. Chestnut-collared Kingfisher	2·00	2·25
	a. Horiz pair. Nos. 514/15	4·00	4·50
515	50c. Pair of Three-toed Kingfishers	2·00	2·25
512/15	*Set of 4*	6·75	7·75

Nos. 512/13 and 514/15 were printed together, *se-tenant*, in horizontal pairs throughout the sheets.

191 SME MD3-160M Light Aircraft

192 Jeriau Waterfalls

(Des A. Hassan. Litho Security Printers (M), Malaysia)

1993 (7 Dec). Langkawi International Maritime and Aerospace Exhibition '93. T **191** and similar horiz designs. Multicoloured. W **138** (sideways on 30c.). P 12.

516	30c. Type **191**	50	20
	a. Wmk inverted	4·25	
517	50c. Eagle X-TS light aircraft	80	90
	w. Wmk inverted	80	
518	1r. *Kasturi* (frigate)	1·50	2·75
	a. Wmk sideways	4·25	
516/18	*Set of 3*	2·50	3·50
MS519	120×80 mm. 2r. Map of Langkawi. Wmk upright	1·60	2·50
	a. Wmk sideways	22·00	

(Des Mega Dot. Litho Security Printers (M), Malaysia)

1994 (1 Jan). Visit Malaysia. T **192** and similar horiz designs. Multicoloured. W **138** (inverted). P 12.

520	20c. Type **192**	50	10
521	30c. Flowers	50	25
522	50c. Turtle and fishes	75	65
523	1r. Orang-utan and other wildlife	1·60	2·50
520/3	*Set of 4*	3·00	3·25

Nos. 520/3 were re-issued on 8 November 1994 with the ASEANPEX '94 Stamp Exhibition logo incorporated in the designs. Such stamps were only available from the Malaysian stand at the exhibition and in very limited quantities from the philatelic bureaux.

193 Planetarium and Planets

194 *Spathoglottis aurea*

(Des CD Advertising and DeArt Forms. Litho Security Printers (M), Malaysia)

1994 (7 Feb). National Planetarium, Kuala Lumpur. T **193** and similar horiz designs. Multicoloured. W 138 (inverted on 30c.). P 12.

524	30c. Type **193**	50	25
	w. Wmk upright		
525	50c. Static displays	65	80
526	1r. Planetarium auditorium	1·50	2·50
524/6	*Set of 3*	2·40	3·25

(Des P. Ket. Litho Security Printers (M), Malaysia)

1994 (17 Feb). Orchids. T **194** and similar multicoloured designs. W **138** (sideways). P 12.

527	20c. Type **194**	40	15
528	30c. *Paphiopedilum barbatum*	50	25
529	50c. *Bulbophyllum lobbii*	85	90
530	1r. *Aerides odorata*	1·40	2·75
527/30	*Set of 4*	2·75	3·75
MS531	120×82 mm. 2r. *Grammatophyllum speciosum* (horiz)	2·50	4·00

No. **MS**531 also commemorates the Hong Kong '94 International Stamp Exhibition.

195 Decorative Bowl

196 Flock of Chickens and Vet examining Cat

(Des Assist Ad. Litho Security Printers (M), Malaysia)

1994 (17 June). World Islamic Civilisation Festival '94, Kuala Lumpur. T **195** and similar vert designs. Multicoloured. W **138**. P 12.

532	20c. Type **195**	20	10
	w. Wmk inverted	18·00	
533	30c. Celestial globe	30	20
	w. Wmk inverted	18·00	
534	50c. Dinar coins	50	65
	w. Wmk inverted	20·00	
535	1r. Decorative tile	95	2·00
532/5	*Set of 4*	1·75	2·75

Nos. 532/5 were re-issued on 16 August 1994 with the Philakorea '94 Stamp Exhibition logo incorporated in the designs. Such stamps were only available from the Malaysia stand at the exhibition and in very limited quantities from the philatelic bureaux.

(Des TIARA CDP. Litho Security Printers (M), Malaysia)

1994 (26 July). Centenary of Veterinary Services. T **196** and similar vert designs. Multicoloured. W **138** (inverted on 30c.). P 12.

536	30c. Type **196**	50	25
537	50c. Vet in abattoir	70	55
538	1r. Herd of cows and veterinary equipment	1·00	2·25
	w. Wmk inverted	9·00	
536/8	*Set of 3*	2·00	2·75

197 Workers laying Electric Cable

198 Expressway from the Air

(Des Mega Dot. Litho Security Printers (M), Malaysia)

1994 (3 Sept). Centenary of Electricity Supply. T **197** and similar horiz designs. Multicoloured. W **138** (sideways). P 12.

539	30c. Type **197**	40	65
	a. Horiz pair. Nos. 539/40	80	1·25
540	30c. Illuminated city	40	65
541	1r. City of the future	1·00	2·00
539/41	*Set of 3*	1·60	3·00

Nos. 539/40 were printed together, *se-tenant*, in horizontal pairs throughout the sheet.

(Des The Sharper Image. Litho Security Printers (M), Malaysia)

1994 (8 Sept). Opening of North-South Expressway. T **198** and similar horiz designs. Multicoloured. W **138** (sideways). P 12.

542	30c. Type **198**	30	20
543	50c. Expressway junction	45	50
544	1r. Expressway bridge	90	2·00
542/4	*Set of 3*	1·50	2·50

Nos. 542/4 were also prepared incorporating the Philakorea '94 Stamp Exhibition logo as recorded beneath Nos. 532/5, but these stamps were not placed on sale.

199 Sultan Tuanku Ja'afar

200 Map of Malaysia and Logo

(Des R. Yaacob. Litho Security Printers (M), Malaysia)

1994 (22 Sept). Installation of Sultan Tuanku Ja'afar as Yang di Pertuan Agong. W **138**. P 12.

545	**199**	30c. multicoloured	30	20
		a. Wmk sideways		
		w. Wmk inverted	2·75	
546		50c. multicoloured	50	50
547		1r. multicoloured	85	2·00
545/7 *Set of 3*			1·50	2·50

(Des Limkokwing Integrated. Litho Security Printers (M), Malaysia)

1994 (29 Oct). 16th Commonwealth Games, Kuala Lumpur (1998) (1st issue). T **200** and similar vert design. Multicoloured. W **138**. P 12.

548	1r. Type **200**	90	1·50
	a. Horiz pair. Nos. 548/9	1·75	3·00
	b. Perf 14½	6·00	
	ba. Horiz pair. Nos. 548b/9b	12·00	
549	1r. Wira (games mascot) holding national flag	90	1·50
	b. Perf 14½	6·00	

Nos. 548/9 were issued together, *se-tenant*, in sheets of 30 (6×5), showing No. 548 in vertical rows 1 and 4, No. 549 in vertical rows 3 and 6, and a stamp-size label, showing the mascot playing rugby, basketball, cricket and hockey, in vertical rows 2 and 5.

See also Nos. 575/6, 627/30, 668/71, **MS**678, 693/708 and **MS**715/16.

201 Tunku Abdul Rahman Putra and National Flag

(Des T. Teh Ching Seng. Litho Leigh-Mardon Ltd, Melbourne, Australia)

1994 (10 Nov). 5th Death Anniv of Tunku Abdul Rahman Putra (former Prime Minister). T **201** and simlar horiz design. Multicoloured. P 14½.

550	30s. Type **201**	30	20
551	1r. The Residency, Kuala Lumpur	1·00	1·75

202 Library Building

203 *Microporus xanthopus*

(Des Image Promotions. Litho Security Printers (M), Malaysia)

1994 (16 Dec). Opening of the New National Library Building. T **202** and similar horiz designs. Multicoloured. W **138** (sideways). P 12.

552	30c. Type **202**	20	25
553	50c. Computer plan on screen	45	50
554	1r. Ancient Koran	1·00	2·00
552/4 *Set of 3*		1·50	2·50

(Des Greenmild Advertising. Litho Enschedé)

1995 (18 Jan). Fungi. T **203** and similar vert designs. Multicoloured. P 14½×14.

555	20c. Type **203**	15	10
556	30c. *Cookeina tricholoma*	25	20
557	50c. *Phallus indusiatus* ("*Dictyophora phalloidea*")	45	55
558	1r. *Ramaria* sp.	90	2·75
555/8 *Set of 4*		1·60	2·75

204 Sea Fans

(Litho Security Printers (M), Malaysia)

1995 (10 Apr). Marine Life (5th series). Corals. T **204** and similar horiz designs. Multicoloured. W **138** (sideways). P 12.

559	20c. Type **204**	1·00	1·50
	a. Booklet pane. Nos. 559/60, each×5	8·00	
560	20c. Feather Stars	1·00	1·50
561	30c. Cup Coral	1·00	1·50
	a. Booklet pane. Nos. 561/2, each×5	9·00	
562	30c. Soft Coral	1·00	1·50
559/62 *Set of 4*		3·50	5·50

Nos. 559/60 and 561/2 were only available from 2r. and 3r. stamp booklets.

205 Clouded Leopard on Branch

(Des A. Robinson. Litho Enschedé)

1995 (18 Apr). Endangered Species. Clouded Leopard. T **205** and similar horiz designs. Multicoloured. Ordinary paper. W w **14** (sideways). P 13½.

563	20c. Type **205**	70	35
	a. Strip of 4. Nos. 563/6	3·50	3·50
564	30c. With cubs	80	40
565	50c. Crouched on branch	1·00	90
566	1r. Climbing tree	1·50	2·25
563/6 *Set of 4*		3·50	3·50

In addition to separate sheets of 50 Nos. 563/6 were also available in sheets of 16 (4×4) with the stamps *se-tenant* both vertically and horizontally.

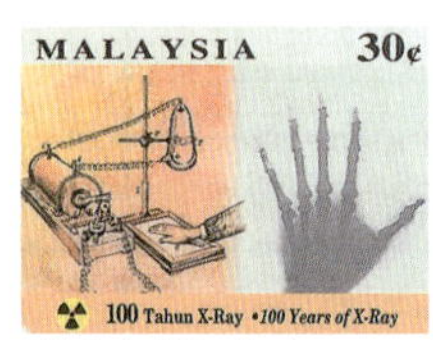

206 Early X-Ray Equipment and X-Ray of Hand

(Des Eka IPR Agensi. Litho Security Printers (M), Malaysia)

1995 (29 May). Centenary of Discovery of X-Rays by Wilhelm Conrad Rontgen. T **206** and similar horiz designs. Multicoloured. W **138**. P 12.

567	30c. Type **206**	65	80
	a. Pair. Nos. 567/8	1·25	1·60
568	30c. Body scanner and brain scan	65	80
569	1r. Chest X-rays	1·50	2·00
567/9 *Set of 3*		2·50	3·25

Nos. 567/8 were printed together, *se-tenant*, in horizontal and vertical pairs throughout the sheet.

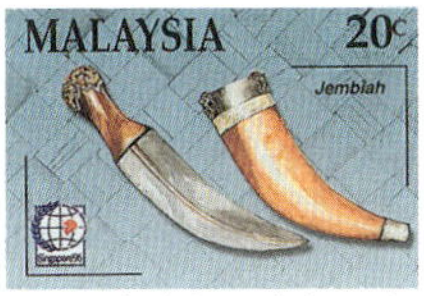

207 Jembiah (curved dagger)

208 Badminton, Cricket, Shooting, Tennis, Hurdling, Hockey and Weightlifting

(Des BJ Image. Litho Quests)

1995 (1 Sept). Singapore '95 International Stamp Exhibition. Traditional Malay Weapons. T **207** and similar horiz designs. Multicoloured. P 14.

570	20c. Type **207**	15	10
571	30c. Keris panjang (sword)	25	20
572	50c. Kerambit (curved dagger)	40	50
573	1r. Keris sundang (sword)	80	2·00
570/3	*Set of 4*	1·40	2·50
MS574	100×70 mm. 2r. Ladig terns (dagger)	3·00	3·50

(Des Limkokwing Integrated. Litho Security Printers (M), Malaysia)

1995 (11 Sept). 16th Commonwealth Games, Kuala Lumpur (1998) (2nd issue). T **208** and similar vert design. Multicoloured. W **138**. P 13½.

575	1r. Type **208**	2·50	2·50
	a. Horiz pair. Nos. 575/6	5·00	5·00
	b. Perf 14½	4·50	5·00
	ba. Horiz pair. Nos. 575b/6b	9·00	10·00
576	1r. Cycling, bowls, boxing, basketball, rugby, gymnastics and swimming	2·50	2·50
	b. Perf 14½	4·50	5·00

Nos. 575/6 were issued together, *se-tenant*, in sheets of 30 (6×5), showing No. 575 in vertical rows 1 and 4, No. 576 in vertical rows 3 and 6, and a stamp-size label, showing the monkey mascot hurdling, boxing and playing badminton, in vertical rows 2 and 5.

209 Leatherback Turtle (*Dermochelys coriacea*)

(Des Chao Beng Teong. Litho Security Printers (M), Malaysia)

1995 (26 Sept). Turtles. T **209** and similar horiz design. Multicoloured. W **138** (sideways). P 14½.

577	30c. Type **209**	1·25	1·25
	a. Booklet pane. Nos. 577/8 each×5	11·00	
578	30c. Green Turtle (*Chelonia mydas*)	1·25	1·25

Nos. 577/8 were only issued in 3r. stamp booklets.

210 Anniversary Emblem and Symbolic People around Globe

211 Boeing 747, Globe, Emblem and Malaysian Scenes

(Des PAC Advertising. Litho Southern Colour Print, Dunedin, New Zealand)

1995 (24 Oct). 50th Anniv of United Nations. T **210** and similar horiz design. Multicoloured. P 13½.

579	30c. Type **210**	30	20
580	1r. United Nations emblem	70	1·50

(Des ISC Bullseye. Litho Enschedé)

1995 (30 Oct). 50th Anniv of International Air Transport Association. T **211** and similar vert designs, each showing Boeing 747 and globe. Multicoloured. P 14½×14.

581	30c. Type **211**	60	70
	a. Horiz pair. Nos. 581/2	1·10	1·40
582	30c. Asian and Australasian scenes	60	70
583	50c. European and African scenes	80	1·00
	a. Horiz pair. Nos. 583/4	1·60	2·00
584	50c. North and South American scenes	80	1·00
581/4	*Set of 4*	2·50	3·00

Nos. 581/2 and 583/4 were printed together, *se-tenant*, in horizontal pairs throughout the sheets.

212 Proton "Saga 1.5" Saloon, 1985

213 "Ariane 4" Launch Rocket

(Des Long's Creative. Litho Southern Colour Print, Dunedin)

1995 (23 Dec). Tenth Anniv of Proton Cars. T **212** and similar horiz designs. Multicoloured. P 14×14½.

585	30c. Type **212**	70	90
	a. Booklet pane. Nos. 585/94	6·25	8·00
586	30c. "Iswara 1.5" aeroback, 1992	70	90
587	30c. "Iswara 1.5" saloon, 1992	70	90
588	30c. "Wira 1.6" saloon, 1993	70	90
589	30c. "Wira 1.6" aeroback, 1993	70	90
590	30c. Proton rally car, 1994	70	90
591	30c. "Satria 1.6" hatchback, 1994	70	90
592	30c. "Perdana 2.0" saloon, 1995	70	90
593	30c. "Wira 1.6" aeroback, 1995	70	90
594	30c. "Wira 1.8" saloon, 1995	70	90
585/94	*Set of 10*	6·25	8·00

Nos. 585/94 were only issued in 3r. stamp booklets with the horizontal edges of the pane imperforate.

(Des Nerve Centre Associates. Litho Southern Colour Print, Dunedin)

1996 (13 Jan). Launch of MEASAT 1 (Malaysia East Asia Satellite). T **213** and similar multicoloured designs. P 13½.

595	30c. Type **213**	25	20
596	50c. Satellite over Eastern Asia	40	45
597	1r. Satellite Earth station, Langkawi	90	2·00
595/7	*Set of 3*	1·40	2·40
MS598	100×70 mm. 5r. Satellite orbiting Globe (hologram) (horiz). P 14×14½	7·00	8·00

214 *Nepenthes sanguinea*

215 Brahminy Kite

(Des P. Ket. Litho Security Printers (M), Malaysia)

1996 (6 Apr). Pitcher Plants. T **214** and similar vert designs. Multicoloured. W **138**. P 13½ (30c.) or 14½×14 (50c.).

599	30c. Type **214**	25	45
	a. Horiz pair. Nos. 599/600	50	90
	b. Perf 14½×14	3·50	4·00
	ba. Horiz pair. Nos. 599b/600b	7·00	8·00
600	30c. *Nepenthes macfarlanei*	25	45
	b. Perf 14½×14	3·50	4·00
601	50c. *Nepenthes rajah*	35	55
	a. Horiz pair. Nos. 601/2	70	1·10
	b. Perf 13½	3·75	4·25
	ba. Horiz pair. Nos. 601b/2b	7·50	8·50
602	50c. *Nepenthes lowii*	35	55
	b. Perf 13½	3·75	4·25
599/602	*Set of 4*	1·10	1·90

(Des Teh Yew Kiang)

1996 (18 May–Dec). Birds of Prey. T **215** and similar multicoloured designs. W **138**. P 13½ (30c.) or 14½×14 (others).

(a) Litho Security Printers (M), Malaysia.

603	20c. Type **215**	45	20
604	30c. Crested Serpent Eagle	60	25
	aw. Wmk inverted	20·00	
	b. Perf 14×14½	5·50	70
605	50c. White-bellied Sea Eagle	90	75
	b. Perf 13½	6·00	
606	1r. Crested Hawk Eagle	1·40	2·50
	aw. Wmk inverted	15·00	
	b. Perf 13½	13·00	
603/6 *Set of 4*		3·00	3·25
MS607 100×70 mm. 2r. Blyth's Hawk Eagle (vert). P 13½×14		3·50	4·00
	a. Perf 13½	8·50	9·00
	b. Perf 14	8·50	9·00
	bw. Wmk inverted	42·00	

(b) Litho Southern Colour Print, Dunedin. No wmk. P 13½

607c	20c. Type **215** (Dec)	2·75	30

No. **MS**607 also includes the "CHINA '96" 9th Asian International Stamp Exhibition logo on the sheet margin.

216 Family, Globe and Burning Drugs

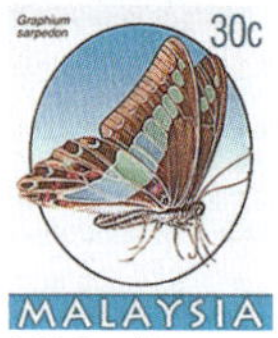

217 *Graphium sarpedon*

(Des CD Advertising. Litho Security Printers (M), Malaysia)

1996 (26 June). International Day against Drug Abuse and Illicit Tracking. T **216** and similar horiz designs. Multicoloured. W **138** (sideways). P 14×14½.

608	30c. Type **216**	65	70
	a. Horiz pair. Nos. 608/9	1·25	1·40
	b. Perf 13½	4·50	5·00
	ba. Horiz pair. Nos. 608b/9b	9·00	10·00
609	30c. Sporting activities	65	70
	b. Perf 13½	4·50	5·00
610	1r. Family and rainbow	1·25	2·00
	b. Perf 13½		
608/10 *Set of 3*		2·25	3·00

Nos. 608/9 were printed together, *se-tenant*, in horizontal pairs throughout the sheet.

(Des P. Chuah. Litho Southern Colour Print, Dunedin)

1996 (27 Sept). ISTANBUL '96 International Stamp Exhibition. Butterflies. T **217** and similar vert designs. Multicoloured. P 14½×14.

611	30c. Type **217**	1·25	1·25
	a. Booklet pane. Nos. 611/15×2	11·00	11·00
612	30c. *Terinos terpander*	1·25	1·25
613	30c. *Melanocyma faunula*	1·25	1·25
614	30c. *Trogonoptera brookiana*	1·25	1·25
615	30c. *Delias hyparete*	1·25	1·25
611/15 *Set of 5*		5·75	5·75

Nos. 611/15 were only issued in 3r. stamp booklets.

218 Kuala Lumpur Tower

219 C.A.P.A. Logo on Kite

(Des The Sharper Image (2r.), Akitek Akiprima (others). Litho Southern Colour Print, Dunedin)

1996 (1 Oct). Opening of Kuala Lumpur Telecommunications Tower. T **218** and similar multicoloured designs. P 13½.

616	30c. Type **218**	20	20
617	50c. Diagram of top of tower	30	35
618	1r. Kuala Lumpur Tower at night	80	1·75
616/18 *Set of 3*		1·10	2·10
MS619 70×100 mm. 2r. Top of Kuala Lumpur Tower (different) (vert)		1·50	2·50

(Des The Sharper Image. Litho Enschedé)

1996 (7 Oct). 14th Conference of the Confederation of Asian and Pacific Accountants. T **219** and similar horiz design. Multicoloured. P 14×14½.

620	30c. Type **219**	25	20
621	1r. Globe and C.A.P.A logo	75	1·40

(Litho Southern Colour Print, Dunedin)

1996 (16 Oct). TAIPEI '96 10th Asian International Stamp Exhibition. As No. **MS**619, but with exhibition logo added to bottom right-hand corner of sheet. P 13½.

MS622 70×100 mm. 2r. Top of Kuala Lumpur Tower (vert)		1·50	2·25

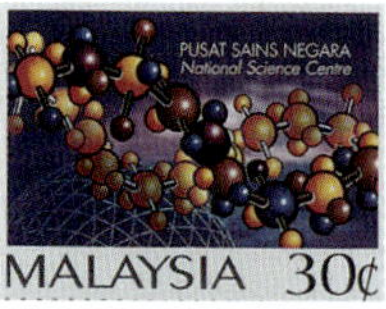

220 Model of D.N.A. Molecule

221 Slow Loris

(Des The Sharper Image. Litho Southern Colour Print, Dunedin)

1996 (29 Nov). Opening of National Science Centre, Kuala Lumpur. T **220** and similar horiz designs. Multicoloured. P 13½.

623	30c. Type **220**	25	20
624	50c. Planetary model and Science Centre	40	40
625	1r. National Science Centre	90	1·50
623/5 *Set of 3*		1·40	1·90

(Des Teh Yew Kiang. Litho Southern Colour Print, Dunedin)

1996 (2 Dec). Stamp Week. Wildlife. Sheet 165×75 mm containing T **221** and similar multicoloured designs. P 14.

MS626 Type **221**; 30s. Prevost's Squirrel; 50s. Atlas Moth; 1r. Rhinoceros Hornbill (60×30 mm); 1r. Whitehanded Gibbon (30×60 mm); 2r. Banded Palm Civet (60×30 mm)		3·25	4·00

A similar sheet, but imperforate and without face values, was also available from the Philatelic Bureau at 1r.5.

222 Running

223 Pygmy Blue Flycatcher

(Des CD Advertising. Litho Southern Colour Print, Dunedin)

1996 (21 Dec). 16th Commonwealth Games, Kuala Lumpur (1998) (3rd issue). T **222** and similar horiz designs. Multicoloured. P 12.

627	30s. Type **222**	35	55
	a. Vert pair. Nos. 627/8	70	1·10
628	30s. Hurdling	35	55
629	50s. High jumping	45	65
	a. Vert pair. Nos. 629/30	90	1·30
630	50s. Javelin	45	65
627/30 *Set of 4*		1·40	2·10

Nos. 627/8 and 629/30 were each printed together, *se-tenant*, in sheets of 20 (5×4) with the first design in rows 1 and 3 and the second in rows 2 and 4. As there are horizontal gutters between rows 1 and 2 and 3 and 4, Nos. 627a and 629a only occur from rows 2 and 3.

(Des P. Chuah. Litho Enschedé)

1997 (4 Jan). Highland Birds. T **223** and similar vert designs. Multicoloured. P 13½×14.

631	20s. Type **223**	45	20
632	30s. Silver-eared Mesia	55	25
633	50s. Black-sided Flower-pecker	70	70
634	1r. Scarlet Sunbird	1·10	1·75
631/4 *Set of 4*		2·50	2·50

(Litho Southern Colour Print, Dunedin)

1997 (12 Feb). HONG KONG '97 International Stamp Exhibition. As No. **MS**626, but with exhibition logo added to top sheet margin. P 14.

MS635 165×75 mm. 20s. Type **221**; 30s. Tree Squirrel; 50s. Attacus atlas (butterfly); 1r. Rhinoceros Hornbill (60×30 mm); 1r. Common Gibbon (30×60 mm); 2r. Banded Palm Civet (60×30 mm)		5·50	6·50

224 Transit Train leaving Station

225 Bowler

(Des The Sharper Image. Litho Southern Colour Print, Dunedin)

1997 (1 Mar). Opening of Kuala Lumpur Light Rail Transit System. T **224** and similar horiz design. Multicoloured. P 14×14½.

636	30s. Type **224**	1·25	1·00
	a. Booklet pane. Nos. 636/7 each×5	11·00	
637	30s. Trains in central Kuala Lumpur	1·25	1·00

Nos. 636/7 were only issued in 3r. stamp booklets.

(Des P. Chuah. Litho Security Printers (M), Malaysia)

1997 (24 Mar). International Cricket Council Trophy, Kuala Lumpur. T **225** and similar vert designs. Multicoloured. W **138**. P 13½ (1r.) or 14½ (others).

638	30s. Type **225**	45	15
639	50s. Batsman	60	55
	a. Perf 13½	4·50	
640	1r. Wicket keeper	1·10	1·75
	a. Perf 14½	9·00	
638/40	*Set of 3*	1·90	2·25

226 Boeing 747-400 over World Map

227 *Schima wallichii*

(Des The Sharper Image. Litho Security Printers (M), Malaysia)

1997 (2 Apr). 50th Anniv of Aviation in Malaysia. T **226** and similar horiz designs. Multicoloured. W **138** (sideways*). P 13½ (30s.) or 14½ (others).

641	30s. Type **226**	65	15
	a. Perf 14½	5·00	
	aw. Wmk top of letters to right	5·50	
642	50s. Boeing 747-400 over Kuala Lumpur	1·10	60
	aw. Wmk top of letters to right		
	b. Perf 13½	3·25	
643	1r. Tail fins of four airliners	1·50	2·25
	a. Perf 13½	3·25	
641/3	*Set of 3*	3·00	2·75

*The normal sideways watermark shows the top of the letters to left, *as seen from the back of the stamp.*

(Des The Sharper Image. Litho Southern Colour Print, Dunedin)

1997 (7 May). Highland Flowers (1st series). T **227** and similar vert designs. Multicoloured. P 14½×14.

644	30s. Type **227**	65	80
	a. Booklet pane. Nos. 644/8 each×2	6·00	
645	30s. *Aeschynanthus longicalyx*	65	80
646	30s. *Aeschynanthus speciosa*	65	80
647	30s. *Phyllagathis tuberculata*	65	80
648	30s. *Didymocarpus quinquevulnerus*	65	80
644/8	*Set of 5*	3·00	3·50

Nos. 644/8 were only issued in 3r. stamp booklets showing the outer edges of the pane imperforate.

See also Nos. 944/58.

228 World Youth Football Championship Mascot

229 Members of First Conference, 1897

(Des The Sharper Image. Litho Harrison (30s., 50s.), Security Printers (M), Malaysia (1r.))

1997 (16 June). Ninth World Youth Football Championship, Malaysia. T **228** and similar vert designs. Multicoloured. W **138** (sideways) (1r.) or no watermark (others). P 12½ (1r.) or 13½×13 (others).

649	30s. Type **228**	30	10
650	50s. Football and players	45	35
651	1r. Map of Malaysia and football	1·00	1·75
649/51	*Set of 3*	1·50	2·00

(Des R. Yaacob. Litho Southern Colour Print, Dunedin)

1997 (31 July). Centenary of Rulers' Conference. T **229** and similar horiz designs. Multicoloured. P 14.

652	30s. Type **229**	20	10
653	50s. State emblems	40	45
654	1r. Seal and press	80	1·75
652/4	*Set of 3*	1·25	2·00

230 A.S.E.A.N. Logo and Ribbons

231 *Tubastrea* sp.

(Des R. Yaacob. Litho Security Printers (M), Malaysia)

1997 (8 Aug). 30th Anniv of Association of South-east Asian Nations. T **230** and similar horiz designs. W **138**. P 13½.

655	30s. Type **230**	65	10
656	50s. "30" enclosing logo	1·00	55
657	1r. Chevrons and logo	1·50	2·00
655/7	*Set of 3*	2·75	2·40

(Des The Sharper Image. Litho Southern Colour Print, Dunedin)

1997 (23 Aug). International Year of the Coral Reefs. T **231** and similar multicoloured designs. P 14½.

658	20s. Type **231**	30	15
	a. Perf 13½	5·50	
659	30s. *Melithaea* sp.	35	15
	a. Perf 13½	5·50	
660	50s. *Aulostomus chinensis*	45	40
	a. Perf 13½	5·50	
661	1r. *Symphillia* sp.	70	1·40
	a. Perf 13½	5·50	
658/61	*Set of 4*	1·60	1·90
MS662	70×100 mm. 2r. Green Turtle (horiz)	2·00	3·00

232 Women Athletes, Scientist and Politician

233 1867 12c. on 4 anna with Malacca Postmark

(Des Eka IPR Agensi. Litho Enschedé)

1997 (25 Aug). 20th International Pan-Pacific and South-east Asia Women's Association Conference, Kuala Lumpur. T **232** and similar vert design. Multicoloured. P 13×13½.

663	30s. Type **232**	40	50
	a. Booklet pane. Nos. 663/4, each×5, with margins all round	3·50	
664	30s. Family and house	40	50

Nos. 663/4 were only available from 3r. stamp booklets.

(Des P. Chuah. Photo Enschedé)

1997 (9 Sept). Malpex '97 Stamp Exhibition, Kuala Lumpur. 50th Anniv of Organised Philately. Sheet, 120×70 mm, containing T **233** and similar diamond-shaped designs. Multicoloured. P 12½.

MS665	20s. Type **233**; 30s. 1997 Highland Birds set; 50s. 1996 Wildlife miniature sheet seen through magnifying glass; 1r. 1867 cover to Amoy	3·00	3·50

234 Group of 15 Emblem

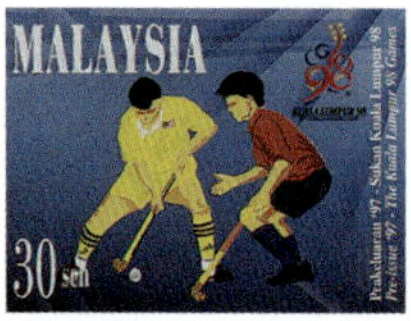

235 Hockey

(Des P. Ket. Litho Security Printers (M), Malaysia)

1997 (3 Nov). Seventh Summit Conference of the Group of 15, Kuala Lumpur. T **234** and similar vert design. Multicoloured. P 12 (30s.) or 13½ (1r.).

666	30s. Type **234**	15	10
	a. Perf 13½	13·00	
667	1r. Flags of member countries	1·25	1·50

(Des CD Advertising. Litho Southern Colour Print, Dunedin)

1997 (15 Nov). 16th Commonwealth Games, Kuala Lumpur (1998) (4th issue). T **235** and similar horiz designs. Multicoloured. P 12.

668	30s. Type **235**	85	85
	a. Vert pair. Nos. 668/9	1·60	1·60
669	30s. Netball	85	85
670	50s. Cricket	1·25	1·25
	a. Vert pair. Nos. 670/1	2·50	2·50
671	50s. Rugby	1·25	1·25
668/71 *Set of 4*		3·75	3·75

Nos. 668/9 and 670/1 were each printed together, *se-tenant*, in sheets of 20 (5×4) with the first design in rows 1 and 3 and the second in rows 2 and 4. As there are horizontal gutters between rows 1 and 2 and 3 and 4, Nos. 668a and 670a only occur from rows 2 and 3.

236 False Gharial

237 Kundang

(Des Teh Yew Kiang. Litho Southern Colour Print, Dunedin)

1997 (1 Dec). Stamp Week '97. Endangered Wildlife. Sheet, 165×75 mm, containing T **236** and similar multicoloured designs. P 14½.

MS672	20s. Type **236**; 30s. Western Tarsier (vert); 50s. Indian Sambar (vert); 2r. Crested Wood Partridge; 2r. Malayan Bony-tongue (fish)	2·50	3·25

A second miniature sheet, incorporating a 2r. tiger design, had no postal validity.

(Photo Enschedé)

1997 (15 Dec). INDEPEX '97 International Stamp Exhibition, New Delhi. As No. **MS**665, but with exhibition logo added to the sheet margin, in gold, at bottom right. P 12½.

MS673	120×70 mm. 20s. Type **233**; 30s. 1997 Highlands Bird set; 50s. 1996 Wildlife miniature sheet seen through magnifying glass; 1r. 1867 cover to Amoy	1·25	2·00

(Des Eka IPR Agensi. Litho Southern Colour Print, Dunedin)

1998 (10 Jan). Rare Fruits of Malaysia (1st series). T **237** and similar vert designs. Multicoloured. P 13½.

674	20s. Type **237**	15	15
675	30s. Sentul	20	15
676	50s. Pulasan	30	25
677	1r. Asam Gelugur	70	1·60
674/7 *Set of 4*		1·25	1·90

See also Nos. 719/26 and1324/7.

238 Swimming Complex

239 Mas (coin) from Trengganu, 1793-1808

(Des CD Advertising. Litho Security Printers (M), Malaysia)

1998 (23 Feb). 16th Commonwealth Games, Kuala Lumpur (5th issue). Venues. Sheet, 120×80 mm, containing T **238** and similar horiz designs. Multicoloured. W **138**. P 13½*.

MS678	20s. Type **238**; 30s. Hockey Stadium; 50s. Indoor Stadium; 1r. Main Stadium	1·75	2·50
	w. Wmk inverted	40·00	

*The 20s. and 30s. designs are perforated 14 at foot.

(Des The Sharper Image. Litho Security Printers (M), Malaysia)

1998 (11 Apr). Gold Coins. T **239** and similar horiz designs. Multicoloured. W **138**. P 13½ (20s., 50s., 1r.) or 14½ (30s.).

679	20s. Type **239**	25	15
	aw. Wmk inverted	2·25	
	b. Perf 14½	2·00	
	bw. Wmk inverted	6·00	
680	30s. Kupang from Kedah, 1661-1687	25	15
681	50s. Kupang from Johore, 1597-1615	45	35
	a. Perf 14½	3·25	
682	1r. Kijang from Kelantan, 1400-1780	60	1·50
679/82 *Set of 4*		1·40	1·90

240 Red Crescent Ambulance Boat and Emblem

241 Transit Train and Boeing 747-400 at Airport

(Des P. Chuah. Litho Security Printers (M), Malaysia)

1998 (8 May). 50th Anniv of Malaysian Red Crescent Society. T **240** and similar vert design. Multicoloured. W **138** (inverted on 1r.). P 13½.

683	30s. Type **240**	40	10
	a. Perf 14½	1·75	
684	1r. Ambulance and casualty	1·25	1·60
	a. Perf 14½	1·25	1·60
	aw. Wmk upright	12·00	

(Des P. Chuah. Litho Security Printers (M), Malaysia)

1998 (27 June). Opening of Kuala. Lumpur International Airport. T **241** and similar multicoloured designs, each showing control tower. W **138**. P 12.

685	30s. Type **241**	50	10
	a. Perf 12½	4·75	
686	50s. Airport Terminals	85	60
687	1r. Airliner in flight	1·75	2·25
	a. Perf 12½		
685/7 *Set of 3*		2·75	2·75
MS688	119×70 mm. 2r. Globe and control tower (22×32 *mm*). P 14½×14	2·25	2·75
	w. Wmk inverted	6·50	

242 Solanum torvum

243 Weightlifting

(Des The Sharper Image. Litho Security Printers (M), Malaysia)

1998 (18 July). Medicinal Plants. T **242** and similar vert designs. W **138**. P 13½ (20s., 30s.) or 14½ (50s., 1r.).

689	20s. Type **242**	20	15
690	30s. *Tinospora crispa*	25	10
691	50s. *Jatropha podagrica*	45	35
	a. P 13½		5·00
692	1r. *Hibiscus rosa-sinensis*	80	1·60
689/92 *Set of 4*		1·50	2·00

(Des P. Chuah. Litho Security Printers (M), Malaysia)

1998 (11 Sept). 16th Commonwealth Games, Kuala Lumpur, Malaysia (6th issue). Sports. T **243** and similar horiz designs. Multicoloured. W **138**. P 13½.

693	20s. Type **243**	35	40

	a. Sheetlet. Nos. 693/708	5·50	6·75
	b. Perf 14½	80	1·00
	ba. Sheetlet. Nos. 693b/708b	13·00	15·00
694	20s. Badminton	35	40
	b. Perf 14½	80	1·00
695	20s. Netball	35	40
	b. Perf 14½	80	1·00
696	20s. Shooting	35	40
	b. Perf 14½	80	1·00
697	30s. Men's hockey	40	45
	b. Perf 14½	95	1·10
698	30s. Women's hockey	40	45
	b. Perf 14½	95	1·10
699	30s. Cycling	40	45
	b. Perf 14½	95	1·10
700	30s. Bowls	40	45
	b. Perf 14½	95	1·10
701	50s. Gymnastics	40	45
	b. Perf 14½	95	1·10
702	50s. Cricket	40	45
	b. Perf 14½	95	1·10
703	50s. Rugby	40	45
	b. Perf 14½*	95	1·10
704	50s. Running	40	45
	b. Perf 14½*	95	1·10
705	1r. Swimming	40	55
	b. Perf 14½	95	1·10
706	1r. Squash	40	55
	b. Perf 14½	95	1·10
707	1r. Boxing	40	55
	b. Perf 14½*	95	1·10
708	1r. Ten-pin bowling	40	55
	b. Perf 14½*	95	1·10
693/708 *Set of* 16		5·50	6·75

*Nos. 703b/4b and 707b/8b, which occur on the bottom row of the sheetlet, are perforated 14 at foot. Nos. 693/708 were printed together, *se-tenant*, in sheetlets of 16 with the designs for each face value arranged as blocks of 4.

244 L.R.T. "Putra" Type Train

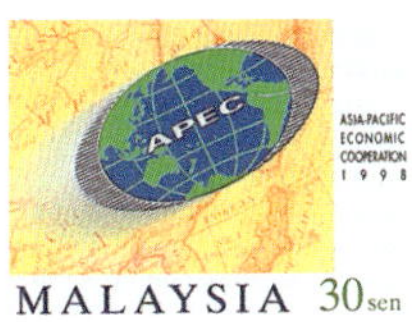

245 Globe and A.P.E.C. Logo

(Des P. Chuah. Litho Security Printers (M), Malaysia)

1998 (31 Oct). Modern Kuala Lumpur Rail Transport. T **244** and similar horiz designs. Multicoloured. W **138**. P 14½.

709	30s. Type **244**	3·25	
	aw. Wmk inverted	4·00	
	b. Perf 13½	65	15
	bw. Wmk inverted	2·75	
710	50s. LRT "Star" type train	1·50	40
	aw. Wmk inverted	4·25	
	b. Perf 13½	55	35
711	1r. KTM commuter train	75	1·50
709/11 *Set of* 3		1·75	1·75

(Des The Sharper Image. Litho Security Printers (M), Malaysia)

1998 (14 Nov). Asia-Pacific Economic Co-operation Conference. T **245** and similar horiz design. Multicoloured. W **138**. P 13½.

712	30s. Type **245**	2·50	10
	aw. Wmk inverted	3·00	
	b. Perf 14½	30	10
	bw. Wmk inverted	4·00	
713	1r. Business meeting and computer office	70	1·25
	b. Perf 14½	3·25	

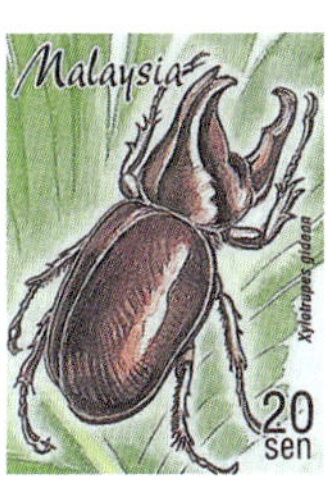

246 *Xylotrupes gideon*

247 Nural Hudda (Women's Air Rifle Shooting)

(Des P. Chuah. Litho Security Printers (M), Malaysia)

1998 (28 Nov). Stamp Week '98. Insects (2nd series). Sheet, 165×75 mm, containing T **246** and similar multicoloured designs. W **138** (sideways). P 12 (2r.) or 12½ (others).

MS714 20s. Type **246**; 30s. *Pomponia imperotoria*; 50s. *Phyllium pulchrifolium*; 2r. *Hymenopus coronatus* (43×27 mm); 2r. *Macrolyristes corporalis* (43×27 mm)	3·00	3·75
a. 50s. value perf 12 at foot	6·50	
b. 20, 30, 50s. values perf 12 at foot	5·50	
c. No wmk. 20s. value perf 12 at foot	7·50	

No. **MS**714 was also available as an imperforate uncut Press Sheet, containing four miniature sheets and sold for 40r.

(Des P. Chuah. Litho Security Printers (M), Malaysia)

1998 (12 Dec). 16th Commonwealth Games, Kuala Lumpur (7th issue). Malaysian Gold Medal Winners. Two miniature sheets, each 160×125 mm, containing multicoloured designs as T **247**. W **138** (sideways). P 14.

MS715 2r. Malaysian badminton team celebrating (128×80 mm)	3·50	4·00
a. Perf 14×15	9·50	
b. No wmk	14·00	
MS716 30s. Type **247**; 30s. Sapok Biki (48 kg Boxing); 30s. G Saravanan (50 km Walk); 30s. Muhamad Hidayat Hamidon (69 kg Weight lifting); 50s. Kenny Ang and Ben Heng (Tenpin Bowling Men's Doubles); 50s. Kenny Ang (Tenpin Bowling Men's Singles); 50s. Choong Tan Fook and Lee Wan Wah (Badminton Men's Doubles); 50s. Wong Choon Hann (Badminton Men's Singles); 1r. Women's Rhythmic Gymnastics team (63×26 mm)	6·00	7·50
a. Wmk upright	3·50	3·50
bw. Wmk inverted	13·00	
c. No wmk. 1r. perf 14½ at top	16·00	
ca. No wmk. Bottom row of stamps perf 14½ at foot	10·00	

Nos. **MS**715/16 were also available as imperforate uncut Press Sheets containing four of the normal items.

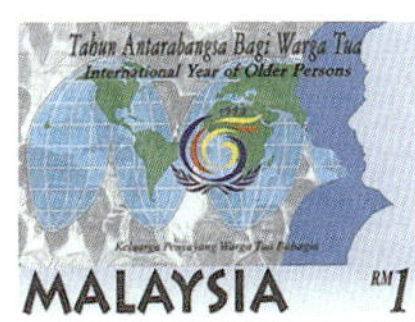

248 Profile of Elderly Couple, World Map and Emblem

249 *Syzygium malaccense*

(Des Bowline Communications. Litho Security Printers (M), Malaysia)

1999 (28 Jan). International Year of the Older Person. T **248** and similar horiz design. Multicoloured. W **138** (sideways). P 14½.

717	1r. Type **248**	70	1·00
718	1r. Four silhouettes of elderly people, world map and emblem	70	1·00

(Des P. Chuah. Litho Security Printers (M), Malaysia)

1999 (27 Feb). Rare Fruits of Malaysia (2nd series). T **249** and similar vert designs. P 12.

(a) W **138** (sideways)

719	20s. Type **249**	25	15
720	30s. *Garcinia prainiana*	30	15
721	50s. *Mangifera caesia*	40	30
722	1r. *Salacca glabrescens*	70	1·25
719/22 *Set of* 4		1·50	1·60

(b) W **138** (upright)

723	20s. Type **249**	20	25
	a. Horiz strip of 4. Nos. 723/6	1·40	1·75
	b. Perf 12½	30	35
	ba. Horiz strip of 4. Nos. 723b/6b*	2·00	2·40
724	30s. *Garcinia prainiana*	25	25
	b. Perf 12½	40	40
725	50s. *Mangifrea caesia*	40	50
	b. Perf 12½	60	70
726	1r. *Salacca glabrescens*	70	90
	b. Perf 12½	90	1·25
723/6 *Set of* 4		1·40	1·75

Horizontal strip No. 723ba shows the final stamp, No. 726b, perforated 12 at right. Nos. 719/22 come from sheets of 50, each of one value. Nos. 723/6 were printed together, *se-tenant*, as horizontal strips of 4 in sheets of 20.

250 Kucing Malaysia Cat

251 Sumatran Rhinoceros

(Des P. Chuah. Litho Security Printers (M), Malaysia)

1999 (1 Apr). Malaysian Cats. T **250** and similar vert designs. Multicoloured. W **138** (sideways*). P 12.

727	30s. Type **250**	30	15
728	50s. Siamese	45	35
729	1r. Abyssinian	80	1·25
	w. Wmk top of SPM to right	5·50	
727/9 *Set of 3*		1·40	1·60
MS730	Two sheets, each 81×90 mm. (a) 1r. British Shorthair; 1r. Scottish Fold. (b) 1r. Birman; 1r. Persian *Set of 2 sheets*	2·00	2·50

*The normal sideways watermark shows the top of SPM to left, *as seen from the back of the stamp.*

(Des P. Chuah. Litho Security Printers (M), Malaysia)

1999 (28 May). Protected Mammals of Malaysia (1st series). T **251** and similar horiz designs. Multicoloured.

(a) W **138**. P 12½

731	20s. Type **251**	50	15
732	30s. Panther	20	15
733	50s. Sun Bear	25	25
734	1r. Indian Elephant	65	1·00
	a. Perf 12½×12	—	8·50
731/4 *Set of 4*		1·40	1·40

(b) W **138** (sideways). P 12

735	20s. Type **251**	45	55
	a. Vert strip of 5. Nos. 735/9	4·50	4·75
736	30s. Panther	50	55
737	50s. Sun Bear	60	70
738	1r. Indian Elephant	1·00	1·40
739	2r. Orang-utan	1·50	2·00
735/9 *Set of 5*		3·50	4·75
MS740	119×80 mm. 2r. No. 739	1·50	2·00
	b. Perf 12		

Nos. 731/4 were printed in individual sheets of 50. Nos. 735/9 were printed together, *se-tenant*, as vertical strips of 5 in sheets of 20. *No. **MS**740a is perforated 12 at right and 12½ on the other three sides.

See also Nos. 922/32 and 1281/5.

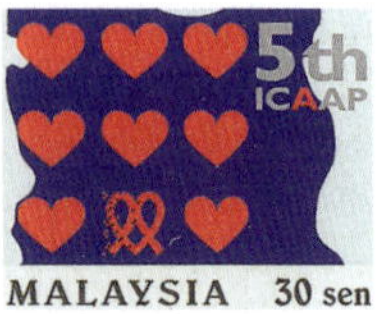

252 Hearts and AIDS - Ribbons

253 P. Ramlee in Traditional Dress

(Des Grey Malaysia. Litho Security Printers (M). Malaysia)

1999 (19 June). Fifth International Conference on AIDS in Asia. and the Pacific, Kuala Lumpur. T **252** and similar horiz designs. Each bright scarlet, bright ultramarine and black. W **138** (sideways). P 14½ (30s.) or 13½ (others).

741	30s. Type **252**	35	15
742	50s. Fragmenting and stylised AIDS ribbons	55	45
743	1r. Two AIDS ribbons	90	1·50
741/3 *Set of 3*		1·60	1·90

(Des Eka IPR Agensi. Litho Security Printers (M), Malaysia)

1999 (24 July). 70th Birth Anniv of P. Ramlee (actor and film director). T **253** and similar vert designs.

(a) Multicoloured. W **138**. P 13½

744	20s. Type **253**	55	15
745	30s. Receiving an award	65	15
746	50s. Playing part of soldier in film	85	55
747	1r. Using film camera	1·40	1·60
	a. Perf 14½	1·10	1·40
MS748	Two sheets, each 100×70 mm. (a) 1r. Wearing check shirt. (b) 1r. In traditional dress. Wmk sideways. P 14½ *Set of 2 sheets*	15·00	15·00
	a. Perf 13½ at left *Set of 2 sheets*	15·00	15·00

(b) Designs each orange-brown, yellow-ochre and black. W **138** (sideways). P 13½

749	30s. In traditional dress	1·25	1·40
	a. Strip of 4. Nos. 749/52	4·50	5·00
	b. Wmk upright	1·25	1·40
	ba. Strip of 4. Nos. 749/52b	4·50	5·00
750	30s. With hands raised	1·25	1·40
	b. Wmk upright	1·25	1·40
751	30s. Singing into microphone	1·25	1·40
	b. Wmk upright	1·25	1·40
752	30s. Wearing army uniform	1·25	1·40
	b. Wmk upright	1·25	1·40
744/7, 749/52 *Set of 8*		7·00	7·00

Nos. 744/7 were printed in individual sheets of 100.

Nos. 749/52b were printed together, *se-tenant*, as horizontal or vertical strips of four, in sheets of 16.

254 *Monochoria hastata* (water plant)

255 *Lagerstroemia floribunda* (tree)

(Des P. Chuah. Litho Security Printers (M), Malaysia)

1999 (31 July). Freshwater Fish (2nd series). T **254** and similar horiz designs. Multicoloured. W **138** (sideways). P 14*.

753	10s. Type **254**	20	30
	a. Vert pair. Nos. 753/4	40	60
	b. Wmk upright	30	40
	ba. Block of 10. Nos. 753b/62b	3·25	4·00
	c. Perf 13½×14		
	ca. Vert pair. Nos. 753c/4c		
	d. Perf 14¼×14¾		
	da. Vert pair. Nos. 753d/4d		
754	10s. *Trichopsis vittatus*	20	30
	b. Wmk upright	30	40
	c. Perf 13½×14		
	d. Perf 14¼×14¾		
755	15s. *Limnocharis flava* (water plant))	20	30
	a. Vert pair. Nos. 755/6	40	60
	b. Wmk upright	30	40
	c. Perf 13½×14		
	ca. Vert pair. Nos. 755c/6c		
	d. Perf 14¼×14¾		
	da. Vert pair. Nos. 755d/6d		
756	15s. *Betta imbellis*	20	30
	b. Wmk upright	30	40
	c. Perf 13½×14		
	d. Perf 14¼×14¾		
757	25s. *Nymphaea pubescens* (water plant)	30	40
	a. Vert pair. Nos. 757/8	60	80
	b. Wmk upright	30	40
	c. Perf 13½×14		
	ca. Vert pair. Nos. 757c/8c		
	d. Perf 14¼×14¾		
	da. Vert pair. Nos. 757d/8d		
758	25s. *Trichogaster trichopterus*	30	40
	b. Wmk upright	30	40
	c. Perf 13½×14		
	d. Perf 14¼×14¾		
759	50s. *Eichhornia crassipes* (water plant)	45	50
	a. Vert strip of 4. Nos. 759/60	1·60	1·75
	b. Wmk upright	45	50
	c. Perf 13½×14		
	ca. Vert strip of 4. Nos. 759c/60c		
	d. Perf 14¼×14¾		
	da. Vert strip of 4. Nos. 759d/60d		
760	50s. *Sphaerichthys osphromenoides*	45	50
	b. Wmk upright	45	50
	c. Perf 13½×14		
	d. Perf 14¼×14¾		
761	50s. *Ipomea aquatica* (water plant)	45	50
	b. Wmk upright	45	50
	c. Perf 13½×14		
	d. Perf 14¼×14¾		
762	50s. *Helostoma temmincki*	45	50
	b. Wmk upright	45	50

c. Perf 13½×14
d. Perf 14¼×14¾
753/62 *Set of* 10 — 3·00 3·50

*Examples of Nos. 754b, 756b, 758b, 760b and 762b from the bottom row of each pane of the sheets of 40 are perforated 14½ at foot.

For Nos. 753/62 the two designs of the 10, 15 and 25s. were printed together, *se-tenant*, as vertical pairs and those for the 50c. as a vertical strip of 4 in sheets of 50.

Nos. 753b/62b were printed together, *se-tenant*, as blocks of ten (5×2) from sheets of 40 containing two panes of 20 (5×4) with a horizontal gutter between. The gutter and sheet margins show a river scene.

No. 760 is inscribed "Sphaerichthys osphronemoides" in error.

(Des M. Chuah. Litho Security Printers (M), Malaysia)

1999 (14 Aug). Trees of Malaysia. T **255** and similar horiz designs. Multicoloured. W **138** (sideways). P 14×13½.

763 30s. Type **255** — 45 70
a. Booklet pane. Nos. 763/7, each×4 — 8·00
764 30s. *Elateriospermum tapos* — 45 70
765 30s. *Dryobalanops aromatics* — 45 70
766 30s. *Alstonia angustiloba* — 45 70
767 30s. *Fagraea fragrans* — 45 70
763/7 *Set of* 5 — 2·00 3·25

Nos. 763/7 were only available from 6r. stamp booklets.

256 Petronas Twin Towers, Kuala Lumpur

257 Peace Hotel and Rickshaw

(Des CBN Worldwide. Litho Southern Colour Print, Dunedin (Nos. 768/70) or Walsall (No. **MS**771))

1999 (30 Aug). Completion of Petronas Twin Towers Building, Kuala Lumpur. T **256** and similar vert designs. Multicoloured (except 50s.). P 14.

768 30s. Type **256** — 35 15
769 50s. Construction sketches (light violet blue, violet and black) — 45 40
770 1r. Twin Towers at night — 80 1·25
768/70 *Set of* 3 — 1·40 1·60
MS771 100×75 mm. 5r. Hologram of Twin Towers (30×50 mm). P 14½×14 — 4·00 4·50

No. **MS**771 also exists imperforate from a limited printing.

(Des P. Chuah. Litho Security Printers (M), Malaysia)

1999 (1 Sept). 125th Anniv of Taiping Perak. T **257** and similar horiz designs. Multicoloured. P 12.

772 20s. Type **257** — 30 15
773 30s. Town Hall and 1930s car — 30 15
774 50s. Railway Station — 1·25 65
775 1r. Airport — 1·50 1·75
772/5 *Set of* 4 — 3·00 2·40
MS776 120×69 mm. 2r. Perak Museum and horse-drawn carriage — 4·50 5·00

258 Power Station at Night

259 New National Theatre and Traditional Characters

(Des Eka IPR Agensi. Litho Security Printers (M), Malaysia)

1999 (9 Sept). 50th Anniv of Tenaga Nasional Berhad (electricity generating company). T **258** and similar multicoloured designs. P 14×14½.

777 30s. Type **258** — 35 15
778 50s. Control room and pylon — 50 35
779 1r. Kuala Lumpur skyline at night — 90 1·50
777/9 *Set of* 3 — 1·60 1·75
MS780 69×99 mm. 1r. Electric cart. P 14½ — 2·00 2·50
MS780*a* 69×99 mm. 1r. Pylon. P 13½
b. Perf 14, 13½ at right — 10·00

(Des P. Chuah. Litho Security Printers (M), Malaysia)

1999 (15 Sept). Opening of New National Theatre, Kuala Lumpur. T **259** and similar vert designs. Multicoloured. W **138** (sideways). P 12.

781 30s. Type **259** — 30 15
782 50s. New National Theatre and horseman — 55 40
783 1r. New National Theatre and traditional musician — 90 1·25
781/3 *Set of* 3 — 1·60 1·60

260 New Yang di-Pertuan Agong and Malaysian Flag

(Des P. Chuah. Litho Security Printers (M), Malaysia)

1999 (23 Sept). Installation of Sultan Salahuddin Abdul Aziz Shah of Selangor as Yang di-Pertuan Agong.

(a) Horiz designs as T **260**. Multicoloured. W **138** (sideways). P 13½ (30s.) or 14×14½ (others).

784 30s. Type **260** — 30 15
w. Wmk top of SPM to right — 12·00
785 50s. Yang di-Pertuan Agong and Palace — 45 30
786 1r. Yang di-Pertuan Agong and Parliament Buildings — 90 1·25
784/6 *Set of* 3 — 1·50 1·50

(b) Vert designs, 24×29 mm, showing portrait only. W **138**. P 14.

787 (30s.) muticoloured (purple frame) — 75 90
aw. Wmk inverted
b. Strip of 3. Nos. 787/9 — 2·00 2·40
bw. Wmk inverted (strip of 3)
788 (30s.) multicoloured (yellow frame) — 75 90
aw. Wmk inverted
789 (30s.) multicoloured (blue frame) — 75 90
aw. Wmk inverted
787/9 *Set of* 3 — 2·00 2·40

The normal sideways watermark on Nos. 784/6 has the top of the letters SPM pointing to the left *as seen from the back of the stamp*.

Nos. 787/9 are inscribed "BAYARAN POS TEMPATAN HINGGA 20GM" and were valid on local mail weighing no more than 20 gm. They were printed together, *se-tenant*, as strips of three in sheets of 21 (7×3) with enlarged illustrated and inscribed right and bottom margins.

261 Motorway Junction outside Kuala Lumpur

(Des Eka IPR Agensi. Litho Security Printers (M), Malaysia)

1999 (3 Oct). 21st World Road Congress, Kuala Lumpur. T **261** and similar horiz designs. Multicoloured. P 12.

790 30s. Type **261** — 35 15
791 50s. Damansara Puchong Bridge at night — 50 30
792 1r. Aerial view of motorway junction, Selatan — 90 1·25
790/2 *Set of* 3 — 1·60 1·50

262 Driver's Helmet and Canopy Tower, Formula 1 Circuit, Sepang

(Des P. Chuah. Litho Security Printers (M), Malaysia)

1999 (17 Oct). Malaysian Grand Prix, Sepang. T **262** and similar horiz designs. Multicoloured. No wmk.

(a) Designs including driver's helmet. P 12.

793	20s. Type **262**	40	20
	a. Wmk W **138**	9·00	
794	30s. Central Grandstand	50	20
795	50s. Formula 1 racing car	75	50
796	1r. Formula 1 racing car from Red Bull team	1·25	1·50
793/6 *Set of 4*		2·50	2·25

(b) Scenes from Sepang Formula 1 Circuit. P 12½.

797	20s. Canopy Tower and Central Grand stand	40	50
	a. Strip of 4. Nos. 797/800	2·40	3·00
	b. Wmk W **138** sideways		
	ba. Strip of 4. Nos. 797b/800b		
798	30s. Pit Building	50	50
	b. Wmk W **138** sideways		
799	50s. Wheel-change in pits	75	90
	b. Wmk W **138** sideways		
800	1r. Race in progress	1·25	1·40
	b. Wmk W **138** sideways		
797/800 *Set of 4*		2·50	3·00

Nos. 797/800 were printed together, *se-tenant*, both horizontally and vertically in sheets of 16 (4×4) with illustrated margins. They also exist imperforate from a limited printing.

263 Sultan Haji Abroad Shah and Rowers

264 World Cup

(Des Eka IPR Agensi. Litho Security Printers (M), Malaysia)

1999 (23 Oct). 25th Anniv of Installation of Sultan of Pahang. T **263** and similar horiz designs. Multicoloured. W **138** (sideways). P 14.

801	30s. Type **263**	55	60
	a. Horiz strip of 5. Nos. 801/5	2·50	2·75
	aw. Wmk top of SPM to right	3·25	
	awa. Horiz strip of 5. Nos. 801aw/5aw	15·00	
	b. Perf 13½	2·75	
	ba. Horiz strip of 5. Nos. 801b/5b	12·00	
802	30s. Butterfly and motorway	55	60
	aw. Wmk top of SPM to right	3·25	
	b. Perf 13½	2·75	
803	30s. Diver and beach	55	60
	aw. Wmk top of SPM to right	3·25	
	b. Perf 13½	2·75	
804	30s. Power station	55	60
	aw. Wmk top of SPM to right	3·25	
	b. Perf 13½	2·75	
805	30s. Mosque	55	60
	aw. Wmk top of SPM to right	3·25	
	b. Perf 13½	2·75	
801/5 *Set of 5*		2·50	2·75

The normal watermark on Nos. 801/5 and 801b/5b shows the tops of SPM pointing to the left *as seen from the back of the stamp.*

Nos. 801/5 were printed together, *se-tenant,* in horizontal strips of 5 throughout the sheet.

(Des P. Chuah. Litho Security Printers (M), Malaysia)

1999 (18 Nov). World Cup Golf Championship, Mines Resort City. T **264** and similar horiz designs. Multicoloured. P 14 (with one elliptical hole on each horizontal side).

(a) W **138** (sideways*) (from sheets of 100)

806	20s. Type **264**	35	15
807	30s. Emblem on golf ball	35	15
	w. Wmk top of SPM to right	13·00	
808	50s. Fairway	60	45
	w. Wmk top of SPM to right	13·00	
809	1r. First hole and club house	1·10	1·40
806/9 *Set of 4*		2·25	1·90

(b) *W* **138** (upright) (from *se-tenant* sheets of 20).

810	20s. Type **264**	50	50
	a. Vert strip of 4. Nos. 810/13	2·40	2·50
	aw. Wmk inverted	20·00	
	b. Perf 13 at right		
	ba. Vert strip of 4. Nos. 810b/13b		
811	30s. Emblem on golf ball	50	50
	b. Perf 13 at right		
812	50s. Fairway	70	80
	b. Perf 13 at right		
813	1r. First hole and club house	1·00	1·10
	b. Perf 13 at right		
810/13 *Set of 4*		2·40	2·50

*The normal sideways watermark shows the top of SPM to left, *as seen from the back of the stamp.*

Nos. 810/13 were printed in *se-tenant* sheets of 20 (5×4), with enlarged illustrated margins, containing five examples of No. 810a. No. 810ba occurs in the final vertical column of some sheets only.

A 2r. miniature sheet was only available as part of a limited edition album costing 25r.

265 *Strelitzia augusta*

266 Letters and Computer Screen

(Litho Security Printers (M), Malaysia)

1999 (29 Nov). Stamp Week '99. Heliconias. T **265** and similar vert designs. Multicoloured. W **138** (sideways). P 12.

814	30s. Type **265**	55	55
	a. Block or horiz strip of 10. Nos. 814/23	5·00	5·00
815	30s. *Heliconia rostrata*	55	55
816	30s. *Heliconia psittacorum* (yellow)	55	55
817	30s. *Heliconia stricta*	55	55
818	30s. *Musa violascens*	55	55
819	30s. *Strelitzia reginae*	55	55
820	30s. *Heliconia colganta*	55	55
821	30s. *Heliconia psittacorum* (white and pink)	55	55
822	30s. *Heliconia latispatha*	55	55
823	30s. *Phaeomeria speciosa*	55	55
814/23 *Set of 10*		5·00	5·00
MS824 198×136 mm. Nos. 814/23		5·00	5·50

Nos. 814/23 were printed in sheets of 50, containing four *se-tenant* blocks of 10 (5×2) and one horizontal strip of 10.

No. **MS**824 was printed in vertical pairs with a row of perforations, measuring 12 or 10½, between them.

(Des The Sharper Image. Litho Security Printers (M), Malaysia)

1999 (18 Dec). 125th Anniv of Universal Postal Union. T **266** and similar horiz designs. Multicoloured. W **138** (sideways). P 13½ (20, 30c.) or 14×14½ (others).

825	20s. Type **266**	20	10
826	30s. Globe and Malaysian stamps	40	10
	a. Perf 14	5·00	
827	50s. World map and mail plane	1·00	70
828	1r. POS Malaysia emblem	1·25	1·60
825/8 *Set of 4*		2·50	2·50

267 Fern, Pitcher Plant and Hornbill

(Des P. Chuah. Litho Security Printers (M), Malaysia)

1999 (31 Dec). New Millennium (1st issue). Land and History. T **267** and similar designs. Multicoloured (except No. **MS**839). W **138** (sideways). P 12½.

829	30s. Type **267**	50	60
	a. Block or horiz strip of 10. Nos. 829/38	4·50	5·50
	ab. Block of 10. Nos. 829/33 and 834b/8b	5·00	6·00
830	30s. Ceramic pots and Mt. Kinabalu	50	60
831	30s. Frog and Tualang (tree)	50	60
832	30s. Rolling rubber and palm trees	50	60
833	30s. Angelfish and sailing barge	50	60
834	30s. Mousedeer and traditional Malay building	50	60
	b. Perf 12 at foot	60	75
835	30s. Ruler on elephant and Straits of Malacca	50	60
	b. Perf 12 at foot	60	75
836	30s. Malay kris (sword) and junks	50	60
	b. Perf 12 at foot	60	75
837	30s. Clock Tower, Kuala Lumpur, and A Famosa ruins	50	60
	b. Perf 12 at foot	60	75
838	30s. Sailing boat and palm trees	50	60
	b. Perf 12 at foot	60	75
829/38 *Set of* 10		4·50	5·50
MS839	120×80 mm. 1r. Traditional Malay sailing ship (horiz) (black & scarlet). Wmk upright	2·50	2·75
	a. Perf 12 at right	5·00	
	w. Wmk inverted	13·00	
	wa. Perf 12 at right	15·00	

Nos. 829/38 were printed either in sheets of 50 containing four *se-tenant* blocks of 10 (5×2) and one horizontal strip of 10, or in sheets of 20 (5×4), with enlarged illustrated margins, containing two *se-tenant* blocks. The stamps from the bottom row of the sheetlet of 20 are perforated 12 at foot.

(Des P. Chuah. Litho Security Printers (M), Malaysia)

2000 (1 Jan). New Millennium (2nd issue). People and Achievements. Multicoloured designs as T **267**. W **138** (sideways). P 12½.

840	30s. Iban playing sape and traditional costumes from East Malaysia	60	60
	a. Block or horiz strip of 10. Nos. 840/9	5·50	5·50
	ab. Block of 10. Nos. 840/4 and 845b/9b	6·00	6·50
841	30s. Hurricane lamp, shell and couple from fishing village	60	60
842	30s. Doctor with patient and toddler with mother	60	60
843	30s. Badminton player and young Malaysians	60	60
844	30s. Man with kite and traditional dancers	60	60
845	30s. Motor cycle, car and motorway	60	60
	b. Perf 12 at foot	70	85
846	30s. Butterfly, Sepang motor racing circuit and airport	60	60
	b. Perf 12 at foot	70	85
847	30s. High speed train and Kuala Lumpur skyline	60	60
	b. Perf 12 at foot	70	85
848	30s. Computer operator and mosque	60	60
	b. Perf 12 at foot	70	85
849	30s. Lorry and container port	60	60
	b. Perf 12 at foot	70	85
840/9 *Set of* 10		5·50	5·50
MS850	120×80 mm. 1r. Modern airliner (horiz). Wmk upright	2·50	2·75
	w. Wmk inverted	17·00	

Nos. 840/9 were printed in a similar sheet format to Nos. 829/38.
MS850 is known imperforate.

268 Pottery Vase (New Stone Age)

(Des P. Chuah. Litho Security Printers (M), Malaysia)

2000 (6 Jan). Chinese New Year. Year of the Dragon. Artefacts and Fish. T **268** and similar multicoloured designs. W **138** (sideways). P 13.

851	30s. Type **268**	60	60
	a. Diagonal strip of 5. Nos. 851/5	2·75	2·75
	b. Block of 10. Nos. 851/60	5·50	5·50
	c. Perf 14 at lower left	65	75
	ca. Diagonal strip of 5. Nos. 851c/5c	3·00	3·25
	d. Perf 14½ at lower left		
852	30s. Dragon eaves tile (Western Han Dynasty)	60	60
	c. Perf 14 at lower left	65	75
	d. Perf 14½ at lower left		
853	30s. Bronze knocker base (Tang Dynasty)	60	60
	c. Perf 14 at lower left	65	75
	d. Perf 14½ at lower left		
854	30s. Jade sword pommel (Western Han Dynasty)	60	60
	c. Perf 14 at lower left	64	75
	d. Perf 14½ at lower left		
855	30s. Dragon statue (Tang Dynasty)	60	60
	c. Perf 14 at lower left	65	75
	d. Perf 14½ at lower left		
856	30s. Arawana (*Osteoglossum bicirrhosum*)	60	60
	a. Diagonal strip of 5. Nos. 856/60	2·75	2·75
	c. Perf 14 at lower left	65	75
	ca. Diagonal strip of 5. Nos. 856c/60c	3·00	3·25
	d. Perf 14½ at lower left		
	e. Perf 12 at lower left		
857	30s. Spotted Barramundi (*Scleropages leichardti*)	60	60
	c. Perf 14 at lower left	65	75
	d. Perf 14½ at lower left		
	e. Perf 12 at lower left		
858	30s. Asian Bonytongue (red) (*Scleropages formosus*)	60	60
	c. Perf 14 at lower left	65	75
	d. Perf 14½ at lower left		
	e. Perf 12 at lower left		
859	30s. Black Arawana (*Osteoglossum ferrerirai*)	60	60
	c. Perf 14 at lower left	65	75
	d. Perf 14½ at lower left		
	e. Perf 12 at lower left		
860	30s. Asian Bonytongue (gold) (*Scleropages formosus*)	60	60
	c. Perf 14 at lower left	65	75
	d. Perf 14½ at lower left		
	e. Perf 12 at lower left		
851/60 *Set of* 10		5·50	5·50
MS861	Two sheets, each 120×65 mm. (a) 1r. Dragon dance (*square*). (b) 1r. Dragon boat (*square*). Wmk upright *Set of* 2 sheets	2·25	3·00

Nos. 851/60 were printed together in sheets of 50, containing either *se-tenant* strips of five or *se-tenant* blocks of ten (5×2), or in sheets of 20 containing either Nos. 851/5 or 856/60. On these sheets the bottom line of perforations is either 14, 14½ or 12 (fish designs only).

269 Table Tennis Bats and Globe

270 Malaysian Climbers on Mt Everest

(Des Eka IPR Agensi. Litho Security Printers (M), Malaysia)

2000 (19 Feb). World Table Tennis Championships, Bukit Jalil. T **269** and similar horiz designs. Multicoloured. W **138** (sideways). P 13½.

862	30s. Type **269**	25	10
	a. Perf 14	8·00	
863	50s. Mascot and logo	45	35
	a. Perf 14	12·00	
864	1r. Table tennis bats and ball	75	1·10
862/4 *Set of* 3		1·25	1·40
MS865	100×70 mm. 1r. Mascot and table tennis table; 1r. Bats and table tennis table. Wmk upright. P 14	1·25	1·75

(Litho Security Printers (M), Malaysia)

2000 (26 Feb). New Millennium (3rd issue). Malaysian Triumphs. Two sheets, each 120×80 mm, containing T **270** and similar vert designs. Multicoloured. W **138**. P 12.

MS866	(a) 50s. Type **270**; 50s. Hikers; 50s. Arctic expedition and Proton car. (b) 50s. Solo yachtsman *Set of* 2 sheets	3·25	3·50

271 Outline Hand on Button

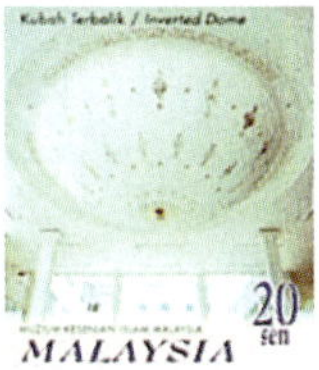

272 Internal Inverted Dome

(Des P. Chuah. Litho Security Printers (M), Malaysia)

2000 (7 Mar). Second Global Knowledge Conference, Kuala Lumpur. T **271** and similar vert designs. Multicoloured. W **138**. P 13½ (30s.) or 14 (50s.).

867 30s. Type **271** ... 55 60
a. Pair. Nos. 867/8 plus label ... 1·10 1·10
b. Perf 14 ... 5·00
ba. Pair. Nos. 867b/8b plus label ... 10·00
868 30s. Outline Globe ... 55 60
b. Perf 14 ... 5·00
869 50s. Woman's silhouette ... 80 90
a. Pair. Nos. 869/70 plus label ... 1·60 1·75
b. Perf 13½ ... 7·00
ba. Pair. Nos. 869b/70b plus label ... 14·00
870 50s. Man's silhouette ... 80 90
b. Perf 13½ ... 7·00
867/70 *Set of 4* ... 1·40 1·60

Nos. 867/8 and 869/70 were each printed together, *se-tenant*, in sheets containing 20 stamps and 10 stamp-size labels showing the Conference logo. The first design for each value occurs in the first and fourth vertical rows, the second design in the third and sixth, with labels in rows two and five.

Two types of 30c.:
I. "30 sen" 5½ mm. high. Thin white outline round figures, central ornament in gold with black inlay (sheets of 100).
II. "30 sen" 6½ mm. high. Thick white outline round figures, central ornament in gold only (sheets of 20).

(Des Eka IPR Agensi. Litho Security Printers (M), Malaysia)

2000 (6 Apr). Islamic Arts Museum, Kuala Lumpur. T **272** and similar vert designs. Multicoloured. W **138**. P 14×13½ (with one elliptical hole on each vertical side).

871 20s. Type **272** ... 40 15
872 30s. Main dome of Museum (I) ... 45 15
a. Type II ... 35 35
873 50s. Ottoman panel ... 65 45
w. Wmk inverted ...
874 1r. Ornate Mihrab ... 1·25 1·75
871/4 *Set of 4* ... 2·40 2·25

Nos. 871/4 were printed in sheets of 100. In addition the 30s. (No. 872a) comes from sheets of 20 containing two blocks of 10 (5×2) separated by an illustrated and inscribed gutter. This sheet format also exists imperforate from a limited printing.

273 Buatan Beret Prahu

274 Unit Trust Emblem and Women with Flags

(Des Eka IPR Agensi. Litho Security Printers (M), Malaysia)

2000 (15 Apr). Traditional Malaysian Prahus (canoes). T **273** and similar horiz designs. Multicoloured. W **138** (sideways). P 14×13½.

875 30s. Type **273** ... 35 45
a. Booklet pane. Nos. 875/8, each×5 ... 6·25
876 30s. Payang prahu (red and blue hull) ... 35 45
877 30s. Payang prahu (red, white and green hull) ... 35 45
878 30s. Burung prahu ... 35 45
875/8 *Set of 4* ... 1·25 1·60

Nos. 875/8 were only issued in 6r. stamp booklets.

(Des Orient Communications. Litho Security Printers (M), Malaysia)

2000 (20 Apr). Unit Trust Week. T **274** and similar vert designs. Multicoloured. No wmk. P 13½.

879 30s. Type **274** ... 50 10
a. Perf 14 ...
880 50s. City skyline and Malaysians in traditional costume ... 70 50
a. Perf 14 ... 7·00
881 1r. Map of South-east Asia and Malaysians in traditional costume ... 1·40 1·75
879/81 *Set of 3* ... 2·40 2·10

275 Badminton Player and Cup Logo

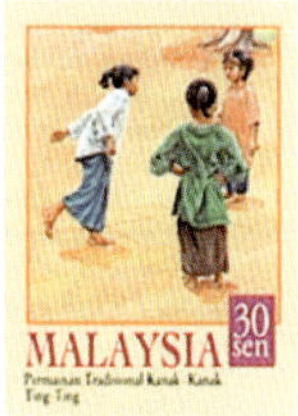

276 Children playing Ting Ting

(Des P. Chuah. Litho Security Printers (M), Malaysia)

2000 (11 May). Thomas Cup Badminton Championships, Bukit Jalil. T **275** and similar multicoloured designs. W **138**. P 12½.

882 30s. Type **275** ... 60 60
a. Horiz strip of 5. Nos. 887/6 ... 2·75 2·75
b. Perf 12 ... 3·25
ba. Horiz strip of 5. Nos. 882b/6b ... 15·00
883 30s. Thomas Cup and flags ... 60 60
b. Perf 12 ... 3·25
884 30s. Championship logo and mascot ... 60 60
b. Perf 12 ... 3·25
885 30s. Uber Cup and flags ... 60 60
b. Perf 12 ... 3·25
886 30s. Badminton player and mascot ... 60 60
b. Perf 12 ... 3·25
882/6 *Set of 5* ... 2·75 2·75
MS887 120×80 mm. 1r. Thomas Cup (vert). Wmk sideways. P 12½ (12 at foot) ... 1·75 2·25
a. Perf 12 ...

Nos. 882/6 were printed together, *se-tenant*, in sheets of 50 (10×5) with enlarged illustrated and inscribed right-hand margin. They also exist imperforate from a limited printing.

(Des Ad Integrated. Litho Security Printers (M), Malaysia)

2000 (24 June). Children's Traditional Games (1st series). T **276** and similar vert designs. Multicoloured. P 13½.

(a) *W* **138** (upright) (from sheets of 50 (5×10))

888 30s. Type **276** ... 80 80
a. Horiz strip of 5. Nos. 888/92 ... 3·50 3·50
b. Perf 14½ ...
ba. Horiz strip of 5. Nos. 888b/92b ...
889 30s. Tarik Upih ... 80 80
b. Perf 14½ ...
890 30s. Kite flying ... 80 80
b. Perf 14½ ...
891 30s. Marbles ... 80 80
b. Perf 14½ ...
892 30s. Bicycle rim racing ... 80 80
b. Perf 14½ ...
888/92 *Set of 5* ... 3·50 3·50

(b) *W* **138** (sideways) (from sheets of 20 (5x4) with enlarged illustrated margins)

893 30s. Type **276** ... 80 80
a. Horiz strip of 5. Nos. 893/7 ... 3·50 3·50
b. Perf 14¼ ... 1·75
ba. Horiz strip of 5. Nos. 893b/7b ... 8·00
c. Perf 14¼, 14 at foot ... 2·10
ca. Horiz strip of 5. Nos. 893c/7c ... 9·50
d. Perf 14¼, 13½ at foot ... 2·10
da. Horiz strip of 5. Nos. 893d/7d ... 9·50
894 30s. Tarik Upih ... 80 80
b. Perf 14¼ ... 1·75
c. Perf 14¼, 14 at foot ... 2·10
d. Perf 14¼, 13½ at foot ... 2·10
895 30s. Kite flying ... 80 80
b. Perf 14¼ ... 1·75
c. Perf 14¼, 14 at foot ... 2·10
d. Perf 14¼, 13½ at foot ... 2·10
896 30s. Marbles ... 80 80
b. Perf 14¼ ... 1·75
c. Perf 14¼, 14 at foot ... 2·10
d. Perf 14¼, 13½ at foot ... 2·10
897 30s. Bicycle rim racing ... 80 80
b. Perf 14¼ ... 1·75
c. Perf 14¼, 14 at foot ... 2·10
d. Perf 14¼, 13½ at foot ... 2·10
893/7 *Set of 5* ... 3·50 3·50

The stamps listed as being perf 14¼ are exactly 14.2. This perforation is described as perf 14 elsewhere in this listing but is differentiated here because the perforation at the foot of No. 893c etc is exactly 14.

Nos. 888/92 and 893/7 were each printed together, *se-tenant*, in horizontal strips of five.

See also Nos. 936/9.

277 Aspects of Computer Technology

(Des Eka IPR Agensi. Litho Security Printers (M), Malaysia)

2000 (26 June). 27th Islamic Foreign Ministers' Conference, Kuala Lumpur. T **277** and similar horiz designs. Multicoloured. W **138** (sideways). P 13½.

898 30s. Type **277** 55 60
a. Horiz strip of 5. Nos. 898/902 .... 2·50 2·75
899 30s. Traditonal Islamic scrollwork 55 60
900 30s. Conference logo 55 60
901 30s. Early coin 55 60
902 30s. Pens and satellite photograph 55 60
898/902 *Set of 5* .... 2·50 2·75

Nos. 898/902 were printed together, *se-tenant*, as horizontal strips of five in sheets of 100. Sheets of 50 imperforate exist from a limited printing with watermark either upright or sideways.

278 Malaysian Family on Map

(Des Eka IPR Agensi. Litho Security Printers (M), Malaysia)

2000 (5 July). Population and Housing Census. T **278** and similar horiz designs. Multicoloured. W **138** (sideways). P 14½.

903 30s. Type **278** 55 60
a. Horiz strip of 5. Nos. 903/7 .... 2·50 2·75
b. Perf 13½ .... 2·75
ba. Horiz strip of 5. Nos. 903b/7b .... 12·00
904 30s. Symbolic house 55 60
b. Perf 13½ .... 2·75
905 30s. Pea on pie chart 55 60
b. Perf 13½ .... 2·75
906 30s. Diplomas and workers 55 60
b. Perf 13½ .... 2·75
907 30s. Male and female symbols 55 60
b. Perf 13½ .... 2·75
903/7 *Set of 5* .... 2·50 2·75

Nos. 903/7 were printed together, *se-tenant*, in horizontal strips of five from sheets of 100. Sheets of 50 imperforate exist from a limited printing with watermark either upright or sideways.

279 Rothschild's Peacock-Pheasant

280 *Hopea odorata* (fruit)

(Des Eka IPR Agensi. Litho Security Printers (M), Malaysia)

2000 (22 July). Pheasants and Partridges. T **279** and similar multicoloured designs. W **138**. P 13.

908 20s. Type **279** 40 20
w. Wmk inverted .... 25·00
909 30s. Crested Argus (*Rheinartia ocellata*) (female) 45 20
a. No wmk ....
910 50s. Great Argue Pheasant (*Argusianus argus*) 65 50
911 1r. Crestless Fireback Pheasant (*Lophura erythropthalma*) .... 1·10 1·50
908/11 *Set of 4* .... 2·40 2·25

MS912 100×40 mm. 2r. Crested Argus (male) (31×26 mm). Wmk sideways. P 13½×14 .... 2·00 2·75

In addition to normal sheets of 100, the 30s. was also available in sheets of 20 with the stamps arranged as a frame around a label showing a male Great Argus. This format also exists imperforate from a limited printing.

No. 909 is inscribed "Rheinardia" and No. 910 "Argisianus", both in error.

(Des P. Chuah. Litho Security Printers (M), Malaysia)

2000 (7 Aug). International Union of Forestry Research Organisations Conference, Kuala Lumpur. T **280** and similar vert designs. Multicoloured. W **138**. P 12.

913 30s. Type **280** 75 75
a. Horiz strip of 5. No 913/17 .... 3·25 3·25
914 30s. *Adenanthera pavonina* (seeds) 75 75
915 30s. *Shorea macrophylla* (seeds) 75 75
916 30s. *Dyera costulata* (fruits) 75 75
917 30s. *Alstonia angustiloba* (seeds) 75 75
913/17 *Set of 5* .... 3·25 3·25

MS918 Four sheets each 92×71 mm. (a) Trees. 10s. *Fagraea fragrans*; 10s. *Dryobalanops aromatica*; 10s. *Terminalia catappa*; 10s. *Samanea saman*; 10s. *Dracontomelon dao*. (b) Leaves. 15s. *Heritiera javanica*; 15s. *Johannesteijsmannia. altifrons*; 15s. *Macaranga gigantea*; 15s. *Licuala grandis*; 15s. *Endospermum diadenum*. (c). Bark. 25s. *Pterocymbium javanicum*; 25s. *Dryobalanops aromatica*; 25s. *Dipterocarpus costulatus*; 25s. *Shorea leprosula*; 25s. *Ochanostachys amentacea* (d) Forest fauna. 50s. Indigo Flycatcher; 50s. Slow Loris; 50s. Marbled cat; 50s. Common Carp; 50s. Pit Viper. P 12×11½ *Set of 4 sheets* .... 6·50 7·50

Nos. 913/17 were printed together, *se-tenant*, in horizontal strips of five. No. **MS**918 contains four sheets each of five 18×22 mm designs, and a label showing the Conference logo. Nos. 913/17 exist imperforate from a limited printing.

281 Institute in 1901, Brugia malayi and Beri-Beri

282 Otter Civet

(Des The Sharper Image. Litho Security Printers (M), Malaysia)

2000 (24 Aug). Centenary of Institute for Medical Research. T **281** and similar horiz designs. Multicoloured. No wmk. P 13½ (30s.) or 14 (others).

919 30s. Type **281** 60 10
920 50s. Institute in 1953, bacteria and mosquito 85 60
921 1r. Institute in 1976, chromatogram and Eurycoma longifolia .... 1·75 2·00
919/21 *Set of 3* .... 3·00 2·40

MS922 120×65 mm. 2r. DNA molecule. W **138**. P 14½ .... 2·75 3·00

The 30s. also exists imperforate from a limited printing.

(Des P. Chuah. Litho Security Printers (M), Malaysia)

2000 (26 Aug). Protected Mammals of Malaysia (2nd series). T **282** and similar square designs. Multicoloured. P 13.

(a) W **138** (sideways*) (from sheets of 50)

923 20s. Type **282** 60 25
924 30s. Young Otter Civet 60 30
w. Wmk top of letters to right ....
925 50s. Binturong on bank 75 50
926 1r. Head of Binturong .... 1·40 1·60

(b) W **138** (upright) (from sheets of 20 (5×4) with illustrated margins).

927 30s. Hose's Palm Civet (*Hemigalus hosei*) 60 70
a. Horiz strip of 5. Nos. 927/31 .... 2·75 3·25
928 30s. Common Palm Civet (*Paradoxurus hermaphroditus*) 60 70
929 30s. Masked Palm Civet (*Paguma larvata*) 60 70
930 30s. Malay Civet (*Viverra tangalunga*) 60 70
931 30s. Three-striped Palm Civet (*Arctogalidia trivirgata*) 60 70
923/31 *Set of 9* .... 2·75 3·25

MS932 140×80 mm. 1r. Banded Palm Civet; 1r. Banded Linsang. Wmk sideways .... 2·75 3·00
a. Wmk top of SPM to right .... 23·00

*The normal sideways watermark on Nos. 923/**MS**932 shows top of letters to left, *as seen from the back of the stamp*. Nos. 927/31 were printed together, *se-tenant*, in horizontal strips of 5. They also exist imperforate from a limited printing.

283 Cogwheels

284 Cyclist and Pedestrians

(Des Eka IPR Agensi. Litho Security Printers (M), Malaysia)

2000 (14 Sept). 50th Anniv of RIDA-MARA (Rural and Industrial Development Authority - Council for Indigenous People). T **283** and similar horiz designs. Multicoloured. W **138** (sideways). P 14.

933 30s. Type **283** 40 10
a. Perf 13½ at foot 1·50 1·75
b. Perf 13½ 40 40
ba. Perf 13½ (14 at foot) 1·50 1·75
934 50s. Compasses and stethoscope 55 40
935 1r. Computer disk, book and mouse 1·00 1·40
933/5 *Set of 3* 1·75 1·60

In addition to normal sheets of 100, the 30s. was also available in sheets of 20 with the stamps arranged as a frame around a bi-lingual label commemorating the anniversary. This format also exists imperforate from a limited printing The sheet of 20 contains eight stamps perforated 14 (Rows 3 to 6), two perforated 14 on three sides, but 13½ at foot (Row 7), eight perforated 13½ (Rows 1 and 8) and two perforated 13½ on three sides, but 14 at foot.

(Des Ad Integrated. Litho Security Printers (M), Malaysia)

2000 (16 Sept). Children's Traditional Games (2nd series). Multicoloured designs as T **276**, but horiz. W **138** (sideways). P 13½.

936 20s. Bailing Tin 50 60
a. Horiz pair. Nos. 936/7 1·00 1·10
b. Perf 14½
ba. Horiz pair. Nos. 936b/7b
c. Perf 14 6·00
ca. Horiz pair. Nos. 936c/7c 12·00
937 20s. Top-spinning 50 60
b. Perf 14½
c. Perf 14 6·00
938 30s. Sepak Raga 60 70
a. Horiz pair. Nos. 938/9 1·10 1·40
939 30s. Letup-Letup 60 70
936/9 *Set of 4* 2·00 2·40

Nos. 936/7 and 938/9 were each printed together, as horizontal *se-tenant* pairs throughout the sheets.

(Des Orient Communications. Litho Security Printers (M), Malaysia)

2000 (24 Sept). World Heart Day. T **284** and similar vert designs. Multicoloured. W **138** (sideways). P 12.

940 30s. Type **284** 60 60
a. Horiz strip of 5. Nos. 940/4 2·75 2·75
941 30s. Family at play 60 60
942 30s. Kite flying, football and no smoking sign 60 60
943 30s. Keep fit class 60 60
944 30s. Farmer, animals and food 60 60
940/4 *Set of 5* 2·75 2·75

Nos. 940/4 were printed together, *se-tenant*, in horizontal strips of 5 with the backgrounds forming a composite design.

285 *Rhododendron brookeanum*

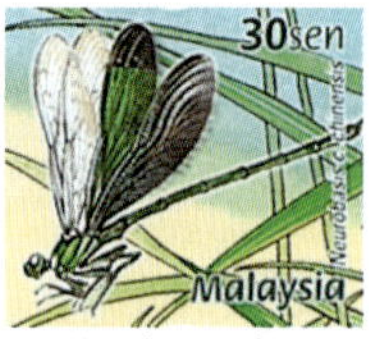

286 *Neurobasis c. chinensis*

(Des P. Chuah. Litho Security Printers (M), Malaysia)

2000 (9 Oct). Stamp Week 2000. Highland Flowers (2nd series). T **285** and similar vert designs. Multicoloured. W **138** (sideways). P 12.

945 30s. Type **285** 40 50
a. Block of 4. Nos. 945/8 1·40 1·75
946 30s. *Rhododendron jasminiflorum* 40 50
947 30s. *Rhododendron scortechinii* 40 50
948 30s. *Rhododendron pauciflorum* 40 50
949 30s. *Rhododendron crassifolium* 40 50
a. Block of 10. Nos. 949/58 3·50 4·50
950 30s. *Rhododendron longiflorum* 40 50
951 30s. *Rhododendron javanicum* 40 50
952 30s. *Rhododendron variolosum* 40 50
953 30s. *Rhododendron acuminatum* 40 50
954 30s. *Rhododendron praetervisum* 40 50
955 30s. *Rhododendron himantodes* 40 50
956 30s. *Rhododendron maxwellii* 40 50
957 30s. *Rhododendron ericoides* 40 50
958 30s. *Rhododendron fallacinum* 40 50
945/58 *Set of 14* 5·00 6·00
MS959 55×90 mm. 1r. *Rhododendron malayanum* 1·25 1·75

Nos. 945/8 and 949/58 were each printed together in sheets of 60, containing *se-tenant* blocks of either four or ten (5×2). No. 955 is inscribed "Rhodadendron" and No. 957 "Rhododendron erocoides", both in error.

(Des Orient Communications. Litho Security Printers (M), Malaysia)

2000 (25 Nov). Dragonflies and Damselflies. T **286** and similar horiz designs. Multicoloured.

(a) Booklet stamps. *W* **138** (sideways). P 13½ (with one elliptical hole on each horizontal side).

960 30s. Type **286** 45 45
a. Booklet pane. Nos. 960/9, each×2 7·50
961 30s. *Aristocypha fenestrella* (blue markings on tail) 45 45
962 30s. *Vestalis gracilis* 45 45
963 30s. *Nannophya pymaea* 45 45
964 30s. *Aristocypha fenestrella* (white markings on tail) 45 45
965 30s. *Rhyothemis p. Phyllis* 45 45
966 30s. *Crocothemis s. servilia* 45 45
967 30s. *Euphaea ochracea* (male) 45 45
968 30s. *Euphaea ochracea* (female) 45 45
969 30s. *Ceriagrion cerinorubellum* 45 45
960/9 *Set of 10* 4·00 4·00

(b) Sheetlet stamps. *W* **138** (upright). P 14×13½ (with one elliptical hole on each horizontal side).

970 (30s.) *Vestalis gracilis* 40 50
a. Sheetlet. Nos. 970/94 9·00 11·00
971 (30s.) *Crocothemis s. servilia* (male) 40 50
972 (30s.) *Trithemis aurora* 40 50
973 (30s.) *Pseudothemis jorina* 40 50
974 (30s.) *Diplacodes nebulosa* 40 50
975 (30s.) *Crocothemis s. servilia* (female) 40 50
976 (30s.) *Neurobasis c. chinensis* (male) 40 50
977 (30s.) *Burmagomphus divaricatus* 40 50
978 (30s.) *Ictinogomphus d. melaenops* 40 50
979 (30s.) *Orthetrum testaceum* 40 50
980 (30s.) *Trithemis festiva* 40 50
981 (30s.) *Brachythemis contaminata* 40 50
982 (30s.) *Neurobasis c. chinensis* (female) 40 50
983 (30s.) *Neurothemis fluctuans* 40 50
984 (30s.) *Acisoma panorpoides* 40 50
985 (30s.) *Orthetrum s. sabina* 40 50
986 (30s.) *Rhyothemis p. phyllis* 40 50
987 (30s.) *Rhyothemis obsolescens* 40 50
988 (30s.) *Neurothemis t. tulia* 40 50
989 (30s.) *Lathrecista a. asiatica* 40 50
990 (30s.) *Aethriamanta gracilis* 40 50
991 (30s.) *Diplacodes trivialis* 40 50
992 (30s.) *Neurothemis fulvia* 40 50
993 (30s.) *Rhyothemis triangularis* 40 50
994 (30s.) *Orthetrum glaucum* 40 50
970/94 *Set of 25* 9·00 11·00

Nos. 960/9 were only issued in 6r. stamp booklets and show the backgrounds forming a composite design.

Nos. 970/94 were only printed in sheetlets of 25, each stamp being inscribed "Bayaran Pos Tempatan Hingga 20gm". They were valid at 30s. for local mail up to 20g. An imperforate version exists from a limited printing.

287 Indian Blue Quail

(Des Teh Yew Kiang. Litho Security Printers (M), Malaysia)

2001 (22 Jan). Quails and Partridges. T **287** and similar horiz designs. Multicoloured. No wmk. P 14½.

995 30s. Type **287** 60 20
a. Wmk W **138** (sideways)

996 50s. Sumatran Hill Partridge (*Arborophila campbelli*) 1·00 65
a. Perf 13½
b. Perf 14 6·00
997 1r. Bustard Quail (*Turnix suscitator*) 1·75 2·00
a. Perf 13½
b. Perf 14 8·00
995/7 *Set of 3* 3·00 2·50
MS998 100×170 mm. 2r. Chestnut-breasted Tree Partridge (*Arborophila charltonii*); 2r. Crimsonheaded Wood Partridge (*Haematortyx sanguiniceps*). W 138 (sideways). P 14 (13½ at foot) 4·00 4·25
a. Without watermark 8·00

288 Federal Government Administrative Centre

(Des Reign Associates. Litho Security Printers (M), Malaysia)

2001 (1 Feb). Formation of Putrajaya Federal Territory. T **288** and similar horiz design. Multicoloured. W **138** (sideways). P 14×14½.
999 30s. Type **288** 50 10
a. Perf 13½
1000 1r. Government buildings and motorway bridge 2·00 2·25
a. Perf 13½ 6·50

289 Beadwork

290 *Cananga odorata*

(Des Ad Integrated. Litho Security Printers (M), Malaysia)

2001 (17 Feb). Sabah and Sarawak Beadwork. T **289** and similar horiz designs showing different styles. Multicoloured. Background colours given. W **138** (sideways). P 14×14½.
1001 30s. apple green 50 55
a. Block of 4. Nos. 1001/4 1·75 2·00
b. Perf 13½ 1·25
ba. Block of 4. Nos. 1001b/4b 4·50
1002 30s. pale blue 50 55
b. Perf 13½ 1·25
1003 30s. buff 50 55
b. Perf 13½ 1·25
1004 30s. carmine-rose 50 55
b. Perf 13½ 1·25
1001/4 *Set of 4* 1·75 2·00
Nos. 1001/4 were printed together, *se-tenant*, in blocks of 4.

(Des Reign Associates. Litho Security Printers (M), Malaysia)

2001 (26 Mar). Scented Flowers. T **290** and similar vert designs. Multicoloured. W **138**. P 13½.
1005 30s. Type **290** 50 10
a. Perf 14 9·00
1006 50s. *Mimusops elengi* 70 50
1007 1r. *Mesua ferrea* 1·40 1·75
1005/7 *Set of 3* 2·40 2·10
MS1008 70×100 mm. 2r. *Michelia champaca* 2·75 3·00

291 Raja Tuanku Syed Sirajuddin

292 Beetle Nut Leaf Arrangement

(Des Hazel design. Litho National Security Printers)

2001 (7 May). Installation of Tuanku Syed Sirajuddin as Raja of Perlis. T **291** and similar multicoloured design. W **138**. P 13½.
1009 **291** 30s. multicoloured 50 15
1010 50s. multicoloured 70 50
1011 1r. multicoloured 1·40 1·75
1009/11 *Set of 3* 2·40 2·25
MS1012 100×70 mm. 2r. Raja Tuanku Syed Sirajuddin and Tengku Fauziah (horiz). Multicoloured. Wmk sideways. P 14×13½ 2·75 3·00

(Des R. Yaacob. Litho National Security Printers)

2001 (11 June). Traditional Malaysian Artefacts (1st series). T **292** and similar vert designs. Multicoloured. W **138**. P 13½.
1013 30s. Type **292** 50 60
a. Horiz pair. Nos. 1013/14 1·00 1·10
1014 30s. Baby carrier 50 60
1015 50s. Quail trap 80 90
a. Horiz pair. Nos. 1015/16 1·60 1·75
1016 50s. Ember container 80 90
1013/16 *Set of 4* 2·40 2·75
Nos. 1013/14 and 1015/16 were each printed together, *se-tenant*, in sheets of 30 (2 panes, 3×5) with the first design listed in vertical rows one, three and five with the other design for each value in vertical rows two, four and six.
See also Nos. 1490/2.

293 Perodua Kancil Car, 1995

(Des Hazel Design. Litho National Security Printers)

2001 (9 July). Malaysia-made Motor Vehicles. T **293** and similar horiz designs. Multicoloured. W **138** (sideways). P 13½.
1017 30s. Type **293** 60 60
a. Block of 10. Nos. 1017/26 5·50 5·50
1018 30s. Proton Tiara, 1995 60 60
1019 30s. Perodua Rusa, 1995 60 60
1020 30s. Proton Putra, 1997 60 60
1021 30s. Inokom Permas, 1999 60 60
1022 30s. Perodua Kembara, 1999 60 60
1023 30s. Proton GTI, 2000 60 60
1024 30s. TD 2000, 2000 60 60
1025 30s. Perodua Kenari, 2000 60 60
1026 30s. Proton Waja, 2000 60 60
1017/26 *Set of 10* 5·50 5·50
Nos. 1017/26 were printed together, *se-tenant*, as blocks of 10 (5×2) throughout the sheet.

294 Serama Bantam Cock

295 Diving

(Des Teh Yew Kiang. Litho National Security Printers)

2001 (1 Aug). Malaysian Bantams. T **294** and similar multicoloured designs. W **138** (sideways on 30s., 1r.). P 12 (50s.) or 12½ (others).
1027 30s. Type **294** 50 15
1028 50s. Kapan Bantam cock 90 60
1029 1r. Serama Bantam hen 1·60 1·75
1027/9 *Set of 3* 2·75 2·25
MS1030 98×70 mm. 3r. Red Junglefowl hens and chicks (44×34 mm). Wmk sideways. P 12½ 4·50 4·75
No. **MS**1030 exists imperforate from a limited printing.

2001 (1 Aug). Philanippon '01 International Stamp Exhibition, Tokyo. As No. **MS**1030 but with exhibition logo added to the sheet margin. P 12½.
MS1030*a* 98×70 mm. 3r. Red Junglefowl hens and chicks (44×34 mm)

(Des Reign Associates. Litho National Security Printers)

2001 (8 Sept). 21st South East Asian Games, Kuala Lumpur. T **295** and similar vert designs. Multicoloured. W **138**. P 13½.

1031	20s. Type **295**	30	35
	aw. Perf 14½. Wmk inverted	12·00	
1032	30s. Rhythmic Gymnastics	35	35
	a. Perf 14		
1033	50s. Bowling	50	70
1034	1r. Weightlifting	85	1·25
	a. Perf 14		
	w. Wmk inverted	9·00	
1035	2r. Cycling	2·00	2·25
	a. Perf 14		
1031/5 *Set of 5*		3·50	4·50
MS1036 110×90 mm. 5r. Running		5·50	6·00

Nos. 1031/5 were each issued in sheets of 20 stamps and five *se-tenant* labels depicting the squirrel mascot. The position of the labels varies for each value.

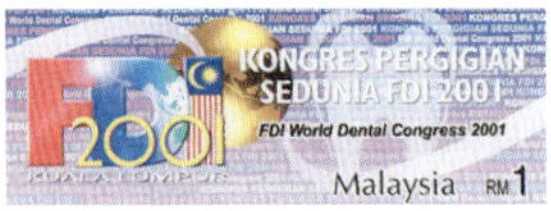

296 "F.D.I. 2001" Logo

(Des Reign Associates. Litho National Security Printers)

2001 (27 Sept). F.D.I. 2001 World Dental Congress, Kuala Lumpur. W **138** (sideways). P 14.

1037	**296**	1r. multicoloured	1·75	1·75

297 KWSP Headquarters, Kuala Lumpur

(Des Hazel Design. Litho National Security Printers)

2001 (1 Oct). 50th Anniv of Employees' Provident Fund (Kumpulan Wang Simpanan Pekerja). T **297** and similar horiz designs. Multicoloured. W **138** (sideways*). P 13½ (1r.) or 14 (others).

1038	30s. Type **297**	30	15
1039	50s. Column chart on coins and banknotes	45	40
1040	1r. Couple with KWSP logo	90	1·25
1038/40 *Set of 3*		1·50	1·60

*The normal sideways watermark on Nos. 1038/9 shows the tops of the letters to left and on No. 1040 to right, *both as seen from the back of the stamp*.

298 Satellite and Rainforest in Shape of Malaya Peninsula

299 *Tridacna gigas* (clam)

(Des Eka IPR Agensi. Litho National Security Printers)

2001 (18 Oct). Centenary of Peninsular Malaysia Forestry Department. T **298** and similar horiz designs. Multicoloured. W **138** (sideways). P 14.

1041	30s. Type **298**	55	15
1042	50s. Cross-section through forest and soil	75	50
1043	1r. Newly-planted forest	1·50	2·00
1041/3 *Set of 3*		2·50	2·40

(Des Hazel Design. Litho National Security Printers)

2001 (10 Nov). Stamp Week. Endangered Marine Life. T **299** and similar horiz designs. Multicoloured. W **138** (sideways). P 13½.

1044	20s. Type **299**	40	15
1045	30s. *Hippocampus* sp (seahorse)	50	15
1046	50s. *Oreaster occidentalis* (starfish)	70	50
	a. Perf 14½	14·00	
1047	1r. *Cassis cornuta* (shell)	1·40	2·00
	a. Perf 14½	14·00	
1044/7 *Set of 4*		2·75	2·50
MS1048 100×70 mm. 3r. Dugong. P 14½		2·75	3·25
	a. Perf 13½ at foot		
	b. As No. **MS**1048, but 110×80 mm and imperf		

No. **MS**1048b was available, at face value, via mail order only.

300 Hockey Player in Orange

301 *Couroupita guianensis*

(Des Hazel Design. Litho National Security Printers)

2002 (2 Jan). 10th Hockey World Cup, Kuala Lumpur. T **300** and similar vert designs. Multicoloured. W **138**. P 13½.

1049	30s. Type **300**	50	15
1050	50s. Goalkeeper	70	55
1051	1r. Hockey player in yellow	1·50	1·50
	a. Perf 14	10·00	
1049/51 *Set of 3*		2·40	2·00
MS1052 100×70 mm. 3r. Hockey player in blue (30×40 mm). Wmk sideways. P 12½ (12 at foot)		3·50	3·50
	a. As No. **MS**1052 but 110×80 mm and imperf		

No. **MS**1052a was available, at face value, via mail order only.

(Des Hazel Design. Litho Secura, Singapore)

2002 (5 Feb). Malaysia–China Joint Issue. Rare Flowers. T **301** and similar multicoloured designs. Multicoloured. W w **15** (sideways). P 12½.

1053	30s. Type **301**	45	10
1054	1r. *Couroupita guianensis*	90	1·25
	a. Horiz pair. Nos. 1054/5	1·75	2·50
1055	1r. *Camellia nitidissima*	90	1·25
1053/5 *Set of 3*		2·00	2·50
MS1056 108×79 mm. 2r. *Schima brevifolia* buds (horiz); 2r. *Schima brevifolia* Blossom		2·25	2·75

Nos. 1054/5 were printed together, *se-tenant*, as horizontal pairs throughout the sheets of 20.

302 *Python reticulates*

303 Stesen Sentral Station, Kuala Lumpur

(Des Chakra Creative. Litho National Security Printers)

2002 (5 Mar). Malaysian Snakes. T **302** and similar vert designs. Multicoloured. W **138** (sideways). P 14.

1057	30s. Type **302**	60	30
1058	30s. *Gonyophis margaritatus*	60	30
1059	50s. *Bungarus candidus*	85	60
	a. Perf 13½	12·00	
1060	1r. *Maticora bivirgata*	1·60	1·75
	a. Perf 13½	12·00	
1057/60 *Set of 4*		3·25	2·75
MS1061 108×78 mm. 2r. *Ophiophagus hannah* (head of adult); 2r. *Ophiophagus hannah* (juvenile). P 13½		3·50	4·00

No. **MS**1061 also exists imperforate from a limited printing.

(Des Reign Associates. Litho National Security Printers)

2002 (13 Apr). Express Rail Link from Central Kuala Lumpur to International Airport. T **303** and similar horiz designs. Multicoloured. W **138** (sideways). P 12.

1062	30s. Type **303**	75	25
1063	50s. Train and Central Station	1·40	1·50
	a. Horiz pair. Nos. 1063/4	2·75	3·00
1064	50s. Train and International Airport	1·40	1·50
1062/4 *Set of 3*		3·25	3·00

MS1065 Two sheets, each 106×76 mm. (a) 1r. KLIA Express and high speed train; 1r. Express and local trains. (b) 2r. KLIA Express. P 12½* ..... 5·50 6·00

Nos. 1063/4 were printed together, *se-tenant*, as horizontal pairs throughout the sheet.

*In No. **MS**1065a the left side of the left-hand stamp and in No. **MS**1065b the left side of the single stamp are perforated 12.

304 *Paraphalaenopsis labukensis*

305 Raja Tuanku Syed Sirajuddin of Perlis

(Des Reign Associates. Litho Secura, Singapore)

2002 (24 Apr). 17th World Orchid Conference. T **304** and similar multicoloured designs. W w **15** (sideways). P 12½.

1066	30s. Type **304**	65	65
	a. Horiz pair. Nos. 1066/7	1·25	1·25
1067	30s. *Renanthera bella*	65	65
1068	50s. *Paphiopedilum sanderianum*	1·00	40
1069	1r. *Coelogyne pandurata*	1·50	1·75
	a. Horiz pair. Nos. 1069/70	3·00	3·50
1070	1r. *Phalaenopsis amabilis*	1·50	1·25
1066/70 *Set of 5*		4·75	4·75
MS1071 76×105 mm. 5r. *Cleisocentron merillianum* (45×40 mm). No wmk. P 13		5·00	6·00

Nos. 1066/7 and 1069/70 were each printed together, *se-tenant*, as horizontal pairs throughout the sheets.

(Des R. Yaacob. Litho Secura, Singapore)

2002 (25 Apr). Installation of Raja Tuanku Syed Sirajuddin as Yang di-Pertuan Agong. W w **15**. P 13.

1072	**305** 30s. multicoloured	65	10
1073	50s. multicoloured	90	50
1074	1r. multicoloured	1·75	2·00
1072/4 *Set of 3*		3·00	2·40

306 *Cryptocoryne purpurea*

307 White-bellied Woodpecker (*Dryocopus javensis*)

(Des Reign Associates. Litho National Security Printers)

2002 (11 May). Aquatic Plants. T **306** and similar multicoloured designs. W **138** (sideways). P 12½ (1r.) or 12 (others).

1075	30s. Type **306**	55	10
1076	50s. *Barclaya kunstleri*	85	30
1077	1r. *Neptunia oleracea*	1·50	2·00
	a. Horiz pair. Nos 1077/8	3·00	4·00
1078	1r. *Monochoria hastate*	1·50	2·00
1075/8 *Set of 4*		4·00	4·00
MS1079 110×80 mm. 1r. *Eichhornia crassipes* (vert); 2r. *Nymphaea pubescens*. P 12½ (12 at foot) (1r.) or 12 (2r.)		5·50	6·00

Nos. 1077/8 were printed together, *se-tenant*, as horizontal pairs throughout the sheets.

(Des T. Kiang. Litho National Security Printers)

2002 (27 June). Malaysia–Singapore Joint Issue. Birds. T **307** and similar multicoloured designs. W **138** (sideways). P 12½.

1080	30s. Type **307**	75	75
	a. Horiz pair. Nos. 1080/1	1·50	1·50
1081	30s. Black-naped Oriole (*Oriolus chinensis*)	75	75
1082	1r. Red-throated Sunbird (*Anthreptes rhodolaema*)	2·00	2·25
	a. Horiz pair. Nos. 1082/3	4·00	4·50
1083	1r. Asian Fairy Bluebird (*Irena puella*)	2·00	2·25
1080/3 *Set of 4*		5·00	5·50
MS1084 99×70 mm. 5r. Orange-bellied Flowerpecker (*Dicaenum trigonostigma*) (60×40 mm). P 12½ (12 at foot)		6·50	7·00

Nos. 1080/1 and 1082/3 were each printed together, *se-tenant*, as horizontal pairs throughout the sheets. Stamps with similar designs were issued by Singapore.

308 Sibu Island, Johore

(Des Reign Associates. Litho Secura, Singapore)

2002 (31 July). Tourist Beaches. T **308** and similar horiz designs. Multicoloured. W w **15**. P 13.

1085	30s. Type **308**	70	60
	a. Horiz pair. Nos. 1085/6	1·40	1·10
	w. Wmk inverted	5·00	
	wa. Horiz pair. Nos. 1085w/6w	10·00	
1086	30s. Perhentian Islands, Trengganu	70	60
	w. Wmk inverted	5·00	
1087	50s. Manukan Island, Sabah	85	85
	a. Horiz pair. Nos. 1087/8	1·60	1·60
	w. Wmk inverted	5·00	
	wa. Horiz pair. Nos. 1087w/8w	10·00	
1088	50s. Tioman Island, Pahang	85	85
	w. Wmk inverted	5·00	
1089	1r. Singa Besar Island, Kedah	1·60	1·75
	a. Horiz pair. Nos. 1089/90	3·00	3·50
	w. Wmk inverted	5·00	
	wa. Wmk inverted. Nos. 1089w/90w	10·00	
1090	1r. Pangkor Island, Perak	1·60	1·75
	w. Wmk inverted	5·00	
1085/90 *Set of 6*		5·75	5·75
MS1091 110×80 mm. 1r. Ferringhi Bay, Penang; 1r. Port Dickson, Negri Sembilan. Wmk sideways		3·75	4·00

Nos. 1085/6, 1087/8 and 1089/90 were each printed together, *se-tenant*, as horizontal pairs throughout the sheets.

309 Ethnic Musicians and Dancers

(Des Reign Associates. Litho Secura, Singapore)

2002 (24 Aug). Malaysian Unity. T **309** and similar horiz designs. Multicoloured. W w **15**. P 13.

1092	30s. Type **309**	70	70
	a. Horiz pair. Nos. 1092/3	1·40	1·40
1093	30s. Children playing mancala (game)	70	70
1094	50s. Children from different races (82×30 mm)	1·00	1·00
1092/4 *Set of 3*		2·25	2·25
MS1095 68×99 mm. 1r. Children playing tug-of-war. Wmk sideways		2·50	2·75

Nos. 1092/3 were printed together, *se-tenant*, as horizontal pairs throughout the sheet.

(Litho Security Printers (M), Malaysia)

2002 (Aug–Sept?). Fruits of Malaysia. As T **141** and similar vert designs but redenominated in "sen" and "RM". Multicoloured. W **138**. P 13½×14

1095*a*	40s. Type **141**	1·00	10
	aw. Wmk inverted	12·00	
1095*b*	50s. Pineapple	1·00	10
1095*d*	1r. Mangosteen	1·50	10
	dw. Wmk inverted	21·00	
1095*e*	2r. Star fruit	2·00	80
	ea. Wmk sideways	5·00	3·50
	ewa. Wmk top of SPM to left	16·00	
	ew. Wmk inverted	20·00	
1095*g*	10r. Mango	6·00	1·50
	gw. Wmk inverted	24·00	
1095*h*	20r. Papaya	9·00	2·75
1095*a/h* *Set of 6*		18·50	7·25

*The normal sideways watermark on No. 1095ea shows the top of SPM to the right, *as seen from the back of the stamp.*

310 Zainal Abidin bin Ahmad ("Za'ba") as a Student

311 Green Kebaya Nyonya

(Des Hazel Design. Litho National Security Printers)

2002 (17 Sept). 30th Death Anniv of Zainal Abidin bin Ahmad ("Za'ba") (2003) (scholar). T **310** and similar multicoloured designs. W **138** (sideways). P 13½.

1096	30s. Type **310**	55	10
	a. Perf 12×13½		
	b. Perf 12	3·50	
1097	50s. Za'ba with typewriter	85	95
	a. Horiz pair. Nos. 1097/8	1·60	1·75
	b. Perf 12	5·50	
	ba. Horiz pair. Nos. 1097b/8b	11·00	
1098	50s. Za'ba and traditional Malay building	85	95
	b. Perf 12	5·50	
1096/8 *Set of 3*		2·00	1·75
MS1099 100×70 mm. 1r. Za'ba at desk (vert)		2·50	3·00

Nos. 1097/8 were printed together, *se-tenant*, as horizontal pairs throughout the sheets of 20.

(Des Hazel Design. Litho National Security Printers)

2002 (2 Nov). The Kebaya Nyonya (traditional Malay women's blouse). T **311** and similar vert designs. Multicoloured. W **138**. P 12½ (30s.) or 12½×13 (50s.).

1100	30s. Type **311**	60	45
	a. Perf 12½×13	2·50	
1101	30s. Red kebaya nyonya	60	45
	a. Perf 12½×13	2·50	
	aw. Wmk inverted	12·00	
1102	50s. Yellow kebaya nyonya	90	1·00
	aw. Wmk inverted	10·00	
	b. Perf 12½	4·25	
1103	50s. Pink kebaya nyonya	90	1·00
	a. Perf 12½	4·25	
1100/3 *Set of 4*		2·75	2·50
MS1104 70×100 mm. 2r. Kebaya nyonya and sarong (34×69 mm). P 13		3·00	3·25

312 Suluh Budiman Building, Sultan Idris University of Education

313 Leopard Cat with Kittens

(Des Amber Communications. Litho National Security Printers)

2002 (29 Nov). 80th Anniv of Sultan Idris University of Education. T **312** and similar horiz designs. Multicoloured. W **138** (sideways*). P 13½ (30s.) or 12 (50s.).

1105	30s. Type **312**	60	10
	aw. Wmk top of SPM to right	2·75	
	bw. Perf 12 (wmk top of SPM to right)	2·75	
1106	50s. Tadahan Selatan Building	90	1·00
	a. Horiz pair. Nos. 1106/7	1·75	2·00
	bw. Wmk top of SPM to right	2·75	
	bwa. Horiz pair. Nos. 1106bw/7bw	5·50	
	cw. Perf 13½ (wmk top of SPM to right)	2·75	
	cwa. Horiz pair. Nos. 1106cw/7cw	5·50	
1107	50s. Chancellery Building	90	1·00
	bw. Wmk top of SPM to right	2·75	
	cw. Perf 13½ (wmk top of SPM to right)	2·75	
1105/7 *Set of 3*		2·25	2·00

*The normal sideways watermark on Nos. 1105/7 shows the top of the SPM to the left, *as seen from the back of the stamp.*

Nos. 1106/7 were printed together, *se-tenant*, as horizontal pairs throughout the sheet.

No. 1107 is inscribed "Chancellory" in error.

(Des Teh Yew Kiang. Litho National Security Printers)

2002 (17 Dec). Stamp Week. Wild and Domesticated Animals. T **313** and similar multicoloured designs. W **138** (sideways). P 12½.

1108	30s. Type **313**	70	70
	a. Horiz pair. Nos. 1108/9	1·40	1·40
1109	30s. Domestic cat and kittens	70	70
1110	1r. Lesser Sulphur-crested Cockatoo	1·90	2·25
	a. Horiz pair. Nos. 1110/11	3·75	4·50
1111	1r. Malay Fish Owl	1·90	2·25
1108/11 *Set of 4*		4·75	5·50
MS1112 Two sheets, each 105×76 mm. (a) 1r. Goldfish (horiz); 1r. Porcupinefish (horiz). Wmk sideways. P 13½ (12 at foot). (b) 1r. Giant Squirrel; 1r. Domestic rabbit with young. Wmk upright. P 13½ (12 at right) *Set of 2 sheets*		5·00	5·50
	aa. Goldfish design p 13½ at foot		

Nos. 1108/9 and 1110/11 were each printed together, *se-tenant*, as horizontal pairs in sheets of 20 containing two panes of 10 (2×5) separated by a vertical gutter.

Nos. **MS**1112 (a) and (b) also exist imperforate.

314 Southern Serow

315 Peace Doves and Emblem

(Des Reign Associates. Litho National Security Printers)

2003 (25 Jan). Southern Serow. T **314** and similar vert designs. Multicoloured. W **138** (sideways). P 12½.

1113	30s. Type **314**	80	10
1114	50s. Southern Serow lying down	1·00	1·25
	a. Horiz pair. Nos. 1114/15	2·00	2·50
1115	50s. Young Southern Serow	1·00	1·25
1113/15 *Set of 3*		2·50	2·50

Nos. 1114/15 were printed together, *se-tenant*, as horizontal pairs in sheets of 20.

(Des Chakra Creative. Litho National Security Printers)

2003 (6 Feb). 13th Conference of Heads of State or Government of the Non-Aligned Movement, Kuala Lumpur. T **315** and similar horiz designs. Multicoloured. W 138. P 12½.

1116	30s. Type **315**	50	50
	a. Horiz pair. Nos. 1116/17	1·00	1·00
1117	30s. Conference emblem in cupped hands	50	50
1118	50s. Emblem and outline map of Malaysia	1·00	1·00
	a. Horiz pair. Nos. 1118/19	2·00	2·00
1119	50s. "2003" with noughts containing Malaysian flag and emblem	1·00	1·00
1116/19 *Set of 4*		2·75	2·75

Nos. 1116/17 and 1118/19 were each printed together, *se-tenant*, in horizontal pairs throughout the sheets, each pair forming a composite background design of a Malaysian flag and world map (Nos. 1116/17) or a globe (Nos. 1118/19).

316 Pale Pink Hybrid Tea Rose

317 Tunku Abdul Rahman

(Des Hazel Design. Litho Secura, Singapore)

2003 (22 Feb). Roses in Malaysia. T **316** and similar multicoloured designs. W w **15**. Phosphor background. P 13½.

1120	30s. Type **316**	55	40
1121	30s. Red hybrid tea	55	40
1122	50s. Apricot hybrid tea	90	1·25
	a. Horiz pair. Nos. 1122/3	1·75	2·50

1123 50s. Pink and white striped floribunda........... 90 1·25
1120/3 *Set of 4*................ 2·50 3·00
MS1124 70×100 mm. 1r. Miniature floribunda (29×40 mm); 2r. Rosa centifolia (29×81 mm). P 12½.................. 2·75 3·25
Nos. 1122/3 were printed together, *se-tenant*, as horizontal pairs in sheets of 20.

(Des Hazel Design. Litho National Security Printers)

2003 (3 Mar). Birth Centenary of Tunku Abdul Rahman (first Prime Minister of Federation of Malaya (1957–63) and of Malaysia (1963–70)). T **317** and similar vert designs. Multicoloured. W **138** (sideways). Phosphorised paper. P 12½.
1125 30s. Type **317**................ 55 15
1126 50s. Tunku Abdul Rahman (different)............. 85 30
1127 1r. Tunku Abdul Rahman in ceremonial dress................ 1·25 1·50
a. Horiz pair. Nos. 1127/8................ 2·50 3·00
1128 1r. Tunku Abdul Rahman wearing topi hat 1·25 1·50
1125/8 *Set of 4*................ 3·50 3·00
MS1129 100×70 mm. 1r. Tunku Abdul Rahman reading Proclamation of Independence, 1957. Wmk upright. P 13½................ 2·00 2·00
w. Wmk inverted................ 7·00
Nos. 1127/8 were printed together, *se-tenant*, in horizontal pairs as sheets of 20.

318 Sultan Sharafuddin Idris Shah

319 Siamese Fighting Fish

(Des Prof. Raja Zahabuddin Raja Yaacob. Litho National Security Printers)

2003 (8 Mar). Coronation of Sultan of Selangor. T **318** and similar vert designs. Multicoloured. W **138** (sideways). Phosphorised paper. P 12½.
1130 30s. Type **318**................ 60 15
a. Perf 12................ 5·00
1131 50s. Sultan in uniform................ 1·00 45
a. Perf 12................ 7·00
w. Wmk top of letters to right................
1132 1r. Sultan of Selangor (wearing crown)....... 1·75 2·00
a. Perf 12................ 11·00
1130/2 *Set of 3*................ 3·00 2·40
*The normal sideways watermark on Nos. 1130/2 shows the tops of the letters to left, *as seen from the back of the stamp*.

(Des Hazel Design. Litho National Security Printers)

2003 (26 Apr). Siamese Fighting Fish (*Betta splendens*). T **319** and similar horiz designs. Multicoloured. W **138** (sideways*). Phosphorised paper. P 13½ (50s.) or 12½ (30s., 1r.).
1133 30s. Type **319**................ 60 15
b. Perf 12................ 3·50
c. Perf 13½................ 3·00
1134 50s. Siamese Fighting Fish (yellow)................ 3·00
ax. Wmk reversed................ 4·50
bx. Perf 12 (wmk reversed)................ 5·50
by. Wmk top of SPM to right and reversed 1·00 35
cx. Perf 12 (wmk reversed)................ 3·50
1135 1r. Siamese Fighting Fish (blue)................ 1·40 1·75
a. Horiz pair. Nos. 1135/6................ 2·75 3·50
aw. Wmk top of SPM to right................ 3·50
awa. Horiz pair. Nos. 1135aw/6aw................ 7·00
ay. Wmk top of SPM to right and reversed 4·00
aya. Horiz pair. Nos. 1135ay/6ay................ 8·00
b. Perf 12................ 1·75
ba. Horiz pair. Nos. 1135b/6b................ 3·50
bw. Wmk top of SPM to right................ 3·50
bwa. Horiz pair. Nos. 1135bw/6bw................ 7·00
cw. Perf 12½ (wmk top of SPM to right)...... 3·00
cwa. Horiz pair. Nos. 1135cw/6cw................ 6·00
cy. Wmk top of SPM to right and reversed 3·50
cya. Horiz pair. Nos. 1135cy/6cy................ 7·00
1136 1r. Siamese Fighting Fish (red with fringed fins)................ 1·40 1·75
aw. Wmk top of SPM to right................ 3·50
ay. Wmk top of SPM to right and reversed 4·00
b. Perf 12................ 1·75
bw. Wmk top of SPM to right................ 3·50
cw. Perf 12½ (wmk top of SPM to right)...... 3·00
cy. Wmk top of SPM to right and reversed 3·50
1133/6 *Set of 4*................ 4·00 3·50
MS1137 99×70 mm. 50s. *Betta imbellis* (Local Fighting Fish) (33×28 mm); 50s. *Betta coccina* (Red Fighting Fish) (33×28 mm). P 13½×14 (with one elliptical hole on each horiz side)................ 2·00 2·25
w. Wmk top of SPM to right................ 16·00
*The normal sideways watermark on Nos. 1133/6 shows the top of the letters to the left, *as seen from the back of the stamp*.
Nos. 1135/6 were printed together, *se-tenant*, as horizontal pairs in sheets of 20.

320 Christ Church Clock Tower, Malacca

321 Malaysian Flag and Sultan Abdul Samad Building, Kuala Lumpur

(Des Warna Ilham. Litho National Security Printers)

2003 (24 May). Clock Towers. T **320** and similar vert designs. Multicoloured. Phosphorised paper. P 12½.

(a) No wmk.

1138 30s. Type **320**................ 55 55
a. W **138** (upright). P 12................
aw. W **138** (inverted). P 12................
1139 30s. Jubilee Clock Tower, Penang................ 55 55
1140 30s. Sungai Petani Clock Tower, Jalan Ibrahim................ 55 55
ax. W **138** (sideways reversed)................
1141 30s. Teluk Intan Clock Tower................ 55 55
1142 30s. Sarawak State Council Monument.......... 55 55
ax. W **138** (sideways reversed)................
1138/42 *Set of 5*................ 2·50 2·50
MS1143 99×70 mm. 1r. Sultan Abdul Samad Building; 1r. Taiping Clock Tower, Perak. W 138 (sideways). P 12×12½................ 2·25 2·50

(b) W **138** (sideways*).

1144 30s. Type **320**................ 50 60
a. Booklet pane. Nos. 1144/8, each ×2....... 4·50
w. Wmk top of letters to right................ 1·10
wa. Booklet pane. Nos. 1144w/8w, each×2. 10·00
1145 30s. Jubilee Clock Tower, Penang................ 50 60
w. Wmk top of letters to right................ 1·10
1146 30s. Sungai Petani Clock Tower, Jalan Ibrahim................ 50 60
w. Wmk top of letters to right................ 1·10
1147 30s. Teluk Intan Clock Tower................ 50 60
w. Wmk top of letters to right................ 1·10
1148 30s. Sarawak State Council Monument.......... 50 60
w. Wmk top of letters to right................ 1·10
Nos. 1138/42 were each issued in sheetlets of 20 containing two panes of ten (2×5) separated by an illustrated vertical gutter.
The normal sideways watermark on Nos. 1144/8 has the top of the letters SPM pointing to the left *as seen from the back of the stamp*.
Nos. 1144/8 and 1144w/8w only come from 3r. booklets, Nos. SB13/a.
See also Nos. 1404/6.

(Des Reign Associates. Litho and embossed (Nos. 1145, 1147 and **MS**1148 only) Secura, Singapore)

2003 (28 June). Islands and Beaches of Malaysia (2nd series). Multicoloured designs as T **308**. W w **15**. Phosphorised paper. P 13½.
1149 30s. Aerial view of Ligitan Island................ 55 55
a. Horiz pair. Nos. 1149/50................ 1·10 1·10
1150 30s. Outline map of Ligitan Island................ 55 55
1151 50s. Sipadan Island................ 90 1·00
a. Horiz pair. Nos. 1151/2................ 1·75 2·00
1152 50s. Outline map of Sipadan Island................ 90 1·00
1149/52 *Set of 4*................ 2·50 2·75
MS1153 70×100 mm. 50s. Aerial view of Sipadan Island (vert); 50s. Relief map of Ligitan Island (vert). Wmk sideways. P 12½................ 2·25 2·50
Nos. 1149/50 and 1151/2 were each printed together, *se-tenant*, in horizontal pairs in sheets of 20 (4×6) which also contain a block of four stamp-size labels at top right.

(Des Hazel Design. Litho Secura, Singapore)

2003 (19 Aug). 46th Independence Celebration. T **321** and similar designs. W w **15**. Phosphorised paper. P 12½.

1154	**321**	30s. multicoloured	65	15
1155	–	1r. multicoloured	1·75	1·75
MS1156 70×100 mm. 1r. black and grey			2·25	2·50

Designs: 59×40 mm—No. 1155, Malaysian flag; No. **MS**1156, Independence delegation in motorcade, Malacca, 1956.

322 Modenas Jaguh 175

323 Putrajaya Convention Centre

(Des Reign Associates (Nos. 1157/61) or Hazel Design (**MS**1162). Litho Secura, Singapore)

2003 (27 Sept). Malaysian made Motorcycles and Scooters. T **322** and similar horiz designs. Multicoloured. W w **15**. Phosphorised paper. P 12½.

1157	30s. Type **322**	70	15
1158	50s. Modenas Karisma 125	90	1·00
	a. Horiz pair. Nos. 1158/9	1·75	2·00
1159	50s. Modenas Kriss 1	90	1·00
1160	50s. Modenas Kriss 2	90	1·00
	a. Horiz pair. Nos. 1160/1	1·75	2·00
1161	50s. Modenas Kriss SG	90	1·00
1157/61 *Set of 5*		3·75	3·75
MS1162 Four sheets, each 100×70 mm. (a) 1r. Comel Turbulence RG125; 1r. Comel Cyclone GP150. (b) 1r. Demak Adventurer; 1r. Demak Beetle. (c) 1r. MZ 125SM; 1r. MZ Perintis 120S Classis. (d) 1r. Gagiva Momos 125R; 1r. Nitro NE150 Windstar		6·50	7·00

Nos. 1158/9 and 1160/1 were each printed together, *se-tenant*, in horizontal pairs in sheets of 20 (4×6) which also contain a block of four blank stamp-size labels at top right.

(Des Reign Associates. Litho Secura, Singapore)

2003 (3 Oct). Tenth Session of Islamic Summit Conference, Putrajaya. T **323** and similar vert designs. Multicoloured. W w **15**. Phosphorised paper. P 12½.

1163	30s. Type **323**	50	50
	a. Horiz pair. Nos. 1163/4	1·00	1·00
1164	30s. Emblem	50	50
1165	50s. Putrajaya Mosque, modern Kuala Lumpur buildings and flag	90	1·00
	a. Horiz pair. Nos. 1165/6	1·75	2·00
1166	50s. Sultan Abdul Samad Building, Kuala Lumpur and Federal Government Administrative Centre, Putrajaya	90	1·00
1163/6 *Set of 4*		2·50	2·75

Nos. 1163/4 and 1165/6 were each printed together, *se-tenant*, in horizontal pairs in sheets of 20. Nos. 1165/6 form a composite design.

2003 (4 Oct). Bangkok 2003 World Stamp Exhibition, Thailand. Nos. 1157/61 additionally inscr with "Bangkok" and exhibition logo.

1167	30s. Type **322**	60	20
1168	50s. Modenas Karisma 125	80	1·00
	a. Horiz pair. Nos. 1168/9	1·60	2·00
1169	50s. Modenas Kriss 1	80	1·00
1170	50s. Modenas Kriss 2	80	1·00
	a. Horiz pair. Nos. 1170/1	1·60	2·00
1171	50s. Modenas Kriss SG	80	1·00
1167/71 *Set of 5*		3·50	3·75

324 Children in Circle and World Map

325 Red Leaf Monkey feeding

(Des Reign Associates. Litho National Security Printers)

2003 (11 Oct). 50th World Children's Day. T **324** and similar horiz designs. Multicoloured. W **138** (sideways)*. Phosphorised paper. P 12.

1172	20s. Type **324**	50	10
	a. Perf 13½		
	b. Perf 12½	70	75
	ba. Booklet pane. Nos. 1172b/6b, each ×2	6·00	
	w. Wmk top of letters to right. Perf 12½	1·40	1·50
	wa. Booklet pane. Nos. 1172w/6w, each ×2	12·00	
	wb. W w **15** (sideways). Perf 12½	3·00	
1173	30s. Family outside their home	70	75
	a. Horiz pair. Nos. 1173/4	1·40	1·50
	b. Perf 12½	70	75
	w. Wmk top of letters to right. Perf 12½	1·40	1·50
1174	30s. Girl flying kite and children with computer	70	75
	b. Perf 12½	70	75
	w. Wmk top of letters to right. Perf 12½	1·40	1·50
1175	30s. "Sambutan 50 tahun Hari kanak-kanak Sedunia" in child's writing	70	75
	a. Horiz pair. Nos. 1175/6	1·40	1·50
	b. Perf 12½	70	75
	w. Wmk top of letters to right. Perf 12½	1·40	1·50
1176	30s. Open book, house, Malaysian flag, rainbow, car and flower	70	75
	b. Perf 12½	70	75
	w. Wmk top of letters to right. Perf 12½	1·40	1·50
1172/6 *Set of 5*		3·25	3·50

Nos. 1173/4 and 1175/6 were printed together, *se-tenant*, in horizontal pairs throughout sheets of 20, Nos. 1173/4 forming a composite design.

*The normal sideways watermark on Nos. 1172/6 shows the top of the letters to the left, *as seen from the back of the stamp.*

Nos. 1172b/6b and 1172w/6w only come from 2r.80 stamp booklets, Nos. SB14/a.

(Des Reign Associates. Litho Secura, Singapore)

2003 (16 Dec). Stamp Week. Primates of Malaysia. T **325** and similar vert designs. Multicoloured. W w **15**. Phosphorised paper. P 12½.

1177	30s. Type **325**	60	60
1178	30s. Red Leaf Monkey sat on branch	60	60
1179	50s. Proboscis Monkey	90	90
	a. Horiz pair. Nos. 1179/80	1·75	1·75
1180	50s. Female Proboscis Monkey with baby	90	90
1177/80 *Set of 4*		2·75	2·75

Nos. 1179/80 were printed together, *se-tenant*, in horizontal pairs in sheets of 20.

326 One Fathom Bank Lighthouse

327 Fauna at Seashore and in Forest

(Des Reign Associates. Litho National Security Printers)

2004 (31 Jan). Lighthouses. T **326** and similar vert designs. Multicoloured. W **138** (sideways). Phosphorised paper. P 12½.

1181	30s. Type **326**	70	60
1182	30s. Muka Head Lighthouse, Pulau Pinang	70	60
1183	30s. Pulau Undan Lighthouse, Melaka	70	60
1184	30s. Althingsburg Lighthouse, Selangor	70	60
1181/4 *Set of 4*		2·50	2·25
MS1185 70×100 mm. 1r. Tanjung Tuan Lighthouse. Wmk upright. P 13½		2·75	3·00

(Des Hazel Design. Litho Secura, Singapore)

2004 (9 Feb). Seventh Conference of Convention on Biological Diversity and First Meeting of Cartagena Protocol on Biosafety. T **327** and similar horiz designs. Multicoloured. W w **15**. Phosphorised paper. P 12½.

1186	30s. Type **327**	70	15
1187	50s. Conference logo	90	95
1188	50s. DNA, leaf and test tube	90	95
1186/8 *Set of 3*		2·25	1·90

328 Sultan of Kelantan

(Des Reign Associates. Litho National Security Printers)

2004 (29 Feb). Silver Jubilee of Sultan Ismail Petra Ibni Almarhum of Kelantan. T **328** and similar horiz designs. Multicoloured. W **138** (sideways). Phosphorised paper. P 13½ (30s, 1r.) or 12 (50s.).

1189 30s. Type **328** 60 15
1190 50s. Sultan and Istana Jahar, Museum of Royal Traditions and Customs 90 40
1191 1r. Sultan and Khota Bharu .... 1·75 2·00
1189/91 *Set of* 3 .... 3·00 3·25

329 Golf Ball, City Skyline and World Map

330 Emblem

(Des Hazel Design. Litho Secura, Singapore)

2004 (19 Mar). First Commonwealth Tourism Ministers Meeting, Kuala Lumpur. T **329** and similar multicoloured designs. W w **15**. Phosphorised paper. P 13.

1192 30s. Type **329** 65 20
1193 50s. World map and seashore 90 40
1194 1r. Logo and montage of images of Malaysia (vert) .... 1·60 1·75
1192/4 *Set of* 3 .... 2·75 2·10

(Des Creative & Communications House. Litho Secura (Nos. 1195/7) or National Security Printers (**MS**1198))

2004 (22 May). National Service Programme. T **330** and similar vert designs. Multicoloured. W w **15**. Phosphorised paper. P 12½.

1195 30s. Type **330** 30 15
1196 50s. Abseiling 55 30
1197 1r. Three youths with Malaysian flag .... 1·25 1·50
1195/7 *Set of* 3 .... 1·75 1·75
MS1198 70×100 mm. 2r. Saluting. W **138**. P 13½ .... 2·25 2·50
w. Wmk inverted .... 6·00

331 *Lanchara* (Malayan sailing ship)

332 Banteng

(Des Hazel Design. Litho National Security Printers)

2004 (31 May). 30th Anniv of Malaysia-China Diplomatic Relations. T **331** and similar multicoloured designs. W **138** (sideways). Phosphorised paper. P 12½.

1199 30s. Type **331** 30 30
a. Horiz pair. Nos. 1199/1200 .... 60 60
1200 30s. Chinese junk 30 30
1201 1r. Handshake and sailing ship .... 1·00 1·40
a. Horiz pair. Nos. 1201/2 .... 2·00 2·75
1202 1r. Sailing ship and flags of Malaysia and China .... 1·00 1·40
1199/202 *Set of* 4 .... 2·40 3·00
MS1203 100×70 mm. 2r. Niujie Mosque, Beijing and Kampung Hulu Mosque, Malacca (59×39 mm) .... 1·90 2·50

Nos. 1199/200 and 1201/2 were each printed together, *se-tenant*, in horizontal pairs in sheets of 20.

(Des Reign Associates. Litho National Security Printers (Nos. 1204/7) or Secura (**MS**1208))

2004 (14 June). Wildlife in the Malaysian Forest. T **332** and similar horiz designs. Multicoloured. W **138** (sideways*). Phosphorised paper. P 13½.

1204 30s. Type **332** 50 50
a. Horiz pair. Nos. 1204/5 .... 1·00 1·00
1205 30s. Gaur ("SELADANG") 50 50
1206 1r. Tiger .... 1·75 1·75
a. Horiz pair. Nos. 1206/7 .... 3·50 3·50
w. Wmk top of letters to left .... 2·50
wa. Horiz pair. Nos 1206w/7w .... 5·00
1207 1r. Indian Elephant .... 1·75 1·75
w. Wmk top of letters to left .... 2·50
1204/7 *Set of* 4 .... 4·00 4·00
MS1208 101×70 mm. 2r. Malayan Tapir (vert). W w **15**. P 13 .... 2·00 2·50

*The normal sideways watermark on Nos. 1204/5 shows the top of the SPM to the left and on Nos. 1206/7 to the right, *both as seen from the back of the stamp.*

Nos. 1204/5 and 1206/7 were each printed together, *se-tenant*, in horizontal pairs in sheets of 20.

333 Multimedia Super Corridor Entrance

(Des Reign Associates. Litho Secura, Singapore (Nos. 1209/11) or National Security Printers (No. **MS**1212))

2004 (1 July). Multimedia Super Corridor. T **333** and similar multicoloured designs. W w **15**. Phosphorised paper. P 13.

1209 30s. Type **333** 30 15
1210 50s. Globe, binary code and Petronas Towers 50 30
1211 $1 ID card, computer terminals and brain linked to Multimedia Super Corridor .... 90 1·25
1209/11 *Set of* 3 .... 1·50 1·50
MS1212 70×100 mm. $2 Map of Multimedia Super Corridor. W **138** (sideways). P 12½ .... 2·75 3·00

No. **MS**1212 also exists imperforate.

334 Johor

(Des Reign Associates. Litho National Security Printers)

2004 (24 July). Ports of Malaysia. T **334** and similar horiz designs. Multicoloured. W **138** (sideways). Phosphorised paper. P 12 (1213/1216) or 13½ (1217).

1213 30c. Type **334** 60 40
1214 30c. Kota Kinabalu 60 40
1215 50c. Kuantan 90 90
1216 50c. Penang 90 90
1217 $1 Bintulu .... 1·75 1·75
1213/17 *Set of* 5 .... 4·25 4·00
MS1218 100×70 mm. $2 Northport. P 13½ .... 2·75 3·00

335 Trishaw

336 Long-tailed Macaque

(Des Reign Associates. Litho Secura, Singapore)

2004 (18 Aug). Traditional Transportation. T **335** and similar multicoloured designs. W **138** (sideways*). Phosphorised paper. P 12 (1219/20), 13½ (1221) or 14 (**MS**1222).

1219	30s. Type **335**	45	15
	a. Wmk upright	6·00	
	b. Perf 13½	1·50	
	c. Wmk top of letters to right. Perf 12	3·00	
	d. Wmk top of letters to right. Perf 13½	3·00	
1220	50s. Rickshaw	65	30
1221	1r. Padi horse	1·10	1·40
1219/21	*Set of 3*	2·00	1·60
MS1222	100×70 mm. 2r. Bullock cart (39×49 mm). Wmk upright	2·75	3·00

(b) Booklet stamps. W w **15**. P 12½

1223	30s. Type **335**	45	15
	a. Booklet pane. No. 1223×10	4·50	

*The normal sideways watermark on Nos. 1219/21 shows the top of the letters SPM pointing to the left, *as seen from the back of the stamp.*

No. **MS**1222 was also issued imperforate.

No. **MS**1222 was also issued with "Kuala Lumpur Stamp Show 2004" optd on the margin in the bottom right corner.

No. 1223 was only available from 3r. stamp booklets, No. SB15.

2004 (28 Aug). World Stamp Championship, Singapore. As No. **MS**1203 but with exhibition logo and numbering added to the sheet margin. P 12½.

MS1224	100×70 mm. 2r. Niujie Mosque, Beijing and Kampung Hulu Mosque, Malacca (59×39 mm)	2·50	3·00

(Des Hazel Design. Litho Secura, Singapore)

2004 (4 Oct). Centenary of Matang Mangroves, Perak. T **336** and similar vert designs. Multicoloured. Phosphorised paper. P 13.

1225	30s. Type **336**	50	45
	a. Horiz pair. Nos. 1225/6	1·00	90
1226	30s. *Sonneratia ovata* (Mangrove apple) and moth	50	45
1227	1r. Fishing boat at jetty and cockle	1·50	1·75
	a. Horiz pair. Nos. 1227/8	3·00	3·50
1228	1r. Lesser Adjutant stork and Brahminy kite	1·50	1·75
1225/8	*Set of 4*	3·50	4·00
MS1229	100×69 mm. 2r. Tall-stilted Mangrove	2·25	2·75

Nos. 1225/6 and 1227/8 were each printed together, *se-tenant*, in horizontal pairs in sheets of 20.

337 Humpback Whales

(Des Hudacorp. Litho Secura, Singapore)

2004 (9 Oct). Marine Life. T **337** and similar horiz designs. Multicoloured. Phosphorised paper. W w **15** (sideways on **MS**1233). P 13.

1230	30s. Type **337**	60	25
1231	50s. Octopus	80	35
1232	1r. Bottlenose dolphins	1·50	1·75
1230/2	*Set of 3*	2·50	2·10
MS1233	101×71 mm. 2r. Thornback ray	2·75	3·00

338 Tongkat Ali

339 *Rhododendron stenophyllum*

(Des Warna Ilham. Litho Secura, Singapore)

2004 (11 Dec). Medicinal Plants. T **338** and similar horiz designs. Multicoloured. Phosphorised paper. W w **15**. P 13.

1234	30s. Type **338**	40	20
1235	50s. Kacip Fatimah	60	30
1236	1r. Kerdas	1·10	1·40
	a. Horiz pair. Nos. 1236/7	2·10	2·75
1237	1r. Buah Keras	1·10	1·40
1234/7	*Set of 4*	3·00	3·00
MS1238	100×71 mm. 2r. Mas Cotek	2·50	3·00

Nos. 1236/7 were printed together, *se-tenant*, as horizontal pairs in sheets of 20.

(Des Reign Associates. Litho Secura Singapore)

2005 (11 Jan). Rare Flowers. T **339** and similar multicoloured designs. Phosphorised paper. W w **15**. P 13.

1239	30s. Type **339**	50	30
1240	30s. *Rhododendron nervulosum*	50	30
1241	50s. *Rhododendron rugosum*	90	50
1242	1r. *Rhododendron stapfianum*	1·75	1·90
1239/42	*Set of 4*	3·25	2·75
MS1243	100×70 mm. 2r. *Rhododendron lowii* (horiz)	2·50	3·00

340 Kuala Lumpur Skyline

(Des Reign Associates. Litho Secura, Singapore)

2005 (24 Jan). Fifth Ministers Forum in the Asia Pacific. T **340** and similar horiz designs. Multicoloured. Phosphorised paper. W **138** (sideways). P 12.

1244	30s. Type **340**	40	15
	a. Perf 13½	4·00	
1245	50s. Putrajaya International Convention Centre and Parliament Building	70	40
1246	1r. Kuala Lumpur International Airport	2·00	2·00
1244/6	*Set of 3*	2·75	2·25

341 Crested Honey Buzzard

(Des Reign Associates. Litho National Security Printers)

2005 (3 Feb). Migratory Birds. T **341** and similar horiz designs. Multicoloured. Phosphorised paper. W **138** (sideways*). P 13½.

1247	30s. Type **341**	60	25
	a. Perf 12. Wmk top of letters to right		
1248	50s. Purple heron	95	50
1249	1r. Lesser crested tern	1·75	1·90
1247/9	*Set of 3*	3·00	2·40
MS1250	70×100 mm. 2r. Dunlin	3·25	3·25

*The normal sideways watermark on Nos. 1247/9 shows the top of the letters SPM to the left, *as seen from the back of the stamp.*

342 Proton Gen. 2

(Des M. Erickson. Litho National Security Printers)

2004 (7 Mar). Proton Gen. 2. T **342** and similar multicoloured designs. Phosphorised paper. W **138** (sideways). P 13½.

1251	30s. Type **342**	40	20
	a. Perf 12	40	50
	ab. Booklet pane. No. 1251a ×10	3·50	
	aw. Wmk top of letters to right	1·25	1·25
	awb. Booklet pane. No. 1251aw×10	12·00	
1252	50s. Proton Gen. 2 (blue)	65	35
1253	1r. Proton Gen. 2 (red)	1·60	2·00
1251/3	*Set of 3*	2·40	2·25
MS1254	100×70 mm. 2r. Proton Gen. 2 (purple) (vert). Wmk upright	2·25	2·75

Nos. 1251a/awb were only available from 3r. booklets, No. SB16. The normal sideways watermark on Nos. 1251/3 shows the top of the letters SPM pointing to the left, *as seen from the back of the stamp.*

343 Bharata Natyam and Kathak

344 Pucuk Rebung Gigi Yu

(Des Reign Associates. Litho National Security Printers)

2005 (9 Apr). Traditional Dances. T **343** and similar horiz design. Multicoloured. Phosphorised paper. W **138** (sideways). P 12.

1255	30s. Type **343**	35	15
	a. Perf 13½	2·50	
1256	50s. Kipas and Payung	55	35
1257	1r. Zapin and Asyik	1·00	1·40
1255/7	*Set of 3*	1·75	1·75
MS1258	100×70 mm. 2r. Datun julud and Sumazau. P 13½	2·75	3·00
	w. Wmk top of letters to right	9·00	

*The normal sideways watermark on No. **MS**1258 shows the top of the letters SPM pointing to the left *as seen from the back of the stamp*

2005 (21 Apr). Pacific Explorer 2005 World Stamp Expo, Sydney. No. **MS**1249 additionally inscr with "PACIFIC EXPLORER 2005 WORLD STAMP EXPO 21-24 APRIL SYDNEY CONVENTION AND EXHIBITION CENTRE" and emblem on sheet margin. Phosphorised paper. W **138** (sideways*). P 13½.

MS1259	70×100 mm. 2r. Dunlin	2·50	3·00
	w. Wmk top of letters to left	14·00	

*The normal sideways watermark on No. **MS**1259 shows the top of the letters SPM pointing to the right *as seen from the back of the stamp.*

(Des TV3. Litho National Security Printers)

2005 (29 Apr). Songket (designs on brocade textiles). T **344** and similar vert designs. Multicoloured. W **138** (sideways). Phosphorised paper. P 13×12½.

1260	30s. Type **344**	35	10
1261	50s. Bunga Bertabur Pecah Lapan	55	35
1262	1r. Pucuk Rebung Gigi Yu dan Bunga Kayohan	90	1·25
	a. Horiz pair. Nos. 1262/3	1·75	2·50
1263	1r. Teluk Berantai Bunga Pecah Empat	90	1·25
1260/3	*Set of 4*	2·40	2·75
MS1263a	100×70 mm. 2r. Potong Wajik Bertabur	2·00	2·50

Nos. 1262/3 were printed together, *se-tenant* , as horizontal pairs in sheetlets of 20, each sheetlet containing two columns of horizontal pairs separated by an illustrated vertical gutter.

345 Spotted-necked Dove

346 Tunku Canselor Hall, University of Malaya

(Des HudaCorp Sdn. Bhd. Litho National Security Printers)

2005 (14 May). Birds. T **345** and similar vert designs. Multicoloured. W **138** (inverted). P 13½×14.

1264	20s. Type **345**	35	10
	w. Wmk upright	70	20
1265	30s. Ochraceous bulbul	40	10
1266	40s. Long-tailed parakeet	50	20
1267	50s. White-rumped shama	60	25
	w. Wmk upright	70	20
1268	75s. Yellow-bellied ("Olive-backed") sunbird	80	40
1269	1r. Emerald dove (Green-winged Pigeon)	90	55
1270	2r. Blue-tailed ("Banded") pitta	1·75	1·50
1271	5r. Imperial pigeon	3·50	3·50
1264/71	*Set of 8*	8·00	6·00

(Des Hazel Design. Litho National Security Printers)

2005 (9 June). Centenary of University of Malaya. T **346** and similar horiz designs. Multicoloured. W **138** (sideways) (inverted on **MS**1275). P 12.

1272	30s. Type **346**	30	10
	a. Perf 13½	30	30
	ab. Booklet pane. No. 1272a×10	2·75	
1273	50s. Library, University of Malaya	50	30
1274	1r. Medical Centre, University of Malaya	90	1·25
1272/4	*Set of 3*	1·50	1·50
MS1275	70×100 mm. 1r. Botanic Gardens, University of Malaya; 1r. Museum of Asian Arts, University of Malaya	1·75	2·25

No. 1272ab was only available from 3r. stamp booklets, No. SB17.

347 *Kapal Dagang* (Merchant Ship)

348 Yellow-throated Marten

(Des Reign Associates. Litho National Security Printers)

2005 (21 July). 600th Anniv of Trade between Malaysia and China. T **347** and similar vert designs. Multicoloured. Phosphorised paper. W **138** (sideways). P 13×12½.

1276	30s. Type **347**	30	20
1277	30s. Royal Seal of the Emperor of China	30	20
1278	50s. Merchants	45	30
1279	1r. Nyonya ceramic plate	85	1·10
1276/9	*Set of 4*	1·75	1·60
MS1280	100×70 mm. 2r. Tin animal and copper coins	1·50	2·00

(Des Reign Associates. Litho National Security Printers)

2005 (27 July). Protected Mammals of Malaysia (3rd series). T **348** and similar multicoloured designs. Phosphorised paper. W **138** (sideways). P 13½ (Nos. 1281/3) or 12 (No. 1284).

1281	30s. Type **348**	40	25
	a. Perf 12		
1282	30s. Malay weasel	40	25
1283	50s. Hairy-nosed otter	70	35
	a. Perf 12		
1284	1r. Large spotted civet	1·25	1·50
1281/4	*Set of 4*	2·50	2·10
MS1285	100×70 mm. 2r. Long-tailed porcupine (vert). P 13×12½	2·00	2·25

349 Box Boat (Perahu Kotak)

(Des Reign Associates. Litho National Security Printers)

2005 (9 Aug). Traditional Water Transport. T **349** and similar multicoloured designs. Phosphorised paper. W **138** (sideways on Nos. 1286/8). P 13½.

1286	30s. Type **349**	35	10
1287	50s. Sampan	60	35
1288	1r. Bamboo raft (Rakit buluh)	1·00	1·25
1286/8	*Set of 3*	1·75	1·50
MS1289	70×100 mm. 2r. Long boat (Perahu batang) (40×50 mm). P 14×13½	2·25	2·50
	a. Perf 14	2·25	2·50
	w. Wmk inverted	9·00	9·00

2005 (19 Aug). Taipei 2005 International Stamp Exhibition. No. **MS**1285 additionally inscr with "TAIPEI 2005" and emblem on sheet margin.

MS1290	100×70 mm. 2r. Long-tailed porcupine (vert). P 13×12½	1·50	2·00

350 Big School and Playing Field

(Des Reign Associates. Litho National Security Printers)

2005 (30 Aug). Centenary of Malay College, Kuala Kangsar. T **350** and similar multicoloured designs. Phosphorised paper. W **138** (sideways on 1291/3). P 13½.

1291 30s. Type **350** 35 10
1292 50s. Prep School 65 70
1293 50s. Big Tree 65 70
1291/3 *Set of 3* .... 1·50 1·40
MS1294 100×70 mm. 50s.×4 (22×51 mm), Sultan Idris Murshidul'Adzam Shah; Sultan Alaiddin Sulaiman Shah; Yam Tuan Tuanku Muhamad Shah; Sultan Ahmad Al-Mu'adzam Shah. P 12 .... 1·75 2·25

351 *Varanus rudicollis*

(Des Reign Associates. Litho National Security Printers)

2005 (28 Sept). Endangered Reptiles. T **351** and similar multicoloured designs. Phosphorised paper. W **138** (sideways on 1295/8). P 13½.

1295 30s. Type **351** 35 25
1296 30s. *Varanus dumerilii* 35 25
1297 50s. *Gonocephalus grandis* 65 35
1298 1r. *Crocodylus porosus* .... 1·25 1·50
1295/8 *Set of 4* .... 2·40 2·10
MS1299 70×100 mm. 2r. *Draco quinquefasciatus* (40×50 mm). P 14 .... 1·75 2·25

352 Wau Jala Budi

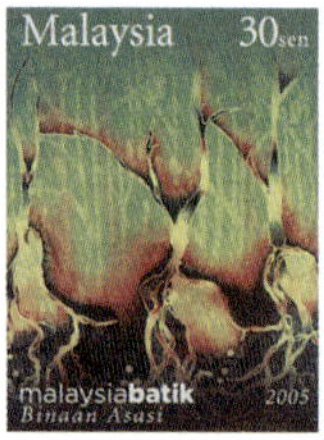

353 "Binaan Asasi" (Masrina Abdullah)

(Des Reign Associates. Litho National Security Printers)

2005 (10 Oct). Traditional Kites. T **352** and similar horiz designs. Multicoloured. Phosphorised paper. W **138** (sideways). P 13½ (30s.) or 12 (others).

1300 30s. Type **352** 35 10
a. Perf 12 .... 2·75
1301 50s. Wau Bulan 65 35
a. Perf 13½ 75 40
1302 1r. Wau Kucing .... 1·25 1·40
a. Perf 13½ .... 1·50 1·50
1300/2 *Set of 3* .... 2·00 1·60
MS1303 100×70 mm. 2r. Wau Merak. P 13½ .... 1·75 2·25

(Des Gempita Maju Sdn Bhd. Litho National Security Printers)

2005 (2 Dec). Stamp Week. Malaysian Batik Designs. T **353** and similar vert designs showing motifs produced by winners of Piala Seri Endon Batik Design Competition. Multicoloured. Phosphorised paper. W **138** (sideways). P 13×12½.

1304 30s. Type **353** 25 10
1305 50s. "Pesona Sutera" (Nazari Maarus) 45 35
1306 1r. "Malaysia Bersatu" (Mohd Nizamuddin Ambia) .... 80 1·10
1304/6 *Set of 3* .... 1·40 1·40
MS1307 100×70 mm. 2r. "Penyatuan" (Mohd Azizi Hassan) .... 1·50 2·00

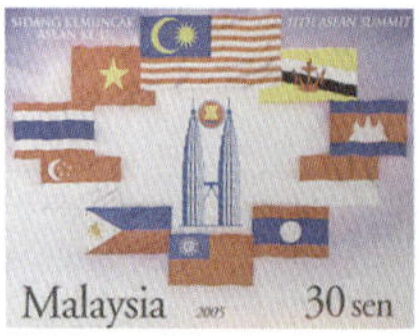

354 Flags of Member Countries

(Des Reign Associates. Litho National Security Printers)

2005 (12 Dec). 11th ASEAN Summit, Kuala Lumpur. T **354** and similar horiz designs, each showing summit emblem. Multicoloured. Phosphorised paper. W **138**. P 12½×13.

1308 30s. Type **354** 25 10
1309 50s. "ONE VISION IDENTITY COMMUNITY" 45 35
1310 1r. Petronas Twin Towers and city of Kuala Lumpur .... 80 1·10
1308/10 *Set of 3* .... 1·40 1·40

355 Mariveles Reef and *Synapta media* (sea cucumber)

(Des Reign Associates. Litho National Security Printers)

2005 (22 Dec). Malaysia's Five Islands and Reefs in the South China Sea. T **355** and similar horiz designs. Multicoloured. Phosphorised paper. W **138** (sideways on 1, 2r). P 12½×13 (30s.) or 12 (1r.).

1311 30s. Type **355** 25 20
1312 30s. Erica Reef and *Chromodoris magnifica* (nudibranch) 25 20
1313 1r. Investigator Reef and *Chlamys rastellum* (bivalve) .... 80 1·10
a. Perf 13½ .... 1·10 1·10
1314 1r. Swallow Island and *Echinaster callosus* (sea star) .... 80 1·10
a. Perf 13½ .... 3·50
1311/14 *Set of 4* .... 1·90 2·40
MS1315 100×70 mm. 2r. Aerial view of Malaysia's five islands and reefs, South China Sea (50×40 mm). P 13½×14 .... 2·25 2·50

356 Green-winged Teal (*Anas crecca*)

(Des Reign Associates. Litho National Security Printers)

2006 (26 Jan). Wild Duck Species. T **356** and similar horiz designs. Multicoloured. Phosphorised paper. W **138** (sideways). P 13½.

1316 30s. Type **356** 50 30
1317 30s. White-winged wood duck (*Cairina scutulata*) 50 30
a. Perf 12 ....
1318 50s. Northern pintail (*Anas acuta*) 90 90
1319 50s. Northern shoveller (*Anas clypeata*) 90 90
1316/19 *Set of 4* .... 2·50 2·25
MS1320 100×70 mm. 2r. Great cormorant (*Phalacrocorax carbo*) .... 3·00 3·25

No. **MS**1320 also exists imperforate.

357 National Audit Academy, Negri Sembilan

358 *Artocarpus sericicarpus*

(Des Creative & Communications House. Litho National Security Printers)

2006 (14 Feb). Centenary of National Audit Institution. T **357** and similar horiz designs. Multicoloured. Phosphorised paper. W **138**. P 12½×13.

1321 30s. Type **357** 30 20
1322 50s. Arms and logo of National Audit Department 55 55
1323 50s. Auditor General's reports 55 55
1321/3 *Set of 3* .... 1·25 1·10

(Des Hazel Design. Litho National Security Printers)

2006 (28 Mar). Rare Fruits of Malaysia (3rd series). T **358** and similar vert designs. Multicoloured. Phosphorised paper. W **138**. P 14×13½ (with one elliptical hole on each vert side).

1324	30s. Type **358**	30	20
1325	50s. *Phyllanthus acidus*	50	35
1326	1r. *Garcinia hombroniana*	90	1·25
1324/6	*Set of* 3	1·50	1·60
MS1327	100×70 mm. 1r. *Lepisanthes alata*; 1r. *Baccaurea polyneura*. Wmk sideways. P 14 (with one elliptical hole on each vert side)	1·75	1·90

359 Mount Kinabalu, Sabah and Orchid

(Des Reign Associates. Litho (with embossing on Nos. 1328/31) National Security Printers)

2006 (26 Apr). Mountains of Malaysia. T **359** and similar horiz designs. Multicoloured. Phosphorised paper. W **138** (sideways). P 12.

1328	30s. Type **359**	55	45
	a. Horiz pair. Nos. 1328/9	1·10	90
	b. Perf 13½	2·25	
1329	30s. Mount Ledang, Johor and pitcher plant	55	45
	b. Perf 13½	2·25	
1330	50s. Mount Jerai, Kedah and orchid	90	1·00
	a. Horiz pair. Nos. 1330/1	1·75	2·00
	b. Perf 13½	3·50	
1331	50s. Mount Mulu and the Pinnacles, Sarawak	90	1·00
	b. Perf 13½	3·50	
1328/30	*Set of* 4	2·50	2·50
MS1332	100×70 mm. 2r. Mount Tahan, Pahang (49×39 mm). P 13½×14	1·75	2·25

Nos. 1328/9 and 1330/1 were printed together, *se-tenant*, in horizontal pairs in sheets of 20.

360 *Leptobarbus hoevenii* (carp)

(Des Hazel Design. Litho and hologram (**MS**1337) or litho (others) National Security Printers)

2006 (25 May). Freshwater Fish (3rd series). T **360** and similar horiz designs. Multicoloured. Phosphorised paper. W **138**. P 12½×13.

1333	30s. Type **360**	35	15
1334	50s. *Hampala macrolepidota*	65	65
1335	50s. *Pangasius* sp.	65	65
1336	1r. *Probarbus jullieni*	1·10	1·40
1333/6	*Set of* 4	2·50	2·50
MS1337	100×70 mm. 5r. *Clarias batrachus* and *Mystus nemurus* (silver foil hologram) (69×33 mm). Wmk sideways. P 13½	4·00	5·00

361 Mural on Façade of Balai Budaya Tun Syed Nasir

(Des Hazel Design. Litho National Security Printers)

2006 (22 June). 50th Anniv of Dewan Bahasa dan Pustaka (Malay language organization). T **361** and similar horiz designs. Multicoloured. Phosphorised paper. W **138**. P 12½.

1338	50s. Type **361**	55	40
1339	50s. Palmyra palm frond and emblem	55	40
1340	1r. Books and laptop computer	95	1·25
1338/40	*Set of* 3	1·90	1·90

362 Oil Palm and Rubber Trees

(Des Fluorescent Squid. Litho National Security Printers)

2006 (7 July). 50th Anniv of FELDA (Federal Land Development Authority). T **362** and similar horiz designs. Multicoloured. Phosphorised paper. W **138**. P 12½.

1341	30s. Type **362**	35	15
1342	50s. Settler's houses, c. 1956, modern bungalow house and aerial view of oil palm estate	60	35
1343	1r. Old and new FELDA offices and new office tower, Kuala Lumpur	1·00	1·25
1341/3	*Set of* 3	1·75	1·60

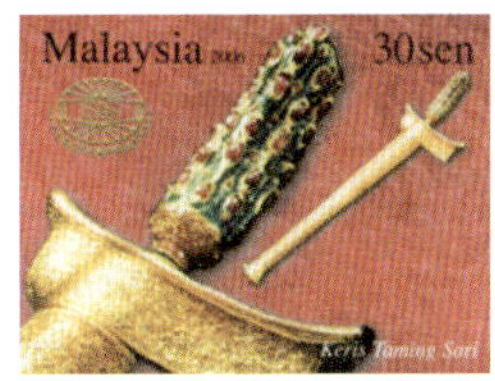

363 Keris Taming Sari (sword from Perak State Regalia)

(Des Prof. Dato'Raja Zahabuddin Raja Yaacob. Litho National Security Printers)

2006 (18 July). Galeri Sultan Azlan Shah. T **363** and similar horiz designs. Multicoloured. Phosphorised paper. W **138** (sideways*). P 12.

1344	30s. Type **363**	35	15
	a. Perf 13½	1·25	1·25
	w. Wmk top of letters to right (p 12)		
1345	50s. Galeri Sultan Azlan Shah	60	35
	a. Perf 13½	2·25	2·25
1346	1r. Royal aigrette	1·00	1·25
	a. Perf 13½	4·50	4·50
1344/6	*Set of* 3	1·75	1·60

*The normal sideways watermark shows the top of the letters pointing to the left, *as seen from the back of the stamp*.

364 Hari Raya Aidil Fitri

365 Malaysian Traditional Costume

(Adapted First Option Resources. Litho National Security Printers)

2006 (15 Aug). Festivals. Children's Paintings. T **364** and similar multicoloured designs. Phosphorised paper. W **138** (sideways). P 13½.

1347	30s. Type **364**	35	15
	a. Perf 12	1·75	1·75
1348	50s. Tahun Baru Cina (Chinese New Year)	60	35
	a. Perf 12	3·00	3·00
1349	1r. Deepavali	1·00	1·25
	a. Perf 12	5·25	5·25
1347/9	*Set of* 3	1·75	1·60
MS1350	70×100 mm. 1r. Tadau Kaamatan (vert); 1r. Pesta Gawai (vert). P 13×12½	1·75	2·00

(Des Hazel Design. Litho National Security Printers)

2006 (29 Aug). Traditional Costumes. T **365** and similar vert designs. Multicoloured. Phosphorised paper. W **138** (sideways). P 12½.

1351	50s. Type **365**	65	65
1352	50s. Chinese	65	65
1353	50s. Indian	65	65
1351/3	*Set of* 3	1·75	1·75

MS1354 70×100 mm. 1r. Iban; 1r. Kadazan. Wmk upright. P 13½ ... 2·50 2·75
w. Wmk inverted ... 7·00

366 *Periophthalmodon schlosseri* (mudskipper)

(Des Hazel Design. Litho National Security Printers)

2006 (9 Oct). Stamp Week. Semi Aquatic Animals. T **366** and similar multicoloured designs. Phosphorised paper. W **138** (sideways). P 13½.

1355 30s. Type **366** ... 40 15
1356 50s. *Pagurus bernhardus* (hermit crab) ... 65 35
1357 1r. *Cnora amboinensis* (Asian box turtle) ... 1·10 1·40
1355/7 *Set of 3* ... 1·90 1·75
MS1358 119×69 mm. 1r. *Polypedates leucomystax* (four-lined tree frog); 1r. *Varanus salvator* (common monitor); 1r. *Cynogale bennettii* (otter civet); 1r. *Xenochrophis trianguligera* (triangle keelback snake) (all 29×34 mm). P 13½×14 (with elliptical hole on each vert side) ... 2·75 3·25

367 FIGO Emblem

368 Wheelchair Race

(Des Dr. T. P. Baskaran. Litho National Security Printers)

2006 (6 Nov). 18th FIGO World Congress of Gynaecology and Obstetrics, Kuala Lumpur. T **367** and similar horiz designs. Multicoloured. Phosphorised paper. W **138**. P 12½.

1359 30s. Type **367** ... 40 15
1360 50s. Congress emblem and map of the Americas ... 75 75
1361 50s. Silhouette of foetus, map of Asia and Congress emblem ... 75 75
1359/61 *Set of 3* ... 1·75 1·50

(Des Reign Associates. Litho National Security Printers)

2006 (25 Nov). Ninth Far East and South Pacific Games for the Disabled (FESPIC), Kuala Lumpur. T **368** and similar vert designs. Multicoloured. Phosphorised paper. W **138** (sideways). P 12½.

1362 30s. Type **368** ... 40 15
1363 50s. Swimming ... 65 35
1364 1r. Wheelchair tennis ... 1·10 1·40
1362/4 *Set of 3* ... 1·90 1·75
MS1365 100×70 mm. 2r. Wheelchair basketball. Wmk inverted. P 13½ ... 3·00 3·00

369 Map with Flags of China and ASEAN Countries

(Des Reign Associates. Litho National Security Printers)

2006 (30 Nov). 15th Anniv of Dialogue between ASEAN Countries and China. T **369** and similar horiz designs. Multicoloured. Phosphorised paper. W **138** (sideways). P 12 (50s.) or 13½ (others).

1366 30s. Type **369** ... 45 15
a. Perf 12 ... 3·00 3·00
1367 50s. Great Wall of China and motorway intersection ... 65 35
a. Perf 13½ ... 3·00 3·00
1368 1r. Red ribbons tied in knot ... 1·10 1·40
a. Perf 12 ... 4·50 4·50
1366/8 *Set of 3* ... 2·00 1·75

370 Emblem

(Des Reign Associates. Litho National Security Printers)

2006 (4 Dec). 25th General Assembly of the World Veterans Association, Kuala Lumpur. T **370** and similar horiz designs. Multicoloured. Phosphorised paper. W **138** (sideways). P 13½ (30s.) or 12 (others).

1369 30s. Type **370** ... 35 15
a. Perf 12 ... 6·00
1370 50s. "25" and Kuala Lumpur Convention Centre ... 65 35
1371 1r. Tugu Negara Independence memorial ... 1·10 1·40
a. Perf 13½ ... 6·00
1369/71 *Set of 3* ... 1·90 1·75

371 Expedition Tent and Sled in Antarctic

(Des Hazel Design. Litho National Security Printers)

2006 (28 Dec). Sharifah Mazlina Syed Abdul Kadir's South Pole Expedition, 2004 T **371** and similar horiz designs. Multicoloured. Phosphorised paper. W **138** (sideways). P 13½.

1372 30s. Type **371** ... 50 20
a. Perf 12 ... 3·00
b. Perf 12, 13½ at foot ... 3·50
1373 50s. Sharifah Mazlina Syed Abdul Kadir on skis with sled ... 90 50
a. Perf 12 ...
1374 1r. Ski sailing from Hercules Inlet to South Pole ... 1·40 1·60
a. Perf 12 ... 3·50
b. Perf 12, 13½ at foot ... 4·50
1372/4 *Set of 3* ... 2·50 2·10

372 *Taenianotus triacanthus* (leaf scorpionfish)

(Des Reign Associates. Litho National Security Printers)

2007 (6 Feb). Marine Life. T **372** and similar horiz designs. Multicoloured. Phosphorised paper. W **138** (sideways). P 13½.

1375 50s. Type **372** ... 75 65
a. Perf 12 ... 3·25
b. Perf 12, 13½ at foot ... 4·50
1376 50s. *Balistapus undulatus* (orange-striped triggerfish) ... 75 65
a. Perf 12 ... 3·25
b. Perf 12, 13½ at foot ... 4·50
MS1377 100×70 mm. 1r. *Nautilus pompilius* (chambered nautilus); 1r. *Ostracion meleagris* (spotted boxfish) ... 2·25 2·50

Stamps in similar designs were issued by Brunei.

373 Hornbill, Flower and Rain Forest

374 Tuanku Mizan Zainal Abidin

(Litho National Security Printers)

2007 (19 Mar). Visit Malaysia Year. T **373** and similar multicoloured designs. Phosphorised paper. W 138 (sideways*).

(a) Sheet stamps. P 12.

1378	30s. Type **373**	45	45
	a. Horiz pair. Nos. 1378/9	90	90
	b. Perf 13½		
	ba. Horiz pair. Nos. 1378b/9b		
1379	30s. Coral reef	45	45
	b. Perf 13½		
1380	50s. Malaysian buildings	80	80
	a. Horiz pair. Nos. 1380/1	1·60	1·60
1381	50s. Malaysian crafts	80	80
1378/81 *Set of 4*		2·25	2·25
MS1382	100×70 mm. 2r. Petronas Twin Towers (29×49 mm). Wmk inverted. P 13½	2·00	2·50

(b) Booklet stamps. Horiz designs as T **373** showing national costumes and dishes. P 13½

1383	30s. Malay (dancer with headdress)	40	50
	a. Booklet pane. Nos. 1383/92	3·50	
	w. Wmk top of letters to right	40	50
	wb. Booklet pane. Nos. 1383w/92w	3·50	
1384	30s. Chinese (dancer with fans)	40	50
	w. Wmk top of letters to right	40	50
1385	30s. Indian (dancer in turquoise)	40	50
	w. Wmk top of letters to right	40	50
1386	30s. Kadazandusun of Sabah (black and gold dress)	40	50
	w. Wmk top of letters to right	40	50
1387	30s. Iban of Sarawak (woman wearing elaborate headdress)	40	50
	w. Wmk top of letters to right	40	50
1388	30s. Satay	40	50
	w. Wmk top of letters to right	40	50
1389	30s. Yee Sang	40	50
	w. Wmk top of letters to right	40	50
1390	30s. Banana leaf rice	40	50
	w. Wmk top of letters to right	40	50
1391	30s. Hinava (raw fish salad)	40	50
	w. Wmk top of letters to right	40	50
1392	30s. Manok Pansuh (chicken meat stuffed in bamboo)	40	50
	w. Wmk top of letters to right	40	50
1383/92 *Set of 10*		3·50	4·50

Nos. 1378/9 and 1380/1 were each printed together, *se-tenant*, in horizontal pairs throughout the sheets.

*The normal sideways watermark on Nos. 1378/92 has the tops of the letters SPM pointing to the left, *as seen from the back of the stamp*.

Nos. 1383/92 were only issued in 3r. booklets, No. SB18.

(Des Prof. Dato Raja Zahabuddin Raja Yaacob. Litho National Security Printers)

2007 (26 Apr). Installation of Tuanku Mizan Zainal Abidin, Sultan of Terengganu as Yang di-Pertuan Agong. Phosphorised paper. W **138** (sideways). P 13×12½.

1393	30s. Type **374**	35	10
1394	50s. Wearing white uniform	65	40
1395	1r. As Type **374** (bright mauve background)	1·10	1·40
1393/5 *Set of 3*		1·90	1·75

375 *Pedostibes hosii* (brown tree toad)

(Des Reign Associates. Litho National Security Printers)

2007 (3 May). Frogs and Toads of Malaysia. T **375** and similar horiz designs. Multicoloured. Phosphorised paper. W **138** (sideways). P 13½.

1396	30s. Type **375**	35	10
	a. Perf 12	1·40	20
1397	50s. *Megophrys nasuta* (horned toad)	65	40
	a. Perf 12	2·00	1·50
1398	50s. *Nyctixalus pictus* (spotted tree frog)	1·10	1·40
	a. Perf 12	2·00	1·50
1396/8 *Set of 3*		1·90	1·75
MS1399	100×70 mm. 1r. *Rana laterimaculata* (lesser swamp frog) (34×33 mm). P 13½	1·50	1·75

376 Shorts SC.7 Skyvan

377 J.W.W. Birch Clock Tower, Ipoh, 1917

(Des Bates Malaysia. Litho National Security Printers)

2007 (24 May). Air Transportation in Malaysia. T **376** and similar horiz designs. Multicoloured. Phosphorised paper. W **138** (sideways). P 12.

1400	30s. Type **376**	40	15
1401	50s. de Havilland Canada DHC 7-110	75	75
1402	50s. GAF N22 Nomad	75	75
1400/2 *Set of 3*		1·75	1·50
MS1403	100×70 mm. 1r. Airspeed Consul; 1r. Douglas DC-3. P 13½	2·00	2·25

(Des Hazel Design. Litho National Security Printers)

2007 (6 June). Clock Towers (2nd series). T **377** and similar vert designs. Multicoloured. Phosphorised paper. W **138** (sideways). P 13½.

1404	30s. Type **377**	35	10
1405	50s. Atkinson Clock Tower, Kota Kinabalu, 1905	65	50
1406	1r. Alor Setar Clock Tower, 1912	1·10	1·40
1404/6 *Set of 3*		1·90	1·75

378 Bawang Merah put to work by her Stepmother and Stepsister

379 *Fulgora pyrorhyncha* (lantern fly)

(Des Reign Associates. Litho National Security Printers)

2007 (26 June). Traditional Children,s Folk Tales. T **378** and similar horiz designs. Multicoloured. W **138** (sideways*). Phosphorised paper. P 13½. (a) Booklet stamps.

1407	30s. Type **378**	50	55
	a. Booklet pane. Nos. 1407/11, each ×2	3·75	
	w. Wmk top of letters to right	1·10	
	wa. Booklet pane. Nos. 1407w/11w, each ×2	10·00	
1408	30s. Badang carrying rock	50	55
	w. Wmk top of letters to right	1·10	
1409	30s. Sang Kancil crossing river on backs of crocodiles	50	55
	w. Wmk top of letters to right	1·10	
1410	30s. Crocodile Sang Bedal seizing Sang Kerbau's leg	50	55
	w. Wmk top of letters to right	1·10	
1411	30s. Mat Jenin daydreaming	50	55
	w. Wmk top of letters to right	1·10	
1407/11 *Set of 5*		2·25	2·50

(b) Sheetlet stamps.

1412	50s. Type **378**	70	70
	a. Horiz strip of 4. Nos. 1412/15	2·50	2·50
1413	50s. As No. 1408	70	70
1414	50s. As No. 1409	70	70
1415	50s. As No. 1410	70	70
1412/15 *Set of 4*		2·50	2·50
MS1416	100×70 mm. 5r. Ship's captain Si Tanggang and his rejected mother (59×38 mm). P 14	4·25	4·50

Nos. 1407/11 were only issued in 3r. stamp booklets, No. SB19.

Nos. 1412/15 were issued as horizontal strips of four in sheetlets of 20. Nos. 1407/8, 1409/10, 1412/13 and 1414/15 each form composite background designs.

*The normal sideways watermark on Nos. 1407/11 has the tops of the letters SPM pointing to the left, *as seen from the back of the stamp.*

(Des Hazel Design. Litho National Security Printers)

2007 (7 July). Insects (3rd series). T **379** and similar vert designs. Multicoloured. W **138** (sideways). Phosphorised paper. P 12½.

1417	30s. Type **379**	35	35
	a. Horiz pair. Nos. 1417/18	70	70
1418	30s. *Dysdercus cingulatus* (fruit bug)	35	35
1419	50s. *Valanga nigricornis* (grasshopper)	65	65
	a. Horiz pair. Nos. 1419/20	1·25	1·25
1420	50s. *Rhaphipodus hopei* (longhorn beetle)	65	65
1417/20 *Set of 4*		1·75	1·75
MS1421	120×70 mm. 5r. Male and female emperor moths (*Antheraea helferi*) (50×40 mm). Wmk upright P 14	4·00	5·00

Nos. 1417/18 and 1419/20 were each printed together, *se-tenant*, as horizontal pairs in sheets of 20.

No. **MS**1421 was re-issued on 3 August 2007 with a "Bangkok 2007" emblem on the top margin. This minature sheet was only sold at Bangkok 2007 International Stamp Exhibition.

380 Peon, Fire Brigade and Hutton Lane Police Station, Penang, 1880

381 Eight Long Keris

(Des Hazel Design. National Security Printers)

2007 (24 July). Bicentenary of the Establishment of the Police Force. T **380** and similar horiz designs. Multicoloured. Phosphorised paper. W **138** (sideways). P 13½.

1422	30s. Type **380**	50	15
1423	50s. Royal Federation of Malaya Policeman, 1958 and "Flying Squad" anti-terrorist police in jungle, 1948	90	90
1424	50s. Modern police officers, police vehicles and Putrajaya District Police Headquarters	90	90
1422/4 *Set of 3*		2·10	1·75

(Des Reign Associates. Litho National Security Printers)

2007 (2 Aug). Royal Heritage of Negri Sembilan. T **381** and similar vert designs. W **138** (sideways). Phosphorised paper. P 13×12½.

1425	30s. Type **381**	35	10
1426	50s. Audience Hall	65	50
1427	1r. Raja of Negri Sembilan	1·10	1·40
1425/7 *Set of 3*		1·90	1·75
MS1428	100×70 mm. 2r. Tuanku Ja'afar and Tuanku Najihah Binti Tuanku Besar Burhanudin	2·00	2·25

382 Secretariat Building, Brunei Darussalam

383 Tunku Abdul Rahman Putra Al-Haj declaring Independence, 31 August 1957

(Des Reign Associates. Litho National Security Printers)

2007 (8 Aug). 40th Anniv of ASEAN (Association of South-east Asian Nations). Ancient and Modern Architecture. T **382** and similar horiz designs. Multicoloured. W **138** (sideways). Phosphorised paper. P 14.

1429	50s. Type **382**	65	65
	a. Block of 10. Nos. 1429/38	6·00	6·00
1430	50s. National Museum of Cambodia	65	65
1431	50s. Fatahillah Museum, Jakarta, Indonesia	65	65
1432	50s. Typical Lao house	65	65
1433	50s. Malayan Railway Headquarters Building, Kuala Lumpur, Malaysia	65	65
1434	50s. Yangon Post Office, Myanmar	65	65
1435	50s. Malacañang Palace, Philippines	65	65
1436	50s. National Museum of Singapore	65	65
1437	50s. Vimanmek Mansion, Bangkok, Thailand	65	65
1438	50s. Presidential Palace, Hanoi, Vietnam	65	65
1429/38 *Set of 10*		6·00	6·00

Nos. 1429/38 were printed together, *se-tenant* , as blocks of ten in sheetlets of 20 stamps containing two blocks of ten (5×2) separated by an enlarged illustrated gutter containing a line of perforations.

Similar designs were issued on the same day by the ten member countries, Indonesia, Philippines, Singapore, Thailand, Brunei, Vietnam, Laos, Myanmar and Cambodia.

(Des Jari Seni Communication. Litho National Security Printers)

2007 (31 Aug). 50th Anniv of Independence. T **383** and similar horiz designs. Multicoloured. Phosphorised paper. W **138** (sideways*). P 13½. (a) Sheet stamps.

1439	30s. Type **383**	35	35
	a. Horiz pair. Nos. 1439/40	70	70
1440	30s. Petronas Twin Towers, Kuala Lumpur Tower, Government administrative building at Putrajaya, Proton car and Penang Bridge	35	35
1441	50s. Tunku Abdul Rahman Putra Al-Haj signing Declaration of Independence	65	65
	a. Horiz pair. Nos. 1441/2	1·25	1·25
	w. Wmk top of SPM to right	65	65
	wa. Horiz pair. Nos. 1441w/2w	1·25	1·25
1442	50s. Golden Jubilee logo	65	65
	w. Wmk top of SPM to right	65	65
1439/42 *Set of 4*		1·75	1·75
MS1442a	100×70 mm. 5r. Malaysian flag (69×33 mm). P 13	2·75	2·75

(b) Booklet stamps. Horiz designs as T **383** showing Malaysian leaders and national flag.

1443	30s. Dato' Onn Jafar (founder of United Malays National Organization)	50	50
	a. Booklet pane. 1443/7, each ×2	4·50	50
1444	30s. Tunku Abdul Rahman Putra Al-Haj (Prime Minister 1957-70)	50	50
1445	30s. Tun Abdul Razak (Prime Minister 1970-6)	50	50
1446	30s. Tun Tan Cheng Lock (founder of Malaysian Chinese Association)	50	50
1447	30s. Tun V. T. Sambanthan (President of Malaysian Indian Congress 1955-73)	50	50
1443/7 *Set of 5*		2·25	2·25

The normal sideways watermark on Nos. 1439/42a shows the top of the letters pointing to the left, *as seen from the back of the stamp.* The normal sideways watermark on Nos. 1443/7 shows the top of the letters pointing to the right, *as seen from the back of the stamp.*

Nos. 1443/7 were only issued in 3r. booklets, No. SB20.

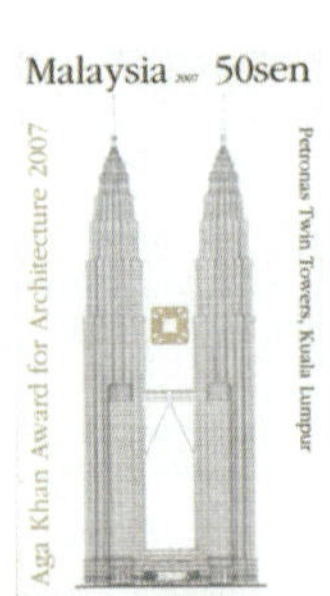

384 Petronas Twin Towers, Kuala Lumpur

385 Arms of Malaysia

(Des Irma Boom. Litho National Security Printers)

2007 (4 Sept). Aga Khan Award for Architecture. Phosphorised paper. W **138** (sideways). P 13½.

1448	**384**	50s. grey, black and gold	4·50	1·75

(Des Prof. Dato' Raja Zahabuddin Raja Yaacob. Litho National Security Printers)

2007 (25 Sept). State Emblems. T **385** and similar vert designs showing arms. Multicoloured. Phosphorised paper. W **138**. P 13½×14.

1449	50s. Type **385**	50	50
	a. Sheetlet. Nos. 1449/62	6·25	6·25
1450	50s. Kedah	50	50
1451	50s. Negri Sembilan	50	50
1452	50s. Pahang	50	50
1453	50s. Kelantan	50	50
1454	50s. Johor	50	50
1455	50s. Perak	50	50
1456	50s. Perlis	50	50
1457	50s. Selangor	50	50
1458	50s. Terengganu	50	50
1459	50s. Sarawak	50	50
1460	50s. Pulau Pinang	50	50
1461	50s. Sabah	50	50
1462	50s. Melaka	50	50
1449/62	*Set of 14*	6·25	6·25

Nos. 1449/62 were printed together, *se-tenant*, in sheetlets of 28 stamps containing two panes of 14 (2×7) separated by a line of rouletting.

386 *Solanum ferox*

387 Oldenburger

(Des Hazel Design. Litho National Security Printers)

2007 (26 Nov). Stamp Week. Rare Vegetables. T **386** and similar vert designs. Multicoloured. Phosphorised paper. W **138** (sideways). P 13½×14 (**MS**1466) or 13½ (others) (both with one elliptical hole on each vert side).

1463	50s. Type **386**	50	50
1464	50s. *Momordica charantia* (bitter melon)	50	50
1465	50s. *Etlingera elatior* (torch ginger)	50	50
1463/5	*Set of 3*	1·40	1·40
MS1466	120×70 mm. 1r.×4 *Luffa aegyptiaca* (smooth petola); *Psophocarpus tetragonolobus* (winged bean); *Sesbania grandiflora; Solanum torvum*	3·00	3·25

(Des La Scheers Co. Litho National Security Printers)

2007 (13 Dec). KL Grand Prix (show-jumping), Kuala Lumpur. T **387** and similar vert designs showing horse breeds as show-jumpers. Multicoloured. Phosphorised paper. W **138** (sideways). P 13½.

1467	30s. Type **387**	40	20
1468	50s. Hanoverian	70	70
1469	50s. Dutch warmblood	70	70
1467/9	*Set of 3*	1·60	1·40

388 Merdeka Bridge, Kedah

(Des Reign Associates. Litho National Security Printers)

2008 (28 Feb). Bridges of Malaysia. T **388** and similar horiz designs. Multicoloured. W **138** (sideways*). Phosphorised paper. P 13½.

1470	30s. Type **388**	30	10
1471	50s. Victoria Bridge, Perak	55	55
	w. Wmk top of letters to right	12·00	
1472	50s. Kota Bridge, Selangor	55	55
1473	1r. Sungai Segamat Bridge, Johor	80	1·00
1470/3	*Set of 4*	2·00	2·00

*The normal sideways watermark on Nos. 1470/3 shows the top of the letters pointing to the left, *as seen from the back of the stamp.*

389 *Echinosorex gymnurus* (moonrat)

(Des Hazel Design. Litho National Security Printers)

2008 (13 Mar). Nocturnal Animals. T **389** and similar multicoloured designs. W **138** (sideways). Phosphorised paper. P 13½.

1474	30s. Type **389**	30	20
1475	30s. *Mydaus javanensis* (Malay badger)	30	20
1476	50s. *Catopuma temminckii* (golden cat)	55	45
1477	1r. *Pteropus vampyrus* (flying fox)	80	1·00
1474/7	*Set of 4*	1·75	1·60
MS1478	120×70 mm. 2r. *Tarsius bancanus* (tarsier) (vert); 3r. *Nycticebus coucang* (slow loris) (59×39 mm). Wmk upright. P 12½	4·00	4·25

No. **MS**1478 also exists imperforate.

390 Smaller Wood Nymph (*Ideopsis gaura perakana*)

(Des Hazel Design. Litho National Security Printers)

2008 (24 Apr). Butterflies of Malaysia. T **390** and similar horiz designs. Multicoloured. Phosphorised paper. W **138** (sideways)*. P 13½.

1479	30s. Type **390**	40	45
	a. Horiz pair. Nos. 1479/80	80	90
	b. Booklet pane. Nos. 1479/83, each ×2	3·50	
	w. Wmk top of letters to right	60	70
	wa. Booklet pane. Nos. 1479w/83w, each ×2	5·50	
1480	30s. Malayan lacewing (*Cethosia hypsea hypsina*)	40	45
	w. Wmk top of letters to right	60	70
1481	30s. Common rose (*Atrophaneura aristolochiae*)	40	45
	w. Wmk top of letters to right	60	70
1482	30s. Blue glassy tiger (*Ideopsis vulgaris*)	40	45
	w. Wmk top of letters to right	60	70
1483	30s. Green dragontail (*Lamproptera meges*)	40	45
	w. Wmk top of letters to right	60	70
1484	50s. Malay red harlequin (*Paralaxita damajanti damajanti*)	65	65
	a. Perf 12×13½	65	65
1485	1r. Glorious begum (*Agatasa calydonia calydonia*)	90	1·00
	a. Perf 12×13½	90	1·00
1479/85	*Set of 7*	3·25	3·50
MS1486	114×66 mm. 5r. Five-bar swordtail (*Graphium antiphates*) (49×38 mm). P 14	4·25	4·25

Nos. 1479/80 were printed together, *se-tenant*, as horizontal pairs in sheets of 20, each pair forming a composite design of butterflies on a hibiscus flower.

Nos. 1479/80 come from sheets and booklets; Nos. 1481/3 and 1479w/83w only come from 3r. stamp booklets, No. SB21/a.

*The normal sideways watermark on Nos. 1479/86 shows the top of the letters pointing to the left, *as seen from the back of the stamp.*

No. **MS**1486 was cut around in the shape of a butterfly and has slits cut into the margins of the miniature sheet to mimic the scales on a butterfly's wing.

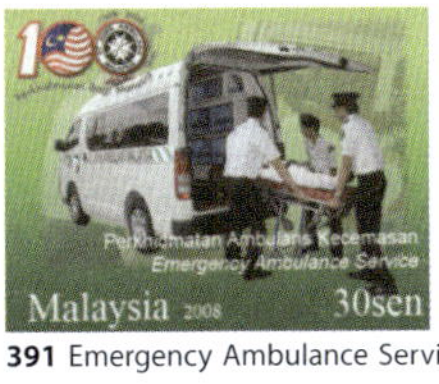

391 Emergency Ambulance Service

(Des Hoo We Tak and Lai See Ming. Litho National Security Printers)

2008 (22 May). Centenary of St. John Ambulance in Malaysia. T **391** and similar horiz designs. Multicoloured. Phosphorised paper. W **138** (sideways). P 13½.

1487	30s. Type **391**	50	20
1488	50s. First aid	95	70
1489	1r. Cardio pulmonary resuscitation	1·60	1·60
1487/9 *Set of* 3		2·75	2·25

392 Batu Giling (stone grinder for chilli or spices)

(Des Hazel Design. Litho National Security Printers)

2008 (10 June). Traditional Malaysian Artefacts (2nd series). T **392** and similar multicoloured designs. Phosphorised paper. W **138** (sideways). P 13½×14 (1492) or 13½ (others).

1490	30s. Type **392**	40	20
1491	50s. Supu (silver tobacco container)	65	65
1492	50s. Kukur Kelapa (wooden coconut grater with metal spur) (triangular 62×31 mm)	65	65
1490/2 *Set of* 3		1·60	1·40

No. 1492 is perforated 13½ on both sides and 14 at foot.

393 Sultan of Kedah, Paddy Field, Zahir Mosque and Alor Setar in early 1950s

(Des Hazel Design. Litho National Security Printers)

2008 (15 July). Golden Jubilee of Sultan Abdul Halim Mu'Adzam Shah of Kedah. T **393** and similar horiz designs. Multicoloured. Phosphorised paper. W **138** (sideways). P 12.

1493	30s. Type **393**	40	20
	a. Perf 13½	1·25	
	b. Perf 13½, 12 at foot	2·75	
1494	50s. Sultan, Jalan Telok Wanjah Water Fountain and old State Secretary's office	65	50
	a. Perf 13½	1·90	
	b. Perf 13½, 12 at foot	4·00	
1495	1r. Sultan, Jubilee emblem and modern Alor Setar	90	1·25
	a. Perf 13½	3·00	
	b. Perf 13½, 12 at foot	6·50	
1493/5 *Set of* 3		1·75	1·75

394 Drummer and Crew on Boat No. 6

(Des Hazel Design. Litho National Security Printers)

2008 (1 Aug). Sixth IDBF Club Crew World Championship, Penang. T **394** and similar horiz designs showing dragon boats. Multicoloured. Phosphorised paper. W **138** (sideways). P 13½×13.

1496	30s. Type **394**	40	20
1497	50s. Boats No. 2 and No. 5	65	50
1498	1r. Boat No. 4 and steerer in stern of other boat	90	1·25
1496/8 *Set of* 3		1·75	1·75
MS1499	120×60 mm. 2r. Dragon boat No. 5 (79×29 mm). Wmk upright	1·75	1·75

No. **MS**1499 also exists imperforate.

395 Scouts Map reading and Lord Baden-Powell (founder of World Scouting)

(Des Zonice Rovers. Litho National Security Printers)

2008 (14 Aug). Centenary of the Scouts Association of Malaysia. T **395** and similar horiz designs. Multicoloured. Phosphorised paper. W **138** (sideways). P 13½.

1500	30s. Type **395**	40	20
1501	50s. Scouts crossing Monkey Bridge	65	65
1502	50s. Sea scouts diving, kayaking and in launch	65	65
1500/2 *Set of* 3		1·50	1·40

396 *Semangat Ledang* (Spirit of Ledang) (Syed Ahmad Jamal) (acrylic on canvas), 2003

(Litho National Security Printers)

2008 (28 Aug). "Treasures of the Nation's Visual Arts". Artwork from the National Art Gallery of Malaysia. T **396** and similar multicoloured designs. Phosphorised paper. W **138** (sideways on 50s., 1r.). P 13 (1r.) or 12½ (others).

1503	30s. Type **396**	40	20
	w. Inverted watermark	1·75	
1504	50s. "Chuah Thean Teng" ("Fruits Season") (Musim Buah) (batik), 1968 (vert)	65	65
1505	1r. "Pago-pago" (Latiff Mohidin) (oil on canvas), 1965 (35×35 mm)	90	1·00
1503/5 *Set of* 3		1·75	1·60

No. 1503 exists with upright and inverted watermarks.

397 Tengkoloks for Yang Di-Pertuan Agong and Sultans of the Nine Malaysian States

(Des Prof. Dato Raja Zahabuddin Raja Yaacob. Litho National Security Printers)

2008 (16 Sept). Royal Headgear. T **397** and similar horiz designs showing official tengkoloks of the Sultans of the Malaysian states. Multicoloured. Phosphorised paper. W **138** (inverted). P 14½.

1506	50s. Type **397**	65	65
	a. Block of 10. Nos. 1506/15	6·50	6·50
	b. Perf 13½	65	65
	ba. Block of 10. Nos. 1506b/15b	6·50	6·50
1507	50s. Black tengkolok with gold embroidery and platinum star and crescent (Yang Di-Pertuan Agong at his Coronation)	65	65
	b. Perf 13½	65	65
1508	50s. Black tengkolok with gold thread design and Kedah crest with diamond paddy stalks (Kedah)	65	65
	b. Perf 13½	65	65
1509	50s. Yellow songket destar (Negri Sembilan)	65	65
	b. Perf 13½	65	65
1510	50s. Purple tengkolok with embroidery (Pahang)	65	65
	b. Perf 13½	65	65
1511	50s. Pale blue destar with crest (Kelantan)	65	65
	b. Perf 13½	65	65
1512	50s. White destar with silver embroidery and crest (Perak)	65	65

	b. Perf 13½	65	65
1513	50s. Embroidered tengkolok with white and yellow crest (Perlis)	65	65
	b. Perf 13½	65	65
1514	50s. Yellow songket destar with crest (Selangor)	65	65
	b. Perf 13½	65	65
1515	50s. Embroidered yellow songket destar with crest (Trengganu)	65	65
	b. Perf 13½	65	65
1506/15 *Set of 10*		6·50	6·50

Nos. 1506/15 were printed together, *se-tenant*, as blocks of ten in sheetlets of 20 stamps containing two blocks of ten (5×2) separated by an enlarged illustrated gutter containing a line of roulettes. Stamps from the top block are perforated 14½ and stamps from the bottom block 13½.

398 *Goniothalamus tapis*

(Des Hazel Design. Litho National Security Printers)

2008 (9 Oct). Unique Flowers. T **398** and similar multicoloured designs. Phosphorised paper. W **138** (sideways). P 13 (Nos. 1516/19) or 14 (**MS**1520).

1516	50s. Type **398**	65	65
	a. Horiz pair. Nos. 1516/17	1·25	1·25
1517	50s. *Gloriosa superba*	65	65
1518	50s. *Quisqualis indica*	65	65
	a. Horiz pair. Nos. 1518/19	1·25	1·25
1519	50s. *Michelia figo*	65	65
1516/19 *Set of 4*		2·50	2·50
MS1520	100×70 mm. 5r. *Epiphyllum oxypetalum* (38×49 mm)	4·25	4·25

Nos. 1516/17 and 1518/19 were each printed together, *se-tenant*, as horizontal pairs in sheets of 20.

No. **MS**1520 has varnish applied to the flower.

399 *Soyuz TMA II* Rocket

(Des Hazel Design. Litho National Security Printers)

2008 (21 Oct). National Astronaut Programme. T **399** and similar vert designs. Multicoloured. Phosphorised paper. W **138**. P 13×13½.

1521	30s. Type **399**	40	20
1522	50s. Dr. Sheikh Muszaphar Syukor Al-Masrie conducting experiments in microgravity	65	50
1523	1r. International Space Station	90	1·25
1521/3 *Set of 3*		1·75	1·75
MS1524	100×70 mm. 1r. Launch of Dr. Al-Masrie aboard rocket, Baikonur Cosmodrome, 2007; 1r. *Soyuz TMA II* rocket in flight	2·00	2·00

400 Horned Helmet (*Cassis cornuta*)

(Des Hazel Design. Litho National Security Printers)

2008 (11 Nov). Seashells of Malaysia. T **400** and similar horiz designs. Multicoloured. Phosphorised paper. W **138** (sideways). P 11½ (Nos. 1525/8) or 12 (**MS**1529).

1525	30s. Type **400**	40	35
1526	30s. Burnt murex (*Chicoreus brunneus*)	40	35
1527	50s. Frog shell (*Tutufa rubeta*)	65	75
1528	50s. Triton's trumpet (*Charonia tritonis*)	65	75
1525/8 *Set of 4*		1·90	1·90
MS1529	90×60 mm. 2r. Venus comb murex (*Murex pecten*) (60×40 mm)	2·00	2·00

No. **MS**1529 also exists imperforate.

401 'The Kampung Boy'

(Des Hazel Design. Litho National Security Printers)

2008 (1 Dec). Malaysian Cartoons by Lat (Dato' Mohd. Nor Khalid). T **401** and similar black and red (Nos. 1530/8) or black and silver (**MS**1539) designs. Phosphorised paper. W **138** (sideways). P 13½×14 (with one elliptical hole on each vertical side) (Nos. 1530/4) or 12½ (**MS**1539).

1530	30s. Type **401**	40	45
	a. Booklet pane. Nos. 1530/4, each ×2	3·50	
1531	30s. Riding the pinang frond ('Permainen Anak Kampung') (58×33 mm)	40	45
1532	30s. Drawing caricature of teacher Mrs. Hew on blackboard ('Guru Sekolah Yang Garang') (58×33 mm)	40	45
1533	30s. Mat and Frankie playing at rock musicians with brush and racket ('Town Boy')	40	45
1534	30s. Lat at easel painting, spilling paint everywhere	40	45
1535	50s. As Type **401**	65	65
	a. Horiz strip of 4. Nos. 1535/8	2·40	2·40
1536	50s. As No. 1531	65	65
1537	50s. As No. 1532	65	65
1538	50s. As No. 1533	65	65
1530/8 *Set of 9*		4·00	4·25
MS1539	120×70 mm. 5r. People on pedestrian crossing ('Malaysian daily life') (60×40 mm)	4·25	4·25

Nos. 1530/4 have red panels at the foot of the stamps and come from 3r. booklets, No. SB22.

Nos. 1535/8 have the red panels omitted. They were printed together, *se-tenant*, as horizontal strips of four stamps in sheets of 20.

402 S.M.K. St. Thomas, Kuching, Sarawak

(Des Hazel Design. Litho National Security Printers)

2008 (16 Dec). Premier Schools. T **402** and similar horiz designs. Multicoloured. Phosphorised paper. W **138** (sideways). P 13½×13.

1540	50s. Type **402**	65	65
1541	50s. SMK Victoria (Victoria Institution), Kuala Lumpur	65	65
1542	50s. SMK Convent Bukit Nanas, Kuala Lumpur	65	65
1543	50s. SM All Saints, Kota Kinabalu, Sabah	65	65
1540/3 *Set of 4*		2·50	2·50

403 *Polyplectron malacense* (Malaysian peacock-pheasant)

(Des Teh Yew Kiang. Litho National Security Printers)

2009 (21 Jan). Unique Birds of Malaysia. T **403** and similar horiz designs. Multicoloured. Phosphorised paper. W **138** (sideways). P 13½×13.

1544 30s. Type **403** ... 50 25
1545 50s. *Mycteria cinerea* (milky stork) ... 90 90
1546 50s. *Myophonus robinsoni* (Malaysian whistling thrush) ... 90 90
1544/6 *Set of 3* ... 2·10 1·90
MS1547 110×70 mm. 5r. *Aceros subruficollis* (wreathed hornbill) (45×35 mm). P 12 ... 4·75 4·75
a. Country name "MALAYSIA" omitted ... 9·50
w. Wmk top of letters to left ... 4·75 4·75

The normal sideways watermark on Nos. 1544/7 has the top of the letters to the right, *as seen from the back of the stamp.*

404 Sultan of Perak and Sultan kissing Ceremonial Sword during Installation Ceremony, 1985

(Des Prof. Dato' Raja Zahabuddin Raja Yaacob. Litho National Security Printers)

2009 (3 Feb). Silver Jubilee of Sultan Azlan Muhibbuddin Shah of Perak. T **404** and similar horiz designs. Multicoloured. W **138** (sideways). P 13½.

1548 30s. Type **404** ... 40 20
1549 50s. Sultan of Perak and Ubudiah Mosque ... 65 50
1550 1r. Sultan Azlan Muhibbuddin Shah and Raja Permaisuri Perak Tuanku Bainun ... 90 1·25
1548/50 *Set of 3* ... 1·75 1·75

405 Malay Bride and Groom and Mosque

(Des Hazel Design. Litho National Security Printers)

2009 (23 Mar). Traditional Wedding Costumes. Multicoloured. Phosphorised paper. W **138**. P 13×13½.

(a) Booklet stamps. T **405** and similar vert designs.

1551 30s. Type **405** ... 40 45
a. Booklet pane. Nos. 1551/5, each ×2 ... 3·50
w. Wmk inverted ... 1·25 1·40
wb. Booklet pane. Nos. 1551w/5w, each ×2 ... 10·00
1552 30s. Chinese bride and groom and dragon and phoenix on temple columns ... 40 45
w. Wmk inverted ... 1·25 1·40
1553 30s. Indian bride and groom and temple ... 40 45
w. Wmk inverted ... 1·25 1·40
1554 30s. Orang Ulu bride and groom and traditional house ... 40 45
w. Wmk inverted ... 1·25 1·40
1555 30s. Bajau bride and groom and traditional house ... 40 45
w. Wmk inverted ... 1·25 1·40
1551/5 *Set of 5* ... 1·75 2·00

(b) Sheetlet stamps. Designs as Nos. 1551/5 but with different backgrounds.

1556 50s. Malay bride and groom and Bunga telur (wedding decoration) ... 65 65
a. Horiz strip of 5. Nos. 1556/60 ... 3·00 3·00
1557 50s. Chinese bride and groom and red "double happiness" symbols ... 65 65
1558 50s. Indian bride and groom and garland ... 65 65
1559 50s. Orang Ulu bride and groom and Bunga Jarau (wooden wedding ornament) ... 65 65
1560 50s. Bajau bride and groom and Tipo serisir (woven silk material and beadwork wedding mat) ... 65 65
1556/60 *Set of 5* ... 3·00 3·00

Nos. 1556/60 were printed together, *se-tenant*, as horizontal strips of five stamps in sheetlets of 20.

406 Stadthuys (former Dutch governor's residence) and Old Town Square, Banda Hilir, Malacca

(Des Hazel Design. Litho National Security Printers)

2009 (9 Apr). UNESCO World Heritage Sites. T **406** and similar horiz designs. Multicoloured. Phosphorised paper. W **138** (sideways). P 13½ (1561/4) or 14×13½ (**MS**1565).

1561 50s. Type **406** ... 65 65
a. Horiz pair. Nos. 1561/2 ... 1·25 1·25
1562 50s. Old City Hall (now Municipal Council building), George Town, Penang ... 65 65
1563 50s. Pinnacles of Gunung Api, Mulu National Park and tarsier ... 65 65
a. Horiz pair. Nos. 1563/4 ... 1·25 1·25
1564 50s. Kinabalu National Park and scarlet minivet (bird) ... 65 65
1561/4 *Set of 4* ... 2·50 2·50
MS1565 70×110 mm. 50s.×4 Banda Hilir, Malacca; Lenticular cloud over mountain peak, Kinabalu National Park; Clock tower and colonial corner building, George Town, Penang; Cave, Mulu National Park (all 59×25 mm) ... 1·75 1·75

Nos. 1561/2 and 1563/4 were each printed together, *se-tenant*, as horizontal pairs in sheetlets of 20.

407 Railway, Harbour, Aircraft and Steam Locomotive ("Transportation and Port – Past")

(Des Reign Associates. Litho National Security Printers)

2009 (20 Apr). "Engineering Excellence in Nation Building". T **407** and similar horiz designs. Multicoloured. Phosphorised paper. W **138**. P 12½.

1566 30s. Type **407** ... 55 55
a. Horiz pair. Nos. 1566/7 ... 1·10 1·10
1567 30s. Modern buildings ("Transportation and Ports – Present") ... 55 55
1568 30s. Switchboard and pylon ("Telecommunication and Power – Past") ... 55 55
a. Horiz pair. Nos. 1568/9 ... 1·10 1·10
1569 30s. Satellite dish and pylons ("Telecommunication and Power – Present") ... 55 55
1570 50s. Bridge and dam ("Road, Bridge and Dam – Past") ... 75 75
a. Horiz pair. Nos. 1570/1 ... 1·50 1·50
1571 50s. Reservoir, roads and bridge ("Road, Bridge and Dam – Present") ... 75 75
1566/71 *Set of 6* ... 3·25 3·25

Nos. 1566/7, 1568/9 and 1570/1 were each printed together, *se-tenant*, as horizontal pairs in sheets of 20, each pair forming a composite design.

408 *Licuala grandis*

(Des Hazel Design. Litho National Security Printers)

2009 (19 May). Palm Trees. T **408** and similar square designs. Multicoloured. Phosphorised paper. P 13 (1572/4) or 12 (**MS**1575).

1572	50s. Type **408**	65	65
1573	50s. *Caryota mitis*	65	65
1574	50s. *Livistona saribus*	65	65
1572/4	*Set of 3*	1·75	1·75
MS1575	80×80 mm. 3r. *Livistona endauensis* and *Johannesteijsmannia altifrons* (69×49 mm)	2·75	2·75

Ths stamp within **MS**1575 is shaped as a rectangle with the top right quarter removed.

STAMP BOOKLETS

B **1** Seafans and Feather Stars

1995 (10 Apr). Marine Life (5th series). Corals. Multicoloured covers as Type B **1**, 92×60 mm. Stamps attached by selvedge.

SB1 2r. booklet containing pane of 10 20s. stamps (No. 559a) (cover showing Type B **1**) ..... 8·00

SB2 3r. booklet containing pane of 10 30s. stamps (No. 561a) (cover showing Cup Coral and Soft Coral) ..... 9·00

B **2** Turtle swimming Underwater

1995 (26 Sept). Turtles. Multicoloured cover as Type B **2**, 92×60 mm. Stamps attached by selvedge.

SB3 3r. booklet containing pane of ten 30s. stamps (No. 577a) ..... 11·00

B **3** Proton Saloon Car and Factory

1995 (23 Dec). 10th Anniv of Proton Cars. Multicoloured cover as Type B **3**, 100×50 mm. Stamps attached by selvedge.

SB4 3r. booklet containing pane of ten 30s. stamps (No. 585a) ..... 6·25

B **4** *Pachliopta aristolochiae*

1996 (27 Feb). "ISTANBUL '96" International Stamp Exhibition. Butterflies. Multicoloured cover as Type B **4**, 85×50 mm. Stamps attached by selvedge.

SB5 3r. booklet containing pane of ten 30s. stamps (No. 611a) ..... 11·00

It is reported that a 3r. booklet for the 16th Commonwealth Games containing Nos. 627/8 each×5 was not issued by the Malaysian postal authorities.

B **5** Train leaving Station

1997 (1 Mar). Opening of Kuala Lumpur Light Rail Transit System. Multicoloured cover as Type B **5**, 99×50 mm. Stamps attached by selvedge.

SB6 3r. booklet containing pane of ten 30s. stamps (No. 636a) ..... 11·00

B **6** Flowers

1997 (7 May). Highland Flowers. Multicoloured cover as Type B **6**, 99×50 mm. Stamps attached by selvedge.

SB7 3r. booklet containing pane of ten 30s. stamps (No. 644a) ..... 4·50

B **7**

1997 (25 Aug). 20th International Pan-Pacific and Southeast Asia Women's Association Conference, Kuala Lumpur, Multicoloured cover as Type B **7**, 110×60 mm. Stamps attached by selvedge.

SB8 3r. booklet containing pane of ten 30s. stamps (No. 663a) ..... 3·50

B **8**

1999 (14 Aug). Trees of Malaysia. Multicoloured cover as Type B **8**, 55×105 mm. Stamps attached by selvedge.

SB9 6r. booklet containing pane of twenty 30s. (No. 763a) ..... 8·00

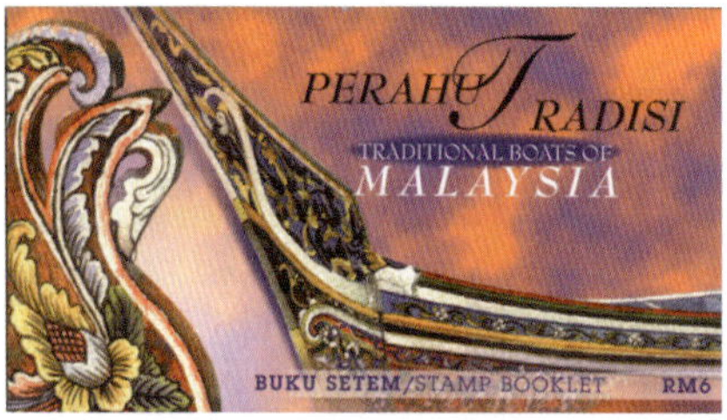

B **9** Prahus Prows

2000 (15 Apr). Traditional Malaysian Prahus (canoes). Multicoloured cover as Type B **9**, 105×55 mm. Stamps attached by selvedge.

SB10 6r. booklet containing pane of twenty 30s. (No. 875a) ..... 6·25

B **10** Dragonfly

2000 (25 Nov). Dragonflies and Damselflies. Multicoloured cover as Type B **10**, 62×110 mm. Stamps attached by selvedge.

SB11 6r. booklet containing pane of twenty 30s. (No. 960a) ..... 7·50

B **11** Proton Waja, 2000

2001 (9 July). Malaysian-made Motor Vehicles. Multicoloured cover as Type B **11**, 115×65 mm. Stamps attached by selvedge.

SB12 3r. booklet containing block of 10 30s. stamps (No. 1017a) ..... 3·50

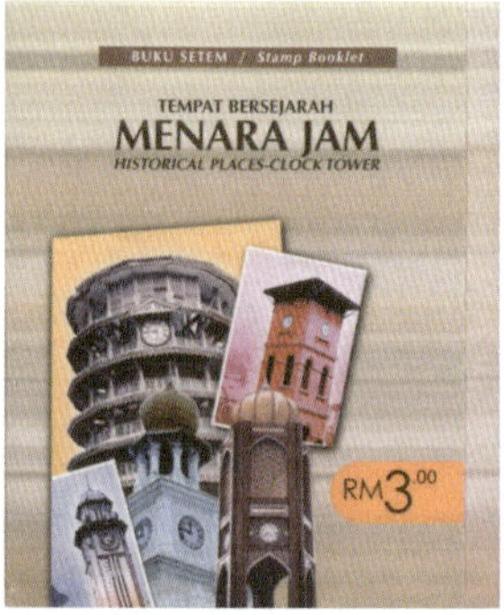

B **12** Clock Towers

2003 (24 May). Clock Towers. Multicoloured cover as Type B **12**, 75×90 mm. Stamps attached by selvedge.

SB13 3r. booklet containing ten 30s. (No. 1144a) ..... 4·50

a. Containing pane No. 1144wa ..... 10·00

B **13** Children gardening

2003 (11 Oct). 50th World Children's Day. Multicoloured cover as Type B **13**. Stamps attached by selvedge.

SB14 2r.80 booklet containing pane of two 20s. and eight 30s. (No. 1172ba) ..... 6·00

a. Containing pane No. 1172wa ..... 12·00

B **14** Rickshaw

2004 (18 Aug). Traditional Transportation. Multicoloured cover as Type B **14**, 100×80 mm. Stamps attached by selvedge.

SB15 3r. booklet containing pane of ten 30s. (No. 1223a) .... 4·50

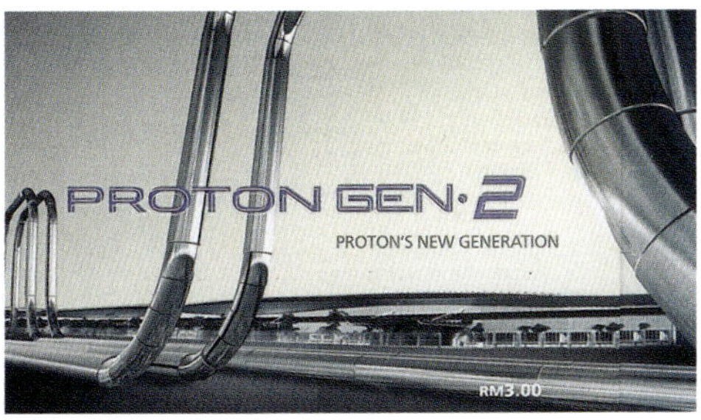

B **15** Race Track

2005 (7 Mar). Proton Gen. 2. Multicoloured cover as Type B **15**, 114×65 mm. Stamps attached by selvedge.

SB16 3r. booklet containing pane of ten 30s. (No. 1251ab) .... 3·50
a. Containing pane No. 1251awb .... 12·00

B **16** University of Malaya

2005 (9 June). Centenary of University of Malaya. Multicoloured cover as Type B **16**, 115×65 mm. Stamps attached by selvedge.

SB17 3r. booklet containing pane of ten 30s. (No. 1272ab) .... 2·75

B **17** National Costumes and Dishes

2007 (19 Mar). Visit Malaysia Year. Multicoloured cover as Type B **17**, 115×65 mm. Stamps attached by selvedge.

SB18 3r. booklet containing pane of ten 30s. (No. 1383a) .... 3·50
a. Containing pane No. 1383wb .... 3·50

B **18** Raja Bersiung

2007 (26 June). Traditional Children's Folk Tales. Multicoloured cover as Type B **18**, 115×65 mm. Stamps attached by selvedge.

SB19 3r. booklet containing pane of ten 30s. (No. 1407a) .... 3·75
a. Containing pane No. 1407wa .... 10·00

B **19** Tunku Abdul Rahman Putra Al-Haj declaring Independence, 31 August 1957

2007 (31 Aug). 50th Anniv of Independence. Multicoloured cover as Type B **19**, 114×65 mm. Stamps attached by selvedge.

SB20 3r. booklet containing pane of ten 30s. (No. 1443a) .... 4·50

B **20** Butterfly

2008 (24 Apr). Butterflies of Malaysia. Multicoloured cover as Type B **20**, 115×70 mm. Stamps attached by selvedge.

SB21 3r. booklet containing pane of ten 30s. (No. 1479b) .... 3·50
a. Containing pane No. 1479wa .... 5·50

B **21** Lat drawing Self Portrait

2008 (1 Dec). Malaysian Cartoons by Lat (Dato' Mohd. Nor Khalid). Multicoloured cover as Type B **21**, 115×75 mm. Stamps attached by selvedge.

SB22 3r. booklet containing pane of ten 30s. (1530a) ..... 3·50

B **22** Wedding Decorations

2009 (23 Mar). Traditional Wedding Costumes. Multicoloured cover as Type B **22**, 99×110 mm. Stamps attached by selvedge.

SB23	3r. booklet containing pane of ten 30s. (No. 1551a)	3·50
	a. Containing pane No. 1551wb	10·00

POSTAGE DUE STAMPS

Until 15 August 1966 the postage due stamps of MALAYAN POSTAL UNION were in use throughout MALAYSIA.

D **1**

D **2**

(Litho Harrison)

1966 (15 Aug)–**71**. Ordinary paper. W w **13** (upright). P 14½×14.

D1	D **1**	1c. rose	20	4·75
D2		2c. indigo	25	2·75
D3		4c. apple-green	1·00	9·00
D4		8c. blue-green	2·00	16·00
		a. Chalk-surfaced paper. *Bright blue green* (1.6.71)	4·50	15·00
D5		10c. bright blue	1·50	2·50
		a. Chalk-surfaced paper (1.6.71)	4·50	13·00
D6		12c. reddish violet	60	4·50
D7		20c. red-brown	2·00	4·75
		a. Chalk-surfaced paper. *Brown purple* (22.4.69)	2·75	15·00
D8		50c. brownish bistre	2·00	8·00
		a. Chalk-surfaced paper. *Olive-bistre* (1.6.71)	4·50	16·00
D1/8 *Set of 8*			8·50	45·00

Later issues in this design were printed on glazed or unwatermarked paper.

1972 (23 May). Glazed paper. W w **13** (sideways). P 14½×14.

D12	D **1**	8c. turquoise-green	7·50	25·00
D13		10c. dull ultramarine	6·00	17·00
D15		20c. pale chocolate	7·50	17·00
D16		50c. pale olive-bistro	8·00	23·00
D12/16 *Set of 4*			26·00	75·00

1980–**88**. No wmk. P 14½×14.

D17	D **1**	2c. indigo	30	3·25
D17*a*		4c. apple-green (1986?)		
D18		8c. blue-green	80	6·50
D19		10c. dull ultramarine	80	3·00
D19*a*		12c. reddish lilac (1986)	12·00	20·00
D20		20c. pale chocolate	1·00	3·50
D21		50c. pale olive-bistre	1·50	4·25
D17/21 (ex 4c.) *Set of 6*			15·00	35·00

(Des Kathy Wong. Litho Security Printers (M), Malaysia)

1986 (15 Sept). P 12×11½.

D22	D **2**	5c. cerise and rose-lilac	20	1·25
D23		10c. brownish black & pale olive-grey	25	60
D24		20c. dull vermilion and cinnamon	45	75
D25		50c. dp turquoise-green & turq-bl	70	1·00
D26		$1 ultramarine and cobalt	1·25	2·25
D22/6 *Set of 5*			2·50	5·25

(Litho Security Printers (M), Malaysia)

1999. W **138**. P 12×11½.

D28	D **2**	10s. brownish black & pale grey-brn	2·00	2·50
D29		20s. yellow-orange and brown-ochre	2·00	2·50

B. FEDERAL TERRITORY ISSUES

Kuala Lumpur, previously part of Selangor state, was established as a Federal Territory on 1 February 1974.

The following stamps were produced for use there, corresponding to the low value definitives provided for the states of the federation.

The island of Labuan, formerly part of Sabah, became the second Federal Territory on 16 April 1984, when Nos. K1/14 replaced the low value definitives of Sabah previously used there.

The city of Putrajaya was declared a Federal Territory on 1 February 2001.

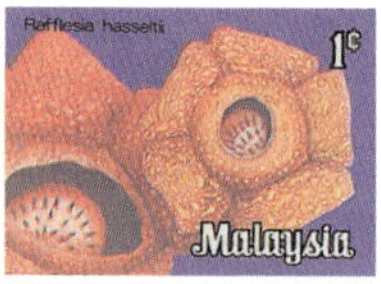

K **1** *Rafflesia Hasseltii*

K **2** Coffee

(Des M. Yusof bin Mohammed; adapted Malaysian Advertising Services. Litho Asher and Co., Melbourne)

1979 (30 Apr). Flowers. Horiz designs as Type K **1**. Multicoloured. W **95** (sideways). P 15×14½.

K1	1c. Type K **1**	10	40
K2	2c. *Pterocarpus indicus*	10	40
K3	5c. *Lagerstroemia speciosa* (Type I)	15	40
K4	10c. *Durio zibethinus*	15	10
K5	15c. *Hibiscus rosa-sinensis*	30	10
	a. *Vert pair, top stamp imperf*		
K6	20c. *Rhododendron scortechinii*	30	10
K7	25c. *Etlingera elatior* (inscr "*Phaeomeria speciosa*")	70	10
K1/7 *Set of 7*		1·60	1·40

For higher values used in conjunction with this series see Nos. 190/7.

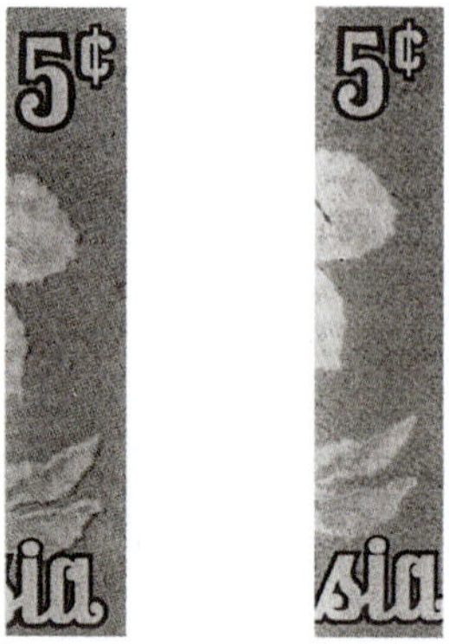

I II

Two types of 5c.:

Type I. "5" over "i" and "c" to right of "a" in "Malaysia" (Nos. K3 and K10).
Type II. "5" over "s" and "c" aligns on "a" of "Malaysia" (No. K10a).

1983–**85**. As Nos. K3/7 but without wmk.

K10	5c. *Lagerstroemia speciosa* (I) (turquoise-green background) (12.12 84)	13·00	3·00
K10*a*	5c. *Lagerstroemia speciosa* (II) (turquoise-blue background) (17.12.84)	2·25	1·00
K11	10c. *Durio zibethinus* (9.84)	75	60
K12	15c. *Hibiscus rosa-sinensis* (5.11.83)	1·00	15
K13	20c. *Rhododendron scortechinii* (blackish brown background) (1983)	19·00	1·25
K13*a*	20c. *Rhododendron scortechinii* (bronze-green background) (1983)	1·00	35
K14	25c. *Etlingera elatior* (inscr "*Phaeomeria speciosa*") (1.85)	4·50	3·00

*There was no official release date for these stamps. Dates shown are the earliest recorded from postmarks and may be revised if earlier examples are reported.

The 10c., 15c. and 20c. (No. K13a) are also from redrawn plates and show the inscriptions or the face value in slightly different positions.

(Des Kathy Wong. Litho Security Printers (M), Malaysia)

1986 (25 Oct)–**96**. Agricultural Products of Malaysia. Vert designs as Type K **2**. Multicoloured. W **138**. P 12.

K15	1c. Type K **2**	10	30
K16	2c. Coconuts	10	30
K17	5c. Cocoa	10	10
	c. Perf 14×13¾ (1994)	3·50	50
	ca. Wmk sideways		
	cw. Wmk inverted	5·00	
	ew. Perf 14×14½. Wmk inverted		
	f. Perf 14¾×14½ (1995)	2·00	10
	fw. Wmk sideways		
K18	10c. Black Pepper	15	10
	aw. Wmk inverted (1995)		
	b. Perf 13½×13¾	17·00	1·50
	c. Perf 14×13¾ (1994)	3·50	50
	cw. Wmk inverted	9·50	
	e. Perf 14×14½ (1994)	5·00	35
	f. Perf 14¾×14½ (1994)	3·00	35
K19	15c. Rubber	20	10
	w. Wmk inverted	5·00	
K20	20c. Oil palm	20	10
	aw. Wmk inverted	20·00	
	c. Perf 14×13¾ (1994)	1·25	10
	f. Perf 14¾×14½ (1994)	6·50	45
K21	30c. Rice	30	15
	aw. Wmk inverted	6·50	
	b. Perf 13½×13¾ (1994)		
	c. Perf 14×13¾ (1994)	2·50	20
	cw. Wmk inverted	9·00	
	e. Perf 14×14½ (1996)	5·00	30
	ew. Wmk inverted	7·00	
	f. Perf 14¼×14½ (1994)	4·50	45
	fw. Wmk inverted (1996)	9·00	
K15/21	*Set of 7*	1·00	1·00

For notes concerning perforation varieties see below Johore Nos. 202/8.

2002 (Aug?). Vert designs as Type K **2** but redenominated in "sen". Multicoloured. W **138** (sideways on 5s.). P 14×13¾.

K22	5s. Cocoa	2·00	10
	w. Wmk top of SPM to left	16·00	
K23	10s. Black Pepper	1·50	10
	aw. Wmk inverted	7·50	
	bw. Perf 14×14½. Wmk inverted	11·00	
K24	20s. Oil Palm	1·50	10
	a. Wmk sideways	5·00	
	aw. Wmk inverted	7·00	
	b. Perf 14×14½	4·50	
	ca. Wmk sideways	5·00	
	c. Perf 14¾×14½	3·25	
	ca. Wmk sideways	5·00	
	caw. Wmk top of SPM to left	9·00	
	cw. Wmk inverted	7·00	
K25	30s. Rice	1·50	10
	a. Wmk sideways		
	aw. Wmk inverted	8·00	
	b. Perf 14×14½	2·75	
	c. Perf 14¾×14½	2·75	
	cw. Wmk inverted	8·00	

The nomal sideways watermark on Nos. K22 and K24 has the top of the letters SPM pointing to the right, *as seen from the back of the stamp.*

K **3** *Nelumbium nelumbo* (sacred lotus)

(Des Prof. Dato Raja Zahabuddin Raja Yaacob. Litho National Security Printers)

2007 (31 Dec). Garden Flowers. Type K **3** and similar vert designs. Multicoloured. W **138**. Phosphorised paper. P 14×13½.

K26	5s. *Type K 3*	10	10
K27	10s. *Hydrangea macrophylla*	15	10
	a. Perf 14½		
K28	20s. *Hippeastrum reticulatum*	25	15
K29	30s. Bougainvillea	40	20
K30	40s. *Ipomoea indica*	50	30
K31	50s. *Hibiscus rosa-sinensis*	65	65
	w. Wmk inverted	6·50	
K26/31	*Set of 6*	1·90	1·10

STAMP BOOKLETS

1979 (1 Dec). Cover as No. SB5 of Johore, but inscr "WILAYAH PERSEKUTUAN". Stitched.

SBK1 $3 booklet containing eight 5c., 10c., and twelve 15c., (Nos. K3/5) in blocks of 4 .... 8·50

No. KSB1 exists with two different versions of the back cover.

1983 (23 May). Stamps attached by selvedge.

SBK2 $1 booklet containing 20c. (No. K6) in strip of 5 .... 5·50

1988. Black on lemon covers. Stamps attached by selvedge.

SBK3 60c. booklet containing 20c. (No. K13) in strip of 3.. 35·00

SBK4 $1.50 booklet containing 15c. (No. K12) in pair and 20c. (No. K13) in strip of 6 .... 60·00

1987 (1 June). Cover as Type B **2** of Johore, but inscr "WILAYAH PERSEKUTUAN". Stapled.

SBK5 $2 booklet containing 5c., 10c., 15c. and 20c. (Nos. K17/20), each in block of 4 .... 11·00

1988. Black on rose cover as Type B **2**. Stamps attached by selvedge.

SBK6 60c. booklet containing 20c. (No. K20) in strip of 3.. 30·00

1992 (1 July). Kuala Lumpur '92 International Philatelic Exhibition. Cover as Type B **3** of Johore, but inscr "Wilayah Persekutuan". Stamps attached by selvedge.

SBK7 $3 booklet containing 30c. (No. K21) in block of 10 .... 8·00

1993 (June). Multicoloured on pale buff covers as Nos. SB8/9 of Johore, but inscr "Wilayah Persekutuan". Stamps attached by selvedge.

SBK8 $2 booklet containing 20c. (No. K20) in block of 10 .... 1·50

SBK9 $3 booklet containing 30c. (No. K21) in block of 10 .... 2·25

1998. Black on buff cover as Type B **2**. Stamps attached by selvedge.

SBK10 60c. booklet containing 10c. (No. K18 in strip of 3 and 15c. (No. K19)) in pair......

VII. MALAYSIAN STATES

PRINTERS. All Malaysian States stamps were printed in typography by De La Rue and Co. Ltd, London, *unless otherwise stated.*

JOHORE

A British adviser was appointed to Johore in 1914. The state joined the Federation of Malaya on 1 February 1948.

Until 1 January 1899 mail for addresses outside Malaya had the external postage paid by stamps of the STRAITS SETTLEMENTS.

PRICES FOR STAMPS ON COVER TO 1945

Nos. 1/2	—
Nos. 3/5	*from* × 15
No. 6	*from* × 20
Nos. 7/8	—
Nos. 9/15	*from* × 25
No. 16	—
Nos. 17/20	*from* × 15
Nos. 21/31	*from* × 10
Nos. 32/8	*from* × 15
Nos. 39/53	*from* × 8
Nos. 54/60	*from* × 6
Nos. 61/74	*from* × 8
Nos. 75/7	—
Nos. 78/87	*from* × 8
No. 88	*from* × 10
Nos. 89/102	*from* × 6
Nos. 103/25	*from* × 5
Nos. 126/8	—
Nos. 129/30	*from* × 6
Nos. D1/5	*from* × 5

(1)

1876 (July). No. 11 of Straits Settlements handstamped with T 1.

1	2c. brown	£18000	£5500

No. 1 is known with the handstamp double.

From September 1878 to August 1884 no overprinted stamps were supplied by Singapore to Johore.

JOHORE
(2)

JOHORE (3) ("H" and "E" wide. "J" raised. Opt 16 mm long)
JOHORE (4) ("H" wide, "E" narrow. Opt 16 mm long)
JOHORE (5) ("H" and "E" wide. Opt 16¾ mm long)

JOHORE. (6)
JOHORE (7)
JOHORE (8)

1884 (June)–86. No. 63 of Straits Settlements optd with T 2/8.

2	**2**	2c. pale rose	£7000	
3	**3**	2c. pale rose (8.84)	£2250	£650
		a. Opt double	£4000	£2000
4	**4**	2c. pale rose (8.84)	£2750	£800
		a. Opt double		
5	**5**	2c. pale rose (8.84)	£2250	£650
		a. Opt double	—	£2000
6	**6**	2c. pale rose (3.85)	£190	£200
		a. Opt double	£1000	
7	**7**	2c. pale rose (1885)	£8000	
8	**8**	2c. pale rose (4.86)	£110	£120

Nos. 3 to 7 were from triplet settings, either 3+4+5 or three examples of the same overprint. Nos. 2 and 8 are probably single unit handstamps.

JOHOR (**9**) (All letters narrow)
JOHOR (**10**)
JOHOR (**11**) ("H" wide)

JOHOR (**12**)
JOHOR (**13**)
JOHOR. (**14**)

JOHOR (**15**)
JOHOR (**16**)

JOHOR
Thin, narrow "J"

1884 (Aug)–**91**. Nos. 63/a of Straits Settlements optd with T **9**/**16**.

9	**9**	2c. pale rose	16·00	20·00
		a. Opt double	£800	
10	**10**	2c. pale rose (10.84)	16·00	12·00
		a. Thin, narrow "J" (R. 6/6)	£225	£180
		b. Opt double	£900	
		c. Bright rose (1890)	14·00	13·00
		ca. Thin, narrow "J" (R. 6/6)	£200	£200
		cb. Opt double	£1200	
11	**11**	2c. pale rose (2.85)	95·00	95·00
12	**12**	2c. pale rose (1886)	60·00	55·00
		a. Opt double	£750	
13	**13**	2c. pale rose (1886)	50·00	55·00
14	**14**	2c. pale rose (1888)	£180	65·00
		a. Thin, narrow "J"	£900	£400
		b. Opt double	£800	
15	**15**	2c. bright rose (9.90)	19·00	19·00
16	**16**	2c. bright rose (1891)	£9000	

Settings:

No. 9 – various triplets with the length of the overprint varying from 12 to 15 mm
No. 10 – triplet or 60 (6×10)
No. 11 – two types, length 13¼ mm and 14¼ mm, from separate printings, both triplets of 11+9+9
No. 12 – triplet
No. 13 – triplet
No. 14 – 30 (3×10)
No. 15 – 60 (6×10)
No. 16 – not known. As no used examples are known it is possible that this stamp was not issued.

JOHOR Two CENTS (17)
JOHOR Two CENTS (18)
JOHOR Two CENTS (19)
JOHOR Two CENTS (20)

1891 (May). No. 68 of Straits Settlements surch as T 17/20.

17	**17**	2c. on 24c. green	27·00	40·00
		a. "CENST" (R. 5/4)	£900	£475
		b. Thin, narrow "J" (R. 5/6)	£450	£450
		w. Wmk inverted	£180	£180
18	**18**	2c. on 24c. green	£130	£140
		a. Thin, narrow "J" (R. 6/6)	£475	£475
		w. Wmk inverted	£475	
19	**19**	2c. on 24c. green	42·00	55·00
		w. Wmk inverted	£300	£300
20	**20**	2c. on 24c. green	£120	£130
		w. Wmk inverted	£475	£475

Nos. 17/20 come from the same setting of 60. Type **17** occurs on horizontal rows 1 to 5, Type **18** on row 6, Type **19** on rows 7, 8 and 9 and Type **20** on row 10.

The setting was altered to remove the "CENST" error and in doing so the thin, narrow "J" was moved from R. 5/6 to 6/6. Otherwise the two settings were the same.

21 Sultan Aboubakar

3 cents.
(22)

KEMAHKOTAAN
(23)

1891 (16 Nov)–**94**. No wmk. P 14.

21	**21**	1c. dull purple and mauve (7.94)	80	50
22		2c. dull purple and yellow	60	1·50
23		3c. dull purple and carmine (7.94)	60	50
24		4c. dull purple and black	2·75	20·00
25		5c. dull purple and green	7·00	21·00
26		6c. dull purple and blue	8·00	21·00
27		$1 green and carmine	80·00	£170
21/7 *Set of 7*			90·00	£200

1894 (Mar). Surch with T **22**.

28	**21**	3c. on 4c. dull purple and black	2·50	50
		a. No stop (R. 5/11)	£100	70·00
29		3c. on 5c. dull purple and green	2·00	3·75
		a. No stop (R. 5/11)	£130	£160
		b. "3 cents." spaced 3½ mm from bar	£160	90·00
30		3c. on 6c. dull purple and blue	3·50	4·50
		a. No stop (R. 5/11)	£180	£200
31		3c. on $1 green and carmine	12·00	75·00
		a. No stop (R. 5/11)	£425	£800
28/31 *Set of 4*			18·00	75·00

No. 29b shows the surcharge spaced 3½ mm from the bar instead of the normal 7½ mm. It appears to come from a separate setting as a cancelled-to-order block of eight is known.

1896 (Mar). Coronation of Sultan Ibrahim. Optd with T **23**.

32	**21**	1c. dull purple and mauve	50	1·00
		a. "KETAHKOTAAN"	3·75	5·00
33		2c. dull purple and yellow	50	1·00
		a. "KETAHKOTAAN"	5·50	7·00
34		3c. dull purple and carmine	55	1·00
		a. "KETAHKOTAAN"	10·00	13·00
35		4c. dull purple and black	80	2·25
		a. "KETAHKOTAAN"	2·75	14·00
36		5c. dull purple and green	5·50	7·50
		a. "KETAHKOTAAN"	3·50	7·50
37		6c. dull purple and blue	3·50	6·50
		a. "KETAHKOTAAN"	8·00	13·00
38		$1 green and carmine	50·00	£120
		a. "KETAHKOTAAN"	38·00	£170
32/8 *Set of 7*			55·00	£130
32a/8a *Set of 7*			65·00	£200

Stamps overprinted "KETAHKOTAAN" (= We mourn) come from the first overprinting. The overprint was subsequently changed to the intended "KEMAHKOTAAN" (= Coronation), but both were issued together some months after the Coronation of Sultan Ibrahim had taken place.

24 Sultan Ibrahim

25 Sultan Ibrahim

26

27

1896 (26 Aug)–**99**. W **27**. P 14.

39	**24**	1c. green	80	2·00
40		2c. green and blue	50	60
41		3c. green and purple	4·00	3·50
		a. Green and dull claret	4·00	3·00
42		4c. green and carmine	1·00	2·50
43		4c. yellow and red (1899)	1·50	1·50
44		5c. green and brown	2·00	3·50
45		6c. green and yellow	2·00	4·50
46	**25**	10c. green and black (1898)	7·00	48·00
47		25c. green and mauve (1898)	9·00	42·00
48		50c. green and carmine (1898)	16·00	45·00
49	**24**	$1 dull purple and green (1898)	32·00	75·00
50	**26**	$2 dull purple and carmine (1898)	45·00	80·00
51		$3 dull purple and blue (1898)	38·00	£110
52		$4 dull purple and brown (1898)	38·00	85·00
53		$5 dull purple and yellow (1898)	85·00	£130
39/53 *Set of 15*			£250	£550

Nos. 42 and 43 were reissued in 1918 to meet a shortage of 4c. stamps.

3 cents.
(28)

10 cents.
(29)

1903 (Apr). Surch with T **28** or **29**.

54	**24**	3c. on 4c. yellow and red	60	1·10
		a. Original value uncancelled	3·75	23·00
55		10c. on 4c. green and carmine	2·50	9·00
		a. Tall "1" in "10" (R. 9/12)	75·00	£130
		b. Original value uncancelled	20·00	70·00
		ba. As b, with tall "1" in "10" (R. 9/12)	£1300	£1800

The bars on these stamps were ruled by hand with pen and ink.

50 Cents.
(30)

One Dollar
(31)

1903 (Oct). Surch with T **30** or **31**.

56	**26**	50c. on $3 dull purple and blue	30·00	85·00
57		$1 on $2 dull purple and carmine	65·00	£120
		a. "e" of "One" inverted (R. 7/9)	£1700	

10 CENTS.
(32)

1904. Surch as T **32**.

58	**24**	10c. on 4c. yellow and red (Apr)	20·00	40·00
		a. Surcharge double	£8000	
59		10c. on 4c. green and carmine (Aug)	9·50	60·00
60	**26**	50c. on $5 dull purple and yellow (May)	75·00	£170
58/60 *Set of 3*			95·00	£225

33

34

35 Sultan Sir Ibrahim

1904 (Sept)–**10**. W **27**. Ordinary paper. P 14.

61	**33**	1c. dull purple and green	2·00	40
		a. Chalk-surfaced paper (10.09)	10·00	10·00
62		2c. dull purple and orange	3·00	4·25
		a. Chalk-surfaced paper (10.10)	12·00	16·00
63		3c. dull purple and olive-black	4·75	60
		a. Chalk-surfaced paper	—	£100
64		4c. dull purple and carmine	8·00	3·25
65		5c. dull purple and sage-green	2·50	3·00
66	**35**	8c. dull purple and blue	4·25	12·00
67	**34**	10c. dull purple and black	50·00	11·00
		a. Chalk-surfaced paper (1910)	£110	80·00
68		25c. dull purple and green	8·50	40·00
69		50c. dull purple and red	45·00	17·00
70	**33**	$1 green and mauve	13·00	65·00
71	**35**	$2 green and carmine	27·00	50·00
72		$3 green and blue	32·00	85·00
73		$4 green and brown	32·00	£120
74		$5 green and orange	55·00	90·00
75	**34**	$10 green and black	90·00	£200
76		$50 green and ultramarine (F.C. £50)	£300	£425
77		$100 green and scarlet (F.C. £50)	£450	£750
61/75 *Set of 15*			£350	£650

1910–**19**. Wmk Mult Rosettes (vertical). Chalk-surfaced paper. P 14.

78	**33**	1c. dull purple and green (1912)	1·25	15
79		2c. dull purple and orange (1912)	6·00	1·00
80		3c. dull purple and olive-black (1912)	10·00	65
		a. Wmk horizontal (1910)	10·00	19·00
81		4c. dull purple and carmine (1912)	16·00	1·00
		a. Wmk horizontal (1910)	20·00	60·00
82		5c. dull purple and sage-green (1912)	7·50	2·75
83	**35**	8c. dull purple and blue (1912)	4·00	9·00
84	**34**	10c. dull purple and black (1912)	60·00	3·00
		a. Wmk horizontal (1911)	26·00	85·00
85		25c. dull purple and green (1912)	16·00	48·00
86		50c. dull purple and red (1919)	65·00	£140
87	**33**	$1 green and mauve (1918)	95·00	£120
78/87 *Set of 10*			£225	£275

3 CENTS.
(36)

37 Sultan Sir Ibrahim and Sultana

1912 (Mar). No. 66 surch with T **36**.

88		3c. on 8c. dull purple and blue	6·50	9·00
		a. "T" of "CENTS" omitted	£1500	
		b. Bars double		

No. 88b shows the bars printed twice with the upper pair partly erased.

1918–**20**. Wmk Mult Crown CA. Chalk-surfaced paper. P 14.

89	**33**	2c. dull purple and green (1919)	50	1·25
		w. Wmk inverted	†	£325
90		2c. purple and orange (1919)	1·00	5·00
91		4c. dull purple and red	1·75	70
92		5c. dull purple and sage-green (1920)	2·00	9·00
		w. Wmk inverted	£180	
		ws. Ditto, optd "Specimen"	70·00	
93	**34**	10c. dull purple and blue	2·00	1·40
94		21c. dull purple and orange (1919)	2·25	2·50
95		25c. dull purple and green (1920)	8·00	28·00
96		50c. dull purple and red (6.18)	24·00	65·00
97	**33**	$1 green and mauve	14·00	75·00
98	**35**	$2 green and carmine	23·00	55·00
99		$3 green and blue	60·00	£130
100		$4 green and brown	75·00	£170
101		$5 green and orange	£110	£200
102	**34**	$10 green and black	£325	£475
89/102 *Set of 14*			£600	£1100
89s/102s Optd "Specimen" *Set of 14*			£550	

1922–41. Wmk Mult Script CA. Chalk-surfaced paper. P 14.

103	**33**	1c. dull purple and black	30	20
104		2c. purple and sepia (1924)	1·25	4·25
105		2c. green (1928)	50	40
106		3c. green (1925)	2·00	4·75
107		3c. purple and sepia (1928)	1·40	1·50
108		4c. purple and carmine (1924)	2·50	20
109		5c. dull purple and sage-green	50	30
		w. Wmk inverted		
110		6c. dull purple and claret	50	50
111	**34**	10c. dull purple and blue	16·00	32·00
		w. Wmk inverted	†	£325
112		10c. dull purple and yellow	50	25
		a. Thin striated paper (1941)	£100	£150
113	**33**	12c. dull purple and blue	1·00	1·25
114		12c. ultramarine (1940)	48·00	2·25
115	**34**	21c. dull purple and orange (1928)	2·00	3·00
116		25c. dull purple and myrtle	3·75	1·00
117	**35**	30c. dull purple and orange (1936)	9·00	9·00
118		40c. dull purple and brown (1936)	9·00	10·00
119	**34**	50c. dull purple and red	3·75	1·60
		a. Thin striated paper (1941)	£150	£150
120	**33**	$1 green and mauve	3·75	1·25
		a. Thin striated paper (1941)	75·00	75·00
121	**35**	$2 green and carmine (1923)	20·00	15·00
		a. Thin striated paper (1941)	10·00	4·00
122		$3 green and blue (1925)	70·00	95·00
123		$4 green and brown (1926)	£110	£190
		w. Wmk inverted	£800	
124		$5 green and orange	60·00	50·00
		a. Thin striated paper (1941)	75·00	
125	**34**	$10 green and black (1924)	£275	£400
		a. Thin striated paper (1941)	£500	
126		$50 green and ultramarine (F.C. £100)	£1100	
		s. Optd "Specimen"	£200	
127		$100 green and scarlet (F.C. £150)	£1700	
		s. Optd "Specimen"	£300	
128	**35**	$500 blue and red (1926) (F.C. £350)	£20000	
		s. Optd "Specimen"	£900	
103/25 *Set of 23*			£550	£700
103s/25s Optd or Perf (12c. ultram, 30c., 40c.) "Specimen" *Set of 23*			£800	

Printings of the 1c., 2c., 6c., 10c., 50c., $1, $2, $5 and $10 on thin striated paper were made in 1941 by Williams, Lea & Co. Ltd. following bomb damage to the De La Rue works on 29 December 1940.

(Recess Waterlow)

1935 (15 May). 50th Anniv of Treaty Relations with Great Britain. Wmk Mult Script CA (sideways). P 12½.

129	**37**	8c. bright violet and slate	4·25	3·00
		s. Perf "Specimen"	65·00	

38 Sultan Sir Ibrahim

39 Sultan Sir Ibrahim

(Recess D.L.R.)

1940 (Feb). Wmk Mult Script CA. P 13½.

130	**38**	8c. black and pale blue	22·00	1·00
		s. Perf "Specimen"	75·00	

38a King George VI and Queen Elizabeth

38b King George VI and Queen Elizabeth

(Des and photo Waterlow (T **38a**). Design recess; name typo B.W. (T **38b**))

1948 (1 Dec). Royal Silver Wedding. Wmk Mult Script CA.

131	**38a**	10c. violet (p 14×15)	20	75
132	**38b**	$5 green (p 11½×11)	25·00	45·00

1949 (2 May)–**55**. Wmk Mult Script CA. Chalk-surfaced paper. P 17½×18.

133	**39**	1c. black	50	10
134		2c. orange	20	20
		a. Orange-yellow (22.1.52)	1·75	2·50
135		3c. green	50	1·00
		a. Yellow-green (22.1.52)	20·00	3·75
136		4c. brown	1·00	10
136*a*		5c. bright purple (1.9.52)	70	30
137		6c. grey	60	20
		a. Pale grey (22.1.52)	60	50
		ac. Error. St. Edward's Crown W **9b**	£2250	£1700
138		8c. scarlet	3·75	1·25
138*a*		8c. green (1.9.52)	6·00	2·25
139		10c. magenta	70	10
		aa. Imperf (pair)	£3250	
139*a*		12c. scarlet (1.9.52)	7·00	6·00
140		15c. ultramarine	3·50	10
141		20c. black and green	1·25	1·00
141*a*		20c. bright blue (1.9.52)	1·00	10
142		25c. purple and orange	3·25	10
142*a*		30c. scarlet and purple (4.9.55)	1·75	2·75
142*b*		35c. scarlet and purple (1.9.52)	7·50	1·25
143		40c. red and purple	6·00	14·00
144		50c. black and blue	3·75	10
145		$1 blue and purple	8·00	2·00
146		$2 green and scarlet	20·00	9·50
147		$5 green and brown	42·00	14·00
133/47 *Set of 21*			£110	50·00

1949 (10 Oct). 75th Anniv of U.P.U. As Nos. 96/9 of Brunei.

148	10c. purple	30	40
149	15c. deep blue	2·00	1·25
150	25c. orange	65	3·50
151	50c. blue-black	1·25	3·75
148/51 *Set of 4*		3·75	8·00

39a Queen Elizabeth II

(Des and eng B.W. Recess D.L.R.)

1953 (2 June). Coronation. Wmk Mult Script CA. P 13½×13..

152	**39a**	10c. black and reddish purple	1·25	10

40 Sultan Sir Ibrahim

41 Sultan Sir Ismail and Johore Coat of Arms

(Recess D.L.R.)

1955 (1 Nov). Diamond Jubilee of Sultan. Wmk Mult Script CA. P 14.

153	**40**	10c. carmine-red	10	10

(Photo Courvoisier)

1960 (10 Feb). Coronation of Sultan. No wmk. P 11½.

154	**41**	10c. multicoloured	20	20

1960. As T **9/19** of Kedah, but with portrait of Sultan Ismail. P 13½ ($1); others 12½×13 (vert) or 13×12½ (horiz).

155	1c. black (7.10.60)	10	50
156	2c. orange-red (7.10.60)	10	1·25
157	4c. sepia (19.8.60)	10	10
158	5c. carmine-lake (7.10.60)	10	10
159	8c. myrtle-green (9.12.60)	1·50	3·00
160	10c. deep maroon (10.6.60)	30	10
161	20c. blue (9.12.60)	2·00	1·00
162	50c. black and bright blue (19.8.60)	50	20
163	$1 ultramarine and reddish purple (9.12.60)	3·00	5·50
164	$2 bronze-green and scarlet (9.12.60)	13·00	20·00
165	$5 brown and bronze-green (7.10.60)	32·00	40·00
155/65 *Set of 11*		48·00	65·00

In No. 161 there are only two figures in the boat, the steersman being missing. In the 20c. value for all the other dates there are three figures.

The 6, 12, 25 and 30c. values used with this issue were Nos. 1/4 of Malayan Federation.

42 *Vanda hookeriana* (Inset portrait of Sultan Ismail)

(Des A. Fraser-Brunner. Photo Harrison)

1965 (15 Nov). T **42** and similar horiz designs. W w **13** (upright). P 14½.

166	1c. Type **42**	10	30
	a. Grey (orchid's name and part of flower) omitted	£375	
	w. Wmk inverted	2·50	
167	2c. *Arundina graminifolia*	10	1·00
168	5c. *Paphiopedilum niveum*	10	10
	b. Yellow (flower) omitted	£110	
169	6c. *Spathoglottis plicata*	40	30
170	10c. *Arachnis flos-aeris*	40	20
	a. Green omitted	£150	
171	15c. *Rhyncostylis retusa*	1·50	10
	b. Green (face value and leaves) omitted	£700	
172	20c. *Phalaenopsis violacea*	1·50	75
	a. Bright purple (blooms) omitted	£300	
166/72 *Set of 7*		3·50	2·25

The 2c. to 15c. exist with both PVA gum and gum arabic.

The 2c. with black (name of state, arms and head) omitted is listed under Sarawak No. 213a as there is some evidence that a sheet was issued there; if it also exists from any of the other states it would, of course, be identical.

The higher values used with this issue were Nos. 20/27 of Malaysia (National Issues).

1970. As No. 166 and 170 but W w **13** (sideways).

173	1c. multicoloured (20.11)	1·75	6·50
174	10c. multicoloured (27.5)	1·75	2·50

44 *Delias ninus* (Inset portrait of Sultan Ismail)

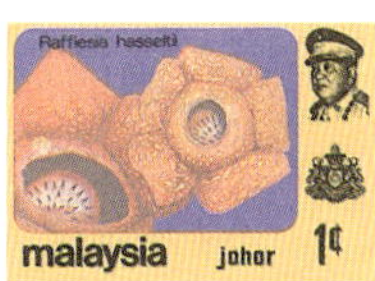

45 *Rafflesia hasseltii* (Inset portrait of Sultan Ismail)

(Des V. Whiteley)

1971 (1 Feb)–**78**. Butterflies. T **44** and similar horiz designs. Multicoloured. No wmk. P 13½×13.

(a) Litho by Bradbury, Wilkinson

175	1c. Type **44**	50	2·00
176	2c. *Danaus melanippus*	1·50	2·75
177	5c. *Parthenos sylvia*	1·50	20
178	6c. *Papilio demoleus*	1·50	2·25
179	10c. *Hebomoia glaucippe*	1·50	20
180	15c. *Precis orithya*	1·75	10
181	20c. *Valeria valeria*	1·75	50
175/81 *Set of 7*		9·00	7·00

(b) Photo Harrison (1977-78)

182	1c. Type **44**	1·50	3·75
183	2c. *Danaus melanippus*	1·50	5·50
184	5c. *Parthenos sylvia*	4·75	80
185	10c. *Hebomoia glaucippe*	3·00	40
186	15c. *Precis orithya*	5·00	25
187	20c. *Valeria valeria*	5·50	1·25
182/7 *Set of 6*		19·00	11·00

The higher values used with this issue were Nos. 64/71 of Malaysia (National Issues).

DIFFERENCES BETWEEN LITHO AND PHOTO PRINTINGS. Stamps from the photogravure printings can be easily identified by the appearance of certain features. The differences are most easily observed on the face values and inscriptions. Stamps printed by lithography show straight edges to letters and figures, but when those produced by photogravure are examined under a magnifying glass it will be seen that these edges are broken by the photogravure screen.

In addition the backgrounds and portraits of those stamps of this series printed by lithography show a regular screen of dots, a feature not visible on those printed by the photogravure process.

A number of instances have come to light of photogravure stamps which have had the top colour "removed" by means of an eraser.

(Des M. Yusof bin Mohammed; adapted Malaysian Advertising Services. Litho Asher and Co., Melbourne)

1979 (30 Apr). Flowers. Horiz designs as T **45**. Multicoloured. W **95** of Malaysia (sideways). P 15×14½.

188	1c. Type **45**	10	1·00
189	2c. *Pterocarpus indicus*	10	1·00
190	5c. *Lagerstroemia speciosa*	10	60
191	10c. *Dario zibethinus*	15	10
192	15c. *Hibiscus roses-sinensis*	15	10
193	20c. *Rhododendron scortechinii*	20	25
194	25c. *Etlingera elatior* (inscr "*Phaeomeria speciosa*")	40	25
188/94 *Set of 7*		1·00	2·75

For higher values used in conjunction with this series see Nos. 190/7 of Malaysia.

1983 (16 June)–**85**. As Nos. 190/3 but without wmk.

197	5c. *Lagerstroemia speciosa* (20.11.83)	1·50	1·60
198	10c. *Durio zibethinus* (11.7.85)	1·50	1·60
199	15c. *Hibiscus roses-sinensis* (12.83)	1·00	20
200	20c. *Rhododendron scortechinii* (blackish brown background)	24·00	1·00
200*a*	20c. *Rhododendron scortechinii* (bronze green background) (23.9.83)	1·60	65

*There was no official release date for these stamps. Dates shown are the earliest recorded from postmarks and may be revised if earlier examples are reported.

On Nos. 197/9 and 200a the "Johore" inscription is in rounded instead of square-ended letters.

WATERMARKED AND UNWATERMARKED PRINTINGS. The first printing of the 20s, value on unwatermarked paper was from the same plates and in the same shades as the original watermarked issue.

Subsequent no watermark printings of the 20c. and all no watermark printings of the other values were in changed shades and can be readily identified as follows:

5c. No watermark printing has the frame in turquoise-blue instead of the dull blue of the watermarked version.

10c. No watermark printing shows a purple-brown background instead of the sepia of the watermarked.

15c. No watermark printing shows stronger highlights in the design and more detail on the flowers and leaves.

20c. Later no watermark printings have a bronze-green background instead of the blackish brown shown on the watermarked and first no watermark stamps.

25c. No watermark printing has a deep background with more detail on the flower. The latin inscription has also been moved downwards to a more central position up the side of the vignette.

Differences also occur in the plates used to apply the state names, rulers' portraits or crests. Notes on these are provided under the individual issues.

46 Coconuts (Inset portrait of Sultan Mahmood)

(Des Kathy Wong. Litho Security Printers (M), Malaysia)

1988 (25 Oct)–**96**. Agricultural Products of Malaysia. Vert designs as T **46**. Multicoloured. W **138**. Phosphorised paper. P 12.

202	1c. Type **46**	10	20
	w. Wmk inverted		
203	2c. Coconuts	10	40
204	5c. Cocoa	15	10
	aw. wmk inverted		
	c. Perf 14×13¾ (1994)	3·25	30
	cw. wmk inverted	6·50	
	e. Perf 14×14½ (1998)	20·00	
	f. Perf 14¾×14½ (1995)	1·50	10
205	10c. Black pepper	15	10
	a. Imperf (pair)	£200	
	c. Perf 14×13¼ (1994)	3·25	30
	e. Perf 14×14½ (1996)	4·50	20
	f. Perf 14¾×14½ (1999)	14·00	
206	15c. Rubber	25	10
207	20c. Oil palm	25	15
	aw. Wmk inverted		
	c. Perf 14×13¾ (1994)	1·75	30
	e. Perf 14×14½ (1996)	15·00	50
	f. Perf 14¾×14½ (1994)	1·75	10

	fw. Wmk inverted (1994)	11·00	
208	30c. Rice	30	15
	c. Perf 14×13¾ (1994)	3·00	30
	cw. wmk inverted (1995)	12·00	
	e. Perf 14×14½	4·00	
	f. Perf 14¾×14½ (1994)	14·00	1·25
202/8	*Set of 7*	1·10	1·00

PERFORATION VARIETIES. Delays in the production of new definitives to replace the Agricultural Products issue led to an extended series of new printings as the postal authorities in the various states indented, on an annual basis, for fresh stocks of those values which were running short. These annual indents were identified by the plate numbers used so that 1A = 1986-87, 2A 1987-88 etc.

Many of these printings show different perforations from the gauge 12 of the original set. Those perforations known to us have been listed. The order of listing may not show the chronological sequence parts of which remain unclear. Other perforations may well exist on these stamps.

Stamps apparently perforated 14 are now believed to result from the dimensional instability of a batch of paper used in 1994-95. These are no longer listed as the variable nature of the paper produces inaccurate perforation readings.

To assist identification the perforations are quoted to the nearest ¼. The exact decimal equivalents are as follows:

13½×13¾ = 13.5×13.75 (used 1991-1993)
14×13¾ = 14.1×13.75 (used 1993-1997)
14×14½ = 14.1×14.4 (used 1994-1999)
14¾×14½ = 14.75×14.4 (used 1994-1996)

2003. Vert designs as T **46** but redenominated in "sen". Multicoloured. W **138**. P 14×13¾.

209	30s. Rice	1·75	10

47 *Nelumbium nelumbo* (sacred lotus) (Inset portrait of Sultan Mahmud Iskandar)

(Des Prof. Dato Raja Zahabuddin Raja Yaacob. Litho National Security Printers)

2007 (31 Dec). Garden Flowers. T **47** and similar vert designs. Multicoloured. W **138**. Phosphorised paper. P 14.

210	5s. Type **47**	10	10
211	10s. *Hydrangea macrophylla*	15	10
212	20s. *Hippeastrum reticulatum*	25	15
213	30s. Bougainvillea	40	20
214	40s. *Ipomoea indica*	50	30
215	50s. *Hibiscus rosa-sinensis*	65	35
210/15	*Set of 6*	1·90	1·10

STAMP BOOKLETS

1928. Black on white card. Interleaved with tissue. Stapled.

SB1	$2 booklet containing ten 1c. and 2c. (Nos. 103, 105), twenty 4c. (No. 108), each in blocks of 10 and eighteen 5c. (No. 109) in blocks of 6	£2000

1929. Black on pink cover. Stapled.

SB2	$1 booklet containing 2c., 3c. and 5c. (Nos. 105, 107, 109) in blocks of 10	

1930. Black on buff cover. Stapled.

SB3	$1 booklet containing ten 1c. and 5c. (Nos. 103, 109) and twenty 2c. (Nos. 105) in blocks of 10..	

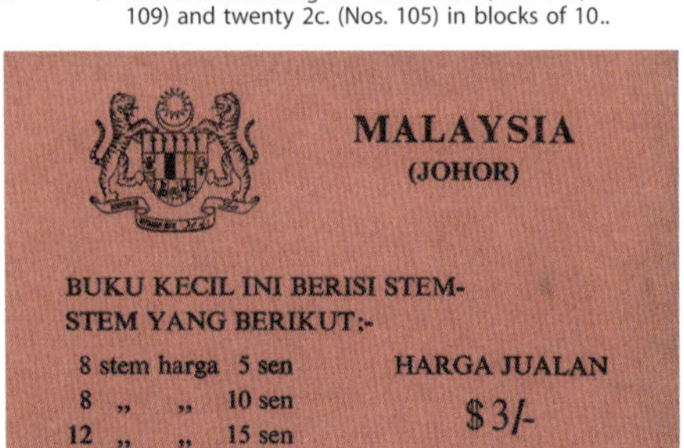

B **1**

1973 (8 Dec). Black on light magenta cover as Type B **1**. Stitched.

SB4	$3 booklet containing eight 5c., 10c. and twelve 15c. (Nos. 177, 179/80) in blocks of 4	35·00

1979 (1 Dec). Black on pink cover as Type B **1**, but 80×50 mm.

SB5	$3 booklet containing eight 5c., 10c. and twelve 15c. (Nos. 190/2) in blocks of 4	10·00

No. SB5 exists with two different versions of the back cover.

B **2** Produce

1987 (1 June). Black on orange-yellow cover as Type B **2**. Stapled.

SB6	$2 booklet containing 5c., 10c., 15c. and 20c. (Nos. 204/7) in blocks of 4	13·00

B **3** Sultan Abdul Samad Building, Kuala Lumpur

1992 (1 July). "Kuala Lumpur '92" International Philatelic Exhibition. Multicoloured cover as Type B **3**. Stamps attached by selvedge.

SB7	$3 booklet containing 30c. (No. 208) in block of 10	8·00

1993. Multicoloured on pale green (No. SB8) or on pale buff (No. SB9) covers as Type B **3**, but with face values and "Kuala Lumpur" logo replaced by postal service emblem and face value, both at bottom right. Stamps attached by selvedge.

SB8	$2 booklet containing 20c. (No. 207) in block of 10	1·50
SB9	$3 booklet containing 30c. (No. 208) in block of 10	2·00

POSTAGE DUE STAMPS

D **1**

(Typo Waterlow)

1938 (1 Jan). Wmk Mult Script CA. P 12½.

D1	D **1**	1c. carmine	17·00	45·00
D2		4c. green	40·00	40·00
D3		8c. orange	48·00	£150
D4		10c. brown	48·00	50·00
D5		12c. purple	55·00	£130
D1/5		*Set of 5*	£180	£375
D1s/5s		Perf "Specimen" *Set of 5*	£160	

KEDAH

The Thai monarchy exercised suzerainty over Kedah and the other northern states of the Malay peninsula from the 16th century onwards. The extent of Thai involvement in its internal affairs was very variable, being dependent on the strength, or otherwise, of the Bangkok administration and the degree of co-operation of the local ruler.

The Thai postal service, which had been inaugurated in 1883, gradually extended into the north of the Malay penninsula and an office was opened at Alor Star in Kedah during 1887 with the earliest known postmark being dated 27 October. Further post offices at Kuala Muda (3 Oct 1907), Kulim (7 July 1907) and Langkawi (16 Feb 1908) followed.

A straight-line obliteration showing "Kedah" between short vertical dashes is not believed to be genuine.

Stamps of Thailand used in Kedah

Types of Thailand (Siam)

1

2

9

๓ อัฐ 1 (12)   ๒ อัฐ 2 (17)   ๒ อัฐ 2 (18)

4 atts (24)   4 atts (25)

1 Atts.

ราคา ๑ อัฐ (27)   2 Atts. (28)   2 (33)

1 Att.   1 Att.

ราคา๑ อัฐ (34)   ราคา ๑ อัฐ (35)   1 Att. (36)

2 Atts.   10 Atts.

ราคา ๒ อัฐ (37)   2 Atts. (38)   ราคา๑๐อัฐ (39)

4 Atts. (40)   4 Atts. (41)

1 Att.

ราคา ๑ อัฐ (42)   2 Atts. (44)   3 Atts. (45)   4 Atts. (46)

2 Atts. (48a)

49

50

1 Att. ๑ อัฐ (51)

53

๔ อัฐ

1att. (56)   9 Atts (59)

The following types of postmark were used on Siamese stamps from the Malay tributary states:

Type A. Single ring with date at foot (examples from 1900 show the year in manuscript)

Type B. Single ring with date in centre

Type C. Double ring. Bilingual

Type D. Double ring. English at top and ornament at foot

PRICES are for stamps showing a large part of the postmark with the inscription clearly visible.

The Siamese post office at Alor Star was opened during 1887 with the first known postmark being dated 27 October. Further post offices at Kuala Muda (3 Oct 1907), Kulim (7 July 1907) and Langkawi (16 Feb 1908) followed.

A straight-line obliteration showing "KEDAH" between short vertical dashes is not believed to be genuine.

Alor Star

Stamps of SIAM cancelled as Type A inscribed "KEDAH".

1883. (Nos. 1/5).

Z2	**1**	1att. rose-carmine	£250
Z3		1sio. red	£450
Z4	**2**	1sik. yellow	£450

1897–91. (Nos. 11/18).

Z6	**9**	1a. green	85·00
Z7		2a. green and carmine	75·00
Z8		3a. green and blue	95·00
Z9		4a. green and brown	85·00
Z10		8a. green and yellow	85·00
Z11		12a. purple and carmine	75·00
Z12		24a. purple and blue	85·00
Z13		64a. purple and brown	£150

1889–91. Surch as T **12** (Nos. Z15, Z19), T **17** (No. Z21) or T **18** (No. Z22) (Nos. 20/30).

Z15	**9**	1a. on 2a. rose-carmine	95·00
Z19		1a. on 3a. red	£110
Z21		2a. on 3a. yellow	£150
Z22		2a. on 3a. green and blue	£180

1892. Surch as T **24/5** (with or without stop) and Siamese handstamp (Nos. 33/6).

Z28	**9**	4a. on 24a. purple and blue (Type **24**)	95·00
Z29		4a. on 24a. purple and blue (Type **25**)	£120
Z30		4a. on 24a. purple and blue (Type **24** with stop)	£120
Z31		4a. on 24a. purple and blue (Type **25** with stop)	£120

1894. Surch as T **27** with variations of English figures as T **28** and **33** (Nos. 37/44).

Z34	**9**	2a. on 64a. purple and brown (Type **28**)	95·00
Z39		2a. on 64a. purple and brown (Type **33**)	95·00

1894. Surch with T **34** (No. 45).

Z41	**9**	1a. on 64a. purple and brown	£120

1894–95. Surch as T **35** with variations of English figures as T **36/9** (Nos. 46/50).

Z42	**9**	1a. on 64a. purple and brown (Type **35**)	95·00
Z43		1a. on 64a. purple and brown (Type **36**)	95·00
Z44		2a. on 64a. purple and brown (Type **37**)	95·00
Z45		2a. on 64a. purple and brown (Type **38**)	95·00
Z46		10a. on 24a. purple and blue (Type **39**)	95·00

1896. Surch as T **39** (Siamese) and T **40** (English) (No. 51).

Z47	**9**	4a. on 12a. purple and carmine	95·00

1897. Surch as T **39** (Siamese) and T **41** (English) (No. 52).

Z48	**9**	4a. on 12a. purple and carmine	95·00

1898–99. Surch as T **42** with variations of English section as T **44/6** (Nos. 53/62).

Z49	**9**	1a. on 12a. purple and carmine (Type **42**–11½ mm long)	£130
Z52		2a. on 64a. purple and brown (Type **44**)	£110
Z53		3a. on 12a. purple and carmine (Type **45**–13½ mm long)	95·00
Z54		3a. on 12a. purple and carmine (Type **45**–11½ to 11¾ mm long)	95·00
Z55		4a. on 12a. purple and carmine (Type **46**–8 mm long)	95·00
Z56		4a. on 12a. purple and carmine (Type **46**–8½ to 9 mm long)	95·00

1899. Surch in Siamese and English with T **48a** (Nos. 63/6).

Z62	**9**	2a. on 64a. purple and brown	£110

1899–1904. (Nos. 67/81).

Z63	**49**	1a. olive-green (wide Siamese characters in face value)	95·00
Z64		2a. grass-green	75·00
Z65		3a. red and blue	80·00
Z66		4a. carmine	75·00
Z67		8a. deep green and orange	75·00
Z69		12a. brown-purple and carmine	£120
Z70		24a. brown-purple and blue	£180
Z71		64a. brown-purple and chestnut	£150

1899. (Nos. 82/6).

Z72	**50**	1a. green	£325
Z73		2a. green and red	£475

Stamps of SIAM cancelled as Type B *inscr* "KEDAH" (*from* March 1901).

1887–91. (Nos. 11/18).

Z74	**9**	12a. purple and carmine	75·00
Z75		24a. purple and brown	75·00

1898–99. Surch with T **42** with variations of English section as T **45/6** (Nos. 53/62).

Z76	**9**	1a. on 12a. purple and carmine (Type **42**–11½ mm long)	95·00
Z81		3a. on 12a. purple and carmine (Type **45**–11½ to 11¾ mm long)	75·00
Z83		4a. on 12a. purple and carmine (Type **46**–8½ to 9 mm long)	75·00
Z84		4a. on 24a. purple and blue (Type **46**)	80·00

1899–1904. (Nos. 67/81).

Z86	**49**	1a. olive-green (wide Siamese characters in face value)	75·00
		a. Narrow Siamese characters in face value	70·00
Z87		2a. grass-green	60·00
Z88		2a. scarlet and pale blue	60·00
Z89		3a. red and blue	70·00
Z90		3a. deep green	70·00
Z91		4a. carmine	60·00
Z92		4a. chocolate and pink	65·00
Z93		8a. deep green and orange	60·00
Z94		10a. ultramarine	60·00
Z95		12a. brown-purple and carmine	70·00
Z96		24a. brown-purple and blue	£150
Z97		64a. brown-purple and chestnut	£140

1905–09. (Nos. 92/105).

Z102	**53**	1a. green and orange	60·00
Z103		2a. grey and deep violet	60·00
Z104		3a. green	70·00
Z105		4a. pale red and sepia	60·00
Z106		5a. carmine	70·00
Z107		8a. olive-bistre and dull black	60·00
Z108		12a. blue	70·00
Z109		24a. red-brown	£180
Z110		1t. bistre and deep blue	£180

Stamps of SIAM cancelled as Type C inscr "Kedah" at foot (from July 1907).

1887–91. (Nos. 11/18).

Z111	**9**	12a. purple and carmine	85·00

1899–1904. (Nos. 67/81).

Z112	**49**	1a. olive-green (wide Siamese characters in face value)	70·00
		a. Narrow Siamese characters in face value	65·00
Z113		2a. scarlet and pale blue	60·00
Z114		3a. red and blue	70·00
Z116		8a. deep green and orange	65·00
Z117		10a. ultramarine	65·00
Z118		12a. brown-purple and carmine	65·00

1905–09. (Nos. 95/105).

Z128	**53**	1a. green and orange	60·00
Z129		2a. grey and deep violet	60·00
Z130		3a. green	70·00
Z131		4a. pale red and sepia	60·00
Z132		4a. scarlet	60·00
Z133		5a. carmine	70·00
Z134		8a. olive-bistre and dull black	60·00
Z135		9a. blue	60·00
Z136		18a. red-brown	95·00
Z137		24a. red-brown	£180
Z138		1t. bistre and deep blue	£180

1907. Surch with T **56** (No. 109).

Z139	**9**	1a. on 24a. purple and blue	70·00

Kuala Muda

Stamps of SIAM cancelled as Type B inscr "KUALA MUDA" (from July 1907).

1887–91. (Nos. 11/18).

Z143	**9**	12a. purple and carmine	£375

1899–1904. (Nos. 67/81).

Z144	**49**	2a. scarlet and pale blue	£375
Z145		24a. brown-purple and blue	£425

1905–09. (Nos. 92/105).

Z146	**53**	1a. green and orange	£375
Z147		2a. grey and deep violet	£375
Z148		3a. green	£400

Z150 5a. carmine £400
Z151 8a. olive-bistre and dull black £375

Stamps of SIAM cancelled as Type C inscr "Kwala Muda" at foot (from 1907).

1887–91. (Nos. 11/18).
Z155 **9** 12a. purple and carmine £170

1899–1904. (Nos. 67/81).
Z156 **49** 8a. deep green and orange £200
Z157 10a. ultramarine £200

1905–09. (Nos. 92/105).
Z158 **53** 1a. green and orange £200
Z159 2a. grey and deep violet £200
Z160 3a. green £225
Z161 4a. pale red and sepia £200
Z162 4a. scarlet £200
Z163 5a. carmine £250
Z164 8a. olive-bistre and dull black £200
Z165 9a. blue £170
Z166 24a. red-brown £425

1907. Surch with T **56** (No. 109).
Z167 **9** 1a. on 24a. purple and blue £170

Kulim

Stamps of SIAM cancelled as Type D inscr "KULIM" (from July 1907).

1887–91. (Nos. 11/18).
Z173 **9** 12a. purple and carmine £375

1899–1904. (Nos. 67/81).
Z174 **49** 8a. deep green and orange £375

1905–09. (Nos. 92/105).
Z175 **53** 1a. green and orange £400
Z176 2a. grey and deep violet £400
Z177 3a. green £425
Z178 4a. pale red and sepia £375
Z179 4a. scarlet £375
Z180 5a. carmine £400
Z181 8a. olive-bistre and dull black £375
Z182 9a. blue £375

1907. Surch with T **56** (No. 109).
Z184 **9** 1a. on 24a. purple and blue £375

Stamps of SIAM cancelled as Type C inscr "Kulim" at foot (from Feb 1908).

1887–91. (Nos. 11/18).
Z190 **9** 12a. purple and carmine £150

1899–1904. (Nos. 67/81).
Z191 **49** 8a. deep green and orange £150
Z192 10a. ultramarine £160

1905–09. (Nos. 92/105).
Z196 **53** 4a. pale red and sepia £150
Z197 4a. scarlet £150
Z198 5a. carmine £160
Z199 9a. blue £160
Z200 24a. red-brown £375
Z201 1t. bistre and deep blue £375

1907. Surch with T **56** (No. 109).
Z202 **9** 1a. purple and blue £160

Langkawi

Stamps of SIAM cancelled as Type D inscr "LANGKAWI" (from Feb 1908).

1899–1904. (Nos. 67/81).
Z208 **49** 8a. deep green and orange £375
Z209 10a. ultramarine £375

1905–09. (Nos. 92/105).
Z212 **53** 3a. green £400
Z213 4a. pale red and sepia £375
Z215 8a. olive-bistre and dull black £375

Stamps of SIAM cancelled as Type C inscr "Langkawi" at foot (from Nov 1908).

1887–91. (Nos. 11/18).
Z219 **9** 12a. purple and carmine £160

1899–1904. (Nos. 67/81).
Z220 **49** 1a. olive-green (Type B) £170
Z221 8a. green and orange £160

1905–09. (Nos. 92/105).
Z222 **53** 2a. grey and deep violet £160
Z223 3a. green £225
Z224 4a. pale red and sepia £160
Z225 4a. scarlet £170
Z226 8a. olive-bistre and dull black £160
Z228 24a. red-brown £425
Z229 1t. bistre and deep blue £425

1907. Surch with T **56** (No. 109).
Z230 **9** 1a. on 24a. purple and blue £170

Suzerainty over Kedah was transferred by Thailand to Great Britain on 15 July 1909 and the following day stamps of the FEDERATED MALAY STATES were placed on sale in post offices in the state.

A Treaty of Friendship between Great Britain and Kedah was signed on 1 November 1923 and the state joined the Federation of Malaya on 1 February 1948.

Stamps of the Federated Malay States used in Kedah

Alor Star

Cancelled as Type C inscribed "Kedah"

1909–12. (Nos. 29/49).
Z231 **3** 1c. green (Die II) 35·00
Z232 3c. carmine 40·00
Z233 4c. black and rose 40·00
Z234 5c. green and carmine/*yellow* 90·00
Z235 8c. grey-brown and ultramarine 90·00
a. Wmk upright 55·00
Z236 10c. black and purple 70·00
Z237 20c. mauve and black (chalk-surfaced paper) 75·00
Z238 50c. grey-brown and orange-brown (chalk-surfaced paper) 85·00
Z239 **4** $1 grey-green and green £190

Type F

Cancelled as Type F

1909–12. (No. 34).
Z241 **3** 3c. carmine 60·00

Type G

Cancelled as Type G

1909–12. (Nos. 34/47cc).
Z242 **3** 1c. green (Die II) 50·00
Z243 3c. carmine 50·00
Z244 4c. black and rose 75·00
Z245 8c. grey-brown and ultramarine
a. Wmk upright 75·00
Z246 10c. black and purple 75·00
Z247 50c. grey-brown and orange-brown (chalk-surfaced paper) 85·00

Kulim

Type H

Cancelled as Type H

1909–12. (Nos. 34/45a).

Z248	**3**	1c. green (Die II)	60·00
Z249		3c. carmine	55·00
Z250		4c. black and rose	60·00
Z251		5c. green and carmine/*yellow*	90·00
Z252		10c. black and purple	90·00
Z253		20c. mauve and black (chalk-surfaced paper)	80·00

Type I

Cancelled as Type I

1909–12. (Nos. 34/43d).

Z254	3c. carmine	55·00
Z255	4c. black and rose	65·00
Z255a	10c. black and purple	£100

Langkawi

Cancelled as Type H inscribed "LANGKAWI"

1909–12. (Nos. 34/49).

Z256	**3**	3c. carmine	90·00
Z256a		5c. green and carmine/*yellow*	£110
Z257		8c. grey-brown and ultramarine (wmk upright)	90·00
Z258	**4**	$1 grey-green and green	£225
Z259		$2 green and carmine	£325

Cancelled as Type I inscribed "LANGKAWI"

1909–12. (Nos. 29/43d).

Z260	**3**	1c. green (Die II)	90·00
Z261		3c. carmine	48·00
Z262		10c. black and purple	90·00

Kuala Muda

Cancelled as Type B inscribed "KUALA MUDA"

1909–12. (Nos. 29/41bb).

Z263	**3**	1c. green (Die II)	75·00
Z264		3c. carmine	48·00
Z265		4c. black and rose	85·00
Z266		5c. green and carmine/*yellow*	85·00
Z267		8c. grey-brown and ultramarine (wmk upright)	85·00

Jitra

The post office in Jitra was opened in 1910.

Type J

Cancelled as Type J

1910–12. (No. 34).

Z268	**3**	3c. carmine	75·00

Cancelled as Type I inscribed "JITRA"

1910–12. (Nos. 29/34).

Z269	**3**	1c. green Die II	45·00
Z270		3c. carmine	40·00

Lunas

The post office in Lunas was opened in 1910.

Type K

Cancelled as Type K

1910–12. (No. 34).

Z271	**3**	3c. carmine	95·00

Cancelled as Type I inscribed "LUNAS"

1910–12. (Nos. 29/36d).

Z272	**3**	1c. green (Die II)	65·00
Z273		3c. carmine	65·00
Z274		4c. black and rose	90·00

Semiling

The post office in Semiling was opened in 1910.

Cancelled as Type I inscribed "SEMILING"

1910–12. (Nos. 29/41b).

Z275	**3**	1c. green (Die II)	50·00
Z276		3c. carmine	85·00
Z277		4c. black and rose	85·00
Z278		8c. grey-brown and ultramarine (wmk upright)	85·00

Sungei Patani

The post office in Sungei Patani was opened in 1911.

Cancelled as Type I inscribed "SUNGEI PATANI"

1911–12. (Nos. 29/34).

Z279	**3**	1c. green (Die II)	£100
Z280		3c. carmine	£100

Yen

The post office in Yen was opened in 1910.

Cancelled as Type I inscribed "YEN"

1910–12. (Nos. 29/34).

Z281	**3**	1c. green (Die II)	£110
Z282		3c. carmine	£110

PRICES FOR STAMPS ON COVER TO 1945

Nos. 1/14	*from* × 15
Nos. 15/23	*from* × 10
Nos. 24/40	*from* × 8
Nos. 41/8	*from* × 12
Nos. 49/51	—
Nos. 52/9	*from* × 4
Nos. 60/8	*from* × 3
Nos. 68*a*/9	*from* × 4

1 Sheaf of Rice

2 Malay ploughing

3 Council Chamber, Alor Star

(Recess D.L.R.)

1912 (16 June). Wmk Mult Crown CA (sideways* on 10c. to $5). P 14.

1	**1**	1c. black and green	60	25
		y. Wmk inverted and reversed	£800	£375
2		3c. black and red	4·50	30
3		4c. rose and grey	10·00	25
4		5c. green and chestnut	2·25	3·00
5		8c. black and ultramarine	3·75	3·50
6	**2**	10c. blue and sepia	2·25	1·00
		w. Wmk Crown to left of CA	†	—
		y. Wmk Crown to left of CA and reversed	†	£350
7		20c. black and green	5·50	4·00
		x. Wmk reversed	£225	
8		30c. black and rose	3·00	11·00
9		40c. black and purple	3·50	17·00
10		50c. brown and blue	9·00	13·00
11	**3**	$1 black and red/*yellow*	16·00	22·00
		w. Wmk Crown to left of CA	55·00	
		x. Wmk reversed	£350	
		y. Wmk Crown to left of CA and reversed		
12		$2 green and brown	22·00	85·00
13		$3 black and blue/*blue*	95·00	£170
		a. "A" of "CA" missing from wmk	£1700	
14		$5 black and red	£100	£170
1/14 *Set of* 14			£250	£450
1s/14s Optd "Specimen" *Set of* 14			£300	

*The normal sideways watermark shows the Crown to right of CA, *as seen from the back of the stamp.*

Due to an increase in postal rates 1c. and 4c. stamps of STRAITS SETTLEMENTS were used in Kedah for some months from March 1919.

Short sheaf (R. 10/1)

(i)

(ii)

DOUBLE AND SINGLE PLATES. (i) Printed from separate plates for frame and centre, with dotted shading extending close to the central sheaf. Soft impression of centre with little clear detail.

(ii) Printed from single plate, with white space around sheaf. Centre more deeply etched with sharp image.

1919 (June)–**21**. New colours and values. Wmk Mult Crown CA (sideways* on 21c., 25c.). P 14.

15	**1**	1c. brown (i) (18.8.19)	55	50
		w. Wmk inverted	£130	£160
		y. Wmk inverted and reversed	†	£375
18		2c. green (ii)	50	30
19		3c. deep purple (i) (1920)	65	2·00
		x. Wmk reversed	£350	
		y. Wmk inverted and reversed	80·00	£130
20		4c. rose (i)	5·00	40
21		4c. red (ii) (18.8.19)	3·50	1·00
		a. Short sheaf	£130	60·00
		w. Wmk inverted		
22	**2**	21c. mauve and purple (18.8.19)	5·50	60·00
		a. "A" of "CA" missing from wmk	—	£700
		w. Wmk Crown to left of CA	£160	£190
		ws. Ditto, optd "Specimen"	£100	
		x. Wmk reversed	£350	
		y. Wmk Crown to left of CA and reversed	£325	
23		25c. blue and purple (1921)	1·75	29·00
		a. "A" of "CA" missing from wmk	£600	
15/23 *Set of* 6			11·00	80·00
15s/23s Optd "Specimen" *Set of* 6			£150	

*The normal sideways watermark shows Crown to right of CA, *as seen from the back of the stamp.*

ONE

DOLLAR

(**4**)

MALAYA-
BORNEO
EXHIBITION.

(**5**)

(Surch by Ribeiro & Co, Penang)

1919 (Mar). Surch as T **4**.

24	**3**	50c. on $2 green and brown	70·00	80·00
		a. "C" of "CENTS" inserted by handstamp (R. 6/4)	£1300	£1500
25		$1 on $3 black and blue/*blue*	20·00	90·00

Nos. 24/5 were surcharged from settings of 30 (5×6).

Two types of centre plate for Type **2** wmkd Mult Script CA:

Type I (Plate 1) (produced by electrotyping)

Type II (Plate 2) (produced by transfer die)

A new common centre plate, 2, was prepared from the original die in 1926. Stamps from Plate 2, produced using a transfer die, show considerably more detail of the ground and have the oxen, ploughman's hat and his clothing much more deeply cut as illustrated in Type II above.

1921–32. Wmk Mult Script CA (sideways* on 10c. to $5). P 14.

26	1	1c. brown (ii)	80	20
		w. Wmk inverted	†	£350
		y. Wmk inverted and reversed	†	£350
27		2c. dull green (ii) (Type I)	1·50	20
28		3c. deep purple (ii)	80	70
		w. Wmk inverted	£325	
29		4c. deep carmine (ii)	5·00	20
		a. Short sheaf	£170	32·00
30	2	10c. blue and sepia (I)	2·75	75
		ax. Wmk reversed	£375	
		ay. Wmk Crown to left of CA and reversed	£130	
		b. Type II (wmk Crown to left of CA) (1927)	55·00	2·75
		by. Wmk Crown to right of CA and reversed	£425	£300
31		20c. black and yellow-green (I)	4·50	2·00
32		21c. mauve and purple (I)	2·25	13·00
33		25c. blue and purple (I)	2·25	9·00
		a. Type II (wmk Crown to left of CA) (1932)	95·00	4·00
34		30c. black and rose (I) (1922)	3·00	11·00
		a. Type II (wmk Crown to left of CA) (1927)	50·00	3·00
35		40c. black and purple (I)	4·50	55·00
		aw. Wmk Crown to left of CA (1924)	42·00	48·00
		b. Type II (wmk Crown to left of CA) (1932)	95·00	26·00
36		50c. brown and grey-blue (I)	3·00	19·00
		aw. Wmk Crown to left of CA (1924)	40·00	21·00
		b. Type II (wmk Crown to left of CA) (1932)	£110	9·50
37	3	$1 black and red/*yellow* (1924)	75·00	80·00
		w. Wmk Crown to left of CA	6·50	9·50
38		$2 myrtle and brown	13·00	£100
		w. Wmk Crown to left of CA (1924)	32·00	90·00
39		$3 black and blue/*blue*	70·00	£100
		w. Wmk Crown to left of CA (1924)	£100	85·00
40		$5 black and deep carmine	85·00	£160
		w. Wmk Crown to left of CA (1926)	£130	£160
26/40 *Set of* 15			£180	£350
26s/40s Optd "Specimen" *Set of* 15			£300	

*The normal sideways watermark shows Crown to right of CA, *as seen from the back of the stamp.*

Nos. 26/40 were produced by De La Rue using the "wet" method of recess-printing during which the stamps contracted when they were dried before gumming. From 1933 the firm adopted the "dry" method, using pre-gummed paper, with the result that stamps were up to 0.5 mm larger in size. Of the low values as Type **1** in this series only the 2c. was still current when the "dry" method was introduced.

Stamps as Type **1** can be found perforated either comb or line. The 1c. and 4c. come comb only, the 3c. line only and the 2c. either way.

Examples of Nos. 37/40 are known with part strikes of a forged Sungei Patang postmark dated "14 JY 1920".

For the 2c. Type II see No. 69.

OVERPRINT SETTINGS FOR NOS. 41/51. The low values in Type **1** were overprinted using Setting II as detailed under Straits Settlements. The three listed constant varieties from the original typeset block of 12 occur in the same positions for these Kedah stamps as does the No Stop variety from R. 1/5 of the left pane.

For the higher values in Type **2**, which were in sheets of 60 (5×12), a further setting was prepared using the first four vertical rows of the typeset block with each horizontal row completed by a single random impression of the overprint. This means that, in addition to their positions in the truncated typeset block, the Oval last "O" additionally occurs on R. 11/5 and the Raised stop on R. 5/5 of the sheet. In this setting, as for the low values, "BORNEO" was 14 mm long.

Further supplies were subsequently required of the 21, 25 and 50c. values and these were produced using a completely different setting of 20 (5×4), applied three times to each sheet, on which "BORNEO" was 15–15½ mm long.

1922 (Apr). Malaya-Borneo Exhibition, Singapore. Optd as T **5** at Singapore.

I. "BORNEO" 14 mm long.

(a) Wmk Mult Crown CA (Nos. 10, 18 and 22/3).

41	1	2c. green (ii)	3·50	25·00
		b. Oval last "O" in "BORNEO"	8·00	45·00
		c. Raised stop after "EXHIBITION"	8·00	45·00
		d. Small second "A" in "MALAYA"	8·00	45·00
		f. No stop	40·00	
42	2	21c. mauve and purple	32·00	80·00
		b. Oval last "O" in "BORNEO"	50·00	£130
		c. Raised stop after "EXHIBITION"	50·00	£130
43		25c. blue and purple	32·00	80·00
		a. Opt inverted	£1500	
		b. Oval last "O" in "BORNEO"	50·00	£130
		c. Raised stop after "EXHIBITION"	50·00	£130
44		50c. brown and blue	32·00	95·00
		b. Oval last "O" in "BORNEO"	50·00	£150
		c. Raised stop after "EXHIBITION"	50·00	£150

(b) Wmk Mult Script CA (Nos. 26 and 28/30).

45	1	1c. brown (ii)	5·00	23·00
		b. Oval last "O" in "BORNEO"	10·00	42·00
		c. Raised stop after "EXHIBITION"	10·00	42·00
		d. Small second "A" in "MALAYA"	10·00	42·00
		f. No stop	45·00	
46		3c. deep purple (ii)	3·50	45·00
		b. Oval last "O" in "BORNEO"	8·00	70·00
		c. Raised stop after "EXHIBITION"	8·00	70·00
		d. Small second "A" in "MALAYA"	8·00	70·00
		f. No stop	40·00	
47		4c. deep carmine (ii)	3·50	25·00
		a. Short sheaf	£130	
		b. Oval last "O" in "BORNEO"	8·00	45·00
		c. Raised stop after "EXHIBITION"	8·00	45·00
		d. Small second "A" in "MALAYA"	8·00	45·00
		f. No stop	40·00	
48	2	10c. blue and sepia (I)	6·50	48·00
		b. Oval last "O" in "BORNEO"	12·00	75·00
		c. Raised stop after "EXHIBITION"	12·00	75·00
41/8 *Set of* 8			£110	£375

II. "BORNEO" 15–15½ mm long. Wmk Mult Crown CA (Nos. 10 and 22/3).

49	2	21c. mauve and purple	24·00	£100
50		25c. blue and purple	24·00	£120
51		50c. brown and blue	55·00	£170
49/51 *Set of* 3			90·00	£350

Examples of all values are known with part strikes of the forged postmark mentioned after Nos. 26/40.

1922–40. New colours, etc. Wmk Mult Script CA (sideways* on 12, 35c.). P 14.

52	1	1c. black (ii) (Type I)	1·00	10
53		3c. green (ii) (1924)	2·25	90
54		4c. violet (ii) (1926)	1·00	10
		a. Short sheaf	55·00	10·00
55		5c. yellow (ii)	1·75	10
		w. Wmk inverted	85·00	£100
		x. Wmk reversed	†	£250
		y. Wmk inverted and reversed	†	£250
56		6c. carmine (ii) (1926)	2·50	65
		a. Carmine-red (1940)	12·00	48·00
57		8c. grey-black (ii) (10.36)	15·00	10
58	2	12c. black and indigo (II) (1926)	6·50	3·50
59		35c. purple (II) (1926)	10·00	35·00
52/9 *Set of* 8			35·00	35·00
52s/9s Optd or Perf (8c.) "Specimen" *Set of* 8			£350	

*The normal sideways watermark shows Crown to left of CA, *as seen from the back of the stamp.*

With the exception of the 6c. and 8c. the printing plates for the Type **1** values listed above were, as for the previous issue, produced by electrotyping with the face values added to the plates by pantograph. The plates for the 6c. and 8c. values were constructed by the more modern method of using a transfer die to enter each impression.

Printings after November 1933 were normally produced by the "dry" method as described beneath Nos. 26/40. There were late "wet" printings of the 1c. (No. 68*a*) and 2c. (No. 27) in August 1938. The 3c. only exists from a "wet" printing, the 6c. (No. 56*a*) and 8c. from dry printings and the remainder from either method.

Stamps as Type **1** can be found perforated either comb or line. The 3c. and 6c. (No. 56) come comb only, the 6c. (No. 56*a*) and 8c. line only and the 1, 4 and 5c. either way.

For the 1c. Type II see No. 68*a*.

6 Sultan Abdul Hamid Halimshah

(Recess Waterlow)

1937 (30 June). Wmk Mult Script CA. P 12½.

60	**6**	10c. ultramarine and sepia	5·00	2·00
61		12c. black and violet	50·00	4·50
		a. "A" of "CA" missing from wmk		
62		25c. ultramarine and purple	10·00	4·50
63		30c. green and scarlet	9·00	10·00
64		40c. black and purple	4·75	16·00
65		50c. brown and blue	9·50	4·50
66		$1 black and green	4·00	10·00
67		$2 green and brown	£130	75·00
68		$5 black and scarlet	35·00	£170
60/8 *Set of 9*			£225	£275
60s/8s Perf "Specimen" *Set of 9*			£300	

I II I II

1938 (May)–**40**. As Nos. 52 and 27, but face values redrawn as Types II.

68*a*	**1**	1c. black	£130	3·00
69		2c. bright green (1940)	£275	6·50

1c. Type II. Figures "1" have square-cut corners instead of rounded, and larger top serif. Larger "C". Line perf. Produced from a new electrotyped Plate 2 with different engraved face values. Printings exist from either the "wet" or "dry" methods.

2c. Type II. Figures "2" have circular instead of oval drops and the letters "c" are thin and tall instead of thick and rounded. Produced from a new plate, made from a transfer die, and printed by the "dry" method.

1948 (1 Dec). Royal Silver Wedding. As Nos. 131/2 of Johore.

70	10c. violet	20	40
71	$5 carmine	28·00	42·00

1949 (10 Oct). 75th Anniv of U.P.U. As Nos. 96/9 of Brunei.

72	10c. purple	25	1·25
73	15c. deep blue	2·00	1·50
74	25c. orange	65	2·50
75	50c. blue-black	1·00	4·25
	a. "A" of "CA" missing from watermark	£800	
72/5 *Set of 4*		3·50	8·50

7 Sheaf of Rice

8 Sultan Badlishah

1950 (1 June)–**55**. Wmk Mult Script CA. Chalk-surfaced paper. P 17½×18.

76	**7**	1c. black	50	30
77		2c. orange	50	15
78		3c. green	2·00	1·00
79		4c. brown	75	10
79*a*		5c. bright purple (1.9.52)	3·00	2·50
		ab. Bright mauve (24.9.53)	3·00	1·00
80		6c. grey	70	15
81		8c. scarlet	1·75	4·00
81*a*		8c. green (1.9.52)	2·50	1·75
		ab. Deep green (24.9.53)	17·00	17·00
82		10c. magenta	70	10
82*a*		12c. scarlet (1.9.52)	2·75	2·50
83		15c. ultramarine	2·75	35
84		20c. black and green	2·50	2·50
84*a*		20c. bright blue (1.9.52)	1·50	10
85	**8**	25c. purple and orange	1·50	30
85*a*		30c. scarlet and purple (4.9.55)	4·00	1·25
85*b*		35c. scarlet and purple (1.9.52)	3·50	1·50
86		40c. red and purple	4·25	7·00
87		50c. black and blue	3·50	35
88		$1 blue and purple	3·50	6·00
89		$2 green and scarlet	22·00	28·00
90		$5 green and brown	45·00	60·00
76/90 *Set of 21*			95·00	£110

1953 (2 June). Coronation. As No. 152 of Johore.

91	10c. black and reddish purple	2·00	60

9 Copra

10 Pineapples

11 Ricefield

12 Masjid Alwi Mosque, Kangar

13 East Coast Railway "Golden Blowpipe" Express

14 Tiger

15 Fishing Prau

16 Aborigines with Blowpipes

17 Government Offices

18 Bersilat

19 Weaving

(Recess D.L.R.)

1957. Inset portrait of Sultan Badlishah. W w **12**. P 13×12½ (1c. to 8c.), 12½×13 (10c., 20c.), 12½ (50c., $2, $5) or 13½ ($1).

92	**9**	1c. black (21.8)	10	60
93	**10**	2c. orange-red (25.7)	30	1·75
94	**11**	4c. sepia (21.8)	30	1·00
95	**12**	5c. carmine-lake (21.8)	30	75
96	**13**	8c. myrtle-green (21.8)	2·00	8·00
97	**14**	10c. deep brown (4.8)	80	40
98	**15**	20c. blue (26.6)	2·75	2·50
99	**16**	50c. black and blue (25.7)	3·25	3·50
100	**17**	$1 ultramarine and reddish purple (25.7)	8·00	14·00
101	**18**	$2 bronze-green and scarlet (21.8)	28·00	42·00
102	**19**	$5 brown and bronze-green (26.6)	48·00	42·00
92/102 *Set of 11*			85·00	£100

The 6, 12, 25 and 30c. values used with this issue were Nos. 1/4 of Malayan Federation.

20 Sultan Abdul Halim Mu'Adzam Shah

21 Sultan Abdul Halim Shah

(Photo Harrison)

1959 (20 Feb). Installation of the Sultan. W w **12**. P 14×14½.

103	**20**	10c. multicoloured	65	10

1959 (1 July)–**62**. As Nos. 92/102 but with inset portrait of Sultan Abdul Halim Shah as in T **21**.

104	**21**	1c. black	10	75
105	**10**	2c. orange-red	10	2·00
106	**11**	4c. sepia	10	75
107	**12**	5c. carmine-lake	10	10
108	**13**	8c. myrtle-green	3·50	3·50
109	**14**	10c. deep brown	1·00	10
109*a*		10c. deep maroon (19.12.61)	8·50	70
110	**15**	20c. blue	1·00	1·00
111	**16**	50c. black and blue (p 12½)	30	1·75
		a. Perf 12½×13 (14.6.60)	30	60
112	**17**	$1 ultramarine and reddish purple	1·75	2·25
113	**18**	$2 bronze-green and scarlet	13·00	18·00
114	**19**	$5 brown and bronze-green (p 12½)	16·00	19·00
		a. Perf 13×12½ (26.11.62)	32·00	16·00
104/14 *Set of 12*			40·00	40·00

22 *Vanda hookeriana*

23 *Danaus melanippus*

1965 (15 Nov). As Nos. 166/72 of Johore but with inset portrait of Sultan Abdul Halim Shah as in T **22**. W w **13** (upright).

115		1c. multicoloured	10	1·50
		a. Grey omitted (orchid's name and part of flower)	£250	
116		2c. multicoloured	10	1·75
		b. Yellow (flower) omitted	£200	
		c. Dark green omitted	£250	
117		5c. multicoloured	10	20
		a. Black (country name and head) omitted	£300	
		c. Red omitted	£100	
118		6c. multicoloured	15	60
119		10c. multicoloured	30	20
		a. Red omitted	£700	
		b. Green (leaves) omitted	£800	
120		15c. multicoloured	1·50	10
121		20c. multicoloured	1·75	1·00
		a. Bright purple (blooms) omitted	£475	
		b. Yellow (leaves) omitted	65·00	
115/21 *Set of 7*			3·50	4·50

The 1c. to 15c. exist with PVA gum as well as gum arabic.

The 6c. value exists with black (country name, arms and head) omitted and is listed under Sarawak where it was issued.

The higher values used with this issue were Nos. 20/27 of Malaysia (National Issues).

1970 (27 May). As Nos. 115 and 119 but W w **13** (sideways).

122	**22**	1c. multicoloured	2·50	5·50
123	–	10c. multicoloured	1·00	4·25

1971 (1 Feb)–**78**. As Nos. 175/87 of Johore but with portrait of Sultan Abdul Halim Shah as in T **23**.

(a) Litho by Bradbury, Wilkinson.

124	1c. multicoloured	30	1·75
125	2c. multicoloured	50	1·75
126	5c. multicoloured	1·25	40
127	6c. multicoloured	1·25	2·00
128	10c. multicoloured	1·25	10
129	15c. multicoloured	1·25	10
130	20c. multicoloured	1·50	70
124/30 *Set of 7*		6·50	6·00

(b) Photo by Harrison (1977-78)

130*a*	2c. multicoloured	15·00	17·00
131	5c. multicoloured	3·25	1·25
132	10c. multicoloured	9·00	65
133	15c. multicoloured	2·50	30
134	20c. multicoloured	3·50	2·25
130*a*/4 *Set of 5*		30·00	19·00

The higher values used with this issue were Nos. 64/71 of Malaysia (National Issues).

24 *Pterocarpus indicus*

25 Sultan Abdul Halim Shah

1979 (30 Apr). As Nos. 188/94 of Johore but with portrait of Sultan Abdul Halim Shah as in T **24**.

135	1c. *Rafflesia hasseltii*	10	90
136	2c. Type **24**	10	90
137	5c. *Lagerstroemia speciosa*	10	60
138	10c. *Durio zibethinus*	15	10
139	15c. *Hibiscus rosa-sinensis*	15	10
140	20c. *Rhododendron scortechinii*	20	10
141	25c. *Etlingera elatior* (inscr "*Phaeomeria speciosa*")	40	20
135/41 *Set of 7*		1·00	2·50

For higher values used in conjunction with this series see Nos. 190/7 of Malaysia (National Issues).

(Des and litho Security Printers (M), Malaysia)

1983 (15 July). Silver Jubilee of Sultan. T **25** and similar multicoloured designs. P 13×13½ (20c.) or 13½×13 (others).

142	20c. Type **25**	70	30
143	40c. Paddy fields (horiz)	1·75	1·75
144	50c. Paddy fields and Mount Jerai (horiz)	2·50	5·25
142/4 *Set of 3*		4·50	6·50

1983 (22 Feb)–**85**. As Nos. 138/40 but without wmk.

148	10c. *Durio zibethinus* (11.5.85)	23·00	3·25
149	15c. *Hibiscus rosa-sinensis* (12.84)	55	50
150	20c. *Rhododendron scortechinii* (blackish brown background)	40·00	1·00
150*a*	20c. *Rhododendron scortechinii* (bronze green background) (16.12.83)	30	30

*There was no official release date for these stamps. Dates shown are the earliest recorded from postmarks and may be revised if earlier examples are reported.

For details of the shade differences between watermarked and unwatermarked printings see after Johore No. 200a.

Nos. 148/9 and 150a show "kedah" nearer to "malaysia" than on Nos. 135/41 and 150.

26 Cocoa

1986 (25 Oct)–**96**. As Nos. 202/8 of Johore, but with portrait of Sultan Abdul Halim Shah as is T **26**. P 12.

152	1c. Coffee	10	30
153	2c. Coconuts	10	30
154	5c. Type **26**	15	10
	c. Perf 14×13¾ (1996)	1·50	20
	f. Perf 14¾×14½ (1994)	4·50	45
155	10c. Black pepper	15	10
	b. Perf 13½×13¾	4·50	35
	c. Perf 14×13¾ (1994)		
	ca. No watermark (1996)	9·00	
156	15c. Rubber	25	10
157	20c. Oil palm	25	15
	aw. Wmk inverted		
	c. Perf 14×13¾ (1994)	1·00	10
	cw. Wmk inverted (1994)	4·00	
	e. Perf 14×14½ (1999)	12·00	
	f. Perf 14¾×14½ (1994)	14·00	30
158	30c. Rice	30	15

b. Perf 13½×13¾ ...
c. Perf 14×13¾ (1994) ... 3·25 30
ca. No watermark (1999) ...
cw. Wmk inverted (1995) ... 7·00
e. Perf 14×14½ (1996) ... 2·50 20
ew. Wmk inverted ... 13·00
f. Perf 14¾×14½ (1996) ... 3·75 30
152/8 *Set of 7* ... 1·10 80

2003 ((?)). Vert designs as Type **26** but redenominated in "sen". Multicoloured. W **138**. P 14×13¾.
159 30s. Rice ... 1·40 10
w. Wmk inverted ... 7·50

27 *Nelumbium nelumbo* (sacred lotus)

2007 (31 Dec). Garden Flowers. As Nos. 210/15 of Johore, but with portrait of Sultan Abdul Halim Shah and Arms of Kedah as in T **27**. Multicoloured. W 138. Phosphorised paper. P 14.
160 5s. Type **47** ... 10 10
161 10s. *Hydrangea macrophylla* ... 15 10
162 20s. *Hippeastrum reticulatum* ... 25 15
163 30s. Bougainvillea ... 40 20
164 40s. *Ipomoea indica* ... 50 30
165 50s. *Hibiscus rosa-sinensis* ... 65 35
160/5 *Set of 6* ... 1·90 1·10

STAMP BOOKLETS

1973 (8 Dec). Cover as Type B **1** of Johore, but inscr "KEDAH". Stitched.
SB1 $3 booklet containing eight 5c., 10c. and twelve 15c. (Nos. 126, 128/9) in blocks of 4 ... 32·00

1979 (1 Dec). Cover as No. SB5 of Johore, but inscr "KEDAH". Stitched.
SB2 $3 booklet containing eight 5c., 10c., and twelve 15c. (Nos. 137/9) in blocks of 4 ... 10·00
No. SB2 exists with two different versions of the back cover.

1987 (1 June). Cover as Type B **2** of Johore, but inscr "KEDAH". Stapled.
SB3 $2 booklet containing 5c., 10c., 15c. and 20c. (Nos. 154/7) in blocks of 4 ... 11·00

1992 (1 July). "Kuala Lumpur '92" International Philatelic Exhibition. Cover as Type B **3** of Johore, but inscr "Kedah". Stamps attached by selvedge.
SB4 $3 booklet containing 30c. (No. 158) in block of 10 ... 9·00

1993. Covers as Nos. SB8/9 of Johore, but inscr "Kedah". Stamps attached by selvedge.
SB5 $2 booklet containing 20c. (No. 157) in block of 10 ... 1·50
SB6 $3 booklet containing 30c. (No. 158) in block of 10 ... 2·00

KELANTAN

The Thai monarchy exercised suzerainty over Kelantan and the other northern states of the Malay peninsula from the 16th century onwards.

The first Siamese post office in Kelantan opened at Kota Bharu in 1895. It appears that in the early years this office only accepted letters franked with stamps for delivery within Kelantan.

The initial cancellation, of which no complete example has been discovered, showed Thai characters only. Partial examples have been reported on the 1887–91 8a. and 1896 4a. on 12a.

The operations of the Duff Development Company in Kelantan from 1903 led to a considerable expansion of the postal service based on the company's river steamers. A further post office opened at Batu Mengkebang in 1908, but may have been preceded by manuscript endorsements of "B.M." and date known from early 1907 onwards.

Type E. Double ring. English at top and bottom

For other stamps and postmark types, See under Kedah.

Kota Bharu

Stamps of SIAM cancelled as Type B inscr "KALANTAN" (from March 1898).

1887–91. (Nos. 11/18).
Z301 **9** 2a. green and carmine ... £110
Z302 3a. green and blue ... £120
Z303 4a. green and brown ... £120
Z304 8a. green and yellow ... £120
Z305 12a. purple and carmine ... £100
Z306 24a. purple and blue ... £110

1894. Surch as T **27** with variation of English figures as T **33** (Nos. 37/44).
Z307 **9** 2a. on 64a. purple and brown ... £160

1894–95. Surch as T **35** with variation of English figures as T **36** (Nos. 46/50).
Z308 **9** 1a. on 64a. purple and brown ... £140

1896. Surch as T **39** (Siamese) and T **40** (English) (No. 51).
Z309 **9** 4a. on 12a. purple and carmine ... £140

1897. Surch as T **39** (Siamese) and T **41** (English) (No. 52).
Z310 **9** 4a. on 12a. purple and carmine ... £140

1898–99. Surch as T **42** with variation of English section as T **46** (Nos. 53/62).
Z311 **9** 3a. on 12a. (11½–11¾ mm long) ... £150
Z312 4a. on 12a. purple and carmine (8 mm long) .. £140

1899–1904. (Nos. 67/81).
Z313 **49** 1a. olive-green (wide Siamese characters in face value) ... £110
Z314 2a. grass-green ... £100
Z315 2a. scarlet and pale blue ... £100
Z316 3a. red and blue ... £120
Z317 4a. carmine ... £100
Z318 4a. chocolate and pink ... £120
Z319 8a. deep green and orange ... £100
Z320 10a. ultramarine ... £110
Z321 12a. brown-purple and carmine ... £110
Z322 64a. brown-purple and chestnut ... £250

1905–09. (Nos. 92/105).
Z323 **53** 1a. green and orange ... £100
Z324 2a. grey and deep violet ... £100
Z325 4a. pale red and sepia ... £100
Z326 4a. scarlet ... £100
Z327 5a. carmine ... £130
Z328 8a. olive-bistre and dull black ... £100
Z329 12a. blue ... £130
Z330 24a. red-brown ... £325
Z331 1t. bistre and deep blue ... £325

1907. Surch with T **56** (No. 109).
Z332 **9** 1a. on 24a. purple and blue ... £140

Stamps of SIAM cancelled as Type E inscr "Kota Bahru/Kelantan" (from July 1908).

1887–91. (Nos. 11/18).
Z333 **9** 12a. purple and carmine ... £100
Z334 24a. purple and blue ... £140

1899–1904. (Nos. 67/81).
Z335 **49** 8a. deep green and orange ... £110
Z336 64a. brown-purple and chestnut ... £160

1905–09. (Nos. 92/105).
Z337 **53** 1a. green and orange ... £110
Z338 2a. grey and deep violet ... £110
Z339 2a. pale yellow-green ... £110
Z340 4a. pale red and sepia ... £110
Z341 4a. scarlet ... £110
Z342 8a. olive-bistre and dull black ... £100

Z343		9a. blue	£120
Z344		18a. red-brown	£180

1907. Surch with T **56** (No. 109).

Z345	**9**	1a. on 24a. purple and blue	£110

1908. Surch as T **59** (Nos. 110/12).

Z346	**9**	2a. on 24a. purple and blue	£160
Z347	**53**	4a. on 5a. carmine	£190
Z348	**49**	9a. on 10a. ultramarine	£130

Batu Mengkebang

Stamps of SIAM cancelled as Type E inscr "Batu Menkebang/Kelantan" (from July 1908).

1887–91. (Nos. 11/18).

Z349	**9**	12a. purple and carmine	£200
Z349*a*		24a. purple and blue	£400

1899–1904. (Nos. 67/81).

Z350	**49**	8a. deep green and orange	£200

1905–09. (Nos. 92/105).

Z351	**53**	1a. green and orange	£190
Z352		2a. grey and deep violet	£190
Z353		2a. pale yellow-green	£200
Z354		4a. pale red and sepia	£200
Z355		4a. scarlet	£190
Z356		8a. olive-bistre and dull black	£160
Z357		9a. blue	£160
Z358		12a. blue	£250
Z359		24a. red-brown	£375
Z360		1t. bistre and deep blue	£400

1907. Surch with T **56** (No. 109).

Z361	**9**	1a. on 24a. purple and blue	£160

1908. Surch as T **59** (Nos. 110/12).

Z362	**49**	9a. on 10a. ultramarine	£250

Suzerainty over Kelantan was transferred by Thailand to Great Britain on 15 July 1909.

Siamese stamps were withdrawn from sale and replaced the following day by stamps of the Federated Malay States.

Stamps of the Federated Malay States used in Kelantan

Kota Bahru

Type M

Cancelled as Type F

1909–11. (Nos. 29/49).

Z367	**3**	1c. green (Die II)	80·00
Z368		3c. carmine	70·00
Z369		4c. black and rose	80·00
Z370		8c. grey-brown and ultramarine	70·00
		a. Wmk upright	85·00
Z373	**4**	$2 green and carmine	£300

Cancelled as Type M

1909–11. (Nos. 29/45a).

Z375	**3**	1c. green (Die II)	60·00
Z376		3c. carmine	60·00
Z377		4c. black and rose	60·00
Z378		5c. green and carmine/*yellow*	90·00
Z379		8c. grey-brown and ultramarine	80·00
		a. Wmk upright	90·00
Z380		10c. black and purple	£100
Z381		20c. mauve and black (chalk-surfaced paper)	£100

Batu Menkebang

Cancelled as Type I inscribed "Batu Menkebang"

1909–11. (Nos. 34/43d).

Z385	**3**	3c. carmine	£110
Z386		5c. green and carmine/*yellow*	£130
Z387		10c. black and purple	£130

Cancelled as Type M inscribed "BATU MENKEBANG" at top

1909–11. (Nos. 29/45a).

Z391	**3**	1c. green (Die II)	85·00
Z392		3c. carmine	55·00
Z393		4c. black and rose	75·00
Z394		5c. green and carmine/*yellow*	£120
Z395		8c. grey-brown and ultramarine (wmk upright)	95·00
Z396		20c. mauve and black (chalk-surfaced paper)	£120

Federated Malay States stamps were replaced by those of Kelantan in January 1911.

A British adviser was appointed to Kelantan in 1923 and the state joined the Federation of Malaya on 1 February 1948.

PRICES FOR STAMPS ON COVER TO 1945	
Nos. 1/11	*from* × 30
No. 12	—
Nos. 14/23	*from* × 30
Nos. 30/8	*from* × 15
Nos. 39/*a*	*from* × 10
Nos. 40/8	*from* × 30
Nos. 49/52	*from* × 20
No. 53	*from* × 3
No. 54	—

1

MALAYA
BORNEO
EXHIBITION

(**2**)

1911 (Jan)–**15**. Wmk Mult Crown CA. Ordinary paper (1c. to 10c.) or chalk-surfaced paper (30c. to $25). P 14.

1	**1**	1c. yellow-green	7·00	1·00
		a. Blue-green	6·00	30
2		3c. red	4·25	15
3		4c. black and red	1·50	15
4		5c. green and red/*yellow*	10·00	1·00
		w. Wmk inverted	†	£500
5		8c. ultramarine	5·50	1·00
6		10c. black and mauve	30·00	75
7		30c. dull purple and red	11·00	2·50
		a. Purple and carmine	27·00	14·00
8		50c. black and orange	8·50	2·50
9		$1 green and emerald	48·00	35·00
9*a*		$1 green and brown (5.15)	70·00	2·00
10		$2 green and carmine	1·50	2·75
11		$5 green and blue	4·00	4·00
12		$25 green and orange	50·00	90·00
1/12 *Set of* 13			£225	£130
1s/12s Optd "Specimen" *Set of* 13			£275	

1921 (5 May)–**28**. Wmk Mult Script CA. Ordinary paper (1c. to 10c.) or chalk-surfaced paper (30c. to $1). P 14.

14	**1**	1c. dull green (7.21)	4·25	60
15		1c. black (24.2.23)	1·00	50
16		2c. brown (29.7.22)	7·50	3·75
16*a*		2c. green (24.7.26)	5·50	40
16*b*		3c. brown (5.3.27)	5·00	1·00
		ba. "C" of "CA" missing from wmk		
17		4c. black and red (15.7.22)	3·50	10
18		5c. green and red/*pale yellow* (12.22)	1·75	10
19		6c. claret (29.7.22)	3·50	1·00
19*a*		6c. scarlet (26.5.28)	4·00	4·50
20		10c. black and mauve	3·00	10
21		30c. purple and carmine (24.7.26)	4·00	5·00
22		50c. black and orange (21.3.25)	6·50	45·00
23		$1 green and brown (9.2.24)	28·00	85·00
14/23 *Set of* 13			70·00	£130
14s/23s Optd "Specimen" *Set of* 13			£375	

Examples of Nos. 22/3 are known showing part strikes of a forged Kota Bharu postmark dated "27 JUL 11".

For the 4c., 5c. and 6c. surcharged, see issues under "Japanese Occupation".

OVERPRINT SETTINGS FOR NOS. 30/8. All values were overprinted using a triplet of three slightly different types. It is not known if this was applied to the sheets three stamps at a time or if a forme to overprint a pane of 60 was constructed from it.

On the normal setting "MALAYA" is 13 mm long. The1c and 5c. only is also known with "MALAYA" 14 mm from a different triplet setting. It has been suggested that this was a trial overprint on one sheet which was subsequently included in postal stocks.

1922 (31 Mar). Malaya-Borneo Exhibition, Singapore. Optd with T **2** ("MALAYA" 13 mm long) by Govt Survey Office, Kkota Bharu.

(a) Wmk Mult Crown CA.

30	**1**	4c. black and red	6·50	50·00
		a. Opt double	£3000	

31		5c. green and red/*pale yellow*	6·50	50·00
		a. "MALAYA" 14 mm long	£275	
32		30c. dull purple and red	6·50	80·00
33		50c. black and orange	9·50	85·00
34		$1 green and brown	32·00	£110
35		$2 green and carmine	90·00	£275
36		$5 green and blue	£225	£475

(b) Wmk Mult Script CA.

37	**1**	1c. green	3·50	55·00
		a. Opt double	£3000	
		b "MALAYA" 14 mm. long		
38		10c. black and mauve	6·50	75·00
30/8 *Set of 9*			£350	£1100

Nos. 30a and 37a show all three lines of the overprint double.

Examples of all values are known showing part strikes of the forged postmark mentioned below Nos. 14/23.

3 Sultan Ismail

4 Sultan Ismail

(Recess Harrison (No. 39) or D.L.R. (No. 39a))

1928–35. Wmk Mult Script CA. P 12.

39	**3**	$1 blue	15·00	80·00
		a. Perf 14 (1935)	55·00	45·00
		s. Perf "Specimen"	95·00	

(Recess B.W.)

1937 (July)–**40.** Wmk Mult Script CA. P 12.

40	**4**	1c. grey-olive and yellow	2·00	55
41		2c. green	6·50	20
42		4c. scarlet	6·50	1·00
43		5c. red-brown	4·75	10
44		6c. lake (10.37)	13·00	10·00
45		8c. grey-olive	4·75	10
46		10c. purple (10.37)	24·00	2·75
47		12c. blue	6·50	6·00
48		25c. vermilion and violet	7·50	3·50
49		30c. violet and scarlet (10.37)	48·00	22·00
50		40c. orange and blue-green	8·50	32·00
51		50c. grey-olive and orange (10.37)	75·00	9·00
52		$1 violet and blue-green (10.37)	48·00	13·00
53		$2 red-brown and scarlet (3.40)	£225	£190
54		$5 vermilion and lake (3.40)	£475	£650
40/54 *Set of 15*			£850	£850
40s/54s Perf "Specimen" *Set of 15*			£650	

For above issue surcharged see issues under "Japanese Occupation".

1948 (1 Dec). Royal Silver Wedding. As Nos. 131/2 of Johore.

55	10c. violet	75	2·75
56	$5 carmine	28·00	50·00

1949 (10 Oct). 75th Anniv of U.P.U. As Nos. 96/9 of Brunei.

57	10c. purple	25	30
58	15c. deep blue	2·25	2·00
59	25c. orange	40	5·00
60	50c. blue-black	70	3·00
57/60 *Set of 4*		3·25	9·25

Due to the exhaustion of certain B.M.A. values PERAK 2c., 3c., 4c., 6c., 15c., 20c. black and green, 25c., 40c. and 50c. stamps were used in Kelantan from 27 November 1950 until the issue of Nos. 61/81.

5 Sultan Ibrahim

Normal

No. 62a Tiny stop (R. 1/2)

1951 (11 July)–**55.** Chalk-surfaced paper. Wmk Mult Script CA. P 17½×18.

61	**5**	1c. black	50	30
62		2c. orange	1·25	35
		a. Tiny stop	29·00	32·00
		b. Orange-yellow (11.5.55)	6·50	3·50
63		3c. green	4·50	1·25
64		4c. brown	1·50	15
65		5c. bright purple (1.9.52)	1·50	50
		a. Bright mauve (9.12.53)	2·75	1·00
66		6c. grey	75	20
67		8c. scarlet	4·00	3·50
68		8c. green (1.9.52)	3·75	1·75
69		10c. magenta	50	10
70		12c. scarlet (1.9.52)	4·00	2·25
71		15c. ultramarine	5·50	60
72		20c. black and green	4·00	10·00
73		20c. bright blue (1.9.52)	1·50	25
74		25c. purple and orange	1·50	55
75		30c. scarlet and purple (4.9.55)	1·25	4·00
76		35c. scarlet and purple (1.9.52)	2·00	1·50
77		40c. red and purple	13·00	18·00
78		50c. black and blue	5·50	40
79		$1 blue and purple	8·50	10·00
80		$2 green and scarlet	30·00	45·00
81		$5 green and brown	55·00	60·00
		a. Green and sepia (8.12.53)	£110	£110
61/81 *Set of 21*			£130	£140

1953 (2 June). Coronation. As No. 152 of Johore..

82	10c. black and reddish purple	1·25	1·40

1957 (26 June)–**63.** As Nos. 92/102 of Kedah but with inset portrait of Sultan Ibrahim.

83	**9**	1c. black (21.8.57)	10	30
84	**10**	2c. orange-red (25.7.57)	75	1·50
		a. *Red-orange* (17.11.59)	9·00	6·00
85	**11**	4c. sepia (21.8.57)	40	10
86	**12**	5c. carmine-lake (21.8.57)	40	10
87	**13**	8c. myrtle-green (21.8.57)	1·50	3·00
88	**14**	10c. deep brown (4.8.57)	2·75	10
89		10c. deep maroon (19.4.61)	13·00	8·50
90	**15**	20c. blue	2·50	30
91	**16**	50c. black and blue (*p* 12½) (25.7.57)	50	70
		a. Perf 12½×13 (28.6.60)	1·00	30
92	**17**	$1 ultramarine and reddish purple (25.7.57)	8·00	1·50
93	**18**	$2 bronze-green and scarlet (*p* 12½) (21.8.57)	14·00	6·50
		a. Perf 13×12½ (9.4.63)	15·00	28·00
94	**19**	$5 brown and bronze-green (*p* 12½)	19·00	12·00
		a. Perf 13×12½ (13.8.63)	26·00	35·00
83/94 *Set of 12*			55·00	30·00

The 6, 12, 25 and 30c. values used with this issue were Nos. 1/4 of Malayan Federation.

6 Sultan Yahya Petra and Crest of Kelantan

(Photo Harrison)

1961 (17 July). Coronation of the Sultan. W w **12.** P 15×14.

95	**6**	10c. multicoloured	40	80

7 Sultan Yahya Petra

8 *Vanda hookerlana*

(Recess D.L.R.)

1961–63. As Nos. 92/8 of Kedah but with inset portrait of Sultan Yahya Petra as in T **7.** W w **13.** P 12½×13 (vert) or 13×12½ (horiz).

96	1c. black (1.3.62)	10	2·50
97	2c. orange-red (1.3.62)	40	2·75
98	4c. sepia (1.3.62)	1·50	1·75
99	5c. carmine-lake (1.3.62)	1·25	20
100	8c. myrtle-green (1.3.62)	12·00	14·00
	a. *Deep green* (15.1.63)	15·00	13·00
101	10c. deep maroon (2.12.61)	1·75	25
102	20c. blue (1.3.62)	8·50	2·25
96/102 *Set of 7*		23·00	20·00

1965 (15 Nov). As Nos. 166/72 of Johore but with inset portrait of Sultan Yahya Petra as in T **8**. W w **13** (upright).

103		1c. multicoloured	10	1·25
		b. Magenta omitted	£275	
104		2c. multicoloured	10	1·75
105		5c. multicoloured	15	30
106		6c. multicoloured	70	2·25
107		10c. multicoloured	30	25
		a. Red omitted	£160	
108		15c. multicoloured	1·50	25
109		20c. multicoloured	1·50	1·75
		a. Bright purple (blooms) omitted	£275	
		b. Yellow (leaves) omitted	80·00	
103/9 *Set of 7*			3·75	7·00

The 5c. and 10c. exist with PVA as well as gum arabic.

The higher values used with tissue were Nos. 20/27 of Malaysia (National Issues).

1970 (20 Nov). As Nos. 103 and 107 but W w **13** (sideways).

110	**8**	1c. multicoloured	1·50	8·00
111	–	10c. multicoloured	3·75	5·00

9 *Parthenos sylvia*

10 *Lagerstroemia speciosa*

1971 (1 Feb)–**78**. As Nos. 175/87 of Johore but with portrait of Sultan Yahya Petra and arms, as in T **9**.

(a) Litho by Bradbury, Wilkinson.

112		1c. multicoloured	30	2·25
113		2c. multicoloured	40	2·25
114		5c. multicoloured	1·50	60
115		6c. multicoloured	1·50	2·50
116		10c. multicoloured	1·50	30
117		15c. multicoloured	1·50	10
		a. Black (state inscription, portrait and arms) omitted	£140	
118		20c. multicoloured	2·00	1·50
112/18 *Set of 7*			7·75	5·50

(b) Photo by Harrison (1977-78)

119		1c. multicoloured	80	4·50
120		5c. multicoloured	5·50	4·00
121		10c. multicoloured	6·00	3·25
122		15c. multicoloured	12·00	75
119/22 *Set of 4*			22·00	11·00

The higher values used with this issue were Nos. 64/71 of Malaysia (National Issues).

For differences between litho and photo printings, see after Johore No. 187.

On No. 117a only the country inscription, portrait and arms are omitted, the remainder of the black printing being as normal. The design was produced using two black plates, one for the main design, value and inscription and the other to apply the state name, head and arms. It is this plate which is omitted from No. 117a.

1979 (30 Apr). As Nos. 188/94 of Johore but with portrait of Sultan Yahya Petra as in T **10**.

123		1c. *Rafflesia hasseltii*	10	1·00
124		2c. *Pterocarpus indicus*	10	1·00
125		5c. Type **10**	10	80
126		10c. *Durio zibethinus*	15	10
127		15c. *Hibiscus rosa-sinensis*	15	10
128		20c. *Rhododendron scortechinii*	20	10
129		25c. *Etlingera elatior* (inscr "*Phaeomeria speciosa*")	40	50
123/9 *Set of 7*			1·00	3·25

For higher values used in conjunction with this series see Nos. 190/7 of Malaysia (National Issues).

11 Sultan Tengku Ismail Petra

12 Black Pepper

(Des M. A. B. bin Saman. Litho Harrison)

1980 (30 Mar). Coronation of Sultan Tengku Ismail Petra. P 14.

130	**11**	10c. multicoloured	40	75
131		15c. multicoloured	40	15
132		50c. multicoloured	90	2·75
130/2 *Set of 3*			1·50	3·25

1983–86. As Nos. 125/6 and 128 but without wmk.

135		5c. Type **10** (1986)	75	1·50
136		10c. *Durio zibethinus* (18.9.84)	30	60
138		20c. *Rhododendron scortechinii* (blackish brown background) (1983)	40·00	2·25
138*a*		20c. *Rhododendron scortechinii* (bronze green background) (5.10.83)	50	50

*There was no official release date for these stamps. Dates shown are the earliest recorded from postmarks and may be revised if earlier examples are reported.

For details of the shade differences between watermarked and unwatermarked printings see after Johore No. 200a.

On Nos. 135/6 and 138a the portrait and state arms have been redrawn smaller.

1988 (25 Oct)–**97**. As Nos. 202/8 of Johore, but with portrait of Sultan Ismail Petra as in T **12**. P 12.

140		1c. Coffee	10	30
		w. Wmk inverted		
141		2c. Coconuts	10	40
		f. Perf 14¾×14½ (1994)	3·25	50
142		5c. Cocoa	50	10
		c. Perf 14×13¾	3·00	40
		cw. Wmk inverted	8·50	
143		10c. Type **12**	20	10
		c. Perf 14×13¾ (1995)	3·25	50
144		15c. Rubber	30	10
145		20c. Oil palm	20	15
		c. Perf 14×13¾ (1995)	3·75	50
		f. Perf 14¾×14½	3·25	
146		30c. Rice	40	15
		c. Perf 14×13¾ (1994)	1·25	25
		cw. Wmk inverted	7·00	
		e. Perf 14×14½ (1997)	2·75	20
		f. Perf 14¾×14½		
140/6 *Set of 7*			1·40	1·10

13 *Nelumbium nelumbo* (sacred lotus)

2007 (31 Dec). Garden Flowers. As Nos. 210/15 of Johore, but with portrait of Sultan Ismail Petra and Arms of Kelantan as in T **13**. Multicoloured. W **138**. Phosphorised paper. P 14.

147		5s. Type **13**	10	10
148		10s. *Hydrangea macrophylla*	15	10
149		20s. *Hippeastrum reticulatum*	25	15
150		30s. Bougainvillea	40	20
151		40s. *Ipomoea indica*	50	30
152		50s. *Hibiscus rosa-sinensis*	65	35
147/52 *Set of 6*			1·90	1·10

STAMP BOOKLETS

1927 (June). Black on white (No. SB1) or black on grey (No. SB2) covers. Stapled.

SB1	36c. booklet containing thirty-six 1c. (No. 15) in blocks of 6	£2750
SB2	96c. booklet containing twenty-four 4c. (No. 17) in blocks of 6	£2750

1927 (Dec). Black on white (No. SB3) or on grey (No. SB4) covers. Stapled.

SB3	40c. booklet containing forty 1c. (No. 15) in blocks of 10	£2750
SB4	80c. booklet containing twenty 4c. (No. 17) in blocks of 10	£2750

1973 (8 Dec). Cover as Type B **1** of Johore, but inscr "KELANTAN". Stitched.

SB5	$3 booklet containing eight 5c., 10c. and twelve 15c. (Nos. 114, 116/17) in blocks of 4	35·00

1979 (1 Dec). Cover as No. SB5 of Johore, but inscr "KELANTAN". Stitched.

SB6	$3 booklet containing eight 5c., 10c., and twelve 15c. (Nos. 125/7) in blocks of 4	12·00

No. SB6 exists with two different versions of the back cover.

1987 (1 June). Cover as Type B **2** of Johore, but inscr "KELANTAN". Stapled.

SB7	$2 booklet containing 5c., 10c., 15c. and 20c. (Nos. 142/5) in blocks of 4	11·00

1992 (1 July). "Kuala Lumpur '92" International Philatelic Exhibition. Cover as Type B **3** of Johore, but inscr "Kelantan". Stamps attached by selvedge.

SB8	$3 booklet containing 30c. (No. 146) in block of 10	10·00

1993. Covers as Nos. SB8/9 of Johore, but inscr "Kelantan". Stamps attached by selvedge.

SB9	$2 booklet containing 20c. (No. 145) in block of 10	1·50
SB10	$3 booklet containing 30c. (No. 146) in block of 10	2·00

MALACCA

One of the Straits Settlements which joined the Federation of Malaya on 1 February 1948.

1948 (1 Dec). Royal Silver Wedding. As Nos. 131/2 of Johore.

1	10c. violet	30	1·75
2	$5 brown	29·00	40·00

1949 (1 Mar)–**52**. As T **58** of Straits Settlements, but inscr "MALACCA" at foot. Wmk Mult Script CA. Chalk-surfaced paper. P 17½×18.

3	1c. black	30	70
4	2c. orange	80	45
5	3c. green	30	1·75
6	4c. brown	30	10
6a	5c. bright purple (1.9.52)	60	1·50
7	6c. grey	75	85
8	8c. scarlet	75	6·00
8a	8c. green (1.9.52)	5·00	4·75
9	10c. purple	30	10
9a	12c. scarlet (1.9.52)	5·00	8·50
10	15c. ultramarine	2·75	60
11	20c. black and green	75	7·00
11a	20c. bright blue (1.9.52)	7·00	2·50
12	25c. purple and orange	75	70
12a	35c. scarlet and purple (1.9.52)	5·00	3·00
13	40c. red and purple	1·50	11·00
14	50c. black and blue	1·50	1·25
15	$1 blue and purple	13·00	25·00
16	$2 green and scarlet	24·00	25·00
17	$5 green and brown	55·00	45·00
3/17 *Set of 20*		£110	£130

1949 (10 Oct). 75th Anniv of U.P.U. As Nos. 96/9 of Brunei.

18	10c. purple	30	50
19	15c. deep blue	2·00	2·75
20	25c. orange	40	7·50
21	50c. blue-black	60	4·75
18/21 *Set of 4*		3·00	14·00

1953. Coronation. As No. 152 of Johore.

22	10c. black and reddish purple	1·00	1·50

1 Queen Elizabeth II

2 Copra

1954 (9 June)–**57**. Chalk-surfaced paper. Wmk Mult Script CA. P 17½×18.

23	**1**	1c. black (27.4.55)	10	60
24		2c. yellow-orange (27.4.55)	30	1·25
25		4c. brown	1·25	10
		a. *Pale brown* (24.4.57)	12·00	4·50
26		5c. bright purple (12.7.54)	30	2·50
27		6c. grey	10	40
28		8c. green (5.1.55)	40	2·75
29		10c. brown-purple (1.7.54)	2·00	10
		a. *Reddish purple* (27.3.57)	4·25	2·00
30		12c. rose-red (5.1.55)	30	3·00
31		20c. bright blue (5.1.55)	20	1·25
32		25c. brown-purple and yellow-orge (27.4.55)	20	1·50
33		30c. rose-red and brown-purple (5.9.55)	20	30
34		35c. rose-red and brown-purple (8.9.54)	20	1·50
35		50c. black and bright blue (5.1.55)	3·00	2·50
36		$1 bright blue and brown-purple (8.9.54)	7·00	10·00
37		$2 emerald and scarlet (27.4.55)	23·00	42·00
38		$5 emerald and brown (27.4.55)	23·00	48·00
23/38 *Set of 16*			55·00	£110

1957. As Nos. 92/102 of Kedah but with inset portrait of Queen Elizabeth II.

39	**9**	1c. black (21.8)	10	40
40	**10**	2c. orange-red (25.7)	10	40
41	**11**	4c. sepia (21.8)	40	10
42	**12**	5c. carmine-lake (21.8)	40	10
43	**13**	8c. myrtle-green (21.8)	1·50	2·50
44	**14**	10c. deep brown (4.8)	30	10
45	**15**	20c. blue (26.6)	2·00	50
46	**16**	50c. black and blue (25.7)	60	1·00
47	**17**	$1 ultramarine & reddish purple (25.7)	5·00	4·25
48	**18**	$2 bronze-green and scarlet (21.8)	18·00	26·00
49	**19**	$5 brown and bronze-green (26.6)	20·00	48·00
39/49 *Set of 11*			42·00	75·00

The 6, 12, 25 and 30c. values used with this issue were Nos. 1/4 of Malayan Federation.

(Recess D.L.R.)

1960 (15 Mar)–**62**. As Nos. 39/49, but with inset picture of Melaka tree and Pelandok (mouse deer) as in T **2**. W w **12**. P 13×12½ (1c. to 8c., $2, $5), 12½×13 (10c. to 50c.) or 13½ ($1).

50	1c. black	10	30
51	2c. orange-red	10	65
52	4c. sepia	10	10
53	5c. carmine-lake	10	10
54	8c. myrtle-green	3·00	3·00
55	10c. deep maroon	30	10
56	20c. blue	2·00	80
57	50c. black and blue	1·25	1·00
	a. *Black and ultramarine* (9.1.62)	3·75	1·00
58	$1 ultramarine and reddish purple	3·75	2·50
59	$2 bronze-green and scarlet	7·00	15·00
60	$5 brown and bronze-green	14·00	14·00
50/60 *Set of 11*		28·00	35·00

3 *Vanda hookeriana*

1965 (15 Nov)–**68**. As Nos. 166/72 of Johore but with Arms of Malacca inset and inscr "MELAKA" as in T **3**. W w **13** (upright).

61	1c. multicoloured	10	1·75
62	2c. multicoloured	10	1·50
63	5c. multicoloured	10	40
	b. Yellow (flower) omitted	75·00	
	c. Red omitted	£130	
64	6c. multicoloured	30	1·00
65	10c. multicoloured	20	10
66	15c. multicoloured	1·75	40
67	20c. multicoloured (purple-brown background)	2·25	1·00
	a. *Red-brown background* (2.4.68)	3·50	2·75
61/7 *Set of 7*		4·00	5·00

The 5c., 6c., 10c. and 20c. exist with PVA gum as well as gum arabic.

The higher values used with this issue were Nos. 20/27 of Malaysia (National Issues).

1970. As Nos. 61 and 65 but W w **13** (sideways)

68	3	1c. multicoloured (27.5.70)	1·75	8·00
69	–	10c. multicoloured (20.11.70)	5·50	8·00

1971 (1 Feb)–**78**. As Nos. 175/87 of Johore but with arms of Malacca and inscr "melaka", as in T **4**.

(a) Litho by Bradbury, Wilkinson.

70	1c. multicoloured	60	2·25
71	2c. multicoloured	1·00	2·25
72	5c. multicoloured	1·50	1·00
73	6c. multicoloured	1·50	3·00
74	10c. multicoloured	1·50	60
75	15c. multicoloured	2·25	20
76	20c. multicoloured	2·25	2·50
70/6 *Set of 7*		9·50	10·50

(b) Photo by Harrison (1977-78)

77	1c. multicoloured	4·75	8·00
78	5c. multicoloured	1·75	2·25
79	10c. multicoloured	5·00	2·00
80	15c. multicoloured	14·00	60
81	20c. multicoloured	4·50	4·00
77/81 *Set of 5*		27·00	15·00

The higher values used with this issue were Nos. 64/71 of Malaysia (National Issues).

For differences between litho and photo printings, see after Johore No. 187.

5 *Durio zibethinus*

6 Rubber

1979 (30 Apr). As Nos. 188/94 of Johore but with Arms of Malacca and inscr "melaka" as in T **5**.

82	1c. *Rafflesia hasseltii*	10	1·25
83	2c. *Pterocarpus indicus*	10	1·25
84	5c. *Lagerstroemia speciosa*	15	1·00
85	10c. Type **5**	20	35
86	15c. *Hibiscus rosa-sinensis*	20	10
87	20e. *Rhododendron scortechinii*	25	10
88	25c. *Etlingera elatior* (inscr "*Phaeomeria speciosa*")	45	80
82/8 *Set of 7*		1·25	4·25

For higher values used in conjunction with this series see Nos. 190/7 of Malaysia (National Issues).

1983 (26 Oct)–**86**. As Nos. 85/7 but without wmk.

92	10c. Type **5** (19.4.85)	1·25	3·00
93	15c. *Hibiscus rosa-sinensis* (9.86)	55	55
94	20c.. *Rhododendron scortechinii* (blackish brown background)	40·00	3·50
94*a*	20c. *Rhododendron scortechinii* (bronze green background) (13.6.84)	75	1·25

There was no official release date for these stamps. Dates shown are the earliest recorded from postmarks and may be revised if earlier examples are reported.

For details of the shade differences between watermarked and unwatermarked printings see after Johore No. 200a.

On Nos. 92/3 and 94a the distance between the coat of arms and the value is greater than on Nos. 85, 87 and 94.

1986 (25 Oct)–**96**. As Nos. 202/8 of Johore, but with Arms of Malacca and inscr "MELAKA" as in T **6**. P 12.

96	1c. Coffee	10	25
	w. Wmk inverted		
97	2c. Coconuts	10	30
98	5c. Cocoa	15	10
	c. Perf 14×13¾ (1995)	1·50	20
	ca. Wmk sideways (1996)	5·00	
99	10c. Black pepper	20	10
	c. Perf 14×13¼ (1995)	1·00	20
	f. Perf 14¾×14½ (1995)	2·00	10
100	15c. Type **6**	30	10
	w. Wmk inverted (1991)	8·00	
101	20c. Oil palm	30	15
	aw. Wmk inverted		
	c. Perf 14×13¾ (1994)	1·00	10
102	30c. Rice	40	15
	c. Perf 14×13¾ (1994)	4·75	30
	cw. Wmk inverted (1996)	7·50	
	e. Perf 14×14½	7·00	30
	ew. Wmk inverted	8·50	
	f. Perf 14¾×14½ (1996)	6·50	40
96/102 *Set of 7*		1·40	1·00

7 *Nelumbium nelumbo* (sacred lotus)

2007 (31 Dec). Garden Flowers. As Nos. 210/15 of Johore, but with Arms of Malacca as in T **7**. Multicoloured. W **138**. Phosphorised paper. P 14.

103	5s. Type **7**	10	10
104	10s. *Hydrangea macrophylla*	15	10
105	20s. *Hippeastrum reticulatum*	25	15
106	30s. Bougainvillea	40	20
107	40s. *Ipomoea indica*	50	30
108	50s. *Hibiscus rosa-sinensis*	65	35
103/8 *Set of 6*		1·90	1·10

STAMP BOOKLETS

1973 (8 Dec). Cover as Type B **1** of Johore, but inter "MELAKA". Stitched.

SB1	$3 booklet containing eight 5c., 10c. and twelve 15c. (Nos. 72, 74/5) in blocks of 4	35·00

1979 (1 Dec). Cover as No. SB5 of Johore, but inscr "MELAKA". Stitched.

SB2	$3 booklet containing eight 5c., 10c. and twelve 15c. (Nos. 84/6) in blocks of 4	13·00

No. SB2 exists with two different versions of the back cover.

1987 (1 June). Cover as Type B **2** of Johore, but inscr "MELAKA". Stapled.

SB3	$2 booklet containing 5c., 10c., 15c. and 20c. (Nos. 98/101) in blocks of 4	14·00

1992 (1 July). "Kuala Lumpur '92" International Philatelic Exhibition. Cover as Type B **3** of Johore, but inscr "Melaka". Stamps attached by selvedge.

SB4	$3 booklet containing 30c. (No. 102) in block of 10	10·00

1993. Covers as Nos. SB8/9 of Johore, but inscr "Melaka". Stamps attached by selvedge.

SB5	$2 booklet containing 20c. (No. 101) in block of 10	1·50
SB6	$3 booklet containing 30c. (No. 102) in block of 10	2·00

NEGRI SEMBILAN

A federation of smaller states reconstituted in 1886. Sungei Ujong, taken under British protection in 1874, was absorbed into Negri Sembilan by Treaty of 8 August 1895. The Negri Sembilan federation joined the Federated Malay States in 1896.

A. SUNGEI UJONG

Until 1 January 1899, when the Federated Malay States joined the U.P.U., mail for addresses outside Malaya was franked with the stamps of the STRAITS SETTLEMENTS.

PRICES FOR STAMPS ON COVER

Nos. 1/14	—
Nos. 15/27	*from* × 25
Nos. 28/36	*from* × 8
Nos. 37/49	*from* × 10
Nos. 50/5	*from* × 25

(**1**)

1878. No. 11 of Straits Settlements handstamped with T **1**.

1	2c. brown	£3500	£3750

This overprint on India No. 54 is bogus.

SUNGEI (**2**) (Narrow letters)

SUNGEI (**3**) ("N" wide)

SUNGEI (**4**) ("S" wide)

UJONG (**5**) ("N" wide)

UJONG (**6**) (Narrow letters, "UJ" close together)

UJONG (**7**) (Narrow letters, evenly spaced)

1881. No. 11 of Straits Settlements optd with T **2/7**.

2	**2+5**	2c. brown	£5000	£3750
3	**3+5**	2c. brown	£3500	£2750
4	**2+6**	2c. brown	£350	
		a. Opt Type **6** double	£1800	
5	**4+6**	2c. brown	£1300	
6	**2+7**	2c. brown	£400	

The two lines of this surcharge were applied as separate operations. On Nos. 2/3 "SUNGEI" was printed as a triplet, probably 2+3+3 "UJONG" being added by a single unit handstamp. Nos. 4 and 5 come from a similar triplet, 4+4+5, completed by another single unit handstamp. No. 6 comes from a single type triplet with the second line added as a triplet instead of by a single unit handstamp.

The 10c. slate overprinted Types **2** + **7** is bogus.

SUNGEI (8) ("N" and "E" wide) SUNGEI (9) ("SUN" and "E" wide) SUNGEI (10) ("SUN" wide)

SUNGEI (11) ("S" wide) SUNGEI (12) (Narrow letters)

UJONG (13) ("U" and "NG" wide) UJONG (14) (Narrow letters)

1881. No. 11 of Straits Settlements optd with T **8/14**.

7	**8+13**	2c. brown	£350	
8	**9+13**	2c. brown	£375	
9	**10+13**	2c. brown	£350	
10	**11+14**	2c. brown	£350	
		a. "S" inverted	£3750	
11	**12+14**	2c. brown	£225	

Nos. 7/11 also had the two lines of the overprint applied at separate operations. "SUNGEI" as a triplet, either 7+8+9 or 10+11+11, and "UJONG" as a single unit.

S.U. (15)

1882. Nos. 50/1 of Straits Settlements optd as T **15**.

12		2c. brown (with stops)	£325	
		a. Opt double	£3250	
13		2c. brown (without stops)	£275	£325
14		4c. rose (with stops)	£3750	£4250

Each of the above was applied by a triplet setting.

Examples of Straits Settlements No. 11 with a similar overprint, including stops, are trials which were not issued.

SUNGEI (16) ("S" and "E" wide) SUNGEI (17) ("E" wide) UJONG (18) ("N" wide)

1882 (Dec)–**84**. Nos. 12, 50, 52/3 and 63 of Straits Settlements optd with T **11/12**, **14** and **16/18**.

15	**12+14**	2c. brown	£1200	£500
16	**11+14**	2c. brown	£1700	£750
17	**12+14**	2c. pale rose (1884)	£225	£225
18	**11+14**	2c. pale rose (1884)	£225	£225
		a. Opt Type **14** double		
19	**16+14**	2c. pale rose (1884)	£120	£120
		a. Opt Type **16** double	†	£1000
20	**17+14**	2c. pale rose (1884)	£130	£140
21	**12+18**	2c. pale rose (1884)	£130	£140
		a. Opt Type **18** double	£1100	
22	**12+14**	4c. rose	£1700	£1800
		a. Opt Type **12** double	†	£4000
23	**11+14**	4c. rose	£2750	£3000
24	**12+14**	8c. orange	£1900	£1400
25	**11+14**	8c. orange	£3250	£2750
26	**12+14**	10c. slate	£600	£475
27	**11+14**	10c. slate	£850	£750

Nos. 15/27 had the two lines of the overprint applied by separate triplets. Settings so far identified are Nos. 15+16+15, 17+18+19, 19+20+21, 22+23+22, 24+25+24 and 26+27+26.

The 4c. rose overprinted Types **16** + **14** is now believed to be a trial.

UJONG. (19) (With stop. Narrow letters) UJONG. (20) (With stop. "N" wide) UJONG (21) (Without stop. Narrow letters)

1883–84. Nos. 50 and 63/4 of Straits Settlements optd with T **12**, **16/17** and **19/21**.

28	**12+19**	2c. brown	50·00	£140
29	**16+19**	2c. brown	50·00	£140
30	**12+20**	2c. brown	50·00	£140
		a. Opt Type **12** double	£1200	
31	**16+21**	2c. pale rose (1884)	£110	£120
32	**17+21**	2c. pale rose (1884)	£110	£120
33	**12+21**	2c. pale rose (1884)	£110	£120
		a. Opt Type **21** double	£1200	
34	**16+21**	4c. brown (1884)	£275	£375
		a. Opt Type **16** double		
		b. Opt Type **21** double	£2250	
35	**17+21**	4c. brown (1884)	£275	£375
36	**12+21**	4c. brown (1884)	£275	£375
		a. Opt Type **21** double	£4000	

Nos. 28/36 had the two lines of the overprint applied by separate triplets. Settings were Nos. 28+29+30, 31+32+33 and 34+35+36.

The 8c. orange overprinted Types **12** + **19** is now believed to be a trial (*Price* £900 *unused*).

Sungei Ujong (22) SUNGEI UJONG (23) SUNGEI UJONG (24)

SUNGEI UJONG (25) SUNGEI UJONG (26) SUNGEI UJONG (27)

SUNGEI UJONG (28) SUNGEI UJONG. (29) SUNGEI UJONG (30)

Antique "G" in "SUNGEI" (R. 6/1)

1885–90. Nos. 63/a of Straits Settlements optd with T **22/30**.

37	**22**	2c. pale rose	80·00	90·00
		a. Opt double	£650	£650
38	**23**	2c. pale rose	42·00	65·00
		a. Opt double	£650	
39	**24**	2c. pale rose (1886)	£100	£120
40	**25**	2c. pale rose (1886)	£140	£150
		a. Opt double		
41	**26**	2c. pale rose (1886)	90·00	£100
		a. Opt double		
42	**27**	2c. pale rose (1887)	23·00	45·00
43	**28**	2c. pale rose (1889)	13·00	15·00
		a. Narrow "E" (2 mm wide) (R. 3/4 and 4/3)	£130	
		c. Opt double	£1400	
		d. Bright rose (1890)	16·00	12·00
		da. Narrow "E" (2 mm wide) (R. 3/4 and 4/3)	£150	
		db. Antique "N" in "UJONG" (R. 10/6)	£250	
44	**29**	2c. pale rose (1889)	95·00	70·00
		a. "UNJOG" (R. 7/3)	£5000	£3500
45	**30**	2c. bright rose (1890)	50·00	20·00
		a. Antique "G" in "SUNGEI" (R. 6/1)	£650	
		b. Antique "G" in "UJONG" (R. 8/3)	£650	
		c. Pale rose		

All the above overprints had both lines applied at the same operation. Nos. 37/42 were from different triplet settings. The first printing of Type **28** was from a triplet (No. 43) but this was followed by two further settings of 60 (6×10), the first containing No. 43a and the second Nos. 43*d*/db. Nos. 44/5 were both from settings of 60.

The antique letter varieties on Types **28** and **30** are similar in style to those on Types **25** and **26**.

SUNGEI UJONG Two CENTS (31) SUNGEI UJONG Two CENTS (32) SUNGEI UJONG Two CENTS (33)

SUNGEI UJONG Two CENTS (34)

1891. No. 68 of Straits Settlements surch with T **31/4**.

46	**31**	2c. on 24c. green	£1000	£1000
47	**32**	2c. on 24c. green	£400	£400
		w. Wmk inverted	£800	£850
48	**33**	2c. on 24c. green	£1000	£1000
49	**34**	2c. on 24c. green	£225	£225
		a. Antique "G" in "SUNGEI" (R. 6/1)	£1300	
		b. Antique "G" in "UJONG" (R. 8/3)	£1300	
		w. Wmk inverted	£500	£600

Nos. 46/9 come from the same setting of 60 on which "SUNGEI UJONG" was from the same type as No. 45. No. 46 occurs in row 1. No. 47 from rows 2 to 4, No. 48 from row 5 and No. 49 from rows 6 to 10.

35

3 CENTS

(36)

37

1891 (Nov)–**94**. Wmk Crown CA. P 14.

50	**35**	2c. rose	32·00	27·00
51		2c. orange (12.94)	1·75	4·25
52		5c. blue (3.93)	5·50	6·50
50/2 *Set of* 3			35·00	35·00
50s/2s Optd "Specimen" *Set of* 3			65·00	

1894 (Dec). Surch as T **36** by De La Rue. Wmk Mult Crown CA. P 14.

53	**35**	1c. on 5c. green	1·00	70
54		3c. on 5c. rose	2·50	5·50

1895 (Oct). Wmk Crown CA. P 14.

55	**37**	3c. dull purple and carmine	16·00	4·50
53s/5s Optd "Specimen" *Set of* 3			65·00	

B. NEGRI SEMBILAN

Stamps of the STRAITS SETTLEMENTS were used in Negri Sembilan during 1891, until replaced by the stamps listed below. Until the Federated Malay States joined the U.P.U. On 1 January 1899 Straits Settlements stamps continued to be used for mail to addresses outside Malaya.

PRICES FOR STAMPS ON COVER TO 1945

No. 1	*from* × 200
Nos. 2/4	*from* × 10
Nos. 5/14	*from* × 8
Nos. 15/20	*from* × 10
Nos. 21/49	*from* × 4

Negri
Sembilan

(1)

2

3

1891 (Aug?). No. 63a of Straits Settlements optd with T **1**.

1		2c. bright rose	3·00	7·50

Short "N" in "SEMBILAN" (Top left pane R. 8/3)

1891 (Nov)–**94**. Wmk Crown CA. P 14.

2	**2**	1c. green (6.93)	3·25	1·00
3		2c. rose	3·25	10·00
		a. Short "N"	85·00	
4		5c. blue (11.94)	30·00	42·00
2/4 *Set of* 3			32·00	48·00
2s/4s Optd "Specimen" *Set of* 3			85·00	

1895–99. Wmk Crown CA. P 14.

5	**3**	1c. dull purple and green (1899)	17·00	8·00
6		2c. dull purple and brown (1898)	35·00	£120
7		3c. dull purple and carmine	15·00	1·50
8		5c. dull purple and olive-yellow (1897)	8·50	11·00
9		8c. dull purple and ultramarine (1898)	29·00	18·00
10		10c. dull purple and orange (1897)	27·00	14·00
11		15c. green and violet (1896)	42·00	80·00
12		20c. green and olive (1897)	70·00	40·00
13		25c. green and carmine (1896)	70·00	95·00
14		50c. green and black (1896)	80·00	70·00
5/14 *Set of* 10			£350	£400
5s/14s Optd "Specimen" *Set of* 10			£225	

Four cents.

(4)

Four cents.

(5)

1898 (Dec)–**1900**.

(a) Surch as T **4**.

15	**3**	1c. on 15c. green and violet (1900)	£100	£300
		a. Raised stop (R. 5/1 and R. 10/1 of each pane)	£425	£1100
		b. Surch double, one albino	£400	
16	**2**	4c. on 1c. green	2·50	19·00
17	**3**	4c. on 3c. dull purple and carmine	3·25	21·00
		a. Horiz pair, one without surch	£11000	£5500
		b. Surch double	£2250	£1000
		ba. Ditto. "Four cents" albino	†	£1000
		c. Surch inverted	£1900	£1300
		d. "cents" repeated at left	£3000	£2500
		e. "Four" repeated at right	£3000	£2500
		f. Without bar	£800	£650
		g. Bar double	†	£800
18	**2**	4c. on 5c. blue	1·25	15·00

On Nos. 15 and 17 the bar is at the top of the stamp.

The surcharges were applied as a setting of 30 (6×5).

(b) Surch as T **5**.

19	**3**	4c. on 8c. dull purple & ultram (G.) (12.98)	8·00	4·25
		a. Vert pair, one without surch	£6500	£4000
		b. Surch double	£2500	£2250
		c. Surch double (G.+R.)	£850	£900
20		4c. on 8c. dull purple & ultramarine (Bk.)	£1300	£1400

Care should be taken in distinguishing the true black surcharge, No. 20, from very deep shades of the green surcharge, No. 19.

Pending the arrival of the permanent Federated Malay States issue the stamps of SELANGOR, FEDERATED MALAY STATES provisional overprints, STRAITS SETTLEMENTS and PERAK were used at various times between October 1899 and April 1901.

The general issues for FEDERATED MALAY STATES were used in Negri Sembilan from 29 April 1901 until 1935.

6 Arms of Negri Sembilan

7 Arms of Negri Sembilan

1935 (2 Dec)–**41**. Wmk Mult Script CA. Ordinary paper (6c. grey, 15c.) or chalk-surfaced paper (others). P 14.

21	**6**	1c. black (1.1.36)	1·00	20
22		2c. green (1.1.36)	1·00	20
23		2c. orange (*Thin striated paper*) (11.12.41)	4·25	70·00
24		3c. green (*ordinary paper*) (21.8.41)	19·00	8·00
		a. Thin striated paper (12.41)	8·00	10·00
25		4c. orange	2·00	10
26		5c. brown (5.12.35)	2·00	10
27		6c. scarlet (1.1.37)	17·00	2·75
		a. Stop omitted at right (R. 10/4)	£550	£160
28		6c. grey (18.12.41)	4·75	£100
		a. Stop omitted at right (R. 10/4)	£225	
29		8c. grey	2·00	10
30		10c. dull purple (1.1.36)	1·25	10
31		12c. bright ultramarine (1.1.36)	3·25	50
32		15c. ultramarine (1.10.41)	11·00	60·00
33		25c. dull purple and scarlet (1.4.36)	1·50	70
		a. Thin striated paper (1941)		
34		30c. dull purple and orange (1.1.36)	3·50	2·00
35		40c. scarlet and dull purple	3·25	2·00
36		50c. black/*emerald* (1.2.36)	6·50	2·25
37		$1 black and red/*blue* (1.4.36)	5·00	4·25
38		$2 green and scarlet (16.5.36)	42·00	17·00
39		$5 green and red/*emerald* (16.5.36)	26·00	90·00
21/39 *Set of* 19			£130	£325
21s/39s Perf "Specimen" *Set of* 19			£400	

The stamps issued in 1941 were printed by Harrison and Sons following bomb damage to the De La Rue works on 29 December 1940. The used prices quoted for Nos. 23, 28 and 32 are for examples with clearly identifiable 1941 cancellations. These stamps, and No. 39, are commonly found with forged cancellations.

An 8c. scarlet on ordinary paper was issued but only with opt during Japanese Occupation of Malaya. Unoverprinted specimens result from leakages.

During shortages in 1941 stamps of STRAITS SETTLEMENTS (2c. green, 25c., 30c.), SELANGOR (2c. green, 2c. orange (both perfs), 8c. grey, 25c.), PERAK (2c. orange, 25c., 50c.) and PAHANG (8c. scarlet) were issued in Negri Sembilan.

1948 (1 Dec). Royal Silver Wedding. As Nos. 131/2 of Johore.

40		10c. violet	40	50
41		$5 green	22·00	32·00

1949 (1 Apr)–**55**. Chalk-surfaced paper. Wmk Mult Script CA. P 17½×18.

42	**7**	1c. black	1·00	10
43		2c. orange	70	10
44		3c. green	50	30
45		4c. brown	30	10
46		5c. bright purple (1.9.52)	1·50	50
		a. Bright mauve (25.8.53)	50	45
47		6c. grey	2·00	10
		a. Pale grey (25.8.53)	6·50	1·75
48		8c. scarlet	80	75
49		8c. green (1.9.52)	4·50	1·60
50		10c. purple	40	10
51		12c. scarlet (1.9.52)	4·50	2·75
52		15c. ultramarine	4·00	10
53		20c. black and green	1·75	1·75
54		20c. bright blue (1.9.52)	1·50	10
55		25c. purple and orange	1·00	10
56		30c. scarlet and purple (4.9.55)	1·25	2·50
57		35c. scarlet and purple (1.9.52)	2·75	1·00
58		40c. red and purple	4·25	4·75
59		50c. black and blue	4·75	20
60		$1 blue and purple	5·50	2·25
61		$2 green and scarlet	17·00	26·00
62		$5 green and brown	55·00	70·00
42/62 *Set of 21*			£100	£100

1949 (10 Oct). 75th Anniv of U.P.U. As Nos. 96/9 of Brunei.

63	10c. purple	20	20
64	15c. deep blue	1·40	3·25
	a. "A" of "CA" missing from wmk	£800	
65	25c. orange	30	2·75
66	50c. blue-black	60	3·25
63/6 *Set of 4*		2·25	8·50

1953 (2 June). Coronation. As No. 152 of Johore.

67	10c. black and reddish purple	1·25	50

1957 (26 June)–**63**. As Nos. 92/102 of Kedah but with inset Arms of Negri Sembilan.

68	**9**	1c. black (21.8.57)	10	10
69	**10**	2c. orange-red (25.7.57)	10	10
70	**11**	4c. sepia (21.8.57)	10	10
71	**12**	5c. carmine-lake (21.8.57)	10	10
72	**13**	8c. myrtle-green (21.8.57)	1·50	1·40
73	**14**	10c. deep brown (4.8.57)	2·00	10
74		10c. deep maroon (10.1.61)	8·50	10
75	**15**	20c. blue	1·00	10
76	**16**	50c. black and blue (*p* 12½) (25.7.57)	30	1·40
		a. Perf 12½×13 (19.7.60)	75	10
77	**17**	$1 ultramarine & reddish pur (25.7.57)	3·75	2·00
78	**18**	$2 bronze-green & scarlet (p 12½) (21.8.57)	12·00	16·00
		a. Perf 13×12½ (15.1.63)	19·00	29·00
79	**19**	$5 brown and bronze-green (p 12½)	14·00	23·00
		a. Perf 13×12½ (6.3.62)	27·00	24·00
		ab. Perf 13×12½. Brown and yellow olive (13.11.62)	£300	90·00
68/79 *Set of 12*			38·00	38·00

The 6, 12, 25 and 30c. values used with this issue were Nos. 1/4 of Malayan Federation.

8 Tuanku Munawir

9 *Vanda hookeriana*

(Photo Enschedé)

1961 (17 Apr). Installation of Tuanku Munawir as Yang di-Pertuan Besar of Negri Sembilan. No wmk. P 14×13.

80	**8**	10c. multicoloured	30	70

1965 (15 Nov)–**69**. As Nos. 166/72 of Johore but with Arms of Negri Sembilan inset and inscr "NEGERI SEMBILAN" as in T **9**. W w **13** (upright).

81	1c. multicoloured	10	1·60
82	2c. multicoloured	10	1·60
	w. Wmk inverted	3·25	
83	5c. multicoloured	40	10
	b. Yellow omitted	80·00	
	c. red omitted	80·00	
84	6c. multicoloured	40	60
85	10c. multicoloured	40	10
86	15c. multicoloured	80	10
87	20c. jet-black and multicoloured	1·25	1·00
	a. Blackish brown & mult (19.12.69)	6·00	1·75
81/7 *Set of 7*		3·00	4·50

The 2c., 6c., 15c. and 20c. exist with PVA gum as well as gum arabic.

The higher values used with this issue were Nos. 20/27 of Malaysia (National Issues).

See also No. 90.

10 Negri Sembilan Crest and Tuanku Ja'afar

(Des Z. Noor. Photo Japanese Govt Ptg Wks)

1968 (8 Apr). Installation of Tuanku Ja'afar as Yang di-Pertuan Besar of Negri Sembilan. P 13.

88	**10**	15c. multicoloured	15	70
89		50c. multicoloured	30	1·40

1970 (27 May). As No. 81 but with W w **13** (sideways).

90	**9**	1c. multicoloured	2·75	7·00

1971 (1 Feb)–**78**. As Nos. 175/87 of Johore but with Arms of Negri Sembilan and inscr "negeri sembilan", as in T **11**.

(a) Litho by Bradbury, Wilkinson

91	1c. multicoloured	40	2·00
92	2c. multicoloured	70	2·00
93	5c. multicoloured	1·00	20
94	6c. multicoloured	1·00	2·00
95	10c. multicoloured	1·00	10
96	15c. multicoloured	1·40	10
97	20c. multicoloured	1·40	50
91/7 *Set of 7*		6·25	6·25

(b) Photo by Harrison (1977-78)

98	2c. multicoloured	1·00	5·00
99	5c. multicoloured	1·00	1·75
100	10c. multicoloured	10·00	1·50
101	15c. multicoloured	13·00	30
102	20c. multicoloured	2·50	2·00
98/102 *Set of 5*		25·00	9·50

The higher values used with issue were Nos. 64/71 of Malaysia (Nations Issues).

For differences between litho and photo printings, see after Johore No. 187.

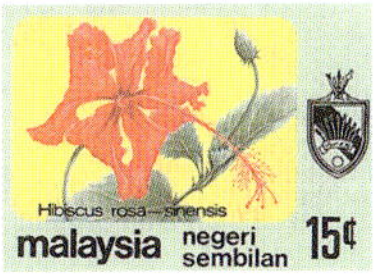

12 *Hibiscus rosa-sinensis*

13 Oil Palm

1979 (30 Apr). As Nos. 188/94 of Johore but with Arms of Negri Sembilan and inscr "negeri sembilan" as in T **12**.

103	1c. *Rafflesia hasseltii*	10	1·25
104	2c. *Pterocarpus indicus*	10	1·25
105	5c. *Lagerstroemia speciosa*	15	40
106	10c. *Durio zibethinus*	20	10
107	15c. Type **12**	20	10
108	20c. *Rhododendron scortechinii*	25	10
109	25c. *Etlingera elatior* (inscr "*Phaeomeria speciosa*")	45	25
103/9 *Set of 7*		1·25	3·00

For higher values used in conjunction with this series see Nos. 190/7 of Malaysia (National Issues).

1983 (1 Oct)–**84**. As Nos. 105/8 but without wmk.

112	5c. *Lagerstroemia speciosa* (25.5.84)	1·00	1·75
113	10c. *Durio zibethinus* (24.10.84)	30	50
114	15c. Type **12** (11.8.84)	50	45
115	20c. *Rhododendron scortechinii* (blackish brown background)	60·00	1·25
115*a*	20c. *Rhododendron scortechinii* (bronze green background) (1983)	50	50

*There was no official release date for these stamps. Dates shown are the earliest recorded from postmarks and may be revised if earlier examples are reported.

For details of the shade differences between watermarked and unwatermarked printings see after Johore No. 200a.

Nos. 112/14 and 115*a* show a larger crest, further from the face value than on Nos. 105/8 and 115.

1986 (25 Oct)–**96**. As Nos. 202/8 of Johore, but with Arms of Negri Sembilan and inscr "NEGERI SEMBILAN" as in T **13**. P 12.

117	1c. Coffee	10	30
	w. Wmk inverted		
118	2c. Coconuts	10	30
119	5c. Cocoa	15	10
	c. Perf 14×13¾ (1996)	1·50	10

	ca. Wmk sideways*	4·75	
	cb. Wmk top of SPM to left	6·00	
	cw. Wmk inverted	5·00	
	f. Perf 14¾×14½ (1998)	10·00	
120	10c. Black pepper	15	10
	c. Perf 14×13¾ (1995)	1·00	10
	e. Perf 14×14½ (1996)	2·75	15
	f. Perf 14¾×14½ (1996)	8·50	40
121	15c. Rubber	25	10
	w. Wmk inverted (1993)	9·50	
122	20c. Type **13**	25	10
	aw. Wmk inverted		
	c. Perf 14×13¼ (1994)	2·50	10
	f. Perf 14¾×14½ (1999)	13·00	
123	30c. Rice	30	10
	c. Perf 14×13¼ (1994)	3·25	20
	cw. Wmk inverted	8·50	
	e. Perf 14×14½	5·50	20
	ew. Wmk inverted	7·50	
	f. Perf 14¾×14½ (1996)	4·00	20
117/23 *Set of 7*		1·10	1·00

*The normal sideways watermark for this value shows the top of SPM to right, as seen from the back of the stamp.

14 *Nelumbium nelumbo* (sacred lotus)

2007 (31 Dec). Garden Flowers. As Nos. 210/15 of Johore, but with portrait of Sultan Tuanku Ja'afar and Arms of Negri Sembilan as in T **14**. Multicoloured. W **138**. Phosphorised paper. P 14.

124	5s. Type **14**	10	10
125	10s. *Hydrangea macrophylla*	15	10
126	20s. *Hippeastrum reticulatum*	25	15
127	30s. Bougainvillea	40	20
128	40s. *Ipomoea indica*	50	30
129	50s. *Hibiscus rosa-sinensis*	65	35
124/9 *Set of 6*		1·90	1·10

STAMP BOOKLETS

1935. Stapled.

SB1	$1 booklet containing twenty 5c. (No. 26) in blocks of 10	£2750
SB2	$1.30 booklet containing 5c. and 8c. (Nos. 26, 29), each in block of 10	£3250

1973 (8 Dec). Cover as Type B **1** of Johore, but inscr "N. SEMBILAN". Stitched.

SB3	$3 booklet containing eight 5c., 10c. and twelve 15c. (Nos. 93, 95/6) in blocks of 4	30·00

Examples of No. SB3 exist with a white label giving revised postage rates.

1979 (1 Dec). Cover as No. SB5 of Johore, but inscr "NEGERI SEMBILAN". Stitched.

SB4	$3 booklet containing eight 5c., 10c., and twelve 15c. (Nos. 105/7) in blocks of 4	10·00

No. SB4 exists with two different versions of the back cover.

1987 (1 June). Cover as Type B **2** of Johore, but inscr "NEGERI SEMBILAN". Stapled.

SB5	$2 booklet containing 5c., 10c., 15c. and 20c. (Nos. 119/22) in blocks of 4	9·00

1992 (1 July). Kuala Lumpur '92 International Philatelic Exhibition. Cover as Type **3** of Johore, but inscr "Negeri Sembilan". Stamps attached by selvedge.

SB6	$3 booklet containing 30c. (No. 123) in block of 10	11·00

1993. Covers as Nos. SB8/9 of Johore, but inscr "Negeri Sembilan". Stamps attached by selvedge.

SB7	$2 booklet containing 20c. (No. 122) in block of 10	1·50
SB8	$3 booklet containing 30c. (No. 123) in block of 10	2·00

PAHANG

The first British Resident was appointed in 1888. Pahang joined the Federated Malay States in 1896.

Until 1 January 1899, when the Federated Malay States joined the U.P.U., mail for addresses outside Malaya was franked with stamps of the STRAITS SETTLEMENTS.

PRICES FOR STAMPS ON COVER TO 1945

No. 1	*from* × 50
Nos. 2/3	—
No. 4	*from* × 100
No. 5	—
No. 6	*from* × 100
Nos. 7/10	*from* × 8
Nos. 11/13	*from* × 25
Nos. 14/16	*from* × 20
Nos. 17/*a*	—
Nos. 18/*d*	*from* × 6
Nos. 19/24	*from* × 8
No. 25	*from* × 20
Nos. 26/7	—
No. 28	*from* × 15
Nos. 29/46	*from* × 6

PAHANG (1) PAHANG (2) PAHANG (**2a**) (Antique letters)

1889 (Jan). Nos. 52/3 and 63 of Straits Settlements optd with T **1**.

1	2c. pale rose	£120	50·00
2	8c. orange	£1800	£1800
3	10c. slate	£225	£250

All three values were overprinted from a triplet setting, but the 2c. also exists from a similar setting of 30 or 60.

1889. No. 63 of Straits Settlements optd with T **2**.

4	2c. pale rose	17·00	21·00
	a. Bright rose	8·50	9·50
	ab. Opt Type **2a**. Antique letters	£850	

No. 4 was overprinted from a setting of 60. No. 4ab usually occurs on R. 10/1, but has also been found on R. 8/1 as the result of revision of the setting.

PAHANG (3) PAHANG (4)

1890. No. 63a of Straits Settlements optd.

5	**3**	2c. bright rose	£8500	£2000
6	**4**	2c. bright rose	£110	14·00
		w. Wmk inverted		

No. 5 may have been overprinted from a triplet setting. No. 6 was from a setting of 60.

PAHANG *Two* CENTS (5) PAHANG *Two* CENTS (6)

PAHANG Two CENTS (7) PAHANG Two CENTS (8)

1891. No. 68 of Straits Settlements surch with T **5/8**.

7	**5**	2c. on 24c. green	£200	£250
8	**6**	2c. on 24c. green	£950	£1100
9	**7**	2c. on 24c. green	£375	£425
10	**8**	2c. on 24c. green	£950	£1100

Nos. 7/10 come from one setting used to surcharge the panes of sixty. No. 7 occurs in rows 1 to 5, No. 8 on row 6, No. 9 on rows 7 to 9 and No. 10 on row 10.

9

10

1891 (Nov)–**95**. Wmk Crown CA. P 14.

11	**9**	1c. green (3.95)	4·25	3·25
12		2c. rose	4·50	3·25
13		5c. blue (6.93)	11·00	45·00
11/13 *Set of 3*			18·00	45·00
11s/13s Optd "Specimen" *Set of 3*			80·00	

Following an increase of postage rates on 1 March 1894 1 cent stamps of STRAITS SETTLEMENTS were used in Pahang until the autumn of the following year.

1895–**99**. Wmk Crown CA. P 14.

14	**10**	3c. dull purple and carmine	8·50	2·75
15		4c. dull purple and carmine (1899)	17·00	14·00
16		5c. dull purple and olive-yellow (1897)	35·00	22·00
14/16 *Set of 3*			55·00	35·00
14s/16s Optd "Specimen" *Set of 3*			65·00	

1897 (2 Aug). No. 13 bisected, surch in red manuscript at Kuala Lipis and initialled "JFO".

(a) Bisected horizontally.

17	2c. on half of 5c. blue (surch "2" and bar across "5")	—	£2500
17*a*	3c. on half of 5c. blue (surch "3")	£6000	£2500

(b) Bisected diagonally.

18	2c. on half of 5c. blue (surch "2" and bar across "5")	£1500	£400
	a. Unsevered pair. Nos. 18 and 18d	£11000	£4000
	b. Se-tenant pair. Nos. 18 and 18d	£4500	£1100
	c. Surch in black manuscript	£9000	£3250
18*d*	3c. on half of 5c. blue (surch "3")	£1500	£400
	dc. Surch in black manuscript	£9000	£3250

The initials are those of John Fortescue Owen, the District Treasurer at Kuala Lipis.

Nos. 17 and 18 only occur on the bottom half of the 5c. and Nos. 17*a* and 18*d* on the top half. No. 18a is a complete example of No. 13 showing the two surcharges. No. 18b is a *se-tenant* pair of bisects from adjoining stamps.

Pahang.
(11)

Pahang.
(12)

1898–**99**.

(a) Nos. 72/5 of Perak optd with T **11**.

19	10c. dull purple and orange (3.98)	23·00	26·00
20	25c. green and carmine	85·00	£160
21	50c. dull purple and greenish black	£450	£500
22	50c. green and black (1899)	£275	£375

(b) Nos. 76 and 79 of Perak optd with T **12**.

23	$1 green and pale green	£375	£550
24	$5 green and ultramarine	£1400	£2250

Pahang
Four cents
(13)

Four cents.
(14)

1898.

(a) No. 71 of Perak surch with T **13**.

25	4c. on 8c. dull purple and ultramarine	7·00	7·00
	a. Surch inverted	£3750	£1500
	b. Surch double	£950	

(b) T **13** on plain paper (no stamp), but issued for postage. Imperf.

26	4c. black	—	£4000
27	5c. black	£2500	

No. 26 also exists pin-perforated.

1899. No. 16 surch with T **14**.

28	**10**	4c. on 5c. dull purple and olive-yellow	19·00	65·00

Pending the arrival of the permanent Federated Malay States issue the stamps of SELANGOR, FEDERATED MALAY STATES provisional overprints and PERAK were used at various times between November 1899 and July 1902.

The general issues for the FEDERATED MALAY STATES were used in Pahang from July 1902 until 1935.

15 Sultan Sir Abu Bakar

16 Sultan Sir Abu Bakar

1935 (2 Dec)–**41**. Chalk-surfaced paper. Wmk Mult Script CA. P 14.

29	**15**	1c. black (1.1.36)	20	40
30		2c. green (1.1.36)	2·25	50
31		3c. green (*ordinary paper*) (21.8.41)	48·00	4·25
		a. Thin striated paper	19·00	18·00
32		4c. orange	70	50
33		5c. brown (5.12.35)	70	10
34		6c. scarlet (1.1.37)	22·00	1·75
35		8c. grey	60	10
36		8c. scarlet (*Thin striated paper*) (11.12.41)	5·00	70·00
37		10c. dull purple (1.1.36)	1·50	10
		a. Thin striated paper (1941)		
38		12c. bright ultramarine (1.1.36)	3·50	1·25
39		15c. ultram (*ordinary paper*) (1.10.41)	24·00	60·00
40		25c. dull purple and scarlet (1.4.36)	2·25	1·50
41		30c. dull purple and orange (1.1.36)	1·25	1·10
		a. Thin striated paper (1941)		
42		40c. scarlet and dull purple	1·00	2·00
43		50c. black/*emerald* (1.2.36)	4·50	1·50
44		$1 black and red/*blue* (1.4.36)	4·00	8·00
45		$2 green and scarlet (16.5.36)	27·00	38·00
46		$5 green and red/*emerald* (16.5.36)	10·00	75·00
29/46 *Set of 18*			£110	£250
29s/46s Perf "Specimen" *Set of 18*			£425	

The stamps issued during 1941 were printed by Harrison and Sons following bomb damage to the De La Rue works on 29 December 1940. The used prices quoted for Nos. 36 and 39 are for examples with clearly identifiable 1941 cancellations.

A 2c. orange and a 6c. grey, both on thin striated paper, were prepared but not officially issued. (*Price mint £4 each*).

During shortages in 1941 stamps of STRAITS SETTLEMENTS (2c., 25c.), SELANGOR (2c. orange, 3c., 8c.), NEGRI SEMBILAN (6c.) and PERAK (2c. orange) were issued in Pahang.

1948 (1 Dec). Royal Silver Wedding. As Nos. 131/2 of Johore..

47	10c. violet	15	60
48	$5 green	25·00	40·00

1949 (10 Oct). 75th Anniv of U.P.U. As Nos. 96/9 of Brunei.

49	10c. purple	30	25
50	15c. deep blue	1·10	1·50
51	25c. orange	35	2·25
52	50c. blue-black	70	2·75
49/52 *Set of 4*		2·25	6·00

1950 (1 June)–**56**. Wmk Mult Script CA. Chalk-surfaced paper. P 17½×18.

53	**16**	1c. black	10	10
54		2c. orange	20	10
55		3c. green	30	80
56		4c. brown	2·00	10
		a. Chocolate (24.3.54)	12·00	2·75
57		5c. bright purple (1.9.52)	50	70
		a. Bright mauve (10.9.53)	50	15
58		6c. grey	50	30
59		8c. scarlet	50	1·50
60		8c. green (1.9.52)	1 00	75
61		10c. magenta	25	10
62		12c. scarlet (1.9.52)	1·25	1·25
63		15c. ultramarine	75	10
64		20c. black and green	60	2·75
65		20c. bright blue (1.9.52)	2·00	10
		a. Ultramarine (8.3.56)	8·00	3·00
66		25c. purple and orange	50	10
67		30c. scarlet and brown-purple (4.9.55)	2·00	35
		a. Scarlet and purple (8.3.56)	23·00	6·00
68		35c. scarlet and purple (1.9.52)	75	25
69		40c. red and purple	1·75	7·50
70		50c. black and blue	1·50	10
71		$1 blue and purple	3·00	3·25
72		$2 green and scarlet	14·00	24·00
73		$5 green and brown	60·00	85·00

		a. Green and sepia (24.3.54)	£110	£110
53/73		*Set of 21*	85·00	£110

1953 (2 June). Coronation. As No. 152 of Johore.

74		10c. black and reddish purple	2·00	10

1957 (26 June)–**62**. As Nos. 92/102 of Kedah but with inset portrait of Sultan Sir Abu Bakar.

75	**9**	1c. black (21.8.57)	10	10
76	**10**	2c. orange-red (25.7.57)	10	10
77	**11**	4c. sepia (21.8.57)	10	10
78	**12**	5c. carmine-lake (21.8.57)	10	10
79	**13**	8c. myrtle-green (21.8.57)	1·50	2·25
80	**14**	10c. deep brown (4.8.57)	1·25	10
81		10c. deep maroon (21.2.61)	3·50	30
82	**15**	20c. blue	2·25	20
83	**16**	50c. black and blue (*p* 12½) (25.7.57)	45	75
		a. Perf 12½×13 (17.5.60)	1·00	20
84	**17**	$1 ultramarine & reddish pur (25.7.57)	9·00	2·25
85	**18**	$2 bronze-grn & scar (*p* 12½) (21.8.57)	6·50	9·00
		a. Perf 13×12½ (13.11.62)	9·00	21·00
86	**19**	$5 brown and bronze-green (*p* 12½)	12·00	15·00
		a. Perf 13×12½ (17.5.60)	13·00	22·00
		b. Perf 13×12½. Brown and yellow olive (23.10.62)	38·00	42·00
75/86		*Set of 12*	35·00	26·00

The 6, 12, 25 and 30c. values used with this issue were Nos. 1/4 of Malayan Federation.

17 *Vanda hookeriana*

1965 (15 Nov). As Nos. 166/72 of Johore but with inset portrait of Sultan Sir Abu Bakar as in T **17**. W w **13** (upright).

87		1c. multicoloured	10	1·25
		c. Grey (flower name, etc) omitted	85·00	
		w. Wmk inverted	6·50	
88		2c. multicoloured	10	1·25
89		5c. multicoloured	15	10
		c. Red (leaves, etc) omitted	£100	
90		6c. multicoloured	30	1·25
91		10c. multicoloured	20	10
		a. Red omitted	£100	
92		15c. multicoloured	1·00	10
93		20c. multicoloured	1·60	40
87/93		*Set of 7*	3·00	3·75

The 2c., 5c. and 6c. exist with PVA gum as well as gum arabic.

The higher values used with this issue were Nos. 20/27 of Malaysia (National Issues).

1970 (27 May). As Nos. 87 and 91 but W w **13** (sideways).

94	**17**	1c. multicoloured	2·50	7·00
95	–	10c. multicoloured	1·00	3·50

(Litho B.W.)

1971 (1 Feb). As Nos. 175/81 of Johore but with portrait of Sultan Sir Abu Bakar and arms, as in T **18**.

96		1c. multicoloured	20	1·75
97		2c. multicoloured	50	2·00
98		5c. multicoloured	1·00	50
99		6c. multicoloured	1·50	2·25
100		10c. multicoloured	1·00	30
101		15c. multicoloured	1·75	10
102		20c. multicoloured	2·00	50
96/102		*Set of 7*	7·25	6·50

The higher values used with this issue were Nos. 64/71 of Malaysia (National Issues).

19 Sultan Haji Ahmed Shah

20 *Rhododendron scortechinii*

(Des Union Advertising. Litho Harrison)

1975 (8 May). Installation of the Sultan. P 14×14½.

103	**19**	10c. slate-green, light lilac and gold	50	1·25
104		15c. greenish black, yellow & dp green	60	10
105		50c. black, light violet-bl & greenish blk	1·75	4·25
103/5		*Set of 3*	2·50	5·00

(Photo Harrison)

1977 (5 Sept)–**78**. As Nos. 97/8, 100/2 but with portraits of Sultan Haji Ahmad Shah.

106		2c. multicoloured (1978)	70·00	65·00
107		5c. multicoloured	70	1·25
108		10c. multicoloured (10.2.78)	1·00	75
109		15c. multicoloured (13.1.78)	1·00	30
		a. Black (face value, etc.)* omitted	£150	
110		20c. multicoloured (1978)	4·00	2·00
106/10		*Set of 5*	70·00	65·00

*There were two black cylinders used for No. 109, one to apply the portrait and state details, the other the face value and parts of the main design.

The higher values used with this issue were Nos. 64/71 of Malaysia (National Issues).

1979 (30 Apr). As Nos. 188/94 of Johore but with portrait of Sultan Haji Ahmad Shah as in T **20**.

111		1c. *Rafflesia hasseltii*	10	1·00
112		2c. *Pterocarpus indicus*	10	1·00
113		5c. *Lagerstroemia speciosa*	10	30
114		10c. *Durio zibethinus*	15	10
115		15c. *Hibiscus rosa-sinensis*	15	10
116		20c. Type **20**	20	10
117		25c. *Etlingera elatior* (inscr "*Phaeomeria speciosa*")	40	40
111/17		*Set of 7*	1·00	2·50

For higher values used in conjunction with this series see Nos. 190/7 of Malaysia (National Issues).

1983 (5 Oct)–**85**. As Nos. 113/16 but without wmk.

120		5c. *Lagerstroemia speciosa* (17.11.83)	55	75
121		10c. *Durio zibethinus* (8.1.85)	1·00	1·50
123		20c. Type **20** (blackish brown background)	60·00	1·25
123*a*		20c. Type **20** (bronze-green background) (20.8.84)	1·25	40

*There was no official release date for these stamps. Dates shown are the earliest recorded from postmarks and may be revised if earlier examples are reported.

For details of the shade differences between watermarked and unwatermarked printings see after Johore No. 200a.

On Nos. 120/1 and 123a "pahang" is one millimetre nearer "malaysia" than on Nos. 113/16 and 123.

21 Rice

1986 (25 Oct)–**96**. As Nos. 202/8 of Johore, but with portrait of Sultan Ahmad Shah as in T **21**. P 12.

125		1c. Coffee	10	25
		aw. Wmk inverted	3·50	
		b. Perf 13½×13¾ (1993)	7·00	40
126		2c. Coconuts	10	35
127		5c. Cocoa	15	10
		c. Perf 14×13¾ (1996)	1·75	10
128		10c. Black pepper	15	10
		aw. Wmk inverted	10·00	
		c. Perf 14×13¾ (1995)	2·00	50
		cw. Wmk inverted		
		f. Perf 14¾×14½ (1994)	9·00	60
129		15c. Rubber	25	10
		w. Wmk inverted (1991)	10·00	
130		20c. Oil palm	25	15
		aw. Wmk inverted		
		c. Perf 14×13¾ (1994)	1·00	10
		e. Perf 14×14½ (1996)	8·00	20
		ew. Wmk inverted	10·00	
		f. Perf 14¾×14½ (1999)	10·00	
131		30c. Type **21**	30	15
		aw. Wmk inverted	11·00	
		c. Perf 14×13¾ (1994)	3·25	20
		ca. Brownish grey (background) omitted	£100	
		cw. Wmk inverted (1995)		
		f. Perf 14¾×14½ (1995)	7·00	60
		fw. Wmk inverted	7·00	
125/31		*Set of 7*	1·10	80

2002 ((?)). Vert designs as Type **21** but redenominated in "sen". Multicoloured. W **138**. P 14×13¾.

132	30s. Rice	2·00	10

22 *Nelumbium nelumbo* (sacred lotus)

2007 (31 Dec). Garden Flowers. As Nos. 210/15 of Johore, but with portrait of Sultan Ahmad Shah and Arms of Pahang as in T **22**. Multicoloured. W **138**. Phosphorised paper. P 14.

133	5s. Type **22**	10	10
134	10s. *Hydrangea macrophylla*	15	10
135	20s. *Hippeastrum reticulatum*	25	15
136	30s. Bougainvillea	40	20
137	40s. *Ipomoea indica*	50	30
138	50s. *Hibiscus rosa-sinensis*	65	35
133/8	*Set of 6*	1·90	1·10

STAMP BOOKLETS

1935. Black on buff covers. Stapled.

SB1	$1 booklet containing twenty 5c. (No. 33) in blocks of 10	£2750
SB2	$1.30 booklet containing 5c. and 8c. (Nos. 33, 35) each in block of 10 and pane of airmail labels.	£3000

1973 (8 Dec). Cover as Type B **1** of Johore, but inscr "PAHANG". Stitched.

SB3	$3 booklet containing eight 5c., 10c. and twelve 15c. (Nos. 98, 100/1) in blocks of 4	30·00

1979 (1 Dec). Cover as No. SB5 of Johore, but inscr "PAHANG". Stitched.

SB4	$3 booklet containing eight 5c., 10c., and twelve 15c. (Nos. 113/15) in blocks of 4	10·00

No. SB4 exists with two different versions of the back cover.

1987 (1 June). Cover as Type B **2** of Johore, but inscr "PAHANG". Stapled.

SB5	$2 booklet containing 5c., 10c., 15c. and 20c. (Nos. 127/30) in blocks of 4	14·00

1992 (1 July). "Kuala Lumpur '92" International Philatelic Exhibition. Cover as Type B **3** of Johore, but inscr "Pahang". Stamps attached by selvedge.

SB6	$3 booklet containing 30c. (No. 131) in block of 10	9·00

1993. Covers as Nos. SB8/9 of Johore, but inscr "Pahang". Stamps attached by selvedge.

SB7	$2 booklet containing 20c. (No. 130) in block of 10	1·50
SB8	$3 booklet containing 30c. (No. 131) in block of 10	2·00

PENANG

One of the Straits Settlements which joined the Federation of Malaya on 1 February 1948.

1948 (1 Dec). Royal Silver Wedding. As Nos. 131/2 of Johore.

1	10c. violet	30	20
2	$5 brown	38·00	38·00

1949 (21 Feb)–**52**. As T **58** of Straits Settlements, but inscr "PENANG" at foot. Wmk Mult Script CA. Chalk-surfaced paper. P 17½×18.

3	1c. black	1·25	20
4	2c. orange	1·25	20
5	3c. green	40	1·00
6	4c. brown	40	10
7	5c. bright purple (1.9.52)	3·75	3·25
8	6c. grey	1·00	20
9	8c. scarlet	1·00	4·75
10	8c. green (1.9.52)	3·25	2·50
11	10c. purple	50	10
12	12c. scarlet (1.9.52)	3·75	8·50
13	15c. ultramarine	1·75	30
14	20c. black and green	2·25	1·50
15	20c. bright blue (1.9.52)	2·50	1·25
16	25c. purple and orange	2·50	1·00
17	35c. scarlet and purple (1.9.52)	2·50	1·25
18	40c. red and purple	3·50	14·00
19	50c. black and blue	4·75	20
20	$1 blue and purple	20·00	2·75
21	$2 green and scarlet	23·00	2·00
22	$5 green and brown	48·00	3·00
3/22	*Set of 20*	£110	42·00

1949 (10 Oct). 75th Anniv of U.P.U. As Nos. 96/9 of Brunei.

23	10c. purple	20	10
24	15c. deep blue	2·50	3·75
25	25c. orange	45	3·75
26	50c. blue-black	1·50	3·50
23/6	*Set of 4*	4·25	10·00

1953 (2 June). Coronation. As No. 152 of Johore.

27	10c. black and reddish purple	1·50	10

1954 (9 June)–**57**. As T **1** of Malacca (Queen Elizabeth II) but inscr "PENANG" at foot. Chalk-surfaced paper. Wmk Mult Script CA. P 17½×18.

28	1c. black (5.1.55)	10	70
29	2c. yellow-orange (8.9.54)	50	30
30	4c. brown (1.9.54)	1·00	10
	a. Yellow-brown (17.7.57)	8·00	8·00
31	5c. bright purple (1.10.54)	2·00	4·00
	a. Bright mauve (17.7.57)	8·00	8·00
32	6c. grey	20	80
33	8c. green (5.1.55)	20	3·50
34	10c. brown-purple (1.9.54)	20	10
35	12c. rose-red (5.1.55)	30	3·50
36	20c. bright blue (1.9.54)	50	10
37	25c. brown-purple & yellow-orange (1.12.54)	30	10
38	30c. rose-red and brown-purple (5.9.55)	30	10
39	35c. rose-red and brown-purple (8.9.54)	70	60
40	50c. black and bright blue (1.12.54)	50	10
41	$1 bright blue and brown-purple (1.10.54)	2·50	30
42	$2 emerald and scarlet (1.10.54)	13·00	3·75
43	$5 emerald and brown (5.1.55)	48·00	3·75
28/43	*Set of 16*	65·00	18·00

1957. As Nos. 92/102 of Kedah, but with inset portrait of Queen Elizabeth II.

44	**9**	1c. black (21.8)	10	1·50
45	**10**	2c. orange-red (25.7)	10	1·00
46	**11**	4c. sepia (21.8)	10	10
47	**12**	5c. carmine-lake (21.8)	10	30
48	**13**	8c. myrtle-green (21.8)	1·75	2·25
49	**14**	10c. deep brown (4.8)	30	10
50	**15**	20c. blue (26.6)	1·00	40
51	**16**	50c. black and blue (25.7)	1·50	70
52	**17**	$1 ultramarine and reddish purple (25.7)	7·50	1·00
53	**18**	$2 bronze-green and scarlet (21.8)	20·00	17·00
54	**19**	$5 brown and bronze-green (26.6)	25·00	14·00
44/54		*Set of 11*	50·00	35·00

The note after No. 86 of Pahang also applies here.

1 Copra

2 *Vanda hookeriana*

(Recess D.L.R.)

1960 (15 Mar). As Nos. 44/54, but with inset Arms of Penang as in T **1**. W w **12**. P 13×12½ (1c. to 8c., $2, $5), 12½×13 (10c. to 50c.) or 13½ ($1).

55	1c. black	10	1·60
56	2c. orange-red	10	1·60
57	4c. sepia	10	10
58	5c. carmine-lake	10	10
59	8c. myrtle-green	2·75	4·50
60	10c. deep maroon	30	10
61	20c. blue	55	10
62	50c. black and blue	30	30
	a. Imperf (pair)	£700	
63	$1 ultramarine and reddish purple	6·50	1·75
64	$2 bronze-green and scarlet	7·00	6·50
65	$5 brown and bronze-green	14·00	8·50
55/65	*Set of 11*	28·00	22·00

No. 62a comes from a sheet purchased at the Penang Post Office which had the upper five horizontal rows imperforate.

1965 (15 Nov)–**68**. As Nos. 166/72 of Johore but with Arms of Penang inset and inscr "PULAU PINANG" as in T **2**. W w **13** (upright).

66	1c. multicoloured	10	1·25

67	2c. multicoloured	10	1·25
68	5c. multicoloured	30	10
	b. Yellow (flower) omitted	75·00	
	c. Red omitted	£140	
	d. Blue (background and inscr) omitted	£750	
	da. Blue and yellow omitted	£750	
	w. Wmk inverted	2·00	
69	6c. multicoloured	30	1·25
	b. Yellow omitted	75·00	
70	10c. grey and multicoloured	20	10
	a. *Jet-black and multicoloured* (12.11.68)	50	20
71	15c. multicoloured	1·00	10
	b. Green (value and leaves) omitted	£600	
	c. Black (country name and arms) omitted (horizontal pair with normal)	£1200	
72	20c. multicoloured	1·60	30
	a. Bright purple (blooms) omitted	£750	
	b. Yellow (leaves) omitted	£750	
66/72 *Set of 7*		3·00	3·75

The 2c., 5c., 6c., 10c. and 20c. exist with PVA gum as well as gum arabic.

The higher values used with this issue were Nos. 20/27 of Malaysia (National Issues).

1970. As Nos. 66 and 70 but W w **13** (sideways).

73	**2**	1c. multicoloured (27.5.70)	1·60	6·00
74	–	10c. multicoloured (20.11.70)	7·00	4·00

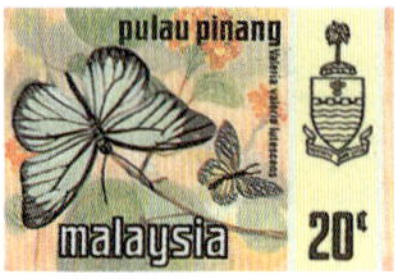

3 Valeria valeria

4 *Etlingera elatior* (inscr "Phaeomeria speciosa")

1971 (1 Feb)–**78**. As Nos. 175/87 of Johore, but with Arms of Penang and inscr "pulau pinang", as in T **3**.

(a) Litho by Bradbury Wilkinson

75	1c. multicoloured	40	2·00
76	2c. multicoloured	70	2·00
77	5c. multicoloured	1·50	40
78	6c. multicoloured	1·50	2·00
79	10c. multicoloured	1·50	15
80	15c. multicoloured	1·50	10
81	20c. multicoloured	1·75	60
75/81 *Set of 7*		8·00	6·50

(b) Photo by Harrison (1977–78).

81*a*	1c. multicoloured	3·50	7·50
82	5c. multicoloured	3·25	60
83	10c. multicoloured	5·50	60
84	15c. multicoloured	16·00	30
85	20c. multicoloured	5·50	1·00
81a/5 *Set of 5*		30·00	9·00

The higher values used with this issue were Nos. 64/71 of Malaysia (National Issues).

For differences between litho and photo printings, see after Johore No. 187.

1979 (30 Apr). As Nos. 188/94 of Johore but with Arms of Penang and inscr "pulau pinang" as in T **4**.

86	1c. *Rafflesia hasseltii*	10	1·00
87	2c. *Pterocarpus indicus*	10	1·00
88	5c. *Lagerstroemia speciosa*	10	35
89	10c. *Durio zibethinus*	15	10
90	15c. *Hibiscus rosa-sinensis*	15	10
91	20c. *Rhododendron scortechinii*	20	10
92	25c. Type **4**	40	30
86/92 *Set of 7*		1·00	2·50

For higher values used in conjunction with this series see Nos. 190/7 of Malaysia (National Issues).

1983–85. As Nos. 88/91, but without wmk.

95	5c. *Lagerstroemia speciosa* (1.84)	30	40
96	10c. *Durio zibethinus* (2.7.85)	6·00	2·50
97	15c. *Hibiscus rosa-sinensis* (27.12.83)	55	40
98	20c. *Rhododendron scortechinii* (blackish brown background) (27.6.84)	55·00	1·25
98*a*	20c. *Rhododendron scortechinii* (bronze green background) (3.84)	1·00	40

*There was no official release date for these stamps. Dates shown are the earliest recorded from postmarks and may be revised if earlier examples are reported.

For details of the shade differences between watermarked and unwatermarked printings see after Johore No. 200a.

On Nos. 95/7 and 98a the state arms are larger than on the watermarked printing and No. 98.

5 Cocoa

1986 (25 Oct)–**95**. As Nos. 202/8 of Johore, but with Arms of Penang and inscr "PULAU PINANG" as in T **5**. P 12.

100	1c. Coffee	10	30
	w. Wmk inverted (1993)	3·75	
101	2c. Coconuts	10	35
102	5c. Type **5**	15	10
	c. Perf 14×13¼ (1994)	2·50	20
	cw. Wmk inverted	5·50	
	f. Perf 14¾×14½ (1995)	1·25	20
103	10c. Black pepper	15	10
	aw. Wmk inverted		
	c. Perf 14×13¾ (1995)	1·00	10
	cw. Wmk inverted	5·50	
	e. Perf 14×14½ (1994)	3·25	20
	f. Perf 14¾×14½ (1995)	2·25	10
	fw. Wmk inverted	4·00	
104	15c. Rubber	25	10
	w. Wmk inverted	9·50	
105	20c. Oil palm	25	15
	aw. Wmk inverted		
	c. Perf 14×13¾ (1994)	1·00	10
	e. Perf 14×14½ (1994)	5·00	10
	f. Perf 14¾×14½ (1994)	4·50	20
106	30c. Rice	30	15
	aw. Wmk inverted	12·00	
	c. Perf 14×13¾ (1994)	1·00	10
	cw. Wmk inverted (1995)	2·50	
	e. Perf 14×14½ (1995)	1·75	20
	f. Perf 14¾×14½ (1994)	2·75	30
	fw. Wmk inverted		
100/6 *Set of 7*		1·10	80

2003 ((?)). Vert dseigns as Type **5** but redenominated in "sen". Multicoloured. W **138**. P 14×13¾.

107	30s. Rice	1·75	10
	a. Perf 14¾×14½	1·75	10

6 *Nelumbium nelumbo* (sacred lotus)

2007 (31 Dec). Garden Flowers. As Nos. 210/15 of Johore, but with Arms of Penang as in T **6**. Multicoloured. W **138**. Phosphorised paper. P 14.

108	5s. Type **6**	10	10
109	10s. *Hydrangea macrophylla*	15	10
110	20s. *Hippeastrum reticulatum*	25	15
111	30s. Bougainvillea	40	20
112	40s. *Ipomoea indica*	50	30
113	50s. *Hibiscus rosa-sinensis*	65	35
108/13 *Set of 6*		1·90	1·10

STAMP BOOKLETS

1973 (8 Dec). Cover as Type B **1** of Johore, but inscr "PULAU PINANG". Stitched.

SB1	$3 booklet containing eight 5c., 10c. and twelve 15c. (Nos. 77, 79/80) in blocks of 4	32·00

1979 (1 Dec). Cover as No. SB5 of Johore, but inscr "PULAU PINANG". Stitched.

SB2	$3 booklet containing eight 5c., 10c., and twelve 15c. (No. 88/90) in blocks of 4	11·00

No. SB2 exists with two different versions of the back cover.

1987 (1 June). Cover as Type B **2** of Johore, but inscr "PULAU PINANG". Stapled.

SB3	$2 booklet containing 5c., 10c., 15c. and 20c. (Nos. 102/5) in blocks of 4	10·00

1992 (1 July). Kuala Lumpur '92 International Philatelic Exhibition. Cover as Type **3** of Johore, but inscr "Pulau Pinang". Stamps attacked by selvedge.

SB4	$3 booklet containing 30c. (No. 106) in block of 10	9·00

1993. Covers as Nos. SB8/9 of Johore, but inscr "Pulau Pinang" Stamps attached by selvedge.

SB5	$2 booklet containing 20c. (No. 105) in block of 10	1·50
SB6	$3 booklet containing 30c. (No. 106) in block of 10	2·00

PERAK

Perak accepted a British Resident in 1874, although he was later murdered.

The state joined the Federated Malay States in 1896.

> The stamps of the STRAITS SETTLEMENTS were used in Perak during 1877/8.
>
> Until 1 January 1899, when the Federated Malay States joined the U.P.U., mail for addresses outside Malaya was franked with stamps of the STRAITS SETTLEMENTS.

PRICES FOR STAMPS ON COVER TO 1945

No. 1	—
Nos. 2/9	*from* × 60
Nos. 10/13	*from* × 30
Nos. 14/16	*from* × 8
Nos. 17/22	*from* × 20
No. 23	—
Nos. 24/5	—
Nos. 26/8	*from* × 15
No. 29	*from* × 75
No. 30	*from* × 20
Nos. 31/2	—
Nos. 33/40	*from* × 15
Nos. 43/60	*from* × 6
Nos. 61/5	*from* × 20
Nos. 66/79	*from* × 12
No. 80	—
Nos. 81/7	*from* × 8
Nos. 88/102	*from* × 4
Nos. 103/21	*from* × 3

The Official stamps of Perak are rare used on cover.

(**1**)

1878. No. 11 of Straits Settlements handstamped with T **1**.

1		2c. brown	£2000	£1600

PERAK (**2**) (14½ mm long) — PERAK (**3**) (11 mm long) — PERAK (**4**) (10¼ mm long)

PERAK (**5**) (17 mm long) — PERAK (**6**) ("RA" narrow) — PERAK (**7**) ("R" narrow)

PERAK (**8**) ("P" and "K" wide) — PERAK (**9**) (12 to 13½ mm long)

1880–81. No. 11 (wmk Crown CC) of Straits Settlements optd with T **2**/**9**.

2	**2**	2c. brown	£3000	£1100
3	**3**	2c. brown	£2500	£750
4	**4**	2c. brown	£1100	£700
5	**5**	2c. brown (1881)	38·00	70·00
		w. Wmk inverted	†	£550
6	**6**	2c. brown (1881)	£300	£325
7	**7**	2c. brown (1881)	£180	£200
8	**8**	2c. brown (1881)	£650	£600
		a. Opt double	†	£2500
9	**9**	2c. brown (1881)	£170	£180

Of the above No. 2 is from a single unit overprint, No. 5 from a setting of sixty and the remainder from settings applied as horizontal strips of three. Nos. 6/8 come from mixed triplets, either 6+7+7 or 7+7+8. No. 4 is believed to come from a single unit overprint in addition to a triplet.

PERAK (**10**) ("A" wide) — PERAK (**11**) ("E" wide)

1882–83. Nos. 50 (wmk Crown CA) and 63 of Straits Settlements optd with T **9**/**11**.

10	**9**	2c. brown	19·00	65·00
		a. Opt double	£650	
11		2c. pale rose (1883)	32·00	55·00
		a. Opt double	£700	
12	**10**	2c. pale rose (1883)	32·00	90·00
13	**11**	2c. pale rose (1883)	32·00	70·00
		a. Opt double	£700	

The above were all overprinted as triplet settings. Those for the 2c. rose were 11+12+13, 13+11+11 and 13+11+12.

2 CENTS PERAK (**12**) — 2 CENTS (**13**)

1883 (July). No. 51 (wmk Crown CA) of Straits Settlements surch.

(a) Surch with T **12**.

14		2c. on 4c. rose	£3250	
		a. On Straits Settlements No. 12 (wmk Crown CC)	£8000	

(b) Optd as T **9** or **11** and surch with T **13**.

15	**11**	2c. on 4c. rose	£1100	£425
16	**9**	2c. on 4c. rose	£650	£250

It is believed that No. 14 occurred on the top row of the sheet with the remaining nine rows surcharged with a triplet containing 15+16+16.

Only one unused example, with defects, of No. 14a is recorded.

PERAK (**14**) ("E" wide) — PFRAK (**15**) ("E" narrow) — PERAK (**16**) (12½–13 mm long)

PERAK (**17**) (12–12½ mm long) — PERAK (**18**) (10½ mm long) — PERAK (**19**) (10 mm long)

PERAK (**20**) (13 mm long)

1884–91. Nos. 63/a of Straits Settlements optd with T **14**/**20**.

17	**14**	2c. pale rose	5·00	3·75
		a. Opt double	£650	£650
		b. Opt inverted	£425	£550
		c. Bright rose	7·00	2·75
18	**15**	2c. pale rose	70·00	70·00
		b. Opt inverted	£1500	£1600
		c. Opt triple	£1500	
		d. Bright rose		
19	**16**	2c. pale rose (1886)	£150	32·00
		a. Bright rose (1891)	2·25	7·50
		ab. Optd "FERAK"	£375	£500
20	**17**	2c. pale rose (1886)	9·00	35·00
		a. Opt double	£1600	
21	**18**	2c. pale rose (1886)	£150	£160
		a. Bright rose		
22	**19**	2c. bright rose (1890)	20·00	55·00
23	**20**	2c. bright rose (1891)	£3500	

Settings:

Nos. 17/18	– triplets (either 17+17+17 or 18+17+17) 30 (3×10) (containing twenty-eight as No. 17 and two as No. 18) 60 (6×10) (containing either fifty-seven as No. 17 and three as No. 18 or all as No. 17)
No. 19	– 60 (6×10) (No. 19ab occurs on one position of the setting, it is often found amended in manuscript)
No. 20	– triplet
No. 21	– triplet
No. 22	– 60 (6×10)
No. 23	– not known

1 CENT

(**21**)

1886. No. 17 surch with T **21**.

24	**14**	1c. on 2c. pale rose	£2750	£2250

ONE CENT PERAK (22) ONE CENT PERAK. (23) ONE CFNT PERAK. (24) ("N" wide in "ONE" and "CENT")

1886. No. 63 of Straits Settlements surch with T **22/4**.

25	**22**	1c. on 2c. pale rose	£650	£700
26	**23**	1c. on 2c. pale rose	65·00	85·00
		a. Surch double	£1100	
27	**24**	1c. on 2c. pale rose	£110	£130

Nos. 26/7 are from a triplet setting, Types **23-24-23**, in which the two Type **23**'s can be differentiated by the height of the right upright of the "N" of "CENT", which is short on one. This triplet was used for the top nine rows of the sheet. Type **22** may have been used on the bottom row.

1 CENT PERAK (25) One CENT PERAK (26) ONE CENT PERAK (27)

1886. No. 63 of Straits Settlements surch with T **25**.

28	1c. on 2c. pale rose	£150	£150
	a. Surch double	£1800	£1800

No. 28 comes from a triplet setting.

1886. No. 63 of Straits Settlements surch with T **26**.

29	1c. on 2c. pale rose	4·00	13·00
	a. "One" inverted	£3000	
	b. Surch double	£1200	

No. 29 comes from a triplet setting. It is believed that No. 29a occurred when the type was dropped and "One" replaced upside down.

1887. No. 63 of Straits Settlements surch with T **27** in blue.

30	1c. on 2c. pale rose	55·00	55·00
	a. Optd in black	£1900	£1400

No. 30 was printed from a setting of 60.

I CENT PERAK (28) 1 CENT PERAK (29)

1887. No. 63 of Straits Settlements surch with T **28**.

31	1c. on 2c. pale rose	£1000	£700

No. 31 comes from a triplet setting.

1887. No. 63 of Straits Settlements surch with T **29**.

32	1c. on 2c. pale rose	£2250	£2250

The size of setting used for No. 32 is not known.

One CENT PERAK (30) One CENT PERAK (31) One CENT PERAK (32) One CENT PERAK (33)

One CENT PERAK (34) One CENT PERAK (35) One CENT PERAK (36) One CENT PERAK (37)

1887–89. No. 63 of Straits Settlements surch with T **30/7**.

33	**30**	1c. on 2c. pale rose	3·75	7·00
		a. Surch double	£1200	
		b. Bright rose	2·75	3·25
34	**31**	1c. on 2c. pale rose (1889)	£130	£160
		b. Bright rose	£180	
35	**32**	1c. on 2c. pale rose (1889)	18·00	48·00
		a. "PREAK" (R. 6/1)	£700	£900
		b. Bright rose	21·00	45·00
		ba. "PREAK" (R. 6/1)	£850	£1200
		w. Wmk inverted	£325	
36	**33**	1c. on 2c. pale rose (1889)	10·00	18·00
		b. Bright rose	4·75	18·00
37	**34**	1c. on 2c. pale rose (1889)	12·00	20·00
		b. Bright rose	4·50	19·00
38	**35**	1c. on 2c. bright rose (1889)	£650	£800
39	**36**	1c. on 2c. bright rose (1889)	£350	£450
40	**37**	1c. on 2c. pale rose (1889)	22·00	42·00
		b. Bright rose	18·00	35·00

Settings. No. 33 originally appeared as a triplet, then as a block of 30 (3×10) and, finally, as part of a series of composite settings of 60. Specialists recognise four such composite settings:

Setting I contained No. 33 in Rows 1 to 4, R. 5/1 to 5/5 and Row 7; No. 34 on R. 5/6, 6/1 and 6/2; No. 35 on R. 6/3–6; No. 36 on Row 8; No. 37 on Rows 9 and 10.

Setting II was similar, but had the example of No. 33 on R. 3/5 replaced by No. 38 and those on R. 7/4 and R. 7/6 by No. 39.

Setting III contained No. 33 in Rows 1 to 5; No. 35 in Row 6 with the "PREAK" error on the first position; No. 36 in Row 7; No. 37 in Rows 8 and 9; No. 40 in Row 10.

Setting IV was similar, but showed the "PREAK" error on R. 6/1 corrected.

ONE CENT. (38) ONE CENT (39)

1889–90. No. 17 surch with T **38/9**.

41	**38**	1c. on 2c. bright rose	£300	£130
42	**39**	1c. on 2c. bright rose (1890)	—	£250

PERAK Two CENTS (40) PERAK One CENT (41)

1891. Nos. 63a, 66 and 68 of Straits Settlements surch.

(a) As T **30**, **32/4** and **37**, but with "PERAK" at top and a bar through the original value.

43	**30**	1c. on 6c. lilac	50·00	28·00
44	**32**	1c. on 6c. lilac	£180	£160
45	**33**	1c. on 6c. lilac	£180	£160
46	**34**	1c. on 6c. lilac	90·00	75·00
47	**37**	1c. on 6c. lilac	£180	£160

(b) With T **40** and as T **32/4** and **37** but with "PERAK" at top, all with a bar through the original value.

48	**40**	2c. on 24c. green	23·00	13·00
		w. Wmk inverted	£325	
49	**32**	2c. on 24c. green	£110	65·00
		w. Wmk inverted		
50	**33**	2c. on 24c. green	£110	65·00
51	**34**	2c. on 24c. green	70·00	35·00
52	**37**	2c. on 24c. green	£110	65·00

(c) With T **41** and as T **30**, **34** and **37**, but with "PERAK" at top.

(i) Without bar over original value.

53	**30**	1c. on 2c. bright rose	£180	
		a. Narrow "O" in "One" (R. 3/3)	£2500	
54	**41**	1c. on 2c. bright rose	£850	
55	**34**	1c. on 2c. bright rose	£375	
56	**37**	1c. on 2c. bright rose	£850	

(ii) With bar through original value.

57	**30**	1c. on 2c. bright rose	2·25	9·50
		a. Narrow "O" in "One" (R. 3/3)	27·00	75·00
58	**41**	1c. on 2c. bright rose	8·50	35·00
59	**34**	1c. on 2c. bright rose	2·25	14·00
60	**37**	1c. on 2c. bright rose	8·50	35·00

Settings. Nos. 43/7 were arranged as Setting IV described under Nos. 33/40.

Nos. 48/52 were similar except that Type **40** replaced Type **30** on the first five rows.

The first printing of the 1c. on 2c. was without a bar through the original face value. Both printings, Nos. 53/60, were from the same setting with Type **30** on Rows 1 to 5, **41** on Row 6, **34** on Rows 7 to 9 and **37** on Row 10.

42

3 CENTS (43)

1892 (1 Jan)–**95**. Wmk Crown CA. P 14.

61	**42**	1c. green	2·25	15
62		2c. rose	1·75	30
63		2c. orange (9.9.95)	50	4·50
64		5c. blue	3·25	7·50
61/4 *Set of 4*			7·00	11·00
61s/4s Optd "Specimen" *Set of 4*			£110	

1895 (26 Apr). Surch with T **43**. Wmk Crown CA. P 14.

65	**42**	3c. on 5c. rose	3·75	3·50
		s. Optd "Specimen"	30·00	

44

45

Malformed "C" in left value tablet (R. 9/3, left pane)

1895 (2 Sept)–**99**. P 14.

(a) Wmk Crown CA.

66	**44**	1c. dull purple and green	2·75	50
		a. Malformed "C"	£140	65·00
67		2c. dull purple and brown	3·25	50
68		3c. dull purple and carmine	3·25	50
69		4c. dull purple and carmine (1899)	13·00	5·00
70		5c. dull purple and olive-yellow	5·00	55
71		8c. dull purple and ultramarine	45·00	65
72		10c. dull purple and orange	15·00	50
73		25c. green and carmine (1897)	£180	12·00
74		50c. dull purple and greenish black	48·00	40·00
75		50c. green and black (12.98)	£225	£170
		(b) Wmk Crown CC.		
76	**45**	$1 green and pale green (1896)	£225	£200
77		$2 green and carmine (1896)	£375	£325
78		$3 green and ochre (1898)	£425	£425
79		$5 green and ultramarine (1896)	£500	£500
80		$25 green and orange (1899?)	£9000	£3250
		s. Optd "Specimen"	£275	
66/76 *Set of 11*			£700	£375
66s/79s Optd "Specimen" *Set of 14*			£425	

Pending the arrival of the permanent Federated Malay States issue the stamps of FEDERATED MALAY STATES provisional overprints, SELANGOR and STRAITS SETTLEMENTS were used at various times between June 1900 and February 1901.
The general issues for the FEDERATED MALAY STATES were used in Perak from 1901 until 1935.

One Cent.
(46)

ONE CENT.
(47)

Three Cent.
(48)

Three Cent.
(49)

Three Cent.
Thinner "t" in "Cent"

1900. Stamps of 1895–99 surch.

81	**46**	1c. on 2c. dull purple & brown (13 July*)	60	2·25
		a. Antique "e" in "One" (R. 5/2)	60·00	£130
		b. Antique "e" in "Cent" (R. 9/4)	60·00	£130
82	**47**	1c. on 4c. dull purple and carmine	1·00	13·00
		a. Surch double	£1100	
83	**46**	1c. on 5c. dull purple & ol-yell (30 June*)	2·75	15·00
		a. Antique "e" in "One" (R. 5/2)	95·00	£275
		b. Antique "e" in "Cent" (R. 9/4)	95·00	£275
84	**48**	3c. on 8c. dull purple & ultram (26 Sept*)	6·50	12·00
		a. Antique "e" in "Cent" (R. 9/4)	£170	£275
		b. No stop after "Cent" (R. 9/5)	£170	£275
		c. Surch double	£500	£550
85		3c. on 50c. green and black (31 Aug*)	4·00	8·00
		a. Antique "e" in "Cent" (R. 9/4)	£130	£200
		b. No stop after "Cent" (R. 9/5)	£130	£200
86	**49**	3c. on $1 green and pale green (21 Oct*)	55·00	£150
		a. Thinner "t" in "Cent"	£300	£550
		b. Surch double	£1500	
		w. Wmk inverted	£400	£600
87		3c. on $2 green and carmine (24 Oct*)	40·00	85·00
81/7 *Set of 7*			£100	£250

*Earliest known postmark date.

With exception of No. 86a, whose sheet position is not known, the remaining surcharge varieties all occur in the left-hand pane.

No. 86b is also known showing the thinner "t" in "Cent" variety. (*Price* £4250 *unused*).

50 Sultan Iskandar

51 Sultan Iskandar

Malformed "2c." (R. 10/10)

1935 (2 Dec)–**37**. Chalk-surfaced paper. Wmk Mult Script CA. P 14.

88	**50**	1c. black (1.1.36)	1·75	10
89		2c. green (1.1.36)	1·75	10
90		4c. orange	2·00	10
91		5c. brown (5.12.35)	75	10
92		6c. scarlet (1.1.37)	11·00	4·25
93		8c. grey	1·00	10
94		10c. dull purple (1.1.36)	80	15
95		12c. bright ultramarine (1.1.36)	3·75	1·00
96		25c. dull purple and scarlet (1.4.36)	2·75	1·00
97		30c. dull purple and orange (1.1.36)	3·75	1·50
98		40c. scarlet and dull purple	5·50	4·50
99		50c. black/*emerald* (1.2.36)	6·50	1·25
100		$1 black and red/*blue* (1.4.36)	2·50	1·25
101		$2 green and scarlet (16.5.36)	28·00	7·00
102		$5 green and red/*emerald* (16.5.36)	£120	35·00
88/102 *Set of 15*			£170	50·00
88s/102s Perf "Specimen" *Set of 15*			£375	

No. 91 exists in coils constructed from normal sheets in 1936.

1938 (2 May)–**41**. Wmk Mult Script CA. Chalk-surfaced paper. P 14.

103	**51**	1c. black (4.39)	13·00	10
104		2c. green (13.1.39)	8·00	10
105		2c. orange (*Thin striated paper*) (30.10.41)	3·50	18·00
		a. Malformed "2c"	85·00	£300
		b. Ordinary paper	5·00	6·00
		ba. Malformed "2c"	£120	£130
106		3c. green (*ordinary paper*) (21.8.41)	—	8·00
		a. Thin striated paper (10.41)	2·75	7·00
107		4c. orange (5.39)	38·00	10
108		5c. brown (1.2.39)	6·50	10
109		6c. scarlet (12.39)	27·00	10
110		8c. grey (1.12.38)	29·00	10
111		8c. scarlet (*Thin striated paper*) (18.12.41)	1·00	75·00
		a. Ordinary paper	2·50	
112		10c. dull purple (17.10.38)	32·00	10
113		12c. bright ultramarine (17.10.38)	24·00	1·00
114		15c. brt ultram (*ordinary paper*) (8.41)	4·25	13·00
115		25c. dull purple and scarlet (12.39)	50·00	3·25
116		30c. dull purple and orange (17.10.38)	9·50	2·25
		a. Thin striated paper (1941)	12·00	20·00
117		40c. scarlet and dull purple	50·00	2·00
118		50c. black/*emerald* (17.10.38)	32·00	75
119		$1 black and red/*blue* (7.40)	£140	21·00
120		$2 green and scarlet (9.40)	£170	65·00
121		$5 green and red/*emerald* (1.41)	£300	£350
103/21 *Set of 19*			£850	£500
103s/21s perf "Specimen" *Set of 19*			£450	

No. 108 exists in coils constructed from normal sheets.

The stamps issued during 1941 were printed by Harrison and Sons following bomb damage to the De La Rue works on 29 December 1940. The used price quoted for No. 111 is for an example with clearly identifiable 1941 cancellation.

During shortages in 1941 stamps of STRAITS SETTLEMENTS (2c. green) and SELANGOR (2c. orange (both perfs), 3c.) were issued in Perak.

1948 (1 Dec). Royal Silver Wedding. As Nos. 131/2 of Johore.

122	10c. violet	15	10
123	$5 green	23·00	35·00

1949 (10 Oct). 75th Anniv of U.P.U. As Nos. 96/9 of Brunei.

124	10c. purple	15	10
125	15c. deep blue	1·50	2·00

126		25c. orange	30	4·50
127		50c. blue-black	1·25	3·50
124/7		*Set of 4*	2·75	9·00

52 Sultan Yussuf 'Izzuddin Shah

53 Sultan Idris Shah

1950 (17 Aug)–**56**. Chalk-surfaced paper. Wmk Mult Script CA. P 17½×18.

128	**52**	1c. black	10	10
129		2c. orange	20	10
130		3c. green	3·50	10
		a. Yellowish green (15.11.51)	14·00	7·50
131		4c. brown	60	10
		a. Yellow-brown (20.6.56)	10·00	30
132		5c. bright purple (1.9.52)	50	2·50
		a. Bright mauve (10.11.54)	1·25	2·50
133		6c. grey	30	10
134		8c. scarlet	1·00	2·25
135		8c. green (1.9.52)	1·00	1·00
136		10c. purple	20	10
		a. Brown-purple (20.6.56)	10·00	55
137		12c. scarlet (1.9.52)	1·00	5·00
138		15c. ultramarine	1·25	10
139		20c. black and green	1·75	65
140		20c. bright blue (1.9.52)	1·00	10
141		25c. purple and orange	75	10
142		30c. scarlet and purple (4.9.55)	2·00	20
143		35c. scarlet and purple (1.9.52)	1·25	25
144		40c. red and purple	5·50	6·00
145		50c. black and blue	5·50	10
146		$1 blue and purple	7·00	1·00
147		$2 green and scarlet	16·00	7·00
148		$5 green and brown	40·00	20·00
128/48		*Set of 21*	80·00	42·00

1953 (2 June). Coronation. As No. 152 of Johore.

149	10c. black and reddish purple	1·50	10

1957 (26 June)–**61**. As Nos. 92/102 of Kedah but with inset portrait of Sultan Yussuf 'Izzuddin Shah.

150	1c. black (21.8.57)	10	20
151	2c. orange-red (25.7.57)	30	1·00
	a. *Red-orange* (15.12.59)	1·75	3·25
152	4c. sepia (21.8.57)	20	10
153	5c. carmine-lake (21.8.57)	20	10
154	8c. myrtle-green (21.8.57)	2·00	3·50
155	10c. deep brown (4.8.57)	2·00	10
156	10c. deep maroon (21.2.61)	5·00	10
157	20c. blue	2·25	10
158	50c. black and blue (*p* 12½) (25.7.57)	40	1·00
	a. Perf 12½×13 (24.5.60)	40	10
159	$1 ultramarine and reddish purple (25.7.57)	6·50	40
160	$2 bronze-green & scar (*p* 12½) (21.8.57)	4·00	4·00
	a. Perf 13×12½ (21.2.61)	6·00	4·00
161	$5 brown and bronze-green (*p* 12½)	14·00	10·00
	a. Perf 13×12½ (24.5.60)	13·00	8·00
150/61	*Set of 12*	32·00	15·00

The 6, 12, 25 and 30c. values used with this issue were Nos. 1/4 of Malayan Federation.

(Photo Harrison)

1963 (26 Oct). Installation of the Sultan of Perak. W w **13**. P 14½.

162	**53**	10c. red, black, blue and yellow	10	10

54 *Vanda hookeriana*

1965 (15 Nov)–**68**. As Nos. 166/72 of Johore but with inset portrait of Sultan Idris as in T **54**. W w **13** (upright).

163	1c. multicoloured	10	50
	w. Wmk inverted	4·50	
164	2c. multicoloured	10	70
	a. Dark green omitted	£100	
	w. Wmk inverted	10·00	
165	5c. pale black and multicoloured	10	10
	a. *Grey-black and multicoloured* (2.4.68)	1·75	30
	b. Yellow (flower) omitted	80·00	
166	6c. multicoloured	15	40
167	10c. multicoloured	15	10
	a. Red omitted	£100	
168	15c. multicoloured	80	10
	a. Black (country name and head) omitted (horizontal pair with normal)	£1200	
	c. Magenta (background) omitted	£1000	
169	20c. multicoloured	1·25	10
	a. Bright purple (blooms) omitted	£150	
163/9	*Set of 7*	2·40	1·60

No. 168a comes from a horizontal strip of three, the centre stamp having the black completely omitted. The two outer stamps show the colour partly omitted.

The 2c. to 15c. exist with PVA gum as well as gum arabic.

The higher values used with this issue were Nos. 20/27 of Malaysia (National Issues).

1970. As Nos. 163 and 167, but W w **13** (sideways).

170	**54**	1c. multicoloured (27.5.70)	2·50	7·00
171	–	10c. multicoloured (20.11.70)	7·00	3·50

1971 (1 Feb)–**78**. As Nos. 175/87 of Johore, but with portrait of Sultan Idris and arms, as in T **55**.

(a) Litho by Bradbury, Wilkinson

172	1c. multicoloured	40	2·00
173	2c. multicoloured	1·00	2·00
174	5c. multicoloured	1·25	10
175	6c. multicoloured	1·25	2·00
176	10c. multicoloured	1·25	10
177	15c. multicoloured	1·00	10
178	20c. multicoloured	1·75	30
172/8	*Set of 7*	7·00	6·00

The higher values used with this issue were Nos. 64/71 of Malaysia (National Issues). For differences between litho and photo printings, see after Johore, No. 187.

(b) Photo by Harrison (1977–78).

179	1c. multicoloured	1·00	3·75
180	5c. multicoloured	4·00	70
181	10c. multicoloured	2·75	65
182	15c. multicoloured	10·00	30
183	20c. multicoloured	3·00	1·25
179/83	*Set of 5*	19·00	6·00

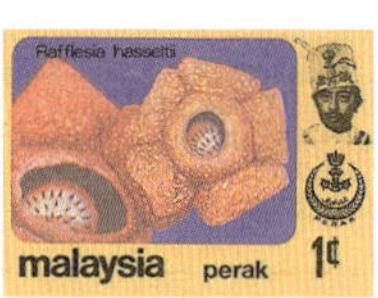

56 *Raffesia hasseltii*

57 Coffee

1979 (30 Apr). As Nos. 188/94 of Johore but with portrait of Sultan Idris as in T **56**.

184	1c. Type **56**	10	85
185	2c. *Pterocarpus indicus*	10	85
186	5c. *Lagerstroemia speciosa*	10	20
187	10c. *Durio zibethinus*	15	10
188	15c. *Hibiscus rosa-sinensis*	15	10
189	20c. *Rhododendron scortechinii*	20	10
190	25c. *Etlingera elatior* (inscr "*Phaeomeria speciosa*")	40	20
184/90	*Set of 7*	1·00	2·00

For higher values used in conjunction with this series see Nos. 190/7 of Malaysia (National Issues).

1983 (15 Oct)–**84**. As Nos. 186/9 but without wmk.

193	5c. *Lagerstroemia speciosa* (9.9.83)	1·00	50
194	10c. *Durio zibenthinus* (1984)	30	50
195	15c. *Hibiscus rosa-sinensis* (9.9.83)	70	30
196	20c. *Rhododendron scortechinii* (blackish brown background)	55·00	1·25
196*a*	20c. *Rhododendron scortechinii* (bronze green background) (20.3.84)	1·00	50

*There was no official release date for these stamps. Dates shown are the earliest recorded from postmarks and may be revised if earlier examples are reported.

For details of the shade differences between watermarked and unwatermarked printings see after Johore No. 200a.

On Nos. 193/5 and 196a the portrait and arms are redrawn smaller.

1986 (25 Oct)–**96**. As Nos. 202/8 of Johore, but with portrait of Sultan Azlan Shah as in T **57**. P 12.

198	1c. Type **57**	10	25
	w. Wmk inverted	6·00	
199	2c. Coconuts	10	35
	f. Perf 14¼×14½ (1994)	3·25	35
200	5c. Cocoa	15	10

	c. Perf 14×13¾ (1994)	3·25	20
	cw. Wmk inverted	8·50	
	f. Perf 14¾×14½ (1996)	3·00	30
201	10c. Black pepper	15	10
	aw. Wmk inverted		
	c. Perf 14×13¼ (1995)	1·00	10
	cw. Wmk inverted	8·00	
	e. Perf 14×14½	14·00	
	f. Perf 14¾×14½ (1996)	2·25	20
202	15c. Rubber	25	10
	w. Wmk inverted	11·00	
203	20c. Oil palm	25	15
	aw. Wmk inverted		
	c. Perf 14×13¾ (1994)	1·50	10
	ca. No wmk	8·50	
	e. Perf 14×14½ (1996)	4·50	40
	f. Perf 14¾×14½ (1996)	3·00	50
204	30c. Rice	30	15
	aw. Wmk inverted		
	c. Perf 14×13¼ (1994)	7·00	40
	cw. Wmk inverted	14·00	
	e. Perf 14×14½	4·00	40
	f. Perf 14¾×14½ (1995)	7·00	1·25
198/204 *Set of 7*		1·10	1·00

58 *Nelumbium nelumbo* (sacred lotus)

2007 (31 Dec). Garden Flowers. As Nos. 210/15 of Johore, but with portrait of Sultan Azlan Shah and Arms of Penang as in T **58**. Multicoloured. W **138**. Phosphorised paper. P 14.

205	5s. Type **58**	10	10
206	10s. *Hydrangea macrophylla*	15	10
207	20s. *Hippeastrum reticulatum*	25	15
208	30s. Bougainvillea	40	20
209	40s. *Ipomoea indica*	50	30
210	50s. *Hibiscus rosa-sinensis*	65	35
205/10 *Set of 6*		1·90	1·10

STAMP BOOKLETS

1935.

SB1	$1 booklet containing twenty 5c. (No. 91) in blocks of 10	
SB2	$1.30 booklet containing 5c. and 8c. (Nos. 91, 93), each in block of 10	

1938.

SB3	$1 booklet containing twenty 5c. (No. 108) in blocks of 10	£3000
SB4	$1.30 booklet containing 5c. and 8c. (Nos. 108, 110), each in block of 10	£3250

1973 (8 Dec). Cover as Type B **1** of Johore, but inscr "PERAK". Stitched.

SB5	$3 booklet containing eight 5c., 10c. and twelve 15c. (Nos. 174, 176/7) in blocks of 4	30·00

1979 (1 Dec). Cover as No. SB5 of Johore, but inscr "PERAK". Stitched.

SB6	$3 booklet containing eight 5c., 10c. and twelve 15c. (Nos. 186/8) in blocks of 4	10·00

No. SB6 exists with two different versions of the back cover.

1987 (1 June). Cover as Type B **2** of Johore, but inscr "PERAK". Stapled.

SB7	$2 booklet containing 5c., 10c., 15c. and 20c. (Nos. 200/3) in blocks of 4	12·00

1992 (1 July). "Kuala Lumpur '92" International Philatelic Exhibition. Cover as Type B **3** of Johore, but inscr "Perak". Stamps attached by selvedge.

SB8	$3 booklet containing 30c. (No. 204) in block of 10	9·00

1993. Covers as Nos. SB8/9 of Johore, but inscr "Perak". Stamps attached by selvedge.

SB9	$2 booklet containing 20c. (No. 203) in block of 10	1·50
SB10	$3 booklet containing 30c. (No. 204) in block of 10	2·00

OFFICIAL STAMPS

P.G.S. (O **1**)   **Service.** (O **2**)

1889 (1 Nov). Stamps of Straits Settlements optd Type O **1**. Wmk Crown CC (Nos. O6 and O8) or Crown CA (others).

O1	2c. bright rose	5·00	7·00
	a. Opt double	£850	£850
	b. Wide space between "G" and "S"	75·00	90·00
	c. No stop after "S"	75·00	90·00
O2	4c. brown	19·00	25·00
	a. Wide space between "G" and "S"	£110	£150
	b. No stop after "S"	£180	£200
	c. Broken oval	£325	
	w. Wmk inverted	£110	
O3	6c. lilac	29·00	50·00
	a. Wide space between "G" and "S"	£160	£200
O4	8c. orange	40·00	65·00
	a. Wide space between "G" and "S"	£180	£275
O5	10c. slate	75·00	75·00
	a. Wide space between "G" and "S"	£325	£325
O6	12c. blue (CC)	£225	£275
	a. Wide space between "G" and "S"	£800	
O7	12c. brown-purple (CA)	£250	£325
	a. Wide space between "G" and "S"	£850	
O8	24c. green (CC)	£750	£850
	a. Wide space between "G" and "S"	£2250	
O9	24c. green (CA)	£190	£225
	a. Wide space between "G" and "S"	£700	

Nos. O1/9 were overprinted from a setting of 30 (3×10). The variety "wide space between G and S" occurs on R. 10/3 and R. 10/6 of the original printing. A later printing of the 2c. and 4c. values had this variety corrected, but was without a stop after "S" on R. 10/1 and R. 10/4.

The broken oval flaw occurs on R. 10/5 (lower right pane) of the basic stamp. For illustration see Straits Settlements.

1894 (1 June). No. 64 optd with Type O **2**.

O10	5c. blue	85·00	1·00
	a. Overprint inverted	£1100	£475

1897. No. 70 optd with Type O **2**.

O11	5c. dull purple and olive-yellow	2·75	50
	a. Overprint double	£650	£400

PERLIS

The Thai monarchy exercised suzerainty over Perlis and the other northern states of the Malay peninsula from the 16th century onwards.

The Siamese post office at Kangar is recorded as opening during 1894. It is believed that the initial cancellation showed Thai characters only, but no complete example has so far been discovered.

Stamps of SIAM cancelled as Type B inscr "PERLIS" (*from* July 1904).

1887–91. (Nos. 11/18).

Z401	9	12a. purple and carmine	£250
Z402		24a. purple and blue	£350

1897. Surch as T **39** (Siamese) and T **41** (English) (No. 52).

Z403	9	4a. on 12a. purple and carmine	£425

1899–1904. (Nos. 67/81).

Z404	49	1a. olive-green (wide Siamese characters in face value)	£275
Z405		2a. grass-green	£250
Z406		2a. scarlet and pale blue	£250
Z407		3a. red and blue	£400
Z408		4a. carmine	£250
Z409		4a. chocolate and pink	£250
Z410		8a. deep green and orange	£250
Z411		10a. ultramarine	£250
Z412		12a. brown-purple and carmine	£225
Z413		24a. brown-purple and blue	£450

1905–09. (Nos. 97/105).

Z416	53	1a. green and orange	£225
Z417		2a. grey and deep violet	£225
Z418		3a. green	£250
Z419		4a. pale red and sepia	£225
Z420		5a. carmine	£250
Z421		8a. olive-bistre and dull black	£225
Z422		12a. blue	£275
Z423		24a. red-brown	£400

Stamps of SIAM cancelled as Type C inscr "Perlis" at foot (from Sept. 1907).

1887–91. (Nos. 11/18).

Z425	9	12a. purple and carmine	£275

1899–1904. (Nos. 67/81).

Z426	**49**	1a. olive-green (narrow Siamese characters in face value)	£275
Z427		8a. deep green and orange	£275
Z428		10a. ultramarine	£275

1905–09. (Nos. 92/105).

Z429	**53**	1a. green and orange	£275
Z430		2a. grey and deep violet	£250
Z431		3a. green	£275
Z432		4a. pale red and sepia	£250
Z433		4a. scarlet	£275
Z434		5a. carmine	£275
Z435		8a. olive-bistre and dull black	£275
Z436		9a. blue	£250
Z437		24a. red-brown	£450

1907. Surch with T **56** (No. 109).

Z438	**9**	1a. on 24a. purple and blue	£275

Suzerainty over Perlis was transferred by Thailand to Great Britain on 15 July 1909, although the use of Siamese stamps appears to have extended into early August. Stamps of the Federated Malay States were used there until 1912.

Stamps of the Federated Malay States used in Perlis

Cancelled as Type C inscribed "Perlis" at foot.

1909–12. (Nos. 29/34).

Z441	**3**	1c. green Die II	£160
Z442		3c. carmine	£160

Cancelled as Type B inscribed "PERLIS".

1909–12. (Nos. 29/36d).

Z443	**3**	1c. green Die II	£150
Z444		3c. carmine	90·00
Z445		4c. black and rose	£150

Federated Malay States stamps were withdrawn on 15 June 1912.

The stamps of Kedah were in use in Perlis between 1912 and 1941.

A Treaty of Friendship between Great Britain and Perlis was signed on 28 April 1930 and the state joined the Federation of Malaya on 1 February 1948.

1948 (1 Dec). Royal Silver Wedding. As Nos. 131/2 of Johore.

1	10c. violet	30	2·75
2	$5 brown	29·00	48·00

1949 (10 Oct). 75th Anniv of U.P.U. As Nos. 96/9 of Brunei2.

3	10c. purple	30	2·00
4	15c. deep blue	1·25	4·25
5	25c. orange	45	3·25
6	50c. blue-black	1·00	3·75
3/6 *Set of 4*		2·75	12·00

1 Raja Syed Putra

2 *Vanda hookariana*

1951 (26 Mar)–**55**. Chalk-surfaced paper. Wmk Mult Script CA. P 17½×18.

7	**1**	1c. black	20	1·00
8		2c. orange	75	50
9		3c. green	1·50	4·00
10		4c. brown	1·50	1·25
11		5c. bright purple (1.9.52)	50	3·50
12		6c. grey	1·50	2·25
13		8c. scarlet	3·25	7·00
14		8c. green (1.9.52)	1·25	3·50
15		10c. purple	1·00	50
		a. Error. St. Edward's Crown W **9b**	£16000	
16		12c. scarlet (1.9.52)	1·50	5·00
17		15c. ultramarine	4·75	7·00
18		20c. black and green	3·25	9·50
19		20c. bright blue (1.9.52)	1·25	1·00
20		25c. purple and orange	2·00	3·50
21		30c. scarlet and purple (4.9.55)	2·00	13·00
22		35c. scarlet and purple (1.9.52)	2·00	7·00
23		40c. red and purple	4·50	26·00
24		50c. black and blue	4·75	6·50
25		$1 blue and purple	8·00	26·00
26		$2 green and scarlet	19·00	55·00
27		$5 green and brown	70·00	£130
7/27 *Set of 21*			£120	£275

1953 (2 June). Coronation. As No. 152 of Johore..

28	10c. black and reddish purple	1·25	3·00

1957 (26 June)–**62**. As Nos. 92/102 of Kedah but with inset portrait of Raja Syed Putra.

29	**9**	1c. black (21.8.57)	10	30
30	**10**	2c. orange-red (25.7.57)	10	30
31	**11**	4c. sepia (21.8.57)	10	30
32	**12**	5c. carmine-lake (21.8.57)	10	10
33	**13**	8c. myrtle-green (21.8.57)	2·00	1·75
34	**14**	10c. deep brown (4.8.57)	1·50	2·25
35		10c. deep maroon (14.3.61)	8·50	3·50
36	**15**	20c. blue	3·00	4·50
37	**16**	50c. black and blue (p 12½) (25.7.57)	1·00	3·75
		a. Perf 12½×13 (8.5.62)	3·00	4·00
38	**17**	$1 ultram & reddish purple (25.7.57)	9·00	13·00
39	**18**	$2 bronze-green and scarlet (25.7.57)	9·00	8·50
40	**19**	$5 brown and bronze-green (21.8.57)	13·00	11·00
29/40 *Set of 12*			42·00	45·00

The 6, 12, 25 and 30c. values used with this issue were Nos. 1/4 of Malayan Federation.

1965 (15 Nov). As Nos. 166/72 of Johore but with inset portrait of Raja Syed Putra as in T **2**.

41	1c. multicoloured	10	1·00
	w. Wmk inverted	16·00	
42	2c. multicoloured	10	1·50
43	5c. multicoloured	15	40
44	6c. multicoloured	65	1·50
45	10c. multicoloured	65	40
46	15c. multicoloured	1·00	40
47	20c. multicoloured	1·00	1·75
41/7 *Set of 7*		3·25	6·25

The 6c. exists with PVA gum as well as gum arabic.

The higher values used with this issue were Nos. 20/27 of Malaysia (National Issues).

3 *Danaus melanippus*

4 Raja Syed Putra

1971 (1 Feb)–**78**. As Nos. 175/87 of Johore but with portrait of Raja Syed Putra and Arms, as in T **3**.

(a) Litho by Bradbury, Wilkinson.

48	1c. multicoloured	20	1·25
49	2c. multicoloured	40	2·25
50	5c. multicoloured	1·25	1·25
51	6c. multicoloured	1·50	3·00
52	10c. multicoloured	1·50	1·25
53	15c. multicoloured	1·50	50
54	20c. multicoloured	1·50	2·50
48/54 *Set of 7*		7·00	11·00

(b) Photo by Harrison (1977–78).

54*a*	10c. multicoloured	£200	8·50
55	15c. multicoloured	6·00	2·50
55*a*	20c. multicoloured	£180	35·00

The higher values used with this issue were Nos. 64/71 of Malaysia (National Issues).

For differences between litho and photo printings, see after Johore No. 187.

(Des Citizen Studio and Engravers. Litho Enschedé)

1971 (28 Mar). 25th Anniv of Installation of Raja Syed Putra. P 13½×13.

56	**4**	10c. multicoloured	30	2·25
57		15c. multicoloured	30	75
58		50c. multicoloured	80	4·25
56/8 *Set of 3*			1·25	6·50

5 *Pterocarpus indicus*

6 Coconuts

1979 (30 Apr). As Nos. 188/94 of Johore but with portrait of Raja Syed Palm as in T **5**.

59	1c. *Rafflesia hasseltii*	10	1·00
60	2c. Type **5**	10	1·00
61	5c. *Lagerstroemia speciosa*	10	1·00
62	10c. *Durio zibethinus*	15	30
63	15c. *Hibiscus rosa-sinensis*	15	10
64	20c. *Rhododendron scortechinii*	20	10
65	25c. *Etlingera elatior* (inscr "*Phaeomeria speciosa*")	40	85
59/65 *Set of 7*		1·00	3·75

For higher values used in conjunction with this series see Nos. 190/7 of Malaysia (National Issues).

1983–84. As No. 64 but without wmk.

71	20c. *Rhododendron scortechinii* (blackish brown background)	90·00	6·00
71*a*	20c. *Rhododendron scortechinii* (bronze green background) (4.12.84)	1·00	1·50

*There was no official release date for these stamps. Dates shown are the earliest recorded from postmarks and may be revised if earlier examples are reported.

For details of the shade differences between watermarked and unwatermarked printings see after Johore No. 200a.

No. 71a shows the Sultan's head larger than on Nos. 64 and 71 and has "perlis" in rounded, instead of square-ended, letters.

1986 (25 Oct)–**94**. As Nos. 202/8 of Johore, but with portrait of Raja Syed Putra as in T **6**. P 12.

73	1c. Coffee	10	50
	w. Wmk inverted	8·50	
74	2c. Type **6**	10	50
75	5c. Cocoa	15	40
	aw. Wmk inverted	10·00	
	c. Perf 14×13¾	8·50	
76	10c. Black pepper	20	15
	e. Perf 14×14½ (1996)	4·50	
	f. Perf 14¾×14½ (1994)	4·50	50
77	15c. Rubber	30	10
78	20c. Oil palm	30	15
	c. Perf 14×13¾ (1995)	10·00	
79	30c. Rice	40	15
	aw. Wmk inverted		
	c. Perf 14×13¾ (1994)	4·50	30
	cw. Wmk inverted	10·00	
	f. Perf 14¾×14½ (1994)	15·00	
	fw. Wmk inverted	17·00	
73/9 *Set of 7*		1·40	1·75

7 Raja Syed Putra and Aspects of Perlis

(Des BJ Image Sdn Bhd. Litho Security (M), Malaysia)

1995 (4 Dec). 50th Anniv of Raja Syed Putra's Accession. T **7** and similar horiz design. Multicoloured. W **138** (sideways). P 14×14½.

80	30c. Type **7**	75	50
	a. Perf 13½	12·00	
81	$1 Raja Syed Putra and Palace	2·25	3·50
	a. Perf 13½	7·00	

8 *Nelumbium nelumbo* (sacred lotus)

2007 (31 Dec). Garden Flowers. As Nos. 210/15 of Johore, but with portrait of Raja Tuanku Syed Sirajuddin and Arms of Perlis as in T **8**. Multicoloured. W **138**. Phosphorised paper. P 14.

82	5s. Type **8**	10	10
83	10s. *Hydrangea macrophylla*	15	10
84	20s. *Hippeastrum reticulatum*	25	15
85	30s. Bougainvillea	40	20
86	40s. *Ipomoea indica*	50	30
87	50s. *Hibiscus rosa-sinensis*	65	35
82/7 *Set of 6*		1·90	1·10

STAMP BOOKLETS

1973 (8 Dec). Cover as Type B **1** of Johore, but inscr "PERLIS". Stitched.

SB1 $3 booklet containing eight 5c., 10c. and twelve 15c. (Nos. 50, 52/3) in blocks of 4 ... 35·00

Examples of No. SB1 exist with a white label giving revised postage rates.

1979 (1 Dec). Cover as No. SB5 of Johore, but inscr "PERLIS". Stitched.

SB2 $3 booklet containing eight 5c., 10c., and twelve 15c. (Nos. 61/3) in blocks of 4 ... 14·00

No. SB2 exists with two different versions of the back cover.

1987 (1 June). Cover as Type B **2** of Johore, but inscr "PERLIS". Stapled.

SB3 $3 booklet containing 5c., 10c., 15c. and 20c. (Nos. 75/8) in blocks of 4 ... 15·00

1992 (1 July). "Kuala Lumpur '92" International Philatelic Exhibition. Cover as Type B **3** of Johore, but inscr "Perlis". Stamps attached by selvedge.

SB4 $3 booklet containing 30c. (No. 79) in block of 10 ... 11·00

1993. Covers as Nos. SB8/9 of Johore, but inscr "Perlis". Stamps attached by selvedge.

SB5 $2 booklet containing 20c. (No. 78) in block of 10 ... 1·50
SB6 $3 booklet containing 30c. (No. 79) in block of 10 ... 2·00

SELANGOR

The first British Resident was appointed in 1874. Selangor joined the Federated Malay States in 1896.

> The stamps of the STRAITS SETTLEMENTS were used in Selangor from 1879 until 1881.
> Until 1 January 1899, when the Federated Malay States joined the U.P.U., mail for addresses outside Malaya was franked with stamps of the STRAITS SETTLEMENTS.

PRICES FOR STAMPS ON COVER TO 1945

Nos. 1/8	—
Nos. 9/19	*from* × 10
Nos. 20/30	*from* × 12
Nos. 31/3	*from* × 25
Nos. 34/6	*from* × 20
Nos. 37/8	*from* × 15
Nos. 38*a*/40	—
Nos. 41/2	*from* × 8
Nos. 43	—
Nos. 44/8	*from* × 8
Nos. 49/53	*from* × 30
Nos. 54/66	*from* × 10
Nos. 66*a*/7	*from* × 4
Nos. 68/85	*from* × 3
Nos. 86/7	*from* × 4

The Straits Settlements 1867 2c. brown with Crown CC watermark (No. 11) has been known since 1881 overprinted in black with a crescent and star over a capital S, all within an oval, similar in style to the overprints listed for Perak and Sungei Ujong.

The status of this item remains unclear, but it may well represent the first issue of distinctive stamps for Selangor. A similar overprint in red on the Straits Settlements 2c. brown with Crown CA watermark also exists and may have been produced for sale to collectors (*Price £350, unused*).

This overprint should not be confused with a somewhat similar cancellation used on Selangor stamps of the same period. This cancellation differs in having a circular frame with the capital S shown above the crescent and star. It is usually struck in red.

SELANGOR
(**1**) ("S" inverted and narrow letters)

SELANGOR
(**2**) ("S" wide)

SELANGOR
(**3**) (narrow letters)

SELANGOR
(**4**) ("N" wide)

SELANGOR
(**5**) ("SE" and "AN" wide)

SELANGOR
(**6**) ("SEL" and "N" wide)

SELANGOR
(**7**) ("SELAN" wide)

1881–82. No. 11 (wmk Crown CC) of Straits Settlements optd with T **1/7**.

1	**1**	2c. brown	£600	£650
2	**2**	2c. brown	£200	£250
3	**3**	2c. brown	£130	£130
4	**4**	2c. brown	£8500	£3000
5	**5**	2c. brown (1882)	£225	£275
6	**6**	2c. brown (1882)	£225	£275
7	**7**	2c. brown (1882)	£225	£275

Nos. 1/3 and 5/7 have been identified as coming from triplet settings, either Nos. 1+2+3, 2+3+3 or 5+6+7. The setting for No. 4 is unknown.

S.
(8)

1882. No. 50 (wmk Crown CA) of Straits Settlements optd with T **8**.

8	**8**	2c. brown	—	£3250

SELANGOR (**9**) ("SEL" and "NG" wide) SELANGOR (**10**) ("E" and "ANG" wide) SELANGOR (**11**) ("ELANG" wide)

SELANGOR (**12**) ("S" and "L" wide) SELANGOR (**13**) ("S" and "A" wide) SELANGOR (**14**) ("E" wide)

SELANGOR (**15**) ("EL" wide) SELANGOR (**16**) ("SE" and "N" wide) SELANGOR (**17**) ("S" and "N" wide)

1882–83. No. 50 (wmk Crown CA) of Straits Settlements optd with T **2/3** and **9/17**.

9	**9**	2c. brown	£300	£400
10	**10**	2c. brown	£300	£400
11	**11**	2c. brown	£300	£400
12	**2**	2c. brown (1883)	£170	£140
13	**3**	2c. brown (1883)	£300	£130
14	**12**	2c. brown (1883)	—	£3500
15	**13**	2c. brown (1883)	£700	£600
16	**14**	2c. brown (1883)	£450	£350
17	**15**	2c. brown (1883)	£450	£350
18	**16**	2c. brown (1883)	£190	£170
		a. Opt double	£1100	
19	**17**	2c. brown (1883)	£190	£170

The above were all printed from triplet settings. Those so far identified are Nos. 9+10+11, 12 (with defective "G") +13+13, 15+16+17 and 18+12+19. No. 14 occurs as the first position of a triplet, but the second and third units are not yet known.

SELANGOR (**18**) ("E" and "A" wide) SELANGOR (**19**) ("A" wide) SELANGOR (**20**) ("L" wide)

SELANGOR (**21**) ("L" narrow) SELANGOR (**22**) ("A" narrow) SELANGOR (**23**) (wide letters)

1883–85. No. 63 of Straits Settlements optd with T **2**, **4**, **12**, **14/15** and **18/23**.

20	**12**	2c. pale rose	£250	£170
21	**14**	2c. pale rose	£140	£110
		a. Opt double		
22	**4**	2c. pale rose (1884)	£200	£170
23	**15**	2c. pale rose (1884)	£120	95·00
		a. Opt double	£1000	
		b. Opt triple		
24	**2**	2c. pale rose (1884)	£150	£110
25	**18**	2c. pale rose (1884)	£150	£110
26	**19**	2c. pale rose (1884)	£450	£180
27	**20**	2c. pale rose (1884)	£600	£250
28	**21**	2c. pale rose (1885)	£120	90·00
29	**22**	2c. pale rose (1885)	£190	£160
30	**23**	2c. pale rose (1885)	£550	£275

The above come from triplet settings with Nos. 20+21+21, 22+22+23, 23+26 (with defective "A") +26, 24+25+23 and 28+29+28 so far identified. The triplets for Nos. 27 and 30 are not known.

SELANGOR (**24**) *Selangor* (**25**) SELANGOR (**26**)

SELANGOR (**27**) SELANGOR (**28**) *SELANGOR* (**29**) SELANGOR (**30**)

SELANGOR (**31**) SELANGOR (**32**) SELANGOR (**33**) *SELANGOR* (**34**)

1885–91. Nos. 63/a of Straits Settlements optd with T **24/34**.

31	**24**	2c. pale rose	15·00	26·00
		a. Opt double	£1100	£900
		w. Wmk inverted	—	£550
32	**25**	2c. pale rose	£1600	£1700
33	**26**	2c. pale rose	38·00	48·00
34	**27**	2c. pale rose (1886)	60·00	65·00
		a. Opt double	†	£800
35	**28**	2c. pale rose (horiz opt without stop) (1887)	15·00	2·75
		a. Opt double	£800	
		b. Bright rose	15·00	2·25
36		2c. pale rose (horiz opt with stop) (1887)	£130	80·00
		a. Bright rose		
37	**29**	2c. pale rose (1889)	£300	85·00
38	**30**	2c. pale rose (vert opt) (1889)	80·00	6·00
		a. Bright rose		
38*b*		2c. bright rose (horiz opt) (1889)	£4000	
39	**31**	2c. pale rose (diagonal opt) (1889)	£3000	
40	**32**	2c. pale rose (1889)	£650	38·00
41	**28**	2c. brt rose (vert opt without stop) (1890)	22·00	38·00
42	**33**	2c. bright rose (1890)	£120	3·00
		a. Opt double		
43	**34**	2c. bright rose (1891)	£350	£150

Settings:

Nos. 31/4	– each in triplet containing three examples of the same stamp
No. 35	– triplet or 60 (6×10)
No. 36	– 60 (6×10)
Nos. 37/8	– 60 (6×10) containing both overprints in an unknown combination, but with No. 38 predominating
Nos. 38*b*/9	– not known
Nos. 40/3	– each in 60 (6×10)

SELANGOR *Two* CENTS (**35**) SELANGOR *Two* CENTS (**36**) SELANGOR Two CENTS (**37**)

SELANGOR Two CENTS (**38**) SELANGOR Two CENTS (**39**)

1891. No. 68 of Straits Settlements, surch with T **35/9**, each with bar obliterating old value.

44	**35**	2c. on 24c. green	38·00	70·00
45	**36**	2c. on 24c. green	£200	£250
46	**37**	2c. on 24c. green	£200	£250
47	**38**	2c. on 24c. green	£110	£140
		a. "SELANGCR"		
48	**39**	2c. on 24c. green	£200	£250

Nos. 44/8 come from the one setting used to surcharge the panes of sixty. No. 44 occurs in rows 1 to 5, No. 45 on row 6, No. 46 on row 7, No. 47 on rows 8 and 9, and No. 48 on row 10.

The error, No. 47a, occurs in the first printing only and is No. 45 (R. 8/3) on the pane.

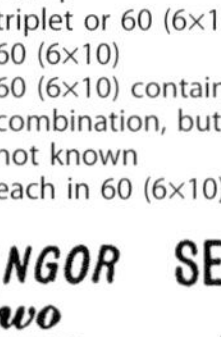

40

3 CENTS
(**41**)

1891 (1 Nov)–**95**. Wmk Crown CA. P 14.

49	**40**	1c. green (5.93)	1·50	25
50		2c. rose	3·50	1·00
51		2c. orange (27.5.95)	2·50	1·00
52		5c. blue (8.92)	24·00	4·75
49/52 *Set of 4*			28·00	6·25
49s/52s Optd "Specimen" *Set of 4*			95·00	

1894 (Dec). Surch with T **41**. Wmk Crown CA. P 14.

53	**40**	3c. on 5c. rose	4·00	50
		s. Optd "Specimen"	35·00	

42

43

Dented frame above "A" of "SELANGOR" (left pane R. 4/5)

1895–99. Wmk Crown CA or Crown CC (dollar values). P 14.

54	**42**	3c. dull purple and carmine	6·50	30
55		5c. dull purple and olive-yellow	8·00	30
56		8c. dull purple and ultramarine (1898)	48·00	7·00
57		10c. dull purple and orange	12·00	2·25
58		25c. green and carmine (1896)	80·00	55·00
59		50c. dull purple and greenish black (1896)	75·00	26·00
		a. Dented frame	£500	
60		50c. green and black (1898)	£425	£120
		a. Dented frame		
61	**43**	$1 green and yellow-green	50·00	£130
62		$2 green and carmine (1897)	£225	£275
63		$3 green and ochre (1897)	£550	£475
64		$5 green and blue	£250	£325
65		$10 green and purple (1899)	£700	£950
		s. Optd "Specimen"	£140	
66		$25 green and orange (1897)	£3500	£3500
		s. Optd "Specimen"	£275	
54/62 *Set of* 9			£850	£550
54s/64s Optd "Specimen" *Set of* 11			£400	

Pending the arrival of the permanent Federated Malay States issue the stamps of STRAITS SETTLEMENTS and PERAK were used at various times between July 1900 and March 1901.

The general issues for the FEDERATED MALAY STATES were used in Selangor from 1901 until 1935.

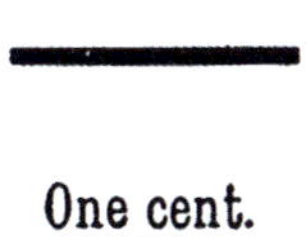

(**44**)

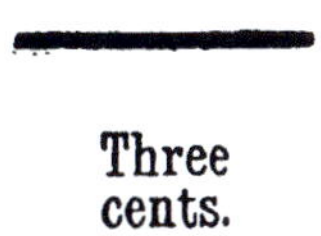

(**45**)

Antique "t" (R. 3/4 and 8/4)

1900 (Oct). Nos. 55 and 59 surch with T **44** or **45**.

66*a*	**42**	1c. on 5c. dull purple & ol-yell (31 Oct*)	60·00	£130
66*b*		1c. on 50c. green and black (22 Oct*)	3·00	27·00
		bc. "cent" repeated at left	£3350	
		bd. Dented frame	£130	
67		3c. on 50c. green and black (30 Oct*)	4·00	25·00
		a. Antique "t" in "cents"	£375	£550
		b. Dented frame	£375	

*Earliest known postmark date.

It is believed that these stamps were surcharged from settings of 30, repeated four times to complete the sheet of 120.

No. 66bc occurred on two separate vertical strips of five stamps where two impressions of the setting overlapped.

46 Mosque at Palace, Klang

47 Sultan Suleiman

Joined script (R. 2/1)

(Des E. J. McNaughton)

1935 (2 Dec)–**41**. Wmk Mult Script CA (sideways on T **46**). Chalk-surfaced paper. P 14 or 14×14½ (No. 70).

68	**46**	1c. black (1.1.36)	30	10
69		2c. green (1.1.36)	90	10
		a. Joined script	55·00	20·00
70		2c. orange (*ordinary paper*) (P 14×14½) (21.8.41)	4·00	75
		aa. Joined script	£130	30·00
		a. Perf 14. Ordinary paper (9.41)	20·00	1·50
		ab. Joined script	£325	55·00
71		3c. green (*ordinary paper*) (21.8.41)	1·50	8·00
		a. Thin striated paper (10.41)	20·00	2·75
72		4c. orange	50	10
73		5c. brown (5.12.35)	70	10
74		6c. scarlet (1.1.37)	6·50	10
75		8c. grey	60	10
76		10c. dull purple (1.1.36)	60	10
77		12c. bright ultramarine (1.1.36)	1·50	10
78		15c. brt ultram (*ordinary paper*) (1.10.41)	12·00	32·00
79		25c. dull purple and scarlet (1.4.36)	1·00	60
		a. Thin striated paper (1941)	4·00	
80		30c. dull purple and orange (1.1.36)	1·00	85
		a. Thin striated paper (1941)	4·00	
81		40c. scarlet and dull purple	1·50	1·00
82		50c. black/*emerald* (1.2.36)	1·00	15
83	**47**	$1 black and rose/*blue* (1.4.36)	9·00	90
84		$2 green and scarlet (16.5.36)	30·00	9·50
85		$5 green and red/*emerald* (16.5.36)	90·00	23·00
68/85 *Set of* 18			£150	65·00
68s/85s Perf "Specimen" *Set of* 18			£450	

The stamps issued during 1941 were printed by Harrison and Sons following bomb damage to the De La Rue works on 29 December 1940.

No. 69 exists in coils constructed from normal sheets.

Supplies of an unissued 8c. scarlet on thin striated paper were diverted to Australia in 1941. Examples circulating result from leakages of this supply (*Price* £800).

48 Sultan Hisamuddin Alam Shah

49 Sultan Hisamud-din Alam Shah

1941. Wmk Mult Script CA. Chalk-surfaced paper. P 14.

86	**48**	$1 black and red/*blue* (15.4.41)	20·00	6·00
87		$2 green and scarlet (7.7.41)	48·00	35·00
		s. Perf "Specimen"	70·00	

A $5 green and red on emerald, T **48**, was issued overprinted during the Japanese occupation of Malaya. Unoverprinted examples are known, but were not issued (*Price* £130).

During shortages in 1941 stamps of STRAITS SETTLEMENTS (2c.) and PERAK (25c.) were issued in Selangor.

1948 (1 Dec). Royal Silver Wedding. As Nos. 131/2 of Johore.

88	10c. violet	20	30
89	$5 green	27·00	22·00

1949 (12 Sept)–**55**. Wmk Mult Script CA. Chalk-surfaced paper. P 17½×18.

90	**49**	1c. black	10	60
91		2c. orange	30	1·25
92		3c. green	3·50	1·50
93		4c. brown	40	10
94		5c. bright purple (1.9.52)	50	2·50
		a. Bright mauve (17.9.53)	30	1·00
95		6c. grey	30	40
96		8c. scarlet	1·50	1·00
97		8c. green (1.9.52)	80	1·75
98		10c. purple	20	10
99		12c. scarlet (1.9.52)	1·25	3·50
		w. Wmk inverted	£550	
100		15c. ultramarine	7·50	10
101		20c. black and green	4·00	35
102		20c. bright blue (1.9.52)	1·00	10

103	25c. purple and orange	2·00	20
104	30c. scarlet and purple (4.9.55)	2·00	2·25
105	35c. scarlet and purple (1.9.52)	1·00	1·50
106	40c. scarlet and purple	10·00	7·00
107	50c. black and blue	3·50	10
108	$1 blue and purple	3·50	60
109	$2 green and scarlet	15·00	60
110	$5 green and brown	48·00	2·25
90/110 *Set of 21*		95·00	23·00

1949 (10 Oct). 75th Anniv of U.P.U. As Nos. 96/9 of Brunei.

111	10c. purple	30	10
112	15c. deep blue	2·50	2·50
113	25c. orange	35	4·50
114	50c. blue-black	1·00	4·50
111/14 *Set of 4*		3·75	10·50

1953 (2 June). Coronation. As No. 152 of Johore.

115	10c. black and reddish purple	1·75	10

1957 (26 June)–**61**. As Nos. 92/102 of Kedah but with inset portrait of Sultan Hisamud-din Alum Shah.

116	1c. black (21.8.57)	10	2·25
117	2c. orange-red (25.7.57)	30	1·00
	a. *Red-orange* (10.11.59)	7·00	5·00
118	4c. sepia (21.8.57)	10	10
119	5c. carmine-lake (21.8.57)	10	10
120	8c. myrtle-green (21.8.57)	2·75	3·00
121	10c. deep brown (4.8.57)	2·25	10
122	10c. deep maroon (9.5.61)	8·00	10
123	20c. blue	2·50	20
124	50c. black and blue (*p* 12½) (25.7.57)	40	10
	a. Perf 12½×13 (10.5.60)	1·00	10
125	$1 ultramarine and reddish purple (25.7.57)	5·00	10
126	$2 bronze-green and scarlet (*p* 12½) (21.8.57)	6·00	2·50
	a. Perf 13×12½ (6.12.60)	7·00	2·50
127	$5 brown and bronze-green (*p* 12½)	13·00	2·50
	a. Perf 13×12½ (10.5.60)	14·00	1·75
116/27 *Set of 12*		35·00	9·75

The 6, 12, 25 and 30c. values used with this issue were Nos. 1/4 of Malayan Federation.

50 Sultan Salahuddin Abdul Aziz Shah

51 Sultan Salahuddin Abdul Aziz Shah

(Photo Harrison)

1961 (28 June). Coronation of the Sultan. W w **12**. P 15×14.

128	**50** 10c. multicoloured	20	10

A sheet exists showing the black printing so misplaced as to produce an effect of a "Double-headed" Sultan (*Price* £160 *un.*).

1961–62. As Nos. 92/8 of Kedah but with inset portrait of Sultan Salahuddin Abdul Aziz as in T **51**. W w **13**. P 12½×13 (vert) or 13×12½ (horiz).

129	1c. black (1.3.62)	60	2·00
130	2c. orange-red (1.3.62)	1·25	2·25
131	4c. sepia (1.3.62)	1·50	10
132	5c. carmine-lake (1.3.62)	1·25	10
133	8c. myrtle-green (1.3.62)	5·00	5·00
134	10c. deep maroon (1.11.61)	1·00	10
135	20c. blue (1.3.62)	8·50	1·25
129/35 *Set of 7*		17·00	9·50

52 *Vanda hookeriana*

1965 (15 Nov). As Nos. 166/72 of Johore but with inset portrait of Sultan Salahuddin Abdul Aziz Shah as in T **52**.

136	1c. multicoloured	10	20
	b. Magenta omitted	£130	
	w. Wmk inverted	1·00	
137	2c. multicoloured	10	1·75
	b. Yellow (flower) omitted	60·00	
138	5c. multicoloured	25	10
	b. Yellow (flower) omitted	65·00	
	c. Red (leaves, etc) omitted	£350	
139	6c. multicoloured	15	10
140	10c. multicoloured	15	10
	a. Red omitted	£140	
141	15c. multicoloured	1·25	10
	b. Green (value and leaves) omitted	£650	
142	20c. multicoloured	1·90	70
	a. Bright purple (blooms) omitted	£140	
	b. Yellow (leaves) omitted	70·00	
136/42 *Set of 7*		3·50	2·50

The 2c. to 20c. values exist with PVA gum as well as gum arabic.

The higher values used with this issue were Nos. 20/27 of Malaysia (National Issues).

1970 (20 Nov). As Nos. 136 etc. but W w **13** (sideways).

143	**52** 1c. multicoloured	1·75	7·50
144	10c. multicoloured	5·00	2·00
145	– 20c. multicoloured	9·00	10·00
143/5 *Set of 3*		14·00	18·00

1971 (1 Feb)–**78**. As Nos. 175/87 of Johore but with portrait of Sultan Salahuddin Abdul Aziz Shah and Arms, as in T **53**.

(a) Litho by Bradbury, Wilkinson.

146	1c. multicoloured	75	2·00
147	2c. multicoloured	1·50	2·00
148	5c. multicoloured	1·50	20
149	6c. multicoloured	1·50	2·00
150	10c. multicoloured	1·50	10
	a. Black (state inscr, portrait and arms) omitted	£140	
151	15c. multicoloured	1·50	10
152	20c. multicoloured	1·50	50
146/52 *Set of 7*		8·75	6·00

(b) Photo by Harrison (1977–78).

153	1c. multicoloured	70	4·50
154	5c. multicoloured	3·50	1·75
155	10c. multicoloured	8·00	1·75
	a. Black (face value etc) omitted	£180	
156	15c. multicoloured	8·00	30
157	20c. multicoloured	4·25	1·00
153/7 *Set of 5*		22·00	8·25

There were two black cylinders used on the photogravure stamps. No. 1553, which occurred on some stamps in the sheet only, shows the "common" black cylinder omitted, but includes the "Selangor" black cylinder.

The higher values used with this issue were Nos. 64/71 of Malaysia (National Issues).

For differences between litho and photo printings see after Johore No. 187.

A used example of No. 150 has been seen with the magenta apparently missing.

For explanation of No. 150a, see note below No. 122 of Kelantan.

54 *Lagerstroemia speciosa*

55 Sultan Salahuddin Abdul Aziz Shah and Royal Crest

1979 (30 Apr). As Nos. 188/94 of Johore but with portrait of Sultan Salahuddin Abdul Aziz Shah as in T **54**.

158	1c. *Rafflesia hasseltii*	10	1·00
159	2c. *Pterocarpus indicus*	10	1·00
160	5c. Type **54**	10	10
161	10c. *Durio zibethinus*	15	10
162	15c. *Hibiscus rosa-sinensis*	15	10
163	20c. *Rhododendron scortechinii*	20	10
164	25c. *Etlingera elatior* (inscr "*Phaeomeria speciosa*")	40	10
158/64 *Set of 7*		1·00	2·00

For higher values used in conjunction with this series see Nos. 190/7 of Malaysia (National Issues).

1983 (6 Oct)–**85**. As Nos. 160/3 but without wmk.

166	5c. Type **54** (20.11.83)	75	1·00
167	10c. *Durio zibethinus* (3.85)	75	1·00
168	15c. *Hibiscus rosa-sinensis* (20.11.83)	70	60
169	20c. *Rhododendron scortechinii* (blackish brown background)	55·00	1·25
169*a*	20c. *Rhododendron scortechinii* (bronze green background) (12.12.83)	1·25	60

*There was no official release date for these stamps. Dates shown are the earliest recorded from postmarks and may be revised if earlier examples are reported.

For details of the shade differences between watermarked and unwatermarked printings see after Johore No. 200a.

On Nos. 166/8 and 1693 the ruler's headdress is bolder than on Nos. 160/3 and 169.

(Des P. Ket. Litho Security Printers (M), Malaysia)

1985 (5 Sept). Silver Jubilee of Sultan. P 13.

173	**55**	15c. multicoloured	1·50	10
174		20c. multicoloured	1·50	15
175		$1 multicoloured	7·00	9·00
173/5 *Set of 3*			9·00	9·00

56 Black Pepper

1986 (25 Oct)–**96**. As Nos. 202/8 of Johore, but with portrait of Sultan Salahuddin Abdul Aziz Shah as in T **56**. P 12.

176	1c. Coffee	10	30
	w. Wmk inverted	11·00	
177	2c. Coconuts	10	30
178	5c. Cocoa	15	10
	c. Perf 14×13¼ (1994)	1·00	10
	cw. Wmk inverted	4·25	
	e. Perf 14×14½ (1999)	14·00	
	f. Perf 14¾×14½ (1994)	4·50	30
179	10c. Type **56**	15	10
	a. Wmk sideways	16·00	
	bw. Wmk inverted		
	c. Perf 14×13¾ (1995)	3·50	20
	cw. Wmk inverted	8·50	
	e. Perf 14×14½ (1994)	6·50	
	f. Perf 14¾×14½ (1994)	1·25	10
180	15c. Rubber	25	10
181	20c. Oil palm	25	15
	aw. Wmk inverted		
	c. Perf 14x13¾ (1994)	1·00	10
	cw. Wmk inverted		
	e. Perf 14×14½ (1999)	9·00	
	f. Perf 14¾×14½ (1996)	3·75	10
	fw. Wmk inverted	9·00	
182	30c. Rice	30	15
	aw. Wmk inverted	1·00	10
	c. Perf 14×13¾ (1994)	1·00	10
	cw. Wmk inverted	6·50	
	e. Perf 14×14½ (1994)	9·00	20
	ew. Wmk inverted		
	f. Perf 14¾×14½ (1995)	4·50	20
176/82 *Set of 7*		1·10	80

2003 ((?)). Vert designs as Type **56** but redenominated in "sen". Multicoloured. W **138**. P 14×13¾.

183	30s. Rice	1·25	10
	aw. Wmk inverted	7·50	
	b. Perf 14¾×14½	1·25	10
	bw. Wmk inverted	7·50	

57 *Nelumbium nelumbo* (sacred lotus)

2007 (31 Dec). Garden Flowers. As Nos. 210/15 of Johore, but with portrait of Sultan Sharafuddin Idris Shah and Arms of Selangor as in T **57**. Multicoloured. W **138**. Phosphorised paper. P 14.

184	5s. Type **57**	10	10
185	10s. *Hydrangea macrophylla*	15	10
186	20s. *Hippeastrum reticulatum*	25	15
187	30s. Bougainvillea	40	20
188	40s. *Ipomoea indica*	50	30
189	50s. *Hibiscus rosa-sinensis*	65	35
184/9 *Set of 6*		1·90	1·10

STAMP BOOKLETS

1935. Stapled.

SB1 $1 booklet containing twenty 5c. (No. 73) in blocks of 10 .... £3000

SB2 $1.30 booklet containing 5c. and 8c. (Nos. 73, 75), each in block of 10 .... £3000

1973 (8 Dec). Cover as Type B **1** of Johore, but inscr "SELANGOR". Stitched.

SB3 $3 booklet containing eight 5c., 10c. and twelve 15c. (Nos. 148, 150/1) in blocks of 4 .... 32·00

1979 (1 Dec). Cover as No. SB5 of Johore, but inscr "SELANGOR". Stitched.

SB4 $3 booklet containing eight 5c., 10c., and twelve 15c. (Nos. 160/2) in blocks of 4 .... 9·50

No. SB4 exists with two different versions of the back cover.

1986. Black on lemon cover as Type B **2** of Federal Territory. Stamps attached by selvedge.

SB5 $1.50 booklet containing 15c. (No. 162) in pair and 20c. (No. 1693) in block of 6 .... 12·00

1986. Cover as No. SB5 but surch with new value and contents. Stamps attached by selvedge.

SB6 60c. booklet containing 20c. (No. 169a) in strip of 3 .... 28·00

1987. Black on buff cover as Type B **2** of Federal Territory. Stamps attached by selvedge.

SB7 60c. booklet containing 20c. (No. 181) in strip of 3.. .... 4·75

1987 (1 June). Cover as Type B **2** of Johore, but inscr "SELANGOR". Stapled.

SB8 $2 booklet containing 5c., 10c., 15c. and 20c. (Nos. 178/81) in blocks of 4 .... 13·00

1991. Black on buff cover as Type B **2** of Federal Territory. Stamps attached by selvedge.

SB9 60c. booklet containing 10c. (No. 179) in strip of 3 and 15c. (No. 180) in pair .... 3·25

1992 (1 July). "Kuala Lumpur '92" International Philatelic Exhibition. Cover as Type B **3** of Johore, but inscr "Selangor". Stamps attached by selvedge.

SB10 $3 booklet containing 30c. (No. 182) in block of 10 .... 11·00

1993 (1 June). Covers as Nos. SB8/9 of Johore, but both on pale buff and inscr "Selangor". Stamps attached by selvedge.

SB11 $2 booklet containing 20c. (No. 181) in block of 10 .... 1·50

SB12 $3 booklet containing 30c. (No. 182) in block of 10 .... 2·00

TRENGGANU

Suzerainty over Trengganu was transferred by Thailand to Great Britain in 1909. A British adviser was appointed in 1919.

The state joined the Federation of Malaya on 1 February 1948.

PRICES FOR STAMPS ON COVER TO 1945

Nos. 1/15	*from* × 12
No. 16/18	—
Nos. 19/22	*from* × 10
Nos. 23/33	*from* × 12
Nos. 34/6	—
Nos. 37/47	*from* × 15
Nos. 48/60	*from* × 6
Nos. D1/4	—

1 Sultan Zain ul ab din

2 Sultan Zain ul ab din

RED CROSS

2c.

(**3**)

1910 (14 Dec)–**19**. Wmk Mult Crown CA. Ordinary paper (1c. to 10c.) or chalk-surfaced paper (20c. to $25). P 14.

1	**1**	1c. blue-green	1·75	1·00
		a. Green	2·75	1·25
2		2c. brown and purple (1915)	1·00	90
3		3c. carmine-red	2·25	2·25
4		4c. orange	3·50	5·50
5		4c. red-brown and green (1915)	2·00	3·75
5a		4c. carmine-red (1919)	1·25	1·75
6		5c. grey	1·25	4·00
7		5c. grey and brown (1915)	2·25	2·00
8		8c. ultramarine	1·25	11·00

9		10c. purple/*yellow*	5·00	14·00
		a. On pale yellow	3·25	9·00
10		10c. green and red/*yellow* (1915)	1·25	2·25
11		20c. dull and bright purple	3·50	5·50
12		25c. green and dull purple (1915)	8·00	38·00
13		30c. dull purple and black (1915)	6·50	65·00
14		50c. black/*green*	4·50	10·00
15		$1 black and carmine/*blue*	17·00	24·00
16		$3 green and red/*green* (1915)	£200	£475
17	2	$5 green and dull purple (1912)	£200	£600
18		$25 rose-carmine and green (1912)	£1100	£2750
		s. Optd "Specimen"	£300	
1/17 *Set of 18*			£425	£1100
1s/17s Optd "Specimen" *Set of 18*			£600	

The 8c. is known used bisected at Kretai in December 1918. Such use was not officially authorised.

1917 (June)–**18**. Surch with T **3**

19	1	3c. + 2c. carmine-red	50	9·00
		a. Comma after "2c."	10·00	42·00
		b. "SS" in "CROSS" inverted	£425	£500
		c. "CSOSS" for "CROSS"	95·00	£200
		d. "2" in thick block type	22·00	70·00
		e. Surch inverted	£1000	£1100
		f. Pair, one without surch	£4500	£4000
		g. "RED CROSS" omitted	£450	
		h. "RED CROSS" twice	£550	
		i. "2c." omitted	£450	
		j. "2c." twice	£550	
20		4c. + 2c. orange	1·50	16·00
		a. Comma after "2c."	18·00	70·00
		b. "SS" in "CROSS" inverted	£2000	£1600
		c. "CSOSS" for "CROSS"	£170	£400
		d. Surch double	£1300	
		e. "RED CROSS" omitted	£500	
		f. "RED CROSS" twice	£750	
		g. "2c." omitted	£500	
		h. "2c." twice	£700	
21		4c. + 2c. red-brown and green (1918)	3·75	45·00
		a. Pair, one without surch	£4000	
		b. "RED CROSS" omitted	£950	
		c. "RED CROSS" twice	£950	
22		8c. + 2c. ultramarine (1917)	1·25	32·00
		a. Comma after "2c."	11·00	85·00
		b. "SS" in "CROSS" inverted	£1000	£1100
		c. "CSOSS" for "CROSS"	£150	£425
		d. "RED CROSS" omitted	£500	
		e. "RED CROSS" twice	£650	
		f. "2c." omitted	£500	
		g. "2c." twice	£600	

Nos. 19/22 were sold at face, plus 2c. on each stamp for Red Cross funds.

The surcharges on Nos. 19/22 were arranged in settings of 18 (6×3) applied three times to cover the top nine rows of the sheet with the tenth row completed by a further impression so that "RED CROSS" from the centre row of the setting appears on the bottom sheet margin. Specialists recognise six different settings:

Setting I – Shows comma after "2" on both R. 1/3 and 1/5, "SS" inverted on R. 1/6 and "CSOSS" for "CROSS" on R. 2/1. Used for 4c. orange and 8c.

Setting Ia – Inverted "SS" on R. 1/6 corrected. Other varieties as Setting I. Used for 3c., 4c. orange and 8c.

Setting II – "CSOSS" on R. 2/1 corrected. Comma varieties as Setting I. Used for 3c., 4c. orange and 8c.

Setting III – Both comma varieties now corrected. Used for 3c., both 4c. and 8c.

Setting IIIa – "SS" inverted on R. 2/5. Used for 3c. only

Setting IV – Thick block "2" on R. 2/2. Inverted "SS" on R. 2/5 corrected. Used for 3c. only.

Nos. 19g/j, 20e/h and 22d/g result from the misplacement of the surcharge.

> During a temporary shortage between March and August 1921 2c., 4c. and 6c. stamps of the STRAITS SETTLEMENTS were authorised for use in Trengganu.

4 Sultan Suleiman

5 Sultan Suleiman

2 CENTS

(**6**)

1921–41. Chalk-surfaced paper P 14.

(a) Wmk Mult Crown CA.

23	4	$1 purple and blue/*blue*	12·00	23·00
24		$3 green and red/*emerald*	£120	£275
25	5	$5 green and red/*pale yellow*	£130	£350
23/5 *Set of 3*			£225	£600
23s/5s Optd "Specimen" *Set of 3*			£150	

(b) Wmk Mult Script CA.

26	4	1c. black (1926)	1·75	1·50
		a. Ordinary paper (1941)	—	75·00
27		2c. green	1·50	2·00
		a. Ordinary paper (1941)	—	75·00
28		3c. green (1926)	2·00	1·00
29		3c. reddish brown (1938)	29·00	14·00
		a. Ordinary paper. *Chestnut* (1941)	—	21·00
30		4c. rose-red	2·50	1·25
		a. Ordinary paper. *Scarlet-vermilion* (1941)	£300	35·00
31		5c. grey and deep brown	2·00	5·00
32		5c. purple/*yellow* (1926)	1·75	1·25
		a. Deep reddish purple/brt yellow (1939)	£250	5·00
33		6c. orange (1924)	4·25	50
		a. Ordinary paper (1941)	—	£180
34		8c. grey (1938)	38·00	6·00
		a. Ordinary paper (1941)	—	32·00
35		10c. bright blue	2·25	1·00
36		12c. bright ultramarine (1926)	4·25	2·75
37		20c. dull purple and orange	2·25	1·50
38		25c. green and deep purple	2·25	2·50
39		30c. dull purple and black	3·25	3·75
40		35c. carmine/*yellow* (1926)	4·75	5·00
41		50c. green and bright carmine	10·00	2·75
42		$1 purple and blue/*blue* (1929)	9·00	3·75
43		$3 green and lake/*green* (1926)	60·00	£170
		a. Green and brown-red/green (1938)	£150	
44	5	$5 green and red/*yellow* (1938)	£500	£3000
45		$25 purple and blue	£800	£1700
		s. Optd "Specimen"	£200	
46		$50 green and yellow	£1900	£3500
		s. Optd "Specimen"	£425	
47		$100 green and scarlet	£6000	£7000
		s. Optd "Specimen"	£800	
26/43 *Set of 18*			£160	£200
26s/44s Optd or Perf (3c. reddish brown, 8c., $1, $5) "Specimen" *Set of 19*			£800	

The used price quoted for No. 44 is for an example with an identifiable cancellation from 1938–41.

Printings of the 2c. yellow-orange, 3c. blue-green, 4c. purple/*yellow*, 6c. slate-grey, 8c. rose, 15c. ultramarine and $1 black and red/*blue* on ordinary paper were despatched to Malaya in late 1941, but did not arrivebefore the Japanese occupation. Unused examples are known of the 2, 3, 6, 8 and 15c. (*Prices*, 3c. £800, *others* £250 *each*, *unused*).

The 12c. bright ultramarine was also printed on ordinary paper, and exists overprinted during the Japanese occupation. See No. J107b.

OVERPRINT SETTINGS FOR NOS. 48/58. The low values in Types **1** and **4** were overprinted using Setting II as detailed under Straits Settlements. The three listed constant varieties from the original typeset block of 12 occur in the same positions for these Trengganu stamps as does the No stop variety from R. 1/5 of the left pane.

A separate setting, believed to be of 30 (6×5), was required for the $5 in the larger design. This was constructed by duplicating the second horizontal row of the original typeset block five times so that the raised stop after "EXHIBITION" variety occurs on all stamps in the second vertical row and the small second "A" in "MALAYA" on all stamps in the sixth.

1922 (Apr). Malaya–Borneo Exhibition, Singapore. optd as T **56** of Straits Settlements at Singapore.

48	4	2c. green	4·75	27·00
		b. Oval last "O" in "BORNEO"	10·00	48·00
		c. Raised stop after "EXHIBITION"	10·00	48·00
		d. Small second "A" in "MALAYA"	10·00	48·00
		f. No stop		
49		4c. rose-red	6·50	42·00
		b. Oval last "O" in "BORNEO"	14·00	75·00
		c. Raised stop after "EXHIBITION"	14·00	75·00
		d. Small second "A" in "MALAYA"	14·00	75·00
		f. No stop		
50	1	5c. grey and brown	3·25	45·00
		b. Oval last "O" in "BORNEO"	7·50	75·00
		c. Raised stop after "EXHIBITION"	7·50	75·00
		d. Small second "A" in "MALAYA"	7·50	75·00
		f. No stop		
51		10c. green and red/*yellow*	5·50	32·00
		b. Oval last "O" in "BORNEO"	12·00	55·00
		c. Raised stop after "EXHIBITION"	12·00	55·00
		d. Small second "A" in "MALAYA"	12·00	55·00
		f. No stop		
52		20c. dull and bright purple	6·00	35·00
		b. Oval last "O" in "BORNEO"	13·00	60·00
		c. Raised stop after "EXHIBITION"	13·00	60·00
		d. Small second "A" in "MALAYA"	13·00	60·00
		f. No stop		
53		25c. green and dull purple	4·75	35·00
		b. Oval last "O" in "BORNEO"	10·00	60·00
		c. Raised stop after "EXHIBITION"	10·00	60·00

		d. Small second "A" in "MALAYA"	10·00	60·00
		f. No stop		
54		30c. dull purple and black	5·50	35·00
		b. Oval last "O" in "BORNEO"	12·00	60·00
		c. Raised stop after "EXHIBITION"	12·00	60·00
		d. Small second "A" in "MALAYA"	12·00	60·00
		f. No stop		
55		50 c. black/*green*	5·50	45·00
		b. Oval last "O" in "BORNEO"	12·00	75·00
		c. Raised stop after "EXHIBITION"	12·00	75·00
		d. Small second "A" in "MALAYA"	12·00	75·00
		f. No stop		
56		$1 black and carmine/*blue*	14·00	75·00
		b. Oval last "O" in "BORNEO"	27·00	£140
		c. Raised stop after "EXHIBITION"	27·00	£140
		d. Small second "A" in "MALAYA"	27·00	£140
		f. No stop		
57		$3 green and red/*green*	£180	£400
		b. Oval last "O" in "BORNEO"	£325	£700
		c. Raised stop after "EXHIBITION"	£325	£700
		d. Small second "A" in "MALAYA"	£325	£700
		f. No stop		
58	**2**	$5 green and dull purple	£300	£650
		c. Raised stop after "EXHIBITION"	£450	£1000
		d. Small second "A" in "MALAYA"	£450	£1000
48/58 *Set of 11*			£475	£1300

1941 (1 May). Nos. 32a and 35 surch as T **6**.

59	**4**	2c. on 5c. deep reddish purple/*bright yellow*	6·50	3·50
60		8c. on 10c. bright blue	7·00	4·25

1948 (2 Dec). Royal Silver Wedding. As Nos. 131/2 of Johore.

61	10c. violet	15	1·75
62	$5 carmine	25·00	42·00

1949 (10 Oct). 75th Anniv of U.P.U. As Nos. 96/9 of Brunei.

63	10c. purple	30	75
64	15c. deep blue	1·90	4·00
65	25c. orange	40	2·75
66	50c. blue-black	1·00	3·50
	a. "C" of "CA" missing from wmk	£800	
63/6 *Set of 4*		3·25	10·00

7 Sultan Ismail

8 Sultan Ismail

1949 (27 Dec)–**55**. Wmk Mult Script CA. Chalk-surfaced paper. P 17½×18.

67	**7**	1c. black	75	75
68		2c. orange	75	75
69		3c. green	3·00	4·00
70		4c. brown	30	60
71		5c. bright purple (1.9.52)	30	1·75
72		6c. grey	1·75	60
73		8c. scarlet	1·00	2·75
74		8c. green (1.9.52)	1·00	1·75
		a. Deep green (11.8.53)	12·00	13·00
75		10c. purple	30	30
76		12c. scarlet (1.9.52)	1·00	2·75
77		15c. ultramarine	4·50	30
78		20c. black and green	4·50	3·75
79		20c. bright blue (1.9.52)	1·00	40
80		25c. purple and orange	2·50	2·00
81		30c. scarlet and purple (4.9.55)	1·25	2·25
82		35c. scarlet and purple (1.9.52)	1·00	2·25
83		40c. red and purple	8·50	18·00
84		50c. black and blue	2·00	2·25
85		$1 blue and purple	7·00	10·00
86		$2 green and scarlet	32·00	35·00
87		$5 green and brown	55·00	60·00
67/87 *Set of 21*			£120	£140

1953 (2 June). Coronation. As No. 152 of Johore.

88	10c. black and reddish purple	2·00	1·25

1957 (26 June)–**83**. As Nos. 92/102 of Kedah, but with inset portrait of Sultan Ismail.

89	1c. black (21.8.57)	10	20
90	2c. orange-red (25.7.57)	1·50	30
	a. *Red-orange* (21.2.61)	28·00	14·00
91	4c. sepia (21.8.57)	10	10
92	5c. carmine-lake (21.8.57)	10	10
93	8c. myrtle-green (21.8.57)	4·00	60
94	10c. deep brown (4.8.57)	1·75	10
94*a*	10c. deep maroon (21.2.61)	6·00	30
95	20c. blue	2·25	1·60
96	50c. black and blue (*p* 12½) (25.7.57)	55	2·50
	a. Perf 12½×13 (17.5.60)	55	1·60
	ab. *Black and ultramarine* (20.3.62)	2·00	1·75
97	$1 ultramarine and reddish purple (25.7.57)	9·00	7·50
98	$2 bronze-green and scarlet (21.8.57)	17·00	7·50
99	$5 brown and bronze-green	22·00	22·00
	a. Perf 13×12½ (13.8.63)	25·00	25·00
89/99 *Set of 12*		55·00	38·00

The 6, 12, 25 and 30c. values used with this issue were Nos. 1/4 of Malayan Federation.

1965 (15 Nov). As Nos. 166/72 of Johore but with inset portrait of Sultan Ismail Nasiruddin Shah as in T **8**.

100	1c. multicoloured	10	2·00
101	2c. multicoloured	10	2·00
102	5c. multicoloured	15	70
	w. Wmk inverted		
103	6c. multicoloured	15	2·00
104	10c. multicoloured	20	25
105	15c. multicoloured	1·50	10
	a. Black (country name and portrait) omitted (horizontal pair with normal)	£1200	
106	20c. multicoloured	1·50	1·25
	a. Bright purple (blooms) omitted	£200	
100/6 *Set of 7*		3·25	7·50

The 5c. value exists with PVA gum as well as gum arabic.

No. 101a, formerly listed here, is now listed as Sarawak No. 213a.

The higher values used with this issue were Nos. 20/27 of Malaysia (National Issues).

9 Sultan of Trengganu

(Des Enche Nik Zainal Abidin. Photo Harrison)

1970 (16 Dec). 25th Anniv of Installation of H.R.H. Tuanku Ismail Nasiruddin Shah as Sultan of Trengganu. P 14½×13½.

107	**9**	10c. multicoloured	1·00	2·50
108		15c. multicoloured	60	1·25
109		50c. multicoloured	1·00	3·00
107/9 *Set of 3*			2·40	6·00

1971 (1 Feb)–**78**. As Nos. 175/87 of Johore but with portrait of Sultan Ismail Nasiruddin Shah and Arms, as in T **10**.

(a) Litho by Bradbury, Wilkinson.

110	1c. multicoloured	40	2·50
111	2c. multicoloured	80	2·50
112	5c. multicoloured	1·00	1·25
113	6c. multicoloured	1·75	2·75
114	10c. multicoloured	1·75	70
115	15c. multicoloured	1·75	20
116	20c. multicoloured	2·00	1·75
110/16 *Set of 7*		8·50	10·50

(b) Photo by Harrison (1977–78).

116*a*	5c. multicoloured	24·00	9·00
117	10c. multicoloured	8·50	3·25
117*a*	15c. multicoloured	4·75	1·25

The higher values used with this issue were Nos. 64/71 of Malaysia (National Issues).

For differences between litho and photo printings, see after Johore No. 187.

11 *Durio zibethinus*

12 Sultan Mahmud

1979 (30 Apr). As Nos. 188/94 of Johore but with portrait of Sultan Ismail Nasiruddin Shah as in T **11**.

118	1c. *Rafflesia hasseltii*	10	1·25
119	2c. *Pterocarpus indicus*	10	1·25
120	5c. *Lagerstroemia speciosa*	10	60
121	10c. Type **11**	15	10
122	15c. *Hibiscus rosa-sinensis*	15	10

123	20c. *Rhododendron scortechinii*	20	10
124	25c. *Etlingera elatior* (inscr "*Phaeomeria speciosa*")	40	50
118/24 *Set of 7*		1·00	3·25

For higher values used in conjunction with this series see Nos. 190/7 of Malaysia (National Issues).

(Des Malaysian Advertising Services. Litho Harrison)

1981 (21 Mar). Installation of Sultan Mahmud. P 14.

125	**12**	10c. black, gold and new blue	35	1·50
126		15c. black, gold and yellow	45	50
127		50c. black, gold and bright purple	1·00	3·00
125/7 *Set of 3*			1·60	4·50

1983 (1 Oct)–**86**. As Nos. 121/4 but without wmk.

131	10c. Type **11** (1.2.86)	14·00	4·50
132	15c. *Hibiscus rosa-sinensis* (24.1.85)	75	1·00
133	20c. *Rhododendron scortechinii* (blackish brown background)	35·00	6·00
133*a*	20c. *Rhododendron scortechinii* (bronze green background) (2.3.84)	2·75	3·00
134	25c. *Etlingera elatior* (inscr "*Phaeomeria speciosa*") (13.11.83)	1·00	1·25

*There was no official release date for these stamps. Dates shown are the earliest recorded from postmarks and may be revised if earlier examples are reported.

For details of the shade differences between watermarked and unwatermarked printings see after Johore No. 200a.

On Nos. 131/2, 133a and 134 the portrait and state arms have been redrawn smaller.

13 Rubber

1986 (25 Oct)–**96**. As Nos. 202/8 of Johore, but with portrait of Sultan Mahmud and inscr "TERENGGANU" as in T **13**. P 12.

135	1c. Coffee	10	30
	b. Perf 13½×13¾ (1993)	4·50	40
136	2c. Coconuts	10	30
137	5c. Cocoa	15	30
	w. Wmk inverted	12·00	
138	10c. Black pepper	20	10
	c. Perf 14×13¾ (1995)	4·75	30
	cw. Wmk inverted	6·50	
139	15c. Type **13**	30	10
	w. Wmk inverted		
140	20c. Oil palm	30	15
	w. Wmk inverted		
	c. Perf 14×13¾ (1995)	7·00	30
141	30c. Rice	40	15
	c. Perf 14×13¾ (1994)	7·50	40
	cw. Wmk inverted		
	f. Perf 14¾×14¾ (1995)	3·75	30
	fw. Wmk inverted		
135/41 *Set of 7*		1·40	1·25

14 Sultan Mizan Zainal Abidin and Maziah Palace in 1999

(Des P. Chuah. Litho Security Printers (M), Malaysia)

1999 (4 Mar). Installation of Sultan Mizan Abidin as Sultan Of Terengganu. T **14** and similar horiz designs. Multicoloured. W **138**. P 13½.

142	30s. Type **14**	50	25
	a. Perf 14½		
143	50s. Maziah Palace in 1903	75	60
	a. Perf 12		
	b. Perf 14		
144	1r. Tengku Tengah Zahara Mosque at night	1·40	2·75
142/4 *Set of 3*		2·40	3·25

1999–2000. As Nos. 137/8 and 140/1, but with portrait of Sultan Mizan. W **138**. P 14×13¾.

147	5s. Cocoa (2000)	3·25	1·50
148	10s. Black Pepper (2000)	3·25	1·50
150	20s. Oil palm (2000)	3·25	1·25
151	30s. Rice	1·00	85
	aw. Wmk inverted	15·00	
	e. Perf 14×14½	5·00	
	f. Perf 14¾×14½	8·50	
	fw. Wmk inverted	15·00	

15 *Nelumbium nelumbo* (sacred lotus)

2007 (31 Dec). Garden Flowers. As Nos. 210/15 of Johore, but with portrait of Sultan Mizan Zainal Abidin and Arms of Trengganu as in T **15**. Multicoloured. W **138**. Phosphorised paper. P 14.

152	5s. Type **15**	10	10
153	10s. *Hydrangea macrophylla*	15	10
154	20s. *Hippeastrum reticulatum*	25	15
155	30s. Bougainvillea	40	20
156	40s. *Ipomoea indica*	50	30
157	50s. *Hibiscus rosa-sinensis*	65	35
152/7 *Set of 6*		1·90	1·10

STAMP BOOKLETS

1973 (8 Dec). Cover as Type B **1** of Johore but inscr "TRENGGANU". Stitched.

SB1	$3 booklet containing eight 5c., 10c. and twelve 15c. (Nos. 112, 114/15) in blocks of 4	32·00	

Examples of No. SB1 exist with a white label giving revised postage rates.

1979 (1 Dec). Cover as No. SB5 of Johore, but inscr "TRENGGANU". Stitched.

SB2	$3 booklet containing eight 5c., 10c., and twelve 15c. (Nos. 120/2) in blocks of 4	11·00	

No. SB2 exists with two different versions of the back cover.

1987 (1 June). Cover as Type SB2 of Johore, but inscr "TERENGGANU". Stapled.

SB3	$2 booklet containing 5c., 10c., 15c. and 20c. (Nos. 137/40) in blocks of 4	13·00	

1992 (1 July). Kuala Lumpur '92 International Philatelic Exhibition. Cover as Type B **3** of Johore, but inscr "Terengganu". Stamps attacked by selvedge.

SB4	$3 booklet containing 30c. (No. 141) in block of 10	11·00	

1993. Covers as Nos. SB8/9 of Johore, but inscr "Terengganu". Stamps attached by selvedge.

SB5	$2 booklet containing 20c. (No. 140) in block of 10	1·25	1·50
SB6	$3 booklet containing 30c. (No. 141) in block of 10	1·50	2·00

POSTAGE DUE STAMPS

D **1**

1937 (10 Aug). Wmk Mult Script CA (sideways). P 14.

D1	D **1**	1c. scarlet	7·50	55·00
D2		4c. green	9·50	60·00
D3		8c. yellow	55·00	£350
D4		10c. brown	£110	95·00
D1/4 *Set of 4*			£160	£500
D1s/4s Perf "Specimen" *Set of 4*			£150	

VIII. JAPANESE OCCUPATION OF MALAYA

PRICES FOR STAMPS ON COVER	
Nos. J1/55	*from* × 10
Nos. J56/76	*from* × 12
Nos. J77/89	*from* × 20
Nos. J90/1	*from* × 15
Nos. J92/115	*from* × 6
Nos. J116/18	—
Nos. J119/32	*from* × 12
Nos. J133/45	*from* × 10
Nos. J146/223	*from* × 6
Nos. J224/58	*from* × 12
No. J259	*from* × 15
Nos. J260/96	*from* × 12
Nos. J297/310	*from* × 20
Nos. J311/17	—
Nos. JD1/10	*from* × 30
Nos. JD11/16	*from* × 12
Nos. JD17/20	*from* × 30
Nos. JD21/7	*from* × 20
Nos. JD28/33	*from* × 30
Nos. JD34/41	*from* × 60

Japanese forces invaded Malaya on 8 December 1941 with the initial landings taking place at Kota Bharu on the east coast. Penang fell, to a force which crossed the border from Thailand, on 19 December, Kuala Lumpur on 11 January 1942 and the conquest of the Malay peninsula was completed by the capture of Singapore on 15 February.

During the Japanese Occupation various small Dutch East Indies islands near Singapore were administered as part of Malaya. Stamps of the Japanese Occupation of Malaya were issued to the post offices of Dabo Singkep, Puloe Samboe, Tanjong Balei, Tanjong Batu, Tanjong Pinang and Terempa between 1942 and 1945. The overprinted issues were also used by a number of districts in Atjeh (Northern Sumatra) whose postal services were administered from Singapore until the end of March 1943.

Malayan post offices were also opened in October 1943 to serve camps of civilians working on railway construction and maintenance in Thailand. Overprinted stamps of the Japanese Occupation of Malaya were used at these offices between October 1943 and the end of the year after which mail from the camps was carried free. Their postmarks were inscribed in Japanese Katakana characters, and, uniquely, showed the Japanese postal symbol.

JOHORE

The postal service in Johore was reconstituted in mid-April 1942 using Nos. J146/60 and subsequently other general issues. Stamps of Johore overprinted "DAI NIPPON 2602" were, however, only used for fiscal purposes. Overprinted Johore postage due stamps were not issued for use elsewhere in Malaya.

POSTAGE DUE STAMPS

(**1**) (Upright)

(**2**)

Second character sideways (R. 6/3)

1942 (1 Apr). Nos. D1/5 of Johore optd as T **1** in brown.

JD1	D **1**	1c. carmine	50·00	85·00
		a. Black opt	20·00	70·00
JD2		4c. green	80·00	95·00
		a. Black opt	65·00	80·00
JD3		8c. orange	£140	£150
		a. Black opt	80·00	95·00
JD4		10c. brown	50·00	70·00
		a. Black opt	16·00	50·00
JD5		12c. purple	95·00	£110
		a. Black opt	45·00	55·00

1943. Nos. D1/5 of Johore optd with T **2**.

JD6	D **1**	1c. carmine	10·00	30·00
		a. Second character sideways	£350	£700
JD7		4c. green	8·00	35·00
		a. Second character sideways	£375	£700
JD8		8c. orange	10·00	35·00
		a. Second character sideways	£425	£750
JD9		10c. brown	9·50	45·00
		a. Second character sideways	£400	£850
JD10		12c. purple	11·00	65·00
		a. Second character sideways	£500	£950
JD6/10 *Set of 5*			45·00	£190

KEDAH

Postal services resumed by 31 January 1942 using unoverprinted Kedah values from 1c. to 8c. which were accepted for postage until 13 May 1942.

During the Japanese occupation Perlis was administered as part of Kedah.

DAI NIPPON

2602

(**3**)

DAI NIPPON

2602

(**4**)

1942 (13 May)–**43**. Stamps of Kedah (Script wmk) optd with T **3** (1c. to 8c.) or **4** (10c. to $5), both in red.

J1	**1**	1c. black (No. 68*a*)	6·50	9·50
J2		2c. bright green (No. 69)	27·00	30·00
J3		4c. violet	7·00	4·00
		a. Short sheaf	£190	£150
J4		5c. yellow	5·50	5·00
		a. Black opt (1943)	£200	£225
J5		6c. carmine (No. 56) (Blk.)	4·25	17·00
		a. *Carmine-red* (No. 56a)	50·00	75·00
J6		8c. grey-black	4·50	3·50
J7	**6**	10c. ultramarine and sepia	15·00	17·00
J8		12c. black and violet	35·00	50·00
J9		25c. ultramarine and purple	11·00	18·00
		a. Black opt (1943)	£325	£275
J10		30c. green and scarlet	70·00	80·00
J11		40c. black and purple	35·00	50·00
J12		50c. brown and blue	35·00	50·00
J13		$1 black and green	£140	£150
		a. Opt inverted	£700	£800
J14		$2 green and brown	£170	£170
J15		$5 black and scarlet	70·00	£100
		a. Black opt (1943)	£1200	£1000
J1/15 *Set of 15*			£550	£650

Nos. J1/15 were gradually replaced by issues intended for use throughout Malaya. Kedah and Perlis were ceded to Thailand by the Japanese on 19 October 1943.

KELANTAN

Postal services resumed on 1 June 1942. Stamps used in Kelantan were overprinted with the personal seals of Sunagawa, the Japanese Governor, and of Handa, the Assistant Governor.

(**5**) Sunagawa Seal

(**6**) Handa Seal

40 CENTS

(**7**)

$1.00

(**8**)

1 Cents

(**9**)

1942 (June). Stamps of Kelantan surch.

(a) As T **7** or **8** (dollar values). Optd with T **5** in red.

J16	**4**	1c. on 50c. grey-olive and orange	£300	£180
J17		2c. on 40c. orange and blue-green	£800	£300
J18		4c. on 30c. violet and scarlet	£2250	£1200
J19		5c. on 12c. blue (R.)	£300	£190
J20		6c. on 25c. vermilion and violet	£350	£190
J21		8c. on 5c. red-brown (R.)	£450	£140
J22		10c. on 6c. lake	80·00	£120
		a. "CENST" for "CENTS"	£8500	
J23		12c. on 8c. grey-olive (R.)	55·00	£110
J24		25c. on 10c. purple (R.)	£1400	£1300
J25		30c. on 4c. scarlet	£2250	£2000
J26		40c. on 2c. green (R.)	65·00	85·00
		a. Surch double (B.+R.)	£4250	
J27		50c. on 1c. grey-olive and yellow	£1700	£1300
J28	**1**	$1 on 4c. black and red (R., bars Blk.)	50·00	80·00
J29		$2 on 5c. green and red/*yellow*	50·00	80·00

J30		$5 on 6c. scarlet	50·00	80·00
		a. Surch double	£475	

(b) As T **7**. Optd with T **6** in red.

J31	**4**	12c. on 8c. grey-olive	£200	£350
		a. Type **6** omitted (in horiz pair with normal)	£4250	

(c) As T **9**. Optd with T **5** in red.

J32	**4**	1c. on 50c. grey-olive and orange	£200	£100
		a. "Cente" for "Cents" (R. 5/1)	£2750	£1200
J33		2c. on 40c. orange and blue-green	£225	£130
		a. "Cente" for "Cents" (R. 5/1)	£2750	£1400
J34		5c. on 12c. blue (R.)	£180	£160
		a. "Cente" for "Cents" (R. 5/1)	£2250	
J35		8c. on 5c. red-brown (R.)	£140	75·00
		a. "Cente" for "Cents" (R. 5/1)	£1800	£1000
J36		10c. on 6c. lake	£450	£475
		a. "Cente" for "Cents" (R. 5/1)	£4000	

(d) As T **9**. Optd with T **6** in red.

J41	**4**	1c. on 50c. grey-olive and orange	£140	£180
		a. "Cente" for "Cents" (R. 5/1)	£1700	
J42		2c. on 40c. orange and blue-green	£150	£190
		a. "Cente" for "Cents" (R. 5/1)	£1800	
J43		8c. on 5c. red-brown (R.)	75·00	£140
		a. "Cente" for "Cents" (R. 5/1)	£1400	
J44		10c. on 6c. lake	£110	£180
		a. "Cente" for "Cents" (R. 5/1)	£1600	

As stamps of the above series became exhausted the equivalent values from the series intended for use throughout Malaya were introduced. Stamps as Nos. J28/30, J32/3 and J35/6, but without Type **5** or **6**, are from remainders sent to Singapore or Kuala Lumpur after the state had been ceded to Thailand (*Price from £16 each unused*). Nos. J19, J21, J23 and J25/6 have also been seen without Type **5** (*Price from £80 each unused*).

The 12c. on 8c., 30c. on 4c., 40c. on 2c. and 50c. on 1c. surcharged with Type **9**, formerly listed as Nos. J37/40, are now believed to exist only as remainders without the Type **5** red handstamp (*Price from £20 each, unused*).

Kelantan was ceded to Thailand by the Japanese on 19 October 1943.

MALACCA

Postal services from Malacca resumed on 21 April 1942, but there were no stamps available for two days.

PRICES. Those quoted are for single stamps. Blocks of four showing complete handstamp are worth from five times the price of a single stamp.

(**10**) "Military Administration Malacca State Government Seal"

1942 (23 Apr). Stamps of Straits Settlements handstamped as T **10**, in red, each impression covering four stamps.

J45	**58**	1c. black	£110	85·00
J46		2c. orange	65·00	70·00
J47		3c. green	70·00	80·00
J48		5c. brown	£160	£160
J49		8c. grey	£250	£130
J50		10c. dull purple	£100	£110
J51		12c. ultramarine	£110	£120
J52		15c. ultramarine	80·00	95·00
J53		40c. scarlet and dull purple	£600	£650
J54		50c. black/*emerald*	£950	£950
J55		$1 black and red/*blue*	£1100	£1000

The 30c., $2 and $5 also exist with this overprint, but these values were not available to the public. (*Price for set of* 3 *£11000 unused*).

POSTAGE DUE STAMPS

1942 (23 Apr). Postage Due stamps of Malayan Postal Union handstamped as T **10**, in red, each impression covering four stamps.

JD11	D **1**	1c. slate-purple	£225	£180
JD12		4c. green	£225	£225
JD13		8c. scarlet	£3000	£1900
JD14		10c. yellow-orange	£475	£450
JD15		12c. ultramarine	£700	£650
JD16		50c. black	£2750	£1700

Nos. J45/55 and JD11/16 were replaced during May 1942 by the overprinted issues intended for use throughout Malaya.

PENANG

Postal services on Penang Island resumed on 30 March 1942 using Straits Settlements stamps overprinted by Japanese seals of the Government Accountant, Mr. A. Okugawa, and his assistant, Mr. Itchiburi.

(**11**) Okugawa Seal

(**12**) Itchiburi Seal

DAI NIPPON
2602
PENANG
(**13**)

1942 (30 Mar). Straits Settlements stamps optd.

(a) As T **11** (three forms of the seal).

J56	**58**	1c. black	9·50	12·00
J57		2c. orange	24·00	23·00
		a. Pair, one without handstamp	£1500	
J58		3c. green	20·00	23·00
J59		5c. brown	24·00	28·00
J60		8c. grey	27·00	38·00
J61		10c. dull purple	50·00	50·00
J62		12c. ultramarine	42·00	50·00
J63		15c. ultramarine	50·00	50·00
J64		40c. scarlet and dull purple	95·00	£110
J65		50c. black/*emerald*	£225	£225
J66		$1 black and red/*blue*	£250	£275
J67		$2 green and scarlet	£850	£700
J68		$5 green and red/*emerald*	£2500	£1500

(b) With T **12**.

J69	**58**	1c. black	£160	£130
J70		2c. orange	£160	£110
J71		3c. green	£100	£100
J72		5c. brown	£2500	£2500
J73		8c. grey	90·00	95·00
J74		10c. dull purple	£160	£170
J75		12c. ultramarine	£100	£120
J76		15c. ultramarine	£120	£130

Straits Settlements 1, 2, 3, 4 and 5c. values exist with a similar but circular seal containing four characters, but these were not available to the public.

1942 (15 Apr). Straits Settlements stamps optd with T **13** by Penang Premier Press.

J77	**58**	1c. black (R.)	6·50	3·00
		a. Opt inverted	£550	£550
		b. Opt double	£300	£300
J78		2c. orange	5·50	4·25
		a. "PE" for "PENANG"	£120	90·00
		b. Opt inverted	£160	
		c. Opt double	£500	
J79		3c. green (R.)	5·50	6·00
		a. Opt double, one inverted	£400	
J80		5c. brown (R.)	3·25	8·00
		a. "N PPON"	£200	
		b. Opt double	£500	£425
J81		8c. grey (R.)	2·25	1·40
		a. "N PPON"	60·00	65·00
		b. Opt double, one inverted	£475	
J82		10c. dull purple (R.)	1·50	2·25
		a. Opt double	£450	£450
		b. Opt double, one inverted	£400	£400
J83		12c. ultramarine (R.)	4·50	17·00
		a. "N PPON"	£550	
		b. Opt double	£400	
		c. Opt double, one inverted	£600	£600
J84		15c. ultramarine (R.)	1·75	4·00
		a. "N PPON"	£110	£120
		b. Opt inverted	£400	£400
		c. Opt double	£550	£550
J85		40c. scarlet and dull purple	5·50	17·00
J86		50c. black/*emerald* (R.)	3·75	30·00
J87		$1 black and red/*blue*	6·00	42·00
		a. Opt inverted	£1100	
J88		$2 green and scarlet	60·00	90·00
J89		$5 green and red/*emerald*	£600	£650
J77/89 *Set of* 13			£650	£800

Nos. J77/89 were replaced by the overprinted issues intended for use throughout Malaya.

SELANGOR

Postal services resumed in the Kuala Lumpur area on 3 April 1942 and gradually extended to the remainder of the state. Stamps of the general overprinted issue were used, but the following commemorative set was only available in Selangor.

SELANGOR
EXHIBITION
DAI NIPPON
2602
MALAYA
(**14**)

1942 (3 Nov). Selangor Agri-horticultural Exhibition. Nos. 294 and 283 of Straits Settlements optd with T **14**.

J90	**58**	2c. orange	12·00	24·00
		a. "C" for "G" in "SELANGOR" (R. 1/9)	£400	£450
		b. Opt inverted	£300	£400
J91		8c. grey	13·00	24·00
		a. "C" for "G" in "SELANGOR" (R. 1/9)	£400	£450
		b. Opt inverted	£300	£400

SINGAPORE

The first post offices re-opened in Singapore on 16 March 1942.

(**15**) "Malaya Military Government Division Postal Services Bureau Seal"

(Handstamped at Singapore)

1942 (16 Mar). Stamps of Straits Settlements optd with T **15** in red.

J92	**58**	1c. black	16·00	19·00
J93		2c. orange	13·00	13·00
		a. Pair, one without handstamp	£2000	
J94		3c. green	50·00	70·00
J95		8c. grey	24·00	18·00
J96		15c. ultramarine	18·00	15·00
J92/6 *Set of 5*			£110	£120

The overprint Type **15** has a double-lined frame, although the two lines are not always apparent, as in the illustration. Three chops were used, differing slightly in the shape of the characters, but forgeries also exist. It is distinguishable from Type **1**, used for the general issues, by its extra width, measuring approximately 14 mm against 12½ mm.

The 6, 10, 30, 40, 50c., $2 and $5 also exist with this overprint, but were not sold to the public.

Nos. J92/6 were replaced on the 3 May 1942 by the stamps overprinted with Type **1** which were intended for use throughout Malaya.

TRENGGANU

Postal services resumed in Trengganu on 5 March 1942 using unoverprinted stamps up to the 35c. value. These remained in use until September 1942.

1942 (Sept). Stamps of Trengganu (Script wmk) optd as T **1** at Kuala Lumpur.

J97	**4**	1c. black (No. 26a)	90·00	90·00
		a. Chalk-surfaced paper (No. 26)	—	£180
		b. Red opt	£225	£225
		c. Brown opt (chalk-surfaced paper)	£475	£275
J98		2c. green (No. 27a)	£140	£140
		a. Chalk-surfaced paper (No. 27)	—	£275
		b. Red opt	£275	£300
		c. Brown opt	£500	£325
J99		2c. on 5c. deep reddish purple/*bright yellow* (No. 59)	40·00	40·00
		a. Red opt	60·00	75·00
J100		3c. chestnut (No. 29a)	£100	85·00
		a. Brown opt	£750	£450
J101		4c. scarlet-vermilion (No. 30a)	£180	£140
J102		5c. dp reddish purple/*bright yellow* (No. 32*a*)	10·00	19·00
		a. Purple/yellow (No. 32)	£150	£160
		b. Red opt	29·00	
J103		6c. orange (No. 33a)	9·50	25·00
		a. Red opt	£300	
		b. Brown opt	£750	£750
J104		8c. grey (No. 34a)	9·00	13·00
		a. Chalk-surfaced paper (No. 34)	£180	
		b. Brown to red opt	55·00	70·00
J105		8c. on 10c. bright blue (No. 60)	13·00	50·00
		a. Red opt	21·00	
J106		10c. bright blue	28·00	50·00
		a. Red opt	£275	
		b. Brown opt	£800	£800
J107		12c. bright ultramarine (No. 36)	8·00	50·00
		a. Red opt	29·00	65·00
		b. Ordinary paper	30·00	
J108		20c. dull purple and orange	9·00	45·00
		a. Red opt	23·00	
J109		25c. green and deep purple	7·50	55·00
		a. Red opt	24·00	
		b. Brown opt	£850	£850
J110		30c. dull purple and black	12·00	45·00
		a. Red opt	35·00	60·00
J111		35c. carmine/*yellow*	29·00	55·00
		a. Red opt	35·00	
J112		50c. green and bright carmine	85·00	£100
J113		$1 purple and blue/*blue*	£4250	£4250
J114		$3 green and brown-red/*green* (No. 43*a*)	75·00	£120
		a. Green and lake/green (No. 43)	£275	
		b. Red opt	75·00	
J115	**5**	$5 green and red/*yellow*	£200	£275
J116		$25 purple and blue	£1500	
		a. Red opt	£6000	
J117		$50 green and yellow	£13000	
J118		$100 green and scarlet	£1700	

DAI NIPPON
2602
MALAYA
(**16**)

1942 (Sept). Stamps of Trengganu (Script wmk) optd with T **16**.

J119	**4**	1c. black (No. 26a)	16·00	12·00
J120		2c. green (No. 27a)	£275	£225
J121		2c. on 5c. deep reddish purple/*bright yellow* (No. 59)	6·00	8·00
J122		3c. chestnut (No. 29a)	15·00	26·00
J123		4c. scarlet-vermilion (No. 30a)	15·00	11·00
J124		5c. dp reddish purple/*bright yellow* (No. 32*a*)	5·50	13·00
J125		6c. orange (No. 33a)	6·00	13·00
J126		8c. grey (No. 34a)	80·00	27·00
J127		8c. on 10c. bright blue (No. 60)	6·00	10·00
J128		12c. bright ultramarine (No. 36)	6·00	32·00
J129		20c. dull purple and orange	18·00	18·00
J130		25c. green and deep purple	8·00	45·00
J131		30c. dull purple and black	8·50	40·00
J132		$3 green and brown-red/*green* (No. 43*a*)	90·00	£170
J119/32 *Set of 14*			£500	£600

1943. Stamps of Trengganu (Script wmk) optd with T **2**.

J133	**4**	1c. black (No. 26a)	18·00	20·00
		a. Chalk-surfaced paper	48·00	
J134		2c. green (No. 27a)	16·00	38·00
J135		2c. on 5c. bright reddish purple/*bright yellow* (No. 59)	9·50	23·00
J136		5c. bright reddish purple/*bright yellow* (No. 32*a*)	14·00	38·00
J137		6c. orange (No. 33a)	15·00	42·00
J138		8c. grey (No. 34a)	70·00	£120
J139		8c. on 10c. bright blue (No. 60)	28·00	55·00
J140		10c. bright blue	95·00	£250
J141		12c. bright ultramarine (No. 36)	18·00	50·00
J142		20c. dull purple and orange	23·00	50·00
J143		25c. green and deep purple	20·00	55·00
J144		30c. dull purple and black	24·00	55·00
J145		35c. carmine/*yellow*	24·00	75·00
J133/45 *Set of 13*			£350	£800

POSTAGE DUE STAMPS

1942 (Sept). Nos. D1/4 of Trengganu optd with T **1** sideways.

JD17	D **1**	1c. scarlet	50·00	85·00
JD18		4c. green	90·00	£130
		a. Brown opt	50·00	90·00
JD19		8c. yellow	14·00	50·00
JD20		10c. brown	14·00	50·00

The Trengganu 8c. postage due also exists overprinted with Type **16**, but this was not issued (*Price* £600 *unused*).

Trengganu was ceded to Thailand by the Japanese on 19 October 1943.

GENERAL ISSUES

The following stamps were produced for use throughout Malaya, except for Trengganu.

1942 (3 Apr). Stamps optd as T **1**.

(a) On Straits Settlements.

J146	**58**	1c. black (R.)	3·25	3·25
		a. Black opt	£400	£400

		b. Violet opt	£1200	£700
J147		2c. green (V.)	£3000	£2000
J148		2c. orange (R.)	3·00	2·25
		a. Black opt	£130	£140
		b. Violet opt	£250	£225
		c. Brown opt	£900	£650
J149		3c. green (R.)	2·75	2·25
		a. Black opt	£400	£400
		b. Violet opt	£1200	£750
J150		5c. brown (R.)	25·00	28·00
		a. Black opt	£550	£550
J151		8c. grey (R.)	5·50	2·25
		a. Pair, one without handstamp	†	£2500
		b. Black opt	£275	£275
J152		10c. dull purple (R.)	55·00	45·00
		a. Brown opt	£1000	£750
J153		12c. ultramarine (R.)	80·00	£130
J154		15c. ultramarine (R.)	3·50	3·75
		a. Violet opt	£750	£550
J155		30c. dull purple and orange (R.)	£3250	£3250
J156		40c. scarlet and dull purple (R.)	£120	95·00
		a. Brown opt	£850	£400
J157		50c. black/*emerald* (R.)	65·00	48·00
J158		$1 black and red/*blue* (R.)	90·00	75·00
J159		$2 green and scarlet (R.)	£150	£180
J160		$5 green and red/*emerald* (R.)	£190	£225

The 2c. green is known with the overprint in red, but this was not available to the public (*Price, £350 unused*).

(b) On Negri Sembilan.

J161	**6**	1c. black (R.)	19·00	13·00
		a. Violet opt	22·00	20·00
		b. Brown opt	13·00	17·00
		c. Black opt	60·00	38·00
		d. Pair. Nos. J161/a	£275	
		e. Pair. Nos. J161 and J161b	£350	
J162		2c. orange (R.)	30·00	21·00
		a. Violet opt	55·00	28·00
		b. Black opt	38·00	29·00
		c. Brown opt	65·00	55·00
J163		3c. green (R.)	42·00	21·00
		a. Violet opt	25·00	29·00
		c. Brown opt	£180	60·00
		d. Black opt	70·00	50·00
J164		5c. brown	42·00	21·00
		a. Pair, one without opt	£2000	
		b. Brown opt	17·00	15·00
		c. Red opt	17·00	11·00
		d. Violet opt	60·00	42·00
		e. Pair. Nos. J164c/d	£375	
J165		6c. grey	£160	£130
		a. Brown opt	£325	£325
J166		8c. scarlet (*ordinary paper*)	£160	£140
J167		10c. dull purple	£275	£250
		a. Red opt	£475	£350
		b. Brown opt	£650	£450
J168		12c. bright ultramarine (Br.)	£1800	£1800
J169		15c. ultramarine (R.)	26·00	8·00
		a. Violet opt	£110	30·00
		b. Brown opt	32·00	12·00
J170		25c. dull purple and scarlet	28·00	38·00
		a. Red opt	65·00	80·00
		b. Brown opt	£600	£450
J171		30c. dull purple and orange	£275	£225
		a. Brown opt	£1500	£1100
J172		40c. scarlet and dull purple	£1700	£1100
		a. Brown opt	£1300	£1000
J173		50c. black/*emerald*	£1400	£1400
J174		$1 black and red/*blue*	£225	£250
		a. Red opt	£180	£200
		b. Brown opt	£425	£425
J175		$5 green and red/*emerald*	£650	£750
		a. Red opt	£1300	£1300

Nos. J161a and J163a exist with the handstamped overprint sideways.

(c) On Pahang.

J176	**15**	1c. black	55·00	50·00
		a. Red opt	60·00	55·00
		b. Violet opt	£400	£275
		c. Brown opt	£300	£225
J177		3c. green	£450	£325
		a. Red opt	£225	£275
		b. Violet opt	£650	£475
J178		5c. brown	16·00	12·00
		a. Red opt	£250	£110
		b. Brown opt	£300	£110
		c. Violet opt	£500	£275
		d. Pair. Nos. J178/b	£850	
J179		8c. grey	£1200	£900
J180		8c. scarlet	21·00	8·00
		a. Red opt	£110	50·00
		b. Violet opt	£100	55·00
		c. Brown opt	£110	65·00
		d. Pair. Nos. J180a/c	£450	
J181		10c. dull purple	£400	£160
		a. Red opt	£350	£225
		b. Brown opt	£400	£250
J182		12c. bright ultramarine	£2250	£2250
		a. Red opt	£1200	£1200
J183		15c. ultramarine	£150	£110
		a. Red opt	£450	£250
		b. Violet opt	£750	£500
		c. Brown opt	£550	£325
J184		25c. dull purple and scarlet	22·00	29·00
J185		30c. dull purple and orange	15·00	29·00
		a. Red opt	£140	£170
J186		40c. scarlet and dull purple	24·00	35·00
		a. Brown opt	£500	£325
		b. Red opt	85·00	90·00
J187		50c. black/*emerald*	£1400	£1400
		a. Red opt	£1500	£1500
J188		$1 black and red/*blue* (R.)	£150	£160
		a. Black opt	£300	£300
		b. Brown opt	£700	£700
J189		$5 green and red/*emerald*	£750	£850
		a. Red opt	£1000	£1100

(d) On Perak.

J190	**51**	1c. black	65·00	40·00
		a. Violet opt	£300	£120
		b. Brown opt	85·00	80·00
J191		2c. orange	30·00	20·00
		a. Violet opt	75·00	70·00
		b. Red opt	60·00	40·00
		c. Brown opt	60·00	55·00
J192		3c. green	28·00	28·00
		a. Violet opt	£550	£325
		b. Brown opt	£180	£150
		c. Red opt	£350	£250
J193		5c. brown	8·50	6·00
		a. Pair, one without opt	£1300	
		b. Brown opt	45·00	32·00
		c. Violet opt	£325	£200
		d. Red opt	£225	£200
J194		8c. grey	85·00	50·00
		a. Red opt	£475	£225
		b. Brown opt	£400	£250
J195		8c. scarlet	42·00	42·00
		a. Violet opt	£600	£325
J196		10c. dull purple	26·00	24·00
		a. Red opt	£400	£225
J197		12c. bright ultramarine	£250	£225
J198		15c. ultramarine	24·00	32·00
		a. Red opt	£250	£200
		b. Violet opt	£550	£325
		c. Brown opt	£400	£275
J199		25c. dull purple and scarlet	14·00	27·00
		a. Red opt	£325	
J200		30c. dull purple and orange (No. 116a)	17·00	32·00
		a. Pair, one without opt	£2000	
		b. Brown opt	£800	£450
		c. Red opt	40·00	60·00
		ca. Pair, one without opt	£2750	
J201		40c. scarlet and dull purple	£600	£375
		a. Brown opt	£550	£450
J202		50c. black/*emerald*	45·00	50·00
		a. Red opt	60·00	65·00
		b. Brown opt	£500	£350
J203		$1 black and red/*blue*	£500	£400
		a. Brown opt	£450	£375
J204		$2 green and scarlet	£4250	£4250
J205		$5 green and red/*emerald*	£500	
		a. Brown opt	£2000	

(e) On Selangor.

J206	**46**	1c. black, S	12·00	27·00
		a. Red opt, SU	45·00	38·00
		b. Violet opt, SU	50·00	48·00
J207		2c. green, SU	£2000	£1300
		a. Violet opt, SU	£2500	£1300
J208		2c. orange (P 14×14½), S	£100	60·00
		a. Red opt, U	£200	£170
		b. Violet opt, U	£225	£160
		c. Brown opt, S	85·00	80·00
J209		2c. orange (P 14), S	£120	80·00
		a. Red opt, U	£225	£170
		b. Violet opt, U	£425	£170
		c. Brown opt, S	—	£170
J210		3c. green, SU	23·00	15·00
		a. Red opt, SU	19·00	15·00
		b. Violet opt, SU	75·00	50·00
		c. Brown opt, SU	18·00	15·00
J211		5c. brown, SU	6·00	5·50
		a. Red opt, SU	15·00	16·00
		b. Violet opt, SU	21·00	22·00
		c. Brown opt, SU	60·00	50·00
J212		6c. scarlet, SU	£425	£425
		a. Red opt, S	£200	£250
		b. Brown opt, S	£950	£950
J213		8c. grey, S	22·00	17·00

		a. Red opt, SU	65·00	40·00
		b. Violet opt, U	40·00	35·00
		c. Brown opt, S	£180	75·00
J214		10c. dull purple, S	15·00	21·00
		a. Red opt, S	85·00	65·00
		b. Brown opt, S	£180	95·00
J215		12c. bright ultramarine, S	70·00	80·00
		a. Red opt, S	£130	£140
		b. Brown opt, S	£140	£130
J216		15c. ultramarine, S	17·00	23·00
		a. Red opt, SU	65·00	65·00
		b. Violet opt, U	£170	£100
		c. Brown opt, S	£120	70·00
J217		25c. dull purple and scarlet, S	90·00	£120
		a. Red opt, S	65·00	85·00
J218		30c. dull purple and orange, S (No. 80a)	11·00	24·00
		a. Brown opt, S	£500	£300
J219		40c. scarlet and dull purple, S	£150	£150
		a. Brown opt, S	£425	£225
		b. Red opt, S	£350	
J220		50c. black/*emerald*, S	£160	£170
		a. Red opt, S	£170	£180
		b. Brown opt, S	£650	£450
J221	**48**	$1 black and red/*blue*	35·00	48·00
		a. Red opt	£120	£150
J222		$2 green and scarlet	38·00	65·00
		a. Pair, one without opt	£2000	
		b. Red opt	£850	£900
J223		$5 green and red/*emerald*	75·00	95·00

On T **46** the overprint is normally sideways (with "top" to either right or left), but on T **48** it is always upright.

S = Sideways.
U = Upright.
SU = Sideways or upright (our prices being for the cheaper).

Specialists recognise nine slightly different chops as Type **1**. Initial supplies with the overprint in red were produced at Singapore. Later overprintings took place at Kuala Lumpur in violet, red or brown and finally, black. No. J155 was from the Kuala Lumpur printing only. Except where noted, these overprints were usedwidely in Malaya and, in some instances, Sumatra.

The following stamps also exist with this overprint, but were not available to the public:

Straits Settlements (in red) 6, 25c.
Kelantan (in black) 10c.
Negri Sembilan 2c. green (Blk. or Brn.), 4c. (Blk.), 6c. scarlet (Blk.), 8c. grey (Blk.), 12c. (Blk.), $2 (Blk. or Brn.).
Pahang (in black, 2c. also in brown) 2, 4, 6c., $2.
Perak 2c. green (R.), 6c. (Blk.).
Selangor 4c. (Blk.).

1942 (May). Optd with T **16**.

(a) On Straits Settlements.

J224	**58**	2c. orange	2·75	60
		a. Opt inverted	15·00	24·00
		b. Opt double, one inverted	55·00	65·00
J225		3c. green	50·00	65·00
J226		8c. grey	8·50	3·75
		a. Opt inverted	21·00	38·00
J227		15c. blue	19·00	12·00
J224/7 *Set of* 4			70·00	75·00

(b) On Negri Sembilan.

J228	**6**	1c. black (*Thin striated paper*)	2·50	60
		a. Opt inverted	9·00	26·00
		b. Opt double, one inverted	35·00	55·00
		c. Chalk-surfaced paper	3·50	1·00
J229		2c. orange	9·00	50
J230		3c. green (No. 24a)	7·00	50
J231		5c. brown	1·75	4·00
J232		6c. grey	4·25	3·25
		a. Opt inverted	†	£1700
		b. Stop omitted at right (R. 10/4)	£130	£140
J233		8c. scarlet (*Ordinary paper*)	9·00	1·25
J234		10c. dull purple	3·25	2·50
J235		15c. ultramarine	18·00	2·50
J236		25c. dull purple and scarlet (*Ordinary paper*)	7·00	20·00
J237		30c. dull purple and orange (*Thin striated paper*)	8·50	3·00
J238		$1 black and red/*blue*	80·00	£100
J228/38 *Set of* 11			£130	£120

(c) On Pahang.

J239	**15**	1c. black (*Thin striated paper*)	3·50	4·00
		a. Opt omitted (in pair with normal)	£550	
J240		5c. brown	1·25	70
J241		8c. scarlet	28·00	2·75
		a. Opt omitted (in pair with normal)	£1600	
J242		10c. dull purple	13·00	8·50
J243		12c. bright ultramarine	3·75	18·00
J244		25c. dull purple and scarlet (*Thin striated paper*)	6·50	26·00
J245		30c. dull purple and orange (No. 41a)	3·75	13·00
J239/45 *Set of* 7			55·00	65·00

(d) On Perak.

J246	**51**	2c. orange (No. 105)	4·50	3·25
		a. Opt inverted	55·00	55·00
J247		3c. green (No. 106a)	1·50	1·50
		a. Opt inverted	18·00	28·00
		b. Opt omitted (in pair with normal)	£600	
J248		8c. scarlet (No. 111)	70	50
		a. Opt inverted	4·50	7·00
		b. Opt double, one inverted	£225	£250
		c. Opt omitted (in horiz pair with normal)	£400	
J249		10c. dull purple (*Thin striated paper*)	18·00	8·00
J250		15c. ultramarine	9·00	2·00
J251		50c. black/*emerald*	4·00	6·00
J252		$1 black and red/*blue*	£500	£550
J253		$5 green and red/*emerald*	50·00	80·00
		a. Opt inverted	£300	£400
J246/53 *Set of* 8			£550	£600

(e) On Selangor.

J254	**46**	3c. green (No. 71a)	2·25	4·50
		a. Ordinary paper		
J255		12c. bright ultramarine	1·50	17·00
J256		15c. ultramarine	9·00	1·50
J257		40c. scarlet and dull purple	2·25	6·00
J258	**48**	$2 green and scarlet	11·00	50·00
J254/8 *Set of* 5			23·00	70·00

On T **46** the overprint is sideways, with "top" to left or right.

The following stamps also exist with this overprint, but were not available to the public.

Perak 1, 5, 30c. (*Price for set of* 3 *£400 unused*).
Selangor 1, 5, 10, 30c., $1, $5 (*Price for set of* 6 *£750 unused*).

DAI NIPPON
2602
MALAYA
2 Cents
(**17**)

DAI NIPPON
YUBIN
2 Cents
(**18**) "Japanese Postal Service"

1942 (Nov). No. 108 of Perak surch with T **17**.

J259	**51**	2c. on 5c. brown	1·75	4·00
		a. Inverted "s" in "Cents" (R. 3/5)	65·00	90·00

1942 (Nov). Perak stamps surch or opt only, as in T **18**.

J260	**51**	1c. black (*Thin striated paper*)	7·00	11·00
		a. Opt inverted	19·00	40·00
J261		2c. on 5c. brown	2·00	6·50
		a. "DAI NIPPON YUBIN" inverted	17·00	40·00
		b. Ditto and "2 Cents" omitted	45·00	65·00
		c. Inverted "s" in "Cents" (R. 3/5)	70·00	£130
J262		8c. scarlet (No. 111)	7·50	2·75
		a. Opt inverted	13·00	25·00
J260/2 *Set of* 3			15·00	18·00

A similar overprint exists on the Selangor 3c. but this was not available to the public (*Price £350 unused*).

On 8 December 1942 contemporary Japanese 3, 5, 8 and 25s. stamps were issued without overprint in Malaya and the 1, 2, 4, 6, 7, 10, 30 and 50s. and 1y. values followed on 15 February 1943.

大日本郵便
(**19**)

6cts. (**20**)   6 cts. (**21**)   2 Cents (**22**)

6 cts. (**23**) $1.00 (**24**)

1942 (4 Dec)–**44**. Stamps of various Malayan territories optd "Japanese Postal Service" in Kanji characters as T **2** or **19**, some additionally surch as T **20** to **24**.

(a) Stamps of Straits Settlements optd with T **2**.

J263	**58**	8c. grey (Blk.) (1943)	1·40	50
		a. Opt inverted	55·00	70·00
		b. Opt omitted (in pair with normal)	£850	
		c. Red opt	2·50	3·50
J264		12c. ultramarine (1943)	1·75	13·00
J265		40c. scarlet and dull purple (1943)	3·25	6·00
J263/5 *Set of* 3			5·75	18·00

(b) Stamps of Negri Sembilan optd with T **2** or surch also.

J266 **6** 1c. black (*Thin striated paper*) 75 3·50
a. Opt inverted 12·00 29·00
b. Sideways second character 32·00 35·00
ba. Opt inverted with sideways second character £750
c. Chalk-surfaced paper 1·25 4·00
J267 2c. on 5c. brown (surch as T **20**) 1·00 2·00
J268 6c. on 5c. brown (surch T **21**) (1943) 40 2·25
a. Opt Type **2** and surch as Type **21** both inverted £225 £225
J269 25c. dull purple and scarlet (*Ordinary paper*) (1943) 1·10 18·00
J266/9 *Set of 4* 3·00 23·00

(c) Stamps of Pahang optd with T **2** and surch also.

J270 **15** 6c. on 5c. brown (surch T **20**) (1943) 50 75
J271 6c. on 5c. brown (surch T **21**) (1943) 1·00 2·00

(d) Stamps of Perak optd with T **2** *or* surch also.

J272 **51** 1c. black (*Thin striated paper*) 1·25 70
a. Sideways second character £225 £250
J273 2c. on 5c. brown (surch as T **20**) 1·00 50
a. Opt Type **2** and surch Type **20** both inverted 20·00 35·00
b. Opt Type **2** inverted 20·00 35·00
c. Sideways second character 50·00 55·00
J274 2c. on 5c. brown (surch T **22**) 60 50
a. Surch Type **22** inverted 18·00 32·00
b. Opt Type **2** and surch Type **22** both inverted 27·00 38·00
c. Sideways second character 25·00 35·00
ca. Surch Type **22** inverted £1400
cb. Opt Type **2** with sideways second character and surch Type **22** both inverted £1400
J275 5c. brown 55 65
a. Opt inverted 42·00 48·00
b. Sideways second character £550 £400
J276 8c. scarlet (No. 111) 75 2·50
a. Opt inverted 17·00 29·00
b. Sideways second character 50·00 70·00
ba. Opt inverted with sideways second character £750
c. Opt omitted (in pair with normal) £1200
J277 10c. dull purple (No. 112) (1943) 75 60
a. Thin striated paper 60 50
J278 30c. dull purple and orange (No. 116a) (1943) 5·50 8·00
J279 50c. black/*emerald* (1943) 4·50 23·00
J280 $5 green and red/emerald (1943) 70·00 £120
J272/80 *Set of 9* 75·00 £140

(e) Stamps of Selangor optd with T 2 (sideways on T **46**).

J281 **46** 1c. black (No. 68) (1943) 1·25 3·50
a. Thin striated paper 1·00 3·50
J282 3c. green (No. 71a) 40 45·00
a. Sideways second character 17·00 27·00
J283 12c. bright ultramarine 45 1·60
a. Sideways second character 70·00 85·00
J284 15c. ultramarine 4·50 3·25
a. Sideways second character 50·00 55·00
J285 **48** $1 black and red/*blue* 3·00 24·00
a. Opt inverted £225 £225
b. Sideways second character £375 £450
J286 $2 green and scarlet (1943) 10·00 50·00
J287 $5 green and red/*emerald* (1943) 22·00 80·00
a. Opt inverted £250 £300
J281/7 *Set of 7* 38·00 £140

(f) Stamps of Selangor optd with T **19** or surch also.

J288 **46** 1c. black (No. 68) (R.) (1943) 50 60
a. Thin striated paper 35 50
J289 2c. on 5c. brown (surch as T **21**) (R.) (1943) 2·00 50
J290 3c. on 5c. brown (surch as T **21**) (1943) 30 5·00
a. "s" in "cts." inverted (R. 4/3) 30·00 75·00
b. Comma after "cts" (R. 9/3) 30·00 75·00
J291 5c. brown (R.) (1944) 2·50 5·50
J292 6c. on 5c. brown (surch T **21**) (1944) 1·25 1·75
J293 6c. on 5c. brown (surch T **23**) (1944) 50 70
a. "6" inverted (R. 7/8) £950
b. Full stop between "6" and "cts" (R. 8/6)
c. Surch and opt double £550
J294 15c. ultramarine 4·00 4·00
J295 $1 on 10c. dull purple (surch T **24**) (18.12.1944) 40 1·25
J296 $1.50 on 30c. dull purple and orange (No. 80a) (surch T **24**) (18.12.1944) 40 1·25
J288/96 *Set of 9* 10·50 18·00

The error showing the second character in Type **2** sideways occurred on R. 6/3 in the first of four settings only.

The 2c. orange, 3c. and 8c. grey of Perak also exist overprinted with Type **2**, but these stamps were not available to the public (*Price for set of 3 £100 unused*).

Examples of No. J275 are known postally used from the Shan States (part of pre-war Burma).

25 Tapping Rubber

26 Fruit

27 Tin dredger

28 War Memorial, Bukit Bartok, Singapore

29 Fishing village

30 Japanese shrine, Singapore

31 Sago Palms

32 Straits of Johore

33 Malay Mosque, Kuala

(Litho Kolff & Co, Batavia)

1943 (29 Apr–1 Oct). P 12½.

J297 **25** 1c. grey-green (1 Oct) 1·75 55
J298 **26** 2c. pale emerald (1 June) 1·00 20
J299 **25** 3c. drab (1 Oct) 1·00 20
J300 **27** 4c. carmine-rose 3·00 20
J301 **28** 8c. dull blue 50 20
J302 **29** 10c. brown-purple (1 Oct) 1·25 20
J303 **30** 15c. violet (1 Oct) 1·75 5·00
J304 **31** 30c. olive-green (1 Oct) 1·50 35
J305 **32** 50c. blue (1 Oct) 5·00 5·00
J306 **33** 70c. blue (1 Oct) 22·00 14·00
J297/306 *Set of 10* 35·00 23·00

The 2c. and 4c. values exist, printed by typography, in paler shades either imperforate or rouletted. It is suggested that these may have been available in Singapore at the very end of the Japanese Occupation.

34 Ploughman

35 Rice-Planting

1943 (1 Sept). Savings Campaign. Litho. P 12½.

J307 **34** 8c. violet 9·50 2·75
J308 15c. scarlet 6·50 2·75

(Des Hon Chin. Litho)

1944 (15 Feb). "Re-birth" of Malaya. P 12½.

J309 **35** 8c. rose-red 17·00 3·25
J310 15c. magenta 4·00 3·25

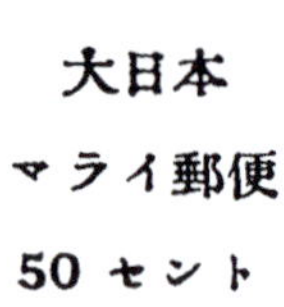

(36)

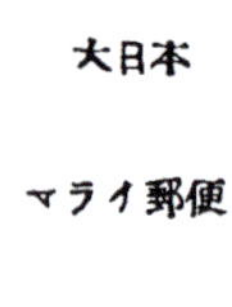

(37)

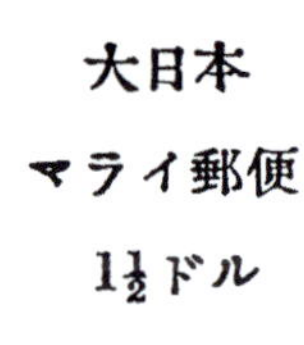

(38)

1944 (16 Dec). Stamps intended for use on Red Cross letters. Surch with T **36/8** in red.

(a) On Straits Settlements.

J311 **58** 50c. on 50c. black/*emerald* 10·00 24·00
J312 $1 on $1 black and red/*blue* 22·00 35·00
J313 $1.50 on $2 green and scarlet 32·00 70·00

(b) On Johore.

J314	**29**	50c. on 50c. dull purple and red (No. 119a)	7·00	20·00
J315		$1.50 on $2 green and carmine (No. 121a)	4·00	12·00

(c) On Selangor.

J316	**48**	$1 on $1 black and red/*blue*	3·50	14·00
J317		$1.50 on $2 green and scarlet	5·00	20·00
J311/17 *Set of 7*			75·00	£180

Nos. J311/17 were issued in Singapore but were withdrawn after one day, probably because supplies of Nos. J295/6 were received and issued on the 18 December.

A similar 6c. surcharge exists on the Straits Settlements 5c. but this was not available to the public (*Price £550 unused*).

STAMP BOOKLETS

1942. Nos. SB3/4 of Perak and SB2 of Selangor with covers optd with T **1**.

SB1	$1 booklet containing twenty 5c. (No. J193) in blocks of 10	£3000
SB2	$1.30 booklet containing 5c. and 8c. (Nos. J193/4), each in block of 10	£3000
SB3	$1.30 booklet containing 5c. and 8c. (Nos. J211 and J213), each in block of 10	£3000

POSTAGE DUE STAMPS

Postage Due stamps of the Malayan Postal Union overprinted.

1942 (3 Apr). Handstamped as T **1** in black.

JD21	D **1**	1c. slate-purple	12·00	29·00
		a. Red opt	£170	£170
		b. Brown opt	£140	£150
JD22		3c. green	75·00	80·00
		a. Red opt	£325	£350
JD23		4c. green	70·00	45·00
		a. Red opt	55·00	55·00
		b. Brown opt	£180	£180
JD24		8c. scarlet	£130	£100
		a. Red opt	£180	£140
		b. Brown opt	£250	£250
JD25		10c. yellow-orange	30·00	50·00
		a. Red opt	£325	£325
		b. Brown opt	90·00	95·00
JD26		12c. ultramarine	25·00	50·00
		a. Red opt	£350	£350
JD27		50c. black	70·00	95·00
		a. Red opt	£550	£600

1942. Optd with T **16**.

JD28	D **1**	1c. slate-purple	3·50	10·00
JD29		3c. green	19·00	25·00
JD30		4c. green	17·00	11·00
JD31		8c. scarlet	28·00	22·00
JD32		10c. yellow-orange	2·00	17·00
JD33		12c. ultramarine	1·75	38·00
JD28/33 *Set of 6*			65·00	£110

The 9c. and 15c. also exist with this overprint, but these were not issued (*Price £700 each unused*).

1943–45. Optd with T **2**.

JD34	D **1**	1c. slate-purple	2·25	4·75
JD35		3c. green	2·25	4·50
		a. Opt omitted (in pair with normal)	£800	
JD36		4c. green	60·00	48·00
JD37		5c. scarlet	1·50	5·00
JD38		9c. yellow-orange	80	8·50
		a. Opt inverted	22·00	28·00
JD39		10c. yellow-orange	2·25	9·00
		a. Opt inverted	80·00	80·00
JD40		12c. ultramarine	2·25	17·00
JD41		15c. ultramarine	2·25	9·00
JD34/41 *Set of 8*			65·00	95·00

IX. THAI OCCUPATION OF MALAYA

Stamps issued for use in the Malay States of Kedah (renamed Syburi), Kelantan, Perlis and Trengganu, ceded by Japan to Thailand on 19 October 1943. British rule was restored on 9 (Kelantan), 18 (Perlis), 22 (Kedah) and 24 September 1945 (Trengganu). Nos. TM1/6 continued to be used for postage until replaced by the overprinted B.M.A. Malaya issues on 10 October 1945.

PRICES FOR STAMPS ON COVER	
Nos. TK1/5	*from* × 30
Nos. TM1/6	*from* × 25
Nos. TT1/35	—

KELANTAN

TK **1**

(Typo Kelantan Ptg Dept, Khota Baru)

1943 (15 Nov). Handstamped with State arms in violet. No gum. P 11.

TK1	TK **1**	1c. black	£200	£300
TK2		2c. black	£250	£250
		a. Handstamp omitted	£700	
TK3		4c. black	£250	£300
		a. Handstamp omitted	£850	
TK4		8c. black	£250	£250
		a. Handstamp omitted	£550	
TK5		10c. black	£350	£450
TK1/5 *Set of 5*			£1200	£1400

Nos. TK1/5 were printed in sheets of 84 (12×7) and have sheet watermarks in the form of "STANDARD" in block capitals with curved "CROWN" above and "AGENTS" below in double-lined capitals. This watermark occurs four times in the sheet.

Sheets were imperforate at top and left so that stamps exist imperforate at top, left or at top and left.

Genuine examples have a solid star at the top centre of the arms, as shown in Type TK **1**. Examples with a hollow outline star in this position are forgeries.

Similar stamps, but with red handstamps, were for fiscal use.

GENERAL ISSUE

TM **1** War Memorial

(Litho Defence Ministry, Bangkok)

1944 (15 Jan–4 Mar). Thick opaque, or thin semi-transparent paper. Gummed or ungummed. P 12½.

TM1	TM **1**	1c. yellow (4 Mar)	30·00	32·00
TM2		2c. red-brown	12·00	20·00
		a. Imperf (pair)	£900	
		b. Perf 12½×11	20·00	20·00
TM3		3c. green (4 Mar)	20·00	38·00
		a. Perf 12½×11	30·00	42·00
TM4		4c. purple (4 Mar)	14·00	28·00
		a. Perf 12½×11	20·00	35·00
TM5		8c. carmine (4 Mar)	14·00	20·00
		a. Perf 12½×11	20·00	20·00
TM6		15c. blue (4 Mar)	38·00	60·00
		a. Perf 12½×11	42·00	60·00
TM1/6 *Set of 6*			£110	£180

5c. and 10c. stamps in this design were prepared, but never issued.

TRENGGANU

TRENGGANU

(TT **1**)

(Overprinted at Trengganu Survey Office)

1944 (1 Oct). Various stamps optd with Type TT **1**.

(a) On Trengganu without Japanese opt.

TT1	**4**	1c. black (26a)		
TT2		30c. dull purple and black (39)		

(b) On Trengganu stamps optd as T **1** of Japanese Occupation.

TT2*a*	**4**	1c. black (J97)	—	£2500
TT3		8c. grey (J104)	£750	£500

(c) On stamps optd with T **16** of Japanese Occupation.

(i) Pahang.

TT4	**15**	12c. bright ultramarine (J243)	£650	£170

(ii) Trengganu.

TT5	**4**	2c. on 5c. deep reddish purple/*bright yellow* (J121)*	£700	£700

TT6		8c. on 10c. bright blue (J127) (inverted)	£600	£600
TT7		12c. bright ultramarine (J128) (inverted)	£650	£650

*This is spelt "TRENGANU" with one "G".

(d) On stamps optd with T **2** of Japanese Occupation.

(i) Straits Settlements.

TT8	**58**	12c. ultramarine (J264)	£650	£650
TT9		40c. scarlet and dull purple (J265)	£650	£650

(ii) Negri Sembilan.

TT9*a*	**6**	25c. dull purple and scarlet (J269)	—	£2500

(iii) Pahang.

TT10	**15**	6c. on 5c. brown (J271)		

(iv) Perak.

TT11	**51**	1c. black (J272)		
TT12		10c. dull purple (J277)		
TT13		30c. dull purple and orange (J278)	£1200	£650
TT13*a*		50c. black/*emerald* (J279)	—	£2500

(v) Selangor.

TT14	**46**	3c. green (J282)	£450	£450
TT15		12c. brt ultramarine (J283) (L. to R.)	£190	£110
TT16		12c. brt ultramarine (J283) (R. to L.)	£180	£110
		a. Sideways second character	£2750	£2750

(e) On Selangor stamps optd with T **19** of Japanese Occupation.

TT16*b*	**46**	1c. black (J288)	—	£2500
TT17		2c. on 5c. brown (J289)	£650	£650
TT18		3c. on 5c. brown (J290)	£650	£650

(f) On pictorials of 1943 (Nos. J297/306).

TT19	**25**	1c. grey-green	£475	£375
TT20	**26**	2c. pale emerald	£475	£190
TT21	**25**	3c. drab	£275	£140
TT22	–	4c. carmine-rose	£425	£190
TT23	–	8c. dull blue	£700	£650
TT24	–	10c. brown-purple	£1500	£800
TT25	**27**	15c. violet	£425	£190
TT26	–	30c. olive-green	£650	£170
TT27	–	50c. blue	£650	£325
TT28	–	70c. blue	£1400	£900

(g) On Savings Campaign stamps (Nos. J307/8).

TT29	**28**	8c. violet	£700	£650
TT30		15c. scarlet	£475	£180

(h) On stamps of Japan.

TT31	–	3s. green (No. 319)		
TT32	–	5s. claret (No. 396)	£650	£475
TT33	–	25c. brown and chocolate (No. 329)	£450	£140
TT34	–	30c. blue-green (No. 330)	£650	£190

(i) On Trengganu Postage Due stamp optd with T **1** of Japanese Occupation.

TT35	D **1**	1c. scarlet (JD17)	£3500	£3500

X. LABUAN

CROWN COLONY

The island of Labuan, off the northern coast of Borneo, was ceded to Great Britain by the Sultan of Brunei in December 1846.

Stamps of STRAITS SETTLEMENTS were used from 1867 until 1879. Covers of 1864 and 1865 are known from Labuan franked with stamps of INDIA or HONG KONG.

PRICES FOR STAMPS ON COVER

Nos. 1/4	—
Nos. 5/10	*from* × 50
Nos. 11/13	—
Nos. 14/21	*from* × 40
Nos. 22/5	—
Nos. 26/35	*from* × 50
Nos. 36/8	—
Nos. 39/47	*from* × 100
Nos. 49/50	*from* × 15
Nos. 51/7	*from* × 60
Nos. 62/74	*from* × 15
Nos. 75/9	*from* × 40
Nos. 80/8	*from* × 20
Nos. 89/97	*from* × 15
Nos. 98/116	*from* × 10
Nos. 117/28	*from* × 30
Nos. 129/37	*from* × 10
Nos. 138/42	—
Nos. D1/9	*from* × 30

1

8
(2)

(3)

(Recess D.L.R.)

1879 (May). Wmk CA over Crown, sideways. P 14.

1	**1**	2c. blue-green	£1300	£850
2		6c. orange-brown	£200	£180
		a. No dot at upper left (R. 2/4)	£475	£425
3		12c. carmine	£1700	£750
		a. No right foot to second Chinese character (R. 2/3)	£3750	£1500
4		16c. blue	65·00	£150

This watermark is always found sideways, and extends over two stamps, a single specimen showing only a portion of the Crown or the letters CA, these being tall and far apart. This paper was chiefly used for long fiscal stamps.

1880 (Jan)–**82**. Wmk Crown CC (reversed on 8c.). P 14.

5	**1**	2c. yellow-green	25·00	38·00
		w. Wnk inverted	£130	
		x. Wmk reversed	50·00	65·00
		y. Wmk inverted and reversed	95·00	95·00
6		6c. orange-brown	£110	£120
		a. No dot at upper left	£225	£225
		w. Wmk inverted	£225	
7		8c. carmine (4.82)	£110	£110
		a. No dot at lower left (R. 2/5)	£200	£200
		x. Wmk normal (not reversed)	£300	£300
8		10c. brown	£170	85·00
		w. Wmk inverted	£130	90·00
		x. Wmk reversed		
9		12c. carmine	£275	£350
		a. No right foot to second Chinese character	£500	£600
		w. Wmk inverted	£450	
		x. Wmk reversed	£325	£350
		y. Wmk inverted and reversed	£475	
10		16c. blue (1881)	90·00	90·00
		w. Wmk inverted	£190	£190
		x. Wmk reversed	£160	£170
		y. Wmk inverted and reversed	£275	
5/10 *Set of* 6			£650	£700

1880 (Aug).

(a) No. 9 surch with T **2** in black and with the original value obliterated by manuscript bar in red or black.

11	8c. on 12c. carmine	£1600	£850
	a. Type **2** inverted	£1900	£1000
	b. "12" not obliterated	£3250	£1800
	c. As b. with Type **2** inverted		
	d. No right foot to second Chinese character	£3250	£1500
	x. Wmk reversed	£1600	£850

(b) No. 4 surch with two upright figures and No. 9 surch with two at right angles as T **3**.

12	6c. on 16c. blue (R.)	£2750	£1000
	a. With one "6" only		
13	8c. on 12c. carmine	£2000	£1200
	a. Both "8's" upright		
	b. Upright "8" inverted	£2000	£1300
	c. No right foot to second Chinese character	£3500	£1900
	w. Wmk inverted	†	£1800
	x. Wmk reversed	£2000	£1200
	y. Wmk inverted and reversed		

EIGHT CENTS
(4)

Eight Cents
(5)

(6)

1881 (Mar). No. 9 handstamped with T **4**.

14	8c. on 12c. carmine	£375	£425
	a. No right foot to second Chinese character	£750	£850
	w. Wmk inverted	£500	
	x. Wmk reversed	£350	£400

1881 (June). No. 9 surch with T **5**.

15	8c. on 12c. carmine	£120	£130
	a. Surch double	£1700	£1700

		b. Surch inverted	£12000	
		c. "Eighr"	£18000	
		d. No right foot to second Chinese character	£275	£325
		w. Wmk inverted	£325	£325
		x. Wmk reversed	£120	£130

The error "Eighr" occurred on R. 2/1 of the first printing, but was soon corrected.

Only one sheet of 10 has been reported of No. 15b, which also shows wmk inverted and reversed.

1883. Wmk Crown CA (reversed on 8c.). P 14.

17	**1**	2c. yellow-green	23·00	32·00
		a. Imperf between (horiz pair)	£13000	
		w. Wmk inverted	65·00	
		x. Wmk reversed	24·00	48·00
		y. Wmk inverted and reversed		
18		8c. carmine	£300	£110
		a. No dot at lower left	£550	£200
		x. Wmk normal (not reversed)	—	£275
19		10c. yellow-brown	42·00	50·00
		w. Wmk inverted	80·00	85·00
		x. Wmk reversed	80·00	85·00
20		16c. blue	£100	£190
21		40c. amber	21·00	£120
		x. Wmk reversed	30·00	£120
17/21 *Set of 5*			£425	£450

1883 (May). No. 10 surch "One Dollar A.S.H." by hand as T **6**.

22	**1**	$1 on 16c. blue (R.)	£4250	

The initials are those of the postmaster, Mr. A. S. Hamilton.

2 CENTS (7) 2 Cents (8) 2 Cents (9)

1885 (June). Nos. 18 and 10 handstamped as T **7**.

23	**1**	2c. on 8c. carmine	£225	£425
		a. No dot at lower left	£400	
		x. Wmk normal (not reversed)	£350	
24		2c. on 16c. blue	£950	£900
		w. Wmk inverted	£1100	
		x. Wmk reversed	†	£900

1885 (July). No. 20 surch as T **8**.

25	**1**	2c. on 16c. blue	£110	£160
		a. Surch double	†	£6500
		b. "2" inserted	£1800	
		w. Wmk inverted		

No. 25b shows a second "2" applied by a separate handstamp to correct indistinct impressions of Type **8**.

1885 (Sept). No. 18 handstamped diag as T **9**.

26	**1**	2c. on 8c. carmine	65·00	£120
		a. No dot at lower left	£150	£300
		x. Wmk normal (not reversed)	£160	

1885 (Sept)–**86**. Wmk Crown CA. P 14.

30	**1**	2c. rose-red	3·75	14·00
		a. Pale rose-red (1886)	3·75	12·00
		w. Wmk inverted	75·00	
		x. Wmk reversed	11·00	
31		8c. deep violet	29·00	8·00
		a. No dot at lower left	65·00	21·00
		b. Mauve (1886)	30·00	9·50
		ba. No dot at lower left	70·00	24·00
		bw. Wmk inverted	85·00	
		bx. Wmk reversed	70·00	
32		10c. sepia (1886)	19·00	50·00
		w. Wmk inverted	45·00	
		x. Wmk reversed	32·00	
33		16c. grey (1886)	£150	
		x. Wmk reversed	£110	£170
30/3 *Set of 4*			£140	£200
30s/3s Optd "Specimen" *Set of 4*			£500	

ISSUES OF BRITISH NORTH BORNEO COMPANY

From 1 January 1890 while remaining a Crown Colony, the administration of Labuan was transferred to the British North Borneo Co, which issued the following stamps.

6 Cents (10) Two CENTS (11) Six CENTS (12)

1891 (July)–**92**. Handstamped with T **10**.

34	**1**	6c. on 8c. deep violet (No. 31)	£150	£130
		a. Surch inverted	£275	£250
		b. Surch double	£500	
		c. Surch double, one inverted	£1000	
		d. "Cents" omitted	£450	£450
		f. Pair, one without surch, one surch inverted	£1800	
		g. No dot at lower left	£325	£300
35		6c. on 8c. mauve (No. 31*b*)	13·00	11·00
		a. Surch inverted	80·00	75·00
		b. Surch double, one inverted	£900	
		c. Surch double, both inverted	£900	
		d. "6" omitted	£500	
		e. Pair, one without surcharge	£1600	£1600
		f. Surch inverted with "Cents" omitted	£500	
		g. Pair, one without surch, one surch inverted	£1800	£1800
		h. Surch double	£325	
		i. No dot at lower left	27·00	27·00
		j. Imperf between (horiz pair)		
		w. Wmk inverted	65·00	65·00
		x. Wmk reversed	40·00	
36		6c. on 8c. mauve (R.) (No. 31*b*) (2.92)	£1100	£550
		a. Surch inverted	£1600	£700
		b. No dot at lower left	£2500	
37		6c. on 16c. blue (No. 4) (3.92)	£2250	£1800
		a. Surch inverted	£10000	£7000
38		6c. on 40c. amber (No. 21)	£12000	£5000
		a. Surch inverted	£11000	£8000

There are two different versions of Type **10** with the lines of the surcharge either 1 mm or 2 mm apart.

(Recess D.L.R.)

1892–93. No wmk. P 14.

39	**1**	2c. rose-lake	6·50	3·50
40		6c. bright green	9·00	4·50
		a. No dot at upper left	22·00	15·00
41		8c. violet	7·50	13·00
		a. Pale violet (1893)	8·00	13·00
43		10c. brown	17·00	8·00
		a. Sepia-brown (1893)	17·00	15·00
45		12c. bright blue	9·00	6·50
		a. No right foot to second Chinese character	21·00	18·00
46		16c. grey	9·00	13·00
47		40c. ochre	21·00	38·00
		a. Brown-buff (1893)	48·00	25·00
39/47 *Set of 7*			70·00	65·00

The 6c., 12c., 16c. and 40c. are in sheets of 10, as are all the earlier issues. The other values are in sheets of 30.

1892 (Dec). Nos. 47 and 46 surch locally as T **11** or **12**.

49	**1**	2c. on 40c. ochre (13 December)	£170	90·00
		a. Surch inverted	£450	£550
50		6c. on 16c. grey (20 December)	£375	£150
		a. Surch inverted	£550	£300
		b. Surch sideways	£550	£300
		c. Surch "Six Cents"	£1900	

There are 10 slightly different versions of each of these surcharges which were applied in settings of 5×2, although instances of single handstamps are known.

A "SIX CENTS" handstamp with Roman "I" in "SIX" (without dot) is a clandestine surcharge, although it can be found with genuine postmarks. It also exists sideways or inverted.

The "Six Cents" surcharge of No. 50c was handstamped onto examples where the Type **12** surcharge had failed to print or where it was partially or completely albino.

CANCELLED-TO-ORDER. Prices are separately indicated, in a third price column, for stamps showing the recognisable black bars remainder cancellation. Earlier issues of the Company administration were also so treated, but, as similar postal cancellations were used, these cannot be identified.

(Litho D.L.R.)

1894 (Apr). No wmk. P 14.

51	**1**	2c. carmine-pink	1·60	15·00	50
52		6c. bright green	18·00	42·00	50
		a. Imperf between (horiz pair)	£8000		
		b. No dot at upper left	32·00	80·00	1·25
53		8c. bright mauve	18·00	42·00	50
54		10c. brown	50·00	55·00	50
55		12c. pale blue	25·00	75·00	70

		a. No right foot to second Chinese character	50·00	£130	1·60
56		16c. grey	29·00	£130	50
57		40c. orange-buff	55·00	£140	50
51/7 *Set of 7*			£180	£450	3·25
51s/7s H/S "Specimen" *Set of 7*			£120		

Collectors are warned against forgeries of this issue.

PERFORATION. There are a number of small variations in the perforation of the Waterlow issues of 1894 to 1905 which we believe to be due to irregularity of the pins rather than different perforators.

In the following lists, stamps perf 12, 12½, 13 or compound are described as perf 12–13, stamps perf 13½, 14 or compound are described as perf 13½–14 and those perf 14½, 15 or compound are listed as perf 14½–15. In addition the 13½–14 perforation exists compound with 14½–15 and with 12–13, whilst perf 16 comes from a separate perforator.

13

LABUAN

40

CENTS

(14)

1894 (May)–**96**. T **24/32** of North Borneo (colours changed), with "LABUAN" engraved on vignette plate as T **13** (8, 12, 24c.) or horizontally (others). P 14½–15.

(a) Name and central part of design in black.

62	**24**	1c. grey-mauve	1·50	10·00	50
		a. Imperf between (vert pair)	†	†	£650
		b. Perf 13½–14	11·00	10·00	—
		ba. Imperf between (vert pair)	£1200	—	£475
		c. Perf 13½–14, comp 14½–15	27·00		
		d. Perf 13½–14, comp 12–13	26·00	13·00	90
		e. Perf 12–13			
63	**25**	2c. blue	2·50	10·00	50
		a. Imperf (pair)	£600		
		b. Perf 13½–14	4·50	10·00	—
		c. Perf 13½–14, comp 14½–15	28·00		
		d. Perf 13½–14, comp 12–13			
		e. Perf 12–13	£130		
64	**26**	3c. ochre	3·75	19·00	50
		a. Perf 13½–14	12·00	9·00	—
		b. Perf 13½–14, comp 14½–15			
		c. Perf 13½–14, comp 12–13	42·00		
		d. Perf 12–13			
65	**27**	5c. green	32·00	28·00	75
		a. Perf 13½–14	38·00	18·00	—
		ab. Imperf between (horiz pair)	£1200		
		b. Perf 13½–14, comp 12–13	55·00		
		c. Perf 12–13	£150		
67	**28**	6c. brown-lake	2·50	18·00	50
		a. Imperf (pair)	£600	†	£300
		b. Perf 13½–14	—	—	1·75
		c. Perf 13½–14, comp 14½–15	—	—	1·25
		d. Perf 13½–14, comp 12–13			
		e. Perf 12–13			
68	**29**	8c. rose-red	26·00	30·00	1·00
		a. Perf 13½–14	30·00	50·00	—
69		8c. pink (1896)	7·50	26·00	50
		a. Perf 13½–14	32·00	32·00	80
70	**30**	12c. orange-vermilion	23·00	48·00	50
		a. Imperf between (vert pair)	†	†	£3250
		b. Perf 13½–14	65·00	70·00	2·00
		c. Perf 12–13	£225		
		d. Perf 13½–14, comp 12–13	80·00	85·00	—
71	**31**	18c. olive-brown	22·00	55·00	50
		a. Perf 13½–14	70·00		
72		18c. olive-bistre (1896)	55·00	70·00	50
		a. Perf 13½–14	27·00	65·00	—
		b. Perf 13½–14, comp 12–13			
		c. Imperf between (vert pair)	†	†	£2000
		d. Perf 13½–14, comp 14½–15	†	†	1·75

(b) Name and central part in blue.

73	**32**	24c. pale mauve	26·00	60·00	50
		a. Perf 13½–14	25·00	55·00	—
		b. Perf 13½–14 comp 14½–15			
74		24c. dull lilac (1896)	15·00	48·00	50
		a. Perf 13½–14	14·00	48·00	50
62/74 *Set of 9*			95·00	£225	4·00
62s/74s Optd "Specimen" *Set of 9*			£150		

1895 (June). No. 83 of North Borneo ($1 inscr "STATE OF NORTH BORNEO") surch as T **14**.

75	**32c**	4c. on $1 scarlet	1·50	3·00	40
76		10c. on $1 scarlet	6·50	1·40	40
77		20c. on $1 scarlet	35·00	12·00	50
78		30c. on $1 scarlet	38·00	50·00	85
79		40c. on $1 scarlet	38·00	40·00	85
75/9 *Set of 5*			£110	95·00	2·75
75s/9s Optd "Specimen" *Set of 5*			80·00		

No. 76 exists with the figures of the surcharge 2½ mm away from "CENTS". The normal setting has a space of 4 mm. Examples of the narrow setting have, so far, only been seen on cancelled-to-order stamps (*Price* £20 *c.t.o.*).

LABUAN (15)

1846 JUBILEE 1896 (16)

4 CENTS (17)

1896. T **32a** to **32c** of North Borneo (as Nos. 81 to 83, but colours changed) optd with T **15**.

80	25c. green	28·00	35·00	60
	a. Opt omitted	25·00	—	1·50
	b. Imperf (pair)	—	—	60·00
	ba. Opt omitted	48·00		
81	50c. maroon	28·00	35·00	60
	a. Opt omitted	23·00	—	1·50
	b. Imperf (pair)	—	—	60·00
	ba. Opt omitted	45·00		
82	$1 blue	70·00	65·00	60
	a. Opt omitted	35·00	—	1·50
	b. Imperf (pair)	—	—	60·00
	ba. Opt omitted	50·00		
80s/2s Optd "Specimen" *Set of 3*		60·00		

Nos. 80/1 showing stamps either printed double or double, one inverted, are from waste sheets subsequently sold by the British North Borneo Company to collectors.

1896 (24 Sept). Jubilee of Cession of Labuan to Gt Britain. Nos. 62 to 68 optd with T **16**. P 14½–15.

83	1c. black and grey-mauve	21·00	22·00	80
	b. Opt in orange	£200	£200	20·00
	c. "JEBILEE" (R. 8/7)	£1200	£550	£300
	d. "JUBILE" (R. 3/10)	£2500		
	e. Perf 13½–14	27·00	22·00	—
	ea. Opt double	£375	£375	—
	eb. Opt in orange	£275	£200	†
	f. Perf 13½–14, comp 12–13	32·00	20·00	—
	fa. Opt in orange	—	£200	†
	g. Perf 12–13			
84	2c. black and blue	45·00	27·00	1·00
	a. Imperf horiz (vert pair)	£950	£1000	†
	b. "JEBILEE" (R. 8/7)	£1500	£1200	—
	c. "JUBILE" (R. 3/10)	£2750	£2750	
	d. Perf 13½–14	42·00	20·00	—
	e. Perf 13½–14, comp 14½–15	—	40·00	—
	f. Perf 13½–14 comp 12–13	48·00		
85	3c. black and ochre	42·00	22·00	80
	a. "JEBILEE" (R. 8/7)	£1900	£1500	£700
	b. "JUBILE" (R. 3/10)			
	d. Perf 13½–14	48·00	28·00	90
	db. Opt treble	£650		
	e. Perf 13½–14, comp 14½–15			
	f. Perf 13½–14, comp 12–13			
	fa. Opt double	£375	£375	£160
	fb. Opt treble	£650		
86	5c. black and green	65·00	16·00	1·00
	a. Opt double	£800	£500	—
	b. Perf 13½–14	65·00	22·00	1·00
	c. Perf 13½–14, comp 12–13			
	d. Perf 13½–14, comp 14½–15	—	—	3·00
87	6c. black and brown-lake	32·00	24·00	80
	a. Opt double	£850	£500	†
	b. "JUBILE" (R. 3/10)	£3000		
	c. Perf 13½–14, comp 14½–15			
	d. Perf 13½–14	—	85·00	—
88	8c. black and pink	50·00	16·00	80
	a. Opt double	†	£3000	†
	b. Perf 13½–14	48·00	15·00	80
	c. Perf 13½–14, comp 14½–15	50·00	18·00	—
83/8 *Set of 6*		£225	£100	4·75
83s/8s Optd "Specimen" *Set of 6*		£150		

The normal overprint on the 1c. varies in appearance from pure black to brownish black due to a mixing of the inks. The orange overprint on this value is in a clear, bright, unadulterated ink.

No. 84b is known in a vertical strip of 3 imperf horizontally except at the base of the bottom stamp (*Price £6500 unused*).

No. 87 also exists with error "JEBILEE", but only with additional "SPECIMEN" overprint. (*Price*, £1800).

1897 (Apr)–**1901**. T **34/45** of North Borneo (colours changed), with "LABUAN" engraved on vignette plate as T **13** (8, 10, 12, 24c.) or horizontally (others). Name and central part in black (24c. in blue). P 13½–14.

89	**34**	1c. dull claret (P 14½–15)	4·25	4·75	50
		a. Perf 13½–14, comp 14½–15			
		ab. Perf 16	—	—	2·00
		b. *Brown* (1901)	20·00	22·00	65
		ba. Perf 14½–15	3·00		
		bb. Perf 16	16·00	14·00	—
90	**35**	2c. blue	19·00	4·75	65
		a. Imperf between (vert pair)	†	†	£850
		b. Imperf between (horiz pair)	†	†	£900
		c. Perf 14½–15	26·00	—	75
		d. Perf 13½–14, comp 12–13	48·00	22·00	—
		e. Perf 16	—	—	7·00
91	**36**	3c. ochre	8·50	23·00	50
		a. Imperf between (vert pair)	£1000	†	£550
		b. Perf 14½–15	8·50	6·50	50
		c. Perf 13½–14, comp 12–13	20·00	30·00	1·50
		d. Perf 12–13	90·00		
92	**38**	5c. green	55·00	55·00	70
		a. Perf 14½–15	50·00	55·00	70
		b. Perf 13½–14, comp 12–13			
93	**39**	6c. brown-lake	6·50	40·00	1·00
		b. Perf 14½–15	9·00	21·00	50
		ba. Imperf between (vert pair)	†	†	£700
		c. Perf 13½–14, comp 12–13	—	—	6·50
94	**40**	8c. rose-red	50·00	—	50
		a. Perf 14½–15	19·00	12·00	—
		b. Perf 13½–14, comp 12–13	40·00	—	2·75
		c. *Vermilion*	12·00	—	50
		ca. Perf 16	—	—	5·50
95	**42**	12c. vermilion	95·00	£110	1·75
		a. Perf 14½–15	32·00	50·00	1·50
96	**44**	18c. olive-bistre	85·00	85·00	1·00
		a. Perf 16	12·00	45·00	50
		ab. Imperf between (vert pair)	†	†	£3250
97	**45**	24c. grey-lilac	50·00	85·00	1·00
		a. Perf 14½–15	12·00	50·00	50
89/97 *Set of 9*			£140	£225	5·25
89s/97s Optd "Specimen" *Set of 9*			£160		

The 12, 18 and 24c. above were errors; in the 12c., "LABUAN" is over the value at the top; the 18c. has "POSTAL REVENUE" instead of "POSTAGE AND REVENUE", and the 24c. is without "POSTAGE AND REVENUE".

1897 (Nov)–**98**.

(a) Types of North Borneo (colours changed), with "LABUAN" engraved on the vignette plate as in T **13**. P 13½–14.

98	**42**	12c. black and vermilion (3.98)	†	—	3·25
		a. Perf 14½–15	42·00	50·00	—
		b. Perf 13½–14, comp 14½–15			
		c. Perf 16	55·00	60·00	—
99	**46**	18c. black and olive-bistre			
		a. Perf 14½–15	85·00	60·00	2·00
		b. Perf 13½–14, comp 12–13	£110		
		c. Perf 16	†	—	9·00
100	**47**	24c. blue and lilac-brown	38·00	55·00	2·00
		a. Perf 14½–15	38·00	55·00	—
		b. Perf 13½–14, comp 12–13	—	65·00	—
		c. Perf 16	40·00		
		d. *Blue and ochre* (P 14½–15)	—	—	3·50

In the 12c. "LABUAN" is now correctly placed at foot of stamp. The 18c. and 24c. have the inscriptions on the stamps corrected, but the 18c. still has "LABUAN" *over* the value at foot, and was further corrected as follows.

(b) As No. 99, but "LABUAN" at top.

101	**46**	18c. black and olive-bistre (3.98)	60·00	60·00	—
		a. Perf 14½–15	30·00	70·00	2·75
		b. Perf 13½–14, comp 12–13	45·00	55·00	—
		c. Perf 12–13			
98s, 100s/1as Optd "Specimen" *Set of 3*			70·00		

1899 (July). Surch with T **17**.

(a) P 14½–15.

102	**38**	4c. on 5c. (No. 92a)	42·00	26·00
103	**39**	4c. on 6c. (No. 93b)	24·00	19·00
		a. Perf 13½–14	32·00	38·00
		b. Perf 13½–14 comp 12–13	50·00	60·00
104	**40**	4c. on 8c. (No. 94a)	60·00	40·00
		a. Perf 13½–14	38·00	32·00
		b. Perf 13½–14, comp 12–13	29·00	35·00
		c. Perf 12–13		
105	**42**	4c. on 12c. (No. 98a)	48·00	35·00
		a. Perf 13½–14	48·00	42·00
		b. Perf 16	48·00	40·00
		c. Perf 13½–14, comp 12–13	55·00	65·00
106	**46**	4c. on 18c. (No. 101a)	28·00	18·00
		a. Surch double	£425	£500
107	**47**	4c. on 24c. (No. 100a)	28·00	30·00
		a. Perf 13½–14	23·00	25·00
		b. Perf 13½–14, comp 12–13	35·00	30·00
		c. Perf 16	48·00	50·00

(b) P 14.

108	**32a**	4c. on 25c. (No. 80)	6·00	7·50
109	**32b**	4c. on 50c. (No. 81)	6·50	7·50
110	**32c**	4c. on $1 (No. 82)	6·50	7·50
102/10 *Set of 9*			£190	£160
102s/10s Optd "Specimen" *Set of 9*			£150	

A new setting of the surcharge with closer spacing (2½ mm) between "4" and "CENTS" was used for the Specimen overprints, including unissued surcharges on the 1c., 2c. and 3c. values (*price* £140 *for the set of three*).

1900–02. Types of North Borneo with "LABUAN" engraved on the vignette plate as in T **13**, in green on 16c. P 13½–14.

111	**35**	2c. black and green	3·75	2·50	30
		a. Imperf between (horiz pair)	£2750		
		b. Perf 13½–14, comp 12–13			
112	**37**	4c. black and yellow-brown	8·50	50·00	60
		a. Imperf between (vert pair)	£1200		
		b. Perf 13½–14, comp 12–13	40·00		
113		4c. black and carmine (8.1900)	14·00	3·00	75
		a. Perf 14½–15	5·00	11·00	50
		b. Perf 13½–14, comp 12–13	38·00	9·00	75
		c. Perf 16			
114	**38**	5c. black and pale blue	20·00	18·00	65
		a. Perf 13½–14, comp 12–13	—	85·00	—
		b. Perf 12–13	£150		
115	**41**	10c. brown and slate-lilac (P 14½–15) (1902)	55·00	90·00	60
116	**43**	16c. green and chestnut (1902)	50·00	£120	2·50
		a. Perf 13½–14, comp 12–13	85·00	£120	—
		b. Perf 12–13	£300		
		c. Perf 14½–15	£140		
111/16 *Set of 6*			£130	£250	4·75
111s/16s Optd "Specimen" *Set of 6*			£150		

No. 112 was printed in an incorrect frame colour and was not issued for postal purposes in Labuan. Used examples come from dealers' stock sent to the island for cancellation.

18

Line through "B" (R. 5/10)

(Recess Waterlow)

1902 (Sept)–**03**. P 13½–14.

117	**18**	1c. black and purple (10.03)	4·75	7·00	50
		a. Perf 14½–15	90·00	7·50	—
		b. Perf 13½–14 comp 12–13	85·00	50·00	
		c. Line through "B"	70·00	90·00	8·00
118		2c. black and green	4·25	5·00	30
		a. Perf 14½–15	£110	5·00	—
		aa. Perf 13½–14, comp 12–13	£110		
		b. Line through "B"	65·00	75·00	8·00
119		3c. black and sepia (10.03)	3·25	16·00	30
		a. Line through "B"	65·00	£130	8·00
120		4c. black and carmine	3·25	3·50	30
		a. Perf 14½–15	7·00	10·00	—
		b. Perf 13½–14 comp 12–13	75·00	50·00	—
		c. Line through "B"	65·00	65·00	8·00
121		8c. black and vermilion	14·00	9·00	50
		a. Perf 14½–15	8·00		
		b. Line through "B"	90·00	£100	8·00
122		10c. brown and slate-blue	3·25	16·00	30
		b. Perf 14½–15	7·00	18·00	50
		ba. Imperf between (vert pair)	†	†	£750
		c. Line through "B"	65·00	£150	8·00
123		12c. black and yellow	9·50	18·00	30
		a. Imperf between (vert strip of 3)	†	†	£3500
		b. Perf 16	9·50	22·00	50
		c. Line through "B"	£100	£170	8·00
124		16c. green and brown	4·75	24·00	30
		a. Imperf between (vert pair)	†	†	£2000
		b. Line through "B"	85·00	£200	8·00
125		18c. black and pale brown	3·25	26·00	30
		a. Line through "B"	75·00	£225	8·00
126		25c. green and greenish blue	7·50	21·00	50

		a. Perf 14½–15	15·00	38·00	60
		b. Error. Black and greenish blue	—	†	£500
		c. Line through "B"	£100	£200	9·00
127		50c. dull purple and lilac	11·00	50·00	1·75
		a. Perf 13½–14 comp 12–13	16·00	60·00	—
		b. Line through "B"	£180	£450	16·00
128		$1 claret and orange	8·50	50·00	1·75
		a. Perf 14½–15	10·00	—	1·75
		b. Line through "B"	£170	£475	16·00
117/28 *Set of 12*			65·00	£225	6·50
117s/28s Optd "Specimen" *Set of 12*			£200		

4

cents

(**19**)

1904 (Dec). Issues of 1896, 1897–8 and 1897/1901 surch with T **19**.

(a) P 14½–15.

129	**38**	4c. on 5c. (No. 92a)	48·00	40·00	14·00
130	**39**	4c. on 6c. (No. 93b)	12·00	38·00	14·00
131	**40**	4c. on 8c. (No. 94a)	25·00	45·00	14·00
132	**42**	4c. on 12c. (No. 98a)	25·00	42·00	14·00
		a. Perf 16	35·00	45·00	—
133	**46**	4c. on 18c. (No. 101) (P 13½–14)	23·00	45·00	14·00
		a. Perf 13½–14, comp 12–13	29·00	45·00	—
		b. Perf 12–13			
134	**47**	4c. on 24c. (No. 100a)	16·00	50·00	14·00
		a. Perf 13½–14	30·00	38·00	—
		b. Perf 13½–14, comp 12–13	42·00	48·00	—
		c. Perf 16	26·00	40·00	14·00

(b) P 14.

135	**32a**	4c. on 25c . (No. 80)	8·50	25·00	14·00
136	**32b**	4c. on 50c. (No. 81)	8·50	25·00	14·00
		a. Surch double	£350		
137	**32c**	4c. on $1 (No. 82)	8·50	25·00	14·00
129/37 *Set of 9*			£150	£300	£110

No. 136a usually shows one complete surcharge and parts of two further examples due to the position of the second impression.

The barred cancels can be found used on "philatelic" covers of this issue.

LABUAN (**20**) **LABUAN** (**21**)

1904 (12 Oct)–**05**. Nos. 81, 83 (in Labuan colour), and 84/6 of North Borneo optd locally with T **20** (25c. $2) or **21** (others).

138	**32a**	25c. indigo (2.05)	£1100	†	£900
139	**32c**	$1 blue (2.05)	†	†	£850
140	**32d**	$2 dull green	£3250	£3250	—
141	**14**	$5 bright purple (2.05)	£6000	†	£1400
		a. Dull purple	£6000	£6500	—
142	**15**	$10 brown (11.05)	£30000	†	£10000

Dangerous forgeries exist.

The overprint on No. 140 is 12 mm long.

POSTAGE DUE STAMPS

POSTAGE DUE

(D **1**)

1901. Optd with Type D **1**, reading vertically upwards. P 13½–14.

D1	**35**	2c. black and green (111)	20·00	32·00	50
		a. Opt double	£350		
		b. Perf 13½–14, comp 12–13	90·00	95·00	10·00
D2	**36**	3c. black and ochre (91)	26·00	£110	70
		a. Perf 13½–14, comp 12–13	85·00	—	2·75
D3	**37**	4c. black and carmine (113)	45·00	—	2·00
		a. Opt double	†	†	£750
		b. Perf 14½–15	45·00	£100	50
D4	**38**	5c. black and pale blue (114)	50·00	£130	1·00
		a. Perf 14½–15	—	—	1·00
		b. Perf 13½–14, comp 12–13	95·00	£180	—
D5	**39**	6c. black and brown-lake (93)	42·00	£110	85
		a. Perf 14½–15	55·00	£100	—
		b. Perf 16	70·00	—	65
D6	**40**	8c. black and vermilion (94c)	80·00	£110	1·75
		b. Perf 14½–15	90·00	£150	85
		ba. Frame inverted	†	†	£9500
		c. Perf 16	90·00	£110	—
		d. Black and rose-red (94)	95·00	£140	—
		da. Perf 14½–15	£130	—	7·50
		db. Perf 13½–14, comp 12–13	£130		
D7	**42**	12c. black and vermilion (98)	£120	—	4·75
		a. Opt reading downwards	†	†	£850
		b. Perf 14½–15	£110	£150	12·00
D8	**46**	18c. black and olive-bistre (101) (P 14½–15)	28·00	£120	1·25
D9	**47**	24c. blue and lilac-brown (100)	60·00	£130	5·50
		a. Perf 13½–14, comp 12–13	90·00		
		b. Perf 14½–15	40·00		
		ba. Blue and ochre	90·00	—	1·25
		c. Perf 16	65·00	£110	—
D1/9 *Set of 9*			£400	£900	10·50

No. D6ba only exists cancelled-to-order.

The administration of Labuan reverted to Colonial Office control, as part of an agreement with Brunei on 1 January 1906. By Letters Patent dated 30 October 1906 Labuan was incorporated with Straits Settlements and ceased issuing its own stamps. In 1946 it became part of the Colony of North Borneo.

XI. SABAH (formerly North Borneo)

NORTH BORNEO

PRICES FOR STAMPS ON COVER TO 1945

No. 1	*from* × 100
Nos. 2/3	*from* × 10
Nos. 4/5	—
Nos. 6/19	*from* × 10
Nos. 19*b*/21*b*	—
Nos. 22/8	*from* × 50
Nos. 29/35	—
Nos. 36/44	*from* × 100
Nos. 45/50	—
Nos. 51/2	*from* × 10
No. 54	—
Nos. 55/65	*from* × 10
Nos. 66/79	*from* × 4
Nos. 81/6	—
Nos. 87/91	*from* × 12
Nos. 92/111	*from* × 4
Nos. 112/26	*from* × 10
Nos. 127/40	*from* × 6
Nos. 141/5	—
Nos. 146/57	*from* × 5
Nos. 158/79	*from* × 8
Nos. 181/5	—
Nos. 186/8	*from* × 10
Nos. 189/230	*from* × 4
Nos. 231/4	—
Nos. 235/49	*from* × 3
Nos. 250/2	—
Nos. 253/75	*from* × 12
Nos. 276/92	*from* × 7
Nos. 293/4	—
Nos. 295/300	*from* × 6
Nos. 301/2	—
Nos. 303/17	*from* × 3
Nos. 318/19	*from* × 20
Nos. 320/34	*from* × 3
Nos. D1/30	*from* × 25
Nos. D31/6	*from* × 12
No. D37	—
Nos. D38/84	*from* × 40
Nos. D85/9	*from* × 8

BRITISH NORTH BORNEO COMPANY ADMINISTRATION

PRINTERS. The stamps of this country up to 1894 were designed by T. Macdonald and printed in lithography by Blades, East and Blades, London.

1

8 Cents. (**2**)

EIGHT CENTS (**3**)

1883 (Mar). P 12.

1	**1**	2c. red-brown	32·00	65·00
		a. Imperf between (horiz pair)	£20000	

The figure "2" varies in size.

1883 (June). No. 1 surch as T **2** or **3**.

2	**2**	8c. on 2c. red-brown	£1300	£800
3	**3**	8c. on 2c. red-brown	£500	£190
		a. Surch double	†	£5000

Type **2** was handstamped and stamps without stop are generally forgeries. Type **3** was a setting of 50 (10×5) providing ten varieties; it normally has a stop which sometimes failed to print.

CANCELLED-TO-ORDER—Prices are separately indicated in a third price column, for stamps showing the recognisable black bars remainder cancellation. The issues since 1916 have not been thus cancelled.

It should be noted, however, that a postmark of this form was in use for postal purposes up to this period, and was used at one or two of the smaller post-offices until 1949. A small oval with five bars was used to mark railway mail during 1945/55 and also as a paquebot mark at Jesselton *c.* 1950.

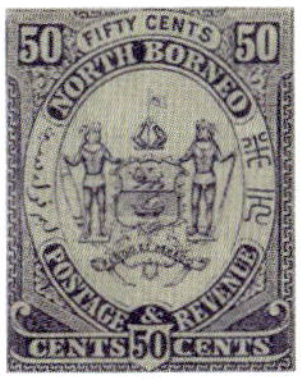
4

5

and Revenue
(**6**)

1883. P 14.

4	**4**	50c. violet	£160	—	30·00
		a. Inverted "L" for first "F" in "FIFTY" (R. 5/2)	£1500	—	£250
5	**5**	$1 scarlet	£140	—	14·00

1883 (July). P 12.

6	**1**	4c. pink	55·00	60·00
		a. Imperf (horiz pair)	†	—
7		8c. green	80·00	60·00

1886. P 14.

8	**1**	½c. magenta	95·00	£180
9		1c. orange	£180	£325
		a. Imperf (pair)	£275	£275
		b. Imperf horiz (vert pair)	£1500	
10		2c. brown	32·00	29·00
		a. Imperf between (horiz pair)	£650	
11		4c. pink	17·00	50·00
12		8c. green	19·00	50·00
		a. Imperf between (horiz pair)	£850	
13		10c. blue	38·00	55·00
		a. Imperf (pair)	£350	
8/13 *Set of 6*			£350	£600

Imperforate examples of the 4c. pink are listed under No. 6a.

1886 (Sept). Nos. 8 and 13 optd with T **6**.

14	½c. magenta	£170	£250
15	10c. blue	£225	£275

3 CENTS
(**7**)

5 CENTS
(**8**)

3 CENTS
Small "3" variety (R. 3/1, 3/4, 3/7)

(Surchd by *North Borneo Herald*, Sandakan)

1886 (Sept). T **1** surch as T **7**/**8**.

(a) P 12.

16	**7**	3c. on 4c. pink	£250	£300
		a. Small "3"	—	£7500
17	**8**	5c. on 8c. green	£250	£300

(b) P 14.

18	**7**	3c. on 4c. pink	£120	£130
		a. Small "3"	£1800	
19	**8**	5c. on 8c. green	£130	£130
		a. Surch inverted	£2500	

9

10

11

12

13

1886–87.

(a) P 14.

21*b*	**9**	½c. magenta	16·00	50·00
22		½c. rose	3·75	15·00
		a. Imperf (pair)	48·00	
23		1c. orange-yellow	14·00	32·00
		a. Imperf between (vert pair)	£400	
		b. Imperf (pair)	60·00	
24		1c. orange	2·00	11·00
		a. Imperf (pair)	45·00	
25		2c. brown	2·00	9·50
		a. Imperf (pair)	45·00	
26		4c. pink	3·75	15·00
		a. Imperf (pair)	48·00	
		b. Imperf between (horiz or vert pair)	£350	
		c. Imperf vert (horiz pair)	£325	
		d. Error. 1c. pink (R. 2/3) (centre stamp of strip of 3)	£300	£850
		da. Imperf between (pair)		
		db. Imperf (pair)	£5000	
27		8c. green	20·00	24·00
		a. Imperf (pair)	48·00	
28		10c. blue	9·00	32·00
		a. Imperf between (vert pair)	£425	
		b. Imperf (pair)	48·00	
29	**10**	25c. indigo	£325	19·00
		a. Imperf between (vert pair)		
		b. Imperf (pair)	£400	42·00
30	**11**	50c. violet	£375	21·00
		a. Imperf (pair)	£450	42·00
31	**12**	$1 scarlet	£350	20·00
		a. Imperf (pair)	£500	42·00
32	**13**	$2 sage-green	£475	26·00
		a. Imperf (pair)	£425	45·00
22/32 *Set of 10*			£1400	£170

(b) P 12.

34	**9**	½c. magenta	£250	£425
35		1c. orange	£190	£275

Nos. 21*b*/32 are known to have been sold as cancelled remainders, but these are difficult to distinguish from postally used. Values above 10c. are infrequently found postally used so that the used prices quoted are for the remainders.

14

15

16

17

18

1888–92. T **14** (as T **9** but inscr "POSTAGE & REVENUE") and T **15/18** (T **10/13** redrawn). P 14.

36	**14**	½c. magenta (1889)	4·00	27·00	2·25
		a. Imperf vert (horiz pair)	†	†	£250
		b. Rose	1·50	6·00	60
		ba. Imperf between (horiz pair)	£400		
		c. Imperf (pair)	45·00	—	11·00
37		1c. orange (1892)	3·75	4·75	50
		a. Imperf vert (horiz pair)	£375		
		b. Imperf (pair)	45·00	—	9·50
38		2c. brown (1889)	12·00	19·00	90
		a. Imperf between (horiz pair)	†	†	£400
		b. Lake-brown	5·00	19·00	50
		c. Imperf (pair)	45·00	—	9·00
39		3c. violet (1889)	2·50	12·00	50
		b. Imperf (pair)	30·00	—	9·00
40		4c. rose-pink (1889)	8·00	38·00	50
		a. Imperf vert (horiz pair)	†	†	£250
		b. Imperf (pair)	48·00	—	9·50
41		5c. slate (1889)	2·75	25·00	50
		a. Imperf between (pair)			
		b. Imperf (pair)	48·00	—	9·50
42		6c. lake (1892)	11·00	25·00	50
		a. Imperf (pair)	48·00	—	12·00
43		8c. blue-green (1891)	32·00	40·00	1·00
		a. Yellow-green	23·00	29·00	50
		c. Imperf (pair)	48·00	—	12·00
44		10c. blue (1891)	8·00	30·00	1·00
		a. Imperf between (vert pair)	†	†	£275
		b. Dull blue	6·50	21·00	50
		ba. Imperf between (horiz pair)			
		d. Imperf (pair)	45·00	—	11·00
45	**15**	25c. indigo	70·00	85·00	75
		a. Imperf (pair)	£350	†	20·00
		b. Imperf vert (horiz pair)	†	†	£275
46	**16**	50c. violet	95·00	£130	75
		a. Imperf (pair)	£450	20·00	20·00
		b. Chalky blue	£120	£130	†
47	**17**	$1 scarlet	38·00	£110	75
		a. Imperf (pair)	£350	†	20·00
48	**18**	$2 dull green	£160	£190	1·50
		a. Imperf (pair)	£500	†	23·00
36b/48 *Set of* 13			£375	£600	7·50

Nos. 39, 43 and 44 showing stamps printed double or triple, one inverted, are from waste sheets subsequently sold by the British North Borneo Company to collectors.

These stamps to the 10c. value were forged on several occasions. Most forgeries of the ½c. value can be identified by the presence of a diagonal line joining the top two horizontal strokes of the uppermost Chinese character.

The new 25c. has the inscription "BRITISH NORTH BORNEO" in taller capitals. In the 50c. the "0" of the numerals "50" in the two upper corners is square-shaped at the top and bottom instead of being oval. The 1 dollar has 14 pearls instead of 13 at each side, and on the 2 dollars the word "BRITISH" measures 10½ to 11 mm in length in place of 12 mm.

19

20

1889. P 14.

49	**19**	$5 bright purple	£275	£300	8·50
		a. Imperf (pair)	£700	†	50·00
50	**20**	$10 brown	£300	£375	12·00
		a. Imperf (pair)	£900	†	60·00
		b. "DOLLAPS" for "DOLLARS" (R. 2/1)	£1500	£2000	£325
		ba. Ditto. Imperf (pair)	£3500	†	£750

Two Cents. (21) **6 cents.** (22) **1 cent.** (23)

1890 (Dec). Surch as T **21**, in red.

51	**15**	2c. on 25c. indigo	70·00	90·00
		a. Surch inverted	£450	£450
52		8c. on 25c. indigo	95·00	£120

The first printing of Nos. 51/2 had the two lines of the surcharge 3.5 mm apart. On a second printing of both values this gap widened to 5 mm.

1891–92. Surch with T **22**.

54	**9**	6c. on 8c. green (1892)	£9000	£4500
		a. Large "s" in "cents"	£16000	
55	**14**	6c. on 8c. yellow-green	25·00	10·00
		a. Surch inverted	£450	£500
		b. Inverted "c" in "cents" (R. 5/4)	£550	£650
		c. "cetns." for "cents" (R. 3/7)	£550	£650
		d. Large "s" in "cents" (R. 2/9 or 3/7)	£250	£200
56	**9**	6c. on 10c. blue	60·00	22·00
		a. Surch inverted	£300	£300
		b. Surch double		
		c. Surch treble	£550	
		d. Large "s" in "cents"	£300	£170
57	**14**	6c. on 10c. blue	£180	26·00
		a. Large "s" in "cents"	£750	£225

Unused examples of Nos. 55 and 57 are normally without gum.

There were three settings of the surcharge for No. 55. On the first two the large "s" in "cents" occurred on R. 2/9 with the other two listed varieties also included. Nos. 55b/c were corrected on the third setting and the large "s" in cents occurred on R. 3/7.

1892 (Mar–Nov). Surch as T **23** ("Cents." with capital "C" as in T **21** on No. 65), in red.

63	**14**	1c. on 4c. rose-pink	23·00	14·00
		a. Surch double	£1500	
		b. Surch on back and on front	†	£600
		ba. As b, but with surch double on front		
64		1c. on 5c. slate (Nov)	7·00	6·00
65	**15**	8c. on 25c. indigo (date?)	£150	£160

Unused examples of Nos. 63/5 are normally without gum.

24 Dyak Chief

25 Sambar Stag (*Cervus unicolor*)

26 Sago Palm

27 Great Argus Pheasant

28 Arms of the Company

29 Malay Dhow

30 Estuarine Crocodile

31 Mount Kinabalu

32 Arms of the Company with Supporters

PERFORATION. There are a number of small variations in the perforation of the Waterlow issues of 1894 to 1922 which we believe were due to irregularity of the pins rather than different perforators.

In the following lists, stamps perf 12, 12½, 13 or compound are described as perf 12–13, stamps perf 13½, 14 or compound are described as perf 13½–14 and those perf 14½, 15 or compound are listed as perf 14½–15. In addition the 13½–14 perforation exists compound with 14½–15 and with 12–13, whilst perf 15½–16 comes from a separate perforator.

(Recess Waterlow)

1894 (Feb). P 14½–15.

66	**24**	1c. black and olive-bistre	1·25	9·50	50
		a. Imperf between (horiz or vert pair)	£900		
		b. Perf 13½–14	1·75	12·00	50
		c. Perf 13½–14, comp 14½–15	45·00	55·00	—
		d. Perf 13½–14, comp 12–13	24·00	50·00	—
		e. Perf 12–13			
67		1c. black and bistre-brown	2·25	17·00	50
		a. Perf 13½–14	3·00	17·00	50
		b. Perf 13½–14, comp 12–13	27·00	55·00	—
		c. Perf 12–13			
68	**25**	2c. black and rose-lake	5·50	4·75	50
		a. Imperf between (horiz or vert pair)	£900	£900	†
		b. Perf 13½–14	40·00	45·00	75
		c. Perf 13½–14, comp 14½–15			
69		2c. black and lake	5·50	4·75	50
		a. Perf 13½–14	40·00	40·00	1·50
		b. Perf 13½–14, comp 12–13	32·00	35·00	—
		c. Imperf between (horiz pair)			
70	**26**	3c. olive-green and dull purple	2·75	8·50	50
		a. Imperf between (horiz pair)	—	£850	†
		aa. Perf 13½–14, comp 14½–15			
		b. Bronze-green and dull purple	5·50	—	50
		c. Perf 13½–14			
71		3c. olive-green and violet (P 13½–14)	25·00	50·00	1·50
		a. Imperf between (horiz pair)			
72	**27**	5c. black and vermilion	14·00	11·00	60
		a. Imperf between (horiz or vert pair)	£800		
		b. Perf 13½–14	45·00	60·00	1·25
		c. Perf 13½–14, comp 12–13	—	65·00	5·50
		d. Perf 13½–14, comp 14½–15			
		e. Perf 12-13			
73	**28**	6c. black and bistre-brown	60·00	80·00	60
		a. Perf 13½–14	4·50	18·00	60
		b. Perf 13½–14, comp 12–13	—	65·00	5·50
		c. Perf 13½–14, comp 14½–15	60·00		
		d. Imperf between (horiz pair)			
74	**29**	8c. black and dull purple	6·50	11·00	60
		a. Imperf between (vert pair)	£750		
		b. Perf 13½–14	9·50	38·00	1·00
		ba. Imperf between (vert pair)	£500	†	£300
		d. Perf 13½–14, comp 12–13			
75	**30**	12c. black and blue	28·00	85·00	2·50
		a. Perf 13½–14	29·00	80·00	2·50
		b. Imperf between (horiz pair)	£1300	†	£650
		c. Perf 13½–14, comp 14½–15	—	—	5·00
76		12c. black and ultramarine	48·00	85·00	3·00
		a. Perf 13½–14	45·00	85·00	3·00
		b. Imperf between (pair)			
78	**31**	18c. black and deep green	27·00	50·00	2·00
		a. Perf 13½–14	35·00	50·00	2·00
		b. Perf 13½–14, comp 14½–15	—	—	5·00
		c. Perf 13½–14 comp 12–13	—	—	5·00
79	**32**	24c. blue and rose-lake	23·00	85·00	2·00
		a. Imperf between (vert pair)	—	—	£400
		b. Imperf between (vert strip of 3)	†	†	£550
		c. Perf 13½–14	23·00	70·00	2·00
		d. Perf 13½–14, comp 14½–15			
66/79 *Set of 9*			£100	£225	9·00

32a

32b

32c

32d

32e

32f

(Litho Blades, East & Blades, London)

1894 (Feb). T **32a** to **32f**. P 14.

81	**32a**	25c. indigo	9·00	30·00	1·00
		a. Imperf (pair)	55·00	†	11·00
		b. Imperf between (horiz or vert pair)	£850	—	£110
82	**32b**	50c. deep slate-purple	35·00	60·00	2·00
		a. Imperf (pair)	—	†	11·00
		b. Imperf between (horiz pair)			
		d. Chalky blue	—	60·00	—
83	**32c**	$1 scarlet	12·00	26·00	1·25
		a. Perf 14×11	£300		
		b. Imperf (pair)	45·00	†	11·00
84	**32d**	$2 dull green	21·00	75·00	2·50
		a. Imperf (pair)	—	†	17·00
85	**32e**	$5 bright purple	£250	£300	16·00
		a. Imperf (pair)	£600	†	55·00
		b. Dull purple	£300	£300	10·00
86	**32f**	$10 brown	£275	£350	15·00
		a. Imperf (pair)	£600	†	55·00
81/6 *Set of 6*			£550	£700	29·00
81s/6s Optd "Specimen" *Set of 6*			£150		

For Nos. 81 to 83 in other colours, see Labuan 80*a*, 81*a* and 82*a*.

Nos. 81/4 showing stamps printed double, double, one inverted, or on both sides, are from waste sheets subsequently sold by the British North Borneo Company to collectors.

4

CENTS

(**33**) 3½ mm between lines of surcharge)

(Surcharged by Waterlow)

1895 (June). No. 83 surch as T **33**.

87	**32c**	4 cents on $1 scarlet	7·00	1·50	50
		a. Surch double, one diagonal	£950		
88		10 cents on $1 scarlet	25·00	1·75	50
89		20 cents on $1 scarlet	45·00	17·00	50
90		30 cents on $1 scarlet	38·00	29·00	1·00
91		40 cents on $1 scarlet	42·00	50·00	1·00
87/91 *Set of 5*			£140	90·00	3·25
87s/91s Optd "Specimen" *Set of 5*			85·00		

For 4c. on $1 with wider spacing see No. 121.

No. 88 exists with the figures of the surcharge 2½ mm away from "CENTS". The normal setting has a space of 3½ mm. Examples of the narrow setting have, so far, only been seen on cancelled-to-order stamps.

34

35

36

37 Orang-Utan

38

39

40

41 Sun Bear

42

43 Borneo Railway Train

44

45

(Recess Waterlow)

1897 (Mar)–**1902**. T **34** to **45**. New frames. P 13½–14.

92	**34**	1c. black and bistre-brown	22·00	4·25	40
		aa. Perf 16			
		a. Perf 14½–15	11·00	2·75	40
		b. Perf 13½–14, comp 12–13	65·00	50·00	—
		c. Imperf between (horiz pair)	†	†	£550
		d. Perf 12–13	£160		
93		1c. black and ochre	55·00	15·00	50
		a. Perf 14½–15	40·00	14·00	50
		ab. Imperf between (horiz pair)	†	†	£550
		b. Perf 13½–14 comp 12–13			
94	**35**	2c. black and lake	48·00	3·50	40
		a. Perf 14½–15	23·00	2·00	40
		ab. Imperf between (horiz pair)	†	†	£600
		b. Perf 13½–14, comp 12–13	—	18·00	1·25
		c. Perf 12–13			
		d. Imperf between (vert pair)	†	†	£650
		e. Perf 13½–14, comp 14½–15	—	—	3·00
95		2c. black and green (1900)	55·00	2·00	60
		a. Perf 14½–15	£100	19·00	2·25
		b. Perf 13½–14, comp 12–13	£140	30·00	—
		c. Perf 12–13			
		d. Imperf between (horiz pair)	—	£1100	†
96	**36**	3c. green and rosy mauve	60·00	16·00	40
		a. Perf 14½–15	65·00	50·00	1·00
		b. Perf 13½–14, comp 12–13	90·00	75·00	—
97		3c. green and dull mauve (P 14½–15)	22·00	3·00	50
98	**37**	4c. black and green (1900)	9·00	—	1·50
		a. Perf 13½–14, comp 12–13			
99		4c. black and carmine (1900)	38·00	10·00	50
		a. Perf 16	90·00	48·00	50
		b. Perf 14½–15	65·00	2·25	50
		c. Perf 13½–14, comp 12–13	38·00	45·00	2·25
		d. Perf 12–13			
100	**38**	5c. black and orange-vermilion	£100	3·50	70
		a. Perf 14½–15	£100	2·50	70
		ab. Imperf between (horiz pair)	†	£1600	†
		b. Perf 13½–14, comp 12–13	£130	14·00	80
		c. Perf 12–13			
101	**39**	6c. black and bistre-brown	60·00	27·00	50
		a. Perf 14½–15	42·00	4·00	50
		b. Perf 13½–14, comp 12–13	—	—	3·00
102	**40**	8c. black and brown-purple	80·00	50·00	—
		a. Perf 16	£110	21·00	70
		ab. Imperf between (vert pair)	£450	£425	—
		b. Perf 14½–15	48·00	2·75	60
103		8c. black and brown	12·00	32·00	75
		a. Perf 14½–15	65·00	80·00	—
		b. Perf 16			
104	**41**	10c. brown and slate-lilac (1902)	£120	48·00	2·75
		a. Imperf between (vert pair)			
105		10c. brown and slate-blue (1902)	£275	95·00	1·50
106	**42**	12c. black and dull blue	£160	48·00	1·75
		a. Imperf between (vert pair)	†	†	£700
		b. Perf 14½–15	£120	35·00	1·50
		c. Perf 13½–14, comp 12–13	£190	55·00	—
		d. Perf 12–13			
107	**43**	16c. green and chestnut (1902)	£130	90·00	3·25
		a. Perf 14½–15	£180	£140	10·00
108	**44**	18c. black and green (P 16)	26·00	75·00	2·75
		a. Imperf vert (horiz pair)	†	†	85·00
		b. Imperf between (vert pair)	†	†	£350
		c. Imperf (pair)	†	†	£180
		d. Perf 14½–15	—	—	10·00
109	**45**	24c. blue and lake	23·00	90·00	2·75
		a. Perf 13½–14, comp 12–13	50·00	£100	2·75
		b. Perf 12–13	£190		
92/109 (*one of each value*) *Set of* 12			£550	£325	13·00
92s/109s (*excl* 93, 97, 103, 105) Optd "Specimen" *Set of* 14			£300		

No. 98 was printed in an incorrect frame colour and it is doubtful if it was issued for postal purposes in North Borneo. Used examples come from dealers' stock sent to the territory for cancellation.

In the above the 18c. has "POSTAL REVENUE" instead of "POSTAGE AND REVENUE" and the 24c. has those words omitted. These stamps were replaced by others with corrected inscriptions; see Nos. 110 and 111.

46

47

1897. Corrected inscriptions. P 13½–14.

110	**46**	18c. black and green	£140	32·00	3·00
		a. Imperf between (horiz pair)	†	†	£600
		b. Perf 14½–15	95·00	12·00	1·50
		c. Perf 13½–14, comp 12–13	—	—	2·75
111	**47**	24c. blue and lake	95·00	50·00	2·25
		a. Perf 16	£150	£120	2·00
		b. Perf 14½–15	45·00	55·00	2·50
		c. Perf 13½–14, comp 12–13	—	—	3·75
		d. Perf 12–13			
110s/11s Optd "Specimen" *Set of* 2			50·00		

4 CENTS
(**48**) (4½ mm between lines of surcharge)

BRITISH PROTECTORATE.
(**49**)

4 cents
(**50**)

1899 (22 July–Oct). Surch with T **48**. P 14½–15 (Nos. 112/17) or 14 (Nos. 118/26).

(a) 4½ mm between lines of surch.

112	4c. on 5c. (No. 100a)	48·00	48·00
	a. Perf 13½–14	35·00	10·00
	asa. Surch inverted, optd "Specimen"	£650	
	b. Perf 13½–14, comp 12–13	45·00	32·00
113	4c. on 6c. (No. 101a) (date?)	19·00	24·00
	a. Perf 13½–14	20·00	48·00
	b. Perf 13½–14 comp 14½–15		
114	4c. on 8c. (No. 102b) (Oct)	15·00	10·00
115	4c. on 12c. (No. 106b) (Oct)	27·00	13·00
	a. Imperf between (horiz pair)	£800	
	b. Imperf between (vert pair)	—	£900
	c. Perf 13½–14	48·00	50·00
	d. Perf 12–13		
	e. Perf 13½–14, comp 12–13	45·00	42·00
116	4c. on 18c. (No. 110b) (Oct)	15·00	14·00
	a. Perf 13½–14	38·00	38·00
117	4c. on 24c. (No. 111b) (Oct)	27·00	18·00
	a. Perf 16	50·00	50·00
	b. Perf 13½–14	24·00	38·00
	c. Perf 13½–14, comp 12–13	40·00	40·00
	d. Perf 12–13	£110	£120
118	4c. on 25c. indigo (No. 81)	5·50	8·50
	a. Imperf between (horiz strip of 3)	£1300	
119	4c. on 50c. deep slate-purple (No. 82)	15·00	16·00
	a. Chalky blue	28·00	38·00
121	4c. on $1 scarlet (No. 83)	5·50	12·00
122	4c. on $2 dull green (No. 84)	5·50	13·00
123	4c. on $5 bright purple (No. 85)	£160	£250
	a. Dull purple	£275	£300
124	4c. on $10 brown (No. 86)	£120	£250
112/24 *Set of* 12		£400	£550
112s/24s Optd "Specimen" *Set of* 12		£200	

(b) 8½ mm between lines of surch. P 14.

125	4c. on $5 (No. 85)	6·50	15·00
126	4c. on $10 (No. 86)	6·50	15·00

No. 121 differs only from No. 87 in having the "4" and "cents" wider apart.

Examples of the Kudat postmark dated "AU 15 1899" struck on Nos. 112/26 are generally considered to be faked.

A new setting of the surcharge, with 2½ mm between "4" and "CENTS" for values to $2 and 3½ mm on the $5 and $10, was used for the Specimen overprints, including unissued surcharges on the 1c., 2c. and 3c. values (*price* £120 *the set of three*).

(Optd by Waterlow)

1901 (8 Oct)–**05**. Optd as T **49**.

	(a) P 13½–14.			
127	1c. (No. 92) (R.)	3·50	1·50	30
	a. Perf 14½–15	2·50	1·75	30
128	2c. (No. 95) (R.)	4·25	1·25	30
	a. Perf 16	3·50	16·00	40
	b. Perf 14½–15	14·00	12·00	30
129	3c. (No. 96)	1·75	5·50	30
	a. Imperf between (vert pair)	†	†	£1200
	b. Perf 14½–15	9·00	2·75	30
	c. Perf 13½–14, comp 14½–15	50·00	—	1·00
130	4c. (No. 99) (G.)	9·00	1·50	30
	a. Perf 14½–15	26·00	1·50	50
131	5c. (No. 100) (G.)	50·00	3·75	30
	a. Perf 14½–15	14·00	2·50	30
132	6c. (No. 101) (R.)	50·00	65·00	1·25
	a. No stop after "Protectorate"	85·00	85·00	1·25
	b. Perf 16	4·00	15·00	70
133	8c. (No. 103) (B.)	3·75	3·75	50
	a. No stop after "Protectorate"	3·00	24·00	1·50
	b. Perf 13½–14, comp 12–13	70·00	28·00	—
	c. Imperf horiz (vert pair)	†	†	£350
134	10c. (No. 104) (R.) (7.02)	70·00	5·00	1·00
	a. Perf 14½–15	£120	32·00	1·75
	c. Perf 13½–14. No stop after "Protectorate"	£225	—	9·50
	d. Opt double	£850	†	£325
	e. (No. 105)	£275	—	1·00
	f. Imperf vert (horiz pair)	†	†	£650
135	12c. (No. 106) (R.)	55·00	12·00	1·50
136	16c. (No. 107) (7.02)	£150	30·00	2·25
	a. Perf 14½–15	£140	55·00	2·25
	b. Perf 13½–14 comp 12–13	£275	90·00	—
137	18c. (No. 110) (R.)	14·00	25·00	1·25
	a. No stop after "Protectorate"			
	b. Perf 13½–14, comp 12–13	60·00	—	1·50
138	24c. (No. 111)	16·00	40·00	1·50
	a. Perf 14½–15	70·00	95·00	1·75
	b. Imperf between (horiz pair)			
	(b) P 14.			
139	25c. (No. 81) (R.)	2·00	10·00	50
	a. No stop after "Protectorate"	£170	£225	25·00
	b. Overprints *tête-bêche* (horiz pair)			
	c. Overprint inverted	£650		
140	50c. (No. 82) (R.)	2·75	11·00	55
	a. No stop after "Protectorate"	95·00	£160	—
	b. Chalky blue			
141	$1 (No. 83) (R.) (1.04)	10·00	65·00	—
142	$1 (No. 83)	6·50	38·00	2·50
	a. Imperf horiz (vert pair)	£800		
	b. Opt double	†	†	£375
	c. Opt treble			
143	$2 (No. 84) (R.) (1903)	32·00	95·00	3·50
	a. Opt double	£1500	†	£450
144	$5 (No. 85*b*) (R.) (2.05)	£275	£500	8·00
145	$10 (No. 86) (R.) (2.05)	£475	£800	11·00
	a. Opt inverted	£2500	†	£450
127/45 *Set of* 18		£1000	£1400	30·00
127s/40s Optd "Specimen" *Set of* 14		£300		

There was more than one setting of the overprint for some of the values. Full sheets of the 6c. and 8c. are known, without stop throughout.

1904–**05**. Surch locally with T **50**.

	(a) P 14½–15.			
146	4c. on 5c. (No. 100a)	45·00	50·00	12·00
	a. Surch omitted (in pair with normal)			
147	4c. on 6c. (No. 101a)	7·00	21·00	12·00
	a. Surch inverted	£225		
148	4c. on 8c. (No. 102b)	14·00	26·00	12·00
	a. Surch inverted	£300		
149	4c. on 12c. (No. 106b)	35·00	40·00	12·00
	a. Perf 13½–14	50·00	60·00	12·00
	b. Perf 13½–14 comp 12–13	35·00	60·00	—
	c. Surch omitted (in pair with normal)			
150	4c. on 18c. (No. 110b)	14·00	38·00	12·00
	a. Perf 13½–14			
151	4c. on 24c. (No. 111b)	28·00	50·00	12·00
	a. Perf 16	18·00	50·00	12·00
	b. Perf 13½–14	27·00	50·00	12·00
	c. Perf 12–13			
	(b) P 14.			
152	4c. on 25c. (No. 81)	4·50	25·00	12·00
153	4c. on 50c. (No. 82)	5·50	38·00	12·00
154	4c. on $1 (No. 83)	6·00	48·00	12·00
155	4c. on $2 (No. 84)	6·00	48·00	12·00
156	4c. on $5 (No. 85)	12·00	48·00	12·00
	a. Surch on No. 85*b*	30·00	50·00	—
157	4c. on $10 (No. 86)	12·00	48·00	12·00
	a. Surch inverted	£2750		
	b. Surch omitted (in pair with normal)			
146/57 *Set of* 12		£160	£425	£130

51 Malayan Tapir

52 Travellers' Tree

53 Jesselton Railway Station

54 The Sultan of Sulu, his staff and W. C. Cowie, Managing Director of the Company

55 Indian Elephant

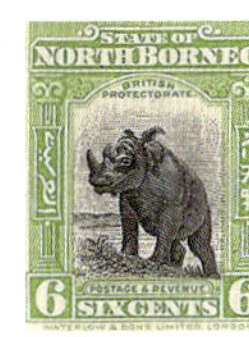

56 Sumatran Rhinoceros

57 Ploughing with Buffalo

58 Wild Boar

59 Palm Cockatoo

60 Rhinoceros Hornbill

61 Banteng

62 Dwarf Cassowary

(Recess Waterlow)

1909 (1 July)–**23**. Centres in black. P 13½–14.

158	**51**	1c. chocolate-brown	7·00	2·50	30
		a. Perf 14½–15	50·00	15·00	40
159		1c. brown	23·00	1·60	30
		a. Perf 14½–15	45·00	4·50	30
		b. Imperf between (vert pair)	£1800		
160	**52**	2c. green	1·00	70	30
		a. Imperf between (pair)			

		b. Perf 14½–15	3·00	70	30
161	**53**	3c. lake	3·25	2·75	30
162		3c. rose-lake	3·25	2·75	50
		a. Perf 14½–15	40·00	—	55
163		3c. green (1923)	35·00	1·50	—
164	**54**	4c. scarlet	2·75	30	30
		a. Imperf between (vert pair)			
		b. Perf 14½–15	20·00	2·00	35
165	**55**	5c. yellow-brown	15·00	6·50	40
		a. Perf 14½–15			
166		5c. dark brown	28·00	5·50	—
167	**56**	6c. olive-green	13·00	2·25	30
		a. Perf 14½–15	80·00	6·50	60
168		6c. apple-green	38·00	3·50	60
169	**57**	8c. lake	4·00	1·75	60
		a. Perf 14½–15	—	—	11·00
170	**58**	10c. greyish blue	45·00	8·00	1·25
		a. Perf 14½–15	95·00	38·00	—
171		10c. blue	55·00	3·75	—
172		10c. turquoise-blue	42·00	2·00	2·00
		a. Perf 14½–15	65·00	5·50	—
173	**59**	12c. deep blue	38·00	3·50	1·00
		a. Perf 14½–15	—	—	11·00
		b. Imperf between (horiz pair)	†	†	£600
173*c*		12c. deep bright blue			
174	**60**	16c. brown-lake	26·00	7·00	1·00
175	**61**	18c. blue-green	£110	32·00	1·00
176	**62**	24c. deep rose-lilac	28·00	3·50	1·75
		a. Deep lilac	45·00	6·00	—
158/76 *Set of 13*			£300	55·00	—
158s/76s Optd "Specimen" *Set of 13*			£300		

For this issue perf 12½ see Nos. 277, etc.

20
CENTS
(63)

64

65

1909 (7 Sept). No. 175 surch with T **63** by Waterlow. P 13½–14.

177	20c. on 18c. blue-green (R.)	7·00	1·00	30
	a. Perf 14½–15	£200	65·00	—
	s. Optd "Specimen"	45·00		

Re-entry. Doubled oars and dots behind lion (R. 4/9).

(Recess Waterlow)

1911 (7 Mar). P 13½–14.

178	**64**	25c. black and yellow-green	16·00	4·75	2·00
		a. Perf 14½–15	17·00	38·00	—
		b. Imperf (pair)	55·00		
		c. Re-entry	60·00	25·00	
178*d*		25c. black and blue-green	50·00		
		e. Re-entry	£150		
179		50c. black and steel-blue	16·00	4·50	2·25
		a. Perf 14½–15	23·00	23·00	—
		ab. Imperf between (horiz pair)	£3250		
		c. Imperf (pair)	90·00		
		d. Re-entry	60·00	25·00	
180		$1 black and chestnut	17·00	4·00	3·75
		a. Perf 14½–15	60·00	16·00	7·50
		b. Imperf (pair)	£170		
		c. Re-entry	65·00	25·00	
181		$2 black and lilac	70·00	17·00	4·75
		a. Re-entry	£200	65·00	
182	**65**	$5 black and lake	£140	£130	32·00
		a. Imperf (pair)	£200		
183		$10 black and brick-red	£475	£550	85·00
		a. Imperf (pair)	£475		
178/83 *Set of 6*			£650	£650	£110
178s/83s Optd "Specimen" *Set of 6*			£325		

BRITISH
PROTECTORATE
(66)

2
cents
(67)

(68)

1912 (July). Nos. 85b and 86 optd with T **66**.

184	$5 dull purple (R.)	£1200	£1400	8·50
185	$10 brown (R.)	£1800	—	8·50
	a. Opt inverted	†	†	—

1916 (Feb). Nos. 162, 167 and 173 surch as T **67** by Govt Printing Office, Sandakan. P 13½–14.

186	**53**	2c. on 3c. black and rose-lake	27·00	15·00
		a. "s" inverted (R. 2/5)	£100	95·00
		b. Surch double	£2000	
187	**56**	4c. on 6c. black and olive-green (R.)	26·00	19·00
		a. "s" inverted (R. 2/5)	£100	£100
		b. "s" inserted by hand	—	£1700
		c. Perf 14½–15	£190	£190
		ca. "s" inverted		
188	**59**	10c. on 12c. black and deep blue (R.)	60·00	70·00
		a. "s" inverted (R. 2/5)	£180	£190
		b. "s" inserted by hand	£1500	
186/8 *Set of 3*			£100	95·00
186s/8s Optd "Specimen" *Set of 3*			£120	

Nos. 186/8 were surcharged from a setting of 25 (5×5) on which the required face values were inserted.

1916 (May). Stamps of 1909–11 optd with T **68** by Waterlow. Centres in black. P 13½–14.

(a) Cross in vermilion (thick shiny ink).

189	**51**	1c. brown	7·50	35·00
190	**52**	2c. green	50·00	80·00
		a. Perf 14½–15	32·00	80·00
		ab. Opt double, one albino	£350	
191	**53**	3c. rose-lake	27·00	50·00
		a. Nos. 191 and 204 *se-tenant* (vert pair)	£3500	
192	**54**	4c. scarlet	5·50	32·00
		a. Perf 14½–15	£250	£170
193	**55**	5c. yellow-brown	48·00	55·00
		a. Perf 14½–15		
194	**56**	6c. apple-green	65·00	70·00
		a. Perf 14½–15	£225	£225
195	**57**	8c. lake	23·00	60·00
196	**58**	10c. blue	48·00	70·00
197	**59**	12c. deep blue	£100	£100
198	**60**	16c. brown-lake	£100	£100
199	**61**	20c. on 18c. blue-green	50·00	£100
200	**62**	24c. dull mauve	£130	£130
		a. Imperf between (vert pair)		
201	**64**	25c. green (P 14½–15)	£350	£425
		a. Re-entry	£1000	
189/201 *Set of 13*			£850	£1100

(b) Cross in shades of carmine (matt ink).

202	**51**	1c. brown	26·00	65·00
		a. Perf 14½–15	£250	
203	**52**	2c. green	27·00	50·00
		b. Perf 14½–15	£180	
		ba. Opt double	†	£1600
204	**53**	3c. rose-lake	50·00	65·00
204*a*	**54**	4c. scarlet	£750	£850
205	**55**	5c. yellow-brown	60·00	75·00
206	**56**	6c. apple-green	60·00	75·00
		a. Perf 14½–15	£200	£225
207	**57**	8c. lake	29·00	55·00
208	**58**	10c. blue	55·00	75·00
209	**59**	12c. deep blue	95·00	£110
210	**60**	16c. brown-lake	£100	£110
211	**61**	20c. on 18c. blue-green	95·00	£100
212	**62**	24c. dull mauve	£120	£140
213	**64**	25c. green	£800	
		a. Perf 14½–15	£425	£475
		ab. Re-entry	£1200	
202/13a (*ex* 4c.) *Set of 12*			£1000	£1200

The British North Borneo Company donated a proportion of the above issue to be sold by the National Philatelic War Fund for the benefit of the Red Cross and St. John's Ambulance Brigade.

RED CROSS
+
TWO CENTS
(69)

FOUR CENTS
(70)

1918 (Aug). Stamps of 1909–11 surch as T **69**. P 13½–14.

(a) Lines of surcharge 9 mm apart.

214	**51**	1c. +2c.brown	3·50	12·00
		a. Imperf between (horiz pair)	£2750	
215	**52**	2c. +2c.green	1·00	8·50
		a. Imperf between (horiz or vert pair)	£3750	
		b. Imperf (pair)		
		c. Perf 14½–15		
216	**53**	3c. +2c.rose-red	14·00	19·00
		a. Imperf between (horiz pair)	£3750	
		b. Perf 14½–15	28·00	65·00
217		3c. +2c.dull rose-carmine	£150	
		a. Perf 14½–15	£190	
218	**54**	4c. +2c.scarlet	70	5·00
		a. Surch inverted	£425	
219	**55**	5c. +2c.deep brown	8·00	26·00
220		5c. +2c.pale brown	9·50	28·00
221	**56**	6c. +2c.olive-green	5·00	25·00
		a. Perf 14½–15	£225	£250
221*b*		6c. +2c.apple-green	5·00	25·00
		c. Perf 14½–15	£275	
222	**57**	8c. +2c.lake	5·50	11·00
		a. Inverted figure "3" for "C" in "CENTS"		
223	**58**	10c. +2c.blue	8·00	25·00
224	**59**	12c. +2c.deep bright blue	21·00	50·00
		a. Surch inverted	£700	
225	**60**	16c. +2c.brown-lake	22·00	45·00
226	**62**	24c. +2c.mauve	22·00	45·00

(b) Lines of surch 13–14 mm apart.

227	**52**	2c. +2c. green	85·00	£180
228	**56**	6c. +2c. olive-green	£475	£850
229	**64**	25c. +2c. green	10·00	42·00
		a. Re-entry	45·00	
230		50c. +2c. steel-blue	12·00	42·00
		a. Re-entry	55·00	
231		$1 +2c. chestnut	48·00	50·00
		a. Surcharge double, one albino	£300	
		b. Re-entry	£140	
232		$2 +2c. lilac	75·00	95·00
		a. Re-entry	£225	
233	**65**	$5 +2c.lake	£375	£600
234		$10 +2c. brick-red	£425	£650
214/34 *Set of 17*			£950	£1600

The above stamps were dispatched from London in three consignments, of which two were lost through enemy action at sea.

No. 218a normally shows a second inverted albino surcharge.

Only one sheet was found of No. 228.

These stamps were sold at a premium of 2c. per stamp, which went to the Red Cross Society.

1918 (Oct). Stamps of 1909–11 surch with T **70**, in red. P 13½–14.

235	**51**	1c. +4c. chocolate	60	5·00
		a. Imperf between (horiz pair)	£2750	
236	**52**	2c. +4c. green	65	8·00
237	**53**	3c. +4c. rose-lake	1·00	3·75
238	**54**	4c. +4c. scarlet	40	4·75
239	**55**	5c. +4c. brown	2·00	22·00
240	**56**	6c. +4c. apple-green	1·90	12·00
		a. Imperf between (vert pair)	£2500	
241	**57**	8c. +4c. lake	1·25	9·50
242	**58**	10c. +4c. turquoise-blue	3·75	12·00
242*a*		10c. +4c. greenish blue	9·00	42·00
243	**59**	12c. +4c. deep blue	14·00	14·00
		a. Surch double	£1300	
244	**60**	16c. +4c. brown-lake	8·00	16·00
245	**62**	24c. +4c. mauve	11·00	20·00
246	**64**	25c. +4c. yellow-green	8·00	50·00
		a. Re-entry	38·00	
247		25c. +4c. blue-green	25·00	75·00
		a. Re-entry	85·00	
248		50c. +4c. steel-blue	15·00	45·00
		a. Perf 14½–15	60·00	
		b. Re-entry	60·00	
249		$1 +4c. chestnut	21·00	60·00
		a. Perf 14½–15	£160	
		b. Re-entry	70·00	
250		$2 +4c. lilac	50·00	80·00
		a. Re-entry	£140	
251	**65**	$5 +4c. lake	£300	£400
252		$10 +4c. brick-red	£350	£425
235/52 *Set of 17*			£700	£1100

Nos. 235/52 were sold at face, plus 4c. on each stamp for Red Cross Funds.

Examples of a double-ring "SANDAKAN N. BORNEO" postmark dated "1 NOV 1918" on these stamps are generally considered to be faked.

MALAYA-BORNEO
EXHIBITION
1922.
(71)

THREE
CENTS
(72)

1922 (31 Mar). Malaya–Borneo Exhibition, Singapore. Stamps of 1909–22 some in different shades, optd as T **71** by Govt Printing Office, Sandakan. P 13½–14.

253	**51**	1c. brown (R.)	17·00	70·00
		a. "BORHEO"	£325	£750
		b. "BORNEQ"	£500	£850
		c. Stop after "EXHIBITION."	90·00	
		d. Raised stop after "1922"	£850	£1100
		e. "EXHIBITICN." with stop	£850	
		f. Perf 14½–15	38·00	75·00
		fa. "BORHEO"	£550	
		fb. "BORNEQ"	£850	£1100
		fc. Raised stop after "1922"	£800	
		fd. "EXHIBITICN." with stop	£800	
		fe. "MHLAYA" and "EXHIBITION." with stop	£6000	
		ff. Stop after "EXHIBITION."	£160	
253*g*		1c. brown (B.) (P 14½–15)	£1400	
		ga. Vert pair, with and without opt	£8000	
		gb. Raised stop after "1922."	£6500	
		gc. "BORHEO"	£4500	
		gd. "BORNEQ"	£6500	
		gg. "MHLAYA" and "EXHIBITION." with stop	£6500	
		gh. "EXHIBITIOH"	£6500	
254		1c. orange-brown (R.)	40·00	70·00
255	**52**	2c. green (R.)	2·25	25·00
		a. Stop after "EXHIBITION."	35·00	£150
		b. No hyphen	65·00	
256	**53**	3c. rose-lake (B.)	16·00	65·00
		a. Stop after "EXHIBITION."	80·00	£250
		b. "EXHIBITICN." with stop	£4500	
		c. Raised stop after "1922"	£4500	
257	**54**	4c. scarlet (B.)	3·75	42·00
		a. Stop after "EXHIBITION."	42·00	
		b. Perf 14½–15	95·00	
		ba. Stop after "EXHIBITION."	£600	
258	**55**	5c. orange-brown (B.)	9·50	65·00
		a. Imperf between (vert pair)	£1700	£2500
		b. Stop after "EXHIBITION."	70·00	£275
		c. Opt double	£2500	
		d. Opt double (with stop)	£8500	
259		5c. chestnut (B.)	20·00	70·00
		a. Stop after "EXHIBITION."	£100	
260	**56**	6c. apple-green (R.)	9·50	70·00
		a. Stop after "EXHIBITION."	60·00	
		b. Opt double	£2500	
		c. Opt double (with stop)	£8500	
261	**57**	8c. dull rose (B.)	8·00	42·00
		a. Stop after "EXHIBITION."	85·00	
262		8c. deep rose-lake (B.)	9·00	50·00
		a. Stop after "EXHIBITION."	£100	
263	**58**	10c. turquoise-blue (R.)	17·00	65·00
		a. Stop after "EXHIBITION."	£100	
		b. Perf 14½–15	42·00	
		ba. Stop after "EXHIBITION."	£300	
264		10c. greenish blue (R.)	18·00	80·00
		a. Stop after "EXHIBITION."	£110	
265	**59**	12c. deep blue (R.)	11·00	21·00
		a. Stop after "EXHIBITION."	95·00	£170
266		12c. deep bright blue (R.)	40·00	
		a. Stop after "EXHIBITION."	£250	
267	**60**	16c. brown-lake (B.)	23·00	70·00
		a. Stop after "EXHIBITION."	£120	
		b. Opt in red	£11000	
268	**61**	20c. on 18c. blue-green (B.)	25·00	85·00
		a. Stop after "EXHIBITION."	£200	
269		20c. on 18c. blue-green (R.)	26·00	£150
		a. Stop after "EXHIBITION."	£350	£700
270	**62**	24c. mauve (R.)	45·00	75·00
		a. Stop after "EXHIBITION."	£200	£325
271		24c. lilac (R.)	45·00	75·00
		a. Stop after "EXHIBITION."	£200	£325
272		24c. reddish lilac (R.)	50·00	85·00
		a. Stop after "EXHIBITION."	£275	
273	**64**	25c. blue-green (R.)	26·00	80·00
		a. Stop after "EXHIBITION."	£275	
		b. Re-entry	£170	
274		25c. yellow-green (R.)	9·50	65·00
		a. Stop after "EXHIBITION."	£140	

		b. Re-entry	90·00	
		c. Opt double	£3500	
		d. Perf 14½–15	15·00	75·00
		da. Stop after "EXHIBITION."	£225	
		db. Re-entry	£130	
275		50c. steel-blue (R.)	15·00	65·00
		a. Stop after "EXHIBITION."	£170	
		b. Re-entry	£130	
		c. Perf 14½–15	26·00	85·00
		ca. Stop after "EXHIBITION."	£225	
		cb. Re-entry	£160	
253/75 *Set of* 14			£190	£750
253s/75s Optd "Specimen" *Set of* 14			£450	

These overprints were applied from a number of settings covering 10, 20, 25 or 30 stamps at a time.

Of the ten settings known for the horizontal stamps the earliest were only used for the 1c. on which most of the varieties occur. Of the others the vast majority come from settings of 20 (10×2) with the stop after "EXHIBITION" variety on R. 2/7 or R. 2/9, or 25 (5×5) on which the same variety can be found on R. 5/4. In addition the 3c. comes from a different setting of 20 (10×2) on which there is a raised stop after "1922" on R. 2/8 and "EXHIBITICN." on R. 2/9.

The 1c. sequence is complicated, but additionally includes a setting of 10 with "BORHEO" on stamps 3 and 10, BORNEQ" on stamp 4, raised stop on stamp 8 and "EXHIBITICN." on stamp 9. A setting of 20 repeats this sequence on its bottom line as does one of 30, although in this instance "MHLAYA" joins "EXHIBITICN" as the variety on stamp 9.

For the vertical stamps (2, 6, 10, 12, 16 and 20c. on 18c.) the settings were of 20 (10×2) or 25 (5×5). The stop after "EXHIBITION" occurs on R. 2/7 or R. 2/9 of the former and R. 5/4 of the latter.

The 25c. and 50c. high values were overprinted from a setting of 10×1 or 25 (5×5), with the stop after "EXHIBITION" on R. 5/4 of the latter.

1923 (Oct). T **54** surch with T **72**.

276		3c. on 4c. black and scarlet	1·75	6·00
		a. Surch double	£1300	
		s. Optd "Specimen"	50·00	

1925–28. Designs as 1909–22 issue with centres in black and some frame colours changed. P 12½.

277	**51**	1c. chocolate-brown	1·00	70
		a. Imperf between (horiz pair)	£1600	
278	**52**	2c. claret	85	60
		a. Imperf between (vert pair)	—	£1300
		b. Imperf between (horiz pair)		
279	**53**	3c. green	3·00	75
		a. Imperf between (horiz pair)	†	£1700
280	**54**	4c. scarlet	50	10
		a. Imperf between (vert pair)	£275	£425
		b. Imperf between (horiz pair)	£750	
		c. Imperf between (vert strip of three)	£1100	
281	**55**	5c. yellow-brown	6·00	2·75
		a. Imperf between (vert pair)	£1000	
282	**56**	6c. olive-green	8·50	90
283	**57**	8c. carmine	4·00	50
		a. Imperf between (vert pair)	£500	
		b. Imperf between (horiz pair)		
		c. Imperf between (vert strip of four)	£1700	
284	**58**	10c. turquoise-blue	4·00	90
		a. Imperf between (horiz pair)	£1000	£1500
		b. Imperf between (vert pair)		
285	**59**	12c. deep blue	22·00	80
286	**60**	16c. red-brown	32·00	£190
287	**61**	20c. on 18c. blue-green (R.)	14·00	3·00
288	**62**	24c. violet	60·00	£160
289	**64**	25c. green	14·00	4·25
		a. Re-entry	60·00	25·00
290		50c. steel-blue	22·00	14·00
		a. Re-entry	75·00	50·00
291		$1 chestnut	23·00	£500
		a. Re-entry	80·00	
292		$2 mauve	75·00	£600
		a. Re-entry	£200	
293	**65**	$5 lake (1928)	£180	£1100
294		$10 orange-red (1928)	£475	£1300
277/94 *Set of* 18			£850	£3500

Examples of No. 278 were supplied for U.P.U. distribution punched with a 3½ mm diameter hole.

Examples of the 16c., 24c., $1, $2, $5 and $10 in this perforation were not supplied to the territory for postal purposes. Used examples exist from covers prepared by stamp dealers.

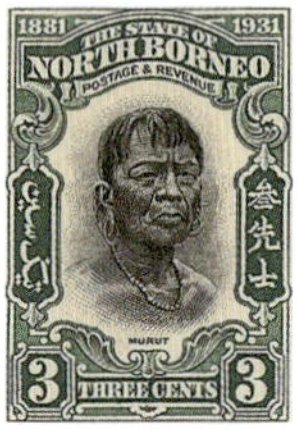
73 Head of a Murut

74 Orang-Utan

75 Dyak warrior

76 Mount Kinabalu

77 Clouded Leopard

78 Badge of the Company

79 Arms of the Company

80 Arms of the Company

(Eng J. A. C. Harrison. Recess Waterlow)

1931 (1 Jan). 50th Anniv of British North Borneo Company. T **73/80**. P 12½.

295	**73**	3c. black and blue-green	1·25	80
296	**74**	6c. black and orange	16·00	3·25
297	**75**	10c. black and scarlet	4·25	13·00
298	**76**	12c. black and ultramarine	4·75	8·00
299	**77**	25c. black and violet	38·00	35·00
300	**78**	$1 black and yellow-green	27·00	£100
301	**79**	$2 black and chestnut	48·00	£110
302	**80**	$5 black and purple	£150	£475
295/302 *Set of* 8			£250	£700
295s/302s Optd "Specimen" *Set of* 8			£300	

Examples of all values are known showing a forged Jesselton postmark dated "22 AUG 1931".

81 Buffalo Transport

82 Palm Cockatoo

83 Native

84 Proboscis Monkey

85 Mounted Bajaus

86 Eastern Archipelago

87 Orang-Utan

88 Murut with blowpipe

89 Dyak

90 River scene

91 Native boat

92 Mt. Kinabalu

93 Badge of the Company

94 Arms of the Company

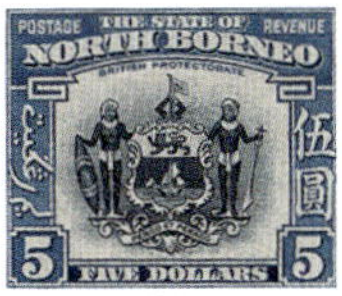

95 Arms of the Company

(Eng J. A. C. Harrison. Recess Waterlow)

1939 (1 Jan). T **81**/**95**. P 12½.

303	**81**	1c. green and red-brown	4·00	2·00
304	**82**	2c. purple and greenish blue	5·00	2·00
305	**83**	3c. slate-blue and green	5·00	2·25
306	**84**	4c. bronze-green and violet	12·00	50
307	**85**	6c. deep blue and claret	11·00	12·00
308	**86**	8c. scarlet	15·00	1·75
309	**87**	10c. violet and bronze-green	38·00	6·50
310	**88**	12c. green and royal blue	38·00	7·00
		a. Green and blue	60·00	10·00
311	**89**	15c. blue-green and brown	30·00	11·00
312	**90**	20c. violet and slate-blue	22·00	6·00
313	**91**	25c. green and chocolate	27·00	14·00
		a. Vignette printed double, one albino	£190	
314	**92**	50c. chocolate and violet	30·00	12·00
315	**93**	$1 brown and carmine	£100	21·00
316	**94**	$2 violet and olive-green	£160	£130
317	**95**	$5 indigo and pale blue	£475	£300
303/17 *Set of* 15			£900	£475
303s/17s Perf "Specimen" *Set of* 15			£500	

Examples of most values are known showing forged Jesselton postmarks dated "22 AUG 1941" or "15 JA 48".

No. 313a has the albino impression sideways.

WAR TAX (**96**)   WAR TAX (**97**)

1941 (24 Feb). Nos. 303/4 optd at Sandakan with T **96**/**7**.

318	1c. green and red-brown	2·25	4·00
	a. Optd front and back	£550	
319	2c. purple and greenish blue	9·00	4·25

The 1c. was for compulsory use on internal mail and the 2c. on overseas mail, both in addition to normal postage.

BRITISH MILITARY ADMINISTRATION

North Borneo, including Labuan, was occupied by the Japanese in January 1942. Australian forces landed on Labuan on 10 June 1945 and by the end of the war against Japan on 14 August had liberated much of western North Borneo. The territory was placed under British Military Administration on 5 January 1946.

BMA (**98**)

(**99**)

1945 (17 Dec). Nos. 303/17 optd with T **98**.

320	**81**	1c. green and red-brown	12·00	2·00
321	**82**	2c. purple and greenish blue	14·00	2·00
		a. Opt double	£8000	
322	**83**	3c. slate-blue and green	1·25	1·25
323	**84**	4c. bronze-green and violet	17·00	16·00
324	**85**	6c. deep blue and claret	1·25	1·25
325	**86**	8c. scarlet	3·00	75
326	**87**	10c. violet and bronze-green	3·00	40
327	**88**	12c. green and blue	6·00	3·25
		a. Green and royal blue	10·00	2·25
328	**89**	15c. blue-green and brown	1·50	1·00
329	**90**	20c. violet and slate-blue	6·00	2·00
330	**91**	25c. green and chocolate	6·50	1·50
331	**92**	50c. chocolate and violet	4·00	2·25
332	**93**	$1 brown and carmine	48·00	40·00
333	**94**	$2 violet and olive-green	50·00	38·00
		a. Opt double	£4000	
334	**95**	$5 indigo and pale blue	26·00	16·00
320/34 *Set of* 15			£180	£110

These stamps and the similarly overprinted stamps of Sarawak were obtainable at all post offices throughout British Borneo (Brunei, Labuan, North Borneo and Sarawak), for use on local and overseas mail.

CROWN COLONY

North Borneo became a Crown Colony on 15 July 1946.

Lower bar broken at right (R. 8/3)

Lower bar broken at left (R. 8/4 and R. 8/8)

1947 (1 Sept–22 Dec). Nos. 303 to 317 optd with T **99** and bars obliterating words "THE STATE OF" and "BRITISH PROTECTORATE".

335	**81**	1c. green and red-brown (15.12)	15	1·00
		b. Lower bar broken at right	22·00	40·00
		c. Lower bar broken at left	20·00	35·00
336	**82**	2c. purple and greenish blue (22.12)	1·75	90
337	**83**	3c. slate-blue and green (R.) (22.12)	15	90
338	**84**	4c. bronze-green and violet	70	90
339	**85**	6c. deep blue and claret (R.) (22.12)	25	20
340	**86**	8c. scarlet	30	20
		b. Lower bar broken at right	23·00	22·00
341	**87**	10c. violet and bronze-green (15.12)	1·50	40
342	**88**	12c. green and royal blue (22.12)	2·50	2·75
		a. Green and blue	9·50	8·50

343	**89**	15c. blue-green and brown (22.12)	2·25	30
344	**90**	20c. violet and slate-blue (22.12)	3·50	85
		b. Lower bar broken at right	55·00	32·00
345	**91**	25c. green and chocolate (22.12)	3·00	50
		b. Lower bar broken at right	75·00	32·00
346	**92**	50c. chocolate and violet (22.12)	3·00	85
		b. Lower bar broken at right	75·00	32·00
		c. Lower bar broken at left	70·00	30·00
347	**93**	$1 brown and carmine (22.12)	11·00	1·75
348	**94**	$2 violet and olive-green (22.12)	17·00	17·00
349	**95**	$5 indigo and pale blue (R.) (22.12)	28·00	21·00
		b. Lower bar broken at right	£200	£180
335/49 *Set of* 15			65·00	45·00
335s/49s Perf "Specimen" *Set of* 15			£300	

1948 (1 Nov). Royal Silver Wedding. As Nos. 131/2 of Johore.

350	8c. scarlet	30	80
351	$10 mauve	27·00	35·00

1949 (10 Oct). 75th Anniv of U.P.U. As Nos. 96/9 of Brunei.

352	8c. carmine	60	30
353	10c. brown	3·25	1·75
354	30c. orange-brown	1·25	1·75
355	55c. blue	1·25	2·75
352/5 *Set of* 4		5·50	6·00

100 Mount Kinabalu

101 Native musical instrument

102 Coconut Grove

103 Hemp drying

104 Cattle at Kota Belud

105 Map

106 Log pond

107 Malay prau, Sandakan

108 Bajau Chief

109 Suluk river canoe, Lahad Datu

110 Clock Tower Jesselton

111 Bajau horsemen

112 Murut with blowpipe

113 Net-fishing

114 Arms of North Borneo

(Photo Harrison)

1950 (1 July)–**52**. T **100/114**. Chalk-surfaced paper. Wmk Mult Script CA. P 13½×14½ (horiz), 14½×13½ (vert).

356	**100**	1c. red-brown	15	1·25
357	**101**	2c. blue	15	50
358	**102**	3c. green	15	15
359	**103**	4c. bright purple	15	10
360	**104**	5c. violet	15	10
361	**105**	8c. scarlet	1·25	85
362	**106**	10c. maroon	1·50	15
363	**107**	15c. ultramarine	2·00	65
364	**108**	20c. brown	2·25	10
365	**109**	30c. olive-brown	5·50	30
366	**110**	50c. rose-carmine ("JESSLETON")	1·50	4·00
366*a*		50c. rose-carmine ("JESSELTON") (1.5.52)	14·00	3·25
367	**111**	$1 red-orange	5·00	1·00
368	**112**	$2 grey-green	11·00	18·00
369	**113**	$5 emerald-green	19·00	27·00
370	**114**	$10 dull blue	50·00	80·00
356/70 *Set of* 16			£100	£120

1953 (3 June). Coronation. As No. 152 of Johore.

371	10c. black and bright scarlet	1·75	1·00

115 Log Pond

(Photo Harrison)

1954 (1 Mar)–**59**. Designs previously used for King George VI issue, but with portrait of Queen Elizabeth II as in T **115**. Chalk-surfaced paper. Wmk Mult Script CA. P 14½×13½ (vert) or 13½×14½ (horiz).

372	**100**	1c. red-brown (1.10.54)	10	30
373	**101**	2c. blue (1.6.56)	1·00	15
374	**102**	3c. green (1.2.57)	3·25	2·00
		a. Deep green (14.1.59)	6·00	4·25
375	**103**	4c. bright purple (16.5.55)	1·25	20
376	**104**	5c. reddish violet (1.7.54)	75	10
377	**105**	8c. scarlet (1.10.54)	75	30
378	**115**	10c. maroon	30	10
379	**107**	15c. bright blue (16.5.55)	1·00	10
380	**108**	20c. brown (3.8.54)	50	15
381	**109**	30c. olive-brown (3.8.54)	2·50	20
382	**110**	50c. rose-carmine ("JESSELTON") (10.2.56)	5·00	20
		a. Rose (9.12.59)	17·00	1·50
		aw. Wmk inverted	—	£300
383	**111**	$1 red-orange (1.4.55)	6·50	20
384	**112**	$2 deep green (1.10.55)	12·00	1·25
		a. Grey-green (22.1.58)	28·00	6·50
385	**113**	$5 emerald-green (1.2.57)	10·00	29·00
386	**114**	$10 deep blue (1.2.57)	26·00	35·00
372/86 *Set of* 15			65·00	60·00

Plate 2 of the 30c., released 10 August 1960, had a finer, 250 screen, instead of the previous 200 (*price £3 mint*).

116 Borneo Railway, 1902

117 Malay prau

118 Mount Kinabalu

119 Arms of Chartered Company

(Recess Waterlow)

1956 (1 Nov). 75th Anniv of British North Borneo Co. T **116/19**. Wmk Mult Script CA. P 13×13½ (horiz) or 13½×13 (vert).

387	**116**	10c. black and rose-carmine	1·00	40
388	**117**	15c. black and red-brown	30	30
389	**118**	35c. black and bluish green	30	1·50
390	**119**	$1 black and slate	65	2·50
387/90 *Set of 4*			2·00	4·25

120 Sambar Stag

121 Sun Bear

122 Clouded Leopard

123 Dusun woman with gong

124 Map of Borneo

125 Banteng

126 Butterfly orchid

127 Sumatran Rhinoceros

128 Murut with blow-pipe

129 Mount Kinabalu

130 Dusun and buffalo transport

131 Bajau horsemen

132 Orang-Utan

133 Rhinoceros Hornbill

134 Crested Wood Partridge

135 Arms of North Borneo

(Des Chong Yun Fatt. Recess Waterlow (until 1962), then D.L.R.)

1961 (1 Feb). T **120/35**. W w **12**. P 13.

391	**120**	1c. emerald and brown-red	20	10
392	**121**	4c. bronze-green and orange	20	90
393	**122**	5c. sepia and violet	30	10
394	**123**	6c. black and blue-green	50	40
395	**124**	10c. green and red	60	10
396	**125**	12c. brown and grey-green	30	10
397	**126**	20c. blue-green and ultramarine	3·50	10
398	**127**	25c. grey-black and scarlet	1·00	1·25
399	**128**	30c. sepia and olive	85	20
400	**129**	35c. slate-blue and red-brown	2·25	2·00
401	**130**	50c. emerald and yellow-brown	2·00	20
402	**131**	75c. grey-blue and bright purple	14·00	90
403	**132**	$1 brown and yellow-green	13·00	80
404	**133**	$2 brown and slate	32·00	3·25
405	**134**	$5 emerald and maroon	38·00	20·00
406	**135**	$10 carmine and blue	40·00	42·00
391/406 *Set of 16*			£130	65·00

(Des M. Goaman. Photo Harrison)

1963 (4 June). Freedom from Hunger. As No. 117 of Brunei.

407	12c. ultramarine	1·50	75

SABAH

(**136**)

(**137**)

1964 (1 July)–**65**. Nos. 391/406 of North Borneo (D.L.R. printings), optd with T **136** (Nos. 408/19) or T **137** (Nos. 420/3).

408	1c. emerald and brown-red	10	10
409	4c. bronze-green and orange	15	50
410	5c. sepia and violet	30	10
	a. Light sepia and deep violet (17.8.65)	4·75	3·00
411	6c. black and blue-green	1·25	10
412	10c. green and red	2·25	10
413	12c. brown and grey-green	20	10
414	20c. blue-green and ultramarine	4·50	10
415	25c. grey-black and scarlet	1·00	90
416	30c. sepia and olive	30	10
417	35c. slate-blue and red-brown	30	20
418	50c. emerald and yellow-brown	30	10
419	75c. grey-blue and bright purple	4·00	65
420	$1. brown and yellow-green	10·00	1·50
421	$2. brown and slate	16·00	2·50
422	$5. emerald and maroon	16·00	12·00
423	$10. carmine and blue	16·00	30·00
408/23 *Set of 16*		65·00	45·00

Old stocks bearing Waterlow imprints of the 4c., 5c., 20c. and 35c. to $10 were used for overprinting, but in addition new printings of all values by De La Rue using the original plates with the De La Rue imprint replacing the Waterlow imprint were specially made for overprinting.

138 *Vanda hookeriana*

1965 (15 Nov)–**68**. As Nos. 166/72 of Johore, but with Arms of Sabah inset as in T **138**. W w **13** (upright).

424	1c. multicoloured	10	1·25
425	2c. multicoloured	10	1·75
	a. Dark green omitted	£150	
426	5c. multicoloured	10	10
427	6c. multicoloured	30	1·50
428	10c. multicoloured	30	10
429	15c. multicoloured (pale black panel)	2·00	10
	a. Brown-black panel (20.2.68)	3·25	35
430	20c. multicoloured	2·75	75
424/30 *Set of 7*		5·00	5·00

The 5c. to 15c. exist with PVA gum as well as gum arabic.
The higher values used with this issue were Nos. 20/27 of Malaysia (National Issues).

1970 (20 Nov). As No. 428, but W w **13** (sideways).

431	10c. multicoloured	5·00	5·00

1971 (1 Feb)–**78**. As Nos. 175/87 of Johore but with Arms of Sabah, as in T **139**.

(a) Litho by Bradbury, Wilkinson.

432	1s. multicoloured	65	2·50
433	2s. multicoloured	75	2·50
434	5s. multicoloured	80	50
435	6s. multicoloured	1·00	2·00
436	10s. multicoloured	80	15
437	15s. multicoloured	1·00	10
438	20s. multicoloured	1·10	1·25
432/8 *Set of 7*		5·50	8·00

(b) Photo by Harrison (1977–78).

439	1s. multicoloured	1·25	4·75
440	2s. multicoloured	1·25	4·75
441	5s. multicoloured	10·00	2·75
442	10s. multicoloured	1·50	1·25
443	15s. multicoloured	2·50	30
444	20s. multicoloured	£250	11·00
439/44 *Set of 6*		£250	22·00

For differences between litho and photo printings, see after Johore No. 187.
The higher values used with this issue were Nos. 64/71 of Malaysia (National Issues).

140 *Hibiscus rosa-sinensis*

141 Coffee

1979 (30 Apr). As Nos. 188/94 of Johore but with Arms of Sabah as in T **140**.

445	1s. *Rafflesia hasseltii*	10	1·60
446	2s. *Pterocarpus indicus*	10	1·60
447	5s. *Lagerstroemia speciosa*	15	50
448	10s. *Durio zibethinus*	30	10
449	15s. Type **140**	50	10
450	20s. *Rhododendron scortechinii*	30	10
451	25s. *Etlingera elatior* (inscr "*Phaeomeria speciosa*")	80	20
445/51 *Set of 7*		2·00	3·75

For higher values used in conjunction with this series see Nos. 190/7 of Malaysia (National Issues).

1983–85. As Nos. 447/50, but without wmk.

454	5s. *Lagerstroemia speciosa* (1.85)	1·50	2·00
455	10s. *Durio zibethinus* (28.7.84)	5·00	7·50
456	15s. Type **140** (5.85)	2·25	1·00
457	20s. *Rhododendron scortechinii* (blackish brown background) (1983)	65·00	2·00
457*a*	20s. *Rhododendron scortechinii* (bronze green background) (29.11.83)	18·00	2·00
454/7a *Set of 5*		80·00	13·00

*There was no official release date for these stamps. Dates shown are the earliest recorded from postmarks and may be revised if earlier examples are reported.

For details of the shade differences between watermarked and unwatermarked printings see after Malaysia-Johore, No. 200a.
On Nos. 454/6 and 457a the state crest is redrawn larger.

1986 (25 Oct)–**97**. As Nos. 202/8 of Johore, but with Arms of Sabah as in T **141**. P 12.

459	1s. Type **141**	10	30
460	2s. Coconuts	10	30
	f. Perf 14¾×14½ (1994)	3·50	40
461	5s. Cocoa	15	15
	c. Perf 14×13¾ (1998)	6·00	
462	10s. Black pepper	15	10
	c. Perf 14×13¾ (1997)	80	10
	cw. Wmk inverted	9·00	
463	15s. Rubber	25	10
464	20s. Oil palm	25	10
	w. Wmk inverted	16·00	
465	30s. Rice	35	15
	aw. Wmk inverted		
	c. Perf 14×13¾ (1994)	1·00	20
	cw. Wmk inverted	12·00	
	e. Perf 14×14½ (1996)	5·00	30
	ew. Wmk inverted	11·00	
	f. Perf 14¾×14½ (1994)	5·00	30
459/65 *Set of 7*		1·10	1·00

142 *Nelumbium nelumbo* (sacred lotus)

2007 (31 Dec). Garden Flowers. As Nos. 210/15 of Johore, but with Arms of Sabah as in T **142**. Multicoloured. W **138**. Phosphorised paper. P 14×13½.

466	5s. Type **142**	10	10
467	10s. *Hydrangea macrophylla*	15	10
468	20s. *Hippeastrum reticulatum*	25	15
469	30s. Bougainvillea	40	20
470	40s. *Ipomoea indica*	50	30
471	50s. *Hibiscus rosa-sinensis*	65	35
	w. Wmk inverted	22·00	
466/71 *Set of 6*		1·90	1·10

POSTAL FISCALS

Three Cents. Revenue
(F **1**) (Raised stop)

Ten Cents. Revenue
(F **2**)

1886. Regular issues surch as Type F **1** or F **2**.

F1	1	3c. on 4c. pink (No. 6)	£130	£180
		a. Raised stop after "Cents"	£110	£170
F2		5c. on 8c. green (No. 7)	£130	£180
		a. Raised stop after "Cents"	£110	£170
F3	4	10c. on 50c. violet (No. 4)	£180	£200
		a. Surch double	—	£1400
		b. No stop after "Cents" and stop after "Revenue."	£475	£500
		c. Inverted "L" for first "F" in "FIFTY" (R. 5/2)	—	£1100

It is believed that Nos. F1/2 were each surcharged from a horizontal setting of five so that the raised stop variety occurs on every stamp in the first, second, third, sixth, seventh and eighth vertical columns in the sheets of 50 (10×5).

POSTAGE DUE STAMPS

POSTAGE DUE
(D **1**)

1895 (1 Aug)–**97**. Nos. 68/79 optd with Type D **1** horizontally (8, 12, 18 and 24c.) or vertically, reading upwards (others). P 14½–15.

D1	25	2c. black and rose-lake	27·00	40·00	2·75
		a. Opt double*	†	†	£300
		b. Opt vertical, reading downwards*	†	†	£425
D2		2c. black and lake	22·00	24·00	2·25
		a. Perf 13½–14			
		b. Perf 13½–14, comp 12–13*	†	†	10·00

		c. Opt omitted (in vert pair with normal)*	†	†	£1900
D3	**26**	3c. olive-green and dull purple	6·00	16·00	1·00
		a. Bronze-green and dull purple			
		b. Opt vertical, reading downwards*	†	†	—
D4		3c. olive-green and violet			
		a. Perf 13½–14			
		b. Opt double*	†	†	£425
D5	**27**	5c. black and vermilion	55·00	27·00	3·00
		a. Printed double	†	—	—
		b. With stop after "DUE" in opt (1897)	£250		
		c. Opt double	£800	£850	†
		d. Perf 13½–14	—	50·00	2·50
		e. Perf 13½–14, comp 12–13	—	60·00	—
D6	**28**	6c. black and bistre-brown	60·00	70·00	2·50
		a. Perf 13½–14	19·00	48·00	2·50
		b. Perf 12–13*	†	†	—
		c. Perf 13½–14, comp 12–13			
		d. Opt vertical, reading downwards*	†	†	£425
D7	**29**	8c. black and dull purple	50·00	50·00	2·75
		a. Opt double*	†	†	£350
		b. Perf 13½–14			
		ba. Opt inverted*	†	†	£190
		c. Perf 13½–14, comp 12–13	75·00		
D8	**30**	12c. black and blue	—	50·00	2·75
		a. Opt double*	†	†	£375
		b. Perf 13½–14	70·00	50·00	2·75
		c. Perf 13½–14, comp 14½–15	90·00		
D9		12c. black and ultramarine (P 13½–14)	80·00	60·00	—
D10	**31**	18c. black and deep green	70·00	60·00	4·00
		a. Opt inverted	£375	£400	†
		b. Perf 13½–14	85·00	80·00	4·00
		ba. Opt double*	†	†	£300
		c. Opt vertical, reading upwards (1897)	75·00	95·00	5·00
		ca. Opt vertical, reading downwards	£500	£350	†
D11	**32**	24c. blue and rose-lake	80·00	85·00	4·00
		a. Opt double*	†	†	£325
		b. Perf 13½–14	32·00	55·00	4·00
		c. Perf 13½–14, comp 14½–15			
D3s, D5s, D8s, D10cs, D11s Optd "Specimen" *Set of 5*			£150		

There were two local overprintings of these stamps which show variations in the distance between the two words. Further overprints were produced in London for sale to dealers by the British North Borneo Company. Those listings marked with an * only exist from the London overprinting and are usually only known cancelled-to-order.

No. D5b comes from at least one sheet which was included in a later overprinting.

1897–99. Nos. 94/7, 99/103, 106, 108/11 optd with Type D **1** horizontally (8c.) or vertically reading upwards (others). P 14½–15.

D12	**35**	2c. black and lake (1898)	8·50	9·00	1·50
		a. Perf 13½–14	45·00		
		b. Opt horizontal*	£250		
		s. Optd "Specimen"	27·00		
D13		2c. black and green (P 13½–14)*	65·00	†	70
		a. Perf 13½–14, comp 12–13*	—	†	90
		b. Perf 16*			
		c. Perf 12–13*			
		d. Opt vertical, reading downwards*			
		e. Opt horizontal*	£200		
D14	**36**	3c. green and rosy mauve*	28·00	†	50
		a. Perf 13½–14*	48·00	†	2·00
		b. Perf 13½–14, comp 14½–15*			
		c. Opt double*			
D15		3c. green and dull mauve	30·00	48·00	†
D16	**37**	4c. black and carmine*	—	†	1·00
		a. Perf 13½–14	60·00	†	50
D17	**38**	5c. black and orange-vermilion (1899)	65·00	60·00	90
		a. Perf 13½–14	22·00	50·00	1·75
D18	**39**	6c. black and bistre-brown	6·00	35·00	70
		a. Perf 13½–14	—	42·00	50
		b. Perf 13½–14, comp 12–13*	—	†	2·00
		s. Optd "Specimen"	27·00		
D19	**40**	8c. black and brown-purple (1898)	65·00	80·00	†
		a. Opt vertical, reading upwards (P 16)*	†	†	£350
		s. Optd "Specimen"	27·00		
D20		8c. black and brown (opt vert, reading upwards)*	8·50	†	50
		a. Opt vertical, reading downwards*	†	†	£600
		b. Perf 13½–14*			
D21	**42**	12c. black and dull blue*	—	†	5·00
		a. Perf 13½–14*	£150	†	4·00
D22	**44**	18c. black and green (P 16)*	†	†	£850
D23	**46**	18c. black and green (P 13½–14)*	75·00	†	4·00
		a. Perf 13½–14, comp 12–13*	£130	†	4·00
D24	**45**	24c. blue and lake*	—	†	£500
D25	**47**	24c. blue and lake*	45·00	†	2·25
		a. Perf 13½–14*			

In addition to local overprints, stamps from the 1897–1902 series were also overprinted by Waterlow on two occasions for sale by the British North Borneo Company to dealers from London. These Waterlow overprints were not supplied to North Borneo for postal purposes and are indicated by an * in the above listing.

1901–02. Nos. 96/7, 100 and 102/3 optd locally as Type D **1**, but with stop after "DUE", horizontally (8c.) or vertically reading upwards (others). P 13½–14.

D26	**36**	3c. green and rosy mauve (1902)	70·00	70·00
		a. Opt double	£325	
D27		3c. green and dull mauve (P 14½–15) (1902)	65·00	70·00
		a. Opt double	£275	£300
D28	**38**	5c. black and orange-vermilion (P 14½–15)	80·00	
D29	**40**	8c. black and brown-purple (P 14½–15)	23·00	75·00
D30		8c. black and brown (P 14½–15)	£200	£225

1902 (10 Oct)–**12**. Stamps of 1901–05 (optd "BRITISH PROTECTORATE") further optd with Type D **1** locally (No. D31) or by Waterlow (others). P 13½–14.

(a) Optd horizontally showing stop after "DUE".

D31	**34**	1c. black and bistre-brown	4·50	55·00
		a. With raised stop after "DUE"	4·75	60·00

(b) Optd vertically reading upwards.

D32	**35**	2c. black and green (P 16)	£500	£250
D33	**36**	3c. green and rosy mauve	£130	£140
D34	**38**	5c. black & orange-verm (P 14½–15)	£225	£150
D35	**40**	8c. black and brown	£180	£100
D36	**47**	24c. blue and lake	£300	£130

(c) Optd horizontally at centre of stamp.

D37	**34**	1c. black and bistre-brown*	—	†	29·00
		a. Perf 14½–15*	£225	†	29·00
D38	**35**	2c. black and green (1909)	23·00	3·75	30
		a. Perf 14½–15 (1903)	50·00	45·00	†
D39	**36**	3c. green and rosy mauve (1912)	6·50	3·50	30
		a. Perf 14½–15 (1904)	50·00	42·00	†
		ab. Type D **1** opt double	£450		
D40	**37**	4c. black and carmine (1912)	19·00	6·50	30
		a. Type D **1** opt double*	£550	†	£160
		b. Perf 14½–15 (1.3.03)	9·00	20·00	1·75
D41	**38**	5c. black and orange-vermilion (1905)	38·00	4·50	30
		a. Perf 14½–15 (1905)	80·00	32·00	†
D42	**39**	6c. black and bistre-brown (1912)	22·00	11·00	40
		a. Type D **1** opt inverted*	£475	†	£120
		b. Type D **1** opt double	£700	—	—
		c. No stop after "PROTECTORATE" (1912)			
		d. Perf 16 (1906)	85·00	38·00	†
D43	**40**	8c. black and brown (1912)	23·00	4·25	40
		a. No stop after "PROTECTORATE" (1903)	60·00	60·00	†
D44	**41**	10c. brown and slate-lilac (1906)	£275	80·00	5·00
		a. No stop after "PROTECTORATE" (1906)	—	—	†
D45		10c. brown and slate-blue (1912)	£110	23·00	1·40
D46	**42**	12c. black and dull blue (2.12.10)	35·00	20·00	3·25
D47	**43**	16c. green and chestnut (2.12.10)	70·00	25·00	3·25
D48	**46**	18c. black and green (2.12.10)	14·00	19·00	1·50
		a. Type D **1** opt double*	£500	†	80·00
		b. Imperf between (vert pair)	—	†	£850
D49	**47**	24c. blue and lake (1905)	14·00	29·00	3·25
		a. Perf 14½–15 (1909)	—	—	†
		b. Type D **1** opt double*	£350	†	£100

(d) Optd horizontally at top of stamp.

D50	**35**	2c. black and green (P 16) (1906)	90·00	42·00
		a. Perf 14½–15 (1908)	70·00	48·00

D51 **37** 4c. black and carmine (1906) 65·00 25·00

Items marked * only occur in stocks obtained from the British North Borneo Company in London.

(D **2**)

(D **3**)

Type D **2**. Thick letters. Ends of "S" and top of "G" straight. Pointed beard to "G".

Type D **3**. Thinner letters. Ends of "S" and top of "G" slanted. Square beard to "G".

1918–30. Opt with Type D **2** locally.

(a) On stamps of 1909–23. P 13½–14.

D52	**52**	2c. black and green (opt at foot) (1.24)	11·00	75·00
		a. Perf 14½–15	25·00	80·00
		s. Optd "Specimen"	28·00	
D53	**53**	3c. black and green (opt at foot) (1.9.23)	4·50	45·00
D54	**54**	4c. black and scarlet (opt at top) (10.18)	95·00	17·00
D55		4c. black and scarlet (opt at foot) (1.22)	1·00	1·25
D56		4c. black and scarlet (opt in centre) (5.23)	—	17·00
D57	**55**	5c. black and yellow-brown (opt at foot) (1.22)	9·50	27·00
D58		5c. black and yellow-brown (opt in centre) (1.23)	22·00	27·00
D59	**56**	6c. black and olive-green (opt at foot) (1.9.23)	14·00	15·00
D60		6c. black and olive-green (opt in centre) (6.23)	26·00	7·50
D61	–	6c. black and apple-green (opt at foot) (1.9.23)	10·00	16·00
D62	**57**	8c. black and rose-lake (opt at foot) (1.9.23)	1·50	1·50
		a. Opt double	£1100	
D63	**58**	10c. black and turquoise-blue (opt at foot) (1.8.24)	14·00	19·00
		a. Perf 14½–15	£100	£180
D64	**59**	12c. black and deep blue (1.8.24)	65·00	50·00
		a. Horiz pair, one without opt	£13000	
D65	**60**	16c. black and brown-lake (2.29)		
		a. Black and red-brown	22·00	50·00
		s. Optd "Specimen"	32·00	

(b) On stamps of 1925–28 with opt at foot. P 12½ (1928–30).

D66	**52**	2c. black and claret (3.30)	75	1·75
D67	**53**	3c. black and green (1926)	10·00	30·00
D68	**54**	4c. black and scarlet (1926)	1·50	2·00
D69	**55**	5c. black and yellow-brown (1926)	8·50	90·00
D70	**56**	6c. black and olive-green (3.28)	10·00	2·75
D71	**57**	8c. black and carmine (2.28)	7·00	21·00
D72	**58**	10c. black and turquoise-blue (1926)	11·00	90·00
D73	**59**	12c. black and deep blue (1926)	32·00	£160

Dates given as month and year only indicate first known postmark where recorded.

1930–38. Optd with Type D **3**, locally, at foot of stamp.

(a) On stamps of 1909–23. P 13½–14.

D74	**57**	8c. black and carmine (1931)	—	1·50
D75	**60**	16c. black and brown-lake (11.31)	17·00	75·00
		a. Black and red-brown	6·50	

(b) On stamps of 1925–28. P 12½.

D76	**52**	2c. black and claret (5.31)	50	2·00
D77	**53**	3c. black and green (11.38)	8·00	30·00
D78	**54**	4c. black and scarlet (6.36)	—	3·00
D79	**55**	5c. black and yellow-brown	17·00	
D80	**56**	6c. black and olive-green (12.30)	7·50	2·50
D81	**57**	8c. black and carmine (9.31)	3·75	22·00
D82	**58**	10c. black and turquoise-blue (12.32)	19·00	90·00
D83	**59**	12c. black and deep blue	45·00	
D84	**60**	16c. black and red-brown	70·00	£225

Dates given are those of earliest postmark where recorded.

D **4** Crest of the Company

(Recess Waterlow)

1939 (1 Jan). P 12½.

D85	D **4**	2c. brown	6·50	80·00
D86		4c. scarlet	6·50	£110
D87		6c. violet	25·00	£140
D88		8c. green	29·00	£275
D89		10c. blue	70·00	£425
D85/9 *Set of 5*			£120	£950
D85s/9s Perf "Specimen" *Set of 5*			£180	

The stamps of North Borneo were withdrawn on 30 June 1964. For later issues see Malaysia/Sabah.

STAMP BOOKLETS

1973 (8 Dec). Cover as Type B **1** of Johore, but inscr "SABAH". Stitched.

SB1 $3 booklet containing eight 5c., 10c. and twelve 15c. (Nos. 434, 436/7) in blocks of 4 32·00

1979 (1 Dec). Cover as No. SB5 of Johore, but inscr "SABAH". Stitched.

SB2 $3 booklet containing eight 5c., 10c., and twelve 15c. (Nos. 447/9) in blocks of 4 11·00

No. SB2 exists with two different versions of the back cover.

1987 (1 June). Cover as Type B **2** of Johore, but inscr "SABAH". Stapled.

SB3 $2 booklet containing 5c., 10c., 15c. and 20c. (Nos. 461/4) in blocks of 4 11·00

1992 (1 July). "Kuala Lumpur '92" International Philatelic Exhibition. Cover as Type B3 of Johore, but inscr "Sabah". Stamps attached by selvedge.

SB4 $3 booklet containing 30c. (No. 465) in block of 10. 9·00

1993. Covers as Nos. SB8/9 of Johore, but inscr "Sabah". Stamps attached by selvedge.

SB5 $2 booklet containing 20c. (No. 464) in block of 10. 1·50

SB6 $3 booklet containing 30c. (No. 465) in block of 10. 2·00

XII. JAPANESE OCCUPATION OF NORTH BORNEO

Japanese forces landed in Northern Borneo on 15 December 1941 and the whole of North Borneo had been occupied by 19 January 1942.

Brunei, North Borneo, Sarawak and, after a short period, Labuan, were administered as a single territory by the Japanese. Until 12 December 1942, previous stamp issues, without overprint, continued to be used in conjunction with existing postmarks. From November 1942 onwards unoverprinted stamps of Japan were made available and examples can be found used from the area for much of the remainder of the War. Japanese Occupation issues for Brunei, North Borneo and Sarawak were equally valid throughout the combined territory but not, in practice, equally available.

PRICES FOR STAMPS ON COVER	
Nos. J1/17	*from* × 5
Nos. J18/19	*from* × 6
Nos. J20/32	*from* × 25
Nos. J33/4	*from* × 2
Nos. J35/48	*from* × 12

(**1**)

2 Mt. Kinabalu

3 Borneo Scene

1942 (30 Sept). Stamps of North Borneo handstamped with T **1**.

(a) In violet on Nos. 303/17.

J1	1c. green and red-brown	£160	£225
	a. Black opt	£275	£200
	ab. Pair, one without opt	£3750	
J2	2c. purple and greenish blue	£170	£225
	a. Black opt	£425	£225
J3	3c. slate-blue and green	£130	£225
	a. Black opt	£450	£325
J4	4c. bronze-green and violet	£225	£275
	a. Black opt	50·00	£130
J5	6c. deep blue and claret	£150	£275
	a. Black opt	£450	£350
J6	8c. scarlet	£190	£190
	a. Pair, one without opt	£3750	
	b. Black opt	£250	£190
J7	10c. violet and bronze-green	£180	£300
	a. Black opt	£425	£300
J8	12c. green and bright blue	£190	£450
	a. Black opt	£700	£450
J9	15c. blue-green and brown	£170	£450
	a. Pair, one without opt	£3750	
	b. Black opt	£750	£450
J10	20c. violet and slate-blue	£200	£550
	a. Black opt	£850	£550

J11		25c. green and chocolate	£200	£550
		a. Black opt	£850	£550
J12		50c. chocolate and violet	£275	£650
		a. Black opt	£950	£650
J13		$1 brown and carmine	£325	£800
		a. Black opt	£1100	£800
J14		$2 violet and olive-green	£475	£1000
		a. Pair, one without opt	£5000	
		b. Black opt	£1500	£950
J15		$5 indigo and pale blue	£600	£1100
		a. Black opt	£2000	£1300

(b) In black on Nos. 318/19 ("WAR TAX").

J16		1c. green and red-brown	£600	£300
		a. Pair, one without opt	†	£3750
		b. Violet opt	—	£850
J17		2c. purple and greenish blue	£1600	£550
		a. Pair, one without opt	†	£6000
		b. Violet opt	—	£1100

(Litho Kolff & Co., Batavia)

1943 (29 Apr). P 12½.

J18	**2**	4c. red	22·00	48·00
J19	**3**	8c. blue	18·00	45·00

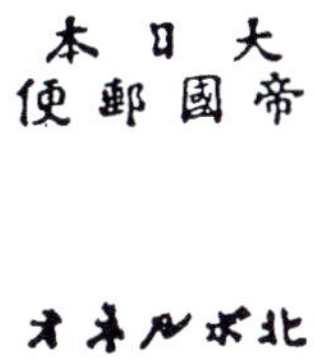

(4)

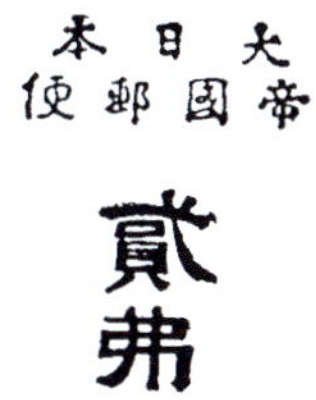

(5)

("Imperial Japanese Postal Service North Borneo")

1944 (30 Sept). Nos. 303/15 of North Borneo optd with T **4** at Chinese Press, Kuching.

J20		1c. green and red-brown	5·50	12·00
J21		2c. purple and greenish blue	7·50	9·00
		a. Optd on No. J2	£425	
J22		3c. slate-blue and green	6·00	10·00
		a. Optd on No. J3	£425	
J23		4c. bronze-green and violet	11·00	19·00
J24		6c. deep blue and claret	8·00	6·50
J25		8c. scarlet	9·50	17·00
		a. Optd on No. J6	£425	
J26		10c. violet and bronze-green	8·50	13·00
		a. Optd on No. J7	£425	
		b. Optd on No. J7a	£200	£400
J27		12c. green and bright blue	14·00	13·00
		a. Optd on No. J8	£425	
J28		15c. blue-green and brown	13·00	16·00
		a. Optd on No. J9	£425	
J29		20c. violet and slate-blue	27·00	45·00
		a. Optd on No. J10	£2250	
J30		25c. green and chocolate	27·00	45·00
		a. Optd on No. J11	£2250	
J31		50c. chocolate and violet	70·00	£120
		a. Optd on No. J12	£3000	
J32		$1 brown and carmine	90·00	£150
J20/32 *Set of* 13			£250	£425

The spacing between the second and third lines of the overprint is 12 mm on the horizontal stamps, and 15 mm on the upright.

1944 (11 May). No. J1 surch with T **5**.

J33	**81**	$2 on 1c green and red-brown	£4500	£3750

(6)

7 Girl War-worker

(**8**) ("North Borneo")

1944 (11 May). North Borneo No. 315 surch with T **6**.

J34		$5 on $1 brown and carmine	£4000	£3000
		a. Surch on No. J13	£7000	£4500

1944 (2 Oct)–**45**. Contemporary stamps of Japan as T **7** (various subjects) optd with T **8** at Chinese Press, Kuching.

J35		1s. red-brown (No. 391) (1.45)	8·50	26·00
J36		2s. scarlet (No. 392b) (10.44)	7·50	23·00
J37		3s. emerald-green (No. 316) (8.45)	8·00	26·00
J38		4s. yellow-green (No. 395) (10.44)	14·00	22·00
J39		5s. claret (No. 396) (1.45)	11·00	25·00
J40		6s. orange (No. 319) (8.45)	16·00	26·00
		a. Opt double, one inverted	£500	£500
J41		8s. violet (No. 321) (11.44)	6·50	26·00
		a. Opt double	£350	
J42		10s. carmine and pink (No. 399) (1.45)	9·50	26·00
J43		15s. blue (No. 401) (11.44)	11·00	26·00
J44		20s. blue-slate (No. 325) (11.44)	80·00	90·00
J45		25s. brown and chocolate (No. 326) (2.45)	55·00	75·00
J46		30s. turquoise-blue (No. 327)	£170	95·00
J47		50s. olive and bistre (No. 328) (8.45)	70·00	70·00
J48		1y. red-brown and chocolate (No. 329) (5.45)	70·00	£100
J35/48 *Set of* 14			£475	£600

Designs:—2s. General Nogi; 3s. Hydro-electric Works; 4s. Hyuga Monument and Mt Fuji; 5s. Admiral Togo; 6s. Garambi Lighthouse, Formosa; 8s. Meiji Shrine; 10s. Palms and map of S.E. Asia; 15s. Airman; 20s. Mt Fuji and cherry blossoms; 25s. Horyu Temple; 30s. Torii, Itsukushima Shrine at Miyajima; 50s. Kinkaku Temple; 1y. Great Buddha, Kamakura.

Examples of some values have been found with hand-painted forged overprints.

POSTAGE DUE STAMPS

1942 (30 Sept). Nos. D85/6 and D88 of North Borneo handstamped with T **1** in black.

JD1	D **2**	2c. brown	—	£4000
JD2		4c. scarlet	—	£4000
JD3		8c. green	—	£4000

XIII. SARAWAK

Sarawak was placed under British protection in 1888. It was ceded to Great Britain on 1 July 1946 and was administered as a Crown Colony until 16 September 1963 when it became a state of the Federation of Malaysia.

From 1859 letters from Sarawak to overseas addresses, other than to other British possessions in Borneo and Singapore, were franked by stamps of INDIA and, after 1867, STRAITS SETTLEMENTS, a stock of which was kept by the Sarawak Post Office. The stamps of Sarawak continued to have this limited validity until 1 July 1897 when the country joined the U.P.U.

PRICES FOR STAMPS ON COVER TO 1945	
No. 1	—
Nos. 2/7	*from* × 50
Nos. 8/21	*from* × 8
Nos. 22/6	*from* × 6
No. 27	*from* × 40
Nos. 28/35	*from* × 6
Nos. 36/47	*from* × 8
No. 48	†
No. 49	*from* × 10
Nos. 50/61	*from* × 6
No. 62	†
Nos. 63/71	*from* × 4
Nos. 72/3	*from* × 8
Nos. 74/5	—
Nos. 76/90	*from* × 7
Nos. 91/105	*from* × 5
Nos. 106/25	*from* × 3
Nos. 126/45	*from* × 2

BROOKE FAMILY ADMINISTRATION

Sir James Brooke. 1842–11 June 1868

Sir Charles Brooke. 11 June 1868–17 May 1917

UNUSED PRICES. Nos. 1/7, 27 and 32/5 in unused condition are normally found without gum. Prices in the unused column are for stamps in this state. Examples of these issues with original gum are worth considerably more.

1 Sir James Brooke

2 Sir Charles Brooke

The initials in the corners of T **1** and **2** stand for "James (Charles) Brooke, Rajah (of) Sarawak".

(T **1** and **2**. Die eng Wm. Ridgeway. Litho Maclure, Macdonald & Co, Glasgow)

1869 (1 Mar). P 11.

1	**1**	3c. brown/*yellow*	50·00	£225

Similar stamps are known printed from the engraved die in orange-brown on orange surface-coloured paper, and perf 12. These are specimens submitted to the Sarawak authorities and exist both with and without obliterations.

1871 (1 Jan). P 11 (irregular).

2	**2**	3c. brown/*yellow*	1·75	3·50
		a. Stop after "THREE"	48·00	65·00
		b. Imperf between (vert pair)	£550	
		c. Imperf between (horiz pair)	£900	

The "stop" variety, No. 2a, which occurs on R. 10/7 of printing stone is of no more philatelic importance than any of the numerous other variations, such as narrow first "A" in "SARAWAK" (R. 2/7) and "R" with long tail in left lower corner (R. 9/10), but it has been accepted by collectors for many years, and we therefore retain it. The papermaker's wmk "L N L" appears once or twice in sheets of No. 2.

Specimens are known, recess-printed, similar to those mentioned in the note after No. 1.

TWO CENTS

Copies of No. 2 surcharged as above were first reported in 1876 but following the discovery of dies for forgeries and faked postmarks in 1891 it was concluded that the issue was bogus, especially as the availability of the 2c. of 1875 made it unnecessary to issue a provisional. It has now been established that a 2c. postal rate was introduced from 1 August 1874 for the carriage of newspapers. Moreover four examples are known with a stop after "CENTS." and showing other minor differences from the forgery illustrated. This version could be genuine and if others come to light we will reconsider listing it.

1875 (1 Jan). P 11½–12.

3	**2**	2c. mauve/*lilac* (*shades*)	14·00	17·00
4		4c. red-brown/*yellow*	4·25	3·00
		a. Imperf between (vert pair)	£800	£900
5		6c. green/*green*	3·75	3·75
6		8c. bright blue/*blue*	3·75	4·50
7		12c. red/*pale rose*	8·00	6·50
3/7 *Set of 5*			30·00	32·00

Nos. 3, 4, 6 and 7 have the watermark "L N L" in the sheet, as No. 2. No. 5 is watermarked "L N T".

All values exist imperf and can be distinguished from the proofs by shade and impression. Stamps rouletted, pin-perf, or roughly perf 6½ to 7 are proofs clandestinely perforated.

The 12c. "laid" paper, formerly listed, is not on a true laid paper, the "laid" effect being accidental and not consistent.

The lithographic stones for Nos. 3 to 7 were made up from strips of five distinct impressions hence there are five types of each value differing mainly in the lettering of the tablets of value. There are flaws on nearly every individual stamp, from which they can be plated.

4 Sir Charles Brooke

(Typo D.L.R.)

1888 (10 Nov)–**97**. No wmk. P 14.

8	**4**	1c. purple and black (6.6.92)	3·50	1·00
9		2c. purple and carmine (11.11.88)	4·25	2·75
		a. Purple and rosine (1897)	12·00	4·75
10		3c. purple and blue (11.11.88)	6·00	4·50
11		4c. purple and yellow	28·00	55·00
12		5c. purple and green (12.6.91)	23·00	3·75
13		6c. purple and brown (11.11.88)	21·00	55·00
14		8c. green and carmine (11.11.88)	14·00	4·25
		a. Green and rosine (1897)	24·00	15·00
15		10c. green and purple (12.6.91)	38·00	14·00
16		12c. green and blue (11.11.88)	13·00	10·00
17		16c. green and orange (28.12.97)	48·00	80·00
18		25c. green and brown (19.11 88)	50·00	45·00
19		32c. green and black (28.12.97)	40·00	60·00
20		50c. green (26.7.97)	55·00	£100
21		$1 green and black (2.11.97)	90·00	95·00
8/21 *Set of 14*			£400	£475

Prepared for use but not issued.

21*a*	$2 green and blue	£950
21*b*	$5 green and violet	£950
21*c*	$10 green and carmine	£950

On No. 21 the value is in black on an uncoloured ground.

The tablet of value in this and later similar issues is in the second colour given.

One Cent. (5) one cent. (6)

2c. (7) 5c (8) 5c. (9)

1889 (3 Aug)–**92**. T **4** surch. P 14.

22	**5**	1c. on 3c. purple and blue (12.1.92)	55·00	35·00
		a. Surch double	£750	£650
23	**6**	1c. on 3c. purple and blue (2.92)	3·00	2·75
		a. No stop after "cent" (R. 2/6)	£250	
24	**7**	2c. on 8c. green and carmine (3.8.89)	3·00	7·00
		a. Surch double	£475	
		b. Surch inverted	£3750	
		c. Surch omitted (in pair with normal)	£7000	
25	**8**	5c. on 12c. green and blue (with stop after "C") (17.2.91)	25·00	48·00
		a. No stop after "C"	32·00	50·00
		b. "C" omitted (in pair with normal)	£650	£700
		c. Surch double	£1300	
		d. Surch double, one vertical	£4000	
		e. Surch omitted (in pair with normal)	£11000	
26	**9**	5c. on 12c. green and blue (17.2.91)	£250	£275
		a. No stop after "C"	£120	£130
		b. "C" omitted (in pair with normal)	£850	£900
		c. Surch double	£1400	

ONE
CENT

(**10**)

1892 (23 May). No. 2 surch with T **10**.

27	**2**	1c. on 3c. brown/*yellow*	1·40	2·00
		a. Stop after "THREE."	42·00	45·00
		b. Imperf between (vert pair)	£750	
		c. Imperf horiz (vert pair)	£700	
		d. Bar omitted (1st ptg)	£225	£250
		e. Bar at top and bottom (1st ptg)	£375	
		f. Surch double (2nd ptg)	£450	£500

No. 27 was surcharged with a setting of 100 (10×10). It was originally intended that there should be no bar at foot, but this was then added at a second operation before the stamps were issued. Subsequent supplies were surcharged with "ONE CENT" and bar at one operation.

Varieties with part of the surcharge missing are due to gum on the face of the unsurcharged stamps receiving part of the surcharge, which was afterwards washed off.

11

12

13 Sir Charles Brooke

14

(Die eng Wm. Ridgeway. Recess P.B.)

1895 (12 Feb–Sept). No wmk. P 11½–12.

28	**11**	2c. brown-red	12·00	9·00
		a. Imperf between (vert pair)	£550	
		b. Imperf between (horiz pair)	£425	
		c. Second ptg. Perf 12½ (Sept)	18·00	4·50
		ca. Perf 12½. Imperf between (horiz pair)	£650	
29	**12**	4c. black	12·00	3·50
		a. Imperf between (horiz pair)	£750	
30	**13**	6c. violet	15·00	9·00
31	**14**	8c. green	32·00	6·00
28/31 *Set of 4*			65·00	21·00

Stamps of these types, printed in wrong colours, are trials and these, when surcharged with values in "pence", are from waste sheets that were used by Perkins, Bacon & Co as trial paper when preparing an issue of stamps for British South Africa.

4
CENTS.
(15)

16

1899 (29 June–16 Nov). Surch as T **15**.

32	**2**	2c. on 3c. brown/*yellow* (19 Sept)	2·25	1·75
		a. Stop after "THREE"	65·00	65·00
		b. Imperf between (vert pair)	£900	
33		2c. on 12c. red/*pale rose*	3·00	3·25
		a. Surch inverted	£900	£1300
34		4c. on 6c. green/*green* (R.) (16 Nov)	38·00	80·00
35		4c. on 8c. bright blue/*blue* (R.)	4·75	9·00
32/5 *Set of* 4			42·00	85·00

A variety of surcharge with small "S" in "CENTS" may be found in the 2c. on 12c. and 4c. on 8c. and a raised stop after "CENTS" on the 4c. on 6c.

The omission of parts of the surcharge is due to gum on the surface of the stamps (see note after No. 27).

A block of 50 of No. 35 from the right of the pane is known line perforated 12.7 between the stamps and the margins at top and right.

(Typo D.L.R.)

1899 (10 Nov)–**1908**. Inscribed "POSTAGE POSTAGE". No wmk. P 14.

36	**4**	1c. grey-blue and rosine (1.1.01)	1·25	1·25
		a. Grey-blue and red	4·75	1·75
		b. Ultramarine and rosine	8·00	2·75
		c. Dull blue and carmine	15·00	4·50
37		2c. green (16.12.99)	2·00	90
38		3c. dull purple (1.2.08)	14·00	65
39		4c. rose-carmine (10.11.99)	12·00	2·50
		a. Aniline carmine	2·50	15
40		8c. yellow and black (6.12.99)	2·25	80
41		10c. ultramarine (10.11.99)	2·75	1·00
42		12c. mauve (16.12.99)	4·75	4·50
		a. Bright mauve (1905)	29·00	8·50
43		16c. chestnut and green (16.12.99)	4·75	1·75
44		20c. bistre and bright mauve (4.00)	5·50	5·00
45		25c. brown and blue (16.12.99)	6·50	5·00
46		50c. sage-green and carmine (16.12.99)	27·00	28·00
47		$1 rose-carmine and green (16.12.99)	80·00	£120
		a. Rosine and pale green	90·00	£130
36/47 *Set of* 12			£140	£150

Prepared for use but not issued.

48	**4**	5c. olive-grey and green	12·00	

The figures of value in the $1 are in colour on an uncoloured ground.

1902. Inscribed "POSTAGE POSTAGE". W **16**. P 14.

49	**4**	2c. green	35·00	17·00

Sir Charles Vyner Brooke. 17 May 1917–1 June 1946

17 Sir Charles Vyner Brooke

ONE
cent
(**18**)

(Typo D.L.R.)

1918 (24 Mar–Apr). Chalk-surfaced paper. No wmk. P 14.

50	**17**	1c. slate-blue and red	2·25	3·00
		a. Dull blue and carmine	2·25	3·00
51		2c. green	2·50	1·50
52		3c. brown-purple (Apr)	3·25	2·75
53		4c. rose-carmine (Apr)	5·50	3·25
		a. Rose-red	7·00	3·00
54		8c. yellow and black (Apr)	12·00	60·00
55		10c. blue (*shades*) (Apr)	4·00	4·00
56		12c. purple (Apr)	15·00	35·00
57		16c. chestnut and green (Apr)	5·50	7·50
58		20c. olive and violet (*shades*) (Apr)	7·00	6·50
59		25c. brown and bright blue (Apr)	4·00	17·00
60		50c. olive-green and carmine (Apr)	10·00	15·00
61		$1 bright rose and green (Apr)	27·00	29·00
50/61 *Set of* 12			90·00	£160
50s/61s Optd "Specimen" *Set of* 12			£275	

Prepared for use but not issued.

62	**17**	1c. slate-blue and slate	22·00	

On the $1 the figures of value are in colour on an uncoloured ground.

Most values are known with part strikes of a forged Kuching postmark dated "12 MAR 90".

1922 (Jan)–**23**. New colours and values. Chalk-surfaced paper. No wmk. P 14.

63	**17**	2c. purple (5.3.23)	2·00	2·75
64		3c. dull green (23.3.22)	2·75	1·25
65		4c. brown-purple (10.4.23)	1·50	1·00
66		5c. yellow-orange	1·75	1·75
67		6c. claret	1·50	1·40
68		8c. bright rose-red (1922)	4·50	32·00
69		10c. black (1923)	2·75	4·25
70		12c. bright blue (12.22)	11·00	18·00
		a. Pale dull blue	11·00	22·00
71		30c. ochre-brown and slate	3·75	4·25
63/71 *Set of* 9			28·00	60·00

1923 (Jan). Surch as T **18**.

		(a) First printing. Bars 1¼ mm apart.		
72	**17**	1c. on 10c. dull blue	10·00	55·00
		a. "cnet" for "cent" (R. 9/5)	£400	£900
73		2c. on 12c. purple	6·50	42·00
		a. Thick, narrower "W" in "TWO"	20·00	£100
		(b) Second printing. Bars ¾ mm apart.		
74	**17**	1c. on 10c. dull blue	£425	
		b. "cnet" for "cent" (R. 9/5)	£17000	
		c. Bright blue	£140	£400
		ca. "en" of "cent" scratched out and "ne" overprinted (R. 9/5)	£6500	
75		2c. on 12c. purple	80·00	£250
		a. Thick, narrower "W" in "TWO"	£150	

In the 2c. on 12c. the words of the surcharge are about 7½ mm from the bars.

The "cnet" error occurred on R. 9/5 of all sheets from the first printing of the 1c. on 10c. A single example of the error, No. 74b, is known from the second printing, but the error was then corrected, as shown by the evidence of a surviving plate block, only to have the correct spelling scratched out by a local employee, and "ne" substituted (No. 74ca).

The thick "W" variety occurs on all stamps of the last two horizontal rows of the first printing (12 stamps per sheet), and in the last two vertical rows of the second (20 stamps per sheet).

1928 (7 Apr)–**29**. Chalk-surfaced paper. W **16** (Multiple). P 14.

76	**17**	1c. slate-blue and carmine	1·50	35
77		2c. bright purple	2·25	1·25
78		3c. green	2·75	5·00
79		4c. brown-purple	1·75	10
80		5c. yellow-orange (7.8.29)	12·00	5·00
81		6c. claret	1·25	30
82		8c. bright rose-red	3·25	22·00
83		10c. black	1·75	1·25
84		12c. bright blue	3·25	29·00
85		16c. chestnut and green	3·25	4·00
86		20c. olive-bistre and violet	3·25	6·50
87		25c. brown and bright blue	5·50	8·50
88		30c. bistre-brown and slate	4·50	10·00
89		50c. olive-green and carmine	8·50	20·00
90		$1 bright rose and green	15·00	24·00
76/90 *Set of* 15			65·00	£120
76s/90s Optd or Perf (5c.) "Specimen" *Set of* 15			£275	

In the $1 the value is as before.

19 Sir Charles Vyner Brooke

20

(Recess Waterlow)

1932 (1 Jan). W **20**. P 12½.

91	**19**	1c. indigo	80	1·00
92		2c. green	1·00	2·00
93		3c. violet	4·00	1·00
94		4c. red-orange	6·00	75
95		5c. deep lake	6·50	1·25
96		6c. scarlet	7·00	9·50
97		8c. orange-yellow	9·00	8·50
98		10c. black	2·25	3·25
99		12c. deep ultramarine	4·00	9·50
100		15c. chestnut	6·50	8·50
101		20c. red-orange and violet	6·50	8·00
102		25c. orange-yellow and chestnut	10·00	22·00
103		30c. sepia and vermilion	9·50	30·00
104		50c. carmine-red and olive-green	14·00	13·00
105		$1 green and carmine	22·00	35·00
91/105 *Set of* 15			95·00	£140
91s/105s Perf "Specimen" *Set of* 15			£325	

21 Sir Charles Vyner Brooke

B M A

(22)

(Recess B.W.)

1934 (1 May)–**41**. No wmk. P 12.

106	**21**	1c. purple	1·25	10
107		2c. green	1·50	10
107*a*		2c. black (1.3.41)	3·75	1·60
108		3c. black	1·25	10
108*a*		3c. green (1.3.41)	7·00	4·50
109		4c. bright purple	2·00	15
110		5c. violet	2·00	10
111		6c. carmine	2·75	60
111*a*		6c. lake-brown (1.3.41)	7·50	8·00
112		8c. red-brown	2·25	10
112*a*		8c. carmine (1.3.41)	8·00	10
113		10c. scarlet	3·25	40
114		12c. blue	3·00	25
114*a*		12c. orange (1.3.41)	6·00	4·75
115		15c. orange	6·50	10·00
115*a*		15c. blue (1.3.41)	8·50	15·00
116		20c. olive-green and carmine	5·50	1·25
117		25c. violet and orange	5·50	1·50
118		30c. red-brown and violet	5·50	2·50
119		50c. violet and scarlet	7·50	75
120		$1 scarlet and sepia	2·50	75
121		$2 bright purple and violet	20·00	20·00
122		$3 carmine and green	40·00	42·00
123		$4 blue and scarlet	40·00	70·00
124		$5 scarlet and red-brown	55·00	75·00
125		$10 black and yellow	27·00	75·00
106/25 *Set of 26*			£250	£300
106s/25s Perf "Specimen" *Set of 26*			£600	

For the 3c. green, wmkd Mult Script CA, see No. 152a.

BRITISH MILITARY ADMINISTRATION

Following the Japanese surrender, elements of the British Military Administration reached Kuching on 11 September 1945. From 5 November 1945 current Australian 1d., 3d., 6d. and 1s. stamps were made available for civilian use until replaced by Nos. 126/45. Other Australian stamps were also accepted as valid for postage during this period.

1945 (17 Dec). Optd with T **22**.

126	**21**	1c. purple	1·25	60
127		2c. black (R.)	2·50	1·25
		a. Opt double	£8000	£8000
128		3c. green	1·25	1·50
129		4c. bright purple	2·25	30
		a. Opt double, one albino	£2000	
130		5c. violet (R.)	3·75	1·00
131		6c. lake-brown	3·00	75
132		8c. carmine	13·00	15·00
133		10c. scarlet	1·50	70
134		12c. orange	3·00	3·75
135		15c. blue	6·50	40
136		20c. olive-green and carmine	3·50	3·25
137		25c. violet and orange (R.)	4·00	2·75
138		30c. red-brown and violet	7·00	2·75
139		50c. violet and scarlet	1·25	35
140		$1 scarlet and sepia	2·50	3·25
141		$2 bright purple and violet	9·00	16·00
142		$3 carmine and green	25·00	80·00
143		$4 blue and scarlet	26·00	55·00
144		$5 scarlet and red-brown	£170	£225
145		$10 black and yellow (R.)	£160	£225
126/45 *Set of 20*			£400	£550

These stamps, and the similarly overprinted stamps of North Borneo, were obtainable at all post offices throughout British Borneo (Brunei, Labuan, North Borneo and Sarawak), for use on local and overseas mail.

The administration of Sarawak was returned to the Brooke family on 15 April 1946, but the Rajah, after consulting the inhabitants, ceded the territory to Great Britain on 1 June 1946. Values from the 1934–41 issue were used until replaced by Nos. 150/64.

23 Sir James Brooke, Sir Charles Vyner Brooke and Sir Charles Brooke

(24)

(Recess B.W.)

1946 (18 May). Centenary Issue. P 12.

146	**23**	8c. lake	2·00	1·00
147		15c. blue	2·50	2·00
148		50c. black and scarlet	2·50	2·50
149		$1 black and sepia	2·50	28·00
146/9 *Set of 4*			8·50	30·00
146s/9s Perf "Specimen" *Set of 4*			£170	

CROWN COLONY

1947 (16 Apr). Optd with T **24**, typo by B.W. in blue-black or red. Wmk Mult Script CA. P 12.

150	**21**	1c. purple	20	30
151		2c. black (R.)	25	15
152		3c. green (R.)	25	15
		a. Albino opt	£7000	
153		4c. bright purple	25	15
154		6c. lake-brown	35	90
155		8c. carmine	1·00	10
156		10c. scarlet	35	20
157		12c. orange	70	1·00
158		15c. blue (R.)	50	40
159		20c. olive-green and carmine (R.)	2·25	50
160		25c. violet and orange (R.)	65	30
161		50c. violet and scarlet (R.)	1·25	40
162		$1 scarlet and sepia	1·50	90
163		$2 bright purple and violet	3·00	3·25
164		$5 scarlet and red-brown	3·00	3·25
150/64 *Set of 15*			14·00	10·50
150s/64s Perf "Specimen" *Set of 15*			£300	

No. 152a shows an uninked impression of T **24**.

1948 (25 Oct). Royal Silver Wedding. As Nos. 131/2 of Johore.

165	8c. scarlet	30	30
166	$5 brown	42·00	48·00

1949 (10 Oct). 75th Anniv of U.P.U. As Nos. 96/9 of Brunei.

167	8c. carmine	1·25	60
168	15c. deep blue	3·50	2·50
169	25c. deep blue-green	2·00	1·50
170	50c. violet	2·00	6·50
167/70 *Set of 4*		8·00	10·00

25 *Trogonoptera brookiana*

26 Western Tarsier

27 Kayan tomb

28 Kayan girl and boy

29 Bead work

30 Dyak dancer

31 Malayan Pangolin

32 Kenyan boys

33 Fire making

34 Kelemantan rice barn

35 Pepper vines

36 Iban woman

37 Kelabit Smithy

38 Map of Sarawak

39 Arms of Sarawak

(Recess; $5 Arms typo B.W.)

1950 (3 Jan). T **25/39**. Wmk Mult Script CA. P 11½×11 (horiz) or 11×11½ (vert).

171	**25**	1c. black	40	30
172	**26**	2c. red-orange	30	40
173	**27**	3c. green	30	60
174	**28**	4c. chocolate	40	20
175	**29**	6c. turquoise-blue	40	15
176	**30**	8c. scarlet	1·00	30
177	**31**	10c. orange	2·00	5·00
178	**32**	12c. violet	3·50	1·50
179	**33**	15c. blue	2·50	15
180	**34**	20c. purple-brown and red-orange	2·75	30
181	**35**	25c. green and scarlet	3·75	30
182	**36**	50c. brown and violet	5·50	30
183	**37**	$1 green and chocolate	23·00	4·50
184	**38**	$2 blue and carmine	32·00	16·00
185	**39**	$5 black, yellow, red and puple	26·00	16·00
171/85 *Set of* 15			90·00	40·00

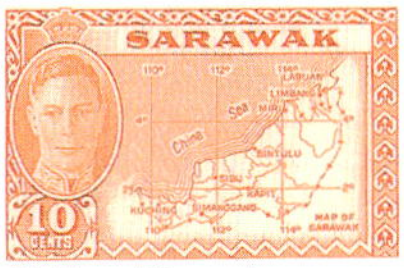

40 Map of Sarawak

(Recess B.W.)

1952 (1 Feb). Wmk Mult Script CA. P 11½×11.

186	**40**	10c. orange	1·75	50

1953 (3 June). Coronation. As No. 152 of Johore.

187	10c. black and deep violet-blue	1·25	1·50

41 Logging

44 Malabar Pied Hornbill

51 Queen Elizabeth II

52 Queen Elizabeth II (after Annigoni)

(Des M. Thoma (1, 2c.), R. Turrell (4c.), J. D. Hughes (6, 12c.) A. Hakim bin Moliti (8c.), J. Woodcock (10c.), J. Browning (15c.), G. Gundersen (20c.), K. Munich (25c.), Recess, Arms typo ($5). B.W.)

1955 (1 June)–**59**. T **41**, **44**, **51/2** and similar designs. Wmk Mult Script CA. P 11×11½ (1c., 2c., 4c.), 12×13 (30c., 50c., $1, $2) or 11½×11 (others).

188	**41**	1c. green (1.10.57)	10	30
189	–	2c. red-orange (1.10.57)	30	55
190	–	4c. lake-brown (1.10.57)	1·00	60
		a. *Brown-purple* (18.3.59)	10·00	6·50
191	**44**	6c. greenish blue (1.10.57)	3·75	3·25
192	–	8c. rose-red (1.10.57)	40	30
193	–	10c. deep green (1.10.57)	30	10
194	–	12c. plum (1.10.57)	3·75	55
195	–	15c. ultramarine (1.10.57)	1·25	30
196	–	20c. olive and brown (1.10.57)	1·00	10
197	–	25c. sepia and green (1.10.57)	6·50	20
198	**51**	30c. red-brown and deep lilac	8·00	30
199	–	50c. black and carmine (1.10.57)	2·50	30
200	**52**	$1 myrtle-green and orange-brown (1.10.57)	11·00	2·00
201		$2 violet and bronze-green (1.10.57)	18·00	3·75
202	–	$5 multicoloured (1.10.57)	27·00	19·00
188/202 *Set of* 15			75·00	28·00

Designs: *Horiz*—8c. Shield with spears; 10c. Kenyah ceremonial carving; 12c. Barong panau (sailing prau); 15c. Turtles; 20c. Melanau basket-making; 25c. Astana, Kuching; $5 Arms of Sarawak. *Vert* (as T **41**)—2c. Young Orang-Utan; 4c. Kayan dancing.

1963 (4 June). Freedom from Hunger. As No. 117 of Brunei.

203	12c. sepia	1·50	1·25

STATE OF MALAYSIA

1964–65. As 1955–57 but wmk w **12**. Perfs as before.

204	**41**	1c. green (8.9.64)	10	75
205	–	2c. red-orange (17.8.65)	75	13·00
206	**44**	6c. greenish blue (8.9.64)	6·00	4·75
207	–	10c. deep green (8.9.64)	1·75	1·25
208	–	12c. plum (8.9.64)	2·50	10·00
209	–	15c. ultramarine (17.8.65)	1·25	14·00
210	–	20c. olive and brown (9.6.64)	50	1·00
211		25c. deep sepia and bluish green (8.9.64)	3·00	5·00
204/11 *Set of* 8			14·00	45·00

53 *Vanda hookeriana*

1965 (15 Nov). As Nos. 166/72 of Johore but with Arms of Sarawak inset as in T **53**.

212	1c. multicoloured	10	1·10
	c. Grey omitted	£120	
213	2c. multicoloured	30	2·00
	a. Black (country name and shield) omitted	£200	
	b. Dark green omitted	£130	
	c. Yellow-olive (stems) omitted	£160	
214	5c. multicoloured	60	10
215	6c. multicoloured	60	2·00
	a. Black (country name and shield) omitted	£200	
216	10c. multicoloured	80	10
	a. Red omitted	£130	
	b. *Intense black*	1·00	20
217	15c. multicoloured	1·50	10
218	20c. multicoloured	2·00	50
212/18 *Set of* 7		5·25	5·25

The 1c., 6c., 10c. and 15c. exist with PVA gum as well as gum arabic.

No. 213a was formerly listed with Trengganu No. 101 but there is evidence that it was issued in Sarawak.

A used example of No. 218 is known with the bright purple (blooms) omitted.

The higher values used with this issue were Nos. 20/7 of Malaysia (National Issues).

(Litho B.W.)

1971 (1 Feb). As Nos. 175/81 of Johore but with Arms of Sarawak inset as in T **54**.

219	1c. multicoloured	65	2·25
220	2c. multicoloured	70	2·25
221	5c. multicoloured	1·75	10
222	6c. multicoloured	1·75	2·50
223	10c. multicoloured	1·75	10
224	15c. multicoloured	2·75	10
225	20c. multicoloured	2·75	1·25
219/25 *Set of 7*		11·00	7·75

The higher values used with this issue were Nos. 64/71 of Malaysia (National Issues).

55 *Precis orithya* (different crest at right)

56 *Rhododendron scortechinii*

(Photo Harrison)

1977 (12 Feb)–**78**. As Nos. 219/21 and 223/5 but ptd in photogravure showing new State Crest as T **55**.

226	1c. multicoloured (1978)	6·50	13·00
227	2c. multicoloured (1978)	13·00	9·50
228	5c. multicoloured	80	70
230	10c. multicoloured (4.4.77)	50	30
231	15c. multicoloured (19.4.77)	1·25	20
232	20c. multicoloured (1978)	3·50	2·25
226/32 *Set of 6*		23·00	23·00

1979 (30 Apr). As Nos. 188/94 of Johore but with Arms of Sarawak as in T **56**.

233	1c. *Rafflesia hasseltii*	10	50
234	2c. *Pterocarpus indicus*	10	50
235	5c. *Lagerstroemia speciosa*	20	70
236	10c. *Durio zibethinus*	20	10
237	15c. *Hibiscus rosa-sinensis*	20	10
238	20c. Type **56**	60	10
239	25c. *Etlingera elatior* (inscr "*Phaeomeria speciosa*")	65	70
233/9 *Set of 7*		1·75	2·40

For higher values used in conjunction with this series see Nos. 190/7 of Malaysia (National Issues).

1983 (11 Oct)–**86**. As Nos. 235/6 and 238 but without wmk.

242	5c. *Lagerstroemia speciosa* (4.4.86)	1·25	1·75
243	10c. *Durio zibethinus* (9.9.85)	85	1·60
245	20c. Type **56** (blackish brown background)	90·00	3·50
245*a*	20c. Type **56** (bronze-green background) (2.8.84)	1·00	1·40
242/5a *Set of 4*		90·00	7·50

*There was no official release date for these stamps. Dates shown are the earliest recorded from postmarks and may be revised if earlier examples are reported.

For details of the shade differences between watermarked and unwatermarked printings see after Malaysia-Johore No. 200a.

On Nos. 242/3 and 245a the crest is closer to the face value than on Nos. 235/6, 238 and 245.

57 Coffee

A

B

Two types of Arms at right.

Type A. Shield divided into three

Type B. Shield with diagonal bars

1988 (25 Oct)–**96**. As Nos. 202/8 of Johore, but with Arms of Sarawak as in T **57**. P 12.

(a) Arms as Type A.

247	1c. Type **57**	10	30
248	2c. Coconuts	10	30
249	5c. Cocoa	15	20
250	10c. Black pepper	15	10
	w. Wmk inverted		
251	15c. Rubber	25	10
	w. Wmk inverted	20·00	
252	20c. Oil palm	25	10
	w. Wmk inverted		
253	30c. Rice	35	15
247/53 *Set of 7*		1·10	1·10

(b) Arms as Type B (1.9.93).

254	1c. Type **57**	10	30
255	2c. Coconuts	10	30
	f. Perf 14¾×14½ (1994)	3·50	30
256	5c. Cocoa	15	20
	aw. Wmk inverted	13·00	
	c. Perf 14×13¾ (1996)	1·50	10
	cw. Wmk inverted	6·00	
257	10c. Black pepper	15	10
	aw. Wmk inverted	10·00	
	c. Perf 14×13¾ (1995)	1·50	20
	e. Perf 14×14½ (1996)	5·00	30
	f. Perf 14¾×14½ (1995)	2·00	20
	fw. Wmk inverted	5·50	
258	15c. Rubber	25	10
259	20c. Oil palm	25	15
	w. Wmk inverted	4·50	
260	30c. Rice	35	15
	aw. Wmk inverted	4·00	
	c. Perf 14×13¾ (1994)	1·75	20
	cw. Wmk inverted (1996)	7·00	
	e. Perf 14×14½ (1994)	4·75	40
	f. Perf 14¾×14½ (1994)	3·25	30
254/60 *Set of 7*		1·10	1·10

58 *Nelumbium nelumbo* (sacred lotus)

2007 (31 Dec). Garden Flowers. As Nos. 210/15 of Johore, but with Arms of Sarawak as in T **58**. Multicoloured. W **138**. Phosphorised paper. P 14.

261	5s. Type **58**	10	10
262	10s. *Hydrangea macrophylla*	15	10
263	20s. *Hippeastrum reticulatum*	25	15
264	30s. Bougainvillea	40	20
265	40s. *Ipomoea indica*	50	30
266	50s. *Hibiscus rosa-sinensis*	65	35
261/6 *Set of 6*		1·90	1·10

STAMP BOOKLETS

1973 (8 Dec). Cover as Type B **1** of Johore, but inscr "SARAWAK". Stitched.

SB1 $3 booklet containing eight 5c., 10c. and twelve 15c. (Nos. 221, 223/4) in blocks of 4 ... 35·00

Examples of No. SB1 exist with a white label giving revised postage rates.

1979 (1 Dec). Cover as No. SB5 of Johore, but inscr "SARAWAK". Stitched.

SB2 $3 booklet containing eight 5c., 10c., and twelve 15c. (Nos. 235/7) in blocks of 4 ... 11·00

No. SB2 exists with two different versions of the back cover.

1987 (1 June). Cover as Type B **2** of Johore, but inscr "SARAWAK". Stapled.

SB3 $2 booklet containing 5c., 10c., 15c. and 20c. (Nos. 249A/52A) in blocks of 4 ... 11·00

1992 (1 July). "Kuala Lumpur '92" International Philatelic Exhibition. Cover as Type B **3** of Johore, but inscr "Sarawak". Stamps attached by selvedge.

SB4 $3 booklet containing 30c. (No. 253A) in block of 10 ... 9·00

1993. Covers as Nos. SB8/9 of Johore, but inscr "Sarawak". Stamps attached by selvedge.

SB5	$2 booklet containing 20c. (No. 252B) in block of 10	1·50
SB6	$3 booklet containing 30c. (No. 253B) in block of 10	2·00

XIV. JAPANESE OCCUPATION OF SARAWAK

Japanese forces landed in North Borneo on 16 December 1941 and Sarawak was attacked on 23 December 1941.

Brunei, North Borneo, Sarawak and after a short period, Labuan, were administered as a single territory by the Japanese. Until September–October 1942, previous stamp issues, without overprint, continued to be used in conjunction with existing postmarks. From 1 October 1942 onwards unoverprinted stamps of Japan were made available and examples can be found used from the area for much of the remainder of the War. Japanese Occupation issues for Brunei, North Borneo and Sarawak were equally valid throughout the combined territory but not, in practice, equally available.

PRICES FOR STAMPS ON COVER

Nos. J1/21	*from* × 8
Nos. J22/6	—

(**1**) ("Imperial Japanese Government")

1942 (Oct). Stamps of Sarawak handstamped with T **1** in violet.

J1	**21**	1c. purple	32·00	80·00
		a. Pair, one without opt	£3000	
J2		2c. green	£140	£190
		a. Black opt	£120	
J3		2c. black	£130	£140
		a. Black opt	£190	£225
J4		3c. black	£450	£450
J5		3c. green	75·00	£100
		a. Black opt	£170	
J6		4c. bright purple	90·00	£100
		a. Black opt	£170	
J7		5c. violet	£110	£120
		a. Black opt	£170	
J8		6c. carmine	£160	£160
J9		6c. lake-brown	£100	£110
		a. Black opt	£160	£170
J10		8c. red-brown	£400	£400
		a. Black opt	£700	
J11		8c. carmine	75·00	£120
		a. Black opt	£325	£400
J12		10c. scarlet	£100	£120
		a. Black opt	£170	
J13		12c. blue	£180	£190
		a. Black opt	£325	
J14		12c. orange	£180	£200
J15		15c. orange	£475	£475
		a. Black opt	£600	
J16		15c. blue	£130	£140
J17		20c. olive-green and carmine	80·00	£110
		a. Black opt	£170	
J18		25c. violet and orange	£120	£130
		a. Black opt	£180	
J19		30c. red-brown and violet	80·00	£110
		a. Black opt	£170	
J20		50c. violet and scarlet	70·00	£110
		a. Black opt	£325	
		b. Blue opt	£600	
J21		$1 scarlet and sepia	£130	£150
		a. Blue opt	£400	
J22		$2 bright purple and violet	£275	£350
		a. Blue opt	£450	
J23		$3 carmine and green	£2250	£2250
		a. Black opt	£3000	
J24		$4 blue and scarlet	£300	£425
J25		$5 scarlet and red-brown	£300	£425
J26		$10 black and yellow	£275	£425

The overprint, being handstamped, exists inverted or double on some values. Those on Nos. J20b, J21a and J22a are diagonal. The remainder are horizontal.

Stamps of T **21** optd with Japanese symbols within an oval frame are revenue stamps, while the same stamps overprinted with three Japanese characters between two vertical double rules, were used as seals.

Nos. J1/26 have been extensively forged. Recent research indicates that complete or part sets on cover cancelled by Japanese circular postmarks in violet dated "17 11 21" (21 Nov 1942) or "18 3 1" (1 Mar 1943) have forged overprints.

Singapore

A Crown Colony until the end of 1957. From 1 August 1958, an internally self-governing territory designated the State of Singapore. From 16 September 1963, part of the Malaysian Federation until 9 August 1965, when it became an independent republic within the Commonwealth.

Stamps in the Crown Colony Victory design with face values of 8c. and 15c. were prepared for Singapore in 1946, but were not issued.

(Currency. 100 cents = 1 Malayan, dollar)

CROWN COLONY

(Typo D.L.R.)

1948 (1 Sept)–**52**. As T **58** of Malaysia (Straits Settlements), but inscribed "SINGAPORE" at foot. Chalk-surfaced paper. Wmk Mult Script CA.

(a) P 14.

1	1c. black	15	1·25
2	2c. orange	15	1·00
3	3c. green	50	1·75
4	4c. brown	20	1·75
5	6c. grey	40	1·00
6	8c. scarlet (1.10.48)	50	1·00
7	10c. purple	30	10
8	15c. ultramarine (1.10.48)	11·00	10
9	20c. black and green (1.10 48)	5·50	1·00
10	25c. purple and orange (1.10.48)	7·00	40
11	40c. red and purple (1.10.48)	9·50	5·00
12	50c. black and blue (1.10.48)	3·25	10
13	$1 blue and purple (1.10.48)	10·00	4·25
14	$2 green and scarlet (25.10.48)	48·00	5·00
15	$5 green and brown (1.10.48)	£110	6·50
1/15	*Set of* 15	£180	27·00

(b) P 17½×18.

16	1c. black (21.5.52)	1·50	4·25
17	2c. orange (31.10.49)	1·50	2·00
19	4c. brown (1.7.49)	1·75	10
19*a*	5c. bright purple (1.9.52)	3·00	2·00
21	6c. grey (10.12.52)	2·00	2·00
21*a*	8c. green (1.9.52)	7·50	4·25
22	10c. purple (9.2.50)	60	10
22*a*	12c. scarlet (1.9.52)	13·00	14·00
23	15c. ultramarine (9.2.50)	19·00	10
24	20c. black and green (31.10.49)	10·00	3·50
24*a*	20c. bright blue (1.9.52)	8·00	10
25	25c. purple and orange (9.2.50)	2·50	10
25*a*	35c. scarlet and purple (1.9.52)	8·00	1·00
26	40c. red and purple (30.4.51*)	45·00	19·00
27	50c. black and blue (9.2.50)	8·50	10
28	$1 blue and purple (31.10.49)	17·00	20
	a. Error. St. Edward's Crown, W **9b**	£12000	£4000
29	$2 green and scarlet (24.5.51)	90·00	1·25
	a. Error. St. Edward's Crown. W **9b**	£15000	
	w. Wmk inverted		
30	$5 green and brown (19.12.51)	£190	1·50
	w. Wmk inverted		
16/30	*Set of* 18	£375	50·00

*Earliest known postmark date.

Single-colour values were from single plate printings (Die II) and all bi-colour, except the 25c., from separate head and duty plates (Die I). For differences between the Dies see after Nos. 278/98 of Malaysia (Straits Settlements). The 25c. is unique in this series in that it combines a Die II frame with a separate head plate.

Nos. 28a and 29a occur on rows in the watermark in which the crowns and letters "CA" alternate.

Postal forgeries of the 50c., $1 and $2 exist on unwatermarked paper and perforated 14×14½.

1948 (25 Oct). Royal Silver Wedding. As Nos. 131/2 of Johore.

31	10c. violet	75	1·00
32	$5. brown	£110	50·00

1949 (10 Oct). 75th Anniv of U.P.U. As Nos. 96/9 of Brunei.

33	10c. purple	75	70
34	15c. deep blue	6·00	4·25
35	25c. orange	6·00	3·00
36	50c. blue-black	6·00	3·25
33/6	*Set of* 4	17·00	10·00

1953 (2 June). Coronation. As No. 152 of Johore.

37	10c. black and reddish purple	2·25	30

1 Chinese Sampan

2 Malay kolek

3 Twa-kow lighter

4 Lombok sloop

5 Trengganu pinas

6 Palari schooner

7 Timber tongkong

8 Hainan junk

9 Cocos-Keeling schooner

10 Douglas DC-4M2 "Argonaut" aircraft

11 Oil tanker

12 *Chusan III* (liner)

13 Raffles Statue

14 Singapore River

15 Arms of Singapore

(Des Dr. C. A. Gibson-Hill, except 25c., 30c., 50c. and $5 (from photographs, etc.). Photo Harrison (1c. to 50a.). Recess (centre typo on $5) B.W. (others)

1955–59. T **1/15**. Wmk Mult Script CA. P 13½×14½ (1e. to 50c.) or 14 (others).

38	**1**	1c. black	10	1·00
39	**2**	2c. yellow-orange	2·00	1·25
40	**3**	4c. brown	1·00	15
		w. Wmk inverted	£250	£275
41	**4**	5c. bright purple	65	50
42	**5**	6c. deep grey-blue	65	70
43	**6**	8c. turquoise-blue	1·25	1·00
44	**7**	10c. deep lilac	3·00	10
45	**8**	12c. rose-carmine	4·25	2·75
46	**9**	20c. ultramarine	2·25	10
		a. *Blue* (13.3.58)	7·00	30
47	**10**	25c. orange-red and bluish violet	7·00	1·50
		a. Orange-red and purple (21.1.59)	27·00	3·75
48	**11**	30c. violet and brown-purple	3·75	10
49	**12**	50c. blue and black	2·25	10
50	**13**	$1 blue and deep purple	30·00	30
		a. Deep purple (Queen's head) omitted	£14000	
51	**14**	$2 blue-green and scarlet	42·00	1·75
52	**15**	$5 yellow, red, brown and slate-black	42·00	5·00
38/52 *Set of* 15			£120	14·50

Plate 2A and 2B of the 10c. (12 April 1960) and the blue "3A" and "3B" plates of the 50c. "3A-2A" "3B-2B" (part of the 24 January 1961 issue and later printings) were printed with a finer screen (250 dots per inch, instead of the normal 200) (*Price* 10c. £3.75 *un*, 20p *us*. 50c. £3.50 *un*, 10p *us*).

No. 50a was caused by a paper fold.

INTERNAL SELF-GOVERNMENT

16 The Singapore Lion

17 State Flag

(Photo Harrison)

1959 (1 June). New Constitution. W w **12.** P 11½×12.

53	**16**	4c. yellow, sepia and rose-red	65	75
54		10c. yellow, sepia and reddish purple	1·00	40
55		20c. yellow, sepia and bright blue	2·25	3·00
56		25c. yellow, sepia and green	2·50	2·25
57		30c. yellow, sepia and violet	2·50	3·25
58		50c. yellow, sepia and deep slate	3·25	3·25
53/8 *Set of* 6			11·00	11·50

(Litho Enschedé)

1960. National Day. W w **12** (sideways*). P 13½.

59	**17**	4c. red, yellow and blue	1·50	1·50
		w. Wmk Crown to right of CA	80·00	
60		10c. red, yellow and grey	2·75	30
		w. Wmk Crown to right of CA	75·00	

*The normal sideways watermark shows Crown to left of CA, *as seen from the back of the stamp.*

18 Clasped Hands

(Photo Enschedé)

1961 (3 June). National Day. W w **12**. P 13½.

61	**18**	4c. black, brown and pale yellow	1·00	1·75
62		10c. black, deep green and pale yellow	1·25	10

19 *Arachnis "Maggie Oei"* (orchid)

20 Yellow Seahorse

21 Six-banded Tiger Barb

24 *Vanda "Tan Chay Yan"* (orchid)

26a Black-naped Tern

30 White-rumped Shama

(Photo Harrison orchids, fish and 15c. bird) D.L.R. (birds, except 15c.)

1962 (31 Mar)–**66**. T **19/21**, **24**, **26a**, **30** and similar designs. W w **12**. P 12½ (i), 14½×13½ (ii), 13½×14½ (iii), 13½×13 (iv) or 13×13½ (v).

63	1c. multicoloured	30	1·00
64	2c. brown and green	30	2·00
65	4c. black and orange-red	30	1·25
	a. Black omitted	£750	
66	5c. red and black	20	10
	a. Red omitted	£650	
67	6c. black and greenish yellow	55	1·25
68	8c. muticoloured (i) (10.3.63)	1·25	3·50
69	10c. red-orange and black (iii)	40	10
	a. Red-orange omitted	£375	£300
	b. Black omitted	£4250	
70	12c. multicoloured (i) (10.3.63)	1·25	3·50
70*a*	15c. multicoloured (i) (9.11.66)	4·50	10
	ab. Orange (eye) omitted	70·00	
	ac. Stone (shading in wings) omitted	£325	
	aw. Wmk inverted	25·00	
71	20c. orange and blue (ii)	40	10
	a. Orange omitted	£800	
72	25c. black and orange (iii)	75	10
	a. Black omitted	£900	
73	30c. multicoloured (i) (10.3.63)	1·25	10
	a. Yellow (flowers) omitted	£130	
	w. Wmk inverted	80·00	
74	50c. multicoloured (iv) (10.3.63)	1·25	10
75	$1 multicoloured (iv) (10.3.63)	19·00	60
76	$2 multicoloured (iv) (10.3.63)	9·00	1·00
77	$5 multicoloured (v) (10.3.63)	18·00	7·00
	w. Wmk inverted	£160	
63/77 *Set of* 16		50·00	19·00

Designs: Horiz (as T **21**)—5c. Orange Clownfish; 10c. Harlequinfish; 25c. Three-spotted Gorami. (As T **30**)—$1 White-breasted Kingfisher. Vert (as T **20**)—6c. Archerfish; 20c. Copper-banded Butterflyfish. (As T **24**)—12c. *Grammatophyllum speciosum* (orchid); 30c. *Vanda* "Miss Joaquim" (orchid). (As T **26a**)—$2 Yellow-bellied Sunbird; $5 White-bellied Sea Eagle.

The 10c. exists in coils, constructed from normal sheets.

The 15c., 30c., $2 and $5 exist with PVA gum as well as gum arabic. The errors, Nos. 70ab, 70ac and 73a, also exist with both gums.

See also Nos. 83/8.

34 "The Role of Labour in Nation-Building"

35 Blocks of Flats, Singapore

(Photo Courvoisier)

1962 (3 June). National Day. P 11½×12.

78	**34**	4c. yellow, rose-carmine and black	1·25	2·25
79		10c. yellow, blue and black	1·50	75

(Photo Harrison)

1963 (3 June). National Day. W w **12**. P 12½.

80	**35**	4c. orange-red, black, blue and turquoise-blue	50	80
81		10c. orange-red, black, yellow-olive and turquoise-blue	1·75	20
		w. Wmk inverted	55·00	

36 Dancers in National Costume

37 Workers

(Photo Harrison)

1963 (8 Aug). South East Asia. Cultural Festival. W w **12**. P 14×14½.

82	**36**	5c. multicoloured	50	50

INDEPENDENT REPUBLIC

1966 (1 Mar)–**67**. As Nos. 63, 66, 69, 72, 74/5, but W w **12** (sideways*).

83	1c. multicoloured (22.6.67)	10	2·00
84	5c. red and black (30.5.67)	4·00	2·75
85	10c. red-orange and black (19.5.67†)	2·00	1·25
86	25c. black and orange (9.66†)	70	2·00
	w. Wmk Crown to right of CA	3·75	
87	50c. multicoloured (11.1.66†)	4·50	3·00
	a. Imperf (pair)	£600	
88	$1 multicoloured (18.5.67)	16·00	13·00
83/8 *Set of 6*		24·00	22·00

*The normal sideways watermark show Crown to left of CA, *as seen from the back of the stamp.*

†The 25 and 50c. values were not released in London until 30.5.67 and 9.6.66. The 25c. value, however, is known used in September 1966 and the 50c. on 11.1.66. The 10c., released in London on 30 May 1967, is known used locally on 19 May.

The 1c. and 25c. exist with PVA gum as well as gum arabic.

(Photo D.L.R.)

1966 (9 Aug). First Anniv of Republic. (30c.) or no wmk (others). W w **12**. P 12½×13.

89	**37**	15c. multicoloured	75	30
90		20c. multicoloured	1·00	1·25
91		30c. multicoloured	1·25	2·00
89/91 *Set of 3*			2·75	3·25

38 Flag Procession

(Photo D.L.R.)

1967 (9 Aug). National Day. P 14×14½.

92	**38**	6c. rosine, brown and slate	50	90
93		15c. reddish purple, brown and slate	80	10
94		50c. bright blue, brown and slate	1·50	1·60
92/4 *Set of 3*			2·50	2·25

Nos. 92/4 are respectively inscribed "Build a Vigorous Singapore" in Chinese, Malay and Tamil in addition to the English inscription.

39 Skyscrapers and Afro-Asian Map

40 Symbolical Figure wielding Hammer, and Industrial Outline of Singapore

(Photo D.L.R.)

1967 (7 Oct). 2nd Afro-Asian Housing Congress. P 14×13.

95	**39**	10c. multicoloured	30	10
		a. Opt omitted	£1200	£1200
96		25c. multicoloured	75	1·00
97		50c. multicoloured	1·40	1·60
95/7 *Set of 3*			2·25	2·40

The above were originally scheduled for release in 1966, and when finally issued were overprinted with the new date and a black oblong obliterating the old date.

(Photo Harrison)

1968 (9 Aug). National Day. Inscription at top in Chinese (6c.), Malay (15c.) or Tamil (50c.). P 13½×14.

98	**40**	6c. orange-red, black and gold	35	65
99		15c. apple-green, black and gold	45	15
100		50c. greenish blue, black and gold	1·00	1·25
98/100 *Set of 3*			1·60	1·90

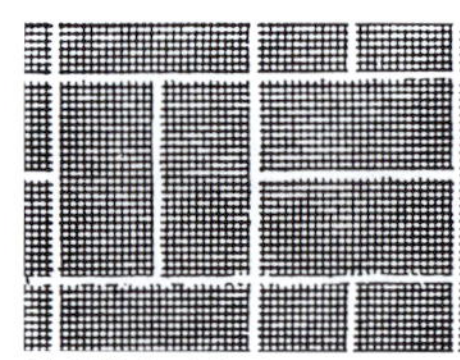

41 Half check Pattern

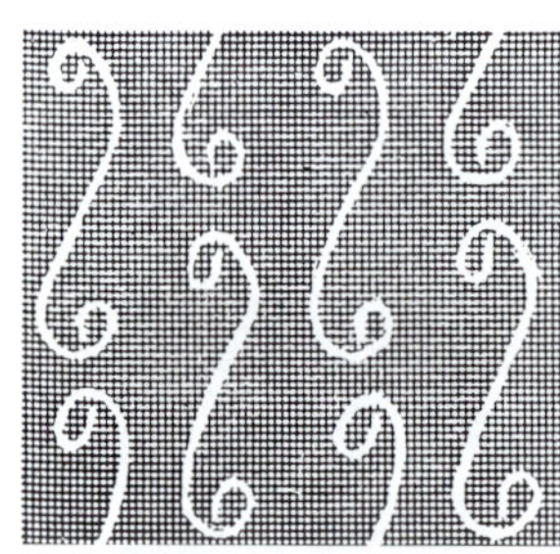

42 Scrolled "S" multiple

43 Mirudhangam

44 Pi Pa

45 Sword Dance

51 Dragon Dance

(Photo D.L.R. (5c. to $1), Japanese Govt Printing Bureau, Tokyo

1968 (1 Dec)–**73**. T **43/5**, **51** and similar designs. (5c. to $1) or W **42** (upright on 1c., $5; sideways on 4c., $2, $10). Chalk-surfaced paper (5c. to $1). W **41**. P 14 (5c. to $1) or 13½ (others).

101	1c. multicoloured (10.11.69)	15	2·25
102	4c. multicoloured (10.11.69)	60	3·00
103	5c. multicoloured (29.12.68)	60	1·75
	a. Glazed unsurfaced paper (16.12.70)	14·00	14·00
	b. Perf 13 (27.6.73)	7·50	10·00
104	6c. black, lemon and orange	1·75	2·25
105	10c. multicoloured (29.12.68)	20	10
	a. Glazed unsurfaced paper (16.12.70)	15·00	10·00
	b. Perf 13 (14.7.73*)	16·00	8·50
106	15c. multicoloured (29.12.68)	60	10
107	20c. multicoloured	1·00	1·75
	a. Perf 13 (12.9.73)	12·00	17·00
108	25c. multicoloured (29.12.68)	1·25	1·75
	a. Perf 13 (27.6.73)	7·50	13·00
109	30c. multicoloured	40	1·50
	a. Perf 13 (12.9.73)	12·00	18·00
110	50c. black, orange-red and light yellow-brown	50	1·00
	a. Perf 13 (12.9.73)	12·00	32·00
111	75c. multicoloured	3·00	4·25
112	$1 multicoloured (29.12.68)	4·50	1·25
	a. Perf 13 (12.9.73)	22·00	25·00
113	$2 multicoloured (10.11.69)	3·50	1·00
114	$5 multicoloured (10.11.69)	14·00	1·50
115	$10 multicoloured (6.12.69)	38·00	15·00
101/15 *Set of 15*		60·00	35·00
103b/12a *Set of 7*		75·00	£110

Designs: Vert (as T **45**)—6c. Lion dance; 10c. Bharatha Natyam; 15c. Tari Payong; 20c. Kathak Kali; 25c. Lu Chih Shen and Lin Chung; 50c. Tari Lilin; 75c. Tarian Kuda Kepang; $1 Yao Chi. (As T **44**—$2, Rebab; $10 Ta Ku. Horiz (as T **43**)—$5 Vina.

*Earliest known date of use.

58 E.C.A.F.E. Emblem

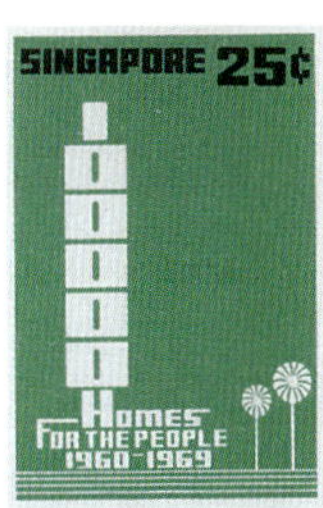

59 "100000" and Slogan as Block of Flats

(Des Eng Sisk Loy. Photo Japanese Govt Ptg Bureau, Tokyo)

1969 (15 Apr). 25th Plenary Session of the U.N. Economic Commission for Asia and the Far East. P 13.

116	**58**	15c. black, silver and pale blue	35	20
117		30c. black, silver and red	65	1·25
118		75c. black, silver and violet-blue	1·00	2·50
116/18 *Set of 3*			1·75	3·50

(Des Tay Siew Chiah. Litho B. W.)

1969 (20 July). Completion of "100,000 Homes for the People" Project. P 13½.

119	**59**	25c. black and emerald	1·00	50
120		50c. black and deep blue	1·25	1·25

60 Aircraft over Silhouette of Singapore Docks

61 Sea Shells

(Des Eng Siak Loy and Han Kuan Cheng. Litho B.W.)

1969 (9 Aug). 150th Anniv of Founding of Singapore. T **60** and similar vert designs. P 14×14½.

121	15c. black, vermilion and yellow	2·50	70
122	30c. black, blue and new blue	2·50	1·00
123	75c. multicoloured	4·50	1·00
124	$1 black and vermilion	9·00	10·00
125	$5 vermilion and black	18·00	45·00
126	$10 black and bright green	27·00	45·00
121/6 *Set of 6*		55·00	90·00
MS127 120×120 mm. Nos. 121/6. P 13½		£375	£400

Designs:—30c. U.N. emblem and outline of Singapore; 75c. Flags and outline of Malaysian Federation; $1 Uplifted hands holding crescent and stars; $5 Tail of Japanese aircraft and searchlight beams; $10 Bust from statue of Sir Stamford Raffles.

(Des Tay Siew Chiah (15c.), Eng Siak Loy (others). Litho Rosenbaum Bros, Vienna)

1970 (15 Mar). World Fair, Osaka. T **61** and similar vert designs. Multicoloured. P 13½.

128	15c. Type **61**	1·25	15
129	30c. Veil-tailed Guppys	1·75	70
130	75c. Greater Flamingo and Helmeted Hornbill	5·00	2·75
131	$1 Orchid	5·00	5·50
128/31 *Set of 4*		11·50	8·25
MS132 94×154 mm. Nos. 128/31		24·00	24·00

62 "Kindergarten"

63 Soldier charging

(Des Choy Weng Yang. Litho B.W.)

1970 (1 July). Tenth Anniv of People's Association. T **62** and similar square designs. P 13½.

133	15c. agate and bright orange	85	20
134	50c. ultramarine and yellow-orange	2·25	2·75
135	75c. bright, purple and black	3·50	4·50
133/5 *Set of 3*		6·00	6·75

Designs:—50c. "Sport"; 75c. "Culture".

(Des Choy Weng Yang. Litho Rosenbaum Bros, Vienna)

1970 (9 Aug). National Day. T **63** and similar vert designs. Multicoloured. P 13½.

136	15c. Type **63**	1·25	20
137	50c. Soldier on assault course	3·75	3·50
138	$1 Soldier jumping	5·00	11·00
136/8 *Set of 3*		9·00	13·00

64 Sprinters

(Des Choy Weng Yang. Photo Japanese Govt Ptg Bureau, Tokyo)

1970 (23 Aug). Festival of Sports. T **64** and similar horiz designs. P 13×13½.

139	10c. magenta, black and ultramarine	2·00	3·25
	a. Horiz strip of 4. Nos. 139/42	9·00	13·00
140	15c. black, ultramarine and red-orange	2·50	3·50
141	25c. black, red-orange and bright green	2·75	3·75
142	50c. black, bright green and magenta	3·00	3·75
139/42 *Set of 4*		9·25	12·50

Designs:—15c. Swimmers; 25c. Tennis-players; 50c. Racing cars.

Nos. 139/42 were issued together *se-tenant* in horizontal strips of four within the sheet.

65 *Neptune Aquamarine* (freighter)

(Des W. Lee. Litho Rosenbaum Bros, Vienna)

1970 (1 Nov). Singapore Shipping. T **65** and similar horiz designs. P 12.

143	15c. multicoloured	2·75	65
144	30c. yellow-ochre and ultramarine	6·00	5·50
145	75c. yellow-ochre and vermillion	10·00	10·00
143/5 *Set of 3*		17·00	14·50

Designs:—30c. Container berth; 75c. Shipbuilding.

66 Country Names forming Circle

(Des W. Lee. Litho D.L.R.)

1971 (14 Jan). Commonwealth Heads of Government Meeting, Singapore. T **66** and similar horiz designs. Multicoloured. P 14 (1r.) or 15×14½ (others).

146	15c. Type **66**	90	20
147	30c. Flags in circle	1·25	80
148	75c. Commonwealth flags	2·25	4·00
149	$1 Commonwealth flags linked to Singapore (63×61 mm)	3·00	7·00
146/9 *Set of 4*		6·75	11·00

Imperforate examples of Nos. 146/7 overprinted "Specimen" are from printer's sample sheets.

67 Bicycle Rickshaws

68 Chinese New Year

(Des Eng Siak Loy (15, 20 and 30c.), W. Lee (others). Litho B.W.)

1971 (4 Apr). Visit A.S.E.A.N. Year (A.S.E.A.N. = Association of South East Asian Nations). T **67** and similar designs. P 13×13½ (50, 75c.) or 11½ (others).

150	15c. black, deep bluish violet and orange	80	25
151	20c. indigo, orange and turquoise-blue	1·10	1·00
152	30c. vermilion and deep maroon	1·40	1·75
153	50c. multicoloured	3·75	7·00
154	75c. multicoloured	5·00	9·00
150/4 *Set of 5*		10·50	17·00

Designs:—As T **67**—20c. Houseboat "village" and sampans; 30c. Bazaar. Horiz (68×18 mm)—50c. Modern harbour skyline; 75c. Religious buildings.

(Des W. Lee. Litho Rosenbaum Bros, Vienna)

1971 (9 Aug). Singapore Festivals. T **68** and similar vert designs. Multicoloured. P 14.

155	15c. Type **68**	1·25	15
156	30c. Hari Raya	2·50	2·50
157	50c. Deepavali	3·50	6·50
158	75c. Christmas	4·00	7·50
155/8 *Set of 4*		10·00	15·00
MS159 150×125 mm. Nos. 155/8		75·00	48·00

69 "Dish" Aerial

(Des W. Lee. Litho BW.)

1971 (23 Oct). Opening of Satellite Earth Station. P 13½.

160	**69**	15c. multicoloured	3·00	1·50
161	–	30c. multicoloured	7·50	9·00
		a. Block of 4. Nos. 161/4	30·00	32·00
162	–	30c. multicoloured	7·50	9·00
163	–	30c. multicoloured	7·50	9·00
164	–	30c. multicoloured	7·50	9·00
160/4 *Set of 5*			30·00	32·00

Designs:—Nos. 161/4 were printed in *se-tenant* blocks of four throughout the sheet, the four stamps forming a composite design similar to T **69**. They can be identified by the colour of the face value which is: yellow (No. 161), green (No. 162), magenta (No. 163) or orange (No. 164).

70 "Singapore River and Fort Canning, 1843–7" (Lieut. E. A. Porcher)

(Des W. Lee. Litho B.W.)

1971 (5 Dec). Art. T **70** and similar horiz designs. Multicoloured. P 12½×13 (50c. and $1) or 13 (others).

165	10c. Type **70**	2·00	2·00
166	15c. "The Padang, 1851" (J. T. Thomson)	2·50	3·00
167	20c. "Singapore Waterfront, 1848–9"	3·00	3·75
168	35c. "View from Fort Canning, 1846" (J. T. Thomson)	6·50	8·00
169	50c. "View from Mt Wallich, 1857" (P. Carpenter) (69×47 mm)	9·00	13·00
170	$1 "Singapore Waterfront, 1861" (W. Gray) (69×47 mm)	11·00	17·00
165/70 *Set of 6*		30·00	42·00

71 One Dollar of 1969

(Des W. Lee. Litho B.W.)

1972 (4 June). Coins. T **71** and similar horiz designs. P 13½.

171	15c. orange, black and deep green	1·25	35
172	35c. black and vermilion	2·25	3·25
173	$1 yellow, black and bright blue	4·00	8·50
171/3 *Set of 3*		6·75	11·00

Designs:—15c. One-cent coin of George V; $1 One hundred and fifty dollar gold coin of 1969.

72 "Moon Festival" (Sean Kim Joo)

73 Lanterns and Fish

(Des W. Lee. Litho State Bank Note Printing Works, Helsinki)

1972 (9 July). Contemporary Art. T **72** and similar multicoloured designs. P 12½.

174	15c. Type **72**	70	30
175	35c. "Complimentary Forces" (Thomas Yeo) (36×54 mm)	1·25	2·00
176	50c. "Rhythm in Blue" (Yusman Aman) (36×54 mm)	1·50	3·50
177	$1 "Gibbons" (Chen Wen Hsi)	3·25	6·50
174/7 *Set of 4*		6·00	11·00

(Des Eng Siak Loy. Litho State Bank Note Printing Works, Helsinki)

1972 (9 Aug). National Day. T **73** and similar vert designs symbolising Festivals. Multicoloured. P 12½.

178	15c. Type **73**	75	20
179	35c. Altar and candles	1·00	2·00
180	50c. Jug, bowl and gifts	1·25	3·00
181	75c. Candle	2·00	4·50
178/81 *Set of 4*		4·50	8·75

74 Student Welding

75 *Maria Rickmers* (barque)

(Des Eng Siak Loy. Photo Kultura, Budapest)

1972 (1 Oct). Youth. T **74** and similar horiz designs. P 12.

182	15c. multicoloured	80	30
183	35c. multicoloured	1·50	3·00
184	$1 red-orange, blue-violet & yellowish grn.	3·25	7·50
182/4 *Set of 3*		5·00	9·75

Designs:—35c. Sport; $1 Dancing.

(Des Choy Weng Yang (Nos. 185/7), Eng Siak Loy (**MS**188). Litho Harrison)

1972 (17 Dec). Shipping. T **75** and similar multicoloured designs. P 14×14½.

185	15c. *Neptune Ruby* (container ship) (42×29 mm)	2·00	80
186	75c. Type **75**	6·00	8·00
187	$1 Chinese junk	6·50	9·00
185/7 *Set of 3*		13·00	16·00
MS188 152×84 mm. Nos. 185/7		45·00	45·00

76 P.Q.R. Slogan

77 Jurong Bird Park

(Des W. Lee. Litho B.W.)

1973 (25 Feb). "Prosperity through Quality and Reliability" Campaign. T **76** and similar vert designs. P 14.

189	**76**	15c. multicoloured	50	15
190	–	35c. multicoloured	1·25	2·75
191	–	75c. multicoloured	1·40	3·25
192	–	$1 multicoloured	1·40	4·50
189/92 *Set of 4*			4·00	9·50

Nos. 190/2 show various P.Q.R. emblems.

(Des Han Kuan Cheng. Litho Harrison)

1973 (29 Apr). Singapore Landmarks. T **77** and similar vert designs. P 12½.

193	15c. black and red-orange	80	15
194	35c. black and myrtle-green	1·50	2·50
195	50c. black and red-brown	2·25	3·25
196	$1 black and purple	3·00	5·00
193/6 *Set of 4*		6·75	9·75

Designs:—35c. National Theatre; 50c. City Hall; $1 Fullerton Building and Singapore River.

78 Aircraft Tail-fins

79 "Culture"

(Des W. Lee. Litho B.W.)

1973 (24 June). Aviation. T **78** and similar horiz designs. Multicoloured. P 13½×13.

197	10c. Type **78**	50	10
198	35c. Emblem of Singapore Airlines and destinations	1·50	2·00
199	75c. Emblem on tail-fin	1·75	2·50
200	$1 Emblems encircling the globe	2·25	3·50
197/200 *Set of 4*		5·50	7·25

(Des Eng Siak Loy. Litho Harrison)

1973 (9 Aug). National Day. T **79** and similar vert designs. P 13½.

201	**79**	10c. orange and black	1·00	2·00
		a. Block of 4. Nos. 201/4	4·25	8·50
202	–	35c. orange and black	1·00	2·25
203	–	50c. orange and black	1·25	2·50
204	–	75c. orange and black	1·40	2·75
201/4 *Set of 4*			4·25	8·50

Nos. 201/4 were printed in *se-tenant* blocks of four within the sheet, and form a composite design representing Singapore's culture.

80 Athletics, Judo and Boxing

81 Agave

82 Mangosteen

(Des C. Lim. Photo Heraclio Fournier)

1973 (1 Sept). Seventh S.E.A.P.* Games. T **80** and similar designs. P 14 (10 to 35c.) or 13×14 (others).

205	10c. gold, silver and indigo	55	20
206	15c. gold and grey-black	1·75	1·50
207	25c. gold, silver and black	1·25	1·50
208	35c. gold, silver and deep blue	2·75	3·00
209	50c. multicoloured	1·50	3·75
210	$1 silver, royal blue and yellow-green	2·75	6·50
205/10 *Set of 6*		9·50	15·00
MS211 130×111 mm. Nos. 205/10. P 13×14		32·00	35·00

Designs: As T **80**—15c. Cycling, weight-lifting, pistol-shooting and sailing; 25c. Footballs; 35c. Table-tennis bat, shuttlecock, tennis ball and hockey stick. Horiz (41×25 mm):—50c. Swimmers; $1 Stadium.

*S.E.A.P. = South East Asian Peninsula.

(Des W. Lee (1c. to 75c.), Eng Siak Loy (others). Photo Heraclio Fournier)

1973 (30 Sept). Various multicoloured designs as T **81/2**. With fluorescent security markings.

(a) Stylized flowers and plants, size as T **81**. P 13.

212	1c. Type **81**	1·00	1·50
213	5c. *Coleus blumei*	10	50
	a. Booklet pane. Nos. 213×4, 214×4, 216×2	12·00	
214	10c. *Vinca rosea*	15	10
215	15c. *Helianthus angustifolius*	1·50	10
	a. Green printed double		
216	20c. *Licuala grandis*	45	60
217	25c. *Wedelia trilobata*	3·75	55
218	35c. *Chrysanthemum frutescens*	1·00	1·00
219	50c. *Costus malorticanus*	1·00	55
220	75c. *Gerbera jamesonii*	2·50	1·00

(b) Fruits, size as T **82**. P 12½×13 (1.11.73).

221	$1 Type **82**	1·50	40
222	$2 Jackfruit	1·75	1·25
223	$5 Coconut	1·75	4·50
224	$10 Pineapple	3·00	7·00
212/24 *Set of* 13		17·00	17·00

Booklet pane No. 213a has the upper and lower edges imperforate and there are margins at left and right.

83 Tiger and Orang-Utans

84 Delta Guppy

(Des Eng Siak Loy. Litho BW.)

1973 (16 Dec). Singapore Zoo. T **83** and similar vert designs. Multicoloured. P 13.

225	5c. Type **83**	85	85
226	10c. Leopard and Waterbuck	90	45
227	35c. Leopard and Thamin	3·00	5·00
228	75c. Horse and Lion	4·50	7·50
225/8 *Set of* 4		8·75	12·50

(Des Eng Siak Loy. Photo Heraclio Fournier)

1974 (21 Apr). Tropical Fish. T **84** and similar vert designs. Multicoloured. P 14.

229	5c. Type **84**	70	60
230	10c. Half-black Delta Guppy	70	15
231	35c. Delta Guppy (*different*)	2·25	3·50
232	$1 Black Delta Guppy	3·00	8·50
229/32 *Set of* 4		6·00	11·50

85 Scout Badge within "9"

86 U.P.U. Emblem and Multiple "Centenary"

(Des W. Lee. Litho Harrison)

1974 (9 June). Ninth Asia-Pacific Scout Conference. P 13½×14½.

233	**85**	10c. multicoloured	30	10
234		75c. multicoloured	1·00	2·00

(Des W. Lee. Litho Harrison)

1974 (7 July). Centenary of Universal Postal Union. T **86** and similar vert designs. P 14×13½.

235	10c. orange-brown, purple-brown and gold.	15	10
	a. Gold (U.P.U. symbol) omitted	£475	
236	35c. new blue, deep blue and gold	40	1·60
237	75c. multicoloured	80	2·75
235/7 *Set of* 3		1·25	3·75

Designs:—35c. U.P.U. emblem and multiple U.N. symbols; 75c. U.P.U. emblem and multiple peace doves.

87 Family Emblem

88 "Tree and Sun" (Chia Keng San)

1974 (9 Aug). World Population Year. T **87** and similar horiz designs. Multicoloured. P 12½×13½.

238	10c. Type **87**	30	10
239	35c. Male and female symbols	80	1·40
	a. Emerald (male symbol) omitted	£700	
240	75c. World population map	1·25	2·75
238/40 *Set of* 3		2·10	3·75

(Des Eng Siak Loy. Photo Heraclio Fournier)

1974 (1 Oct). Universal Children's Day. T **88** and similar vert designs showing children's paintings. Multicoloured. P 13½.

241	5c. Type **88**	40	65
242	10c. "My Daddy and Mummy" (Angeline Ang)	40	20
243	35c. "A Dump Truck" (Si-Hoe Yeen Joong)	1·25	2·75
244	50c. "My Aunt" (Raymond Teo)	1·40	3·50
241/4 *Set of* 4		3·00	6·25
MS245	138×100 mm. Nos. 241/4.	23·00	28·00

89 Street Scene

(Des Loy Chin. Litho Secura, Singapore)

1975 (26 Jan). Singapore Views. T **89** and similar horiz designs. Multicoloured. P 14.

246	15c. Type **89**	80	20
247	20c. Singapore River	1·50	1·25
248	$1 "Kelong" (fish-trap)	3·00	7·00
246/8 *Set of* 3		4·75	7·75

90 Emblem and Lighters' Prows

91 Satellite Earth Station, Sentosa

(Des Choy Weng Yang. Litho Secura, Singapore)

1975 (10 Mar). Ninth Biennial Conference of International Association of Ports and Harbours, Singapore. T **90** and similar horiz designs. Multicoloured. P 14.

249	5c. Type **90**	30	15
250	25c. Freighter and ship's wheel	1·75	1·50
251	50c. Oil-tanker and flags	2·25	3·00
252	$1 Container-ship and propellers	3·50	6·50
249/52 *Set of* 4		7·00	10·00

(Des Sim Tong Khern. Photo Heraclio Fournier)

1975 (29 June). "Science and Industry". T **91** and similar multicoloured designs. P 13½.

253	10c. Type **91**	35	10
254	35c. Oil refineries (vert)	2·25	3·00
255	75c. "Medical Sciences"	2·50	4·25
253/5 *Set of* 3		4·50	6·50

92 "Homes and Gardens"

93 South African Crowned Cranes

(Des Tay Siew Chiah. Litho Secura, Singapore)

1975 (9 Aug). Tenth National Day. T **92** and similar square designs. Multicoloured. P 13½.

256	10c. Type **92**	20	10
257	35c. "Shipping and Ship-building"	1·25	1·75
258	75c. "Communications and Technology"	1·40	2·75
259	$1 "Trade, Commerce and Industry"	1·40	2·75
256/9	*Set of 4*	3·75	6·50

(Des Eng Siak Loy. Litho Harrison)

1975 (5 Oct). Birds. T **93** and similar vert designs. Multicoloured. P 14½×13½.

260	5c. Type **93**	1·75	80
261	10c. Great Indian Hornbill	1·75	30
262	35c. White-breasted Kingfisher and White-collared Kingfisher	7·00	7·00
263	$1 Sulphur-crested Cockatoo and Blue and Yellow Macaw	10·00	14·00
260/3	*Set of 4*	18·00	20·00

94 "Equality"

95 Yellow Flame

(Des Tay Siew Chiah. Litho Secura, Singapore)

1975 (7 Dec). International Women's Year. T **94** and similar square designs. Multicoloured. P 13½.

264	10c. Type **94**	25	10
265	35c. "Development"	1·40	2·50
266	75c. "Peace"	1·60	5·00
264/6	*Set of 3*	3·00	6·75
MS267	128×100 mm. Nos. 264/6	15·00	20·00

(Des Tay Siew Chiah. Litho Secura, Singapore)

1976 (18 Apr). Wayside Trees. T **95** and similar vert designs. Multicoloured. P 14.

268	10c. Type **95**	60	10
269	35c. Cabbage Tree	1·50	2·50
270	50c. Rose of India	1·75	2·50
271	75c. Variegated Coral Tree	2·25	4·75
268/71	*Set of 4*	5·50	8·75

96 *Arachnis hookeriana* × Vanda Hilo Blue

97 Festival Symbol and Band

(Des Eng Siak Loy. Litho Secura, Singapore)

1976 (20 June). Singapore Orchids. T **96** and similar vert designs. Multicoloured. P 14.

272	10c. Type **96**	1·25	10
273	35c. *Arachnis Maggie Oei* × *Vanda insignis*	3·00	3·50
274	50c. *Arachnis Maggie Oei* × *Vandu Rodman*	3·50	4·00
275	75c. *Arachnis hookeriana* × *Vanda* Dawn Nishimura	4·50	7·00
272/5	*Set of 4*	11·00	13·00

(Des Han Kuan Cheng. Litho Harrison)

1976 (9 Aug). Tenth Anniv of Singapore Youth Festival. Horiz designs showing festival symbol as T **97**. Multicoloured. P 12½.

276	10c. Type **97**	20	10
277	35c. Athletes	1·25	1·75
278	75c. Dancers	1·40	2·75
276/8	*Set of 3*	2·50	4·25

98 "Queen Elizabeth Walk"

(Des H. Weepaul. Litho Secura, Singapore)

1976 (14 Nov). Paintings of Old Singapore, circa 1905–10, by A. L. Watson. T **98** and similar horiz designs. Multicoloured. With fluorescent security markings. P 14.

279	10c. Type **98**	50	20
280	50c. "The Padang"	2·00	4·00
281	$1 "Raffles Place"	3·75	6·00
279/81	*Set of 3*	5·75	9·25
MS282	164×91 mm. Nos. 279/81. P 13½	15·00	23·00

99 Chinese Costume

100 Radar, Missile and Soldiers

(Des Margaret Heng. Litho Harrison)

1976 (19 Dec). Bridal Costumes. T **99** and similar vert designs. Multicoloured. P 14½.

283	10c. Type **99**	65	10
284	35c. Indian costume	1·25	2·00
285	75c. Malay costume	2·25	4·75
283/5	*Set of 3*	3·75	6·00

(Des Eng Siak Loy. Litho Harrison)

1977 (12 Mar). Tenth Anniv of National Service. T **100** and similar vert designs. Multicoloured. P 14½.

286	10c. Type **100**	65	10
287	50c. Tank and soldiers	2·50	2·50
288	75c. Soldiers, wireless operators, pilot and Douglas A-4 Skyhawk aircraft	3·50	4·50
286/8	*Set of 3*	6·00	6·50

101 Lyrate Cockle (*Lyrocardium lyratum*)

102 Spotted Hermit Crab

1977 (9 Apr–4 June). Multicoloured designs as T **101/2**. With fluorescent security markings. P 13×13½.

(a) Shells as T **101**.

289	**101**	1c. Type **101**	1·00	2·00
290		5c. Folded or Plicate Scallop (*Decatopecten plicus*)	20	10
		a. Booklet pane. Nos. 290×4 and 291×8 *se-tenant*	3·75	

291	10c. Marble Cone (*Conus marmoreus marmoreus*)	20	10
	a. Imperf (pair)	£500	
292	15c. Scorpion Conch (*Lambis scorpius*)	1·00	40
293	20c. Amplustre or Royal Paper Bubble (*Aplustrum amplustre*)	1·00	10
294	25c. Spiral Babylon (*Babylonia spirata*)	1·25	2·50
295	35c. Royal Thorny or Spiny Oyster (*Spondylus regius*)	1·50	1·50
296	50c. Maple-leaf Triton or Winged Frog Shell (*Biplex perca*)	2·00	10
297	75c. Troschel's Murex (*Murex troscheli*)	3·00	20

(b) Fish and Crustaceans as T **102** (4.6.77).

298	$1 Type **102**	2·00	15
299	$2 Zuge's Stingray	2·00	75
300	$5 Cuttlefish	2·00	3·00
301	$10 Lionfish	3·00	5·50
289/301	*Set of* 13	18·00	15·00

Booklet pane No. 290a has the upper and lower edges imperforate and there are margins at left and right.

103 Shipbuilding

104 Keyhole and Banknotes

(Des W. Lee. Litho Secura, Singapore)

1977 (1 May). Labour Day. T **103** and similar horiz designs. Multicoloured. P 13×12½.

302	10c. Type **103**	30	10
303	50c. Building construction	1·25	2·00
304	75c. Road construction	1·75	2·50
302/4	*Set of* 3	3·00	4·25

(Des Tay Siew Chiah. Litho Secura, Singapore)

1977 (16 July). Centenary of Post Office Savings Bank. T **104** and similar vert designs. Multicoloured. P 13.

305	10c. Type **104**	30	10
	a. Perf 14		
306	35c. On-line banking service	75	50
	a. Perf 14		
307	75c. GIRO service	1·75	1·50
	a. Perf 14		
305/7	*Set of* 3	2·50	1·90

105 Flags of Member Nations

106 "Chingay Procession" (Liang Yik Yin)

(Des Eng Siak Loy. Litho Secura, Singapore)

1977 (8 Aug). Tenth Anniv of A.S.E.A.N. (Association of South East Asian Nations). T **105** and similar vert designs. Multicoloured. P 14.

308	10c. Type **105**	30	10
309	35c. "Agriculture"	75	75
310	75c. "Industry"	1·75	1·75
308/10	*Set of* 3	2·50	2·30

(Des H. Weepaul. Litho Secura, Singapore)

1977 (1 Oct). Children's Art. T **106** and similar horiz designs. Multicoloured. P 12½.

311	10c. Type **106**	30	10
312	35c. "At the Bus Stop" (Chong Khing Ann)	1·00	50
313	75c. "Playground" (Yap Li Hwa)	2·25	2·75
311/313	*Set of* 3	3·25	3·00
MS314	160×97 mm. Nos. 311/13	11·00	18·00

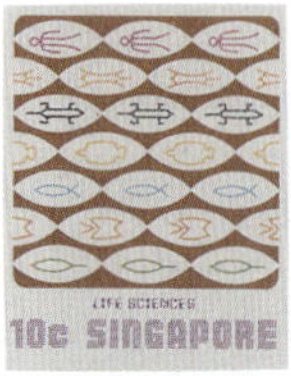

107 "Life Sciences"

108 Botanical Gardens and Esplanade Jurong Bird Park

(Des Tay Siew Chiah. Litho Format)

1977 (10 Dec). Singapore Science Centre. T **107** and similar vert designs. Multicoloured. P 14½×14.

315	10c. Type **107**	20	10
316	35c. "Physical sciences"	45	30
	a. Deep green and brown omitted	£550	
317	75c. "Science and technology"	1·25	1·75
318	$1 Singapore Science Centre	1·50	1·75
315/18	*Set of* 4	3·00	3·50

(Des C. Kiat. Litho Harrison)

1978 (22 Apr). Parks and Gardens. T **108** and similar multicoloured designs. P 14½.

319	10c. Type **108**	20	10
320	35c. Lagoon, East Coast Park (vert)	80	80
321	75c. Botanical Gardens (vert)	1·50	2·25
319/21	*Set of* 3	2·25	2·75

109 Red-whiskered Bulbul

111 Map of South East Asia showing Cable Network

110 Thian Hock Keng Temple

(Des Eng Siak Loy. Litho Secura, Singapore)

1978 (1 July). Singing Birds. T **109** and similar vert designs. Multicoloured. P 13½×14.

322	10c. Type **109**	60	20
323	35c. Oriental White Eye	1·75	1·50
324	50c. White-rumped Shama	2·00	2·50
325	75c. White-crested Laughing Thrush and Hwamei	2·25	3·50
322/5	*Set of* 4	6·00	7·00

(Des Eng Siak Loy. Litho Secura, Singapore)

1978 (9 Aug). National Monuments. T **110** and similar horiz designs. Multicoloured. P 13½.

326	10c. Type **110**	55	80
327	10c. Hajjah Fatimah Mosque	55	80
328	10c. Armenian Church	55	80
329	10c. Sri Mariamman Temple	55	80
326/9	*Set of* 4	2·00	3·00
MS330	173×86 mm. 35c.×4, as Nos. 326/9	3·50	3·75

Stamps from No. **MS**330 are similar in design to Nos. 326/9 but have no borders and the inscriptions are slightly larger.

(Des J. Heng. Litho Secura, Singapore)

1978 (3 Oct). A.S.E.A.N. (Association of South East Asian Nations) Submarine Cable Network (1st issue). Completion of Philippines–Singapore section. P 14 (around design as well as stamp).

331	**111**	10c. multicoloured	15	10
332		35c. multicoloured	60	85
333		50c. multicoloured	80	1·50
334		75c. multicoloured	90	2·00
331/334		*Set of* 4	2·25	4·00

See also Nos. 385/8 and 458/62.

112 *Neptune Spinel* (bulk carrier)

(Des P. Wee Hui Hong. Litho Secura, Singapore)

1978 (18 Nov). Tenth Anniv of Neptune Orient Shipping Lines. T **112** and similar horiz designs. Multicoloured. P 13½×14.

335	10c. Type **112**	70	20
336	35c. *Neptune Aries* (tanker)	1·75	1·75
337	50c. *Anro Temasek* (container ship)	2·00	2·75
338	75c. *Neptune Pearl* (container ship)	2·50	4·25
335/8	*Set of* 4	6·25	8·00

113 Concorde

114 10 Kilometre Marker

(Des P. Wee Hui Hong. Litho Secura, Singapore)

1978 (16 Dec). Aviation. T **113** and similar horiz designs. Multicoloured. P 13½.

339	10c. Type **113**	1·00	30
340	35c. Boeing 747-200	1·00	1·25
341	50c. Vickers Vimy	1·25	2·50
342	75c. Wright Brothers' Wright Flyer I	1·50	4·00
339/42	*Set of* 4	4·25	7·25

(Des W. Lee. Litho Secura, Singapore)

1979 (24 Feb). Metrication. T **114** and similar vert designs. Multicoloured. P 13½.

343	10c. Type **114**	15	10
344	35c. Tape measure	30	50
345	75c. Weighing scales	65	1·25
343/345	*Set of* 3	1·75	1·00

115 Vanda Hybrid

116 Envelope with new Singapore Postcode

(Des P. Wee Hui Hong. Litho Harrison)

1979 (14 April). Orchids. T **115** and similar designs showing different varieties of Vanda Hybrid. P 15×14 (10, 35c.) or 14×15 (others).

346	10c. multicoloured	30	10
347	35c. multicoloured	60	75
348	50c. multicoloured (vert)	70	1·00
349	75c. multicoloured (vert)	80	1·40
346/9	*Set of* 4	2·25	2·75

(Des P. Wee Hui Hong. Litho Secura, Singapore)

1979 (1 July). Postal Code Publicity. P 13.

350	**116**	10c. multicoloured	10	10
351	–	50c. multicoloured	60	90

The 50c. design is as Type **116** but the envelope is addressed to the Philatelic Bureau, General Post Office and has the postcode "Singapore 0104".

117 Early Telephone and Overhead Cables

118 "Lantern Festival" (Eng Chun-Ngan)

(Des Eng Siak Loy. Litho J. W.)

1979 (5 Oct). Centenary of Telephone Service. T **117** and similar horiz designs. P 13½×13.

352	10c. yellow-brown and new blue	15	10
353	35c. bright orange, blue and reddish violet	30	40
354	50c. blue, dp turquoise-grn & yellowish grn	45	70
355	75c. yellowish green and bright orange	65	1·25
352/5	*Set of* 4	1·40	2·25

Designs:—35c. Telephone dial and world map; 50c. Modern tele phone and city scene; 75c. Latest computerised telephone and circuit diagram.

(Des Han Kuan Cheng. Litho Secura, Singapore)

1979 (10 Nov). International Year of the Child. Children's Drawings. T **118** and similar horiz designs. Multicoloured. P 13.

356	10c. Type **118**	10	10
357	35c. "Singapore Harbour" (Wong Chien Chien)	30	40
358	50c. "Use Your Hands" (Leong Choy Yeen)	40	70
359	75c. "Soccer" (Tan Cheong Hin)	60	1·25
356/9	*Set of* 4	1·25	2·25
MS360	154×98 mm. Nos. 356/9	3·75	4·25

119 View of Gardens

120 Hainan Junk

(Des Eng Siak Loy. Litho Secura, Singapore)

1979 (15 Dec). 120th Anniv of Botanic Gardens. T **119** and similar horiz designs showing different views of the gardens. P 13½.

361	10c. multicoloured	30	10
	a. Imperf (pair)	£800	
362	50c. multicoloured	1·00	1·50
363	$1 multicoloured	1·50	2·50
361/3	*Set of* 3	2·50	3·50

(Des Eng Siak Loy. Litho J. W.)

1980 (5 Apr)–**84**. Ships. Multicoloured designs as T **120**. Ordinary paper (1c., 10c.), phosphorised paper ($1 to $10) and ordinary or phosphorised paper (others). P 14 (1 to 75c.) or 13½ ($1 to $10).

364	1c. Type **120** (26.4.80)	1·00	2·00
365	5c. Full-rigged clipper (26.4.80)	30	55
366	10c. Fujian junk (26.4.80)	30	10
	p. One narrow (4 mm) phosphor band (12.81)	45	30
	pa. One wide (10 mm) phosphor band (2.84)	2·50	3·00
367	15c. Golekkan (sailing craft) (26.4.80)	40	15
368	20c. Palari (sailing craft) (26.4.80)	70	40
369	25c. East Indiaman (26.4.80)	80	50
370	35c. Galleon (26.4.80)	90	50
371	50c. Caravel (26.4.80)	60	70
372	75c. Jiangsu trading junk (26.4.80)	1·00	1·50
373	$1 *Kedah* (coaster) (42×25 mm)	70	1·00
	a. Imperf (pair)	£300	
374	$2 *Murex* (tanker) (42×25 mm)	1·00	1·60
375	$5 *Chusan* (screw steamer) (42×25 mm)	1·50	2·75
376	$10 *Braganza* (paddle-steamer) (42×25 mm)	2·50	5·00
364/76	*Set of* 13	10·50	15·00

121 Straits Settlements 1867 1½c. Stamp and Map of Singapore, 1843

122 C.P.F. Emblem and "Keys to Retirement Benefits"

(Des P. Wee Hui Hong. Litho Secura, Singapore)

1980 (6 May). London 1980 International Stamp Exhibition. T **121** and similar vert designs. Multicoloured. P 13.

377	10c. Type **121**	20	10
378	35c. Straits Settlements 1906 $500 stamp and treaty between Johore and British Colony of Singapore	35	25
379	$1 1948 $2 stamp and map of Malaysia	60	1·10
380	$2 1969 150th Anniversary of Singspore $10 commemorative and letter to Col. Addenbrooke from Sir Stamford Raffles	1·00	2·25
377/80 *Set of 4*		1·90	3·25
MS381 148×104 mm. Nos. 377/80		2·00	4·50

(Des P. Wee Hui Hong. Litho Secura, Singapore)

1980 (1 July). 25th Anniv of Central Provident Fund Board. T **122** and similar vert designs showing C.P.F. emblem. Multicoloured. P 13.

382	10c. Type **122**	10	10
383	50c. "C.P.F. savings for home ownership"	40	40
384	$1 "C.P.F. savings for old-age"	75	1·25
382/4 *Set of 3*		1·10	1·60

123 Map of South East Asia showing Cable Network

124 A.S.E.A.N. Trade Fair Emblem

(Des J. Heng. Litho Secura, Singapore)

1980 (8 Aug). A.S.EA.N. (Association of South East Asian Nations) Submarine Cable Network (2nd issue). Completion of Indonesia–Singapore Section. P 14 (around design as well as stamp).

385	**123**	10c. multicoloured	10	10
386		35c. multicoloured	50	50
387		50c. multicoloured	60	1·10
388		75c. multicoloured	75	2·00
385/8 *Set of 4*			1·75	3·25

(Des P. Wee Hui Hong. Litho Secura; Singapore)

1980 (3 Oct). A.S.E.A.N. (Association of South East Asian Nations) Trade Fair. P 13.

389	**124**	10c. multicoloured	15	10
		a. Perf 13½×14	35·00	
390		35c. multicoloured	35	30
		a. Perf 13½×14	11·00	
391		75c. multicoloured	60	1·00
		a. Perf 13½×14	16·00	
389/91 *Set of 3*			1·00	1·25

125 Ixora

126 International Currency Symbols

(Des S. Tan and Chua Ban Har. Litho J.W.)

1980 (8 Nov). National Tree Planting Day. Flowers. T **125** and similar horiz designs. Multicoloured. P 13½×13.

392	10c. Type **125**	10	10
393	35c. Allamanda	40	45
394	50c. Sky Vine	50	70
395	75c. Bougainvillea	60	1·10
392/5 *Set of 4*		1·40	2·00

(Des P. Wee Hui Hong. Litho Secura, Singapore)

1981 (24 Jan). 10th Anniv of Monetary Authority of Singapore. P 14.

396	**126**	10c. black, vermilion & greenish yellow	10	10
397		35c. multicoloured	30	30
398		75c. multicoloured	55	1·25
396/8 *Set of 3*			80	1·50

(**127**)

128 Woodwork

1981 (4 Mar). No. 65 surch with T **127**.

399	**21**	10c. on 4c. black and orange-red	30	40

(Des Sng Tong Beng. Litho J.W.)

1981 (11 Apr). Technical Training. T **128** and similar vert designs. Multicoloured. P 13×13½.

400	10c. Type **128**	10	10
401	35c. Building construction	25	25
402	50c. Electronics	40	60
403	75c. Precision machining	50	1·10
400/3 *Set of 4*		1·10	1·75

129 Figures representing various Sports

130 "The Rights to Environmental Aids"

(Des Lim Ching San. Litho J.W.)

1981 (25 Aug). "Sports for All". T **129** and similar vert designs showing figures representing various sports. P 14.

404	10c. multicoloured	30	10
405	75c. multicoloured	2·00	2·50
406	$1 multicoloured	2·50	3·50
404/6 *Set of 3*		4·25	5·50

(Des Chua Ban Har. Litho Harrison)

1981 (24 Nov). International Year for Disabled Persons. T **130** and similar vert designs. Multicoloured. One centre phosphor band (10c.). or phosphorised paper (others). P 14½.

407	10c. Type **130**	10	10
408	35c. "The right to social integration"	30	25
409	50c. "The right to education"	45	50
410	75c. "The right to work"	60	90
407/10 *Set of 4*		1·25	1·60

Nos. 407/10 were printed with phosphor bands or on phosphorised paper similar to that used on contemporary Great Britain issues.

131 Control Tower and Passenger Terminal Building, Changi Airport

132 *Parthenos sylvia*

(Des J. Heng. Litho Secura, Singapore Ltd)

1981 (29 Dec). Opening of Changi Airport. P 14×13½.

411	**131**	10c. multicoloured	10	10
412		35c. multicoloured	20	30
413		50c. multicoloured	30	75
414		75c. multicoloured	40	1·50
415		$1 multicoloured	45	1·60
411/15 *Set of 5*			1·25	3·75
MS416 154×105 mm. Nos. 411/15			2·25	4·50

The five values show different background emblems representing the Parks and Recreation Dept, Public Works Dept, Telecommunications Authority, Port of Singapore and Dept of Civil Aviation.

(Des Eng Siak Loy. Litho J.W.)

1982 (3 Mar). Butterflies. T **132** and similar horiz designs. Multicoloured. One centre phosphor band (10c.) or phosphorised paper (others).

417	**14**	10c. Type **132**	40	15
418		50c. *Danaus vulgaris*	1·00	75
419		$1 *Trogonoptera brookiana*	1·40	1·75
417/19 *Set of 3*			2·50	2·40

133 A.S.E.A.N. Emblem

134 Football and Stylised Player

(Des P. Wee Hui Hong. Litho Secura, Singapore)

1982 (14 June). 15th Anniv of A.S.E.A.N. (Association of South East Asian Nations). One centre phosphor band (10c.) or phosphorised paper (others). P 14½×14.

420	**133**	10c. multicoloured	10	10
421		35c. multicoloured	30	35
422	–	50c. multicoloured	40	65
423	–	75c. multicoloured	60	1·00
420/3 *Set of 4*			1·25	1·90

The 50 and 75c. values are as Type **133**, but are inscribed "15th ASEAN Ministerial Meeting".

(Des P. Wee Hui Hong. Litho Secura, Singapore)

1982 (9 July). World Cup Football Championship, Spain. T **134** and similar vert designs. One centre phosphor band (10c.) or phosphorised paper (others). P 12.

424	10c. black, bright blue and greenish blue	20	10
425	75c. multicoloured	75	1·50
426	$1 multicoloured	95	1·50
424/6 *Set of 3*		1·75	2·75

Designs:—75c. Football and World Cup, Asian Zone Four emblem; $1 Football and globe.

135 Sultan Shoal Lighthouse, 1896

136 Yard Gantry Cranes

(Des Eng Siak Loy. Litho Secura, Singapore)

1982 (7 Aug). Lighthouses of Singapore. T **135** and similar horiz designs. Multicoloured. One centre phosphor band (10c.) or phosphorised paper (others). P 12.

427	10c. Type **135**	50	15
428	75c. Horsburgh Lighthouse, 1855	1·40	1·75
429	$1 Raffles Lighthouse, 1855	1·50	2·00
427/9 *Set of 3*		3·00	3·50
MS430 148×104 mm. Nos. 427/9		5·50	5·50

No. **MS**430 was printed on plain paper without phosphor.

NEW INFORMATION

The editor is always interested to correspond with people who have new information that will improve or correct this catalogue

(Des Goh Seng Lim. Litho Secura, Singapore)

1982 (15 Sept). Tenth Anniv of Container Terminal. T **136** and similar horiz designs. Multicoloured. One centre phosphor band (10c.) or phosphorised paper (others). P 13½.

431	10c. Type **136**	10	10
432	35c. Computer	25	40
433	50c. Freightlifter	35	85
434	75c. Straddle carrier	65	1·75
431/4 *Set of 4*		1·25	2·75

137 Scouts on Parade

138 Productivity Movement Slogans

(Des Poh Siew Wah. Litho Secura, Singapore)

1982 (15 Oct). 75th Anniv of Boy Scout Movement. T **137** and similar vert designs. Multicoloured. One centre phosphor band (10c.) or phosphorised paper (others). P 14×13½.

435	10c. Type **137**	15	10
436	35c. Scouts hiking	30	25
437	50c. Scouts building tower	50	35
438	75c. Scouts canoeing	60	80
435/8 *Set of 4*		1·40	1·25

(Des M. Gan. Litho Secura, Singapore)

1982 (17 Nov). Productivity Movement. T **138** and similar diamond-shaped designs. One centre phosphor band (10c.) or phosphorised paper (others). P 13½.

439	10c. orange and emerald	10	10
440	35c. yellow-ochre and deep dull blue	25	50
441	50c. maroon, bistre-yellow and brownish grey	40	90
442	75c. maroon and lemon	55	1·25
439/42 *Set of 4*		1·10	2·50

Designs:—35c. Family and housing ("Benefits of Productivity") 50c. Works meeting ("Quality Control Circles" 75c. Aspects of Singapore business ("Everybody's Business").

139 Commonwealth Logo and Country Names

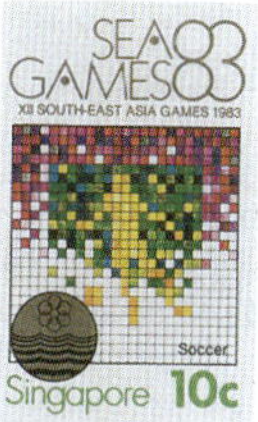

140 Soccer

(Des Eng Siak Loy. Litho Secura, Singapore)

1983 (14 Mar). Commonwealth Day. One centre phosphor band (10c.) or phosphorised paper (others). P 13×13½.

443	**139**	10c. multicoloured	10	10
444		35c. multicoloured	20	35
445		75c. multicoloured	45	1·10
446		$1 multicoloured	65	1·40
443/6 *Set of 4*			1·25	2·75

(Des Lim Ching San. Litho Secura, Singapore)

1983 (28 May). 12th South-East Asia Games. T **140** and similar vert designs. Multicoloured. One centre phosphor band (10c.) or phosphorised paper (others). P 13½×13.

447	10c. Type **140**	10	10
448	35c. Racket games	20	25

449	75c. Athletics	45	50
450	$1 Swimming	65	70
447/50	*Set of 4*	1·25	1·40

141 Policeman and Family

142 1977 ASEAN Stamps and Statue of King Chulalongkorn

(Des Lim Ching San. Litho J.W.)

1983 (24 June). Neighbourhood Watch Scheme. T **141** and similar horiz designs. Multicoloured. One wide centre phosphor band (10c.) or phosphorised paper (others). P 14.

451	10c. Type **141**	15	10
452	35c. Policeman and children	55	55
453	75c. Policeman and inhabitants with linked arms	1·00	2·00
451/3	*Set of 3*	1·50	2·40

(Des Sylvia Tan and Ko Hui-Huy. Litho J.W.)

1983 (4 Aug). Bangkok International Stamp Exhibition. T **142** and similar vert designs. Multicoloured. One wide centre phosphor band (10c.), phosphorised paper (35c., $1) or ordinary paper (miniature sheet). P 14.

454	10c. Type **142**	20	10
455	35c. 1980 ASEAN stamps and map of South-East Asia	55	50
456	$1 1982 ASEAN stamps and signatures of Heads of State	1·25	1·60
454/6	*Set of 3*	1·75	2·00
MS457	147×104 mm. Nos. 454/6	4·25	6·50

143 Map of South-East Asia showing Cable Network

(Des J. Heng. Litho Secura, Singapore)

1983 (27 Sept). A.S.E.A.N. (Association of South-East Asian Nations) Submarine Cable Network (3rd issue). Completion of Malaysia-Singapore-Thailand section. One centre phosphor band (10c.), phosphorised paper (35c. to 75c.) or ordinary paper (miniature sheet). P 13½ (around design as well as stamp).

458	**143**	10c. multicoloured	15	10
459		35c. multicoloured	55	75
460		50c. multicoloured	80	1·25
461		75c. multicoloured	1·25	2·00
458/61		*Set of 4*	2·50	3·75
MS462		146×100 mm. Nos. 331, 388, 458/61	4·75	6·00

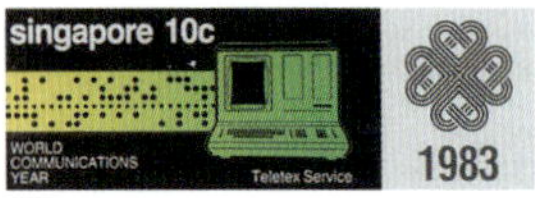

144 Teletex Service

(Des Sylvia Tan and Ko Hui-Huy. Litho Enschedé)

1983 (10 Nov). World Communications Year. T **10** and similar horiz designs. Phosphorised paper. P 12½×13.

463	10c. greenish yellow, light emerald and black	20	15
464	35c. greenish yellow, brt rose-red & chocolate	55	75
465	75c. bright yellow-green, greenish blue and deep violet-blue	1·10	1·75
466	$1 greenish yell, olive-brn & brownish blk..	1·50	2·75
463/6	*Set of 4*	3·00	4·75

Designs:—35c. World telephone numbering plan; 75c. Satellite transmission; $1 Sea communications.

145 Blue-breasted Banded Rail

146 House of Tan Yeok Nee

(Des Poh Siew Wah. Litho Harrison)

1984 (15 Mar). Coastal Birds. T **145** and similar horiz designs. Multicoloured. One wide centre phosphor band (10c.) or phosphorised paper (others). P 14½×13½.

467	10c. Type **145**	60	15
468	35c. Black Bittern	1·50	1·50
469	50c. Brahminy Kite	1·75	2·25
470	75c. Moorhen	2·00	3·25
467/70	*Set of 4*	5·25	6·50

(Des Poh Siew Wah. Litho Secura, Singapore)

1984 (7 June). National Monuments. T **146** and similar vert designs. Multicoloured. One centre phosphor band (10c.) or phosphorised paper (others). P 12.

471	10c. Type. **146**	15	10
472	35c. Thong Chai building	40	65
473	50c. Telok Ayer market	55	1·10
474	$1 Nagore Durgha shrine	80	2·50
471/4	*Set of 4*	1·75	4·00

147 1970 $1 National Day Stamp

148 School children

(Des P. Hong. Litho Secura, Singapore)

1984 (9 Aug–23 Nov). "25 Years of Nation Building." T **147** and similar vert designs showing various Singapore stamps. Multicoloured. One centre phosphor band (10c.) or phosphorised paper (others). P 14×14½.

475	10c. Type **147**	15	10
476	35c. 1981 $1 "Sports for All" stamp	50	70
477	50c. 1969 25c. "100,000 Homes for the People" stamp	60	1·00
478	75c. 1976 10c. Wayside Trees stamp	70	1·25
479	$1 1981 $1 Opening of Changi Airport stamp	80	1·75
480	$2 1981 10c. Monetary Authority stamp	1·40	4·00
475/80	*Set of 6*	3·75	8·00
MS481	132×106 mm. Nos. 475/80. P 12½ (23 Nov)	6·00	7·50

No. **MS**481 is on ordinary paper without a phosphor band on the 10c. stamp.

(Des Lim Ching San. Litho Secura, Singapore)

1984 (26 Oct). "Total Defence". T **148** and similar vert designs. One centre phosphor band. P 12.

482	10c. brown and orange-vermilion	15	40
	a. Horiz strip of 5. Nos. 482/6	65	1·75
483	10c. brown, yellow-olive and new blue	15	40
484	10c. brown, bright violet and pale salmon	15	40
485	10c. brown, orange-brown and mauve	15	40
486	10c. brown, yellow and yellow-olive	15	40
482/6	*Set of 5*	65	1·75

Designs:—No. 482 Type **148**; 483, People of Singapore; 484, Industrial workers; 485 Civil Defence first aid worker; 486, Anti-aircraft gun crew.

Nos. 482/6 were printed together, *se-tenant*, in horizontal strips of five throughout the sheet.

149 Coleman Bridge

150 *Ceriagrion cerinorubellum* (damselfly)

(Des Eng Siak Loy. Recess Harrison)

1985 (15 Mar). Bridges of Singapore. T **149** and similar horiz designs. One phosphor band (10c.) or phosphorised paper (others). P 14½×14.

487	10c. black (Type **149**)	15	10
488	35c. black (Cavenagh Bridge)	30	40
489	75c. black (Elgin Bridge)	55	70
490	$1 black (Benjamin Sheares Bridge)	70	90
487/90 *Set of* 4		1·50	1·90

(Des Eng Siak Loy. Litho Japanese Govt Ptg Bureau, Tokyo, to 1986, thereafter Leigh-Mardon Ltd, Melbourne (5c. to 75c.). Recess and photo Japanese Govt Ptg Bureau, Tokyo ($1 to $10))

1985 (24 Apr)–**89**. Insects. T **150** and similar horiz designs. Multicoloured. One narrow (5 mm) phosphor band (10c.) or phosphorised paper (others). P 13×13½.

491	5c. Type **150**	1·25	50
	a. Leigh-Mardon ptg (5.88)	2·25	1·25
492	10c. *Apis javana* (bee)	1·25	65
	a. Leigh-Mardon ptg (on phosphorised paper) (10.88)	2·25	75
493	15c. *Delta arcuata* (wasp)	1·50	1·50
	a. Leigh-Mardon ptg (2.88)	13·00	1·50
494	20c. *Xylocopa caerulea* (bee)	1·00	1·75
	a. Leigh-Mardon ptg (6.88)	15·00	1·75
495	25c. *Donacia javana* (water beetle)	1·00	1·50
	a. Leigh-Mardon ptg (8.88)	16·00	2·00
496	35c. *Heteroneda reticulata* (ladybird)	1·50	30
	a. Leigh-Mardon ptg (5.88)	18·00	1·50
497	50c. *Catacanthus nigripes* (bug)	1·50	1·25
	a. Leigh-Mardon ptg (1.89)	55·00	2·75
498	75c. *Chremistica pontianaka* (cicada)	1·50	2·50
	a. Leigh-Mardon ptg (7.89)	65·00	4·75
499	$1 *Homoexipha lycoides* (cricket) (5.6.85)	2·75	60
500	$2 *Traulia azureipennis* (grasshopper) (5.6.85)	1·50	1·50
501	$5 *Trithemis aurora* (dragonfly) (5.6.86)	2·00	3·50
502	$10 *Scambophyllum sanguinolentum* (grasshopper) (5.6.85)	3·50	7·00
491/502 *Set of* 12		18·00	20·00
491a/8a *Set of* 8		£170	14·00

Nos. 499/502 are larger, 35×30 mm.

Although the work of the two printers is very similar as far as shade, paper and perforation are concerned Leigh-Mardon used new printing plates taken from the original colour separations and, in consequence, each value does differ from its predecessor printed by the Japanese Government Printing Bureau.

It can be misleading to sort stamps by the paper thickness. Although most Tokyo printings were on paper noticeably thinner than that used by Leigh-Mardon there were Japanese printings of the 5, 15, 20 and 25c., released in the first half of 1987, which were on thick paper.

J.G.P.B. L.-M.

5c. On the J.G.P.B. printing the tail of the insect is ½ mm from the bottom edge of the vignette. On the L.-M. printing the distance is 1 mm.

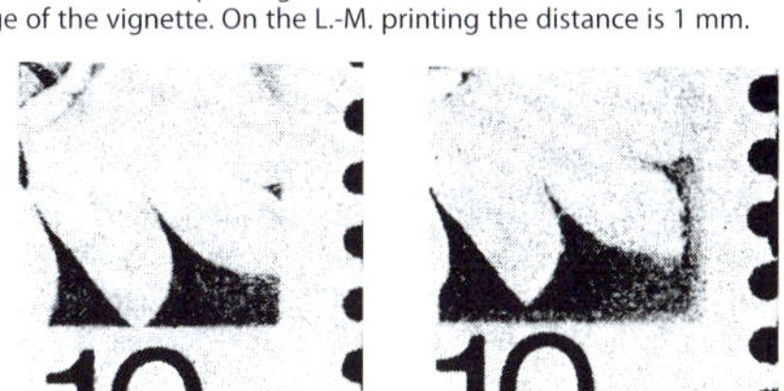

J.G.P.B. L.-M.

10c. The J.G.P.B. printing shows the petals at bottom right cut by the edge of the design. On the L.-M. printing all three petals are complete.

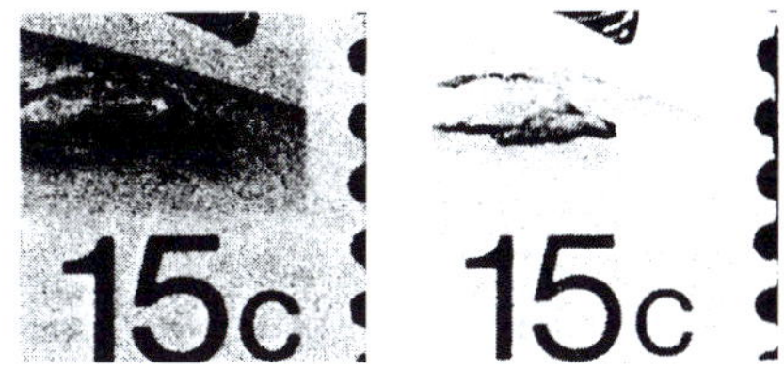

J.G.P.B. L.-M.

15c. The J.G.P.B. printing shows the rock at bottom right 1½ mm from the right-hand edge. On the L.-M. stamp this distance is 2 mm.

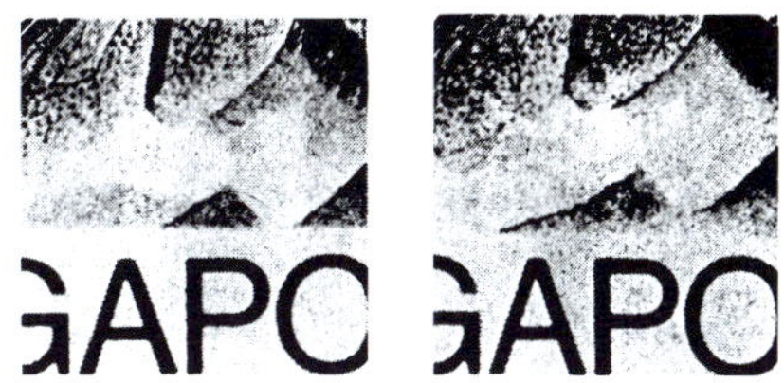

J.G.P.B. L.-M.

20c. On the J.G.P.B. stamp the pink flowers above "SINGAPORE" touch the edge of the vignette. For the L.-M. printing the right-hand petal is clear of the edge.

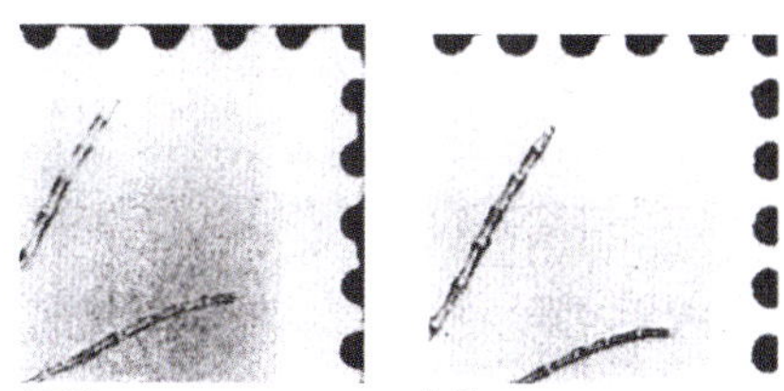

J.G.P.B. L.-M.

25c. The J.G.P.B. printing shows the uppermost feeler of the water beetle touching the top of the design. On the L.-M. stamp the feeler does not reach the edge of the design.

J.G.P.B. L.-M.

35c. On the J.G.P.B. printing the vein on the leaf at bottom left stops just short of the corner of the design. The L.-M. stamp shows this vein reaching the left-hand edge of the design above the corner.

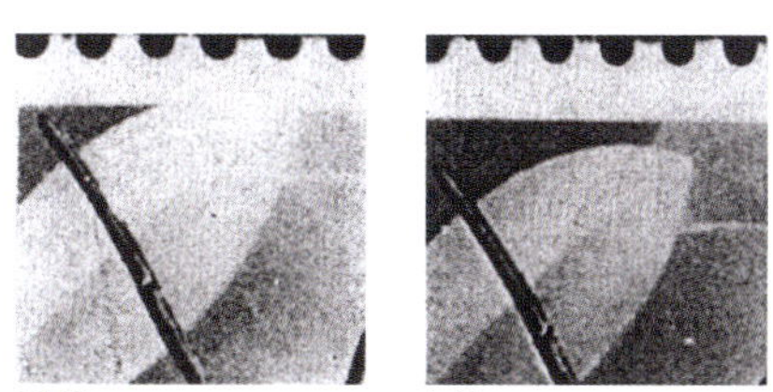

J.G.P.B. L.-M.

50c. The J.G.P.B. stamp has the uppermost leaf cut by the top edge of the design. On the L.-M. printing the leaf is complete.

J.G.P.B.

L.-M.

75c. On the J.G.P.B. printing the shadow of the wings is 1½ mm above the bottom edge of the vignette. For the L.-M stamp the shadow touches the bottom edge.

151 Tennis, Canoeing, Judo and Children Playing

(Des M. Chiew. Litho Secura, Singapore)

1985 (1 July). 25th Anniv of the People's Association. T **151** and similar horiz designs. Multicoloured. One phosphor band (10c.) or phosphorised paper (others). P 14½×14.

503	10c. Type **151**	25	10
504	35c. Lion dance, martial arts and athletes with flags	30	35
505	50c. Tae-kwon-do, Indian dance and Dragon dance	40	50
506	75c. Boxing, table tennis, basketball and dancing	75	1·00
503/6	*Set of* 4	1·50	1·75

152 Modern Housing Estate and Squatter Settlement

153 Brownies

(Des Eng Siak Loy. Litho Secura, Singapore)

1985 (9 Aug). 25th Anniv of Housing and Development Board. Horiz designs as T **152** with different aspects of housing shown at left. Multicoloured. One phosphor band (10c.) or phosphorised paper (others). P 13½×14.

507	10c. Type **152**	15	10
508	35c. Singapore family (Home-ownership)	30	45
509	50c. Group of residents (Community development)	40	1·00
510	75c. Construction workers (Building technology)	55	1·75
507/10	*Set of* 4	1·25	3·00
MS511	126×105 mm. Nos. 507/10	3·25	5·00

(Des Foo Lye Lin. Litho J.W.)

1985 (6 Nov). 75th Anniv of Girl Guide Movement. T **153** and similar vert designs. One phosphor band (10c.) or phosphorised paper (others). Multicoloured. P 14.

512	10c. Type **153**	15	10
513	35c. Guides practising first aid	35	40
514	50c. Senior Branch	45	60
515	75c. Adult leaders and guides	65	90
512/15	*Set of* 4	1·40	1·80

154 Badges and Emblems of Singapore Youth Organizations

155 Guava

(Des Eng Siak Loy. Litho Secure, Singapore)

1985 (18 Dec). International Youth Year. T **154** and similar horiz designs. Multicoloured. One phosphor band (10c.) or phosphorised paper (others). P 12.

516	10c. Type **154**	15	10
517	75c. Hand protecting sapling	80	65
518	$1 Stylised figures and dove	1·00	85
516/18	*Set of* 3	1·75	1·40

(Des Poh Siew Wah. Litho J.W.)

1986 (26 Feb). Singapore Fruits. T **155** and similar vert designs. Multicoloured. One centre phosphor band (10c.) or phosphorised paper (others). P 14.

519	10c. Type **155**	30	10
520	35c. Jambu Air	85	65
521	50c. Rambutan	1·10	1·25
522	75c. Ciku	1·40	2·00
519/22	*Set of* 4	3·25	3·50

156 Laboratory Technician and Salesmen with Bar Graph

157 Calligraphy

(Des W. Lee. Litho Secura, Singapore)

1986 (1 May). 25th Anniv of National Trades Union Congress. T **156** and similar vert designs. Multicoloured. One phosphor band. P 13½.

523	10c. Type **156**	30	50
	a. Horiz strip of 4. Nos. 523/6	1·00	1·75
524	10c. Computer operator and welder	30	50
525	10c. Draughtsmen and surveyors	30	50
526	10c. Group of workers	30	50
523/6	*Set of* 4	1·00	1·75
MS527	148×100 mm. As Nos. 523/6, but each stamp with a face value of 35c. Phosphorised paper	4·00	6·00

Nos. 523/6 were printed together, *se-tenant*, in horizontal strips of 4 throughout the sheet, forming a composite design.

(Des Chua Ban Har. Litho (50c. also die-stamped) Leigh Mardon Ltd, Melbourne)

1986 (2 May). Expo 86 World Fair, Vancouver. T **157** and similar horiz designs. Multicoloured. "All-over" phosphor. P 14×14½.

528	50c. Type **157**	55	75
	a. Horiz strip of 3. Nos. 528/30	1·90	2·75
529	75c. Garland maker	70	95
530	$1 Batik printer	85	1·25
528/30	*Set of* 3	1·90	2·75

Nos. 528/30 were printed together, *se-tenant*, in horizontal strips of 3 throughout the sheet.

158 Industrial Automation

159 Map showing Route of Cable and *Vercors* (cable ship)

(Des Eng Siak Loy. Litho J.W.)

1986 (1 Aug). 25th Anniv of Economic Development Board. T **158** and similar vert designs. Multicoloured. Phosphorised paper. P 15×14½.

531	10c. Type **158**	10	10
532	35c. Manufacture of aircraft components	25	30
533	50c. Electronics industry	30	50
534	75c. Biotechnology industry	50	90
531/4	*Set of* 4	1·00	1·60

(Des J. Heng. Litho Secura, Singapore)

1986 (8 Sept). SEA–ME–WE Submarine Cable Project. Phosphorised paper. P 13½.

535	**159**	10c. multicoloured	40	10
536		35c. multicoloured	85	55
537		50c. multicoloured	1·10	90
538		75c. multicoloured	1·40	2·00
535/8 *Set of 4*			3·25	3·25

160 Stylized Citizens

161 Peace Doves and People of Different Races

(Des W. Lee. Litho Secura, Singapore)

1986 (15 Oct). 21st Anniv of Citizens' Consultative Committees. T **160** and similar vert designs showing citizens. Phosphorised paper. P 12.

539	10c. multicoloured	30	45
	a. Block of 4. Nos. 539/42	1·90	2·25
540	35c. multicoloured	45	60
541	50c. multicoloured	55	70
542	75c. multicoloured	75	85
539/42 *Set of 4*		1·90	2·25

Nos. 539/42 were printed together, *se-tenant*, in blocks of 4 throughout the sheet, each block forming a composite design.

(Des Eng Siak Loy. Litho Secura, Singapore)

1986 (17 Dec). International Peace Year. T **161** and similar horiz designs. Multicoloured. Phosphorised paper. P 14×13½.

543	10c. Type **161**	15	10
544	35c. Doves and map of ASEAN countries	50	70
545	$1 Doves and globe	1·25	3·00
543/5 *Set of 3*		1·75	3·50

162 Orchard Road

163 Flags of Member Nations and Logo

(Des Chua Ban Har. Litho Secura, Singapore)

1987 (25 Feb). Singapore skyline. T **162** and similar horiz designs. Multicoloured. Phosphorised paper. P 12.

546	10c. Type **162**	15	10
547	50c. Central Business District	50	65
548	75c. Marina Centre and Raffles City	75	1·50
546/48 *Set of 3*		1·25	2·00

(Des Chua Ban Har. Litho Secura, Singapore)

1987 (15 June). 20th Anniv, of Association of South-east Asian Nations. Phosphorised paper. P 12.

549	**163**	10c. multicoloured	15	10
550		35c. multicoloured	35	40
551		50c. multicoloured	55	65
552		75c. multicoloured	65	90
549/52 *Set of 4*			1·50	1·80

164 Soldier with Rocket Launcher and Tank

165 Singapore River and Dragon Boats

(Des M. Ng Puay Chiew. Litho Questa)

1987 (1 July). 20th Anniv of National Service. T **164** and similar vert designs. Multicoloured. Phosphorised paper. P 15×14.

553	10c. Type **164**	55	70
	a. Horiz strip of 4. Nos. 553/6	2·00	2·50
554	10c. Radar operator and patrol boat	55	70
555	10c. Fighter pilot, General Dynamics F-16 Fighting Falcon and Douglas A-4 Skyhawk aircraft	55	70
556	10c. Servicemen pledging allegiance	55	70
553/6 *Set of 4*		2·00	2·50
MS557	148×100 mm. 35c.×5. As Nos. 553/6 and Singapore lion symbol (scarlet and black)	4·75	6·00

Nos. 553/6 were printed together, *se-tenant*, in horizontal strips of 4 throughout the sheet.

(Des Ng Keng Seng. Litho Secura, Singapore)

1987 (2 Sept). River Conservation. T **165** and similar square designs. Multicoloured. Phosphorised paper. P 13½.

558	10c. Type **165**	30	10
559	50c. Kallang Basin, canoe and fishing punt	80	1·25
560	$1 Kranji Reservoir, athletes and cyclist	2·25	4·25
558/60 *Set of 3*		3·00	5·00

166 Majapahit Gold Bracelet and Museum

(Des M. Ng Puay Chiew. Litho Secura, Singapore)

1987 (12 Oct). Centenary of National Museum. T **166** and similar horiz designs, each showing different drawings of Museum. Multicoloured. Phosphorised paper. P 13½×14.

561	10c. Type **166**	30	10
562	75c. Ming fluted kendi (water vessel)	1·25	1·75
563	$1 Patani hula pekakak keris (sword)	1·40	3·00
561/3 *Set of 3*		2·75	4·25

167 Omni-theatre

(Des Eng Siak Loy. Litho Leigh-Mardon Ltd, Melbourne)

1987 (10 Dec). Tenth Anniv of Singapore Science Centre. T **167** and similar horiz designs. Multicoloured. Phosphorised paper. P 14½.

564	10c. Type **167**	15	10
565	35c. Omni-planetarium	1·50	1·25
566	75c. Model of body cell	1·50	2·75
567	$1 Physical sciences exhibits	1·50	3·25
564/7 *Set of 4*		4·25	6·50

168 Modern Anti-aircraft Gun

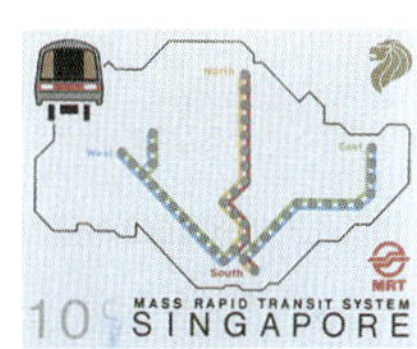

169 Route Map

(Des L. Teck Chong. Litho Secura, Singapore)

1988 (22 Feb). Centenary of Singapore Artillery. T **168** and similar horiz designs. Multicoloured. Phosphorised paper. P 13½×14.

568	10c. Type **168**	55	15
569	35c. 25-pounder field gun firing salute	1·40	1·25
570	50c. Gunner and 12-pounder gun, c. 1920	1·50	2·00
571	$1 Gunner and Maxim gun, 1889	2·25	4·50
568/71 *Set of 4*		5·25	7·00

(Des Ng Keng Seng. Litho Secura, Singapore)

1988 (12 Mar). Singapore Mass Rapid Transit System. T **169** and similar horiz designs. Multicoloured. Phosphorised paper. P 13½×14.

572	10c. Type **169**	1·25	15
573	50c. Train on elevated section	2·50	2·25
574	$1 Train in tunnel	4·00	5·00
572/4 *Set of 3*		7·00	6·75

170 Camera, Film and Outside Broadcast Van

(Des E. Soriano. Litho CPE Australia Ltd, Melbourne)

1988 (4 Apr). 25th Anniv of Television in Singapore. T **170** and similar horiz designs. Multicoloured. Phosphorised paper. P 13½×14.

575	10c. Type **170**	40	10
576	35c. Camera, studio lights and microphone..	80	75
577	75c. Television set and transmitter	1·25	1·50
578	$1 Globe on TV screen and dish aerial	1·75	2·25
575/8 *Set of 4*		3·75	4·25

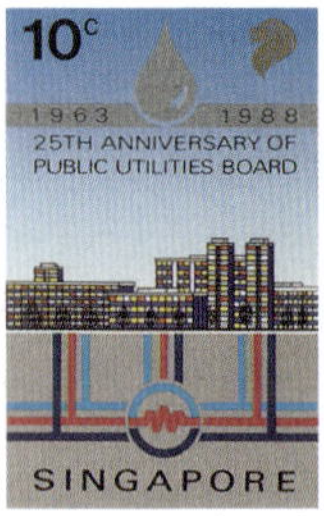

171 Water Droplet and Blocks of Flats

172 Greeting Neighbours

(Des Ng Keng Sung. Litho CPE Australia Ltd, Melbourne)

1988 (4 May). 25th Anniv of Public Utilities Board. T **171** and similar vert designs, each showing a different skyline. Multicoloured. Phosphorised paper. P 13½.

579	10c. Type **171**	20	10
580	50c. Electric light bulb and city centre	1·10	1·00
581	$1 Gas flame and factories	2·00	2·50
579/81 *Set of 3*		3·00	3·25
MS582 116×75 mm. Nos. 579/81		4·75	6·50

(Des M. Ng Puay Chiew. Litho Leigh-Mardon Ltd, Melbourne)

1988 (6 July). Tenth Anniv of National Courtesy Campaign. T **172** and similar horiz designs, each showing campaign mascot "Singa". Multicoloured. Phosphorised paper. P 14½.

583	10c. Type **172**	20	10
584	30c. Queueing at checkout	50	55
585	$1 Helping the elderly	1·50	2·75
583/5 *Set of 3*		2·00	3·00

173 Modern 30 Metre Turntable Fire Appliance

174 Container Ships and Warehouses

(Des Eng Siak Loy. Litho Secura, Singapore)

1988 (1 Nov). Centenary of Fire Service T **173** and similar horiz design. Multicoloured. Phosphorised paper. P 13½.

586	10c. Type **173**	1·00	25
587	$1 Steam fire engine c. 1890	3·25	3·25

(Des Ng Keng Sen, Litho Secura, Singapore)

1989 (3 April). 25th Anniv of Singapore Port Authority. T **174** and similar vert designs. Multicoloured. P 14×13½.

588	10c. Type **174**	55	10
589	30c. Shipping and oil storage depot	1·00	50
590	75c. Container ships and Singapore skyline..	1·50	1·50
591	$1 Container port at night	1·60	1·60
588/591 *Set of 4*		4·25	3·25

175 "Sago Street"

176 North-west Singapore City, 1920

(Litho Questa)

1989 (17 May). Paintings of Chinatown by Choo Keng Kwang. T **175** and similar square designs. Multicoloured. Phosphorised paper.

592	**141**	10c. Type **175**	40	15
593		35c. "Pagoda Street"	1·25	1·00
594		75c. "Trengganu Street"	2·00	2·75
595		$1 "Temple Street"	2·25	3·25
592/5 *Set of 4*			5·25	6·50

(Des L. Teck Chong. Litho Harrison)

1989 (26 July). Maps of Singapore. T **176** and similar multicoloured designs. Phosphorised paper. P 14×14½ (15c.) or 12½×13 (others).

596	15c. Type **176** (top left)	1·50	1·75
	a. Block of 4. Nos. 596/9	5·50	6·25
597	15c. North-east Singapore (top right)	1·50	1·75
598	15c. South-west Singapore (bottom left)	1·50	1·75
599	15c. South-east Singapore (bottom right)	1·50	1·75
600	50c. Singapore Island and Dependencies, 1860s	2·25	2·00
601	$1 British Settlement of Singapore, 1820s..	3·00	3·50
596/601 *Set of 6*		10·00	11·00

Nos. 596/9 were printed together, *se-tenant*, in blocks of 4 throughout the sheet, each block forming a composite design. Individual stamps can be identified by the position of the lion emblem which is quoted in brackets.

177 Clown Triggerfish

178 "Hari Raya Puasa" (Loke Yoke Yun)

(Des Eng Siak Loy. Litho Harrison)

1989 (6 Sept). Fish. T **177** and similar horiz designs. Multicoloured. Phosphorised paper. P 13½.

602	15c. Type **177**	1·75	20
603	30c. Blue-girdled Angelfish	2·75	1·50
604	75c. Emperor Angelfish	4·25	5·00
605	$1 Regal Angelfish	4·75	6·50
602/5 *Set of 4*		12·00	12·00

(Adapted S. Ang Woon Beng. Litho Harrison)

1989 (25 Oct). Festivals of Singapore. Children's Drawings T **178** and similar vert designs. Multicoloured. Phosphorised paper. P 14½.

606	15c. Type **178**	40	10
607	35c. "Chinese New Year" (Simon Koh)	70	65
608	75c. "Thaipusam" (Henry Setiono)	1·40	1·40
609	$1 "Christmas" (Wendy Ang Lin Min)	1·75	1·75
606/9 *Set of 4*		3·75	3·50
MS610 126×75 mm. Nos. 606/9. P 14		4·00	4·00

179 North Entrance of Stadium

180 "Singapore River, 1839" (Louis le Breton)

(Des Lim Ching San. Litho Harrison)

1989 (27 Dec). Opening of Singapore Indoor Stadium. T **179** and similar horiz designs. Multicoloured. Phosphorised paper. P 14.

611	30c. Type **179**	85	30
612	75c. Arena	1·75	1·50
613	$1 East entrance	2·00	1·75
611/13	*Set of* 3	4·25	3·25
MS614	104×104 mm. Nos. 611/13	4·50	4·50

(Des Choy Weng Yang. Litho Leigh-Mardon Ltd, Melbourne)

1990 (21 Mar). Lithographs of 19th-century Singapore. T **180** and similar horiz designs. Multicoloured. Phosphorised paper. P 13.

615	15c. Type **180**	70	15
	a. Booklet pane. No. 615×10	10·00	
616	30c. "Chinatown, 1837" (Barthelemy Lauvergne)	1·25	70
617	75c. "Singapore Harbour, 1837" (Barthelemy Lauvergne)	2·25	2·25
618	$1 "View from the French Resident's House, 1824" (Deroy)	2·50	2·75
615/18	*Set of* 4	6·00	5·25

The upper and lower edges of booklet pane No. 615a are imperforate.

181 1969 150th Anniv of Singapore Stamp Issue

(Des Sylvia Tan. Litho Leigh-Mardon Pty Ltd, Melbourne)

1990 (3 May). 150th Anniv of the Penny Black. T **181** and similar horiz designs, each showing a different map in the background. Multicoloured. Phosphorised paper. P 13½.

619	50c. Type **181**	1·00	60
620	75c. Indian stamps, including bisect, used from Singapore in 1859	1·25	1·50
621	$1 Indian stamps used from Singapore in 1854	1·90	1·90
622	$2 Penny Black and Two Pence Blue	3·00	5·00
619/22	*Set of* 4	6·50	8·00
MS623	134×90 mm. Nos. 619/22	8·50	7·50

No. **MS**623 also commemorates the "Stamp World London 90" international stamp exhibition.

182 Zoological Gardens

183 Chinese Opera Singer and Siong Lim Temple

(Des Ng Keng Seng (5 to 75c.), Lim Ching San ($1 to $10). Photo (5 to 75c.) or recess and photo ($1 to $10) Harrison)

1990 (4 July)–**91**. Tourism. Multicoloured. Phosphorised paper.

(a) T **182** and similar square designs. P 14½.

624	5c. Type **182**	30	40
625	15c. Sentosa Island	30	10
	a. Booklet pane. No. 625×10	17·00	
626	20c. Singapore River	30	20
	a. Booklet pane. No. 626×10 (6.3.91)	7·00	
627	25c. Dragon Boat Festival	55	75
628	30c. Raffles Hotel	70	30
629	35c. Coffee shop bird singing contest	1·25	75
630	40c. Jurong Bird Park	2·00	1·00
631	50c. Chinese New Year boat float	1·25	45
632	75c. Peranakan Place	1·75	70

(b) T **183** and similar horiz designs. P 15×14 (19.10.90).

633	$1 Type **183**	4·50	1·25
634	$2 Malay dancer and Sultan Mosque	6·00	2·25
635	$5 Indian dancer and Sri Mariamman Temple	8·00	7·00
636	$10 Ballet dancer and Victoria Memorial Hall	12·00	11·00
624/36	*Set of* 13	35·00	23·00

The upper and lower edges of booklet panes Nos. 625a and 626a are imperforate.

184 Armed Forces Personnel

185 Stag's Horn Fern

(Des Chua Ban Har. Litho Harrison)

1990 (16 Aug). 25th Anniv of Independence. T **184** and similar horiz designs. Multicoloured. Phosphorised paper. P 14×15.

637	15c. Type **184**	1·25	20
	a. Perf 14	1·25	1·25
	ab. Booklet pane. No. 637a×10	12·00	
638	35c. Inhabitants of Singapore	1·75	1·00
639	75c. Workers and technological achievements	2·50	2·75
640	$1 Cultural activities	3·25	5·00
637/40	*Set of* 4	8·00	8·00

No. 637a only comes from $1.50 stamp booklets in which the pane, No. 637ab, has margins at left and right.

(Des Poh Siew Wah. Litho Questa)

1990 (14 Nov). Ferns. T **185** and similar horiz designs. Multicoloured. Phosphorised paper. P 14.

641	15c. Type **185**	25	10
642	35c. Maiden Hair Fern	60	75
643	75c. Bird's Nest Fern	1·25	2·00
644	$1 Rabbit's Foot Fern	1·60	2·50
641/4	*Set of* 4	3·25	4·75

186 Carved Dragon Pillar, Hong San See Temple

187 *Vanda* "Miss Joaquim"

(Des L. Teck Chong. Litho Leigh-Mardon Ltd, Melbourne)

1991 (23 Jan). National Monuments. T **186** and similar multicoloured designs. Phosphorised paper. P 14½.

645	20c. Type **186**	50	80
	a. Vert pair. Nos. 645/6	1·00	1·60
646	20c. Hong San See Temple (40×25 mm)	50	80
647	50c. Interior of dome, Abdul Gaffoor Mosque	80	1·10
	a. Vert pair. Nos. 647/8	1·60	2·10
648	50c. Abdul Gaffoor Mosque (40×25 mm)	80	1·10
649	75c. Statue of Vishnu, Sri Perumal Hindu Temple	1·10	1·50
	a. Vert pair. Nos. 649/50	2·10	3·00
650	75c. Sri Perumal Temple (40×25 mm)	1·10	1·50
651	$1 Stained glass window, St Andrew's Cathedral	1·25	1·75
	a. Vert pair. Nos. 651/2	2·50	3·50
652	$1 St. Andrew's Cathedral (40×25 mm)	1·25	1·75
645/52	*Set of* 8	6·50	9·25

The two designs for each value were printed together, *se-tenant*, in vertical pairs throughout the sheets.

(Des Chua Ban Har. Litho Leigh-Mardon Ltd, Melbourne)

1991 (24 Apr). Singapore '95 International Stamp Exhibition. Orchids (1st issue). T **187** and similar horiz design. Multicoloured. Phosphorised paper. P 14.

653	$2 Type **187**	4·00	5·00
	a. Horiz pair. Nos. 653/4	8·00	10·00
654	$2 *Dendrobium* "Anocha"	4·00	5·00
MS655	123×80 mm. Nos. 653/4	11·00	12·00

Nos. 653/4 were issued together, *se-tenant*, in sheets of 30 (6×5), showing No. 653 in vertical rows 1 and 4, Nos. 654 in vertical rows 3 and 6, and stamp-size labels with exhibition emblem in vertical rows 2 and 5.

See also Nos. 674/6, 725/7, 755/7, 795/7 and **MS**817.

188 Changi Airport Terminal II, 1991, and Boeing 747-400

189 *Arachnopsis* "Eric Holttum"

(Des L. Teck Chong. Recess and litho Harrison)

1991 (1 June). Singapore Civil Aviation. T **188** and similar horiz designs. Multicoloured. Phosphorised paper. P 13½×14½.

656	20c. Type **188**	1·25	25
657	75c. Changi Airport Terminal I, 1981, and Boeing 747-200	2·50	2·00
658	$1 Paya Lebar Airport, 1955–1981, and Concorde	2·50	2·25
659	$2 Kallang Airport, 1937–1955, and Douglas DC-2	3·75	6·00
656/9	*Set of 4*	9·00	9·50

(Des Chou Ban Har. Litho Questa)

1991 (7 Aug). Orchid Dress Motifs. T **189** and similar horiz designs. Multicoloured. Phosphorised paper. P 14½×14.

660	20c. Type **189**	1·00	25
661	30c. *Cattleya meadii*	1·25	1·50
662	$1 *Calanthe vestita*	3·00	5·00
660/2	*Set of 3*	4·75	6·00

190 Long-tailed Tailor Bird

191 Productivity Discussion

(Des M. Ng Puay Chiew. Litho Leigh-Mardon Ltd, Melbourne)

1991 (19 Sept). Garden Birds. T **190** and similar horiz designs. Multicoloured. Phosphorised paper. P 14.

663	20c. Type **190**	45	25
	a. Booklet pane. No. 663×10	16·00	
664	35c. Scarlet-backed Flowerpecker	1·50	1·50
665	75c. Black-naped Oriole	2·25	3·25
666	$1 Common Iora	2·50	3·75
663/6	*Set of 4*	6·00	7·75

Booklet pane No. 663a has the upper and lower edges imperforate and there are margins at left and right.

(Des Foo Lye Lin. Litho Questa)

1991 (1 Nov). Tenth Anniv of Productivity Movement. T **191** and similar vert design. Multicoloured. Phosphorised paper. P 14×14½.

667	20c. Type **191**	40	30
668	$1 Construction workers	1·10	2·50

192 Railway Creeper

193 "Singapore Waterfront" (Georgette Chen Liying)

(Des Eng Siak Loy. Litho Leigh-Mardon Ltd, Melbourne)

1991 (16 Nov). Phila Nippon '91 International Stamp Exhibition Tokyo. Wild Flowers. T **192** and similar vert designs. Multicoloured. Phosphorised paper. P 14½×14.

669	30c. Type **192**	75	25
670	75c. Asystasia	1·25	1·25
671	$1 Singapore Rhododendron	1·50	2·00
672	$2 Coat Buttons	2·50	5·25
669/72	*Set of 4*	5·50	7·75
MS673	132×90 mm. Nos. 669/72	7·50	8·50

(Des Chou Ban Har. Litho Leigh-Mardon Ltd, Melbourne)

1992 (22 Jan). Singapore '95 International Stamp Exhibition. Orchids (2nd issue). Horiz designs as T **187**. Multicoloured. Phosphorised paper. P 14.

674	$2 *Dendrobium* "Sharifah Fatimah"	2·75	4·25
	a. Horiz pair. Nos. 674/5	5·50	8·50
675	$2 *Phalaenopsis* "Shim Beauty"	2·75	4·25
MS676	123×80 mm. Nos. 674/5	11·00	12·00

Nos. 674/5 were printed in the same sheet format as Nos. 653/4.

(Des Lim Ching San. Litho Secura, Singapore)

1992 (11 Mar). Local Artists (1st series). T **193** and similar square designs. Multicoloured. Phosphorised paper. P 14.

677	20c. Type **193**	40	20
678	75c. "Kampung Hut" (Lim Cheng Hoe)	85	1·25
679	$1 "The Bridge" (Poh Siew Wah)	1·10	1·40
680	$2 "Singapore River" (Lee Boon Wang)	2·25	4·50
677/680	*Set of 4*	4·25	6·50

See also Nos. 818/21.

194 Football

195 Chinese Family and Samfu Pattern

(Des L. Teck Chong. Litho Leigh-Mardon Ltd, Melbourne)

1992 (24 Apr). Olympic Games, Barcelona. T **194** and similar horiz designs. Multicoloured. Phosphorised paper. P 14.

681	20c. Type **194**	25	20
682	35c. Athletics	35	30
683	50c. Swimming	55	65
684	75c. Basketball	1·25	1·25
685	$1 Tennis	1·50	1·50
686	$2 Yachting	2·00	2·75
681/6	*Set of 6*	5·50	6·00
MS687	132×90 mm. Nos. 681/6	9·50	11·00

(Des Chun Ban Har. Litho Leigh-Mardon Ltd, Melbourne)

1992 (22 May). Singapore Costumes of 1910. T **195** and similar vert designs. Multicoloured. Phosphorised paper. P 14½.

688	20c. Type **195**	40	20
689	35c. Malay family and sarong pattern	50	45
690	75c. Indian family and sari pattern	1·00	1·25
691	$2 Straits Chinese family and belt pattern	2·00	3·50
688/91	*Set of 4*	3·50	4·75

196 Infantryman, Air Force Pilot and Navy Gunner

197 Crafts from A.S.E.A.N. Countries

(Des T. Koh. Litho Leigh-Mardon Ltd, Melbourne)

1992 (1 July). 25th Anniv of National Service. T **196** and similar horiz designs. Multicoloured. Phosphorised paper. P 14½.

692	20c. Type **196**	60	30
693	35c. Navy diver, General Dynamics F-16 Fighting Falcon and FH-88 155 mm howitzer	85	75
694	$1 General Dynamics F-16 Fighting Falcon in flight, corvette and AMX-13SM1 tank	2·50	4·00
692/4	*Set of 3*	3·50	4·50

(Des Chua Ban Har. Litho Questa)

1992 (8 Aug). 25th Anniv of A.S.E.A.N (Association of South East Asian Nations). T **197** and similar horiz designs. Multicoloured. Phosphorised paper. P 14×14½.

695	20c. Type **197**	40	20

696	35c. National dances	90	1·00
697	$1 National landmarks	2·00	3·75
695/7	*Set of 3*	3·00	4·50

198 Mosaic Crab

199 Coins

(Des Chua Ban Har. Litho Leigh-Mardon Ltd, Melbourne)

1992 (21 Aug). Crabs. T **198** and similar horiz designs. Multicoloured. Phosphorised paper. P 14½.

698	20c. Type **198**	55	25
	a. Booklet pane. No. 698×10	10·00	
699	50c. Johnson's Freshwater Crab	1·00	1·25
700	75c. Singapore Freshwater Crab	1·50	2·25
701	$1 Swamp Forest Crab	1·75	3·00
698/701	*Set of 4*	4·25	6·00

The upper and lower edges of booklet pane No. 698a are imperforate.

(Des Lim Ching San. Litho Leigh-Mardon Ltd, Melbourne)

1992 (2 Oct). 25th Anniv of Singapore Currency. T **199** and similar square designs. Multicoloured. Phosphorised paper. P 14½.

702	20c. Type **199**	1·00	1·75
	a. Block of 4. Nos. 702/5	7·00	9·75
703	75c. Currency note from "orchid" series	1·75	2·75
704	$1 Currency note from "ship" series	2·25	3·00
705	$2 Currency note from "bird" series	2·75	3·25
702/5	*Set of 4*	7·00	9·75

Nos. 702/5 were printed together, *se-tenant*, as blocks of four throughout the sheet of 20, each block forming a composite design.

200 Sun Bear

201 "Thank You"

(Des Eng Siak Loy. Litho Leigh-Mardon Ltd, Melbourne)

1993 (13 Jan). South-East Asian Mammals. T **200** and similar horiz designs. Multicoloured. Phosphorised paper. P 14½.

706	20c. Type **200**	30	20
707	30c. Orang-utan	60	65
708	75c. Slow Loris	1·10	1·40
709	$2 Greater Malay Chevrotain ("Large Mouse Deer")	2·25	3·75
706/9	*Set of 4*	3·75	5·50

(Des N. Loh Fook Chee. Litho Printset Cambec Pty Ltd, Australia)

1993 (10 Feb). Greetings Stamps. T **201** and similar square designs. Multicoloured. Phosphorised paper. P 14½×14.

710	20c. Type **201**	60	90
	a. Booklet pane. Nos. 710/14×2	5·50	90
711	20c. "Congratulations"	60	90
712	20c. "Best Wishes"	60	90
713	20c. "Happy Birthday"	60	90
714	20c. "Get Well Soon"	60	90
710/14	*Set of 5*	2·75	4·00

Nos. 710/14 were only available from $2 booklets. The upper and lower edges of booklet pane No. 710a are imperforate and there are margins at both left and right.

202 Shophouses

203 "Cranes" (painting) (Chen Wen Hsi)

(Des Ng Keng Seng ($2), W. Kee (others). Litho Leigh-Mardon Ltd, Melbourne)

1993 (10 Mar). Conservation of Tanjong Pagar District. T **202** and similar horiz designs. Multicoloured. Phosphorised paper. P 14.

715	20c. Type **202**	50	20
716	30c. Jinrikisha Station	2·50	70
717	$2 View of Tanjong Pagar	3·75	4·00
715/17	*Set of 3*	6·00	4·50

(Des L. Teck Chong. Photo Courvoisier)

1993 (28 May). Indopex '93 International Philatelic Exhibition, Surabaya. Phosphorised granite paper. P 12.

718	**203** $2 multicoloured	2·75	4·25

204 Football

205 *Danaus chrysippus*

(Des L. Teck Chong. Litho Questa)

1993 (12 June). 17th South-East Asia Games Singapore. T **204** and similar vert designs. Multicoloured. Phosphorised paper. P 14.

719	20c. Type **204**	30	20
720	35c. Basketball	70	60
721	50c. Badminton	90	1·25
722	75c. Athletics	1·00	1·50
723	$1 Waterpolo	1·40	2·00
724	$2 Yachting	2·25	4·00
719/24	*Set of 6*	6·00	8·50

(Des Chou Ban Har. Litho Leigh-Mardon Ltd, Melbourne)

1993 (13 Aug). Singapore '95 International Stamp Exhibition. Orchids (3rd issue). Multicoloured designs as T **187**, but each 25×35 mm. Phosphorised paper. P 14½.

725	$2 *Phalaenopsis amabilis*	3·00	4·00
	a. Horiz pair. Nos. 725/6	6·00	8·00
726	$2 *Vanda sumatrana*	3·00	4·00
MS727	123×80 mm. Nos. 725/6	7·50	8·00

Nos. 725/6 were printed in the same sheet format as Nos. 653/4.

No. **MS**727 also commemorates Taipei '93 Asian International Stamp Exhibition, Taiwan.

(Des Eng Siak Loy. Litho Leigh-Mardon Ltd, Melbourne)

1993 (21 Aug). Butterflies. T **205** and similar horiz designs. Multicoloured. Phosphorised paper. P 14½.

728	20c. Type **205**	30	30
	a. Booklet pane. No. 728×10	7·50	
729	50c. *Cethosia hypsea*	65	65
730	75c. *Amathusia phidippus*	90	1·50
731	$1 *Papilio demolion*	1·25	2·00
728/31	*Set of 4*	2·75	4·00

The upper and lower edges of booklet pane No. 728a are imperforate.

206 Papaya

207 Egrets drinking

(Des Poh Siew Wah. Litho Leigh-Mardon Ltd, Melbourne)

1993 (1 Oct). Bangkok '93 International Stamp Exhibition. Local Fruits. T **206** and similar vert designs. Multicoloured. Phosphorised paper. P 14½×14.

732	20c. Type **206**	40	20
733	35c. Pomegranate	60	50
734	75c. Starfruit	1·25	1·50
735	$2 Durian	2·25	4·00
732/5 *Set of* 4		4·00	5·50
MS736 120×89 mm. Nos. 732/5		4·00	5·50

(Des Eng Siak Loy. Litho Enschedé)

1993 (10 Nov). Endangered Species. Swinhoe's Egret ("Chinese Egret"). T **207** and similar square designs. Multicoloured. Phosphorised paper. P 13½.

737	20c. Type **207**	50	95
	a. Horiz strip of 4. Nos. 737/40	2·25	3·75
738	25c. Egrets eating	55	1·00
739	30c. Egrets searching for fish	65	1·10
740	35c. Egrets in flight	70	1·10
737/40 *Set of* 4		2·25	3·75

Nos. 737/40 were printed together, *se-tenant*, in horizontal strips of 4 throughout the sheet, with the background forming a composite design.

208 Palm Tree

209 Tiger Cowrie

(Des Eng Siak Loy. Photo Avery Dennison, Pasadena)

1993 (24 Nov). Self adhesive Automatic Cash Machine Stamps. Phosphorised polyester film. Die-cut.

741	**208** (20c.) multicoloured	30	50

No. 741 was issued, in sheets of 15 (5×3), from bank automatic cash machines and philatelic centres. It was only valid for use on mail to local addresses and was initially sold at 20c. Advertising on the backing paper originally featured Speedpost, but this was subsequently changed to details of Singapore '95 on 20 January 1995.

(Des Sylvia Tan)

1994 (12 Jan)–**97**. Reef Life (1st series). T **209** and similar horiz designs. Multicoloured. Phosphorised paper. P 13×13½ (5c. to 75c.) or 14* ($1 to $10).

(a) Litho (5c. to 75c.) or recess and litho ($1 to $10) Leigh-Mardon Ltd. Melbourne.

742	5c. Type **209**	30	30
743	20c. Sea-fan	60	75
	a. Booklet pane. No. 743×10	8·00	
744	25c. Tunicate	65	25
745	30c. Clown Anemonefish	70	50
746	35c. Ruppell's Nudibranch	75	75
747	40c. Sea-urchin	1·00	1·50
748	50c. Soft coral	1·00	50
749	75c. Pin Cushion Star	1·50	70
750	$1 Knob coral (31×27 mm) (23.3.94)	4·50	1·75
	a. Silver (country name and value omitted)		
751	$2 Mushroom coral (31×27 mm) (23.3.94)	7·00	3·50
752	$5 Bubble coral (31×27 mm) (23.3.94)	10·00	7·50
753	$10 Octopus coral (31×27 mm) (23.3.94)	15·00	12·00
742/53 *Set of* 12		38·00	27·00

(b) Photo Enschedé (5c. to 50c.) or litho and embossed Questa ($1 to $10).

753*a*	5c. Type **209** (27.1.97)	6·00	3·00
753*b*	25c. Tunicate (4.4.96)	50·00	1·00
753*c*	30c. Clown Anemonefish (22.3.96)	3·50	1·00
753*d*	35c. Ruppell's Nudibranch (13.1.97)	4·00	1·75
753*e*	40c. Sea-urchin (9.9.96)	4·00	2·00
753*f*	50c. Soft coral (23.2.96)	4·75	1·25
753*g*	$1 Knob coral (31×27 mm) (4.11.96)	15·00	2·50
753*h*	$2 Mushroom coral (31×27 mm) (2.12.97)	8·00	9·50
753*i*	$5 Bubble coral (31×27 mm) (5.5.97)	35·00	18·00
753*j*	$10 Octopus coral (31×27 mm) (13.1.97)	45·00	22·00
753*a/j Set of* 10		£160	55·00

The upper and lower edges of booklet pane No. 743a are imperforate and there are margins at left and right.

*Nos. 750/3 and 753*g/j* include a large elliptical hole in both the top and bottom perforations. On the Questa printings this is more elongated than on those produced by Leigh-Mardon.

Nos. 750/3 show a large central lion emblem printed in yellow fluorescence as a security marking. On Nos. 753*g/j* this is replaced by lines of smaller images, also in yellow fluorescence, and by a larger lion emblem in colourless embossing.

On the Leigh-Mardon printings of the $1 to $10 "SINGAPORE" and the face value are shaded. On the Questa printings of these values they are white.

For similar design inscribed "FOR LOCAL ADDRESSES ONLY" see Nos. 784/5c.

(Des Chua Ban Har. Litho Leigh-Mardon Ltd, Melbourne)

1994 (18 Feb). Singapore '95 International Stamp Exhibition. Orchids (4th issue). Multicoloured designs as T **187** but each *25×35* mm. Phosphorised paper. P 14½.

755	$2 Paphiopedilum victoriaregina	4·00	4·50
	a. Horiz pair. Nos. 755/6	8·00	9·00
756	$2 Dendrobium smillieae	4·00	4·50
MS757 123×80 mm. Nos. 755/6		7·50	8·00

Nos. 755/6 were printed in the same sheet format as Nos. 653/4.

No. **MS**757 also commemorates Hong Kong '94 International Stamp Exhibition.

210 Dancers

(Des Elsie Koh. Litho Questa)

1994 (18 May). Singapore Festival of Arts. T **210** and similar horiz designs. Multicoloured. Phosphorised paper. P 13½×14.

758	20c. Type **210**	45	20
759	30c. Actors and puppet	65	55
760	50c. Musicians	1·00	1·00
761	$1 Artists	1·75	3·00
758/61 *Set of* 4		3·50	4·25

211 Civilian taking Pledge, National Day Parade and Soldier with Anti-tank Missile.

212 Black-crowned Night Heron.

(Des D. Kuah. Litho Enschedé)

1994 (1 July). 25th Anniv of Operationally-ready National Servicemen. T **211** and similar horiz designs. Multicoloured. Phosphorised paper. P 13½.

762	20c. Type **211**	90	30
763	30c. Serviceman on beach with family and on jungle patrol	1·10	1·25
764	35c. Serviceman relaxing at home and with machine gun	1·25	1·25
765	75c. National Service officer at work and commanding patrol	2·00	3·00
762/5 *Set of* 4		4·75	5·25

(Des Eng Siak Loy. Litho Leigh-Mardon Ltd, Melbourne)

1994 (16 Aug). Herons. T **212** and similar square designs. Multicoloured. Phosphorised paper. P 14.

766	20c. Type **212**	50	60
	a. Block of 4. Nos. 766/9	2·75	3·25
	b. Booklet pane. No. 766×10	9·50	
767	50c. Green Heron ("Little Heron")	70	85
768	75c. Purple Heron	85	1·00
769	$1 Grey Heron	95	1·25
766/9 *Set of* 4		2·75	3·25

Nos. 766/9 were printed together, *se-tenant*, in blocks of four throughout the sheet, each block forming a composite design.

The upper and lower edges of booklet pane No. 766b are imperforate and there are margins at left and right.

213 Traditional and Modern Education

214 Balloons

(Des Lim Ching San. Litho Enschedé)

1994 (31 Aug). 175th Anniv of Modern Singapore. T **213** and similar horiz designs. Multicoloured. Phosphorised paper. P 13½×14.

770	20c. Type **213**	25	25
771	50c. Rickshaws and Mass Rapid Transit train	70	75
772	75c. Sampans and modern container port	1·00	1·40
773	$1 Victorian buildings and modern skyline	1·25	2·00
770/3 *Set of 4*		2·75	4·00
MS774 135×95 mm. Nos. 770/3		3·50	4·00

No. **MS**774 also exists with the "Singpex '94" logo added in gold for sale at this philatelic exhibition.

(Des Chua Ban Har. Litho Printset-Cambec Pty Ltd, Australia)

1994 (14 Sept). Self-adhesive Greetings Stamps. T **214** and similar vert designs. Multicoloured. Phosphorised paper. P 11½.

775	(20c.) Type **214**	55	80
	a. Booklet pane. Nos. 775/9, each×2	5·00	
776	(20c.) Fireworks	55	80
777	(20c.) Gift-wrapped parcel	55	80
778	(20c.) Bouquet of flowers	55	80
779	(20c.) Birthday cake	55	80
775/9 *Set of 5*		2·50	3·50

Nos. 775/9 are inscribed "For Local Addresses Only" and were available from booklets of 10 sold for $2.

215 Logo and Globe

(Des N. Loh Fook Chee. Litho Questa)

1994 (5 Oct). 50th Anniv of International Civil Aviation Organization. T **215** and similar horiz designs. Phosphorised paper. P 14.

780	20c. Type **215**	20	20
781	35c. Boeing 747 and Changi Airport control tower	60	60
782	75c. Projected hypersonic aircraft over airport	85	1·25
783	$2 Control tower, satellite and Boeing 747	2·00	3·25
780/3 *Set of 4*		3·25	4·75

(Des Sylvia Tan)

1994 (16 Nov)–**97**. Reef Life (2nd series). Multicoloured design as T **209**, but inscr "FOR LOCAL ADDRESSES ONLY".

(a) Litho Leigh-Mardon Ltd, Melbourne. Phosphorised paper. P 13×13½.

784	(20c.) Blue-spotted Stingray	25	30

(b) Litho Leigh-Mardon Ltd, Melbourne. Self adhesive. Phosphor frame. P 9.

785	(20c.) As No. 784	45	45
	a. Booklet pane. No. 785×10	4·00	
	b. Broad phosphor band (12.4.95)	70	70
	ba. Booklet pane. No. 785b×10	7·00	

(c) Photo Enschedé. Phosphorised paper. P 13×13½.

785*c*	(22c.) As No. 784 (2.12.97)	3·00	2·50

Booklet panes Nos. 785a and 785ba are arranged as two blocks of four and a pair with backing card forming the booklet cover.

Nos. 784/5 were initially sold at 20c., but this was increased to 22c. on 1 April 1995.

The inscriptions on No. 785*c* are redrawn so that the "SINGAPORE" is 26 mm long instead of 26½ and the others are also smaller. On No. 784 the "y" of "stingray" is to the right of the "A" in "SINGAPORE"; on No. 785*c* it is under the left leg of the "A".

216 Singapore International Convention and Exhibition Centre, Suntec City

217 "Love, LOVE, Love"

(Des M. Ng Puay Chiew. Litho Enschedé)

1995 (11 Jan). Opening of Singapore International Convention and Exhibition Centre. T **216** and similar horiz designs. Multicoloured. Phosphorised paper. P 13½.

786	(20c.) Type **216**	20	20
787	75c. Suntec City skyline	85	85
788	$1 Temasek Boulevard	1·10	1·40
789	$2 Fountain Terrace	1·75	2·75
786/9 *Set of 4*		3·50	4·75

No. 786 is inscribed "FOR LOCAL ADDRESSES ONLY".

Nos. 786 and 789 also exist in miniature sheets issued at the Singapore '95 exhibition. A different marginal illustration was used for each of the ten days of the exhibition.

(Des Design Objectives. Litho Printset-Cambec Pty Ltd, Australia)

1995 (8 Feb). Self-adhesive Greeting Stamps. T **217** and similar vert designs. Phosphor frame. P 11½.

790	**217** (20c.) multicoloured	90	1·00
	a. Booklet pane. Nos. 790/4, each×2	8·00	
791	– (20c.) vermilion and black	90	1·00
792	– (20c.) multicoloured	90	1·00
793	– (20c.) multicoloured	90	1·00
794	– (20c.) multicoloured	90	1·00
790/4 *Set of 5*		4·00	4·50

Designs:—No. 791, "LOVE" forming spiral around heart; No. 792, "LOVE, LOVE"; No. 793, "Love" in four different languages; No. 794, Geometric symbols.

Nos. 709/4 are inscribed "For Local Addresses Only" and were available from booklets of 10 initially sold for $2, but increased to $2.20 from 1 April 1995.

(Des Chua, Ban Har. Litho Leigh-Mardon Ltd, Melbourne)

1995 (15 Mar). Singapore '95 International Stamp Exhibition. Orchids (5th issue). Horiz designs as T **187**. Multicoloured. Phosphorised paper. P 14.

795	$2 *Vanda* "Marlie Dolera"	2·00	3·00
	a. Horiz pair. Nos. 795/6	4·00	6·00
796	$2 *Vanda limbata*	2·00	3·00
MS797 123×80 mm. Nos. 795/6 with sheet margins showing animals from Singapore Zoo		10·00	10·00

Nos. 795/6 were printed in the same sheet format as Nos. 653/4.

No. **MS**797 also exists imperforate from the Singapore '95 exhibition catalogue.

For further miniature sheet containing these stamps see No. **MS**817.

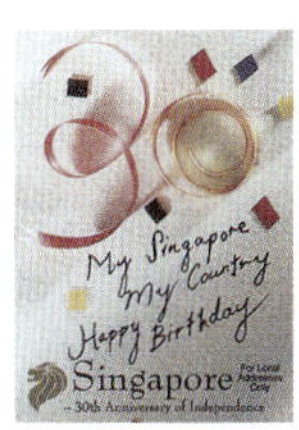

218 Ribbons and "My Singapore, My Country,Happy Birthday"

219 Rejoicing Crowd and 1945 B.M.A. $5 Stamp

(Des L. Teck Chong. Litho Enschedé)

1995 (19 Apr). 30th Anniv of Independence. T **218** and similar multicoloured designs. Phosphorised paper. P 13½.

798	(22c.) Type **218**	20	20
799	50c. Chinese inscr and 1985 Housing and Development 50c. stamp (horiz)	65	80
800	75c. National anthem, Civil Aviation 20c. and inscr in Malay (horiz)	90	1·50
801	$1 National flag, 1986 Economic Development Board $1 and inscr in Tamil	1·25	2·25
798/801 *Set of 4*		2·75	4·25
MS802 120×78 mm. Nos. 798/801		5·50	6·50

No. 798 is inscribed "For Local Addresses Only".

(Des Chua Ban Har. Litho Enschedé)

1995 (21 June). 50th Anniv of End of Second World War. T **219** and similar multicoloured designs. Phosphorised paper. P 14×13½ (vert) or 13½×14 (horiz).

803	(22c.) Type **219**	30	20
804	60c. Lord Mountbatten accepting Japanese surrender at Singapore and 1945 B.M.A. 15c. stamp	1·00	1·00
805	70c. Emergency food kitchen (horiz)	80	1·25
806	$2 Police road block during State of Emergency (horiz)	2·75	4·00
803/6	*Set of 4*	4·25	5·75

No. 803 is inscribed "For Local Addresses Only".

220 Yellow-faced Angelfish

221 Envelope, Stamps and Museum

(Des Sylvia Tan. Litho Enschedé)

1995 (19 July). Marine Fish. T **220** and similar horiz designs. Multicoloured. Phosphorised paper. P 13½×14.

807	(22c.) Type **220**	35	25
808	60c. Harlequin Sweetlips	80	1·00
809	70c. Lionfish	90	1·50
810	$1 Pennant Coralfish ("Longfin Bannerfish")	1·25	2·25
807/10	*Set of 4*	3·00	4·50

No. 807 is inscribed "For Local Addresses Only".

(Des Poh Siew Wah. Litho Japanese Govt Ptg Bureau, Tokyo)

1995 (19 Aug). Opening of Singapore Philatelic Museum. T **221** and similar vert designs, each showing Museum. Multicoloured. Phosphorised paper. P 13×13½.

811	(22c.) Type **221**	50	25
812	50c. Stamps and stamp booklet	1·10	65
813	60c. Stamps and philatelic equipment	1·25	1·25
814	$2 Museum displays	3·25	5·50
811/14	*Set of 4*	5·50	7·00

No. 811 is inscribed "FOR LOCAL ADDRESSES ONLY".

222 Two, Four and Six Digit Post Codes

(Des L. Huei Hoon. Litho Printset-Cambec Pty Ltd, Australia)

1995 (1 Sept). Introduction of Six Digit Postal Codes. T **222** and similar horiz design. Multicoloured. Phosphorised paper. P 14×14½.

815	(22c.) Type **222**	30	25
816	$2 Six empty post code boxes	2·25	3·50

No. 815 is inscribed "For local addresses only".

(Des Chua Ban Har. Litho Leigh-Mardon Ltd, Melbourne)

1995 (1 Sept). Singapore '95 International Stamp Exhibition. Orchids (6th issue). Sheet 123×80 mm, containing Nos. 795/6 with sheet margins showing Sentosa Gardens. Phosphorised paper. P 14.

MS817	$2×2 multicoloured	8·00	9·00

No. **MS**817 also exists either with the marginal illustration in a single colour or with the stamps imperforate, both showing an additional gold embossed inscription. Such miniature sheets were distributed to individual collectors contributing to exhibition funds.

NEW INFORMATION

The editor is always interested to correspond with people who have new information that will improve or correct this catalogue

223 "Tropical Fruits" (Georgette Chen Liying)

(Des Poh Siew Wah. Litho Japanese Govt Ptg Bureau, Tokyo)

1995 (20 Oct). Local Artists (2nd series). T **223** and similar multicoloured designs. Phosphorised paper ($2) or 12½ (others). P 13½×13.

818	(22c.) Type **223**	30	25
819	30c. "Bali Beach" (Cheong Soo Pieng)	40	40
820	70c. "Gibbons" (Chen Wen Hsi)	80	1·25
821	$2 "Shi (Lion)" (Pan Shou) (22½×38½ mm)	2·25	3·75
818/21	*Set of 4*	3·25	5·00

No. 818 is inscribed "FOR LOCAL ADDRESSES ONLY".

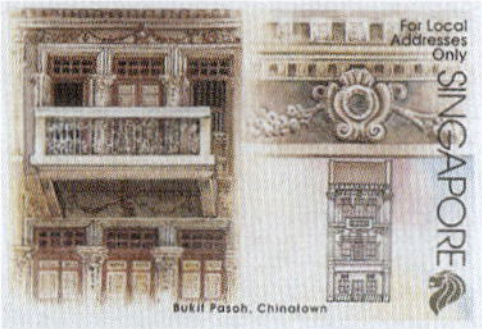

224 Bukit Pasoh, Chinatown

225 Pair of Rats

(Des Poh Siew Wah. Litho Enschedé)

1996 (17 Jan). Architectural Conservation. T **224** and similar horiz designs. Multicoloured. Phosphorised paper. P 13½×14.

822	(22c.) Type **224**	35	25
823	35c. Jalan Sultan, Kampong Glam	50	50
824	70c. Dalhousie Lane, Little India	80	1·25
825	$1 Supreme Court, Civic District	1·10	2·25
822/5	*Set of 4*	2·50	3·75

No. 822 is inscribed "FOR LOCAL ADDRESSES ONLY".

Two Types of No. 826:

Type I (sheets of 50) – Top left emblem cut by curved "FOR LOCAL ADDRESSES ONLY" label. Bottom right emblem clear of right edge of design.

Type II (*se-tenant* sheetlets of 18) – Top left emblem clear of curved label. Bottom right emblem cut by right edge of design.

(Des N. Loh Fook Chee. Litho, Southern Colour Print, Dunedin)

1996 (9 Feb). Chinese New Year ("Year of the Rat"). T **225** and similar vert design. Multicoloured. Phosphorised paper. P 12.

826	(22c.) Type **225** (I)	30	25
	b. Type II	50	75
	ba. Pair. Nos. 826b/7	3·25	4·25
827	$2 Rat holding orange	3·00	4·00

No. 826 is inscribed "FOR LOCAL ADDRESSES ONLY". In addition to separate sheets of 50, the stamps were also issued in sheetlets of 18 horizontally and vertically *se-tenant*.

For these stamps in miniature sheets see Nos. **MS**832/3 and **MS**838.

226 The Straits of Singapore, 1794 (Thomas Jefferys)

227 17th-century Chinese Calligraphy by Zhang Ruitu and Museum Building

(Des D. Kuah. Litho Southern Colour Print, Dunedin, New Zealand)

1996 (13 Mar). Old Maps. T **226** and similar horiz designs. Multicoloured. Phosphorised paper. P 12.

828	(22c.) Type **226**	35	25
829	60c. Singapore (19th-century)	65	75
830	$1 Singapore by James Duncan, 1835	1·00	1·50
831	$2 Singapore by J. B. Tassin, 1839	2·00	3·25
828/31	*Set of* 4	3·50	5·25

No. 828 is inscribed "FOR LOCAL ADDRESSES ONLY" and was sold for 22c.

(Litho Southern Colour Print, Dunedin)

1996 (21 Mar). Indonesia '96 International Youth Stamp Exhibition, Bandung. Sheet 123×80 mm. Phosphorised paper. P 12.

MS832 22c. As Type **225**; $2 No. 827 ... 11·00 12·00

(Litho Southern Colour Print, Dunedin)

1996 (18 May). CHINA '96 9th Asian International Stamp Exhibition, Peking. Sheet 123×80 mm. Phosphorised paper. P 12.

MS833 22c. As Type **225**; $2 No. 827 ... 11·00 12·00

(Des M. Ng Puay Chiew. Litho Enschedé)

1996 (5 June). Inauguration of Asian Civilizations Museum. T **227** and similar horiz designs, each including museum building. Multicoloured. Phosphorised paper. P 13½.

834	(22c.) Type **227**	35	25
835	60c. Javanese divination manuscript, 1842	70	70
836	70c. 19th-century temple hanging, South India	80	1·00
837	$2 17th to 19th-century calligraphic implements, Iran and Turkey	2·00	3·50
834/7	*Set of* 4	3·50	5·00

No. 834 is inscribed "FOR LOCAL ADDRESSES ONLY" and was sold for 22c.

(Litho Southern Colour Print, Dunedin)

1996 (8 June). CAPEX '96 International Stamp Exhibition, Toronto. Sheet 123×80 mm. Phosphorised paper. P 12.

MS838 22c. As Type **225**; $2 No. 827 ... 13·00 14·00

228 "Children in Library" (Ivan Chang)

229 Wind Surfing and Dinghy Sailing

(Adapted Design Business Ltd. Litho SNP Cambec, Australia)

1996 (10 July). Self adhesive Greetings Stamps. "Courtesy". Children's Drawings. T **228** and similar horiz designs. Multicoloured. Phosphorised paper. P 11½.

839	(22c.) Type **228**	30	30
	a. Booklet pane. No. 839×10	2·75	
	b. Booklet pane. No. 839×5, No. 840×2 and Nos. 841/3	5·00	
840	35c. "Children crossing Road" (Cheong Kah Yin)	50	60
841	50c. "Waiting for Bus" (Jeannie Fong)	65	80
842	60c. "In the Rain" (Liew Cai Yun)	75	95
843	$1 "On the Train" (Yong Wan Quan)	1·25	1·60
839/43	*Set of* 5	3·00	3·25
MS844	200×130 mm. 22c. As Type **228** and Nos. 840/3. Phosphor frame	4·75	5·50

No. 839 is inscribed "For Local Addresses Only".

Nos. 839/43 were only issued in $2.20 and $3.90 stamp booklets or as No. **MS**844.

(Des N. Loh Fook Chee. Litho Southern Colour Print, Dunedin)

1996 (19 July). Olympic Games, Atlanta. T **229** and similar vert designs. Multicoloured. Phosphorised paper. P 14½.

845	(22c.) Type **229**	35	25
846	60c. Tennis and football	90	80
847	70c. Pole vaulting and hurdling	90	1·10
848	$2 Diving and swimming	2·25	4·00
845/8	*Set of* 4	4·00	5·50
MS849	120×70 mm. 22c. As Type **229** and Nos. 846/8	4·00	5·50

No. 845 is inscribed "For Local Addresses Only".

230 *Cinnamomum iners*

231 Panmen Gate, Suzhou, China

(Des Poh Siew Wah. Litho Southern Colour Print, Dunedin)

1996 (11 Sept). Singapore Trees. T **230** and similar vert designs. Multicoloured. Phosphorised paper. P 13½.

850	(22c.) Type **230**	30	25
851	60c. *Hibiscus tiliaceus*	70	90
852	70c. *Parkia speciosa*	80	1·25
853	$1 *Terminalia catappa*	1·25	1·75
850/3	*Set of* 4	2·75	3·75

No. 850 is inscribed "FOR LOCAL ADDRESSES ONLY".

(Des Jiang Zhi Nan, adapted Sylvia Tan. Litho Enschedé)

1996 (9 Oct). Singapore–China Joint Issue. T **231** and similar horiz design. Multicoloured. Phosphorised paper. P 13×13½.

854	(22c.) Type **231**	30	25
855	60c. Singapore waterfront	80	1·25
MS856	120×78 mm. 22c. As T **231** and No. 855	1·40	2·00

No. 854 is inscribed "FOR LOCAL ADDRESSES ONLY".

No. **MS**856 also exists overprinted "SINGAPORE–CHINA STAMP EXHIBITION 9–13 OCT '96" for sale at this exhibition.

232 Conference Logo

(Des Design Objectives. Litho Harrison)

1996 (20 Nov). Inaugural Ministerial Conference of World Trade Organization. Phosphorised paper. P 13½.

857	**232** (22c.) multicoloured	30	30
858	60c. multicoloured	70	1·25
859	$1 multicoloured	1·25	1·90
860	$2 multicoloured	2·25	3·75
857/60	*Set of* 4	4·00	6·50

No. 857 is inscribed "For local addresses Only".

233 Ox

234 Shuttlecock

(Des N. Loh Fook Chee. Litho Enschedé)

1997 (10 Jan). Chinese New Year ("Year of the Ox"). T **233** and similar horiz design showing stylised ox. Phosphorised paper. P 13½×14.

861	(22c.) multicoloured	15	20
	a. Pair. Nos. 861/2	1·90	2·75
862	$2 multicoloured	1·75	2·50

No. 861 is inscribed "FOR LOCAL ADDRESSES ONLY" and was sold for 22c.

In addition to separate sheets of 50 Nos. 861/2 were also issued in sheetlets of 18 with the stamps horizontally and vertically *se-tenant*.

(Litho Enschedé)

1997 (12 Feb). HONG KONG '97 International Stamp Exhibition. Chinese New Year ("Year of the Ox"). Sheet 123×80 mm. Phosphorised paper. P 13½×14.
MS863 22c. As Type **233**; $2 No. 862 ..... 6·00 7·00

(Des Chua Ban Har. Litho Southern Colour Print, Dunedin)

1997 (21 Feb). SINGPEX '97 International Stamp Exhibition. Traditional Games. T **234** and similar vert designs. Multicoloured. Phosphorised paper. P 14½×15.
864 (22c.) Type **234** 20 20
865 35c. Marbles 40 40
866 60c. Tops 55 75
867 $1 Fivestones ..... 80 1·50
864/7 *Set of* 4 ..... 1·75 2·50
MS868 140×75 mm. 22c. As Type **234** and Nos. 865/7.. 1·75 2·50
No. 864 is inscribed "For Local Addresses Only" and was sold for 22c.

235 Bullock Cart

236 Taxi

(Des Design Business Ltd. Eng C. Slania ($1 to $10))

1997 (19 Mar–23 April). Transportation. Multicoloured. Phosphorised paper.

(a) Litho Ashton-Potter Canada. T **235** and similar designs. P 13½.
869 5c. Type **235** 15 50
870 20c. Bicycle (vert) ..... 1·00 60
871 (22c.) Jinrickshaw (vert) 40 20
872 30c. Electric tram ..... 1·00 30
873 35c. Trolley bus ..... 1·25 30
874 40c. Trishaw (vert) 70 50
875 50c. Vintage car (vert) ..... 1·00 45
876 60c. Horse-drawn carriage ..... 1·50 50
877 70c. Fire engine ..... 2·00 60
MS878 132×76 mm. 22c. As No. 871 and Nos. 869/70, 872/7 ..... 8·00 8·00

(b) Recess and litho Enschedé. T **236** and similar designs. P 13 (23 Apr).
879 $1 Type **236** ..... 1·50 80
880 $2 Bus (43×24 mm) ..... 3·50 1·60
881 $5 Mass Rapid Transit train ..... 6·00 4·50
882 $10 Light Rapid Transit carriages (43×24 mm) ..... 8·50 9·50
869/77, 879/82 *Set of* 13 ..... 25·00 18·00
MS883 119×71 mm. Nos. 879/82 ..... 17·00 20·00

(c) Litho Ashton-Potter Canada. Self-adhesive. P 11½.
884 (22c.) As No. 871 ..... 20 35
a. Booklet pane. No. 884×10 ..... 2·00
Nos. 871 and 884 are inscribed "For Local Addresses Only". In addition to booklets, containing No. 884a, the self-adhesive version was also available in sheets of 20 (2 panes 5×2).
The original printings of No. 884, both in sheets and booklets, showed the phosphor printed over the designs. Printings of both sheets and booklets from 2000 onwards were on phosphorised paper. These differences cannot be distinguished without a U.V. lamp.

237 Man's Head

238 Family with Car

(Des L. Teck Chong. Litho Enschedé)

1997 (14 May). Self-adhesive Greeting Stamps. "Friends". T **237** and similar vert designs. Multicoloured. Phosphorised paper. P 15.
885 (22c.) Type **237** 45 60
a. Booklet pane. Nos. 885/9, each×2 ..... 4·00
886 (22c.) Hands holding umbrella 45 60
887 (22c.) Two penguins 45 60
888 (22c.) Two butterflies 45 60
889 (22c.) Cup and saucer 45 60
890 (22c.) Large flower 45 60
a. Booklet pane. Nos. 890/4, each×2 ..... 4·00
891 (22c.) Candle 45 60
892 (22c.) Tree 45 60
893 (22c.) Jar with stars 45 60
894 (22c.) Simple telephone 45 60
885/94 *Set of* 10 ..... 4·00 5·50
Nos. 885/94 are inscribed "FOR LOCAL ADDRESSES ONLY" and were available from two different booklets of 10, each sold for $2.20.

(Litho Enschedé)

1997 (29 May). Pacific '97 International Stamp Exhibition, San Francisco. Sheet 123×80 mm, containing designs as Nos. 861/2. Phosphorised paper. P 13½×14.
MS895 22c. As Type **233**; $2 No. 862 ..... 8·00 9·00

(Des D. Kuah. Litho Southern Colour Print, Dunedin)

1997 (16 July). Renovation of Housing and Development Board Estates. T **238** and similar vert designs. Multicoloured. Phosphorised paper. P 14.
896 (22c.) Type **238** 20 20
897 30c. Family at playground 30 35
898 70c. Couple walking through garden 60 80
899 $1 Family on balcony ..... 80 1·50
896/9 *Set of* 4 ..... 1·75 2·50
No. 896 is inscribed "FOR LOCAL ADDRESSES ONLY" and was sold for 22c.

239 Globe and Hand Clasp

240 Flower and Tree
lean Environment")

(Des M. Chiew. Litho Southern Colour Print, Dunedin)

1997 (8 Aug). 30th Anniv of A.S.E.A.N. (Association of Southeast Asian Nations). T **239** and similar semi-circular designs. Multicoloured. Phosphorised paper. P 15 (and 14 around design).
900 (22c.) Type **239** 20 20
901 35c. Dancers, kite flying and decorated truck 35 40
902 60c. Dish aerial and map 55 70
903 $1 National landmarks ..... 80 2·00
900/3 *Set of* 4 ..... 1·75 3·00
No. 900 is inscribed "FOR LOCAL ADDRESSES ONLY" and was sold for 22c.

(Des Design Objectives. Litho Enschedé)

1997 (13 Sept). 25th Anniv of the Ministry of the Environment. T **240** and similar vert designs. Multicoloured. Phosphorised paper. P 13½.
904 (22c.) Type **240** 20 20
a. Booklet pane. No. 904×10 with margins all round ..... 2·00
905 60c. Fish and river ("Clean Waters") 55 60
906 70c. Bird and sky ("Clean Air") 60 70
907 $1 Dustbin and block of flats ("Clean Homes") ..... 80 1·25
904/7 *Set of* 4 ..... 1·90 2·50
No. 904 is inscribed "FOR LOCAL ADDRESSES ONLY" and was sold for 22c.

241 *Drupa morum*

242 Tiger

(Des R., Saichumdee. Adapted Elsie Koh. Litho Enschedé)

1997 (9 Oct). Singapore–Thailand Joint Issue. Sea Shells. T **241** and similar horiz designs. Multicoloured. Phosphorised paper. P 13½×14.

908	(22c.) Type **241**	20	20
909	35c. *Nerita chamaeleon*	30	40
910	60c. *Littoraria melanostoma*	45	60
911	$1 *Cryptospira elegans*	1·50	2·00
908/11	*Set of* 4	1·50	2·10
MS912	125×80 mm. 22c. As Type **241** and Nos. 909/11	1·75	2·50

No. 908 is inscribed "FOR LOCAL ADDRESSES ONLY" and was sold for 22c.

1997 (19 Nov). Shanghai '97 International Stamp and Coin Exhibition. Sheet 123×80 mm. Phosphorised paper. P 13½×14.

MS913	22c. As Type **233**; $2 No. 862	4·25	5·50

(Des N. Loh Fook Chee. Litho Enschedé)

1998 (9 Jan). Chinese New Year ("Year of the Tiger"). T **242** and similar horiz design showing stylised tigers. Phosphorised paper. P 13½×14.

914	(22c.) multicoloured	15	20
	a. Pair. Nos. 914/15	1·50	2·25
915	$2 multicoloured	1·50	2·00

No. 914 is inscribed "FOR LOCAL ADDRESSES ONLY" and was sold for 22c.

In addition to separate sheets of 50 Nos. 914/15 were also issued in sheetlets of 18 (3×6) with the stamps horizontally and vertically *se-tenant*.

243 Pentaceratops

244 Lesser Green Leafbird

(Des N. Loh Fook Chee and Elsie Koh. Litho Avery Dennison, U.S.A.)

1998 (22 Apr). Self-adhesive Automatic Cash Machine Stamps. Dinosaurs. T **243** and similar vert designs. Multicoloured. Phosphorised paper. Die-cut.

916	(22c.) Type **243**	35	45
	a. Horiz strip of 3. Nos. 916/18	1·00	1·25
917	(22c.) Apatosaurus	35	45
918	(22c.) Albertosaurus	35	45
916/18	*Set of* 3	1·00	1·25

Nos. 916/18 are inscribed "For Local Addresses Only" and were sold at 22c. They were printed together, *se-tenant*, in sheetlets of 15 (3×6) available from bank automatic cash machines and philatelic centres. The advertisement on the backing paper was changed from financial services to Singapore stamps showing fauna and flora on 29 December 2000.

(Des Sylvia Tan. Photo Courvoisier)

1998 (6 May). Songbirds. T **244** and similar horiz designs. Multicoloured. P 11½.

919	(22c.) Type **244**	35	20
920	60c. Magpie Robin	70	65
921	70c. Straw-crowned Bulbul	80	80
922	$2 Yellow-bellied Prinia	1·60	2·25
919/22	*Set of* 4	3·00	3·50

No. 919 is inscribed "For Local Addresses Only" and was sold for 22c.

1998 (13 May). Israel '98 International Stamp Exhibition. Sheet 122×80 mm. Phosphorised paper. P 13½×14.

MS923	22c. As Type **242**; $2 No. 915	2·25	3·25

245 "Hello" in Yellow and Orange Bubble

246 Rhino Beetle

(Des Design Objectives. Litho SNP Cambec, Melbourne)

1998 (20 May). Self-adhesive Greetings Stamps. T **245** and similar vert designs, each showing different coloured bubbles. Multicoloured. Phosphorised paper. P 11½.

924	(22c.) Type **245**	50	65
	a. Booklet pane. Nos. 924/8, each×2	4·50	
925	(22c.) "hello" in red and yellow bubble	50	65
926	(22c.) "hello" in yellow and green bubble	50	65
927	(22c.) "Hello" in bluish violet and blue bubble	50	65
928	(22c.) "Hello" in black, red and yellow bubble	50	65
924/8	*Set of* 5	2·25	3·00

Nos. 924/8 are inscribed "FOR LOCAL ADDRESSES ONLY" and were only available in booklets of 10 stamps sold for $2.20.

(Des Design Business Ltd. Photo Enschedé)

1998 (5 June). 25th Anniv of Singapore Zoological Gardens and Launch of New "Fragile Forest" Display. T **246** and similar horiz designs. Multicoloured. Phosphorised paper. Self-adhesive. P 12×11.

929	(22c.) Type **246**	50	65
	a. Booklet pane. Nos. 929/33, each×2	4·50	
	ab. Imperf (booklet pane)		
930	(22c.) Surinam Horned Frog	50	65
931	(22c.) Green Iguana	50	65
932	(22c.) Atlas Moth	50	65
933	(22c.) Giant Scorpion	50	65
934	(22c.) Hissing Cockroach	50	65
	a. Booklet pane. Nos. 934/8, each×2	4·50	
935	(22c.) Two-toed Sloth	50	65
936	(22c.) Cobalt Blue Tarantula	50	65
937	(22c.) Archer Fish	50	65
938	(22c.) Greater Mousedeer	50	65
929/38	*Set of* 10	4·50	5·75

Nos. 929/38 are inscribed "FOR LOCAL ADDRESSES ONLY" and were available from two different booklets of 10, each sold for $2.20.

247 Students and Workers Demonstrating, 1965–69

248 *Phalaenopsis rosenstromii*

(Des Chou Ban Har. Litho Enschedé)

1998 (7 July). "The Singapore Story" Exhibition. T **247** and similar horiz designs. Multicoloured. Phosphorised paper. P 13×13½.

939	(22c.) Type **247**	25	20
940	60c. Self-government, 1959–63	55	55
941	$1 Creation of Malaysian Federation, 1961–65	80	90
942	$2 Celebrating Independence, 1965	1·60	2·25
939/42	*Set of* 4	2·75	3·50
MS943	214×105 mm. 22c. As Type **247** and Nos. 940/2 (sold at $7)	9·00	10·00

No. 939 is inscribed "FOR LOCAL ADDRESSES ONLY" and was sold for 22c.

The stamps in No. **MS**943 show the main features of each design printed in varnish ink. No. **MS**943, which also commemorates "SINGPEX '98" National Stamp Exhibition, was only available in a special folder.

(Des Clare Kaegi and C. Willie. Photo Courvoisier)

1998 (6 Aug). Singapore–Australia Joint Issue. Orchids. T **248** and similar vert designs. Multicoloured. Phosphorised granite paper. P 11½.

944	(22c.) Type **248**	35	20
945	70c. *Arundina graminifolia*	80	65
946	$1 *Grammatophyllum speciosum*	85	90
947	$2 *Dendrobium phalaenopsis*	1·60	2·25
944/7	*Set of* 4	3·25	3·50
MS948	134×73 mm. 22c. As Type **248** and Nos. 945/7	3·75	4·50

No. 944 is inscribed "For Local Addresses Only" and was sold for 22c.

249 *Canna* Hybrid

250 Hari Raya Aidilfitri (Muslim)

(Des Elsie Koh. Litho Ashton Potter Canada)

1998 (9 Sept). Flowers of Singapore. T **249** and similar horiz designs. Phosphorised paper. P 14½×14.

949	(22c.) Type **249**	30	30
	a. Horiz strip of 4. Nos. 949/52	1·10	1·10

b. Booklet pane. Nos. 949/50×3 and 951/2×2 ... 2·75
950 (22c.) *Caesalpinia pulcherrima* ... 30 30
951 (22c.) *Wedilia trilobata* ... 30 30
952 (22c.) *Dillenia suffruticosa* ... 30 30
953 35c. *Zephyranthes rosea* ... 45 50
a. Horiz strip of 4. Nos. 953/6 ... 2·10 2·10
954 35c. *Cassia alata* ... 45 50
955 60c. *Heliconia rostrata* ... 60 70
956 60c. *Allemanda cathartica* ... 60 70
949/56 *Set of 8* ... 3·00 3·25
MS957 206×82 mm. Nos. 949/56 ... 2·25 2·75

Nos. 949/52 are inscribed "FOR LOCAL ADDRESSES ONLY" and were sold at 22c.

Nos. 949/52 and 953/6 were each printed together, *se-tenant*, in horizontal strips of 4 throughout the sheets.

The upper and lower edges of booklet pane No. 949b are imperforate and there are margins at left and right.

Nos. 949/57 and the stamp booklet No. SB36 were impregnated with a flowery scent called "Day Break".

(Des See Pin Pin. Litho Enschedé)

1998 (7 Oct). Festivals. T **250** and similar multicoloured designs. Phosphorised paper.

(a) P 13½×14 (Nos. 958/61) or 13½×13 (others).

958 (22c.) Type **250** ... 35 35
a. Block of 4. Nos. 958/61 ... 1·40 1·40
959 (22c.) Christmas ... 35 35
960 (22c.) Chinese New Year ... 35 35
961 (22c.) Deepavali (Hindu) ... 35 35
962 30c. Boy and decorations (Hari Raya, Aidilfitri) (20×39 mm) ... 45 50
963 30c. Girl with holly (Christmas) (20×39 *mm*) .. 45 50
964 30c. Boy with lanterns (Chinese New Year) (20×39 mm) ... 45 50
965 30c. Girl with oil lamps (Deepavali) (20×39 mm) ... 45 50
958/65 *Set of 8* ... 2·75 3·00

(b) Self-adhesive. P 8.

966 (22c.) Type **250** ... 40 55
967 (22c.) As No. 959 ... 40 55
968 (22c.) As No. 960 ... 40 55
969 (22c.) As No. 961 ... 40 55
966/9 *Set of 4* ... 1·40 2·00

Nos. 958/61 and 966/9 are inscribed "For Local Addresses Only" and were sold at 22c.

Nos. 958/61 were printed together, *se-tenant*, in blocks of four throughout the sheet of 16, each block forming a composite design. Nos. 962/5 and 966/9 were printed in separate sheets of 20.

(Litho Enschedé)

1998 (23 Oct). Italia '98. International Stamp Exhibition, Milan. Sheet 123×80 mm. Phosphorised paper. P 13½×14.

MS970 22c. As Type **242**; $2 No. 915 ... 2·50 3·50

251 Parliament House, 1827

(Des Equinox Art and Design Ltd. Litho Enschedé)

1998 (4 Nov). Historical Buildings. T **251** and similar horiz designs. Multicoloured. Phosphorised paper. P 13½×14.

971 (22c.) Type **251** ... 30 20
972 70c. Chapel of former Convent of the Holy Infant Jesus, 1903 ... 70 65
973 $1 Hill Street Building, 1934 ... 85 95
974 $2 Sun Yat Sen Nanyang Memorial Hall, 1900 ... 1·60 2·25
971/4 *Set of 4* ... 2·75 3·00

No. 971 is inscribed "For Local Addresses Only" and was sold for 22c.

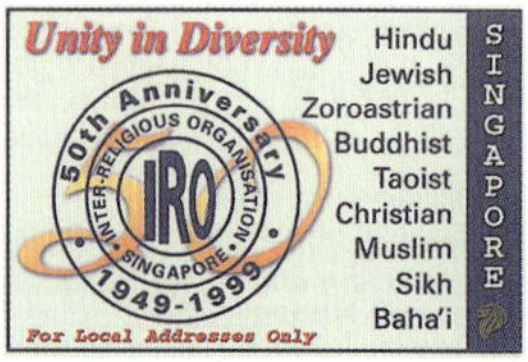

252 Anniversary Logo and List of Religions

(Des L. Chun. Litho Enschedé)

1999 (15 Jan). 50th Anniv of Inter-Religious Organization. Phosphorised paper. P 13×13½.

975 **252** (22c.) multicoloured ... 30 20
976 60c. multicoloured ... 55 55
977 $1 multicoloured ... 85 1·10
975/7 *Set of 3* ... 1·50 1·70

No. 975 is inscribed "For Local Addresses Only" and was sold for 22c.

253 Rabbit

254 Clipper, Tank Locomotive and Tongkang Junk

(Des N. Loh Fook Chee. Litho Southern Colour Print, Dunedin)

1999 (15 Jan). Chinese New Year ("Year of the Rabbit"). T **253** and similar horiz design showing stylized rabbits. Phosphorised paper. P 14.

978 (22c.) multicoloured ... 25 20
a. Pair. Nos. 978/9 ... 1·50 2·25
979 $2 multicoloured ... 1·50 2·00

No. 978 is inscribed "FOR LOCAL ADDRESSES ONLY" and was sold for 22c.

In addition to separate sheets of 50 Nos. 978/9 were also issued in sheetlets of 18 (3×6) with the stamps horizontally and vertically *se-tenant*.

(Des G. Hwee Kheng. Litho Southern Colour Print, Dunedin)

1999 (19 Mar). Maritime Heritage. T **254** and similar multicoloured designs. Phosphorised paper. P 14½.

980 (22c.) Type **254** ... 40 20
981 70c. Twakow (barge) and Sampan Kotek (vert) ... 85 65
982 $1 Fujian junk (vert) ... 1·25 1·10
983 $2 Maduran Golekkan (sailing vessel) ... 1·75 2·25
980/3 *Set of 4* ... 3·75 3·75
MS984 200×67 mm. 22c. As Type **254** and Nos. 981/3.. 3·50 4·00

No. 980 is inscribed "For Local Addresses Only" and was sold for 22c.

No. **MS**984 also includes the "Australia '99" World Stamp Exhibition, Melbourne, emblem on the sheet margin.

1999 (27 Apr). iBRA '99 International Stamp Exhibition, Nuremberg. Sheet 123×80 mm. Phosphorised paper. P 14.

MS985 22c. As Type **253**; $2 No. 979 ... 2·00 2·75

255 Washing Lines ("Think of others")

256 Hong Kong Harbour

(Des Lee Chee Chew. Litho Southern Colour Print, Dunedin)

1999 (12 May). Self-adhesive Greeting Stamps. "Try a Little Kindness". T **255** and similar vert designs. Multicoloured. Fluorescent frame. P 10.

986 (22c.) Type **255** ... 35 55
a. Booklet pane. Nos. 986/90, each×2 ... 3·00
987 (22c.) Man throwing litter ("Do not litter") ... 35 55
988 (22c.) Girl feeding cat and dog ("Be kind to animals") ... 35 55
989 (22c.) Man watching television ("Be considerate") ... 35 55
990 (22c.) Boy putting money in collection tin ("Be generous") ... 35 55
986/90 *Set of 5* ... 1·60 2·50

Nos. 986/90 are inscribed "FOR LOCAL ADDRESSES ONLY" and were only issued in $2.20 stamp booklets.

(Des C. Willie and A. Lam. Litho Enschedé)

1999 (1 July). Singapore–Hong Kong, China Joint Issue. T **256** and similar square designs. Multicoloured. Phosphorised paper. P 14×13½.

991 (22c.) Type **256** ... 25 20

992	35c. Singapore skyline	45	40
993	50c. Giant Buddha, Lantau Island, Hong Kong	60	55
994	60c. Merlion statue, Sentosa Island, Singapore	70	75
995	70c. Street scene, Hong Kong	75	80
996	$1 Bugis Junction, Singapore	1·00	1·10
991/6 *Set of* 6		3·25	3·50
MS997 125×93 mm. 22c. As Type **256** and Nos. 992/6..		3·25	4·00

No. 991 is inscribed "FOR LOCAL ADDRESSES ONLY".

1999 (2 July). Philex France '99 International Stamp Exhibition, Paris. Sheet 123×80 mm. Phosphorised paper. P 14.

MS998 22c. As Type **253**; $2 No. 979	2·00	2·50

257 Peacock Butterfly

258 Pres. Yusof bin Ishak

(Des Olaf Baldursdottir. Eng C. Slania. Recess and litho Stamp Ptg Office, Stockholm)

1999 (12 Aug). Singapore–Sweden Joint Issue. Butterflies. T **257** and similar horiz designs. Multicoloured. Phosphorised paper. P 12½×13.

999	(22c.) Type **257**	55	20
1000	70c. Blue Pansy	1·00	65
1001	$1 Great Egg-fly	1·25	95
1002	$2 Red Admiral	2·00	2·50
999/1002 *Set of* 4		4·25	3·75
MS1003 129×75 mm. 22c. As Type **257** and Nos. 1000/2		4·25	4·50

No. 999 is inscribed "FOR LOCAL ADDRESSES ONLY".

(Litho Southern Colour Print, Dunedin)

1999 (21 Aug). China '99 International Stamp Exhibition, Peking. Sheet 123×80 mm. Phosphorised paper. P 14.

MS1004 22c. As Type **253**; $2 As No. 979	2·25	2·75

(Des Sylvia Tan. Eng C. Slania. Recess and litho Enschedé)

1999 (9 Sept). Yusof bin Ishak (frst President of Singapore) Commemoration. Phosphorised paper. P 13½×14.

1005	**258** $2 multicoloured	2·50	2·00

No. 1005 was printed in sheets of 32 containing eight blocks of four, each surrounded by margins. Examples were available either as blocks of four or as uncut sheets.

259 Green Turtle

(Des L. Teck Chong. Litho Southern Colour Print, Dunedin)

1999 (13 Oct). Amphibians and Reptiles. T **259** and similar horiz designs. Multicoloured. Phosphor bands. P 14.

1006	(22c.) Type **259**	30	20
1007	60c. Green Crested Lizard	60	60
1008	70c. Copper-cheeked Frog	70	70
1009	$1 Water Monitor	90	1·25
1006/9 *Set of* 4		2·25	2·50

No. 1006 is inscribed "For Local Addresses Only". Nos. 1006/9 each show two vertical phosphor bands.

260 New Parliament House from North

(Des Design Objectives. Litho Enschedé)

1999 (17 Nov). Opening of New Parliament House. T **260** and similar horiz designs. Phosphorised paper. Multicoloured. P 13½×14.

1010	(22c.) Type **260**	30	20
1011	60c. North-east view	60	60
1012	$1 South-east view	90	1·00
1013	$2 West view	1·60	2·25
1010/13 *Set of* 4		3·00	3·75

No. 1010 is inscribed "For Local Addresses Only" and was sold for 22c.

The lion's head emblem on these stamps is printed in optically variable ink which changes colour when viewed from different angles.

261 Sir Stamford Raffles and Sir Frank Swettenham (British Governors) and Raffles Museum

262 Dragon

(Des Elsie Koh. Litho Ashton-Potter Canada)

1999 (31 Dec). New Millennium (1st issue). 20th Century Singapore. T **261** and similar horiz designs. Phosphorised paper. Multicoloured. P 13×12½.

1014	(22c.) Type **261**	30	35
	a. Sheetlet. Nos. 1014/23	5·50	6·25
1015	(22c.) Past and present schooling	30	35
1016	35c. Street scene, 1900, and Samsui woman.	45	55
1017	35c. Parliament	45	55
1018	60c. British surrender, 1942, and Lord Mountbatten celebrating Japanese surrender, 1945	60	70
1019	60c. Soldiers firing missile and fighter aircraft	60	70
1020	70c. Singapore River, 1902, and modern forms of transportation	70	80
1021	70c. Festival scenes	70	80
1022	$1 Housing, past and present	95	1·10
1023	$1 Skyscrapers	95	1·10
1014/23 *Set of* 10		5·50	6·25

Nos. 1014/15 are inscribed "for Local addresses only" and were sold for 22c.

Nos. 1014/23 were printed together, *se-tenant*, in sheetlets of 10 as two horizontal strips separated by a gutter margin.

See also Nos. 1027/31.

(Des N. Loh. Litho (No. **MS**1026 also embossed in gold) Cartor)

2000 (1 Jan). Chinese New Year ("Year of the Dragon"). T **262** and similar horiz design. Multicoloured. Phosphorised paper. P 13×13½.

1024	(22c.) Type **262**	25	20
	a. Horiz pair. Nos. 1024/5	2·00	2·40
1025	$2 Dragon curled around spheres	1·75	2·25
MS1026 105×65 mm. $10 As No. 1025. P 13		8·00	9·50

No. 1024 is inscribed "FOR LOCAL ADDRESSES ONLY" and was sold for 22c.

In addition to separate sheets of 50, Nos. 1024/5 were also issued in sheetlets of 18 (3×6) with the stamps horizontally and vertically *se-tenant*.

No. **MS**1026 was only sold in a decorative hongbao (envelope).

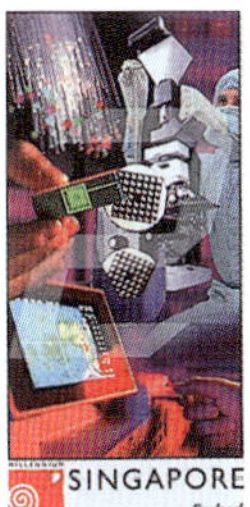

263 Information Technology Equipment

264 Post Office from across Singapore River, 1854

(Des Sylvia Tan. Photo Courvoisier)

2000 (1 Jan). New Millennium (2nd issue). Singapore in 2000. T **263** and similar vert designs. Multicoloured. "All-over" phosphor. Granite paper. P 14×15.

1027	(22c.) Type **263**	25	20
	a. Horiz strip of 4. Nos. 1027/30	3·00	3·75

1028 60c. Symbols of Arts and Culture 60 60
1029 $1 Heritage artifacts 95 1·10
1030 $2 Modern global communications 1·60 2·25
1027/30 *Set of 4* 3·00 3·75
MS1031 140×75 mm. 22c. As Type **263** and Nos. 1028/30 2·75 3·75

No. 1027 is inscribed "For local addresses only" and was sold for 22c.

Nos. 1027/30 were printed together, *se-tenant*, as horizontal strips of 4 in sheetlets of 20 (4×5) with "2000" shown in the phosphor across each strip.

From 8 March 2000 No. 1027 was also available in sheets of 20 (4×5) with each stamp *se-tenant* with a vertical stamp-sized label for use in a "personalised" stamp scheme. Such sheets showing personal photographs on the labels were sold at $20 each.

Two similar sheets, but with the labels showing either 20th-century inventions or festive symbols, were placed on sale to mark the end of the year 2000 at $10 the pair.

(Des Chua Ban Har. Litho Enschedé)

2000 (8 Mar). Opening of Singapore Post Centre. Postal Landmarks. T **264** and similar horiz designs. Multicoloured. Phosphorised paper. P 13½.

1032 (22c.) Type **264** 25 20
a. Booklet pane. Nos. 1032×4 and 1033×2 with margins all round 4·50
1033 60c. General Post Office, *c.* 1873 60 60
1034 $1 G.P.O. Fullerton Building, 1928 95 1·00
a. Booklet pane. Nos. 1034×4 and 1035×2 with margins all round 7·50
1035 $2 Singapore Post Centre, 2000 1·90 2·25
1032/5 *Set of 4* 3·25 3·50
MS1036 119×94 mm. 22c. As Type **264** and Nos. 1033/5 2·75 3·50

No. 1032 is inscribed "FOR LOCAL ADDRESSES ONLY" and was sold for 22c.

(Des N. Loh. Lithe Cartor)

2000. Bangkok 2000 International Stamp Exhibition. Sheet 123×75 mm. Multicoloured. Phosphorised paper. P 13×13½.

MS1037 22c. As Type **262**; $2 No. 1025 1·75 2·25

265 "yipee"

266 Singapore River, 1920s

(Des J. Chuah. Litho Southern Colour Print, Dunedin)

2000 (10 May). Self-adhesive Greetings Stamps. T **265** and similar horiz designs. Multicoloured. Phosphor frame. P 10.

1038 (22c.) Type **265** 45 60
a. Booklet pane. Nos. 1038/42, each×2 4·00
1039 (22c.) "yeah" 45 60
1040 (22c.) "hurray" 45 60
1041 (22c.) "yes" 45 60
1042 (22c.) "happy" 45 60
1038/42 *Set of 5* 2·00 2·75

Nos. 1038/42 are inscribed "For Local Addresses Only" and were only issued in stamp booklets of 10 sold for $2.20.

(Des N. Loh. Lithe Cartor)

2000 (22 May). The Stamp Show 2000 International Stamp Exhibition, London. Sheet 123×75 mm, containing Nos. 1024/5. Multicoloured. Phosphorised paper. P 13×13½.

MS1043 22c. As Type **262**; $2 No. 1025 1·90 2·40

(Des N. Loh. Lithe Cartor)

2000 (21 June). naba 2000 National Stamp Exhibition, St. Gallen, Switzerland. Sheet 123×75 mm, containing Nos. 1024/5. Multicoloured. Phosphorised paper. P 13×13½.

MS1044 22c. As Type **262**; $2 No. 1025 1·90 2·40

(Des C. Willie. Litho Walsall)

2000 (21 June). "A Century on Singapore River". T **266** and similar horiz designs showing scenes and common map section. Multicoloured. Phosphorised paper. P 14.

1045 (22c.) Type **266** 35 40
a. Sheetlet. Nos. 1045/54 3·75 4·50
1046 (22c.) South Boat Quay, 1930s 35 40
1047 (22c.) Social gathering, 1950s 35 40
1048 (22c.) Skyscrapers, 1980s 35 40
1049 (22c.) River Regatta, 1990s 35 40
1050 60c. Sampans at river mouth, 1900s 50 60
1051 60c. Stevedores 1910s 50 60
1052 60c. Lighters, 1940s 50 60
1053 60c. Men at work on junk, 1960s 50 60
1054 60c. Unloading with crane, 1970s 50 60
1045/54 *Set of 10* 3·75 4·50

Nos. 1045/9 are inscribed "For local addresses only" and were sold for 22c.

Nos. 1045/54 were printed together, *se-tenant*, in sheetlets of 10 with the backgrounds forming a composite design.

267 "Future Lifestyle" (Liu Jiang Wen)

(Adapted M. Ng. Lithe Enschedé)

2000 (7 July). "Stampin' the Future" (children's stamp design competition). T **267** and similar square designs. Multicoloured. Phosphorised paper. P 14×13.

1055 (22c.) Type **267** 25 20
1056 60c. "Future Homes" (Shaun Yew Chuan Bin) 60 60
1057 $1 "Home Automation" (Gwendolyn Soh) 90 1·00
1058 $2 "Floating City" (Dawn Koh) 1·60 2·25
1055/8 *Set of 4* 3·00 3·75
MS1059 125×80 mm. Nos. 1055/8 3·00 3·50

No. 1055 is inscribed "FOR LOCAL ADDRESSES ONLY" and was sold for 22c.

268 Archer Fish

(Des Eng Siak Loy. Photo Courvoisier)

2000 (11 Aug). Wetland Wildlife. T **268** and similar horiz designs. Multicoloured. Phosphorised granite paper. P 14½.

1060 (22c.) Type **268** 35 30
a. Block of 4. Nos. 1060/3 3·25 3·25
b. Booklet pane. Nos. 1060/1 each×5 with horizontal edges of pane imperf 4·50
1061 (22c.) Smooth Otter and cubs 35 30
1062 $1 Collared Kingfisher 1·40 1·50
1063 $1 Orange Fiddler Crab 1·40 1·50
1060/3 *Set of 4* 3·25 3·25
MS1064 294×210 mm. Nos. 1060/3, both perf and imperf in *se-tenant* blocks of 4 5·50 6·50

Nos. 1060/1 are inscribed "For Local Addresses Only" and were sold at 22c.

Nos. 1060/3 were printed together, *se-tenant*, as blocks of 4, with the backgrounds forming composite designs.

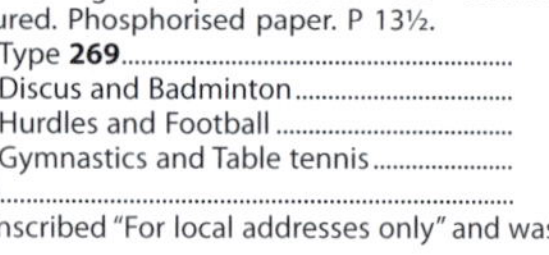

269 High Jump and Swimming

(Des Design Objectives. Litho Cartor)

2000 (15 Sept). Olympic Games, Sydney. T **269** and similar horiz designs showing a sport within the outline of another. Multicoloured. Phosphorised paper. P 13½.

1065 (22c.) Type **269** 25 20
1066 60c. Discus and Badminton 60 60
1067 $1 Hurdles and Football 90 1·00
1068 $2 Gymnastics and Table tennis 1·75 2·25
1065/8 *Set of 4* 3·25 3·75

No. 1065 is inscribed "For local addresses only" and was sold at 22c.

270 Chinese New Year

271 Snake

(Des Merstar Image. Litho Cartor)

2000 (11 Oct). Festivals. T **270** and similar multicoloured designs. Phosphorised paper. P 13.

(a) Normal gum.

1069	(22c.) Type **270**	55	55
1070	(22c.) Hari Raya Aidilfitri	55	55
1071	(22c.) Deepavali	55	55
1072	(22c.) Christmas	55	55
1073	30c. Chinese New Year (*different*) (*diamond*, 36×23 mm)	65	70
1074	30c. Hari Raya Aidilfitri (*different*) (*diamond*, 36×23 mm)	65	70
1075	30c. Deepavali (*different*) (*diamond*, 36×23 mm)	65	70
1076	30c. Christmas (*different*) (*diamond*, 36×23 mm)	65	70

(b) Self-adhesive.

1077	(22c.) Type **270**	75	85
1078	(22c.) As No. 1070	75	85
1079	(22c.) As No. 1071	75	85
1080	(22c.) As No. 1072	75	85
1069/80 *Set of* 12		7·00	8·00

Nos. 1069/72 and 1077/80 are inscribed "FOR LOCAL ADDRESSES ONLY" and were each sold for 22c.

(Des N. Loh. Litho Cartor)

2000 (31 Oct). Guangzhou 2000 International Stamp and Coin Exhibition, China. Sheet 123×75 mm. Multicoloured. Phosphorised paper. P 13×13½.

MS1081 (22c.) As Type **262**; $2 No. 1025 ... 2·25 2·75

(Des N. Loh. Litho Questa)

2001 (12 Jan). Chinese New Year ("Year of the Snake"). T **271** and similar horiz design. Multicoloured. "All-over" phosphor. P 14½×14.

1082	(22c.) Type **271**	30	20
	a. Pair. Nos. 1082/3	2·25	2·50
1083	$2 Two snakes	2·00	2·50

No. 1082 is inscribed "FOR LOCAL ADDRESSES ONLY" and was sold for 22c.

In addition to separate sheets of 50 Nos. 1082/3 were also issued in sheetlets of 18 (3×6) with the stamps horizontally and vertically *se-tenant*.

(Des N. Loh. Litho Questa)

2001 (1 Feb). Hong Kong 2001 Stamp Exhibition. Sheet 123×75 mm. Multicoloured. "All-over" phosphor. P 14½×14.

MS1084 22c. As Type **271**; $2 No. 1083 ... 3·25 3·50

272 Tan Tock Seng

273 People holding Hands ("Co-operation")

(Photo Courvoisier)

2001 (28 Feb). Famous Citizens of Singapore. T **272** and similar vert designs. Granite paper. Multicoloured. P 12.

1085	$1 Type **272**	1·00	1·10
1086	$1 Eunos bin Abdullah	1·00	1·10
1087	$1 P. Govindasamy Pillai	1·00	1·10
1088	$1 Edwin John Tessensohn	1·00	1·10
1085/8 *Set of* 4		3·50	4·00

(Des Design Business. Litho Questa)

2001 (12 Mar). 25th Anniv of Commonwealth Day. T **273** and similar vert designs. Multicoloured. Phosphorised paper. P 14.

1089	(22c.) Type **273**	25	20
1090	60c. People using computers ("Education")	60	60
1091	$1 Sporting activities ("Sports")	1·25	1·00
1092	$2 Dancers and musicians ("Arts and Culture")	1·75	2·25
1089/92 *Set of* 4		3·50	3·75

No. 1089 is inscribed "FOR LOCAL ADDRESSES ONLY" and was sold for 22c.

274 Balloons

275 "Music" ("a")

(Des Design Objectives. Litho Southern Colour Print, Dunedin)

2001 (25 Apr). Self-adhesive Greetings Stamps. "Occasions". T **274** and similar square designs. Multicoloured. Phosphor frame. P 10.

1093	(22c.) Type **274**	40	50
	a. Booklet pane. Nos. 1093/7, each×2	3·50	
1094	(22c.) Stars	40	50
1095	(22c.) Tulips	40	50
1096	(22c.) Parcels	40	50
1097	(22c.) Musical instruments	40	50
1093/7 *Set of* 5		1·75	2·25

Nos. 1093/7 are inscribed "FOR LOCAL ADDRESSES ONLY" and were only issued in stamp booklets of 10, No. SB42, sold for $2.20.

Similar designs, but with traditional gumming, were also issued *se-tenant* in sheets of 20 (4×5) with each horizontal row containing a different design. Such sheets were only available at $11 as part of the "personalised" scheme, incorporating a personal photograph on the blank label accompanying each stamp.

(Des Jasmine Tuan. Litho Questa)

2001 (16 May). Arts Festival. T **275** and similar square designs. Multicoloured. "All-over" phosphor P 14.

1098	(22c.) Type **275**	25	20
	a. Block of 4. Nos. 1098/101	3·00	3·25
1099	60c. "Painting" ("r")	55	45
1100	$1 "Dance" ("t")	90	1·00
1101	$2 "Theatre" ("s")	1·75	2·00
1098/101 *Set of* 4		3·00	3·25

No. 1098 is inscribed "For Local Addresses Only" and was sold for 22c.

Nos. 1098/101 were printed together, *se-tenant*, as blocks of four in sheets of 16.

(Des N. Loh. Litho Questa)

2001 (9 June). BELGICA 2001 International Stamp Exhibition, Brussels. Sheet 123×75 mm. Multicoloured. "All-over" phosphor. P 14½×14.

MS1102 (22c.) Type **271**; $2 No. 1083 ... 3·25 3·50

276 Cockatiels

277

(Des Merstar Image. Litho Enschedé)

2001 (26 July). Singpex '01 National Stamp Exhibition. Pets.

(a) T **276** and similar multicoloured designs. Two phosphor bands. P 13½.

1103	(22c.) Type **276**	25	35
	a. Sheetlet. Nos. 1103/12	3·75	4·75
1104	(22c.) Fish in tank	25	35
1105	(22c.) Tortoise	25	35
1106	(22c.) Ducklings	25	35
1107	(22c.) Cat looking at mouse (24×34 mm)	25	35
1108	(22c.) Dog looking at fish in bowl (24×34 mm)	25	35
1109	50c. West Highland White Terrier and bird (24×41 mm)	55	65
1110	50c. Two cats (24×41 mm)	55	65
1111	$1 Two parrots (24×41 mm)	85	90
1112	$1 Cat in basket and rabbit (24×41 mm)	85	90
1103/12 *Set of* 10		3·75	4·75

(b) T **277** and similar multicoloured frame. Self-adhesive. Phosphor frame. P 15×14½.

1113	(22c.) Type **277** (24×24 mm)	30	30
	a. Sheetlet. No. 1113×6 and No. 1114×4	2·75	
1114	(22c.) As Type **277**, but 24×34 mm	30	30

Nos. 1103/8 and 1113/14 are inscribed "For local addresses only" and were sold for 22c. each.

The phosphor on Nos. 1113/14 reacts greenish yellow under U.V. light.

Nos. 1103/12 were printed together, *se-tenant*, in sheetlets of 10, forming a composite picture of household pets.

Nos. 1113/14 were printed in sheetlets of 10, which also included self-adhesive labels as Nos. 1103/06, each ×3, and Nos. 1117/18, each ×2, which were intended to be applied to the spaces in the centre of the frames. Examples of No. 1114 also show random paw marks.

(Des N. Loh. Litho Questa)

2001 (1 Aug). Philanippon 01 International Stamp Exhibition, Tokyo. Sheet 123×75 mm. Multicoloured. "All-over" phosphor. P 14½×14.

MS1115	(22c.) Type **271**; $2 No. 1083	2·00	2·75

278 Young Ah Meng

279 *Melastoma malabathricum*

(Des Eng Siak Loy. Litho Cartor)

2001 (5 Sept). Orang Utan Conservation. T **278** and similar vert designs showing Ah Meng. Multicoloured.

(a) PVA gum. Phosphorised paper. P 13½×13.

1116	(22c.) Type **278**	25	35
	a. Horiz strip of 4. Nos. 1116/19	2·25	2·50
1117	60c. Ah Meng with mate	55	60
1118	$1 Ah Meng with offspring	85	95
1119	$1 Three generations of Ah Meng's family	85	95
1116/19 *Set of* 4		2·25	2·50
MS1120	190×180 mm. Nos. 1116/19 (sold for $3.90)	4·75	5·00

(b) Self-adhesive. Two phosphor bands. P 12½.

1121	(22c.) Type **278**	50	50
	a. Booklet pane. No. 1121×10 with margins all round	4·50	

Nos. 1116 and 1121 are inscribed "For Local Addresses Only" and were sold for 22c.

Nos. 1116/19 were printed together, *se-tenant*, as horizontal strips of 4 in sheets of 20.

No. **MS**1120 is in the shape of a seated orang utan.

No. 1121 was only available in booklets of 10, No. SB43, on which the surplus self-adhesive paper was retained. The phosphor bands appear greenish-yellow under U.V. light.

(Des N. Loh. Litho Enschedé)

2001 (20 Sept). Singapore–Switzerland Joint Issue. Flowers. T **279** and similar horiz designs. Multicoloured. Phosphorised paper. P 13½×13.

1122	(22c.) Type **279**	25	20
1123	60c. *Leontopodium alpinum*	60	60
1124	$1 *Saraca cauliflora*	90	1·10
1125	$2 *Gentiana clusii*	1·75	2·50
1122/5 *Set of* 4		3·25	4·00
MS1126	98×68 mm. Nos. 1122/5	3·25	4·00

No. 1122 is inscribed "FOR LOCAL ADDRESSES ONLY" and was sold for 22c.

280 Moorish Idol

281 Horse

Two types of the 50c.:

I. Incorrectly inscribed "xanthometapon"
II. Inscribed "xanthometopon"

(Des Eng Siak Loy. Litho Walsall (1142d/da) or Cartor (others))

2001 (24 Oct)–**06**. Tropical Marine Fish. T **280** and similar horiz designs. Multicoloured.

(a) PVA gum. Phosphorised paper. P 13×13½.

1127	5c. Type **280**	15	30
1128	20c. Thread-finned Butterflyfish	45	20
1129	(22c.) Copper-banded Butterflyfish	45	20
1130	30c. Pearl-scaled Butterflyfish	50	25
1130*a*	31c. Eight-banded Butterflyfish (3.2.04)	60	25
1130*b*	(31c.) Eight-banded Butterflyfish (18.3.05)	60	25
1131	40c. Melon Butterflyfish ("Rainbow Butterflyfish")	85	30
1132	50c. Yellow-faced Angelfish (I)	1·00	35
	a. Type II (25.3.02)	1·25	35
1133	60c. Emperor Angelfish	1·25	45
1134	70c. Sail-finned Tang	1·50	50
1135	80c. Palette Surgeonfish ("Palette Tang")	1·60	55
MS1136	149×90 mm. Nos. 1127/30, 1131 and 1132a/5	7·00	8·00

(b) Size 29×24½ mm. PVA gum. Phosphorised paper. P 13½×13.

1137	$1 Blue Turquoise (24.7.02)	2·00	70
1138	$2 Brown Discus (24.7.02)	3·00	1·40
1139	$5 Red Alenquer (24.7.02)	6·00	3·50
1140	$10 Red Turquoise (24.7.02)	11·00	8·00
1127/35, 1137/40 *Set of* 14		28·00	16·00
MS1141	128×75 mm. Nos. 1137/40 (24.7.02)	22·00	24·00

(c) Self-adhesive. Phosphor frame (1142/a) or two phosphor bands (1142c/ca). P 12½.

1142	(22c.) As No 1129	30	35
	a. Booklet pane. No. 1142×10	2·75	
	b. Two phosphor bands (1.3.03)	30	35
	ba. Booklet pane. No. 1142b×10	2·75	
1142*c*	(23c.) As No. 1129 (7.7.04)	30	35
	ca. Booklet pane. No. 1142*c*×10	2·75	
	d. Phosphorised paper (11.12.06)	30	35
	da. Booklet pane. No. 1142d×10	2·75	

Nos. 1129 and 1142 are inscribed "FOR LOCAL ADDRESSES ONLY" and were originally sold for 22c. each.

No. 1130*a* is inscr "31c." and "2nd Local". No. 1130*b* is inscr "2nd Local", and was originally sold for 31c.

Nos. 1142c/d were inscribed "1st Local" and originally sold for 23c. each.

Nos. 1142, 1142b, 1142*c* and 1142d were available either in sheets of 20 (two panes 2×5) or booklets of 10 (Nos. SB44, SB46, SB50 and SB54), all with the self-adhesive paper around each stamp retained.

The issue dates for the sheetlets of 20 (where they differ from the booklet issue dates) were 4 August 2004 (1142*c*) and 8 February 2007 (1142d).

(Des N. Loh. Litho (Nos. 1144 and 1146 also embossed) Cartor)

2002 (10 Jan). Chinese New Year ("Year of the Horse"). T **281** and similar horiz design. Multicoloured. Phosphorised paper. P 13½.

1143	(22c.) Type **281**	25	20
	a. Sheetlet. Nos. 1143 and 1145, each ×8, 1144 and 1146	14·00	17·00
1144	(22c.) As Type **281** but horse embossed in silver	1·00	1·50
1145	$2 Two horses rearing	1·40	1·60
1146	$2 As No. 1145, but horses embossed in gold	3·00	4·00
1143/6 *Set of* 4		5·00	6·50

Nos. 1143/4 are inscribed "FOR LOCAL ADDRESSES ONLY" and were sold for 22c. each.

Nos. 1143/6 were printed together, *se-tenant*, in sheetlets of 18, containing 8 examples each of Nos. 1143 and 1145, and one of each of the embossed designs. Nos. 1143 and 1145 were also available in sheets of 50.

282 Long-tailed Porcupine

(Des W. Kong. Litho Cartor)

2002 (20 Feb). Natural History Drawings from The William Farquhar Collection (*1*st series). Animals, Reptiles, Fruits and Plants. T **282** and similar multicoloured designs.

(a) PVA gum. Phosphorised paper. P 13½.

1147	(22c.) Type **282**	35	40
	a. Sheetlet. Nos. 1147/56	3·25	3·50
1148	(22c.) Tapir	35	40
1149	(22c.) "Landak Kelubu"	35	40
1150	(22c.) Slow Loris	35	40
1151	(22c.) "Biawak Tanah" (lizard)	35	40
1152	(22c.) Flying Fox	35	40
1153	(22c.) Small-clawed Otter	35	40
1154	(22c.) "Biawak Pasir" (lizard)	35	40
1155	(22c.) "Tupai Kerawak" (mouse) (vert)	35	40
1156	(22c.) Mouse Deer (vert)	35	40
1157	(22c.) "Buah Rumenia"	35	40
	a. Sheetlet. Nos. 1157/66	3·25	3·50
1158	(22c.) "Manggis Hutan"	35	40
1159	(22c.) "Cempedak"	35	40
1160	(22c.) "Bunga Dedap"	35	40
1161	(22c.) "Jeringau" (vert)	35	40
1162	(22c.) "Rotang" (vert)	35	40
1163	(22c.) "Tuba" (vert)	35	40
1164	(22c.) "Tebu Gagak" (vert)	35	40
1165	(22c.) "Temu Kunci" (vert)	35	40
1166	(22c.) "Rambutan" (vert)	35	40
1147/66 *Set of* 20		6·50	7·00

(b) Self-adhesive. Phosphor frame. P 12½.

1167	(22c.) Type **282**	40	45
	a. Sheetlet. Nos. 1167/76	3·50	4·00

1168	(22c.) Tapir	40	45
1169	(22c.) "Landak Kelubu"	40	45
1170	(22c.) Slow Loris	40	45
1171	(22c.) "Biawak Tanah" (lizard)	40	45
1172	(22c.) Flying Fox	40	45
1173	(22c.) Small-clawed Otter	40	45
1174	(22c.) "Biawak Pasir" (lizard)	40	45
1175	(22c.) "Tupai Kerawak" (mouse) (vert)	40	45
1176	(22c.) Mouse Deer (vert)	40	45
1177	(22c.) "Buah Rumenia"	40	45
	a. Sheetlet. Nos. 1177/86	3·50	4·00
1178	(22c.) "Manggis Hutan"	40	45
1179	(22c.) "Cempedak"	40	45
1180	(22c.) "Bunga Dedap"	40	45
1181	(22c.) "Jeringau" (vert)	40	45
1182	(22c.) "Rotang" (vert)	40	45
1183	(22c.) "Tuba" (vert)	40	45
1184	(22c.) "Tebu Gagak" (vert)	40	45
1185	(22c.) "Temu Kunci" (vert)	40	45
1186	(22c.) "Rambutan" (vert)	40	45
1167/86	*Set of* 20	7·00	8·00

Nos. 1147/56 (animals and reptiles), 1157/66 (fruits and plants), 1167/76 and 1177/86 were each printed together, *se-tenant*, in sheetlets of 10 and are inscribed "For Local Addresses Only". Each stamp was sold for 22c.

(Des W. Kong. Litho Cartor)

2002 (20 Mar). Natural History Drawings from The William Farquhar Collection (2nd series). Birds and Fish. Multicoloured designs as T **282**.

(a) PVA gum. Phosphorised paper. P 13½.

1187	(22c.) "Burung Gaji-gaji"	35	40
	a. Sheetlet. Nos. 1187/96	3·25	3·50
1188	(22c.) "Kuau Cermin"	35	40
1189	(22c.) "Ayam Kolam"	35	40
1190	(22c.) "Kelengking"	35	40
1191	(22c.) "Burung Kuang"	35	40
1192	(22c.) "Puhung"	35	40
1193	(22c.) "Burung Kunyit (vert)"	35	40
1194	(22c.) "Burung Pacap Sayat Biru" (vert)	35	40
1195	(22c.) "Burung Murai" (vert)	35	40
1196	(22c.) "Burung Berek-Berek" (vert)	35	40
1197	(22c.) "Ikan Tenggiri Papan"	35	40
	a. Sheetlet. Nos. 1197/206	3·25	3·50
1198	(22c.) "Ikan Kertang"	35	40
1199	(22c.) "Ikan Kakatua"	35	40
1200	(22c.) "Ikan Bambangan"	35	40
1201	(22c.) "Ikan Parang"	35	40
1202	(22c.) "Ikan Buntal Pisang"	35	40
1203	(22c.) "Ikan Ketang"	35	40
1204	(22c.) "Pari Hitam"	35	40
1205	(22c.) "Telinga Gajah"	35	40
1206	(22c.) "Ikan Babi"	35	40
1187/206	*Set of* 20	6·50	7·00

(b) Self-adhesive. Phosphor frame. P 12½.

1207	(22c.) "Burung Gaji-gaji"	35	40
	a. Sheetlet. Nos. 1207/16	3·25	3·50
1208	(22c.) "Kuau Cermin"	35	40
1209	(22c.) "Ayam Kolam"	35	40
1210	(22c.) "Kelengking"	35	40
1211	(22c.) "Burung Kuang	35	40
1212	(22c.) "Puhung"	35	40
1213	(22c.) "Burung Kunyit" (vert)	35	40
1214	(22c.) "Burung Pacap Sayat Biru" (vert)	35	40
1215	(22c.) "Burung Murai" (vert)	35	40
1216	(22c.) "Burung Berek-Berek" (vert)	35	40
1217	(22c.) "Ikan Tenggiri Papan"	35	40
	a. Sheetlet. Nos. 1217/26	3·25	3·50
1218	(22c.) "Ikan Kertang"	35	40
1219	(22c.) "Ikan Kakatua"	35	40
1220	(22c.) "Ikan Bambangan"	35	40
1221	(22c.) "Ikan Parang"	35	40
1222	(22c.) "Ikan Buntal Pisang"	35	40
1223	(22c.) "Ikan Ketang"	35	40
1224	(22c.) "Pari Hitam"	35	40
1225	(22c.) "Telinga Gajah"	35	40
1226	(22c.) "Ikan Babi"	35	40
1207/26	*Set of* 20	6·50	7·00

Nos. 1187/96 (birds), 1197/206 (fish), 1207/16 and 1217/26 were each printed together, *se-tenant*, in sheetlets of 10 and are inscribed "For Local Addresses Only". Each stamp was sold for 22c.

283 Lego Town

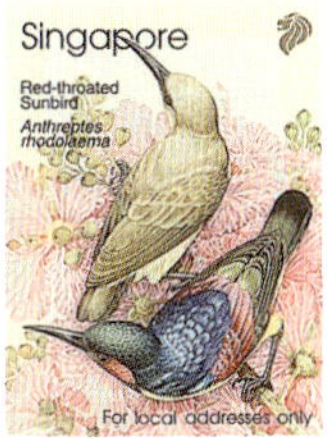

284 Red-throated Sunbird

(Des L. Hoon. Litho Walsall)

2002 (22 May). Toys. T **283** and similar horiz designs. Multicoloured. Two phosphor bands. P 14½.

1227	(22c.) Type **283**	35	20
1228	60c. Cowboy, Indian, soldier and robot	75	55
1229	70c. Dolls	80	95
1230	$1 Racing cars and bike	1·10	1·25
1227/30	*Set of* 4	2·75	2·75

No. 1227 is inscribed "For local addresses only" and was sold for 22c.

(Des T. Kiang. Litho Enschedé)

2002 (27 June). Singapore–Malaysia Joint Issue. Birds. T **284** and similar vert designs. Multicoloured. Phosphor frame. P 13½×14.

1231	(22c.) Type **284**	40	20
1232	40c. Asian Fairy Bluebird	75	50
1233	$1 Black-naped Oriole	1·00	1·00
1234	$2 White-bellied Woodpecker	1·75	2·50
1231/4	*Set of* 4	3·50	3·75
MS1235	135×94 mm. Nos. 1231/4	4·25	4·50

(Des N. Loh. Litho Cartor)

2002 (2 Aug). Philakorea 2002 International Stamp Exhibition, Seoul. Phosphorised paper. P 13×13½.

MS1236	123×75 mm. Nos. 1143 and 1145	2·50	3·00

285 Kolam (doorstep decoration), Deepavali

286 Kolam (doorstep decoration), Deepavali

(Des Wong Wui Kong. Litho Enschedé)

2002 (21 Aug). Festivals. Multicoloured. Phosphor frame.

(a) T **285** and similar vert designs.

(i) PVA gum. P 13½×14.

1237	(22c.) Type **285**	70	70
1238	(22c.) Ketupat (rice cake) wrapper, Hari Raya Aidilfitri	70	70
1239	(22c.) Snowflake in bauble, Christmas	70	70
1240	(22c.) Fish paper decoration, Chinese New Year	70	70

(ii) Self-adhesive. Die-cut perf 13×13½.

1241	(22c.) Type **285**	70	70
1242	(22c.) Ketupat (rice cake) wrapper, Hari Raya Aidilfitri	70	70
1243	(22c.) Snowflake in bauble, Christmas	70	70
1244	(22c.) Fish paper decoration, Chinese New Year	70	70

(b) T **286** and similar horiz designs. PVA gum. P 13½.

1245	50c. Type **286**	90	1·00
1246	50c. Ketupat (rice cake) wrapper, Hari Raya Aidilfitri	90	1·00
1247	50c. Snowflake in bauble, Christmas	90	1·00
1248	50c. Fish paper decoration, Chinese New Year	90	1·00
1237/48	*Set of* 12	8·00	8·50

Nos. 1237/44 are inscribed "For Local Addresses Only" and each stamp was sold for 22c.

The central designs on Nos. 1237/48 are foil holograms.

287 Flame of the Forest

288 Esplanade Performing Arts Centre, Marina Bay

(Des Eng Siak Loy. Litho Cartor)

2002 (25 Sept). Heritage Trees Scheme. T **287** and similar vert designs. Multicoloured.

(a) PVA gum. Phosphorised paper. P 13½×13.

1249	(22c.) Type **287**	30	20
1250	60c. Rain Tree	70	50
1251	$1 Kapok Tree	1·00	1·40
1252	$1 Tembusu	1·00	1·40
1249/52	*Set of 4*	2·75	3·25

(b) Self-adhesive. Two phosphor bands. P 12½.

1253	(22c.) Type **287**	30	35
	a. Booklet pane. No. 1253×10	2·75	

Nos. 1249 and 1253 are inscribed "FOR LOCAL ADDRESSES ONLY" and were sold for 22c.

No. 1253 was only available in $2.20 booklets, No. SB45, on which the surplus self-adhesive paper was retained.

(Des Design Objectives Pte Ltd. Litho Enschedé)

2002 (12 Oct). Opening of Esplanade – Theatres on the Bay Arts Centre. T **288** and similar square designs showing Esplanade Centre from different angles. Two phosphor bands. P 13½×14.

1254	(22c.) multicoloured	30	20
1255	60c. multicoloured	70	50
1256	$1 multicoloured	1·00	1·00
1257	$2 multicoloured	2·00	2·50
1254/7	*Set of 4*	3·50	3·75
MS1258	104×80 mm. Nos. 1254/7	3·50	4·00

289 Two Yachts

290 Goat

(Des Design Objectives. Litho Questa)

2002 (20 Nov). Singapore–A Global City. (1st series). Leisure and Lifestyle. T **289** and similar vert design. Multicoloured. "All-over" phosphor. P 14½×14.

1259	$2 Type **289**	2·00	2·25
	a. Horiz pair. Nos. 1259/60 separated by label	4·00	4·50
1260	$2 Conductor's hands and baton	2·00	2·25
MS1261	135×95 mm. Nos. 1259/60 and double stamp-size label	5·00	6·00

Nos. 1259/60 were printed together, as sheets of 10, the two designs in vertical rows of five separated by a gutter publicising World Stamp Championship 2004.

No. **MS**1261 exists with five different labels advertising Reader's Digest, McDonalds, American Express, Coca-Cola or Swatch.

A set of 15 miniature sheets as Nos. **MS**1261, **MS**1279 and **MS**1407, but optd with Singapore World Stamp Championship logo in silver on the margins, each with the five different labels, was issued on 23 June 2004. They were available from Singapore Post at $68.

(Des N. Loh. Litho Cartor)

2003 (10 Jan). Chinese New Year ("Year of the Goat"). T **290** and similar horiz design. Multicoloured. Phosphorised paper. P 13×13½.

1262	(22c.) Type **290**	30	20
	a. Pair. Nos. 1262/3	2·25	2·50
1263	$2 Goat butting tree	2·00	2·50

No. 1262 is inscribed "FOR LOCAL ADDRESSES ONLY" and was sold for 22c.

In addition to separate sheets of 50 Nos. 1262/3 were also printed together, *se-tenant*, both horizontally and vertically, in sheets of 18 (3×6).

291 Empress Place Building as Government Offices

(Des Sylvia Tan. Litho Questa)

2003 (26 Feb). Opening of Asian Civilizations Museum in Empress Place Building. T **291** and similar horiz designs. Multicoloured. "All-over" phosphor. P 14½.

1264	(22c.) Type **291**	35	20
1265	60c. Empress Place Building as Registrar's Office	80	50
1266	$1 Empress Place Museum	1·25	1·25
1267	$2 Empress Place Building, as Asian Civilizations Museum	2·50	3·00
1264/7	*Set of 4*	4·50	4·50

No. 1264 is inscribed "For local addresses only" and was sold for 22c.

292 Tarsier

293 Community Policewomen and Block of Flats

(Des Wong Wui Kong. Litho Enschedé (miniature sheet also embossed))

2003 (20 Mar). Creatures of the Night. T **292** and similar square designs. Multicoloured. Phosphor frame. P 13½.

1268	(22c.) Type **292**	35	20
1269	40c. Barn Owl	85	50
1270	$1 Babirusa	1·10	1·25
1271	$2 Clouded Leopard	2·25	2·75
1268/71	*Set of 4*	4·00	4·25
MS1272	136×94 mm. Nos. 1268/71	4·00	4·50

No. 1268 is inscribed "FOR LOCAL ADDRESSES ONLY" and was sold for 22c.

No. **MS**1272 has "SINGAPORE", the stars and some facial features of the animals printed in fluorescent ink which is visible in the dark and under U.V. light.

(Des Design Vizio. Litho Cartor)

2003 (23 Apr). Singapore Police Force. T **293** and similar vert designs. Multicoloured. Phosphorised paper. P 13½×13.

1273	(22c.) Type **293**	45	20
1274	40c. Traffic policeman with motor-cycle	80	50
1275	$1 Maritime policeman and launch	1·75	1·50
1276	$2 Singapore police on U.N. peacekeeping duties	2·75	2·75
1273/6	*Set of 4*	5·25	4·50

No. 1273 is inscribed "For Local Addresses Only" and was sold at 22c.

294 Satellite

295 Cheshire Cat ("Joy!")

(Des Design Objectives. Litho DLR)

2003 (21 May). Singapore–A Global City (2nd series). Communications and Technology. T **294** and similar vert design. Multicoloured. "All-over" phosphor. P 14½×14.

1277	$2 Type **294**	2·00	2·25
	a. Horiz pair. Nos. 1277/8 separated by label	4·00	4·50

1278	$2 Robot	2·00	2·25
MS1279	135×95 mm. Nos. 1277/8 and double stamp-size label	4·00	4·50

Nos. 1277/8 were printed together, in sheets of 10, the two designs in vertical rows of five separated by a gutter publicising World Stamp Championship 2004.

No. **MS**1279 exists with five different labels advertising CNN, Creative Technology, Microsoft, Siemens and Singpore Airlines.

(Des Leo Teck Chong. Litho Southern Colour Print, Dunedin)

2003 (25 June). Greetings Stamps. "Joy and Caring". T **295** and similar vert designs. Multicoloured.

(a) PVA gum. Phosphorised paper. P 14½.

1280	(22c.) Type **295**	30	40
	a. Sheetlet. Nos. 1280/9	2·75	3·50
1281	(22c.) Heart with smiling face ("joy!")	30	40
1282	(22c.) Teddy bear ("joy!")	30	40
1283	(22c.) Woman laughing ("joy")	30	40
1284	(22c.) Ostrich ("joy!")	30	40
1285	(22c.) Apple ("caring")	30	40
1286	(22c.) Hand with painted heart ("Helping Hands")	30	40
1287	(22c.) Multicoloured hearts ("Togetherness")	30	40
1288	(22c.) Daisy ("Beauty of a caring heart")	30	40
1289	(22c.) Night sky ("KEEPING IN TOUCH KEEPS US GOING")	30	40
1280/9	*Set of* 10	2·75	3·50

(b) Self-adhesive. Phosphor frame. P 10.

1290	(22c.) As No. 1280	40	50
	a. Booklet pane. Nos. 1290/9	3·50	
1291	(22c.) As No. 1281	40	50
1292	(22c.) As No. 1282	40	50
1293	(22c.) As No. 1283	40	50
1294	(22c.) As No. 1284	40	50
1295	(22c.) As No. 1285	40	50
1296	(22c.) As No. 1286	40	50
1297	(22c.) As No. 1287	40	50
1298	(22c.) As No. 1288	40	50
1299	(22c.) As No. 1289	40	50
1290/9	*Set of* 10	3·50	4·50

Nos. 1280/9 were printed together, *se-tenant*, in sheetlets of 10 with two central stamp-size labels and are inscribed "For local addresses only". Each stamp was sold for 22c.

Nos. 1282 and 1287 were also printed in *se-tenant* sheets of 20 (4×5) containing four vertical rows of stamps alternated with rows of stamp-size labels, either blank or with decorative tabs. Such sheets were only available at $8 and could be "personalised" by incorporating a personal photograph on the blank label accompanying each stamp.

Nos. 1282 and 1287 were re-issued on 25 November 2004 in conjunction with the film *The Polar Express*. They were printed in the same sheet format as before but each vertical row of labels showed a scene from the film. The sheets sold at $10 with one photo or $12 for multiple photos and carried a handling charge of $2.50. Singly the stamps were worth 23c.

Nos. 1290/9 are inscribed "For local addresses only" and were only issued in booklets of 10, No. SB47, sold for $2.20, on which the surplus self-adhesive paper was retained.

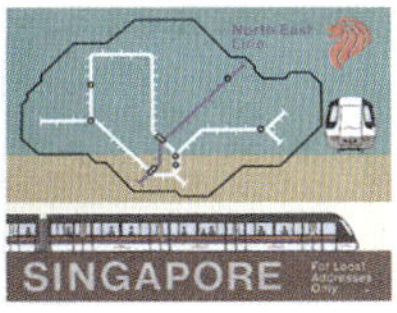

296 Map of Singapore Mass Rapid Transit System

297 National Flag

(Des Ng Keng Seng Ken. Litho Enschedé)

2003 (18 July). Opening of North East Line of Singapore Mass Rapid Transit System. T **296** and similar horiz designs. Multicoloured. Phosphor frame. P 13½×14.

1300	(22c.) Type **296**	40	20
1301	60c. Passengers	80	45
1302	$2 Control centre	2·50	3·00
1300/2	*Set of* 3	3·25	3·25
MS1303	135×93 mm. 10c. Type **169**; 60c. As No. 573; $2 As No. 574 and Nos. 1300/2	5·50	6·00

No. 1300 is inscribed "For Local Addresses Only" and was sold at 22c.

A "For local addresses only" stamp, issued on 8 August 2003, depicting a daisy and inscribed "Beauty of a caring heart" was only available in sheets of 20 containing four vertical rows of stamps alternated with rows of stamp-size labels. These sheets were sold at $8.

(Des Lee Huei Hoon. Litho Cartor)

2003 (9 Aug). National Day. T **297** and similar horiz designs. Multicoloured. Phosphorised paper. P 13½.

1304	(22c.) Type **297**	30	20
1305	60c. Vanda "Miss Joaquim"	75	45
1306	$1 "Merlion" statue and Singapore skyline	1·10	1·00
1307	$2 Children	2·00	2·50
1304/7	*Set of* 4	3·75	3·75
MS1308	140×75 mm. Nos. 1304/7	3·75	4·00

No. 1305 is inscribed "For local addresses only" and was sold for 22c.

No. 1305 was also printed in sheets of 20 (4×5) containing four vertical rows of stamps alternated with rows of stamp-size labels, either blank or with decorative tabs. Such sheets could be "personalised" by incorporating a personal photograph on the blank label accompanying each stamp.

298 Alouette III (helicopter)

299 Singapore Botanic Gardens

(Des W. Chan. Litho Cartor)

2003 (3 Sept). Centenary of Powered Flight. T **298** and similar horiz designs. Multicoloured.

(a) PVA gum. Phosphorised paper. P 13½.

1309	(22c.) Type **298**	40	40
	a. Sheetlet. Nos. 1309/18	3·50	3·50
1310	(22c.) E-2C Hawkeye	40	40
1311	(22c.) Hawker Hunter	40	40
1312	(22c.) Super Puma AS-332M (helicopter)	40	40
1313	(22c.) Hercules C-130H	40	40
1314	(22c.) F-16 C/D Fighting Falcon	40	40
1315	(22c.) AH-64D Apache (helicopter)	40	40
1316	(22c.) KC-135R Stratotanker	40	40
1317	(22c.) Cessna 172	40	40
1318	(22c.) F-5E Tiger II	40	40
1319	(22c.) A340-500	40	40
	a. Sheetlet. Nos. 1319/28	3·50	3·50
1320	(22c.) B747-400	40	40
1321	(22c.) B777-200	40	40
1322	(22c.) B747-400 Freighter	40	40
1323	(22c.) A320	40	40
1324	(22c.) Concorde	40	40
1325	(22c.) B737-100	40	40
1326	(22c.) Comet IV	40	40
1327	(22c.) Viscount	40	40
1328	(22c.) Airspeed Consul	40	40
1309/28	*Set of* 20	7·00	7·00
MS1329	282×188 mm. Nos. 1309/28	7·00	7·00

(b) Self-adhesive. Two phosphor bands. P 12½.

1330	(22c.) Type **298**	40	45
	a. Sheetlet. Nos. 1330/9	3·50	4·00
1331	(22c.) E-2C Hawkeye	40	45
1332	(22c.) Hawker Hunter	40	45
1333	(22c.) Super Puma AS-332M (helicopter)	40	45
1334	(22c.) Hercules C-130H	40	45
1335	(22c.) F-16 F/D Fighting Falcon	40	45
1336	(22c.) AH-64D Apache (helicopter)	40	45
1337	(22c.) KC-135R Stratotanker	40	45
1338	(22c.) Cessna 172	40	45
1339	(22c.) F-5E Tiger II	40	45
1340	(22c.) A340-500	40	45
	a. Sheetlet. Nos. 1340/9	3·50	4·00
1341	(22c.) B747-500	40	45
1342	(22c.) B777-200	40	45
1343	(22c.) B747-400 Freighter	40	45
1344	(22c.) A320	40	45
1345	(22c.) Concorde	40	45
1346	(22c.) B737-100	40	45
1347	(22c.) Comet IV	40	45
1348	(22c.) Viscount	40	45
1349	(22c.) Airspeed Consul	40	45
1330/49	*Set of* 20	7·00	8·00

Nos. 1309/18, 1319/28, 1330/9 and 1340/9 were each printed together, *se-tenant*, in sheetlets of ten. All stamps were inscribed "For local addresses only" and sold at 22c.

2003 (4 Oct). Bangkok 2003 World Stamp Exhibition, Thailand. Sheet 123×75 mm. Multicoloured. Phosphorised paper. P 13×13½.

MS1350	(22c.) Type **290**; $2 No. 1263	2·75	3·50

(Des Lee Huei Hoon. Litho Southern Colour Print, Dunedin)

2003 (22 Oct). Parks and Gardens. T **299** and similar vert designs. Multicoloured.

(a) PVA gum. Phosphorised paper. P 13½.

1351 (22c.) Type **299** ... 40 20
1352 60c. Fort Canning Park ... 75 50
1353 $1 Marina City Park ... 1·40 1·60
1354 $1 Stork's nest, Sungei Buloh Wetland Reserve ... 1·40 1·60
1351/4 *Set of 4* ... 3·50 3·50

(b) Self-adhesive. Phosphor frame. P 10×9½.

1355 (22c.) Type **299** ... 40 45
a. Booklet pane. No. 1355×10 ... 3·50

Nos. 1351 and 1355 are inscribed "FOR LOCAL ADDRESSES ONLY" and were sold for 22c.

No. 1355 was only available in $2.20 booklets, No. SB48, on which the surplus self-adhesive paper was retained.

2003 (20 Nov). China 2003 International Stamp Exhibition, Mianyang. Sheet 122×75 mm. Phosphorised paper. P 13×13½.

MS1356 (22c.) Type **290**; $2 No. 1263 ... 2·75 3·50

300 Monkey with Heart

301 "Farmer's House" (Liu Kang)

(Des N. Loh. Litho Enschedé)

2004 (9 Jan). Chinese New Year ("Year of the Monkey"). T **300** and similar horiz design. Multicoloured. Phosphor frame. P 14×13½.

1357 (22c.) Type **300** ... 40 30
a. Pair. Nos. 1357/8 ... 2·50 2·75
1358 $2 Two monkeys ... 2·25 2·50

No. 1357 is inscribed "FOR LOCAL ADDRESSES ONLY" and was sold for 22c.

In addition to separate sheets of 50 Nos. 1357/8 were also printed together, *se-tenant*, both horizontally and vertically, in sheets of 18 (3×6).

2004 (30 Jan). Hong Kong 2004 International Stamp Exhibition. Sheet 123×75 mm. Multicoloured. Phosphor frame. P 14×13½.

MS1359 (22c.) Type **300**; $2 No. 1358 ... 3·00 3·50

(Des Sylvia Tan. Litho Cartor)

2004 (18 Feb). Paintings by Liu Kang and Ong Kim Seng. T **301** and similar multicoloured designs.

(a) PVA gum. Phosphorised paper. P 13½.

1360 (23c.) Type **301** ... 40 40
a. Sheetlet. Nos. 1360/9 ... 3·50 3·50
1361 (23c.) "Artist and Model" (Liu Kang) ... 40 40
1362 (23c.) "Lanterns Galore" (Liu Kang) ... 40 40
1363 (23c.) "Enjoying a Smoke, Kashmir" (Liu Kang) 40 40
1364 (23c.) "Life by the River" (Liu Kang) ... 40 40
1365 (23c.) "Tenth Trip up to Huangshan" (Liu Kang) ... 40 40
1366 (23c.) "My Young Wife" (Liu Kang) (vert) ... 40 40
1367 (23c.) "Kek Lok Si, Penang" (Liu Kang) (vert) ... 40 40
1368 (23c.) "Souri" (Liu Kang) (vert) ... 40 40
1369 (23c.) "Siesta in Bali" (Liu Kang) (vert) ... 40 40
1370 (23c.) "Kampong Tengah, Singapore" (Ong Kim Seng) ... 40 40
a. Sheetlet. Nos. 1370/9 ... 3·50 3·50
1371 (23c.) "Gyantse Market" (Ong Kim Seng) ... 40 40
1372 (23c.) "Sebatu Spring, Bali" (Ong Kim Seng) ... 40 40
1373 (23c.) "Jetty, Bangkok" (Ong Kim Seng) ... 40 40
1374 (23c.) "Resort, Bali" (Ong Kim Seng) ... 40 40
1375 (23c.) "Dance Studio, Bali" (Ong Kim Seng) ... 40 40
1376 (23c.) "Telok Ayer Market" (Ong Kim Seng) ... 40 40
1377 (23c.) "Kathmandu, Nepal" (Ong Kim Seng) ... 40 40
1378 (23c.) "Portofino, Italy" (Ong Kim Seng) (vert).. 40 40
1379 (23c.) "Boats at Rest" (Ong Kim Seng) (vert) ... 40 40
1360/79 *Set of 20* ... 7·00 7·00

(b) Self-adhesive. Phosphor frame. P 12½.

1380 (23c.) Type **301** ... 40 45
a. Sheetlet. Nos. 1380/9 ... 3·50 4·00
1381 (23c.) "Artist and Model" (Liu Kang) ... 40 45
1382 (23c.) "Lanterns Galore" (Liu Kang) ... 40 45
1383 (23c.) "Enjoying a Smoke, Kashmir" (Liu Kang) 40 45
1384 (23c.) "Life by the River" (Liu Kang) ... 40 45
1385 (23c.) "Tenth Trip up to Huangshan" (Liu Kang) 40 45
1386 (23c.) "My Young Wife" (Liu Kang) (vert) ... 40 45
1387 (23c.) "Kek Lok Si, Penang" (Liu Kang) (vert) ... 40 45
1388 (23c.) "Souri" (Liu Kang) (vert) ... 40 45
1389 (23c.) "Siesta in Bali" (Liu Kang) (vert) ... 40 45
1390 (23c.) "Kampong Tengah, Singapore" (Ong Kim Seng) ... 40 45
a. Sheetlet. Nos. 1390/9 ... 3·50 4·00
1391 (23c.) "Gyantse Market" (Ong Kim Seng) ... 40 45
1392 (23c.) "Sebatu Spring, Bali" (Ong Kim Seng) ... 40 45
1393 (23c.) "Jetty, Bangkok" (Ong Kim Seng) ... 40 45
1394 (23c.) "Resort, Bali" (Ong Kim Seng) ... 40 45
1395 (23c.) "Dance Studio, Bali" (Ong Kim Seng) ... 40 45
1396 (23c.) "Telok Ayer Market" (Ong Kim Seng) ... 40 45
1397 (23c.) "Kathmandu, Nepal" (Ong Kim Seng) ... 40 45
1398 (23c.) "Portofino, Italy" (Ong Kim Seng) (vert).. 40 45
1399 (23c.) "Boats at Rest" (Ong Kim Seng) (vert) ... 40 45
1380/99 *Set of 20* ... 7·00 8·00

Nos. 1360/9, 1370/9, 1380/9 and 1390/9 were each printed together, *se-tenant*, in sheetlets of ten. All stamps were inscribed "For local addresses only" and sold at 23c.

The vert designs in these sheetlets were all laid horizontally on their sides.

302 "Harmony" Sculpture and Suzhou Industrial Park

303 Colonial and Modern Buildings

(Des Zhang Lei. Litho Beijing Stamp Printing House)

2004 (1 Mar). Tenth Anniv of Suzhou Industrial Park. Two phosphor bands. P 13×13½.

1400 **302** 60c. multicoloured ... 1·25 1·00

(Des Leo Teck Chong. Eng C. Slania. Recess and litho ($5), litho (others) Walsall)

2004 (24 Mar). Singapore Skyline. T **303** and similar horiz designs. Multicoloured. Phosphorised paper. P 14×14½.

1401 (23c.) Type **303** ... 40 20
1402 60c. Merlion statue and waterfront ... 1·00 60
1403 70c. Singapore skyline ... 1·10 1·40
1401/3 *Set of 3* ... 2·25 2·00

MS1404 Two sheets, each 113×80 mm. (a) $1 Singapore from the Roads, c. 1900 (95×35 mm). (b) $5 Singapore skyline, 2004 (95×35 mm). P 14 ... 7·50 8·50

No. 1401 is inscribed ""1st Local"" and was sold for 23c.

304 Containers

(Des Design Objectives. Litho DLR)

2004 (21 Apr). Singapore–A Global City (3rd series). Trade and Industry. T **304** and similar horiz design. Multicoloured. "All-over" phosphor. P 14½.

1405 $2 Type **304** ... 2·50 2·75
a. Horiz pair. Nos. 1405/6 separated by label ... 5·00 5·50
1406 $2 Oil refinery ... 2·50 2·75

MS1407 135×95 mm. Nos. 1405/6 and double stamp-size label ... 5·00 5·50

Nos. 1405/6 were printed together in sheets of ten, the two designs in vertical rows of five separated by a gutter publicising World Stamp Championship 2004.

No. **MS**1407 exists with five different labels advertising American International Assurance, GlaxoSmithKline, HSBC, Shell and Sony.

305 Football Field

306 Three Candles (Deepavali)

(Des Wong Wui Kong. Litho and embossed Cartor)

2004 (21 May). Centenary of FIFA (Fédération Internationale de Football Association). T **305** and similar square designs. Multicoloured. Flocked paper. P 13.

1408	30c. Type **305**	40	25
1409	60c. Football	80	50
1410	$1 Football shirt	1·25	1·00
1411	$2 World map	3·00	3·25
1408/11	*Set of* 4	5·00	4·50

(Des T. Ngan. Litho Cartor)

2004 (7 July). Festivals. T **306** and similar vert designs. Multicoloured.

(a) PVA gum. Phosphorised paper. P 13.

1412	(23c.) Type **306**	35	35
1413	(23c.) One candle (Hari Raya Aidilfitri)	35	35
1414	(23c.) Toy Father Christmas and Rudolph (Christmas)	35	35
1415	(23c.) Plum blossom and oranges (Chinese New Year)	35	35
1416	50c. Woman and oil lamp (Deepavali)	65	75
1417	50c. Girl holding sparkler (Hari Raya Aidilfitri)	65	75
1418	50c. Carol singers (Christmas)	65	75
1419	50c. Woman wearing orange kimono	65	75
1412/19	*Set of* 8	3·50	4·00

(b) Self-adhesive. Two phosphor bands. P 12½

1420	(23c.) Type **306**	35	45
1421	(23c.) One candle (Hari Raya Aidilfitri)	35	45
1422	(23c.) Toy Father Christmas and Rudolph (Christmas)	35	45
1423	(23c.) Plum blossom and oranges (Chinese New Year)	35	45
1420/3	*Set of* 4	1·25	1·60

Nos. 1412/23 were each sold in sheets of 10.

Nos. 1412/15 and 1420/23 were inscribed "1st Local" and sold at 23c. each.

307 Column, City Hall

308 Running

(Des L. Teck Chong. Litho Cartor)

2004 (9 Aug). National Day. Monuments. T **307** and similar multicoloured designs. Phosphorised paper. P 13½.

1424	(23c.) Type **307**	40	50
	a. Vert pair. Nos. 1424/5	80	1·00
1425	(23c.) City Hall (41×27 mm)	40	50
1426	30c. Concert Hall bell tower	50	60
	a. Vert pair. Nos. 1426/7	1·00	1·10
1427	30c. Victoria Theatre and Concert Hall (41×27 mm)	50	60
1428	60c. Dome of courthouse	90	1·25
	a. Vert pair. Nos. 1428/9	1·75	2·50
1429	60c. Supreme Court (41×27 mm)	90	1·25
1430	$1 Detail of gate, the Istana	1·40	1·75
	a. Vert pair. Nos. 1430/1	2·75	3·50
1431	$1 The Istana (41×27 mm)	1·40	1·75
1424/31	*Set of* 8	5·75	7·25
MS1432	140×70 mm. Nos. 1425, 1427, 1429 and 1431	2·75	3·50

Nos. 1424/5, 1426/7, 1428/9 and 1430/1, respectively, were each printed together, *se-tenant*, as vertical pairs throughout sheets of ten stamps.

Nos. 1424/5 were inscribed "1st Local" and sold for 23c.

(Des Design Objectives. Litho Secura, Singapore)

2004 (13 Aug). Olympic Games, Athens, Greece. T **308** and similar horiz designs showing Olympic sports depicted on pebbles. Multicoloured. Phosphorised paper. P 13½.

1433	(23c.) Type **308**	40	20
1434	30c. Swimming	55	25
1435	$1 Weight-lifting	1·40	1·10
1436	$2 Sailing	2·75	3·25
1433/6	*Set of* 4	4·50	4·25

2004 (28 Aug). World Stamp Championship, Singapore. Sheet 161×85 mm containing Nos. 1259/60, 1277/8 and 1405/6. Litho. Multicoloured. "All-over" phosphor. P 14½ (horiz) or 14½×14 (others).

MS1437	$2 Containers; $2 Oil refinery; $2 Two yachts; $2 Conductor's hands and baton; $2 Satellite; $2 Robot	14·00	16·00

309 Linked Wrists and Singapore Post Centre

310 Seashore Nutmeg

(Des Sylvia Tan. Litho Beijing Stamp Printing House)

2004 (28 Aug). 150th Anniv of Introduction of Stamps. T **309** and similar horiz designs, each showing early Singapore stamps and postmarks. Multicoloured. Two phosphor bands. P 12×11½.

1438	(23c.) Type **309**	40	20
1439	60c. King George VI and General Post Office, Fullerton Building	90	55
1440	$1 King Edward VII and General Post Office	1·40	1·10
1441	$2 Queen Victoria and the Post Office, Singapore River	2·25	2·75
1438/41	*Set of* 4	4·50	4·25
MS1442	135×94 mm. Nos. 1438/41	4·50	4·75

No. 1438 is inscribed "1st Local" and was sold for 23c.

The stamps and postmarks in each design are overprinted in red fluorescence visible under U.V. light.

(Des Eng Siak Loy. Litho Southern Colour Print, Dunedin)

2004 (20 Oct). Wildlife of Chek Jawa. T **310** and similar vert designs. Multicoloured. (a) PVA gum. Phosphorised paper. P 14.

1443	(23c.) Type **310**	65	65
	a. Horiz strip of 4. Nos. 1443/6	3·75	3·75
1444	(23c.) Oriental Pied Hornbill	65	65
1445	$1 Knobbly Sea Stars	1·50	1·50
1446	$1 Common Seahorses	1·50	1·50
1443/6	*Set of* 4	3·75	3·75

(b) Self-adhesive. One side phosphor band. P 10×9½.

1447	(23c.) Type **310**	40	50
	a. Booklet pane. Nos. 1447/8 both ×5	3·50	
1448	(23c.) Oriental Pied Hornbill	40	50

Nos. 1443/6 were printed together, *se-tenant*, as horizontal rows of four stamps, the backgrounds of which form a composite design, in sheets of 20.

Nos. 1447/8 were available from $2.30 booklets (No. SB51) on which the surplus self-adhesive paper around each stamp is retained.

Nos. 1443/4 and 1447/8 were each inscribed "1st Local" and sold for 23c. each.

311 Rooster

312 Balloon Dog

(Des N. Loh. Litho Secura, Singapore)

2005 (14 Jan). Chinese New Year ("Year of the Rooster"). T **311** and similar horiz design. Multicoloured. Phosphorised paper. P 13½.

1449	(23c.) Type **311**	40	20
	a. Pair. Nos. 1449/50	3·00	3·50
1450	$2 Rooster and hen	2·75	3·25

No. 1449 is inscribed ""1st Local"" and was sold for 23c.

In addition to separate sheets of 50, Nos. 1449/50 were also printed together, *se-tenant*, both horizontally and vertically, in sheets of 18 (3×6).

(Des L. H. Hoon. Litho SNP Sprint)

2005 (23 Feb). Greetings. T **312** and similar horiz designs. Multicoloured. Phosphor frame. (a) PVA gum. P 13½×14.

1451	(23c.) Type **312**	40	45
	a. Vert strip of 5. Nos. 1451/5	1·75	2·00
1452	(23c.) Lily	40	45
1453	(23c.) Gift box	40	45

1454	(23c.) Love heart and bears flower arrangement	40	45
1455	(23c.) Candle	40	45
1451/5	*Set of 5*	1·75	2·00

(b) Size 30×25 mm. Self-adhesive. P 11.

1456	(23c.) Candle	35	45
	a. Booklet pane. Nos. 1456/60, each ×2	3·25	
1457	(23c.) Love heart and bears flower arrangement	35	45
1458	(23c.) Gift box	35	45
1459	(23c.) Lily	35	45
1460	(23c.) Balloon dog	35	45
1456/60	*Set of 5*	1·60	2·00

Nos. 1451/60 were each inscribed "1st Local" and sold for 23c.

Nos. 1451/5 were printed together, *se-tenant*, in two vertical rows in sheets of ten stamps.

Nos. 1456/60 were only available from $2.30 stamp booklets (No. SB53). The surplus self-adhesive paper around each stamp is retained and two thirds of the backing paper contains labels inscribed with fragmented greetings and flowers.

Nos. 1453/4 were re-issued on 25 April 2007 in a "MyStamp" Mothers Day sheetlet containing four of each stamp and four stamp-size labels surrounding a large central label. The sheetlet was cut in the shape of a flower and sold for $10.

313 "Thumbelina"

(Des Wong Wui Kong. Litho Beijing Stamp Printing House)

2005 (30 Mar). Birth Bicentenary of Hans Christian Anderson (artist and children's writer). T **313** and similar horiz designs. Multicoloured. Two phosphor bands. P 13.

1461	(23c.) Type **313**	40	20
1462	60c. "The Ugly Duckling"	70	55
1463	$1 "The Emperor's New Clothes"	1·25	1·25
1464	$2 "The Little Mermaid"	2·25	2·75
1461/4	*Set of 4*	4·25	4·25
MS1465	200×67 mm. Nos. 1461/4	4·25	4·50

No. 1461 was inscribed ""1st Local"" and initially sold for 23c.

314 National University of Singapore Monument and Globe

(Des M. Ng Puay Chiew. Litho Secura, Singapore)

2005 (20 Apr). Centenary of National University of Singapore. T **314** and similar horiz designs. Multicoloured. P 12½.

1466	(23c.) Type **314**	40	20
1467	60c. Students	70	55
1468	70c. Dancers and sculpture outside building	80	90
1469	$1 Science student and equipment	1·25	1·40
1466/9	*Set of 4*	2·75	2·75

2005 (21 Apr). Pacific Explorer 2005 World Stamp Expo, Sydney. Sheet 123×75 mm. Multicoloured. P 13.

MS1469*a*	(23c.) Type **311**; $2 Rooster and hen	4·50	4·75

315 Istana Kampong Gelam (Malay Heritage Centre)

316 Admiral Zheng He

(Des Elsie Koh. Litho Secura, Singapore)

2005 (31 May). Malay Heritage Centre. T **315** and similar square designs. Multicoloured. Phosphorised paper. P 14.

1470	(2nd) Type **315**	40	20
1471	60c. Fountain pen and seal	70	55
1472	$1 Mandolin	1·25	1·25
1473	$2 Sail boat	2·25	2·75
1470/3	*Set of 4*	4·25	4·25

No. 1470 was inscribed "2nd Local" and initially sold for 31c.

(Des Eng Siak Loy. Litho Secura, Singapore)

2005 (28 June). 600th Anniv of the Voyages of Admiral Zheng He. T **316** and similar horiz designs. Multicoloured. Phosphorised paper. P 13½.

1474	(23c.) Type **316**	40	35
	a. Perf 13	40	50
	ab. Horiz pair. Nos. 1474/5	80	1·00
1475	(23c.) Three sailing ships	40	35
	a. Perf 13	40	50
1476	60c. Four sailing ships	80	70
1477	$1 Sailing ships near port	1·40	1·60
1474/7	*Set of 4*	2·75	2·75

Nos. 1474/5 were inscribed "1st Local" and initially sold for 23c. each.

Nos. 1474/7 were each printed in separate sheets of ten stamps.

Nos. 1474a/5a were printed together, *se-tenant*, in horizontal pairs in sheetlets of ten stamps.

317 Football, Table Tennis and Cycling

(Des T. Ngan. Litho Beijing Stamp Printing House)

2005 (5 July). 117th International Olympic Committee Session. T **317** and similar horiz designs, each showing the five competing cities and flight paths to Singapore. Multicoloured. Two phosphor bands. P 14½.

1478	(23c.) Type **317**	50	25
1479	50c. Athletics, tennis and basketball	70	50
1480	60c. Football, tennis and javelin throwing	75	65
1481	$1 Gymnastics and athletics	1·10	1·40
1478/81	*Set of 4*	2·75	2·50

No. 1478 was inscribed "1st Local" and initially sold for 23c.

318 Smiling Stickmen (needlework)

319 Belgian Centre for Comic Strip Art, Brussels

(Des Chua Ban Har. Litho Southern Colour Print, Dunedin)

2005 (9 Aug). National Day. "Fabric of the Nation". T **318** and similar vert designs showing needlework by Singaporeans. Multicoloured. Phosphor frame. (a) PVA gum. P 14½.

1482	(23c.) Type **318**	30	40
	a. Sheetlet. Nos. 1482/1501	5·50	7·00
1483	(23c.) Hearts on patches	30	40
1484	(23c.) Smiling yellow flower	30	40
1485	(23c.) Round Tower	30	40
1486	(23c.) Red orchid	30	40
1487	(23c.) Sun, rainbow and cloud	30	40
1488	(23c.) "Peace"	30	40
1489	(23c.) Outline of Singapore with red heart inside	30	40
1490	(23c.) White orchid	30	40
1491	(23c.) Red heart with orange flowers inside	30	40
1492	(23c.) "Happy Birthday"	30	40
1493	(23c.) Two hands	30	40
1494	(23c.) Cats and dogs	30	40
1495	(23c.) Stars	30	40
1496	(23c.) Washing on lines	30	40
1497	(23c.) Plane and patchwork clouds	30	40
1498	(23c.) Patchwork quarters	30	40
1499	(23c.) Plate with food	30	40
1500	(23c.) Hearts	30	40
1501	(23c.) Skyline	30	40
1502	(23c.) "1" and flowers	30	40
	a. Sheetlet. Nos. 1502/21	5·50	7·00
1503	(23c.) Four children and jigsaw pieces	30	40
1504	(23c.) Four heads around flag	30	40
1505	(23c.) Rainbow and clouds	30	40

1506	(23c.) Face upturned amongst bowed heads...	30	40
1507	(23c.) Four butterflies	30	40
1508	(23c.) Cross-stitch	30	40
1509	(23c.) Heart-shaped fruit	30	40
1510	(23c.) Frog	30	40
1511	(23c.) Bird kites	30	40
1512	(23c.) Four hands around yellow heart	30	40
1513	(23c.) Skyline and "Singapore My Home"	30	40
1514	(23c.) Green orchid	30	40
1515	(23c.) Patchwork hearts as tree	30	40
1516	(23c.) "I", heart and outline of Singapore	30	40
1517	(23c.) Hand and buttons	30	40
1518	(23c.) "Singapore", hills and heart	30	40
1519	(23c.) Four hearts in quarters	30	40
1520	(23c.) Hearts, stars and people in quarters	30	40
1521	(23c.) "The Pledge"	30	40
1482/521	*Set of* 40	11·00	14·00
MS1522	62×90 mm. $1 Needlework designs (39×60 mm)	1·40	1·60

(b) Self-adhesive. Die-cut perf 10×9½

1523	(23c.) Type **318**	30	40
	a. Sheetlet. Nos. 1523/42	5·50	7·00
1524	(23c.) Hearts on patches	30	40
1525	(23c.) Smiling yellow flower	30	40
1526	(23c.) Round Tower	30	40
1527	(23c.) Red orchid	30	40
1528	(23c.) Sun, rainbow and cloud	30	40
1529	(23c.) "Peace"	30	40
1530	(23c.) Outline of Singapore with red heart inside	30	40
1531	(23c.) White orchid	30	40
1532	(23c.) Red heart with orange flowers inside	30	40
1533	(23c.) "Happy Birthday"	30	40
1534	(23c.) Two hands	30	40
1535	(23c.) Cats and dogs	30	40
1536	(23c.) Stars	30	40
1537	(23c.) Washing on lines	30	40
1538	(23c.) Plane and patchwork clouds	30	40
1539	(23c.) Patchwork quarters	30	40
1540	(23c.) Plate with food	30	40
1541	(23c.) Hearts	30	40
1542	(23c.) Skyline	30	40
1543	(23c.) "1" and flowers	30	40
	a. Sheetlet. Nos. 1543/62	5·50	7·00
1544	(23c.) Four children and jigsaw pieces	30	40
1545	(23c.) Four heads around flag	30	40
1546	(23c.) Rainbow and clouds	30	40
1547	(23c.) Face upturned amongst bowed heads...	30	40
1548	(23c.) Four butterflies	30	40
1549	(23c.) Cross-stitch	30	40
1550	(23c.) Heart-shaped fruit	30	40
1551	(23c.) Frog	30	40
1552	(23c.) Bird kites	30	40
1553	(23c.) Four hands around yellow heart	30	40
1554	(23c.) Skyline and "Singapore My Home"	30	40
1555	(23c.) Green orchid	30	40
1556	(23c.) Patchwork hearts as tree	30	40
1557	(23c.) "I", heart and outline of Singapore	30	40
1558	(23c.) Hand and buttons	30	40
1559	(23c.) "Singapore", hills and heart	30	40
1560	(23c.) Four hearts in quarters	30	40
1561	(23c.) Hearts, stars and people in quarters	30	40
1562	(23c.) "The Pledge"	30	40
1523/62	*Set of* 40	11·00	14·00

Nos. 1482/1501, 1502/21, 1523/42 and 1543/62 were each printed together in sheetlets of 20 stamps. All were inscribed "1st Local" and initially sold for 23c.

Nos. 1483/4, 1491, 1495, 1505 and 1519 were re-issued on 2 July 2007 in a "MyStamp" Youth Day sheetlet containing two of each stamp and twelve stamp-size labels. The sheetlet was sold for $6.

2005 (19 Aug). TAIPEI 2005 International Stamp Exhibition. Sheet 123×75 mm. Multicoloured. P 13.

MS1562*a*	(23c.) Type **311**; $2 Rooster and hen	4·50	4·75

(Des Sylvia Tan. Litho Secura, Singapore)

2005 (9 Sept). Architecture. T **319** and similar vert designs. Multicoloured. Phosphorised paper. P 13.

1563	(23c.) Type **319**	40	20
1564	60c. Kandahar Street	70	55
1565	$1 Bukit Pasoh Road	1·25	1·25
1566	$2 Museum of Musical Instruments, Belgium	2·25	2·75
1563/6	*Set of* 4	4·25	4·25
MS1567	170×95 mm. Nos. 1563/6	4·25	4·50

No. 1563 was inscribed "1st Local" and initially sold for 23c.

Stamps of the same design were issued by Belgium.

No. 1563 was also issued in sheetlets of eight stamps and eight *se-tenant* labels showing Belgian comics, sold for $5 each.

Nos. 1564/5 were also issued in sheetlets of eight stamps containing four of each design and eight *se-tenant* labels showing line drawings of Singapore shophouses, sold for $9 per sheetlet.

320 Colugo

321 Dog chasing ball

(Des Leo Teck Chong. Litho Southern Colour Print, New Zealand)

2005 (19 Oct). HSBC Tree Top Walk, Central Catchment Nature Reserve. T **320** and similar vert designs. Multicoloured. One side phosphor band. (a) PVA gum. P 14.

1568	(23c.) Type **320**	50	50
	a. Horiz strip of 4. Nos. 1568/71	4·00	4·50
1569	60c. Fruits of Singapore adenia (climbing vine)	90	90
1570	$1 Red-crowned barbet (bird)	1·50	1·75
1571	$1 Common tree nymph (butterfly)	1·50	1·75
1568/71	*Set of* 4	4·00	4·50

(b) Self-adhesive. Die-cut perf 10½×9½.

1572	(23c.) Type **320**	30	35
	a. Booklet pane. No. 1572×10	2·75	

Nos. 1568/71 were printed together, *se-tenant*, in horizontal strips of 4 in sheets of 40, each strip forming a composite background design showing rainforest and tree top walk.

No. 1572 was only available from $2.30 stamp booklets, No. SB55.

(Des Nicodemus Loh. Litho Beijing Stamp Printing House)

2006 (6 Jan). Chinese New Year ("Year of the Dog"). T **321** and similar horiz design. Multicoloured. Two phosphor bands. P 13×13½.

1573	(23c.) Type **321**	45	20
1574	$2 Two dogs	2·25	2·75

In addition to separate sheets of 50, Nos. 1573/4 were also printed together, *se-tenant*, both horizontally and vertically, in sheets of 18 (3×6).

Five $1 stamps, showing five different patterns in grey all with merlion in scarlet and face value in reddish brown, were issued for Asian Aerospace 2006 on 21 February 2006. They were sold in sheetlets of five stamps and ten labels; five inscribed for Asian Aerospace 2006 and five showing aircraft. Each sheetlet was sold for $8.

322 "White Cloud"

323 Indo-Pacific Bottlenose Dolphin

(Des Jin LiJuan. Litho Secura, Singapore)

2006 (22 Feb). Art by Tan Swie Hian. T **322** and similar multicoloured designs. Phosphorised paper. P 12 (Nos. 1575/9) or 13 (Nos. 1580/**MS**1585).

1575	(23c.) Type **322**	40	45
	a. Sheetlet. Nos. 1575/9, each ×2	3·50	4·00
1576	(23c.) "Ganges"	40	45
1577	(23c.) "Soaring over the Flower Field"	40	45
1578	(23c.) "Kuta is a Song"	40	45
1579	(23c.) "The Winged Steed" (sculpture)	40	45
1580	50c. "Black Panther (pine)" (29×59 mm)	55	65
	a. Sheetlet. Nos. 1580/4, each ×2	5·00	6·00
1581	50c. "Gingko (Male)" (29×59 mm)	55	65
1582	50c. "White Elephant" (29×59 mm)	55	65
1583	50c. "Summer Lotus" (29×59 mm)	55	65
1584	50c. "Water Dhyana"(29×59 mm)	55	65
1575/84	*Set of* 10	4·25	5·00
MS1585	62×90 mm. $2 Calligraphy (40×59 mm)	2·75	3·00

Nos. 1575/9 were inscribed "1st Local" and initially sold for 23c.

Nos. 1575/9 and 1580/4 were each printed together, *se-tenant*, in sheetlets of ten stamps containing two of each design.

(Des Chua Ban Har. Litho Beijing Stamp Printing House)

2006 (22 Mar). Undersea World. Sea Mammals. T **323** and similar vert designs. Multicoloured. Two phosphor bands. (a) PVA gum. P 13½.

1586	(23c.) Type **323**	40	20
1587	(31c.) Indo-Pacific hump-backed dolphin	50	30
1588	$1 Finless porpoise	1·25	1·25
1589	$2 Dugong	2·50	3·00
1586/9 *Set of* 4		4·25	4·25
MS1590 140×74 mm. Nos. 1586/9		4·25	4·50

(b) Self-adhesive. Die-cut perf 13.

1591	(23c.) As No. 1586	35	35

No. 1586/7 are inscribed "1ST LOCAL" and "2ND LOCAL" and were initially sold for 23c. and 31c. respectively.

No. 1591 was printed in sheets of ten.

324 Chinese New Year

325 Chinese New Year

(Des Design Objectives. Litho SEP Sprint, Australia)

2006 (19 Apr). Festivals. Multicoloured. Two phosphor bands. P 14½×14. (a) PVA gum. (i) Vert designs as T **324**.

1592	(23c.) Type **324**	35	35
1593	(23c.) Christmas	35	35
1594	(23c.) Deepavali	35	35
1595	(23c.) Hari Raya Aidilfitri	35	35

(ii) Vert designs as T **325**.

1596	50c. Type **325**	60	70
1597	50c. Christmas	60	70
1598	50c. Deepavali	60	70
1599	50c. Hari Raya Aidilfitri	60	70
1592/9 *Set of* 8		3·50	3·75

(b) Self-adhesive. Vert designs as T **324**

1600	(23c.) Type **324**	35	40
1601	(23c.) Christmas	35	40
1602	(23c.) Deepavali	35	40
1603	(23c.) Hari Raya Aidilfitri	35	40
1600/3 *Set of* 4		1·25	1·40

A "1st Local" stamp, issued on 2 May 2006, depicting a traveller's palm in five different colours, was only available in sheets of ten stamps and ten *se-tenant* labels, each sheet sold for $3.

326 Clog Maker

327 Keyboard (Government)

(Des Tze Ngan. Litho Beijing Stamp Printing House)

2006 (24 May). Vanishing Trades. T **326** and similar horiz designs. Multicoloured. Two phosphor bands. (a) PVA gum. P 13.

1604	(23c.) Type **326**	40	40
1605	(23c.) Wooden bucket maker	40	40
1606	(23c.) Spice grinder	40	40
1607	(23c.) Snake charmer	40	40
1608	(23c.) Satay man	40	40
1609	80c. Mama store	95	1·10
1610	80c. Roti man	95	1·10
1611	80c. Backlane barber	95	1·10
1612	80c. Chinese medicinal tea shop	95	1·10
1613	80c. Tin bucket maker	95	1·10
1604/13 *Set of* 10		6·00	6·75

(b) Self-adhesive. P10.

1614	(23c.) Type **326**	30	40
1615	(23c.) As No. 1605	30	40
1616	(23c.) As No. 1606	30	40
1617	(23c.) As No. 1607	30	40
1618	(23c.) As No. 1608	30	40
1614/18 *Set of* 5		1·40	1·75

Nos. 1604/8 and 1614/18 are inscribed "1st Local" and were initially sold for 23c.

2006 (27 May). Washington 2006 International Stamp Exhibition. Sheet 123×75 mm. Multicoloured. Two phosphor bands. P 13×13½.

MS1619 (23c.) Type **321**; $2 No. 1574		3·75	4·00

Five $1 stamps, showing five different patterns in grey and vermilion, were issued for the World Cup Football Championship, Germany. The first sheetlet of five stamps and ten labels showing footballs and Coca Cola advertisements was issued on 17 June 2006. The second sheetlet was issued on 12 July 2006. It contains five stamps, labels showing footballs or Coca Cola advertisements and five labels showing the national flags of the winning nations since 1990 (Germany, Brazil (twice), France and Italy).

Four 50c. stamps, each showing the same orchid motif in four different colour ways, were issued on 6 June 2006, in two different sheets of eight stamps and eight labels. One sheet with labels showing parrots, hornbills, pelican and toucan, was inscribed for the All Star Bird Show, the other, with labels showing carnivorous birds, was inscribed for the Birds of Prey Show.

(Des Blue Apples Consultancy. Litho Secura)

2006 (20 June). 25th Anniv of Infocomm. T **327** and similar vert designs. Multicoloured. P 13.

1620	(23c.) Type **327**	30	30
1621	60c. Trade	75	55
1622	80c. Boy using computer (Education)	1·00	1·00
1623	$1 Satellite dish (Telecommunications)	1·25	1·40
1620/3 *Set of* 4		3·00	3·00

328 SCCCI Building

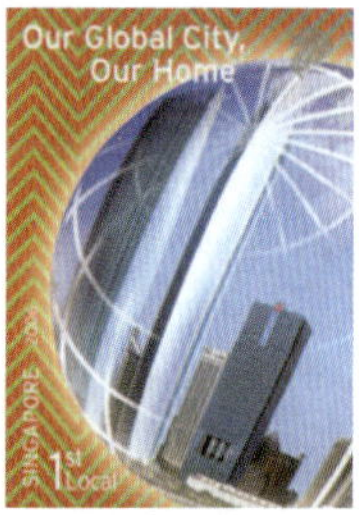

329 City of Singapore

(Des W. Chan. Litho Beijing Stamp Printing House)

2006 (19 July). Centenary of Singapore Chinese Chamber of Commerce and Industry. T **328** and similar fan-shaped designs. Multicoloured. One phosphor band. P 13.

1624	(23c.) Type **328**	40	30
1625	(31c.) *Dendrobium* "Singapore Chinese Chamber of Commerce and Industry"	1·50	80
1626	80c. Logo of World Chinese Entrepreneurs Convention	1·40	1·40
1627	$1 Administration building, Nanyang University	1·40	1·40
1628	$2 War Memorial and Sun Yat Sen Nanyang Memorial Hall	2·25	2·75
1624/8 *Set of* 5		6·25	6·00
MS1629 140×75 mm. Nos. 1624/8		6·00	6·50

Nos. 1624/8 are perforated in a fan-shape contained within an outer perforated rectangle.

No. 1624 is inscribed "1ST LOCAL" and No. 1625 "2ND LOCAL". They were initially sold for 23c. and 31c. respectively.

(Des Design Objectives. Litho Secura, Singapore)

2006 (9 Aug). National Day. T **329** and similar vert designs. Multicoloured. P 13.

1630	(23c.) Type **329**	30	30
1631	60c. People of Singapore	75	55
1632	80c. Containers	1·00	1·00
1633	$1 Entertainers	1·25	1·40
1630/3 *Set of* 4		3·00	3·00
MS1634 113×80 mm. $2 City of Singapore reflected in glass globe (48×48 mm)		2·25	2·50

No. 1630 is inscribed ""1st Local"" and was initially sold for 23c.

330 Orchids

331 One Dollar Coin

(Des Design Objectives. Litho Enschedé)

2006 (13 Sept). International Monetary Fund and World Bank Group Boards of Governors Annual Meetings. Two phosphor bands. (a) Horiz designs as T **330**. Multicoloured. P 13½×14.

1635	50c. Type **330**	70	40
1636	80c. Esplanade–Theatres on the Bay	1·00	80
1637	$1 Singapore skyline	1·25	1·10

(b) Square designs as T **331**. Gold and black ($1) or silver and black ($5). P 13½.

1638	$1 One dollar coin	1·50	1·50
1639	$5 Five dollar coin	6·50	7·50
1635/9	*Set of* 5	9·75	10·00

Nos. 1635/7 have the two phosphor bands in the centre of the stamp.

Nos. 1638/9 were each perforated in a circle contained within an outer perforated square.

Nos. 1638/9 have the two phosphor bands at left and right of the square, only just touching the edges of the circle.

332 "Singapore biennale 06" (illustration reduced. Actual size 97×66 mm)

(Des Work. Litho Enschedé)

2006 (13 Sept). Singapore Biennale 2006. Two phosphor bands. P 14½×14.

1640	**332**	$2 multicoloured	2·25	2·50

333 *Vanda* "Mimi Palmer"

334 Singapore Merlion and St. Peter's Basilica, Rome

(Des M. Motoharu and Sylvia Tan. Litho (and die-stamped **MS**1647) Southern Colour Print, New Zealand)

2006 (3 Oct). Flowers. T **333** and similar multicoloured designs. One phosphor band at right ($1) or one phosphor bar (at left on 70c, right on others). P 14½.

1641	(23c.) Type **333**	40	30
1642	(23c.) *Renanthera* "Singaporeans"	40	30
1643	70c. *Vanda* "Miss Joaquim"	90	90
1644	70c. *Mokara* "Lion's Gold"	90	90
1645	$1 Heron and hollyhocks (48×35 mm)	1·25	1·25
1646	$2 Moorhen and irises (48×35 mm)	2·25	2·75
1641/6	*Set of* 6	5·50	5·75

Nos. 1641/2 are inscribed "1st Local" and were initially sold for 23c. each.

Nos. 1641/6 commemorate the 40th Anniversary of Diplomatic Relations between Singapore and Japan. Stamps in similar designs were issued by Japan.

Nos. 1645/6 depict details from two different screen paintings by Houitsu Sakai both with the title "Flowers and Birds of the Four Seasons".

Stamps as Nos. 1643/6 (but without phosphor bands or bars and perf 13½) were issued in sheetlets of eight stamps (Nos. 1643/4, each ×2 and Nos. 1645/6) and six labels showing Singapore merlion and flower, sold for $8 each.

A miniature sheet containing Nos. 1641/6 was sold at $5.10. The "1st Local" and 70c. stamps from this miniature sheet have the face value and country inscription in gold foil, and the $2 stamp has the country inscription in gold foil.

(Des I. Fantini and Design Business Pte. Ltd. Litho Secura, Singapore)

2006 (12 Oct). 25th Anniv of Diplomatic Relations between Singapore and Vatican City. T **334** and similar vert design. Multicoloured. P 13½.

1647	50c. Type **334**	1·00	45
1648	$2 Flags of Singapore and Vatican City	3·00	3·25
MS1649	123×75 mm. Nos. 1647/8. P 13	4·00	4·00

335 Common Palm Civet

336 Pig

(Des Leo Teck Chong. Litho SEP Sprint, Australia)

2006 (31 Oct). "Fun with Nature" (children's nature education programme). T **335** and similar horiz designs. Multicoloured. Two phosphor bands. (a) P 13×13½.

1650	(23c.) Type **335**	50	50
	a. Block of 4. Nos. 1650/3	4·00	4·50
1651	(23c.) Common flying dragon	50	50
1652	$1 Black-spotted sticky frog	1·75	2·00
1653	$1 Common tiger butterfly	1·75	2·00
1650/3	*Set of* 4	4·00	4·50

(b) Self-adhesive. Die-cut perf 11×11½.

1654	(23c.) Type **335**	40	40
	a. Booklet pane. Nos. 1654/5, each ×5	3·50	
1655	(23c.) As No. 1651	40	40

Nos. 1650/1 and 1654/5 were inscribed "1st Local" and initially sold for 23c. each.

Nos. 1650/3 were printed together, *se-tenant*, as blocks of four stamps in sheets of 32, each block forming a composite background design.

Nos. 1654/5 were only available in $2.30 booklets, No. SB56.

2006 (16 Nov). Belgica 2006 International Stamp Exhibition, Brussels. Sheet 123×75 mm. Multicoloured. Two phosphor bands. P 13×13½.

MS1656	(23c.) Type **321**; $2 Two dogs	2·50	2·75

(Des Nicodemus Loh. Litho Secura, Singapore)

2007 (19 Jan). Chinese New Year ("Year of the Boar"). T **336** and similar vert designs. Multicoloured. P 13½.

1657	(25c.) Type **336**	25	20
	a. Perf 13	50	75
	ab. Pair. Nos. 1657a/8a	2·75	3·25
1658	$2 Two pigs	2·25	2·50
	a. Perf 13	2·25	2·50

No. 1657 is inscribed "1ST LOCAL" and was sold for 25c.

Nos. 1657/8 were each printed in separate sheets of 50 stamps.

Nos. 1657a/8a were printed together, *se-tenant* both horizontally and vertically, in sheets of 18 (6×3).

A collectors sheet containing designs as Nos. 826/7, 861/2, 914/15, 978/9, 1024/5, 1082/3, 1143, 1145, 1262/3, 1357/8, 1449/50, 1573/4 and 1657/8 was issued on the same date and sold for $38. All the stamps within the collectors sheet have the "SINGAPORE" inscription and merlion symbol embossed in gold and are perforated 13. Designs as Nos. 826, 861, 914, 978, 1024, 1082, 1143, 1262 and 1357 are inscribed ""1st Local"" instead of "FOR LOCAL ADDRESSES ONLY".

337 Family with Bicycle and Children holding Hands

338 Korean Wedding Costumes

(Des Haryana Jaafar. Litho SEP Sprint, Australia)

2007 (8 Feb). 10th Anniv of Singapore Kindness Movement. T **337** and similar multicoloured designs showing winning Singapore entries for ASEAN–Japan children's competition. Two phosphor bands. (a) PVA gum. P 13½×13 (horiz) or 13×13½ (vert).

1659	(25c.) Type **337**	30	30
1660	(25c.) Girl catching falling girl (horiz)	30	30
1661	(25c.) Distribution of Red Cross parcels (horiz)	30	30
1662	(25c.) Four people sharing umbrella (horiz)	30	30
1663	(25c.) Children visiting the elderly (horiz)	30	30
1664	(25c.) Boy opening door for woman	30	30
1665	(25c.) People on bus (horiz)	30	30
1666	(25c.) Woman and boy (horiz)	30	30

1667	(25c.) Sighted person helping blind man (horiz)	30	30
1668	(25c.) Zebra crossing (horiz)	30	30
1659/68	*Set of* 10	2·75	2·75

(b) Self-adhesive. P 10½×10 (horiz) or 10×10½ (vert)

1669	(25c.) Type **337**	30	30
	a. Booklet pane. Nos. 1669/78	2·75	
1670	(25c.) As No. 1664	30	30
1671	(25c.) As No. 1660	30	30
1672	(25c.) As No. 1668	30	30
1673	(25c.) As No. 1666	30	30
1674	(25c.) As No. 1663	30	30
1675	(25c.) As No. 1662	30	30
1676	(25c.) As No. 1661	30	30
1677	(25c.) As No. 1667	30	30
1678	(25c.) As No. 1665	30	30
1669/78	*Set of* 10	2·75	2·75

Nos. 1659/78 are all inscribed "1ST LOCAL" and were initially sold for 25c. each.

Nos. 1659/68 were printed together, *se-tenant*, in sheetlets of ten. The two vert designs, Nos. 1659 and 1664, were laid horizontally within the sheetlet.

Nos. 1669/78 were only available in booklets of ten stamps, No. SB57, initially sold for $2.50.

(Des Prof. Yun Yeo-whan and Sylvia Tan. Litho Secura)

2007 (30 Mar). Traditional Wedding Costumes. T **338** and similar vert designs. Multicoloured. P 13½.

1679	(25c.) Type **338**	45	50
	a. Sheetlet. Nos. 1679/86, each ×2	12·00	14·00
1680	(25c.) Korean (man in dark grey)	45	50
1681	65c. Chinese	80	90
1682	65c. Indian	80	90
1683	65c. Malay	80	90
1684	65c. Eurasian	80	90
1685	$1.10 Korean (man in dark blue)	1·25	1·50
1686	$1.10 Korean (man in white)	1·25	1·50
1679/86	*Set of* 8	6·00	7·00
MS1687	170×95 mm. Nos. 1679/86. P 13	5·50	5·75

Nos. 1679/86 were printed together, *se-tenant*, in sheetlets of 16 stamps containing two of each design. Stamps in similar designs were issued by Korea.

339 Chinese Dances

(Des Tze Ngan. Litho Southern Colour Print, New Zealand)

2007 (16 May). Cultural Dances. T **339** and similar horiz designs. Multicoloured. Phosphorised paper. P 15.

1688	(25c.) Type **339**	40	30
1689	(31c.) Indian classical dancer	50	40
1690	$1.10 Eurasian and Western dances	1·25	1·25
1691	$2 Malay dances	2·25	2·50
1688/91	*Set of* 4	4·00	4·00

No. 1688 is inscribed "1ST LOCAL" and was initially sold for 25c.
No. 1689 is inscribed "2ND LOCAL" and was initially sold for 31c.

340 Crimson Sunbird

(Des Wong Wui Kong. Litho Southern Colour Print, New Zealand)

2007 (6 June)–**09**. Flora and Fauna. T **340** and similar horiz designs. Multicoloured. (a) PVA gum. Phosphorised paper. P 14 (5c. to 80c.) or 15×14½ ($1.10, $2, $5, $10).

1692	5c. Type **340**	10	10
1693	20c. Yellow-rumped flycatcher	25	15
1694	(25c.) Frangipani (30×27 mm)	25	20
1694*a*	(26c.) Blue pea vine (30×27 mm) (6.5.09)	25	20
1694*b*	(26c.) Pigeon orchid (30×27 mm) (6.5.09)	25	20
1695	30c. Blue-throated bee-eater	35	25
1696	(31c.) Torch ginger (30×27 mm)	35	25
1697	45c. Yellow wagtail	55	40
1698	50c. Stork-billed kingfisher	65	45
1699	55c. Blue-crowned hanging parrot	70	45
1700	65c. Common goldenback (woodpecker)	90	60
1701	80c. Jambu fruit dove	1·00	70
1702	$1.10 Large Indian civet (49×29 mm)	1·25	1·25
1703	$2 Banded leaf monkey (49×29 mm)	2·50	2·50
1704	$5 Malayan pangolin (49×29 mm)	4·75	4·75
1705	$10 Cream-coloured giant squirrel (49×29 mm)	8·75	8·75
1692/705	*Set of* 16	20·00	19·00

(b) Self-adhesive. Irregular phosphor frame. P 9½×10

1706	(25c.) As No 1694	30	30
	a. Booklet pane. No. 1706×10	2·75	
1706*b*	(26c.) As No. 1694*a* (6.5.09)	40	40
	ba. Booklet pane. No. 1706*b*×10	3·75	
1706*c*	(26c.) As No. 1694*b* (6.5.09)	40	40
	ca. Booklet pane. No. 1706*c*×10	3·75	

Nos. 1694/*b* and 1706/*c* are all inscribed "1st Local". Nos. 1694 and 1706 were initially sold for 25c., and Nos. 1694a/b and 1706b/c for 26c. No. 1696 is inscribed "2ND LOCAL" and was initially sold for 31c.

No. 1706 was issued in sheets of 20 and in booklets of 10, No. SB58, initially sold for $2.50.

Nos. 1706*b*/*c* were issued in separate booklets of ten (Nos. SB62/3), sold for $2.55. They were also issued in sheetlets of 20, containing two panes of ten of each design, separated by a line of rouletting.

A collectors sheet containing Nos. 1692/4 and 1695/705 was issued on 6 June 2007 and sold for $38.

A collectors sheet containing a $5 pigeon orchid stamp with embroidery flowers was issued on 6 May 2009. It was sold in a folder for $8. Imprint dates: Nos. 1692/706 were originally issued on 6 June 2007 with "2007A" imprint date. They were re-issued as follows: "2007B"—No. 1706 (from booklets) 11.7.07; Nos. 1693, 1696/701, 1706 (from sheetlets) 25.7.07; Nos. 1704/5 2.8.07; Nos. 1692, 1702 23.1.08; No. 1695 22.5.09. "2007C"—Nos. 1693, 1696, 1698, 1700/1, 1705, 1706 (from sheetlets and booklets) 23.1.08; Nos. 1697, 1704 25.3.08; No. 1692 28.11.08; No. 1702 22.5.09. "2007D"—No. 1706 (sheetlets and booklets) 25.3.08; Nos. 1693, 1697 23.1.09; No. 1700 22.5.09; No. 1696 7.7.09. "2007E"—No. 1706 (from booklets) 28.11.08.

NOTE: The Singapore "1st Local" postage rate was increased to from 25c. to 26c. from 1 July 2007. Sheets and booklets of ten "1st Local" are currently sold for $2.55, a discount of 10c. off the face value.

341 Singapore Men taking Oath of Allegiance

(Des Design Objectives. Litho Southern Colour Print, New Zealand)

2007 (2 July). 40 Years of National Service. T **341** and similar horiz designs. Multicoloured. P 14½×14.

1707	(26c.) Type **341**	30	20
1708	(32c.) Basic military training exercises	35	25
1709	$1.10 Drill and regimentation	1·40	1·25
1710	$2 Operational training with rifles	2·75	3·00
1707/10	*Set of* 4	4·25	4·25

Nos. 1707 is inscr "1st Local" and was initially sold for 26c.
No. 1708 is inscr "2nd local" and was initially sold for 32c.

2007 (3 Aug). Bangkok 2007 20th Asian International Stamp Exhibition. Sheet 123×75 mm. Multicoloured. Ordinary paper. P 13.

MS1711	(26c.) Type **336**; $2 Two pigs	2·75	2·75

342 Secretariat Building, Brunei

(Des Blue Apples Consultancy. Litho Secura)

2007 (8 Aug). 40th Anniv of ASEAN (Association of South-east Asian Nations). Ancient and Modern Architecture. T **342** and similar horiz designs. Multicoloured. P 13½.

1712	(26c.) Type **342**	45	45
	a. Sheetlet. Nos. 1712/21	4·00	4·00
1713	(26c.) National Museum of Cambodia	45	45
1714	(26c.) Fatahillah Museum, Jakarta, Indonesia	45	45
1715	(26c.) Lao Typical House	45	45
1716	(26c.) Malayan Railway Headquarters Building, Kuala Lumpur, Malaysia	45	45
1717	(26c.) Yangon Post Office, Myanmar	45	45
1718	(26c.) Malacañang Palace, Philippines	45	45

1719	(26c.) National Museum of Singapore	45	45
1720	(26c.) Vimanmek Mansion, Bangkok, Thailand	45	45
1721	(26c.) Presidential Palace, Hanoi, Vietnam	45	45
1712/21	*Set of* 10	4·00	4·00

Nos. 1712/21 are all inscribed "1st Local". They were printed together, *se-tenant*, in sheetlets of ten stamps, sold for $2.55 per sheet, a discount of 10c. off the face value of the stamps. Similar designs were issued on the same day by the ten member countries, Indonesia, Malaysia, Philippines, Thailand, Brunei, Vietnam, Laos, Myanmar and Cambodia.

343 Chinatown

(Des Ong Kim Seng and Sylvia Tan. Litho (**MS**1726 also embossed) Secura)

2007 (9 Aug). National Day. Tourist Landmarks. T **343** and similar multicoloured designs. P 12½.

1722	(26c.) Type **343**	35	25
1723	65c. Kampong glam	80	70
1724	80c. Little India	90	90
1725	$1.10 Orchard Road	1·40	1·60
1722/5	*Set of* 4	3·00	3·00
MS1726	122×80 mm. $5 Merlion statue at Marina Bay (vert)	5·50	6·00

No. 1722 is inscr "1st Local" and was sold for 26c.

344 National Cadet Corps

345 False Clown Anemone Fish and Sea Anemone (*Stichodactyla* sp.)

(Des Eric Kong. Litho SEP Sprint, Australia)

2007 (19 Sept). Uniformed Groups in Schools. T **344** and similar vert designs. Multicoloured. Two phosphor bands. P 13½×13.

1727	(32c.) Type **344**	45	45
1728	(32c.) The Singapore Scout Association	45	45
1729	(32c.) Girl Guides Singapore	45	45
1730	(32c.) The Girls' Brigade Singapore	45	45
1731	(32c.) The Boys' Brigade in Singapore	45	45
1732	(32c.) St. John Ambulance Brigade Singapore.	45	45
1733	(32c.) Red Cross Youth	45	45
1734	(32c.) National Police Cadet Corps	45	45
1735	(32c.) National Civil Defence Cadet Corps	45	45
1727/35	*Set of* 9	3·50	3·50

Nos. 1727/35 were inscr "2nd Local" and sold for 32c. each.

(Des Eng Siak Loy. Litho SEP Sprint, Australia)

2007 (17 Oct). Shores and Reefs. T **345** and similar horiz designs. Multicoloured. Two phosphor bands. (a) P 13×13½.

1736	(26c.) Type **345**	50	50
	a. Block of 4. Nos. 1736/9	4·25	5·00
1737	(26c.) Singapore goby and blind shrimp (*Alpheus* sp)	50	50
1738	$1.10 Hawksbill turtle and remora (*Echeneis naucrates*)	1·90	2·25
1739	$1.10 Razorfish (*Acoliscus strigatus*) and sea urchin (*Diadema* sp)	1·90	2·25
1736/9	*Set of* 4	4·25	5·00

(b) Self-adhesive. P 11×11½.

1740	(26c.) As Type **345**	50	50
	a. Booklet pane. Nos. 1740/1, each ×5	4·50	
1741	(26c.) As No. 1737	50	50

Nos. 1736/9 were printed together, *se-tenant*, as blocks of four stamps in sheets of 20, each block forming a composite background design.

Nos. 1736/7 were inscr "1st Local" and sold for 26c. each.

Nos. 1740/1 were inscr "1st Local" and were only available in booklets of ten stamps, No. SB59, initially sold for $2.55, a discount of 10c. off the face value of the stamps.

346 Profile ("Libraries Spark Imagination")

347 Roof of Terminal 3 with Skylights and Reflector Panels

(Des Jin Li Juan. Litho Beijing Stamp Printing House)

2007 (12 Nov). National Library Board "L2010" Five Year Plan. T **346** and similar horiz designs. Multicoloured. Two phosphor bands. P 13×13½.

1742	(26c.) Type **346**	40	30
1743	80c. Couple dancing ("Libraries Bring Knowledge Alive")	1·10	85
1744	$1.10 Students using computer ("Libraries Create Possibility")	1·60	1·25
1745	$2 Montage of profiles ("Libraries for Life Knowledge for Success")	3·00	3·50
1742/5	*Set of* 4	5·50	5·50

No. 1742 was inscribed "1ST LOCAL" and sold for 26c.

(Des Lew Yen Wei. Litho Southern Colour Print, New Zealand)

2008 (9 Jan). Opening of Terminal 3 at Singapore Changi Airport. T **347** and similar vert designs. Multicoloured. Phosphorised paper. P 14.

1746	(26c.) Type **347**	45	30
1747	65c. Singapore Airlines Airbus A380	1·00	70
1748	$1.10 Palm trees and "Green Wall" vertical garden inside Terminal 3	1·60	1·40
1749	$2 Terminal 3 and Control Tower	3·00	3·50
1746/9	*Set of* 4	5·50	5·50

No. 1746 was inscr "1st Local" and sold for 26c.

348 Rat

349 Chinese New Year

(Des Leo Teck Chong. Litho Southern Colour Print, New Zealand)

2008 (18 Jan). Chinese New Year ("Year of the Rat"). T **348** and similar horiz designs. Multicoloured. (a) PVA gum. Phosphorised paper. P 14½ ($1.10) or 14 (others).

1750	(26c.) Type **348**	40	30
1751	65c. Rat and orange	75	60
1752	$1.10 Two rats (44×34 mm)	1·50	1·75
1750/2	*Set of* 3	2·40	2·40

(b) Self-adhesive. One phosphor band. P 10

1753	(26c.) As Type **348**	30	30

Nos. 1750 and 1753 were inscr "1st Local" and sold for 26c. each.

A collectors sheet containing $5 and $10 stamps in designs as Nos. 1750/1 was issued on the same date and sold in a folder for $16.80. This sheet was printed by Cartor and the stamps within it had silver foil holograms of a pig ($5 stamp) and an ox ($10 stamp).

(Des Neo Lay See. Litho SEP Sprint, Australia)

2008 (29 Feb). Festivals. T **349** and similar horiz designs. Multicoloured. Two phosphor bands. P 14×14½. (a) PVA gum.

1754	(26c.) Type **349**	40	40
1755	(26c.) Christmas (Mary, shepherds and sheep)	40	40
1756	(26c.) Deepavali (people celebrating, fireworks and elephants)	40	40
1757	(26c.) Hari Raya Aidilfitri (women carrying food and lighted lamp)	40	40
1758	(32c.) Easter	45	45
1759	(32c.) Hari Raya Haji	45	45
1760	(32c.) Chinese Mid-Autumn Festival	45	45
1761	(32c.) Pongal	45	45
1762	55c. Chinese New Year (children carrying hong baos)	65	65
1763	55c. Christmas (flying Santas and reindeer)	65	65
1764	55c. Deepavali (people carrying oil lamps and peacocks)	65	65
1765	55c. Hari Raya Aidilfitri (couple, girl kneeling and boy receiving gift)	65	65
1754/65	*Set of* 12	5·50	5·50

(b) Self-adhesive

1766	(26c.) As Type **349**	45	50
1767	(26c.) As No. 1755	45	50
1768	(26c.) As No. 1756	45	50
1769	(26c.) As No. 1757	45	50
1766/9	*Set of 4*	1·60	1·75

Nos. 1754/7 and 1766/9 are inscr "1ST LOCAL" and sold for 26c. each.
Nos. 1758/61 are inscr "2nd LOCAL" and sold for 32c. each.

2008 (7 Mar). Taipei 2008 21st Asian International Stamp Exhibition. Sheet 160×80 mm containing Nos. 1750/2. Phosphorised paper. P 14½ ($1.10) or 13½ (others).

MS1770	(26c.) Type **348**; 65c. Rat and orange; $1.10 Two rats (44×24 mm)	2·40	2·75

350 Porcelain Plate

(Des Nicodemus Loh. Litho Cartor)

2008 (8 Apr). Peranakan Museum Collection. T **350** and similar horiz designs showing Peranakan embroidery, beadwork and porcelain. Multicoloured. Phosphorised paper. P 13×13½.

1771	(26c.) Type **350**	40	40
	a. Horiz pair. Nos. 1771/2	80	80
1772	(26c.) Bird design	40	40
1773	(32c.) Dragon embroidery	50	50
	a. Horiz pair. Nos. 1773/4	1·00	1·00
1774	(32c.) Peony embroidery	50	50
1775	65c. Phoenix and flowers design from vase	90	1·00
	a. Horiz pair. Nos. 1775/6	1·75	2·00
1776	65c. Flying phoenix design from vase	90	1·00
1777	$1.10 Crane design from plate	1·40	1·75
	a. Horiz pair. Nos. 1777/8	2·75	3·50
1778	$1.10 Poppy design porcelain	1·40	1·75
1771/8	*Set of 8*	5·75	6·50

Nos. 1771/2, 1773/4, 1775/6 and 1777/8 were each printed together, *se-tenant*, as horizontal pairs in sheetlets of 10.

Nos. 1771/2 are inscr "1st Local" and sold for 26c. each.

Nos. 1773/4 are inscr "2nd Local" and sold for 32c. each.

A collectors sheet cut in the shape of a wedding purse containing a $5 stamp with a beaded surface was issued on the same date. This sheet was sold in a folder for $8.

351 Crowd celebrating

(Des Tze Ngan. Litho Secura)

2008 (25 June). Youth Olympic Games, Singapore, 2010. T **351** and similar horiz design. Multicoloured. P 13.

1779	(26c.) Type **351**	40	40
	a. Horiz pair. Nos. 1779/80	2·75	3·00
1780	$2 Crowd with flag, schoolchildren and Supreme Court building	2·40	2·75

Nos. 1779/80 were printed together, *se-tenant*, as horizontal pairs in sheetlets of ten, each pair forming a composite design showing a crowd celebrating the announcement that Singapore had been selected as host city.

No. 1779 is inscr "1st Local" and sold for 26c.

352 Carne de porco à Alentejana (pork and clams)

(Des Thomas Au Man Hou and Carlos Goncalves. Litho Enschedé)

2008 (4 July). "Local Delights". Dishes of Singapore and Macao. T **352** and similar multicoloured designs. One side phosphor band. P 14×13½.

1781	(26c.) Type **352**	45	45
	a. Block of 4. Nos. 1781/4	1·60	1·60
1782	(26c.) Lombo de bacalhau braseado em lascas (grilled codfish slices)	45	45
1783	(26c.) Yangzhou fried rice	45	45
1784	(26c.) Crispy fried chicken	45	45
1785	65c. Roti Prata	80	80
	a. Block of 4. Nos. 1785/8	3·00	3·00
1786	65c. Hainanese chicken rice	80	80
1787	65c. Laksa	80	80
1788	65c. Satay	80	80
1781/8	*Set of 8*	4·50	4·50
MS1789	140×90 mm. $2×2 Clay pot rice (vert); Chilli crab (vert). P 13½×14	5·00	5·00

Nos. 1781/4 and 1785/8 were each printed together, *se-tenant*, as blocks of four stamps in sheets of 16, each block forming a composite design of a dish.

Nos. 1781/4 are inscr "1ST LOCAL" and sold for 26c. each.

Stamps in similar designs were issued by Macau.

353 Table Tennis

(Des Teoh Kareen. Litho Secura)

2008 (8 Aug). Olympic Games, Beijing. T **353** and similar horiz designs. Multicoloured. Ordinary paper. P 13.

1790	(26c.) Type **253**	35	35
1791	(32c.) Sailing	40	40
1792	$1.10 Shooting	1·50	1·50
1793	$1.10 Badminton	1·50	1·50
1790/3	*Set of 4*	3·75	3·75

No. 1790 is inscr "1ST LOCAL" and sold for 26c.

No. 1791 is inscr "2ND LOCAL" and sold for 32c.

2008 (8 Aug). Olympex Olympic Stamp Expo, Beijing. Sheet 160×80 mm containing Nos. 1750/2. Phosphorised paper. P 14½ ($1.10) or 13½ (others).

MS1794	(26c.) Type **348**; 65c. Rat and orange; $1.10 Two rats (44×24 mm)	2·75	2·75

354 Parliament House (David Tay Poey Cher)

355 Pilots, Fighter Plane and Helicopter

(Des Willie Chan. Litho Southern Colour Print, New Zealand)

2008 (9 Aug). National Day. "Singapore Today". T **354** and similar square designs showing photographs by Cultural Medallion winning photographers. Multicoloured. Phosphorised paper. P 14½.

1795	(26c.) Type **354**	50	50
1796	(26c.) Tampines North Community Centre (Foo Tee Jun)	50	50
1797	(26c.) Metal sculptures and high-rise buildings of financial sector (Chua Soo Bin)	50	50
1798	(26c.) North Bridge and financial sector (Teo Bee Yen)	50	50
1799	(26c.) People in Temple Street (Si Ma Lu Guanyin) (Tan Lip Seng)	50	50
1800	50c. People at Orchard MRT Station (David Tay Poey Cher)	75	75
1801	50c. Train at Orchard MRT Station (Foo Tee Jun)	75	75
1802	50c. Glass-fronted and other high-rise buildings (Chua Soo Bin)	75	75
1803	50c. Temple within Central Business District (Teo Bee Yen)	75	75
1804	50c. Fish stall at Tekka Market (Tan Lip Seng)	75	75
1795/804	*Set of 10*	5·75	5·75

MS1805	75×75 mm. $2 Montage of photographs of Singapore buildings (60×60 mm)	2·75	2·75

Nos. 1795/9 were all inscr ""1st Local"" and sold for 26c. each.

(Des Sam Hong. Litho Southern Colour Print, New Zealand)

2008 (28 Aug). 40th Anniv of the Republic of Singapore Air Force (RSAF). T **355** and similar horiz designs. Multicoloured. Phosphorised paper. P 14.

1806	(26c.) Type **355**	60	35
1807	(32c.) Weapon Systems Officers monitoring aircraft in Singapore airspace	70	60
1808	65c. Unmanned Aerial Vehicle and pilot (on ground)	1·00	75
1809	80c. Senior Technicians and helicopter	1·50	1·40
1810	$1.10 Weapon Systems Officers and Air Defence Artillery	1·75	2·00
1806/10	*Set of* 5	5·00	4·50

No. 1806 is inscr "1st Local" and sold for 26c.
No. 1807 is inscr "2nd Local" and sold for 32c.

356 Racing Car and City of Singapore

(Des Alynn Teo. Litho Secura)

2008 (26 Sept). First Formula 1 Singapore Grand Prix. T **356** and similar horiz design. Multicoloured. Ordinary paper. P 13½.

1811	$2 Type **356**	2·00	2·25
	a. Horiz pair. Nos. 1811/12	4·00	4·50
1812	$2 Racing car and chequered flag	2·00	2·25

Nos. 1811/12 were each printed together, *se-tenant*, as horizontal pairs in sheets of ten, each pair forming a composite background design.

2008 (23 Oct). Jakarta 2008 International Stamp Exhibition, Jakarta, Indonesia. Sheet 160×80 mm containing Nos. 1750/2. Phosphorised paper. P 14½ ($1.10) or 13½ (others).

MS1813	(26c.) Type **348**; 65c. Rat and orange; $1.10 Two rats (44×24 mm)	3·00	3·25

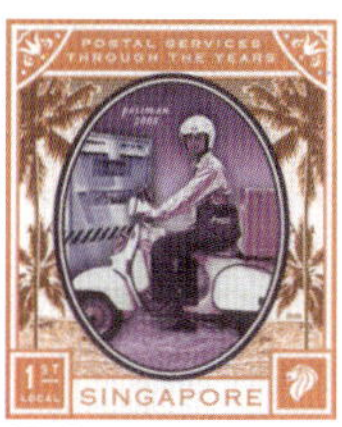

357 Postman, 2008

358 Pepper (*Piper nigrum*)

(Des Sylvia S. H. Tan. Litho Secura)

2008 (29 Oct). Postal Services through the Years. T **357** and similar vert designs. Multicoloured. Ordinary paper. P 13×13½.

1814	(26c.) Type **357**	40	25
1815	(32c.) Postman with motor scooter, c. 1980	55	35
1816	50c. Postman with bicycle, c. 1970	1·25	90
1817	80c. Postman and pillar box, c. 1950	1·40	1·25
1818	$1.10 Postman, c. 1910	1·50	1·75
1814/18	*Set of* 5	4·50	4·00

No. 1814 is inscr "1ST LOCAL" and sold for 26c.
No. 1815 is inscr "2ND LOCAL" and sold for 32c.

(Des Leo Teck Chong. Litho Southern Colour Print, New Zealand)

2008 (12 Nov). Cash Crops of Early Singapore. T **358** and similar vert designs. Multicoloured.

(a) PVA gum. Phosphorised paper. P 13½.

1819	(26c.) Type **358**	55	30
1820	65c. Tapioca (*Manihot esculenta*)	1·25	95
1821	$1.10 Rubber (*Hevea brasiliensis*)	1·75	1·75
1822	$2 Nutmeg (*Myristica fragrans*)	2·75	3·50
1819/22	*Set of* 4	5·75	6·00

(b) Self-adhesive. One side phosphor band. P 10×9½.

1823	(26c.) As Type **358**	40	40
	a. Booklet pane. No. 1823×10	3·75	

No. 1819 and 1823 were inscr "1ST LOCAL" and valid for 26c. each.
No. 1823 was only available in booklets of ten stamps initially sold for $2.55, a discount of 5c. off the face value of the stamps.

359 Dragon Fruit

360 Ox

(Des Nguyen Du (65c.) or Tze Ngan ($1.10). Litho Secura)

2008 (18 Nov). Fruits. T **359** and similar square design. Multicoloured. P 13½.

1824	65c. Type **359**	1·25	1·25
1825	$1.10 Durian	1·75	1·75
MS1826	135×94 mm. Nos. 1824/5	3·00	3·25

Stamps in similar designs were issued by Vietnam.

(Des Leo Teck Chong. Litho Beijing Stamp Printing House)

2009 (9 Jan). Chinese New Year. Year of the Ox. T **360** and similar multicoloured designs. Two phosphor bands.

(a) Ordinary gum. P 13

1827	(26c.) Type **360**	55	35
1828	65c. Ox (facing left)	1·25	1·10
1829	$1.10 Two oxen (34×44 mm)	1·75	2·25
1827/9	*Set of* 3	3·25	3·25

(b) Self-adhesive. Die-cut perf 12

1830	(26c.) Type **360**	45	45

Nos. 1827 and 1830 were inscr "1ST LOCAL" and initially sold for 26c. each.

A collectors sheet containing $5 and $10 stamps in designs as Nos. 1827/8 was issued on the same date and sold in a folder for $16.80. This sheet was printed by Cartor and the stamps within it had silver foil holograms of Chinese letters.

361 Couple's Faces in Champagne Glass

362 Cathay, 1939

(Des Wong Wui Kong. Litho Australia Print Sprintpak)

2009 (11 Feb). Greetings Stamps. "Let's Celebrate". T **361** and similar square designs. Multicoloured.

(a) Ordinary gum. Phosphor background. P 14×14½.

1831	(26c.) Type **361**	45	50
	a. Horiz strip of 5. Nos. 1831/5	2·00	2·25
1832	(26c.) Girl and birthday candles	45	50
1833	(26c.) Couple	45	50
1834	(26c.) Girl with teddy bear and wrapped presents	45	50
1835	(26c.) Boy holding red balloons	45	50
1831/5	*Set of* 5	2·00	2·25

(b) Self-adhesive. Irregular phosphor frames. Die-cut perf 11×10

1836	(26c.) As No. 1831	40	45
	a. Booklet pane. Nos. 1836/40, each ×2	3·50	
1837	(26c.) As No. 1832	40	45
1838	(26c.) As No. 1833	40	45
1839	(26c.) As No. 1834	40	45
1840	(26c.) As Type **361**	40	45
1836/40	*Set of* 5	1·75	2·00

Nos. 1831/40 were all inscribed "1ST LOCAL" and originally sold for 26c. each.

Nos. 1831/5 were printed as horizontal strips of five stamps in sheetlets of ten.

Nos. 1836/40 were issued in booklets of ten stamps, initially sold for $2.55, a discount of 5c. off the face value of the stamps.

(Des Design Objectives Pte Ltd. Litho Southern Colour Print, New Zealand)

2009 (20 Mar). Cinema Theatres of Yesteryear. T **362** and similar vert designs. Multicoloured. P 14.

1841	(26c.) Type **362**	45	25
1842	50c. The Majestic, 1928	75	60
1843	80c. Capitol Building, 1933	1·25	85
1844	$1.10 Queens, c.1920	1·75	2·00
1845	$1.10 Rex, 1946	1·75	2·00
1841/5	*Set of* 5	5·50	5·25

No. 1841 was inscribed "1st Local" and originally sold for 26c.

2009 (10 Apr). China 2009 World Stamp Exhibition, Luoyang, China. Sheet 120×75 mm containing Nos. 1827/9. Two phosphor bands. P 13½.

MS1846	(26c.) Type **360**; 65c. Ox (facing left); $1.10 Two oxen (34×44 mm)	3·00	3·25

2009 (14 May). Hong Kong 2009 International Stamp Exhibition. Sheet 120×75 mm containing Nos. 1827/9. Two phosphor bands. P 13.

MS1847	(26c.) Type **360**; 65c. Ox (facing left); $1.10 Two oxen (34×44 mm)	3·00	3·25

363 Map of Circle Line System on Singapore Map

364 Visitor Centre

(Des SMRT Corporation Ltd. Litho Secura)

2009 (28 May). Launch of SMRT Circle Line. T **363** and similar circular designs. Multicoloured. Ordinary paper. P 13.

1848	(26c.) Type **363**	60	30
1849	80c. New Circle Line station	1·40	1·10
1850	$1.10 Circle Line train	1·75	1·60
1851	$2 Circle Line Operation Control Centre	3·50	4·00
1848/51	*Set of 4*	6·50	6·25

No. 1848 was inscr "1st Local" and originally sold for 26c.

Nos. 1848/51 were each perforated in a circle contained within an outer perforated square.

(Des Eng Siak Loy. Litho Southern Colour Print, New Zealand)

2009 (19 June). 150th Anniv of Singapore Botanic Gardens. T **364** and similar multicoloured designs. Phosphorised paper. P 14.

1852	(26c.) Type **364**	50	50
	a. Horiz strip of 4. Nos. 1852/5	4·00	4·50
1853	(26c.) Rain tree and Band Stand	50	50
1854	$1.10 Orchids, girl on a swing sculpture and pavilion	1·75	2·00
1855	$1.10 Flying swans and heliconias at Swan Lake	1·75	2·00
1852/5	*Set of 4*	4·00	4·50
MS1856	113×80 mm. $2 Black swans (47×47 mm). P 15×14½	3·50	3·50

Nos. 1852/5 were printed together, *se-tenant*, as horizontal strips of four stamps in sheets of 20, each strip forming a composite design.

365 Ice Kacang (shaved ice with red beans)

366 "Standing Figure" (Wee Beng Chong)

(Des Brainwave Design. Litho Secura)

2009 (17 July). Local Desserts. T **365** and similar vert designs. Multicoloured. P 12½.

1857	(26c.) Type **365**	35	35
1858	(32c.) Ondeh-ondeh (dough filled with palm sugar)	45	45
1859	65c. Ang ku kueh (rice flour cake with bean paste or peanut paste filling)	90	90
1860	80c. Lapis sagu (tapioca layer cake)	1·10	1·10
1861	$1.10 Mithai (assorted Indian sweets)	1·50	1·50
1857/61	*Set of 5*	4·25	4·25

No. 1857 was inscr "1ST LOCAL" and originally sold for 26c.

No. 1858 was inscr "2ND LOCAL" and originally sold for 32c.

(Des Willie Chan. Litho Southern Colour Print, New Zealand)

2009 (9 Aug). National Day. Sculptures. T **366** and similar multicoloured designs. P 13×13½ (1862/8) or 14½×14 (**MS**1869).

1862	50c. Type **366**	75	75
1863	50c. "We're Happy. Are You Happy" (Teo Eng Seng)	75	75
1864	50c. "Art Trees" (Han Sai Por)	75	75
1865	50c. "Aspirations" (Anthony Poon)	75	75
1866	50c. "Nude 2" (Tay Chee Toh) (horiz)	75	75
1867	50c. "Signature" (Brother Joseph McNally) (horiz)	75	75
1868	50c. "Wealth" (Ng Eng Teng) (horiz)	75	75
1862/8	*Set of 7*	5·00	5·00
MS1869	113×80 mm. $2 Sculptures (as shown on Nos. 1862/8) (95×37 mm)	2·75	2·75

367 Gymnast ("Excellence")

(Des Leo Teck Chong. Litho Secura)

2009 (14 Aug). Youth Olympic Games, Singapore, 2010 (2nd issue). T **367** and similar horiz designs. Multicoloured. P 13.

1870	(26c.) Type **367**	35	35
1871	65c. Athlete greeting tennis player ("Hello")	90	90
1872	$1.10 Three athletes ("Friendship")	1·50	1·50
1873	$2 Hurdler ("Respect")	2·75	2·75
1870/3	*Set of 4*	5·50	5·50

No. 1870 was inscr "1st Local" and originally sold for 26c.

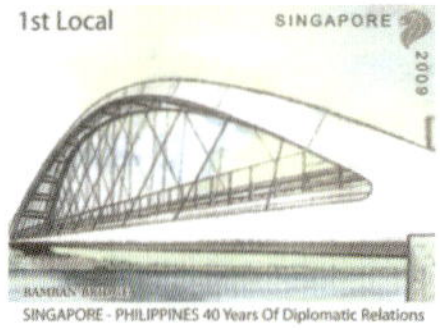

368 Bamban Bridge, Philippines

(Des Victorino Serevo and Willie Chan. Litho Secura)

2009 (28 Aug). 40th Anniv of Diplomatic Relations between Singapore and the Philippines. Bridges. T **368** and similar horiz designs. Multicoloured. P 12½.

1874	(26c.) Type **368**	35	35
1875	65c. Cavenagh Bridge, Singapore	95	95
1876	80c. Henderson Waves and Alexandra Arch, Singapore	1·10	1·10
1877	$1.10 Marcelo B. Fernan Bridge, Cebu, Philippines	1·60	1·60
1874/7	*Set of 4*	4·00	4·00
MS1878	120×75 mm. Nos. 1874/7	4·00	4·00

No. 1874 was inscr "1st Local" and originally sold for 26c.

MACHINE LABELS.

From 19 April 1988 self-adhesive labels in the above design, with the background printed in orange and grey were available from machines situated outside a number of Singapore post offices. Face values between 5c. and $2 could be selected and the location of individual machines is indicated by the code number, from 0001 to 0050, at bottom left.

The designs were changed to three lions' heads in red on 5 June 1989, to the Fullerton Building G.P.O. in brown on 8 September 1990, to haw Par Villa in red on 2 October 1991, to trishaws in brown on 1 December 1192 to the Singapore skyline in turquoise-green on 5 April 1994 and to orchids in red on 1 April 1995.

A new series, showing a family in a park, was introduced on 19 May 1997. These carry code numbers S001 to S094.

Vertical labels inscribed "SINGAPORE POSTAGE" with face values and, in some instances a weight, also exist. These were introduced in January 1983 and come from machines used by P. O. counter clerks to process parcels and registered mail. For a time, 1986–87, these labels were on self-adhesive paper.

A new series of encrypted postage labels was introduced from August 1998 onwards. These come from Pitney Bowes Meter Label Printers which produce white self-adhesive labels 57×40 mm showing a stamp outline enclosing the encrypted information.

STAMP BOOKLETS

1969 (1 Nov). Black on green cover. 69×76 mm. Stapled.
SB1 $1.80 booklet containing twelve 15c. (No. 106) in blocks of 4 .... 50·00

1973 (30 Sept)–**74**. Grey and black printed cover 75×45 mm. Opening hours of Philatelic Counter quoted on back cover as "8 A.M. to 9 P.M. daily". Pane attached by selvedge.
SB2 $1 booklet containing *se-tenant* pane of 10 (No. 213a) .... 12·00
a. Opening hours of Philatelic Counter quoted as "daily except Sundays and Public Holidays"..........

1974 (9 Apr). Blue printed cover 75×45 mm. Pane attached by selvedge.
SB3 $1 booklet containing *se-tenant* pane of 12 (No. 290a) .... 3·75

1980 (26 Apr). Green printed cover 75×45 mm . Stamps attached by selvedge.
SB4 $1 booklet containing 10c. (No. 366) in block of 10. 3·50

B **1** Full-rigged Sailing Ship

1990 (21 Mar). Lithographs of *19*th-century Singapore. Black printed cover as Type B **1**, 92×55 mm. Pane attached by selvedge.
SB5 $1.50 booklet containing pane of ten 15c. (No. 615a).. 10·00

B **2** Mouth of Singapore River

1990 (4 July). Tourism. Deep ultramarine, light greenish blue and light emerald printed cover as Type B **2** 95×69 mm. Pane attached by selvedge.
SB6 $1.50 booklet containing pane of ten 15c. (No. 625a).. 17·00

B **3** National Flag and "Singpex 90" National Stamp Exhibition Emblem

1990 (16 Aug). *25*th Anniv of Independence. Red. black and grey printed cover as Type B **3** 91×76 mm. Pane attached by selvedge.
SB7 $1.50 booklet containing pane of ten 15c. (No. 637ab) .... 12·00

1991 (6 Mar–30 Aug). Tourism. Deep ultramarine, light greenish blue and light emerald printed cover as Type B **2**. "PRODUCED BY SINGAPORE PHILATELIC BUREAU" on outside back cover. Pane attached by selvedge.
SB8 $2 booklet containing pane of ten 20c. (No. 626a).. 17·00
a. "PRODUCED BY SINGAPORE PHILATELIC BUREAU" on inside back cover (30 Aug)..........

B **4** "Mobil 1" Oil Can

1991 (15 May). Tourism. Multicoloured cover as Type B **4**. Pane attached by selvedge.
SB9 $2 booklet containing pane of ten 20c. (No. 626a).. 17·00

B **5** Kingfisher

1991 (19 Sept). Garden Birds. Multicoloured cover as Type B **5**, 95×57 mm. Pane attached by selvedge.
SB10 $2 booklet containing pane of ten 20c. (No. 663a).. 16·00

1991 (11 Nov). Tourism. Multicoloured cover. Pane attached by selvedge.
SB11 $2 booklet containing pane of ten 20c. (No. 626a).. 17·00

B **7** Swamp Forest Crab

1992 (21 Aug). Crabs. Multicoloured cover as Type B **7** 98×60 mm. Pane attached by selvedge.
SB12 $2 booklet containing pane of ten 20c. (No. 698a)... 10·00

B **8** Aspects of Singapore

1992 (1 Sept). Kuala Lumpur '92 International Stamp Exhibition. Multicoloured cover as Type B **8**. Pane attached by selvedge.
SB13 $2 booklet containing pane of ten 20c. (No. 626a).. 7·00

B **9** Children and Party Streamers

1993 (10 Feb). Greetings Stamps. Multicoloured cover as Type B **9**, 80×60 mm. Pane attached by selvedge.
SB14 $2 booklet containing pane of ten 20c. in five different designs (No. 710a) 5·50

B **10** Butterflies and Flowers

1993 (2 Aug). Butterflies. Multicoloured cover as Type B **10**, 93×65 mm. Pane attached by selvedge.
SB15 $2 containing pane of ten 20c. (No. 728a) 7·50

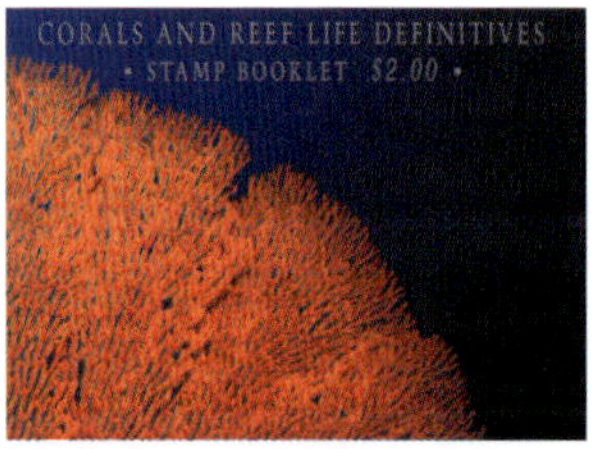

B **11** Sea-fan

1994 (12 Jan–20 May). Reef Life (*1*st series). Multicoloured cover as Type B **11**, 84×56 mm with black bands at top and bottom. Pane attached by selvedge.
SB16 $2 booklet containing pane of ten 20c. (No. 743a).. 8·00
a. Blue bands at top and bottom of cover (31 Mar) 9·50
ab. Revised cover showing silver inscr in three lines with the second and third lines aligned at right (20 May) 9·50

B **12** Grey Heron

1994 (16 Aug). Herons. Multicoloured cover as Type B **12**, 80×60 mm. Pane attached by selvedge.
SB17 $2 booklet containing pane of ten 20c. (No. 766b). 9·50

B **13** Greetings Messages

1994 (14 Sept). Greetings Stamps. Multicoloured cover as Type B **13**, 77×70 mm. Self-adhesive.
SB18 ($2) booklet containing pane of ten self-adhesive stamps (No. 775a) 5·00

The booklet cover, which forms the backing card for the stamps also incorporates 10 self-adhesive labels.

1994 (16 Nov). Reef Life (2nd series). Multicoloured cover as Type B **11**, 87×56 mm, showing Blue-spotted Stingray. Self-adhesive.
SB19 ($2) booklet containing pane of ten self-adhesive stamps (No. 785a) 4·00

B **14** Symbols of Love

1995 (8 Feb). Greetings Stamps. Multicoloured cover as Type B **14** 70×77 mm. Self-adhesive.
SB20 ($2.20) booklet containing pane of ten self-adhesive stamps (No. 790a) 8·00

The booklet cover, which forms the backing card for the stamps also incorporates 10 self-adhesive labels.

B **15** Exhibition Logo and Stamps (inscr "Discover the World through Stamps")

1995 (12 Apr). Singapore '95 International Stamp Exhibition. Multicoloured covers as Type B **15**. Self-adhesive.
SB21 ($2.20) booklet containing pane of ten self-adhesive stamps (No. 785ba) (Type B **15**) 7·00
SB22 ($2.20) booklet containing pane of ten self-adhesive stamps (No. 785ba) (vert design for "POSTECH 1995" Postal Equipment and Machinery Exhibition) (7 June) 7·00
SB23 ($2.20) booklet containing pane of ten self-adhesive stamps (No. 785ba) (horiz cover showing map and inscr "We've Got The Route to Real Excitement!" (5 July) 7·00

B **16** Yellow-faced Angelfish

1995 (19 July). Marine Fish. Multicoloured cover as Type B **16**. Pane attached by selvedge.

SB24 ($2.20) booklet containing ten 22c. stamps (No. 807)... 6·50

B **17** "6 DIGIT POSTAL CODE"

1995 (1 Sept). Introduction of Six Digit Postal Codes. Multicoloured cover as Type B **17**, 87×56 mm. Self-adhesive.

SB25 ($2.20) booklet containing pane of ten self-adhesive stamps (No. 785ba)........ 7·00

B **18** Smiling Flower

1996 (10 July). Greetings Stamps. "Courtesy". Children's Drawings. Multicoloured covers as Type B **18**, 77×70 mm. Self-adhesive.

SB26 ($2.20) booklet containing pane of ten self-adhesive stamps (No. 839a) (Type B **18**)........ 2·75

SB27 $3.90 booklet containing pane of ten self-adhesive stamps (No. 839b) (cover showing smiling flowers)........ 5·00

The booklet covers, which forms the backing card for the stamps also incorporate 10 self-adhesive labels.

B **19** *Cinnamomum iners*

1996 (11 Sept). Singapore Trees. Multicoloured cover as Type B **19**, 55×101 mm. Pane attached by selvedge.

SB28 ($2.20) booklet containing ten 22c. stamps (No. 850).... 4·25

B **20** Jinrickshaw

1997 (19 Mar). Transportation. Multicoloured cover as Type B **20**, 87×56 mm. Self-adhesive.

SB29 ($2.20) booklet containing pane of ten self-adhesive stamps (No. 884a)........ 2·00

B **21** Apple

1997 (14 May). Greetings stamps. "Friends". Multicoloured covers as Type B **21**, 56×87 mm. Self-adhesive.

SB30 ($2.20) booklet containing pane of ten self-adhesive stamps (No. 885a) (Type B **21** "friendship" in vermilion)........ 4·00

SB31 ($2.20) booklet containing pane of ten self-adhesive stamps (No. 890a) (as Type B **21**, but "friendship" in ultramarine)........ 4·00

The booklet covers, which form the backing cards for the stamps each incorporate 10 self-adhesive labels.

B **22** Flowers

1997 (13 Sept). 25th Anniv of the Ministry of the Environment. Multicoloured cover as Type B **22**, 96×60 mm. Pane attached by selvedge.

SB32 ($2.20) booklet containing pane of ten (22c.) (No. 904a)........ 2·00

B **23** "Nice meeting you, it's been a long time" in Bubble

1998 (20 May). Greetings Stamps. Multicoloured cover as Type B **23**, 70×78 mm. Self-adhesive.
SB33 ($2.20) booklet containing pane of ten self-adhesive stamps (No. 924a) .... 4·50
The booklet cover forms the backing card for the stamps and also incorporates 10 self-adhesive labels.

B **24** "Fragile Forest", Twig and Animal Tracks

1998 (5 June). 25th Anniv of Singapore Zoological Gardens and Launch of New "Fragile Forest" Display. Multicoloured covers as Type B **24**, 71×90 mm. Self-adhesive.
SB34 ($2.20) booklet containing pane of ten self-adhesive stamps (No. 929a) .... 4·50
SB35 ($2.20) booklet containing pane of ten self-adhesive stamps (No. 934a) (cover as Type B **24** but showing single leaf) .... 4·50
The covers form the backing for the stamps and also incorporate a scratch card inside each booklet.

B **25** "The Colours of Nature"

1998 (9 Sept). Flowers of Singapore. Multicoloured cover as Type B **25**, 87×61 mm. Pane attached by selvedge.
SB36 ($2.20) booklet containing pane of ten (22c.) stamps (No. 949b) .... 2·75

B **26**

1999 (12 May). Greetings Stamps. "Try a Little Kindness". Multicoloured cover as Type B **26**, 77×71 mm. Self-adhesive.
SB37 ($2.20) booklet containing pane of ten (22c.) (No. 986a) .... 3·00

B **27** Green Turtle

1999 (13 Oct). Amphibians and Reptiles. Multicoloured cover as Type B **27**, 103×60 mm. Stamps attached by selvedge.
SB38 ($2.20) booklet containing block of ten (22c.) (No. 1006) .... 3·00

B **28** Singapore Post Centre (*Illustration further reduced. Actual size* 155×105 *mm*)

2000 (8 Mar). Opening of Singapore Post Centre. Postal Landmarks. Multicoloured cover as Type B **28**. Stitched.
SB39 $10.50 booklet containing two different *se-tenant* panes of 6 (Nos. 1032a and 1034a) .... 12·00

B **29** "Celebrations"

2000 (10 May). Greetings Stamps. Multicoloured cover as Type B **29**, 87×55 mm. Self-adhesive.
SB40 ($2.20) booklet containing pane of ten (22c.) (No. 1038a) .... 4·00
The booklet cover forms the backing card for the stamps and also incorporates 8 self-adhesive labels.

B **30** Smooth Otter and Cubs

2000 (11 Aug). Wetland Wildlife. Multicoloured cover as Type B **30**, 110×56 mm. Pane attached by selvedge.
SB41 ($2.20) booklet containing pane of ten (22c.) (No. 1060b) .... 4·50

B **31** Greetings Emblems

2001 (25 Apr). Greetings Stamps. "Occasions". Multicoloured cover as Type B **31**, 78×70 mm. Self-adhesive.
SB42 ($2.20) booklet containing pane of ten (22c.) (No. 1093a) .... 3·50
The booklet cover forms the backing card for the stamps and also incorporates 10 self-adhesive labels.

B **32** Three Generations of Ah Meng's Family

2001 (5 Sept). Orang Utan Conservation. Multicoloured cover as Type B **32**, 70×90 mm. Self-adhesive.
SB43 ($2.20) booklet containing pane of ten (22c.) stamps (No. 1121a) .... 4·50

B **33** Copper-banded Butterflyfish

2001 (24 Oct). Tropical Marine Fish. Multicoloured cover as Type B **33** Self-adhesive.
SB44 ($2.20) booklet containing pane of ten (22c.) stamps (No. 1142a) .... 2·75

B **34** Flowers, Seeds and Leaves of Tembusu

2002 (25 Sept). Heritage Trees Scheme. Multicoloured cover as Type B **34**, 70×90 mm. Self-adhesive.
SB45 $2.20 booklet containing pane of 10 (22c.) stamps (No. 1253a) .... 2·75

B **35**

2003 (1 Mar). Singapore World Stamp Championship (2004). Multicoloured cover as Type B **35**. Self-adhesive.
SB46 ($2.20) booklet containing pane of ten (22c.) stamps (No. 1142ba) .... 2·75

B **36**

2003 (25 June). Greetings Stamps. "Joy and Caring". Multicoloured cover as Type B **36**, 72×75 mm. Self-adhesive.
SB47 ($2.20) booklet containing pane of ten (22c.) stamps (No. 1290a) .... 3·50

B **37**

2003 (22 Oct). Parks and Gardens. Multicoloured cover as Type B **37**, 71×90 mm. Self-adhesive.
SB48 ($2.20) booklet containing pane of ten (22c.) stamps (No. 1355a) .... 3·50

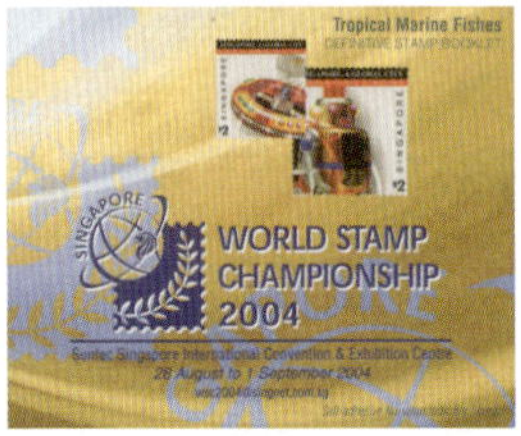

B **38**

2003 (12 Nov). Singapore World Stamp Championship (2004) (2nd issue). Multicoloured cover as Type B **38**. Self-adhesive.
SB49 ($2.20) booklet containing pane of ten (22c.) stamps (No. 1142ba) .... 2·75

B **38a**

2004 (7 July). Singapore World Stamp Championship (2004) (3rd issue). Multicoloured cover as Type B **38a**. Self-adhesive.
SB50 ($2.30) booklet containing pane of ten (23c.) stamps (No. 1142c) .... 2·75

B **39** Underwater Coral Scene

2004 (20 Oct). Wildlife of Chek Jawa. Multicoloured cover as Type B **39**, 70×90 mm. Self-adhesive.
SB51 $2.30 booklet containing pane of ten (23c.) stamps (No. 1447a) .... 3·50

2004 (1 Dec). Tropical Marine Fish. Multicoloured cover as Type B **33**. Self-adhesive.
SB52 ($2.30) booklet containing pane of ten (23c.) stamps (No. 1142c) .... 2·75

B **40** Balloon Dog

2005 (23 Feb). Greetings. Multicoloured cover as Type B **40**, 77×58 mm. Self-adhesive.
SB53 $2.30 booklet containing pane of ten (23c.) stamps (No. 1456a) .... 3·25

B **41**

2005 (15 June)–**06**. Tropical Marine Fish. Multicoloured cover as Type B **41**. Self-adhesive.
SB54 $2.30 booklet containing pane of ten (23c) stamps (No. 1142c) .... 2·75
a. Containing No. 1142da (11.12.06) .... 2·75

B **42** Red-crowned Barbet and Suspension Bridge

2005 (19 Oct). HSBC Tree Top Walk, Central Catchment Nature Reserve. Multicoloured covers as Type B **42**, 71×90 mm. Self-adhesive.
SB55 $2.30 booklet containing pane of ten (23c.) stamps (No. 1572a) .... 2·75

B **43** "Fun with Nature" and Common Palm Civet

2006 (31 Oct). "Fun with Nature" (children's nature education programme). Multicoloured cover as Type B **43**, 89×70 mm. Self-adhesive.
SB56 $2.30 booklet containing pane of ten (23c.) stamps (No. 1654a) .... 3·50

B **44** Singa the Lion Mascot

2007 (8 Feb). 10th Anniv of Singapore Kindness Movement. Multicoloured cover as Type B **44**, 88×78 mm. Self-adhesive.

SB57	($2.50) booklet containing pane of ten (25c.) stamps (No. 1669a)	2·75

B **45** Yellow-rumped Flycatcher

2007 (6 June). Flora and Fauna. Multicoloured cover, 70×60 mm, as Type B **45**. Self-adhesive.

SB58	($2.50) booklet containing pane of ten (25c.) stamps (No. 1706a)	2·75

B **46** Singapore Goby and Blind Shrimp

2007 (17 Oct). Shores and Reefs. Multicoloured cover as Type B **46**, 89×70 mm. Self-adhesive.

SB59	($2.55) booklet containing pane of ten (26c.) stamps (No. 1740a)	4·50

No. SB59 was sold at $2.55, a discount of 10c. off the face value of the stamps.

B **47** Pepper, Tapioca, Rubber and Nutmeg

2008 (12 Nov). Early Cash Crops of Singapore. Multicoloured cover as Type B **47**, 71×90 mm. Self-adhesive.

SB60	($2.55) booklet containing pane of ten (26c.) stamps (No. 1823a)	3·75

B **48** Hand holding Sunflower

2009 (11 Feb). Greetings Stamps. "Let's Celebrate". Multicoloured cover as Type B **48**, 71×78 mm. Self-adhesive.

SB61	($2.55) booklet containing pane of ten (26c.) stamps (No. 1836a)	3·50

2009 (6 May). Flora and Fauna. Multicoloured covers, 70×60 mm, as Type B **45**. Self-adhesive.

SB62	($2.55) booklet containing pane of ten (26c.) stamps (No. 1706ba) (cover showing bird and blue pea vine)	3·75
SB63	($2.55) booklet containing pane of ten (26c.) stamps (No. 1706ca) (cover showing blue-throated bee-eater and pigeon orchid)	3·75

POSTAGE DUE STAMPS

The postage due stamps of Malayan Postal Union were in use in Singapore until replaced by the following issues.

D **1**

D **2**

D **3**

(Litho B.W.)

1968 (1 Feb)–**69**. Toned paper. W w **12**. P 9.

D1	D **1**	1c. green	60	2·00
D2		2c. red	1·60	2·50
D3		4c. yellow-orange	2·00	5·50
D4		8c. chocolate	1·00	2·00
D5		10c. magenta	1·00	90
		a. White paper (16.12.69)	2·25	6·00
D6		12c. slate-violet	2·75	3·25
		a. White paper (16.12.69)	7·00	14·00
D7		20c. new blue	2·00	3·50
		a. White paper (16.12.69)	10·00	14·00
D8		50c. drab	11·00	5·50
D1/8 *Set of* 8			20·00	22·00

In 1973 the 10c. and 50c. were reissued on whiter paper, perf 13×13½. In 1977–8 the 1c., 4c., 10c., 20c. and 50c. were issued on unwatermarked paper, perf 13×13½.

1973. White paper. W w **12**. P 13×13½.

D9	D **1**	10c. bright magenta (27.4)	1·00	4·50
D10		50c. sage-green (24.8)	11·00	12·00

1977–**78**. White paper. No wmk. P 13×13½.

D11	D **1**	1c. green	50·00	38·00
D12		4c. yellow-orange	50·00	80·00
D13		10c. bright magenta	55·00	32·00
D14		20c. new blue	65·00	42·00
D15		50c. sage-green	75·00	48·00
D11/15 *Set of* 5			£275	£225

(Litho Secura, Singapore)

1978 (25 Sept)–**81**. No wmk. P 13×13½.

D16	D **2**	1c. blue-green	65	4·25
		a. Perf 12×11½ (1981)	15	4·50
D17		4c. pale orange	75	6·50
		a. Perf 12×11½ (1981)	20	7·50

D18		10c. cerise	1·00	2·50
		a. Perf 12×11½ (1981)	50	2·50
D19		20c. light blue	1·00	2·75
		a. Perf 12×11½ (1981)	65	2·75
D20		50c. yellow-green	1·60	3·00
		a. Perf 12×11½ (1981)	90	4·00
D16/20 *Set of 5*			4·50	17·00
D16a/20a *Set of 5*			2·25	19·00

(Litho Secura, Singapore)

1989 (12 July)–**97**. P 13×13½.

D21	D **3**	1c. bright emerald (7.11.97)	25·00	25·00
D22		4c. orange-brown (7.11.97)	35·00	35·00
D23		5c. bright mauve	20	50
D24		10c. carmine	20	40
D25		20c. bright greenish blue	30	60
D26		50c. yellow-green	60	1·00
D27		$1 blackish brown (30.4.93)	4·25	5·00

Postage Due stamps were withdrawn on 31 December 1997 and replaced by labels from electronic machines.